ISBN 978-1-333-65462-7
PIBN 10531647

This book is a reproduction of an important historical work. Forgotten Books uses
state-of-the-art technology to digitally reconstruct the work, preserving the original format
whilst repairing imperfections present in the aged copy. In rare cases, an imperfection in
the original, such as a blemish or missing page, may be replicated in our edition. We do,
however, repair the vast majority of imperfections successfully; any imperfections that
remain are intentionally left to preserve the state of such historical works.

1 MONTH OF
FREE
READING

at
www.ForgottenBooks.com

By purchasing this book you are eligible for one month membership to ForgottenBooks.com, giving you unlimited access to our entire collection of over 700,000 titles via our web site and mobile apps.

To claim your free month visit:
www.forgottenbooks.com/free531647

English
Français
Deutsche
Italiano
Español
Português

www.forgottenbooks.com

Mythology Photography **Fiction**
Fishing Christianity **Art** Cooking
Essays Buddhism Freemasonry
Medicine **Biology** Music **Ancient
Egypt** Evolution Carpentry Physics
Dance Geology **Mathematics** Fitness
Shakespeare **Folklore** Yoga Marketing
Confidence Immortality Biographies
Poetry **Psychology** Witchcraft
Electronics Chemistry History **Law**
Accounting **Philosophy** Anthropology
Alchemy Drama Quantum Mechanics
Atheism Sexual Health **Ancient History**
Entrepreneurship Languages Sport
Paleontology Needlework Islam
Metaphysics Investment Archaeology
Parenting Statistics Criminology
Motivational

SAN FRANCISCO

MUNICIPAL REPORTS,

FOR THE

FISCAL YEAR 1866-7, ENDING JUNE 30, 1867.

PUBLISHED BY ORDER OF THE

BOARD OF SUPERVISORS.

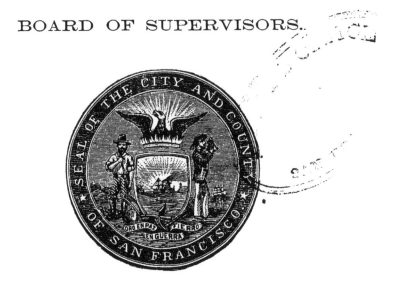

SAN FRANCISCO:

JOSEPH WINTERBURN AND COMPANY, PRINTERS,

No. 417 Clay Street, between Sansome and Battery Streets.

1867.

PRESIDENT,

H. P. COON.

Deputy
Clerk.

Sergeant
at Arms

CLERK.

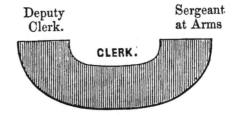

REPORTERS' DESK.

LOBBY.

| CHAS. H. STANYAN | 12 | | 1 | P. H. DALY. |

DIAGRAM

OF THE

CHAMBER

OF THE

BOARD OF

SUPERVISORS,

1867.

| FRANK M'COPPIN | 11 | | 2 | R. P. CLEMENT. |
| J. H. REYNOLDS | 10 | | 3 | EDWARD FLAHERTY |

A. J. SHRADER 9

WM. S. PHELPS. 4

8 F. G. E. TITTEL.

MONROE ASHBURY 5

CHAS. CLAYTON 7

E. N. TORREY. 6

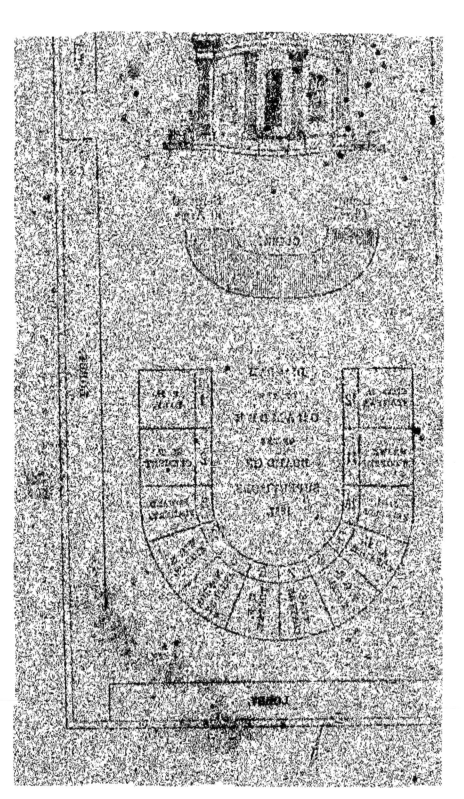

TABLE OF CONTENTS.

APPENDIX TO MUNICIPAL REPORTS.

COMPILED BY JAS. W. BINGHAM.

AUDITOR'S REPORT.

CITY AND COUNTY AUDITOR'S OFFICE, }
San Francisco, August 5, 1867.

To the Honorable Board of Supervisors
of the City and County of San Francisco:

GENTLEMEN—In accordance with Resolution No. 6963, of your Honorable Body, I herewith submit to you my Annual Report for the Fiscal Year ending June 30, 1867.

Remaining your obedient servant,

HENRY M. HALE,

Auditor.

DEMANDS AUDITED DURING THE FISCAL YEAR 1866-7, ENDING JUNE 30TH, 1867.

ON THE GENERAL FUND.

City and County Officers' Salaries....	$181,481 08	
[Items in Appendix of Audited Demands.]		
Extra Deputies' Salaries, under allowance of $3,000 per annum.......	2,960 00	
[Statutes 1861, p. 558; items in Appendix.]		
Police Force Salaries—79 officers at $125, 1 clerk at $150, and 4 captains at $150 per month each, less deductions by Police Commissioners	127,205 89	
[Statutes 1861, p 557; 1863, p. 170; 1863-4, p. 503.]		
Matron for County Jail.............	900 00	
[Statutes 1863-4, p. 474.]		
		$312,546 97
Carried forward........		$312,546 97

2

Brought forward.......		$312,546 97
Fire Department disbursements for expenses and property—		
Old Department, under allowance of $4,000 per month.............	$20,000 50	
[Statutes 1863, p. 168; items in Appendix.]		
Salaries of old officers (Chief, Secretary, and 3 Assistant Engineers, half month December, 1866)	316 66	
[Statutes 1865–6, p. 867.]		
Rents to December 1, 1866........	775 00	
[Statutes 1863, p. 168.],		
New, under Paid Fire Department allowances.		
[Statutes 1865–6, pp. 139, 141.]		
Office rent, stationery, furniture, etc., for Fire Commissioners	1,206 61	
Steam Fire Engines, Hose Reels, Horses, Harness, etc., (Outfit for Paid Fire Department)	34,986 16	
[Items in Appendix.]		
Salaries......................	32,840 28	
[Items in Appendix.]		
Running Expenses..............	21,940 33	
[Items in Appendix.]		
Purchase of Lots, erection and removal of Engine Houses	18,864 10	
[Statutes 1863, p. 171; 1863–4, p. 502; 1865–6, p. 141; items etc., in Appendix.]		
Cisterns and Hydrants	10,001 61	
[Statutes 1863, p. 168; items in Appendix.]		
Appropriation for West End Engine Company....................	1,000 00	
[Statutes 1865–6, p. 83.]		
Extension of, and repairs to, Fire Alarm and Police Telegraph	4,748 42	
[Statutes 1865–6, p. 82; items in Appendix.]		
Salaries Superintendent, Operators, and Repairer Fire Alarm and Police Telegraph	5,100 00	
[Statutes 1863–4, p. 504; 1865–6, p. 82. Salaries of Superintendent and Repairer for one year, $150 and $100 per month, respectively, $3,000; Salaries of 3 Operators after December 1, 1866 (before allowed from allowance for Fire Department expenses), $100 per month each, $2,100.]		
		151,779 67
Carried forward.......		$464,326 64

Brought forward........		$464,326 64
Repairs to Public Buildings		12,000 00
[Statutes 1862, p. 467; items in Appendix.]		
Lighting City Hall, County Jail, Engine Houses, etc...............		7,071 30
[Statutes 1858, p. 46; items in Appendix.]		
Hospital and Almshouse disbursements—expenses of Hospital, New Almshouse and Small Pox Hospital lot and buildings—		
Supplies under allowance of $5,000 per month	$54,721 84	
[Statutes 1863, p. 169; items in Appendix.]		
Salaries of Visiting Physician and Surgeon, $100 per month each...	2,400 00	
[Statutes 1860, p. 274.]		
Supplies for Small Pox Hospital...	1,844 01	
[Statutes 1863, p. 169; items in Appendix.]		
Burials of Indigents.............	1,175 75	
[Statutes 1860, p. 273.]		
Burials and Chemical Analyses by Coroner	1,032 25	
[Statutes 1863-4, p. 161.]		
Almshouse and Pesthouse Lot and Buildings	75,393 01	
[Statutes 1863, p. 170; 1863-4, p. 503; 1865-6, p. 214. 80 acres land, $30,147 27; payments on account of Almshouse, $33,120 62; full payment for Small Pox Hospital, $9,607 50; well, $150; tower, tanks, etc., etc, $2,517 62.]		
		136,566 86
Appropriation for Home for Care of the Inebriate		3,000 00
[Statutes 1863, p. 574.]		
Examination of Insane		1,335 00
[Statutes 1863-4, p. 326.]		
Expense sending Insane to Stockton..		2,058 50
[Statutes 1860, p. 273.]		
Industrial School Expenses—		
Appropriation of $2,000 per month .	24,000 00	
[Statutes 1865-6, p. 304.]		
Medical services.................	300 00	
[Statutes 1863-4, p. 505.]		
Arrest of Runaways..............	368 32	
[Statutes 1863-4, p. 77.]		
		24,668 32
Carried forward.......		$651,026 62

Brought forward.......		$651,026 62
Road Repairs—		
Under allowance of $4,000 per annum for First and Second Districts ...	$4,010 01	
[Statutes 1861, p. 565. Repairs, $3,432 51; Road Masters' Salaries, $577 50.]		
Under allowance of $6,000 for First District	3,147 78	
[Statutes 1865–6, p. 82.]		
New Brannan street Bridge........	4,097 00	
[Statutes 1865–6, p. 83.]		
		11,254 79
Public Parks—		
Inclosing and improving Public Grounds, under allowance of $2,000 per annum....................	1,493 75	
[Statutes 1861, p. 551; items in Appendix.]		
Improvement of Yerba Buena Park.	2,788 00	
[Statutes 1860. p. 274; 1863–4, p. 502.]		
		4,281 75
Registration and Election expenses...		10,946 56
[Statutes 1865–6, pp. 288, 509; see further expenses in items of "Urgent Necessity;" items in Appendix.]		
Subsistence of Prisoners—County Jail, 53,865; City Prison, 19,166; rations 17¼ cents each..........		12,597 83
[Statutes 1856, p. 173; 1862, p. 468.]		
Witnesses expenses		172 50
[Statutes 1856, p. 173.]		
District Court Reporters' services—attendance and transcribing evidence		451 20
[Statutes 1862, p. 253.]		
Special Counsel—see Appendix—		
Under allowance of $5,000 per annum	3,950 00	
[Statutes 1861, p 479.]		
Pueblo Suit....................	4,517 33	
[Statutes 1856, p. 167.]		
City Slip Suits	14,145 30	
[Statutes 1863, p. 169.]		
		22,612 63
Contingent expenses of Mayor's Office, $150 per month................		1,800 00
[Statutes 1860, p. 273.]		
Carried forward........		$715,143 88

Brought forward		$715,143 88
Boat Hire and Office Rent for Harbor Master, $75 per month		900 00
[Statutes 1865–6, p. 663.]		
Copying Assessment Roll		2,100 00
[Statutes 1857, p. 329 ; 1862, p. 510 ; 1863–4, p. 189.]		
Making and copying Military Roll ...		350 00
[Statutes 1863, p. 441.]		
Compiling and publishing Laws and Ordinances		300 00
[Statutes 1861, p. 478.]		
Printing Harbor Police Regulations...		33 00
[Statutes 1863–4, p. 447.]		
Newspapers for Recorder's Office.....		92 13
[Statutes 1862, p. 141.]		
Celebration of Fourth of July, 1866 ..		3,000 00
[Statutes 1863, p. 168.]		
Quarantine expenses		127 50
[Statutes 1865–6, p. 742.]		
Construction and equipment of Iron Clad Steamer "Camanche,"—advanced by Peter Donahue, $60,000. Interest on ditto, from July 11th, 1864, to May 21, 1866, at 10 per cent. per annum, $11,166 66.....		71,166 66
[Statutes 1865–6, p. 809.]		
"Urgent Necessity" allowance, $2,000 per month		23,999 73
[Statutes 1862, p. 467 ; items in Appendix.]		
Military Appropriations—advanced for State of California		21,253 61
[Statutes 1865–6, p. 734 ; items, etc.. in Appendix.]		
Total amount of Demands Audited on the General Fund		$838,466 51

ON THE SPECIAL FEE FUND.

[Statutes 1861, pp. 554–9 ; 1865–6, pp. 66 and 521.]

Salary of Recorder.......... $4,000 00		
Books and Stationery for Office 2,184 38		
	$6,184 38	
Carried forward........	$6,184 38	$838,466 51

Brought forward..........		$6,184 38	$838,466 51
Salary of County Clerk......	4,000 00		
Salaries of Copyists for ditto .	3,079 40		
Books and Stationery for Offices and Courts	2,476 99		
		9,556 39	
Salary of Sheriff......._....	8,000 00		
Books and Stationery for Office	287 10		
		8,287 10	
Salary of Auditor...........	4,000 00		
Books and Stationery for Office	235 45		
		4,235 45	
Salary of Treasurer.........	4,000 00		
Books and Stationery for Office	184 13		
		4,184 13	
Salary of Tax Collector	4,000 00		
Books and Stationery for Office	1,265 00		
Publishing Delinquent Tax List ...._.....	2,513 80		
		7,778 80	
Salary Clerk of Police Court.	2,400 00		
Books and Stationery for Police Court....................	379 71		
		2,779 71	
Books and Stationery for Officers, as follows :			
Clerk Board of Supervisors.		682 39	
District Attorney.........		52 00	
City and County Attorney .		107 97	
Assessor		763 93	
Superintendent of Streets..		694 57	
Coroner		25 00	
Chief of Police		493 62	
Secretary Fire Department.		52 00	
Duplicate Assessment Books of 1867–8...............		340 00	
Total, Special Fee Fund...			46,217 44
Carried forward..........			$884,683 95

Brought forward........ $884,683 95

ON THE STREET LIGHT FUND.

[Statutes 1858, p. 46; 1862. p. 468; 1865-6, p. 437.]

Lighting Streets and repairs Lamps ..   132,646 62
[Items in Appendix.]

ON THE STREET DEPARTMENT FUND.

[Statutes 1865-6, p. 437.]

Repairs Streets—
    In front of Public Property $9,071 11
    Water Front. 2,032 92
    Accepted Streets.......... 12,933 94
    Cases of Urgent Necessity.. 4,647 87
                            ———— $28,685 84
Cleaning Streets and Sewers ..   14,770 50
                                    ————   43,456 34

ON THE POUND FEE FUND.

Salary of Pound Keeper, $75 per month   900 00

[Statutes 1858, p. 237; 1863-4, p. 502.]

ON THE POLICE CONTINGENT FUND.

[Statutes 1859. p. 57.]

Contingent expenses of Police Depart-
    ment—conveyance of Prisoners, Tel-
    egraphing, Traveling expenses, Pho-
    tographing, etc., etc..............   3,048 11

ON THE SCHOOL FUND.

[Statutes 1863, pp. 601-7; 1863-4, pp. 162, 163; 1865-6, p 437.]

Salaries of Teachers.................   209,874 75
Salaries of Janitors 14,795 18
Salary of Clerk of Board of Education   1,800 00
Services of Census Marshals.........   650 00

        Carried forward $227,119 93 $1,064,735 02

Brought forward	$227,119 93	$1,064,735 02
Erection of School House corner of Fifth and Market streets—balance . .	2,130 00	
[Allowed last year, $4,000 ; total for this house, $6,130.]		
Repairs and alterations School Houses	13,214 67	
[Includes Carpenters' salaries.]		
Furniture for Schools	11,161 26	
Fuel and Lights	4,727 31	
Water	272 20	
Books, Stationery, and Advertising . . .	7,698 94	
Rents	11,168 16	
Removal Legal Incumbrances—Lot on Broadway, near Powell street, and Fourth and Harrison streets	2,550 00	
Repairs to Streets front of School Property	3,438 03	
Grading and improving Lots	3,947 56	
Insurance	2,753 59	
Incidental expenses	2,030 60	
		292,212 25

[For urther School expenses see " School Fund, Special," Interest Accounts, and Transfers.]

ON THE SCHOOL FUND, SPECIAL.

[Statutes 1865-6, p. 302.]

Erection of School Houses, etc.		106,376 31
[Items in Appendix.]		

ON INTEREST ACCOUNT—SCHOOL BONDS 1860.

[Statutes 1860, p. 101.]

Remittances to New York to pay Coupons School Bonds, 1860—		
No. 13, due January 1, 1867	2,775 00	
No. 14, due July 1, 1867	2,725 00	
Premium of Exchange, 2¼ per cent. .	123 75	
		5,623 75
Carried forward		$1,468,947 33

Brought forward $1,468,947 33

ON INTEREST ACCOUNT—SCHOOL BONDS 1861.

[Statutes 1861, p. 242.]

Remittances to New York to pay Coupons School Bonds, 1861—

No. 13, due January 1, 1867	$825 00	
No. 14, due July 1, 1867	800 00	
Premium of Exchange, 2¼ per cent..	36 56	
		1,661 56

ON INTEREST ACCOUNT—SCHOOL BONDS 1866-7.

[Statutes 1865-6, p. 303.]

Coupons School Bonds 1866, paid—

No. 1, due Oct 1, 1866, 125 at 35 ..	4,375 00	
No. 2, due April 1, 1867, 125 at 35.	4,375 00	
		8,750 00

ON THE CORPORATION DEBT FUND.

Requisition of Commissioners of Funded Debt of
1851—

[Statutes 1851, p. 287.]

For Interest	$128,990 00	
For Sinking Fund	50,000 00	
		178,990 00

Remittances to New York
to pay Coupons Civil
Bonds, 1855—

[Statutes 1855, p. 286 ; 1856, p. 173.]

No. 23, due Jan. 1, 1867	8,670 00		
No. 24, due July 1, 1867	8,085 00		
Premium of Exchange, 2¼ per cent..........	376 98		
		17,131 98	
			196,121 98

Carried forward 1,675,480 87

Brought forward........ $1,675,480 87

ON COUPON ACCOUNT—BONDS 1858.

[Statutes 1858, p. 187.]

Coupons Bonds 1858, paid—
No. 12, due July 1, 1864, 1 each $15,
  $30 .... $45 00
No. 14, due July 1, 1865, 3 each $15   45 00
No. 15, due January 1, 1866, 9 at
  $15 and 2 at $30 ....   195 00
No. 16, due July 1, 1866, 284 at $15
  and 989 at $30 ....   33,930 00
No. 17, due January 1, 1867, 277 at
  $15 and 981 at $30 ....   33,585 00
                ————————   67,800 00

ON INTEREST ACCOUNT—BONDS 1863 AND 1864.

[Statutes 1862, pp. 265, 266.]

Coupons Bonds 1863, paid—
No. 5, due April 1, 1866, 7 at $17 50,
  and 1 at $35 ....   157 50
No. 6, due October 1, 1866, 841 at
  $17 50 and 496 at $35 ....   32,077 50
No. 7, due April 1, 1867, 836 at
  $17 50 and 471 at $35 ....   31,115 00
Coupons Bonds 1864, paid—
No. 3, due Dec. 1, 1865, 6 at $35...   210 00
No. 4, due June 1, 1866, 6 at $35 ..   210 00
No. 5, due Dec. 1, 1866, 28 at $35..   980 00
No. 6, due June 1, 1867, 28 at $35..   980 00
                ————————   65,730 00

ON INTEREST TAX ACCOUNT—SAN FRANCISCO AND SAN JOSE
RAILROAD BONDS.

[Statutes 1861, p. 201.]

Coupons San Francisco and San Jose
Railroad Bonds, paid—

            Carried forward........ $1,809,010 87

Brought forward........		$1,809,010 87
30 at $17 50 and 15 at $35, due July 1, August 1, 9, Sept. 15, Oct. 13, Nov. 10, Dec. 1, 1866, Jan. 1, Feb. 1, 9, March 15, 1867 (each date), 11 × $1,050..................	$11,550 00	
60 at $17 50 and 30 at $35, due Sept. 14, 1866.................	2,100 00	
23 at $17 50 and 15 at $35, due April 13 and May 10, 1867 (each date), 2 × $927 50	1,855 00	
23 at $17 50 and 11 at $35, due June 1, 1867.................	787 50	
55 at $17 50 and 25 at $35, due March 14, 1867	1,837 50	
21 at $17 50 and 6 at $35, due December 22, 1866...............	577 50	
1 at $17 50, due December 22, 1865, June 1, 1866 (each date), 2 at $17 50......................	35 00	
6 at $17 50, due May 10, 1866	105 00	
18 at $17 50 and 11 at $35, due June 22, 1866.................	700 00	
3 at $17 50 and 2 at $35, due June 22, 1867......	122 50	
		19,670 00

ON INTEREST TAX ACCOUNT—PACIFIC RAILROAD BONDS.

[Statutes 1863, p. 383]

Coupons Central and Western Pacific Railroad Bonds, paid—		
Central No. 4, due July 1, 1866, 400 at $35	14,000 00	
Central No. 5, due January 1, 1867, 400 at $35....................	14,000 00	
Western No. 3, due November 1, 1866, 250 at $35..............	8,750 00	
Western No. 4, due May 1, 1867, 205 at $35....................	7,175 00	
		43,925 00
Carried forward........		$1,872,605 87

Brought forward........ $1,872,605 S7

ON SINKING FUND—SCHOOL BONDS 1860.

[Statutes 1860, p. 102.]

Loans on security of State and City and
  County Bonds..................... $17,200 00
Redemption of 2 Bonds, each $500, =
  $1,000, at 99½ per cent., = $995, less
  Coupon No. 13, not surrendered, $50   945 00
[Nos. of Bonds, 83 and 84.]

                                            18,145 00

ON SINKING FUND—SCHOOL BONDS 1861.]

[Statutes 1861, pp. 242, 243.

Loans on security of City and County
  Bonds 14,400 00
Redemption of 4 Bonds, each $500, =
  $2,000, at par, with interest on $1,500
  July 1 to November 28, at 10 per
  cent. per annum, $61 66, less interest
  November 28 to January 1, on $500,
  $4 58 (Coupon No. 13, on 1 Bond,
  and off 3 Bonds)...................   2,057 08
[Nos. of Bonds, 43, 44, 49, 50.]

                                            16,457 08

ON SINKING FUND—SCHOOL BONDS 1866 AND 1867.

[Statutes 1865–6, p. 303; 1861, p. 242.]

Redemption of 15 Bonds, each $1,000,
  = $15,000, at par...............   15,000 00
[Nos. 71, 72, 73, 74, 75, 76, 77, 78, 86, 87, 88, 89, 90,
91, 92.]

ON SINKING FUND—FIRE BONDS 1854.

Remittance to New York to pay Fire
  Bonds 1854 outstanding, due December 1, 1866, and Coupon attached to same, No. 25—

Carried forward........ $1,922,207 95

Brought forward........		$1,922,207 95
93 Bonds, each $1,000............	$93,000 00	
[Nos. 1 to 20, 22 to 36, 38 to 50, 54 to 62, 89 to 113, 115 to 125, inclusive.]		
163 Bonds, each $500	81,500 00	
[Nos. 63 to 61, 83, 84, 86, 87, 126 to 134, 136, 137, 141 to 154, 156 to 158, 161, 164 to 182, 185, 187 to 191, 193, 194, 197 to 199, 203 to 209, 211, 213 to 220, 222, 225 to 227, 229, 230, 232 to 277, 281, 282, 284, 285, 287, 288, 290 to 292, 297 to 300 inclusive.]		
93 Coupons, No. 25, at $41 67.....	3,875 31	
163 Coupons, No. 25, at $20 83....	3,395 29	
Premium of Exchange, $2\frac{1}{4}$ per cent. on $181,770 60................	4,089 84	
	185,860 44	
Loan on security of State Bonds	58,000 00	
		243,860 44

ON SINKING FUND—BONDS 1855.

[Statutes 1855, p. 286.]

Loans on security of United States and City and County Bonds...........	31,000 00	
Redemption of Bonds—		
2 Bonds, each $500, = $1,000, at $99\frac{1}{2}$ per cent., = $995, with interest from July 1 to November 28, 1866, at 6 per cent. per annum, $24 67......................	1,019 67	
[Nos. 150, 151.]		
70 Bonds, each $500, = $35,000, at $99\frac{7}{8}$ per cent., = $34,956 25, with interest from July 1 to November 28, 1866, at 6 per cent. per annum, $860 58, less 6 Coupons, No. 23, not surrendered, each $15, = $90	35,726 83	
[Nos. 41, 44, 47, 48, 51 to 53, 91, 92, 94 to 99, 116, 169 to 174, 180, 191, 206, 216, 230, 231, 233, 236 to 244, 273, 275, 365, 371, 414, 436, 437, 499, 500, 526, 529, 531, 537, 538, 583 to 585, 586 to 591, 599 to 603, 642, 650, 651, 656.]		
		67,746 50
Carried forward........		$2,233,814 89

Brought forward........ $2,233,814 89

ON SINKING FUND—BONDS 1863 AND 1864.

[Statutes 1863, pp. 265, 266, and Orders 547 and 580, of the Board of Supervisors.]

Loans on security of City and County
  Bonds ....:.... .... $50,975 00
Redemption of Bonds of 1863—
  9, each $1,000, and 70, each $500, =
  $44,000 ($10,000 each at 79½ per
  cent., 80 per cent., 81 per cent.,
  81½ per cent., and $4,000 at 82 per
  cent........ ....   35,480 00
  [Nos. 122, 124, 470, 471, 472, 735, 736, 1,137 to 1,176
  1,181 to 1,192, 1,254 to 1,262, 1,301 to 1,303, 1,313,
  1,315, 1,333 to 1,337, 1,340.]
  21 each $1,000, = $21,000, at 82 per
  cent., = $17,220 with interest from
  October 1 to November 28 at 7
  per cent. per annum, $236 83....   17,456 83
  [Nos. 231, 1,084 to 1,097, 1,099, 1,100, 1,201, 1,202,
  1,244, 1,248.]
Redemption of balance Certificates—
  Bonds 1863 and 1864—
  1863—No. 9, $55 38 at 82 per cent.,
  = $45 41 and interest from Oc-
  tober 1, 1863, to January 1, 1867,
  at 7 per cent. per annum, $12 59 .   58 00
  1863—No. 45, $63 55 at 82 per cent.
  = $52 11, and interest from April
  1, 1864, to January 1, 1867, at 7
  per cent. per annum, $12 23.....   64 34
  1864—No. 40, $7 91 at 82 per cent.
  = $6 48, and interest from June
  1, 1864, to January 1, 1867, at 7
  per cent. per annum, $1 43......   7 91
                                      ———————   104,042 08

       Carried forward........ $2,337,856 97

Brought forward $2,337,856 97

ON SINKING FUND (LOAN FUND ACCOUNT) — SAN FRANCISCO
AND SAN JOSE RAILROAD BONDS.

[Statutes 1861, p. 201.]

Redemption of Bonds issued to San
Francisco and San Jose Railroad
Company—
9, each $1,000, and 11, each $500, =
$14,500 at 75 per cent., = $10,875
with interest on $13,000 from June
22 to December 18, 1866, at 7 per
cent. per annum, $444 90, and on
$1,500 from September 14 to De-
cember 18, 1866, $27 40........ $11,347 30
[Nos. 185, 186, 189 to 195, 205, 209, 211, 213, 216 to
219, 376, 399, 450.]
4, each $1,000, and 2, each $500, =
$5,000 00, at 81⅞ per cent., =
$4,093 75, and 7, each $500, =
$3,500 00, at 81$\frac{19}{20}$ per cent., =
$2,868 25, with interest on $3,500
from October 13 to December 18,
1866, at 7 per cent. per annum,
$44 23, and on $5,000 from September 14 to December 18, 1866,
$91 38.....................   7,097 61
[Nos. 294, 295, 301 to 304, 307, 362, 366 to 368, 400,
401.]
                                            ————   18,444 91

Total demands audited Fiscal Year end-
ing June 30, 1867 .... $2,356,301 88

RECAPITULATION OF DEMANDS AUDITED.

For—

Police Department (including Officers of Police Court)	$147,916 30
School Department (including salary of Superintendent, General Fund), expenditures of every kind, houses included, excepting Interest and Sinking Funds...........................	402,588 56
Fire Department, all expenditures, including houses, outfit, cisterns, and hydrants.................	152,988 25
Hospital and Almshouse Department (including Almshouse lot, 80 acres, and part payment of Almshouse)................................	136,574 37
Lighting Streets, City Hall, and County Jail	138,503 76
Construction and equipment of Monitor, "Camanche "	71,166 66
Interest on Debt..............................	366,716 48
Reduction of Debt............................	354,686 82
Loans from Sinking Funds, advances to State for Armory Rents, etc.........................	192,945 86
Repairs to Streets and Roads.................	71,090 70
[Including expenses of Street Superintendent's Office, $15,194 57.]	
Industrial School Department...................	24,668 32
Registration and Election expenses.............	17,137 81
Subsistence of Prisoners	12,597 83
Special Counsel	22,612 63
Judges County and Probate Courts.............	10,000 00
Repairs to Public Buildings (exclusive of School Houses and Hospital,).....................	12,000 00
Home of Inebriate	3,000 00
Public Squares...............................	4,781 75
Public Offices (Salaries and Incidentals) as follows—	
[Subject to a deduction of $131,009 61, for Fees collected and paid into the Treasury.]	
Mayor's Department	6,600 00
Auditor's Department	6,055 45
Treasurer's Department.......	10,044 30
Tax Collector's Department	19,217 05
Carried forward....................	$2,183,892 90

Brought forward	$2,183,892	90
Sheriff's Department......................	31,987	10
County Clerk's Department	31,031	39
Recorder's Department	30,427	59
City and County Attorney's Department	6,748	42
District Attorney's Department	6,642	00
Assessor's Department......................	19,763	93
Harbor Master's Department	3,900	00
Municipal License Department..............	6,082	00
Coroner's Department	2,532	00
Health Department	5,461	75
Clerk's Department Board of Supervisors......	5,432	39
Porter's Department	2,880	00
Compiling and Printing Municipal Reports, Laws and Orders, and Advertising for Board of Supervisors.	4,837	20
Examination of Insane and sending Insane to Stockton	3,393	50
Copying Assessment Roll and making and copying Military Roll.................................	2,450	00
Celebration of Fourth July, 1866.................	3,000	00
Street Signs	1,575	00
Furniture for City Hall, Pound Expenses, Coal and Wood for City Hall, Fees and Expenses of Witnesses, and District Court Reporters, etc.	4,264	71
Total Demands audited (including Loans of Sinking Funds as well as expenditures)	$2,356,301	88

[See Estimate of Actual Expenditures, forward.]

CONDENSED SUMMARY OF DEMANDS AUDITED.

Ordinary Current Expenses	$1,116,537	31
[Against which apply in reduction Receipts for Fees, etc.; see Statement of Expenditures, forward.]		
Camanche claim................................	71,166	66
Carried forward....................	$1,187,703	97

3

Brought forward......................	$1,187,703	97
Entire new Outfit, Paid Fire Department, and new Hydrants	44,987	77
Permanent Improvements and purchase of Property— Almshouse, Engine Houses, and School Houses ..	209,260	98
[Against which apply Receipts from sale of old Engine Houses and Lots and School Lot.]		
Redemption of Bonds............................	354,686	82
Interest on Bonds.............................	366,716	48
[Against which apply Interest Received]		
Total expended, subject to deductions as stated above................................	2,163,356	02
Loans from Sinking Funds, repayable..............	171,575	00
Loans to State, Armory Rents, $21,253 61, and advanced in the matter of widening Kearny and Merchant streets, $117 25.......................	21,370	86
Total audited as above	$2,356,301	88

AUDITED DEMANDS UNPAID JUNE 30, 1867, WITH PROOF.

UPON WHAT ACCOUNTS OR FUNDS.	Demands outstanding June 30, 1866.	Demands Audited, 1866-7.	TOTAL.	Demands paid, 1866-7.	Demands canceled 1866-7.	Demands outstanding June 30, 1867.
Surplus Fund, 1856-7	$475 20		$475 20			$5 20
Police Fund, 1856-7	65 75		65 75			65 75
General Fund	39,714 86	$838,466 51	878,181 37	$827,480 38		50,700 99
Special Fee Fund	2,867 83	46,017 44	49,085 27	45,764 01		3,321 26
Street Light Fund	10,437 02	132,646 62	143,083 64	131,576 25		11,507 39
Street Department Fund		43,456 34	43,156 34	43,155 94		300 40
Pound Fee Fund	75 00	900 00	95 00	900 00		75 00
Police Contingent Fund	24 95	3,048 11	3,073 06	2,983 50	$67 50	89 56
School Fund	20,195 15	292,212 25	312,407 40	293,097 92		19,241 98
School Fund, Special		106,376 31	106,376 31	101,358 31		5,018 00
Interest Account—School Bonds 1860		5,623 75	5,623 75	5,623 75		
Interest Account—School Bonds 1861		1,661 56	1,661 56	1,661 56		
Interest Account—School Bonds 1866-7		8,750 00	8,750 00	8,750 00		
Corporation Debt Fund	692 50	196,121 98	196,814 48	196,814 48		
Interest Account—Bonds 1858		67,800 00	67,800 00	67,800 00		
Interest Account—Bonds 1863-4		65,730 00	65,730 00	65,730 00		
Interest Tax Account—San Francisco and San José Railroad Bonds		19,670 00	19,670 00	19,670 00		
Interest Tax Account—Pacific Railroad Bonds		43,925 00	43,925 00	43,925 00		
Sinking Fund—School Bonds 1860		18,145 00	18,145 00	18,145 00		
Sinking Fund—School Bonds 1861		16,457 08	16,457 08	16,457 08		
Sinking Fund—School Bonds 1866-7		15,000 00	15,000 00	15,000 00		
Sinking Fund—Fire Bonds 1854		243,860 44	243,860 44	243,860 44		
Sinking Fund—Bonds 1855		67,746 50	67,746 50	67,746 50		
Sinking Fund—Bonds 1863-4		104,042 08	104,042 08	104,042 08		
Sinking Fund Account—San Francisco and San José Railroad Bonds		18,444 91	18,444 91	18,444 91		
	$74,548 26	$2,356,301 88	$2,430,850 14	$2,339,987 11	$67 50	$90,795 53

Of the above amount of demands outstanding, $86,252 48 is for demands of the present year, and $4,543 05 demands of previous years—items of last following.

DEMANDS, JULY 1, 1856, TO JULY 1, 1867, INCLUSIVE, UNPAID.

Fiscal Year.	Number.	Fund.	Name.	Amount.
1856–7	524	..General ..	G. Millett	$20 00
1856–7	872	..General ..	M. Hoadley	12 00
1856–7	1,065	..School ...	M. Hawes .....'............	7 75
1856–7	1,683	..School ...	M. A. Casebolt.............	50 00
1856–7	1,956	..School ...	Dore & Havens	19 75
1856–7	1,957	..School ...	Dore & Havens	16 88
1856–7	1,973	..School ..	B. F. Whitman	3 00
1856–7	2,028	..School ...	W. M. Coy	15 00
1856–7	691	..Police....	H. McNally............	65 75
1856–7	404	..Surplus...	Jos. Norton...............	130 00
1856–7	405	..Surplus...	J. Bolen..................	130 00
1856–7	406	..Surplus...	J. Shelly	130 00
1856–7	523	..Surplus...	Hart & Heaney	85 20
1857–8	17	..General ..	Graves & Smith...........	12 96
1857–8	2,962	..General ..	G. O. Whitney & Co........	9 75
1858–9	3,466	..School ...	T. J. Gangloff	3 50
1859–60	3,261	..General ..	M. G. Searing	8 00
1861–2	409	..General ..	J. H. Dixon	6 50
1861–2	843	..General ..	C. S. Brooks..............	20 00
1861–2	912	..General ..	J. W. Bell................	3 50
1862–3	3,445	..General ..	C. A. Cherry..............	13 20
1863–4	9	..General ..	Jane Miller................	8 00
1863–4	2,363	..General ..	M. O'Brien................	4 60
1863–4	5,296	..General ..	W. Brown.................	12 00
1863–4	5,297	..General ..	L. Stappfer...............	5 00
1864–5	2,026	..General ..	Davis & Jordan...........	3 00
1864–5	2,360	..General ..	J. Van Riper...............	3 86
1864–5	2,686	..General ..	J. Inderstroth.............	55 85
1864–5	145	..School ...	J. D. Farwell & Co.........	1 25
1864–5	216	..School ...	C. V. Gillespie.............	20 00
1864–5	2,584	..School ...	James Stewart	5 00
1864–5	7,822	..School ...	F. Donahue	5 00
1864–5	8,435	..School ...	F. Donahue	5 00
1865–6	1,024	..General ..	B. P. Moore & Co..........	4 50
1865–6	4,770	..General ..	W. J. Stringer.............	12 00
1865–6	4,629	..School ...	Trustees Pacific St. Church...	35 00
1865–6	5,864	..School ...	Henry Comfort.............	4 00
1865–6	8,258	..School ...	L. B. Benchley & Co.	1 75
1865–6	8,451	..School ...	M. L. Jordan..............	27 00
1865–6	9,324	..School ...	S. A. Williams.............	67 50

Demands unpaid of 1861–2, 1863–4, receivable only for delinquent taxes of 1856–7, 1857–8, 1858–9, 35 each $100.......   3,500 00
Demands unpaid of 1866–7, mostly audited June 29, 1867,......   86,252 48

                                                  $90,795 53

APPENDIX TO AUDITED DEMANDS,

SHOWING DETAILS OF SUNDRY EXPENDITURES, VIZ. :

CITY AND COUNTY OFFICERS' SALARIES.

[See list of references forward for laws authorizing same.]

GENERAL FUND.

Salary of—

Mayor, 1 year		$3,000 00
Mayor's Clerk, 1 year		1,800 00
Clerk Board of Health, 14 months, at $25 per month		350 00
Clerk of Board of Supervisors, 1 year		2,400 00
Assistant Clerk Board of Supervisors, 1 year		1,200 00
County Jndge, 1 year		5,000 00
Probate Judge, 1 year		5,000 00
City and County Attorney and Counselor, 1 year		5,000 00
Clerk to ditto, 1 year		1,500 00
District Attorney, 1 year		5,000 00
Clerk to ditto, 1 year		1,500 00
Prosecuting Attorney, 1 year		3,000 00
Police Judge, 1 year		4,000 00
Chief of Police, 1 year		4,000 00
Assessor, 1 year		4,000 00
Deputies of Assessor—		
Chief Deputy, $200 per month, 1 year	2,400 00	
Draughtsman, $150 per month, 1 year, less 1 day	1,795 00	
Carried forward	$4,195 00	$46,750 00

Brought forward........	$4,195 00	$46,750 00
Other Deputies, $150 per month each—		
July, 1866, 5, 1 month, and 1, 22 days	860 00	
August, 1866, 3, 1 month, and 1, 10 days..............	500 00	
September, 1866, 3, 1 month, and 1, half month..........	525 00	
October, 1866, 2, each 25 and 27 days.....................	520 00	
February, 1867, 13, 1 month, and 3, half month..........	2,175 00	
March, 1867, 15, 1 month, and 1, half month	2,325 00	
April, 1867, 12, 1 month, and 1, each 8, 9, 22 days	1,995 00	
May, 1867, 7, 1 month	1,050 00	
June, 1867, 5, 1 month, and 1, 21 days.................	855 00	
		15,000 00
Coroner, 1 year.................		2,500 00
Health Officer, 1 year		2,400 00
Superintendent of Public Schools, 1 year......................		4,000 00
Superintendent of Streets, 1 year...		4,000 00
Deputies of Superintendent of Streets, 3 at $125, and 3 at $150 per month each, 1 year		9,900 00
[See further amount in account of " Extra Deputies' Salaries."]		
Surveyor, 1 year		500 00
Harbor Master, 1 year............		3,000 00
Collector of Licenses, 1 year.......		2,100 00
Deputies of ditto, 2 at $125 each per month		3,000 00
Interpreters for Police Court, 2 at $125 each per month		3,000 00
Carried forward........		$96,150 00

Brought forward			$96,150 00
City Hall Porter, 1 year..........			1,080 00
Assistants of ditto, 2 at $75 each per month, 1 year...................			1,800 00
Auditor's Clerk, 1 year...........			1,800 00
Treasurer's Deputies, 1 each $2,100, $1,500			3,600 00
Tax Collector's Deputies, Clerks, and Auctioneer—			
1 Deputy each, $2,400, $2,100, $1,800, 1 year...............	$6,300 00		
Clerks at $150 per month each—			
July, 1866, 2, 1 month, and 1, 8 days................. ..	340 00		
August, 1866, 2, 1 month, and 1, each 1½, 5, 6, 7, 9 days...	447 50		
September, 1866, 2, ¾ month, and 1, each ¼, ⅓ month, 2 days ..	322 50		
October, 1866, 5, 1 month, and 2, ⅓ month	850 00		
November, 1866, 5, 1 month, and 1, 8 days.................	790 00		
December, 1866, 1, 1 month, and 2, 25 days each	400 00		
January, 1866, to June, 1867, inclusive, 1, 6 months	900 00		
Auctioneer, at Tax Sale	200 00		
		10,550 00	
Sheriff's Deputies—			
Under Sheriff, 1 year...........	2,400 00		
Bookkeeper, 1 year	1,800 00		
7 Deputies, at $150 per month each	12,600 00		
4 Jailkeepers, at $125 per month each	6,000 00		
		22,800 00	

[$900 allowed for Matron for County Jail in addition
to the above.]

Carried forward			$137,780 00

Brought forward........		$137,780 00
County Clerk's Deputies—		
6, at $175, and 3, at $150 per month each, 1 year...........	$18,000 00	
1, at $150 per month, 10 months 10 days	1,550 00	
		19,550 00

[Allowed for 1 Deputy in account of "Urgent Necessity," $1,925, and $3,079 40 for Copyists in Special Fee Fund.]

Recorder's Deputies, Clerks, and Porter—		
1 Deputy, each $2,100, $1,800, 1 year......................	3,900 00	
1 Porter, 1 year	900 00	
Clerks (averaging 13) for copying 161,259 folios at 12 cents	19,351 08	
		24,151 08
Total per Report, page 9..		$181,481 08

[$131,009 61, received from fees of City and County Officers, directly applicable in reduction of the above.]

EXTRA DEPUTIES' SALARIES.

[Allowance $3,000 per annum ; Statutes 1861, p. 558.]

GENERAL FUND.

Salary of—		
Extra Deputies for Treasurer—		
1 License Notice Server, month of June, 1866	75 00	
2 License Notice Servers, July 1 to December 1, 1866, 5 months, at $75 each per month	750 00	
2 License Notice Servers; December 1, 1866, to May 1, 1867, 5 months, at $85 each per month.	850 00	
1 License Notice Server, month of May, 1867..................	85 00	
		1,760 00
Carried forward........		$1,760 00

Brought forward........		$1,760 00
Extra Deputy for Superintendent of Streets, June 1 to October 1, 4 months at $150................		600 00
Clerk Board of Equalization—Personal Property	$150 00	
Clerks Board of Equalization—Real Estate	450 00	
		600 00
Total per Report, page 9.		$2,960 00

RECAPITULATION OF CITY AND COUNTY OFFICERS' SALARIES.

Amounts charged to the accounts of City and County Officers' Salaries, Extra Deputies' Salaries, Matron of County Jail, and Urgent Necessity Allowance on the General Fund.....................	$190,336 08
Amount charged to Special Fee Fund............	33,479 40
	$223,815 48
Deduct Fees received by City and County Officers, and paid into the Treasury...........	131,009 61
Leaving net Salaries of City and County Officers	$92,805 87

STATEMENT OF EXPENSES OF ADMINISTRATIVE DEPARTMENTS (ONLY) OF CITY
AND COUNTY GOVERNMENT, (INCLUDING SALARIES AND CONTINGENT
EXPENSES OF THE SEVERAL OFFICERS), ALSO THE FEES RECEIVED AND
PAID INTO THE TREASURY, DIRECTLY APPLICABLE IN REDUCTION OF THE
SAME.

	Expenses.	Fees Collected and paid over.
Mayor's Department..........................	$6,600 00	
Auditor's Department........................	6,055 45	$2,524 00
[Fees on Licenses.]		
Treasurer's Department......................	10,044 30	13,118 73
[Fees on Licenses and on Moneys paid to State.]		
Tax Collector's Department..................	19,217 05	16,133 30
[Fees on Tax Deeds and on Taxes paid to State.]		
Sheriff's Department........................	31,987 10	16,720 73
[Expenses on Civil and Criminal Business—Fees on Civil Business.]		
County Clerk's Department...................	31,031 39	36,616 95
[Fees on all business.]		
Recorder's Department.......................	30,427 59	43,237 25
[Fees on all business.]		
City and County Attorney's Department........	6,748 42	
District Attorney's Department...............	6,642 00	64 00
[Incidental Fees on Licenses.]		
Assessor's Department.......................	19,763 93	
Harbor Master's Department	3,900 00	
Surveyor's Department	500 00	
Coroner's Department	2,532 00	
Superintendent of Streets' Department	15,194 57	
Municipal License Department..................	6,082 00	
Health Department...........................	5,461 75	
Clerk Board of Supervisor's Department........	5,432 39	854 65
[Incidental Fees.]		
Porter's Department.........................	2,880 00	
	$210,499 94	$129,269 61

The Fees collected by certain officers, as above stated, amounting to $129,269 61 (directly
applicable to expenses), being deducted from the total expenses of administrative officers,
$210,499 94, leaves $81,230 33 as the net total expenses of the administrative departments.

POLICE DEPARTMENT EXPENSES.

Salary of Police Judge	$4,000 00
[See items of City and County Officers' Salaries.]	
Salary of Chief of Police......................	4,000 00
[See items of City and County Officers' Salaries.]	
Salary of Prosecuting Attorney	3,000 00
[See items of City and County Officers' Salaries.]	
Salary of Clerk of Police Court	2,400 00
[See items of City and County Officers' Salaries.]	
Salaries of Interpreters Police Court.............	3,000 00
[See items of City and County Officers' Salaries.]	

Carried forward................... | $16,400 00

Brought forward	$16,400 00
Salaries of 4 Captains, $150 per month each, 1 Clerk, $150 per month, and 79 Officers, at $125 per month each, 1 year, less deductions by Police Commissioners	127,205 89
Rent of Harbor Police Station	108 00
[See items of Urgent Necessity Allowance.]	
Water Pipe, Furniture, etc., for ditto	84 10
[See items of Urgent Necessity Allowance.]	
Repairs to Harbor Boat Eureka	60 50
[See items of Urgent Necessity Allowance.]	
Stationery for Police Court and Chief of Police	873 33
[See items of Special Fee Fund]	
Police Contingent Expenses	3,048 11
[Police Contingent Fund.]	
Lighting Police Stations	136 37
[See items of Lighting Buildings.]	
Total, as per recapitulation of audited demands.	$147,916 30

Fines and fees in Police Court (revenues from Police Department) being deducted from the above, $29,086 75, shows a net expense for Police Department of $118,829 55.

FIRE DEPARTMENT EXPENSES, UNDER ALLOWANCE OF $4,000 PER MONTH,
FROM JULY 1 TO DECEMBER 1, 1866, (VOLUNTEER SYSTEM.)

Salaries—

Chief Engineer, 5 months at $333⅓ per month	$1,666 66
3 Assistants, 5 months at $50 each per month	750 00
Secretary, 5 months at $150 per month	750 00
Telegraph Operators, 5 months at $100 each per month	1,500 00
[Salaries of Operators for balance of year included in account of "Salaries of Superintendent, Operators, and Repairer Fire Alarm and Police Telegraph."]	
Corporation Yard Keeper, 6 months at $30 per month	180 00
Stewards, 20, 4 months, and 19, 1 month at $40 per month each	3,960 00
Carried forward	$8,806 66

Brought forward	$8,806 66	
Engineers for Steam Engines, 4, 5 months at $60 per month	1,200 00	
		$10,006 66
Other Expenses—		
Repairs to Engines, etc.	4,019 82	
Repairs to Corporation Yard (rented building)	101 75	
Rent of Corporation Yard, June 1, 1866, to Jannary 1, 1867, 7 months at $100	700 00	
Wood and Coal for Steam Engines .	379 12	
Cartage	259 50	
Fluid, Oil, Wicks, etc	401 30	
Cotton Waste, Emery Cloth, Rope, etc.	168 99	
Cleaning and Oiling Hydrants	337 50	
Cleaning Vaults	200 00	
Filling Cisterns	30 00	
Telegraphing	167 89	
Horse keeping (Horses bought for Paid Department)	561 47	
Shoeing Horses	44 50	
Cards—location of Signal Boxes . .	12 00	
Horse keeping and payment of Driver for No. 12 Engine Company	450 00	
Lighting Houses, $20 per month each—		
6, month May, 1865, (heretofore omitted)	120 00	
20, July 1 to December 1, 1866, 5 months	2,000 00	
Exempt Engine House, to December 1, 1866	40 00	
		9,993 84
Total, per Report page 10, ...		$20,000 50

MATERIAL (ENGINES, HOSE REELS, HORSES, HARNESS, ETC.) FOR PAID FIRE
DEPARTMENT, (ALLOWANCE, $35,000 IN ALL.)

4 Engines and 1 Hose Reel, and freight on same from
New York $17,655 34
27 Horses 10,154 50
8 Hose Reels 3,205 00
Harness. 2,079 42
Hook and Ladder Truck for Hook and Ladder Company No. 3 .... 750 00
709 feet Hose (balance of cost of Hose charged in account of Running Expenses, this account being
exhausted)..................................... 1,134 40
Alteration of Water Pipe, Engine House Second
Street 7 50

Total, per Report page 10. .... $34,986 16

SALARIES—PAID FIRE DEPARTMENT—FROM DECEMBER 1, 1866, TO JUNE 30,
1867, (ALLOWANCE PER ANNUM, $55,000.)

Salaries of—
Chief Engineer, December 1, 1866, to June 30,
1867, 7 months at $250 per month............ $1,750 00
2 Assistants, December 1, 1866, to June 30, 1867,
7 months at $100 each per month 1,400 00
Clerk, October 1, 1866, to June 30, 1867, 9 months
at $100 per month......................... 900 00
Corporation Yard Keeper, December 1, 1866, to
June 30, 1867, 7 months at $50 per month..... 350 00
Engineers of 6 Steam Engines, $80 per month each,
to June 30, 1867......................... 3,959 13
Drivers of 6 Engines, 3 Hose Carriages, and 2
Trucks, to June 30, 1867, at $60 per month each 5,121 35
Firemen of 6 Steam Engines, at $50 per month each,
to June 30, 1867......................... 2,547 78
Foremen of 6 Engines, 3 Hose Carriages, and 2
Trucks, to June 30, 1867, at $30 per month each 2,310 00
Tillermen of 2 Trucks, to June 30, 1867, at $50
per month each........................... 700 00

Carried forward.................... $19,038 26

Brought forward......................	$19,038	26
Stewards of 3 Hose Companies, to June 30, 1867, at $50 per month each......................	1,065	00
Extra men of 6 Engines, 3 Hose Carriages, and 2 Trucks, to June 30, 1867, at $20 per month each	12,588	00
Men taking charge of Horses, September 19 to December 3, 1866, at $60 per month.............	149	02
Total, per Report page 10.................	$32,840	28

NOTE.—Each Engine Company consists of 1 Engineer, 1 Driver, 1 Fireman, 1 Foreman, and 8 Extra Men.

Each Hook and Ladder Company consists of 1 Driver, 1 Foreman, 1 Tillerman, and 12 Extra Men.

Each Hose Company consists of 1 Driver, 1 Foreman, 1 Steward, and 6 Extra Men.

RUNNING EXPENSES—PAID FIRE DEPARTMENT. (ALLOWANCE $22,000 PER ANNUM, FROM DECEMBER 1, 1866.)

5,074 feet Hose (including freight on that shipped from New York).................................	$8,261	34
Horse Feed..	1,675	20
Shoeing Horses	294	75
Repairs to Engines, etc.........................	3,620	57
730 Tubes, 1,495 pounds..........................	1,016	15
Oil, Wicks, etc. (including 10 barrels Neatsfoot Oil)	1,032	82
Coal and Wood....................................	717	65
Set of Tools of Wm. Free........................	700	00
Beds...	271	00
Pails and Brooms.................................	96	00
Matches, 15 gross	27	00
4 dozen Chairs and 1 dozen Tables...............	167	00
60 Spittoons	126	75
4 Battering Rams.................................	48	00
12 Hose Washers..................................	120	00
6 dozen Fire Belts...............................	63	00
134 Badges, at 80 cents..........................	107	20
Hose for cleaning Engines and Houses.............	261	97
Harness, Blankets, etc...........................	128	00
Soap...	35	48
Carried forward...................	$18,769	88

Brought forward........		$18,769 88
Stoves and Stove Pipe..............		355 75
Hardware		183 52
Rope, Hooks, Thimbles, Castor Oil, Chamois Skin, Sponge, Tripoli, etc.		122 92
Cartage of Engines, rubbish, etc......		149 75
Cleaning Vaults		165 00
Room for Apparatus of Hose Company No. 3 and 2 Men.................		254 66
Rent of Corporation Yard, month of January, 1867...................		100 00
Medical treatment of Horses.........		50 00
Damage to Saloon from running in of Engine No. 5....................		21 00
Salaries not provided for in Salary Allowance of Paid Fire Department Act—		
Of Corporation Yard Drayman, at $75 per month.................	$192 85	
For Oiling Hydrants and Filling Cisterns, 5 months at $75 per month	375 00	
Of Superintendent of Steam Engines, 4 months at $150 per month.....	600 00	
Of Assistant Superintendent of Steam Engines, 4 months at $150 per month	600 00	
		1,767 85
Total, per Report page 10.....		$21,940 33

PURCHASE OF LOTS, ERECTION AND REMOVAL OF ENGINE HOUSES.

Lot on North line of Pacific, 137 feet 6 inches from Jones street, 23 by 60 feet, part 50 vara Lot 877.........	$1,200 00
Deposit of E. Walter for one fourth payment of Engine House and Lot, No. 10, refunded (title defective)...	1,262 50
Carried forward........	$2,462 50

Brought forward		$2,462 50
Purchase of title to same		250 00
Building brick Engine House and Warehouse at Corporation Yard, Sacramento between Drumm and East sts.		13,865 95
Bell Tower and Glass in Engine House No. 9, belonging to old Company . . .		315 00
Commission to Auctioneers on sale of Engine Houses and lots—		
Engine House and Lot No. 3, 1 per cent. on $27,150, United States Tax one-tenth one per cent. $27 15	$298 65	
Engine House and Lot No. 4, 1 per cent. on $16,050	160 50	
Engine House and Lot No. 5, 1 per cent. on $8,000	80 00	
Hose House and Lot No. 1, 1 per cent. on $3,850	38 50	
Hook and Ladder House and Lot No. 1, 1 per cent. on $8,300	83 00	
		660 65
Placing Building purchased of Eureka Hose Company on Lot on Pacific near Jones street (described above)		260 00
Cleaning Engines preparatory to sale .		200 00
House purchased of Rincon Hose Company		850 00
Total, per Report page 10		$18,864 10

NOTE.—Amount at credit of account of purchase of Lots, erection and removal of Engine Houses, June 30, 1865 . . . . $5,921 78

Receipt from sale of Engine House and Lot No. 12, 1865-6 (part payment) 6,325 00

Receipts from sale of Engine Houses and Lots, 1866-7, viz.—

Engine House and Lot No. 3	$27,150 00	
18 inches of Engine Lot No. 1	200 00	
Engine House and Lot No. 4	16,050 00	
Hook and Ladder House and Lot No. 1	8,300 00	
Engine House and Lot No. 5	7,750 00	
Hose House and Lot No. 1	3,850 00	
Carried forward	$63,300 00	$12,246 78

Brought forward	$63,300 00	$12,246 78
Engine Lot on Stockton near Greenwich street..................	300 00	
Engine House and Lot on Sutter street........................	2,075 00	
		65,675 00
Sale of Engine No. 7		1,090 00
		79,011 78
Audited 1865–6...	1,239 43	
Audited 1866–7...	18,864 10	
		20,103 53
Unexpended June 30, 1867		$58,908 25

CISTERNS AND HYDRANTS.

Constructing Cistern corner Pacific and Sansome streets	$1,450 00	
Repairs to Cisterns...	380 71	
		$1,830 71
Setting 60 Hydrants at $60	3,600 00	
Resetting 77 Hydrants at $30	2,310 00	
50 Hydrants purchased............	1,650 00	
Repairs to Hydrants	549 74	
Balance of Bill of $573 80 for setting of Hydrants ($512 64 allowed last year to close appropriation)...........	61 16	
		8,170 90
Total, per Report page 10.		$10,001 61

EXTENSION AND REPAIRS OF FIRE ALARM AND POLICE TELEGRAPH.

3 Bells...	$1,653 15
Bell Tower rear Engine House on Second street....	835 00
Striking Machines, 1, $62 65, 1, $759 60	822 25
Moving and placing Bells.......	356 28
Freight	233 43
Vitriol	110 93
Zinc	72 00
Weights, Hammers, Locks, Keys, Magnets, Armatures, Insulators, Telegraph Wire, etc...........	395 38
Carried forward....................	$4,478 42

4

Brought forward...................	$4,478	42
Fire Alarm Cards.............................	38	00
Sundry disbursements by Superintendent'...... ...	232	00
Total, per Report page 10...................	$4,748	42

Allowance (Statutes 1865-6, page 82)............................		$6,000	00
Audited, 1865-6, on account of said allowance......................	$1,251 58		
Audited, 1866-7..	4,748 42		
		$6,000	00

RECAPITULATION OF ALL DISBURSEMENTS FOR FIRE DEPARTMENT—GENERAL EXPENSES AND PROPERTY PURCHASED.

[Details in previous pages, and in Report. pages 10 and 11.]

Expenses, July 1 to December 1, 1866, under volunteer system...........................:..	$20,000	50
New material—Outfit for Paid Fire Department....	34,986	16
Salaries, December 1, 1866, to July 1, 1867, Paid Fire Department...........................	32,840	28
Running expenses, December 1, 1866, to July 1, 1867, Paid Fire Department......................	21,940	33
Purchase of Lots, erection and removal of Engine Houses	18,864	10
Purchase and erection of Hydrants, etc............	10,001	61
Sundry items in Report, page 10, charged to Fire Department Accounts.......................	13,146	69
Total, as appears by Report page 10,.........	151,779	67
Add amounts for—		
Lighting Engine Houses, December 1, 1866 to June 30, 1867........;. ....:.....	1,110	53
[See Account of Lighting Buildings. Previous to December 1, 1866, charged to Account of Fire Department General Expenses.]		
Sundry items charged to Urgent Necessity Account and Special Fee Fund....................	98	05
Grand total of all accounts incident to Fire Department...........................	$152,988	25

NOTE.—In reduction of the above expenditures, $66,765 was received from sale of Engine Houses and Lots and Engine, making net expenditure for Fire Department, $86,223 25.

REPAIRS TO PUBLIC BUILDINGS.

Repairs to—

City Hall	$5,892	50
Fire Department Buildings......	5,970	50
County Jail	137	00
Total, per Report page 11.	$12,000	00

LIGHTING BUILDINGS.

City Hall, 1 year.............................	$4,959	74
County Jail, 1 year...........................	748	30
Fire Department Buildings, from December 1, 1866, to June 30, 1867, 7 months (balance allowed from allowance for " Fire Department Expenses ").....	1,110	53
Police Stations, 1 year	136	37
City and County Hospital, 1 year...............	7	51
Gas Fixtures..................................	108	85
Total, per Report page 11.	$7,071	30

HOSPITAL SUPPLIES AND EXPENSES, UNDER ALLOWANCE OF $5000 PER MONTH.

[Statutes 1863, p. 169.]

Salaries, 1 year—

Resident Physician, $200 per month	$2,400	00		
Apothecary, $125 per month	1,500	00		
Nurses (10), $30 to $60 per month..	4,555	16		
Interpreter, $30 per month	360	00		
Watchman, $30 per month	360	00		
Waiter, $20 per month	240	00		
Dishwasher, $20 per month	240	00		
Cooks (3), $35, $40, $70 per month.	1,735	47		
Washermen (2), $30, $40 per month.	840	00		
Gatekeeper	308	70		
			$12,539	33
Carried forward........			$12,539	33

Brought forward........		$12,539 33
119,846 Rations, at 24⅝ cents........		29,511 87
Medicines, Surgical Instruments, etc..		3,834 99
Liquors—		
Ale.........................	$210 00	
Claret	38 00	
Brandy	297 50	
Port Wine....................	720 00	
Sherry.......................	168 00	
Whisky.	496 00	
Other Wine..................	51 87	
		1,981 37
Groceries—		
Sugar.......................	110 02	
Soap	333 00	
Lard........................	62 15	
		505 17
Shoes................................		306 00
Pots, Pans, repairs Boilers, Range, etc............		352 00
Coal.................................		73 00
Crockery.............................		60 00
Pulu.................................		171 50
Pails, Brooms, and Brushes		81 00
1 pair Scales, $16, 1 Coffee Mill, $3		19 00
Straw................................		32 75
1 Table and chair and 2 clocks.............		60 00
Matting..............................		24 06
100 Cards "Hospital Regulations"..........		10 65
Horse hire for Hospital Committee..........		10 00
Repairs to Hospital buildings, including gates and lodge for gate keeper.....................		1,557 91
Passage of patient to New York.............		40 00
Flag and halliards....................		42 50
Schedules		80 00
Dry goods, (sheeting, clothing, etc.,).............		2,610 14
Carried forward...................		$53,903 24

Brought forward....................		$53,903 24
Ironing, 12 months, at $35 per month...........		420 00
Sundry disbursements by Resident Physician......		398 60
Total, per Report page 11................		$54,721 84

SUPPLIES FOR SMALL POX HOSPITAL, UNDER ALLOWANCE OF $6,000 PER ANNUM.

[Statutes 1863, p. 169.]

Food		537 40
Wood and axe-helve...............		67 00
Horse feed.......................		25 00
Services of 1 nurse, 1 year, $50 per month	$600 00	
Services of extra nurses...........	36 61	
		636 61
Carriage hire—conveyance of Resident Physician, Hospital Committee and small pox patients..............		513 00
Clothing of Health Inspector destroyed		65 00
Total, per Report page 11.....		$1,844 01

RECAPITULATION OF DISBURSEMENTS FOR HOSPITAL AND ALMSHOUSE PURPOSES.

Supplies for City and County Hospital............	$54,721 84
Salaries of Visiting Physician and Surgeon, City and County Hospital..........................	2,400 00
Supplies for Small Pox Hospital...............	1,844 01
Burials of indigents..........................	1,175 75
Burials and chemical analyses by Coroner.... ...	1,032 25
Land and part payment of buildings for Almshouse and Small Pox Hospital....................	75,393 01
Total, as per Report, page 11............	$136,566 86
Lighting Hospital (in account of Lighting Buildings).	7 51
Grand total..........................	$136,574 37

RECAPITULATION OF DISBURSEMENTS FOR STREET AND ROAD REPAIRS, ETC.

Repairs to streets, (Street Department Fund)......	$28,685 84
Cleaning streets, (Street Department Fund)........	14,770 50
Expenses of office of Superintendent of Streets, (General Fund).............................	15,194 57
City surveying, (General Fund).................	500 00
Road repairs, (General Fund)...................	7,157 79
New Brannan street bridge, (General Fund)........	4,097 00
Removing dead animals from streets, etc., (General Fund, Urgent Necessity account)	685 00
Grand total...........................	$71,090 70

DISBURSEMENTS FOR PUBLIC SQUARES.

Salary of keeper, 3 months at $75 and 10 months at $100 per month............................	$1,225 00
9 Pines..	40 50
5 Barrels lime.................................	13 50
Hose and repairs..............................	18 50
Zinc work on Portsmouth Square...............	75 00
4 Springs for gates...:.......................	35 50
Pipe and labor................................	41 50
500 Pickets, 10 stakes, 50 wire fastenings.........	39 00
Scythe, hay fork, sickle, rake, and hoe...........	5 25
Charged to account of Inclosing and Improving Public Grounds, per Report page 12..............	1,493 75
Charged to account of Improvement of Yerba Buena Park, per Report page 12.....................	2,788 00
Plan and recommendation for a Public Park, (Urgent Necessity Account, page 53)	500 00
	$4,781 75

REGISTRATION AND ELECTION EXPENSES.

Registering 16,550 names, 25c. each..	$4,137 50	
Enrolling 6,955 names, 25c. each....	1,738 75	
		$5,876 25
Carried forward.......		$5,876 25

Brought forward........		$5,876 25
Copying poll lists.................		499 50
250 Copies poll lists...............		1,547 16
Blanks and stationery for registration and election purposes............		424 65
Election expenses under allowance of $75 for each District—election of September 5, 1866..............		1,238 00
Officers of Registration and Election—		
17 Clerks, $18 each..............	306 00	
33 Judges, $15 each, and one $10..	505 00	
35 Extra Clerks, $15 each, and 2 $12 50 each.................	550 00	
		1,361 00
Total, as per Report page 12, under Statutes of 1865-6, pp. 288 and 509		$10,946 56

See items of Urgent Necessity Account, p. 52, for further amounts in excess of the provisions of the Registry and Election Acts of 1865-6. Total, $6,191 25, which, added to the above, makes $17,137 81.

SPECIAL COUNSEL.

Pueblo Suit—		
Fee of J. W. Dwinelle for services commencing in 1863, and including supervision of Transcript on Appeal	$2,000 00	
Fee of T. J. Coffee for services at Washington, procuring dismissal of Appeal	1,000 00	
Printing Brief	1,517 33	
		$4,517 33
City Slip Suits—		
Fee of John W. Dwinelle and Delos Lake, per contract, 7½ per cent. on amount saved to the City by judgments in favor of the same, as per statement following, page 49—on $182,434 89	13,682 60	
Carried forward........	$13,682 60	$4,517 33

Brought forward........	$13,682 60	$4,517 33
Remittiturs from Supreme Court, in cases of Buckley, Des Farges, Herzo, Hoff, and Neuhaus......	462 70	
		14,145 30
O'Neill vs. Kirkpatrick — Tide Land Case—		
Fee of Cornelius Cole and Montgomery Blair.....................	1,000 00	
Fee of Casserly & Barnes	150 00	
		1,150 00
United States vs. De Haro—		
Fee of Cornelius Cole...........		1,000 00
Camanche Claim, on Underwriters—		
Fee of T. N. Cazneau, (retainer)....		800 00
Montgomery Street Extension—		
Fee of Jabish Clement...........		1,000 00
Total paid in 1866–7, per Report page 12		$22,612 63

See Statement of Counsel Fees paid in 11 years ending June 30, 1867, page 50.

STATEMENT OF AMOUNTS SAVED TO THE CITY, BY JUDGMENTS IN FAVOR OF SAME, IN CITY SLIP CASES.

Dates of payments for City Slip Lots.	Suit.	Case decided in Supreme Court.	PRINCIPAL. Amount paid for City Slip Lots.	INTEREST to date of decision 10 per cent. per annum.	TOTAL. Principal and Interest.
1853: Dec. 30	Ainsa vs. City	Mch. 6, 1865	$2,137 50	$2,390 43	
1854 Feb. 27	Ainsa vs. City	Mch. 6, 1865	4,275 00	4,713 18	
April 27	Ainsa vs. City	Mch. 6, 1865	2,137 50	2,320 96	
					$17,974 57
1853 Dec. 27	Des Farges vs. City	July 16, 1866	2,537 50	3,185 26	
1854 Feb. 27	Des Farges vs. City	July 16, 1866	5,075 00	6,285 95	
April 27	Des Farges vs. City	July 16, 1866	2,537 50	3,100 68	
					22,721 89
1853 Dec. 26	Partridge vs. City	Mch. 6, 1865	2,175 00	2,434 79	
1854 Feb. 26	Partridge vs. City	Mch. 6, 1865	4,350 00	4,797 09	
March 8	Partridge vs. City	Mch. 6, 1865	2,175 00	2,391 29	
					18,323 17
1853 Dec. 26	Herzo vs. City	July 16, 1866	4,250 00	5,336 11	
1854 Feb. 1	Herzo vs. City	July 16, 1866	4,250 00	5,294 79	
Feb. 28	Herzo vs. City	July 16, 1866	4,037 50	4,999 77	
March 1	Herzo vs. City	July 16, 1866	4,250 00	5,259 37	
					37,677 54
1853 Dec. 27	Prag vs. City	Mch. 6, 1865	2,275 00	2,546 10	
1854 Jan. 17	Prag vs. City	Mch. 6, 1865	1,848 75	2,058 78	
March 25	Prag vs. City	Mch. 6, 1865	1,144 50	1,252 91	
March 31	Prag vs. City	Mch. 6, 1865	1,556 75	1,702 05	
					14,384 84
1853 Dec. 26	Neuhaus vs. City	July 16, 1866	4,212 50	5,289 02	
1854 Feb. 25	Neuhaus vs. City	July 16, 1866	8,425 00	10,439 98	
					28,366 50

Judgment against City.		Judgment reversed.	Amount of Judgment, 1862.	Interest to date of reversal of Judgment.	
1862 October 2	Hoff vs. City	Dec. 17, 1866	$14,636 89	$6,159 69	20,796 58
October 3	Buckley vs. City	Dec. 17, 1866	15,620 50	6,569 30	22,189 80
			Amount saved.......		182,434 89

Commission of Messrs. Dwinelle & Lake, per contract, 7½ per cent. on amount saved as above (see pages 12 and 47).............. $13,682 60

COUNSEL FEES PAID FROM 1856-7 TO 1866-7, INCLUSIVE.

[Except School Legal Expenses, which have been trifling.]

Pueblo Suit—

1861-2—E. W. F. Sloan and J. W. Dwinelle	$2,000 00	
1863-4—E. W. F. Sloan and J. W. Dwinelle	2,000 00	
1865-6—Cope, Daingerfield & Hambleton	250 00	
1865-6—J. W. Dwinelle..........	250 00	
1866-7—J. W. Dwinelle..........	2,000 00	
1866-7—T. J. Coffee	1,000 00	
		$7,500 00

City Slip Suits—

1857-8—W. Duer and J. P. Hoge	5,000 00	
1859-60—F. M. Haight..........	3,000 00	
1860-1—Shafters & Heydenfeldt .	2,500 00	
1862-3—J. W. Dwinelle and Delos Lake	5,000 00	
1862-3—J. W. Dwinelle and Delos Lake	3,000 00	
1866-7—J. W. Dwinelle and Delos Lake	13,682 60	
		32,182 60

Suits vs. Tax Collector and Commissioners of Funded Debt—

1857-8—Shafters & Heydenfeldt..	2,500 00	
1858-9—Shafters & Heydenfeldt..	2,500 00	
		5,000 00

Suit vs. Tax Collector—1861-2—Guy vs. Washburn		500 00

Suits for Delinquent Taxes—

1862-3—J. B. Felton	6,000 00	
1864-5—D. Lake...............	1,000 00	
		7,000 00

Limantour Suit — 1863-4 — Gregory Yale		3,000 00

Carried forward........	$55,182 60

Brought forward........		$55,182 60
Recovering "Mowry" Property—1863		
–4—J. McHenry		2,000 00
Widening and extending Streets—		
1864–5—Kearny and Third, Alexander Campbell................	$1,000 00	
1866–7—Montgomery street, J. Clement	1,000 00	
		2,000 00
De Haro Suit—		
1865–6—Cope, Daingerfield & Hambleton........................	250 00	
1866–7—Cornelius Cole	1,000 00	
		1,250 00
Suit as to Justices' power to sit as Police Judge during absence of Judge—		
1865–6—N. Bennett.............		150 00
Suit of O'Neill vs. Kirkpatrick—		
1866–7—C.Cole & Montgomery Blair	1,000 00	
1866–7—Casserly & Barnes	150 00	
		1,150 00
Camanche Suit—		
1866–7—T. N. Cazneau		800 00
Total, 11 years...............		$62,532 60

DETAILS OF URGENT NECESSITY ACCOUNT.

[Allowance of $2,000 per month for objects of Urgent Necessity. Statutes 1862, p. 467.]

Salaries—		
Deputy Clerk 15th District Court to June 1, 1867, 11 months, at $175	$1,925 00	
Health Inspector, to June 1, 1867, 11 months, at $120	1,320 00	
Health Officer's Clerk, to July 1, 1867, 1 year	1,200 00	
Sergeant at Arms for Board of Supervisors, to June 1, 1867, 11 months, at $50	550 00	
		$4,995 00

[The above salaries not being provided for by Statute, are allowed by Board of Supervisors out of this account.]

Carried forward........		$4,995 00

Brought forward.......		$4,995 00
Registration and Election Expenses, exceeding statutory allowances—		
17 Clerks' services (extra pay), $100 each	$1,700 00	
30 Judges' services (extra pay), $60 each, extra Judges, $20........	1,820 00	
Expenses bringing Suit to have name enrolled on Poll List—test case ..	14 25	
Advertising....................	1,924 40	
Making duplicate statement of Election Returns	10 00	
Rents of Offices for Boards of Registration	722 60	
[For further amounts see statement of "Registration and Election Expenses."]		
		6,191 25
Advertising—		
For Board of Supervisors, City Printing per contract to December 15, 1866......................	354 15	
For Board of Supervisors, other Printing.....................	636 25	
Auditor's Quarterly Reports.......	20 00	
Treasurer's Monthly Reports	60 00	
Redemption of Bonds, etc., for Treasurer	440 17	
For Tax Collector	888 25	
For Fire Commissioners	7 50	
Advertising and Stationery for Collector of Licenses	336 00	
Advertising and Stationery for Health Office	64 25	
5,000 Municipal License Blanks......	45 00	
		2,851 57
Advertising Kearny Street Notices ...		35 00
Advertising Montgomery Street Notice		82 25
1,000 copies Codified Orders and Consolidation Act..................		1,217 30
Carried forward........		$15,372 37

Brought forward....................	$15,372 37
1,500 copies Municipal Reports, and distributing same (including extra copies of Reports of certain Officers)......................................	2,292 90
Postage for Clerk Board of Supervisors............	3 60
Plan and recommendation for a Public Park.......	500 00
Furniture for City Hall........................	649 50
Furniture for Engine Houses	38 55
Pans, Boilers, repairing Locks, Saws, etc., for County Jail......................................	79 23
2,740 pairs Numbers for Collector of Licenses	411 00
Repairs to Flags and Halliards	26 50
4,500 Street Signs, at 35 cents	1,575 00
Safe for Tax Collector's Office	700 00
Rent of Harbor Police Station, from April 19, 1866, to January 19, 1867, 9 months, at $12	108 00
Water Pipe for Harbor Police Station.............	28 35
Stove Pipe and Furniture for Harbor Police Station..	55 75
Repairs to Harbor Boat Eureka..................	60 50
Cleaning Vaults and removing dead Animals from Streets.....................................	675 00
Rent of Public Pound, 8 months at $10............	80 00
Horse Feed for Horses of Deputy Collectors of Licenses, to June 1, 1867.....................	190 00
Expenses serving Subpœnas and arresting Witnesses in other Counties...........................	111 55
Services of Clerk and serving Subpœnas—Summer street tragedy	20 00
Meals for Jurors	115 50
Expenses bringing a drowned Man from Alcatraz Island..	7 00
Reward for Arrest of Incendiaries	100 00
Cost in Suit for Collection of Delinquent Licenses	90 00
Sundry Law Expenses paid by City and County Attorney, printing Briefs, etc.	120 45
Carried forward....................	$23,410 75

Brought forward....................	$23,410 75
Abstract of Title	20 00
Counting Street Lamps, and making Map for regis-	
tering same................................	40 25
One half expense of moving Building off City Slip	
Lot No. 100, upon which it encroached 7 inches....	20 00
Taxes paid on canceled Mortgage returned.......	55 63
Pumping Water from Redington & Co.'s cellar,	
flooded by grading street adjacent..............	10 00
Coal and Wood for City Hall...................	443 10
Total, per Report page 13...................	$23,999 73

Allowance $24,000 per annum. All Miscellaneous Expenses not provided for by statute, are charged to this account.

MILITARY APPROPRIATIONS ADVANCED FOR STATE OF CALIFORNIA.

Rent of Armory and incidental ex-			
penses—			
Light Battery, April 1, 1866, to June			
30, 1867, 15 months, at $240....			$3,600 00
3 Regiments, April 1, 1866, to June			
30, 1867, 15 months, at $25 each			
per month...................		$1,125 00	
1 Regiment, April 1, 1866, to July			
24, 1866, 3$\frac{24}{31}$ months, at $25......		94 35	
			1,219 35
Companies $50 per month each—			
18, April 1 to October 1, 6 months		$5,400 00	
1, 1$\frac{11}{31}$ months, to October 1......		67 75	
19, October 1 to June 30, 9 months		8,550 00	
1, 2$\frac{8}{30}$ months, April 1 to June 8,			
1866.....................		113 33	
5, 3$\frac{24}{31}$ months, April 1 to July 24,			
1866		943 50	
Carried forward........		$15,074 58	$4,819 35

Brought forward........	$15,074 58	$4,819 35
4, 3$\frac{23}{31}$ months, April 1 to July 23, 1866.....................	748 40	
1, 4 months, April 1 to August 1, 1866......	200 00	
1, 4$\frac{3}{31}$ months, April 1 to August 3, 1866.....................	204 83	
1, 4$\frac{4}{31}$ months, April 1 to August 4, 1866.....................	206 45	
		16,434 26
Total, per Report, page 13....		$21,253 61

Paid by State on account of the above...............	$12,398 61
Balance due June 30, 1867........................	8,855 00
	$21,253 61

ERECTION OF SCHOOL HOUSES, ETC.—SCHOOL FUND—SPECIAL.

Buildings—

Tehama Street..................	$28,324 52
Filbert, between Jones and Taylor Streets......................	17,010 00
Broadway, near Mason Street......	12,470 00
Broadway, between Larkin and Polk Streets......................	5,623 24
Post, between Dupont and Stockton Streets......................	16,095 79
Eighth, between Harrison and Bryant Streets, (part).............	6,185 00
Shotwell, between Twenty-third and Twenty-fourth Streets, (part)....	6,005 00
Union Street...................	2,370 00
Normal, Fifth and Market Streets, (part).......................	1,000 00
West End, (plans)................	18 00
Carried forward........	$95,101 55

Brought forward........	$95,101 55	
Services of architect until buildings were placed under charge of carpenter of School Department, $5\frac{1}{10}$ months, at $150, and 1 month at $100 per month...............	865 00	
		$95,966 55

Lots—

Exchange of school lot 174 for property on Broadway near Mason Street......................	420 00	
Purchase of lot corner Pine and Larkin Streets, 200 feet on Pine by 120 feet on Larkin Street, part W. A. Block No. 14...........	5,989 76	
Purchase of lot on northwest line of Silver, 112 feet southwest from Second, 44 by 70 feet..........	4,000 00	
		$10,409 76
Total, per Report, page 16.....		$106,376 31

EXPENSES INCURRED IN THE MATTER OF WIDENING KEARNY STREET—TO BE RETURNED.

Total July 1, 1866, per report of 1865–6, page 78 (paid in United States coin)..................	$6,866 60
Advertising 1866-7, (see items of Urgent Necessity Account)	35 00
	$6,901 60

EXPENSES INCURRED IN THE MATTER OF WIDENING MERCHANT STREET—TO BE RETURNED.

Total July 1, 1866, per report of 1865-6, page 78— same June 30, 1867, (paid in United States coin) .	$594 00

$792 received in United States Notes, in settlement of the above, July 20.

EXPENSES INCURRED IN THE MATTER OF EXTENDING MONTGOMERY STREET—
TO BE RETURNED.

Counsel Fee $1,000 00
Advertising... .... 82 25

Total, (paid in United States Coin)........ $1,082 25

LIGHTING STREETS, REPAIRS TO LAMPS, ETC.

Month.	Lamps lighted during month equal to, per night, about	Number of Nights.	Amount for Lights, 20 cents each per Night.	Repairs, Lamps, etc.	TOTAL.
July, 1866.	1,820	28	10,192 00	$335 02	$10,527 02
August, 1866.	1,844	28	10,325 40	410 23	10,735 63
September, 1866	1,884	27	10,172 40	414 44	10,586 84
October, 1866.	1,879	28	10,523 60	360 15	10,883 75
November, 1866.	1,886	27	10,186 50	315 31	10,501 81
December, 1866.	1,926	29	11,168 00	489 42	11,657 42
January, 1867.	1,944	28	10,884 20	338 89	11,223 09
February, 1867.	1,953	25	9,767 40	368 47	10,135 87
March, 1867.	1,979	28	11,079 20	462 87	11,542 07
April, 1867.	2,006	27	10,829 80	619 45	11,449 25
May, 1867.	2,026	28	11,342 40	554 08	11,896 48
June, 1867.	2,043	27	11,041 80	465 59	11,507 39
Total, per Report page 15.........			$127,512 70	$5,133 92	$132,646 62

BALANCE OF STREET LIGHT FUND.

Outstanding demand July 1, 1866, p. 27 $10,437 02
Deduct cash on hand July 1, 1866, Re-
    port 1865–6, p. 42...............   10,358 27

                                    78 75
Demands audited, p. 15............   132,646 62

                                   $132,725 37

Receipts, p. 64.................... $111,861 16
Transfer from General Fund, p. 68....   20,864 21
                                   $132,725 37

5

REVENUE FOR THE FISCAL YEAR ENDING JUNE 30, 1867.

APPORTIONED TO THE FOLLOWING FUNDS AND ACCOUNTS.

From	General Fund.	Street Light Fund.	Street Department Fund.	School Fund.	School Fund, Special.	Corporation Debt Fund.	Interest Account, Bonds 1863 & 1864.	Interest Tax Account, S. F. & S. J. R. R. Bonds.	Interest Tax Account, Pacific Railroad Bonds.	Sinking Fund	Total.
Taxes	$516,130 43	$111,861 16	$33,560 26	$261,186 37		$287,829 36	$67,059 67	$29,790 12	$63,331 08	$111,727 86	$1,482,476 31
Poll Taxes	14,003 92			1,932 75							15,936 67
State and County Licenses	93,901 50										93,901 50
Municipal Licenses	21,972 80		9,790 00								31,762 80
Harbor Dues	19,035 30										19,035 30
Sale of City Slip Lots	13,920 00										13,920 00
Sale of Unclaimed Property	1,415 90										1,415 90
Sale of Harbor Boat	350 00										350 00
Quarantine Fees	652 50										652 50
Dog Tax				696 00							696 00
Sale of Bonds				41,318 75	$84,646 63						125,965 38
State School Apportionm't				55,641 60							55,641 60
Total Revenue	$681,382 35	$111,861 16	$43,350 26	$360,775 47	$84,646 63	$287,829 36	$67,059 67	$29,790 12	$63,331 08	$111,727 86	$1,841,753 96

The above Table is made up strictly of Revenues. Cash on hand at the commencement of the year, or received from Loans repaid, or sums which are more properly deductions from Expenditures are not included. These added to revenues make up the sum of money received into the Treasury, as per page 65.

EXPENDITURES DURING THE FISCAL YEAR ENDING JUNE 30, 1867.

CURRENT EXPENSES.

Demands audited on the following
Funds for Current Expenses only—
exclusive of Permanent Improve-
ments, purchase of Lands, etc., and
payment of Debt and Interest—
On General Fund, for all demands
audited except those for entire new
Outfit for Paid Fire Department,
Cisterns and Hydrants, Lots and
Buildings for Fire Department,
Almshouse and Hospital Lot and
Buildings, Camanche Claim, ad-
vance to State for Military Compa-
nies, repayable, and advance in the
matter of Widening Streets $606,684 11
On Special Fee Fund..............   46,217 44
On Street Light Fund............   132,646 62
On Street Department Fund.......   43,456 34
On Pound Fee Fund 900 00
On Police Contingent Fund.......   3,048 11
On School Fund, all demands audit-
ed except those for building and
for improving, and removing legal
incumbrances from Lots.........   283,584 69

  $1,116,537 31

SUMS RECEIVED DIRECTLY APPLICABLE
TO ABOVE EXPENSES.

By Reimbursements—
Fees earned for services, and
paid into the Treasury—
  Fee Officers $131,009 61
  [Salaries paid in lieu of Fees.]
By Pound Keeper.................   496 00
  [Towards Salary.]
Fines, etc., in Police and County
  Courts 30,427 25
  [In reduction of Police Expenses.]

  Carried forward $161,932 86 $1,116,537 61

Brought forward $161,932 86 $1,116,537 31		
Keeping Prisoners of other Counties	1,812 50	
[In reduction of Police Expenses.]		
Sale of Engine No. 7.............	1,090 00	
Lamp Post broken	14 00	
Assessment Expenses—State's pro-		
portion refunded...............	8,424 00	
Hospital Dues—from State towards		
Hospital Expenses	2,533 05	
Rents of School Property..........	1,170 75	
Evening Schools, from pupils, etc.,		
and Fee for changing name	275 10	
Total deductions for Reimbursements.	177,252 26	
Total net Current Expenses.........		$939,285 05

PERMANENT IMPROVEMENTS, PURCHASE OF LANDS, ETC.

[See details in appropriate accounts.]

Demands audited on the following		
Funds—		
General Fund	$139,244 88	
School Fund....................	8,627 56	
School Fund—Special...........	106,376 31	
	254,248 75	
Deduct amount received from Sale of		
Property, viz.—		
Engine Houses and Lots.......... $65,675 00		
School Lot 500 00		
	66,175 00	
Total net Permanent Improve-		
ments, etc.................		188,073 75

CAMANCHE CLAIM.

Construction of iron clad Steamer Ca-		
manche, for Harbor defense.......		71,166 66

REDUCTION OF DEBT.

Demands audited on the following		
Funds and Account—		
Corporation Debt Fund—for Sinking		
Fund Bonds 1851	50,000 00	
Carried forward........	$50,000 00	$1,198,525 26

Brought forward	$50,000 00	$1,198,525 46
Sinking Fund—School Bonds 1860 .	945 00	
Sinking Fund—School Bonds 1861 .	2,057 08	
Sinking Fund—School Bonds 1866 and 1867	15,000 00	
Sinking Fund—Fire Bonds 1854 (exclusive of interest on Bonds redeemed).......................	178,426 25	
Sinking Fund—Bonds 1855........	36,746 50	
Sinking Fund—Bonds 1863 and 1864	53,067 08	
Loan Fund Account—San Francisco and San José Railroad Bonds	18,444 91	
Total		354,686 82

INTEREST ON DEBT.

Demands audited on the following Funds and Accounts—		
Interest Account—School Bonds 1860	$5,623 75	
Interest Account—School Bonds 1861	1,661 56	
Interest Account—School Bonds 1866 and 1867	8,750 00	
Corporation Debt Fund............	146,121 98	
[Including annual Interest paid Fund Commissioners, Debt of 1851, $128,990.)		
Sinking Fund Fire Bonds—Interest due at date of redemption of Bonds.	7,434 19	
Coupon Account—Bonds 1858	67,800 00	
Coupon Account—Bonds 1863 and 1864	65,730 00	
Interest Tax Account—San Francisco and San José Railroad Bonds	19,670 00	
Interest Tax Account—Pacific Railroad Bonds....................	43,925 00	
	366,716 48	
Carried forward........	$366,716 48	$1,553,212 28

Brought forward......		$366,716 48	$1,553,212 28

Deduct Interest received and Profits,
as below—

Interest received by Treasurer......	$17,923 86		
Profits of Fund Commission of 1851—			
The amount of Sinking Fund June 30, 1867, is......... $1,030,588 50			
The amount of Sinking Fund June 30, 1866, was....... 895,148 94			

The difference being profits, or interest received............... 135,439 56

Total Interest and profits for the year,........ 153,363 42

Total net Interest on Debt............... 213,353 06

Total net Expenditures..................... $1,766,565 34

RECAPITULATION OF NET EXPENDITURES.

Current Expenses...	$939,285 05
Permanent Improvements, purchase of Lots, etc..............	188,073 75
Camanche Claim...	71,166 66
Reduction of Debt..	354,686 82
Interest on Debt..	213,353 06
Total net Expenditures as above......................	$1,766,565 34

JOSEPH S. PAXSON, TREASURER, IN CASH ACCOUNT WITH AUDITOR, FOR CITY AND COUNTY MONEYS, FOR THE FISCAL YEAR ENDING JUNE 30, 1867.

Dr.

To Receipts at Credit of the following Funds and Accounts, from the sources named.

GENERAL FUND.

Taxes	$516,130 43
Poll Taxes	14,003 92
State and County Licenses, including Delinquent Licenses collected by District Attorney.................	93,901 50
(See Statement.)	
Municipal Licenses...............	21,972 80
Carried forward.......	$646,008 65

Brought forward........	$646,008 65	
Harbor Dues.....................	19,035 30	
Fines, Police Court................	27,346 75	
Fines, County Court...............	3,075 00	
Sale of City Slip Lots 40, 91, 99, 100,		
111, 112, 113, 114, 115, 116, 118 ..	13,920 00	
Sale of Engine Houses and Lots.....	65,675 00	
(See items of account of "purchase of lots, erection, &c., of engine houses," pages 40 and 41.)		
Sale of Engine No. 7..............	1,090 00	
(See Appendix.)		
Sale of Unclaimed Property in Police Office—sale of 1866..............	1,415 90	
Sale of harbor boat "Eureka".......	350 00	
Keeping Prisoners of other Counties..	1,812 50	
Forfeited Bail....................	5 50	
Lamp Post broken................	14 00	
Assessment expenses, State's proportion	8,424 00	
Rents of Armories and incidental expenses of Military Companies, refunded by State................	12,398 61	
Quarantine Fees..................	652 50	
Hospital Dues, from State..........	2,533 05	
		$803,756 76

SPECIAL FEE FUND.

Fees of City and County Officers—		
Recorder......................	$43,237 25	
County Clerk..................	36,616 95	
Sheriff.......................	16,720 73	
Auditor	2,524 00	
Treasurer.....................	13,118 73	
Tax Collector..................	16,133 30	
Clerk Board of Supervisors.........	854 65	
Clerk Police Court..............	1,740 00	
District Attorney...............	64 00	
		131,009 61

Carried forward........	$934,766 37

Brought forward......		$934,766 37

STREET LIGHT FUND.

Taxes		111,861 16

STREET DEPARTMENT FUND.

Taxes	$33,560 26	
Licenses on Vehicles..............	9,790 00	
		43,350 26

POUND FEE FUND.

Pound Fees......................		496 00

SCHOOL FUND.

Taxes	$261,186 37	
Poll Taxes......................	1,932 75	
Dog Tax.........................	696 00	
Rents of Lots...................	1,170 75	
Evening Schools	257 60	
Sale of Lot.....................	500 00	
Fee for Changing Name............	17 50	
Sale of 50,000 Bonds.............	41,318 75	
State apportionment of School Revenue	55,641 60	
		362,721 32

SCHOOL FUND—SPECIAL.

Sale of Bonds...................		84,646 63

CORPORATION DEBT FUND.

Taxes		287,829 36

INTEREST ACCOUNT—BONDS 1863 AND 1864.

Taxes		67,059 67

INTEREST TAX ACCOUNT—SAN FRANCISCO AND SAN JOSE RAIL-ROAD BONDS.

Taxes		29,790 12

Carried forward....................		$1,922,520 89

Brought forward $1,922,520 89

INTEREST TAX ACCOUNT—PACIFIC RAILROAD BONDS.

Taxes 63,331 08

SINKING FUND—SCHOOL BONDS 1860.

Loans returned....................	$12,350 00	
Interest	2,061 90	
		14,411 90

SINKING FUND—SCHOOL BONDS 1861.

Loans returned....................	$13,500 00	
Interest	767 52	
		14,267 52

SINKING FUND—FIRE BONDS 1854.

Loans returned....................	$234,965 00	
Interest	13,013 20	
		247,978 20

SINKING FUND—BONDS 1855.

Taxes	$37,239 55	
Loans returned....................	31,000 00	
Interest	1,211 83	
		69,451 38

SINKING FUND—BONDS 1863 AND 1864.

Taxes	$55,877 74	
Loans returned....................	47,975 00	
Interest	869 41	
		104,722 15

LOAN FUND ACCOUNT—SAN FRANCISCO AND SAN JOSE RAIL-ROAD BONDS.

Taxes 18,610 57

Total receipts into Treasury.. $2,455,293 69

[Including loans returned.] See Revenue Statement.

To cash on hand July 1, 1866 .... 156,754 11

Grand Total of Debits $2,612,047 80

Cr.

By Payments at debit of the following Funds and Accounts, for demands redeemed.

General Fund.....................	$827,480	38
Special Fee Fund.................	45,764	01
Street Light Fund................	131,576	25
Street Department Fund...........	43,155	94
Pound Fee Fund..................	900	00
Police Contingent Fund...........	2,983	50
School Fund.....................	293,097	92
School Fund—special.............	101,358	31
Interest Account—School Bonds 1860	5,623	75
Interest Account—School Bonds 1861	1,661	56
Interest Account—School Bonds 1866 and 1867......................	8,750	00
Corporation Debt Fund............	196,814	48
Coupon Account—Bonds 1858.......	67,800	00
Interest Account—Bonds 1863 and 1864	65,730	00
Interest Tax Account—San Francisco and San José Railroad Bonds......	19,670	00
Interest Tax Account—Pacific Railroad Bonds...................	43,925	00
Sinking Fund—School Bonds 1860...	18,145	00
Sinking Fund—School Bonds 1861...	16,457	08
Sinking Fund—School Bonds 1866 and 1867......................	15,000	00
Sinking Fund—Fire Bonds 1854.....	243,860	44
Sinking Fund—Bonds 1855.........	67,746	50
Sinking Fund—Bonds 1863 and 1864.	104,042	08
Sinking Fund (Loan Fund Account)— San Francisco and San José Railroad Bonds....................	18,444	91
Total payments from Treasury (including loans from sinking funds)..................	$2,339,987	11

[See Statement of Expenditures.]

Carried forward........ $2,339,987 11

Payments brought forward............ $2,339,987 11

By Cash on hand, June 30, 1867, at credit of the following Funds and Accounts.

General Fund	$132,368	55
Special Fee Fund...............	3,321	26
Street Light Fund	11,507	39
Street Department Fund.........	194	32
Pound Fee Fund	S3	00
• Police Contingent Fund	89	56
School Fund........,............	20,990	67
School Fund—Special...........	3,202	52
Interest Account—School Bonds 1860	51	12
Interest Account—School Bonds 1861	178	94
Interest Account — School Bonds 1866-7	1,750	00
Corporation Debt Fund..........	50,052	73
Coupon Account—Bonds 1858.....	1,095	00
Interest Account—Bonds 1863 and 1864.......................	5,096	38
Interest Tax Account—San Francisco and San José Railroad Bonds .	9,512	21
Interest Tax Account—Pacific Railroad Bonds	26,222	84
Sinking Fund—School Bonds 1860.	1,556	4S
Sinking Fund—School Bonds 1861.·	526	13
Sinking Fund—Bonds 1855.......	2,584	67
Sinking Fund—Bonds 1863 and 1864	903	35
Loan Fund Account—San Francisco and San José Railroad Bonds....	773	57

272,060 69

Grand Total of Credits...... $2,612,047 80

NOTE.—The above balance of Cash on hand is subject to disbursements in July of about $120,000.

TRANSFER ENTRIES—FISCAL YEAR 1866-67.

To General Fund—
From Special Fee Fund.......... $84,792 17

[See balance of Special Fee Fund, page 78.]

Carried forward........ $84,792 17

Brought forward	$84,792 17	
From Police Contingent Fund—		
Amount unexpended of appropriation of $3,600 for 1866-7	551 89	
From Sinking Fund—Fire Bonds—		
Balance after redemption of Fire Bonds	4,260 24	
		$89,604 30
From General Fund—		
To Street Light Fund, to provide for deficiency	20,864 21	
[Statutes 1862, page 468. See page 57.]		
To Pound Fee Fund, to provide for deficiency	441 00	
[Statutes 1863-4, page 502.]		
To Police Contingent Fund—Annual appropriation 1866-67	3,600 00	
		24,905 21
From School Fund—		
To School Fund, Special	$19,914 20	
To Interest Account, School Bonds 1860	5,674 87	
To Interest Account, School Bonds 1861	1,840 50	
To Interest Account, School Bonds 1866-7	10,500 00	
To Sinking Fund, School Bonds 1860	5,000 00	
To Sinking Fund, School Bonds 1861	2,500 00	
To Sinking Fund, School Bonds 1866-7	15,000 00	
		$60,429 57
From Corporation Debt Fund to Coupon Account, Bonds 1858, annual interest...................		$68,010 00
From Interest Tax Account, S. F. and S. J. Railroad Bonds, to Loan Fund Account, S. F. and S. J. Railroad Bonds.............................		$607 91

From Pacific Railroad Loan Fund Account to Pacific
Railroad Interest Tax Account, transfer of amount
at credit July 1, 1866........................ $6,816 76

SUMMARY OF LOAN ACCOUNTS—FISCAL YEAR 1866-7.

[Loans are made on security of United States, State, and City and County Bonds.]

.	Sinking Fund School Bonds 1860.	Sinking Fund School Bonds 1861.	Sinking Fund Fire Bonds.	Sinking Fund Bonds 1855.	Sinking Fund Bonds 1863 and 1864.
Loans outstanding July 1, 1866, per last report	$11,900 00	$6,350	$176,965		$2,000 00
Loans effected during the Fiscal Year 1866-7.......	17,200 00	14,400	58,000	$31,000	50,975 00
	29,100 00	20,750	234,965	31,000	52,975 00
Loans paid during the Fiscal Year 1866-7............	12,350 00	13,500	234,965	31,000	47,975 00
Loans outstanding June 30, 1867....................	$16,750 00	$7,250			$5,000 00
Interest due June 30, 1867..	$11 73				$29 16

STATEMENT OF LOANS FROM SINKING FUNDS, WITH INTEREST, FISCAL YEARS 1865-6 AND 1866-7 COMBINED; INCLUDING LOANS OUTSTANDING JULY 1, 1865.

SINKING FUND—SCHOOL BONDS 1854.

Number of Note.	Date of Note.	Amount of Note.	When Paid.	Interest from	Amount of Interest Paid.
1	June 30, 1862	$2,400	September 14, 1865	December 27, 1863, to September 14, 1865......	$411 30
2	November 29, 1862	2,100	September 14, 1865	December 26, 1863, to September 14, 1865......	360 50
3	September 5, 1864	2,000	September 7, 1865	September 5, 1864, to September 7, 1865......	241 33
4	December 2, 1864	2,000	July 1.	1865 Paid in previous Fiscal Year.	
5	December 23, 1864	1,300	September 16, 1865	April 23, 1865, to September 16, 1865......	62 40
6	May 8, 1865	5,000	September 26, 1865	May 8, 1865, to September 26, 1865......	230 00
7	July 1, 1865	600	September 12, 1865	July 1, 1865, to September 12, 1865......	14 20
8	August 19, 1865	18,360	September 16, 1865	August 19, 1865, to September 16, 1865......	142 80
				Total interest collected during fiscal years 1865-6 and 1866-7 (Sinking Fund School Bonds 1854)............	$1,462 53

Notes and interest paid in full.

Interest accrued and outstanding, July 1, 1865, $966.07. Accrued since July 1, 1865, $496.46.

STATEMENT OF LOANS CONTINUED.—SINKING FUND—SCHOOL BONDS 1860.

Number of Note.	Date of Note.	Amount of Note.	When Paid.	Interest from	Amount of Interest Paid.
1	December 1, 1864	$ 400	*ust 1, 1865	July 1, to August 1, 1865	$ 4 00
2	April 26, 1865	2,700	*er 11, 1866	*ril 26, 1865, to *er 11, 1866	526 50
3	August 19, 1865	4,000	Outstanding.	*ust 19, 1865, to *ust 19, 1867	800 00
4	*er 30, 1865	1,300	{July 19,1866,$650 / Aug. 2, 1866, $650}	Sept. 30, 1865, to July 19, 1866, on $650 / Sept. 30, 1865, to *ust 2, 1866, on $650	133 25
5	October 20, 1865	3,000	*pil 4, 1866	t*0er 20,1865, to *pil 4, 1866	136 67
6	January 22, 1866	400	Jan. 9, 1867, $150. / *ing, $250	H*nary 22,1866, to H*nary 9, 1867, on $150. / *ry 22,1866, to *ary 22, 1867, on $250.	17 25 / 42 50
7	April 9, 1866	3,500	May 25, 1866	*pil 9, to June 22, 1866	40 25
8	J*ne 5, 1866	3,500	*er 31, 1866	*une 5, to May 25, 1866	141 94
9	July 22, 1866	1,000	*ing,	July 22, 1866, to *toher 31, 1867	93 87
10	October 28, 1866	4,700	*er 17, 1866	*er 28, to *er 17, 1866	76 75
11	October 31, 1866	4,500	Outstanding.	*er 31, 1866, to June 30, 1867	283 81
12	December 31, 1866	6,500	Outstanding.	*er 31, 1866, to June 30, 1867	307 03
13	April 23,	500	Outstanding.	Decem'r 31, 1866, to June 30, 1867	
		$16,750			$2,603 82

Total interest collected, fiscal years 1865–6 and 1866–7 (Sinking Fund School Bonds 1860)............ $2,603 82

Of the above amount of interest $450 was due and unpaid July 1, 1865.

NOTES AND INTEREST UNPAID—SINKING FUND SCHOOL BONDS 1860.

Number of Note.	Amount of Note.	When Paid.	Amount accrued interest to June 30, 1867.
3	$4,000	Interest paid to August 19, 1867............	$ 0 58
6	250	Interest June 22 to 30, 1867............	
9	1,000	Interest paid to June 30, 1867............	
11	4,500	Interest paid to June 30, 1867............	
12	6,500	Interest paid to June 30, 1867............	11 15
13	500	Interest April 23 to June 30, 1867............	
	$16,750		$11 73

STATEMENT OF LOANS CONTINUED.—SINKING FUND—SCHOOL BONDS 1861.

Number of Note.	Date of Note.	Amount of Note.	When paid.	Interest from	Amount of Interest paid.
1	May 8, 1865	1,500	...il 4, 1866	April 4, 1865, to May 8, 1866	$135 83
2	...er 4, 1865	1,000	...er 3, 1866	...er 4, 1865, to ...er 3, 1866	149 67
3	...er 12, 1865	600	Mch 1, 1866	...er 12, 1865, to Mch 12, 1866	33 80
4	...er 21, 1865	2,800	...il 4, 1866	...er 21, 1865, to April 4, 1866	126 78
5	April 9, 1866	5,000	...ay 25, 1866	April 9, to May 25, 1866	57 50
6	May 2, 1866	350	Outstanding.	May 2, 1866, to July 2, 1867	49 00
7	June 5, 1866	5,000	...er 31, 1866	...ne 5, 1866, to ...er 31, 1866	202 78
8	...er 31, 1866	7,500	...er 31, 1866	...er 31, 1866, to ...er 31, 1866	118 75
9	...er 31, 1866	1,000	...ng.	...er 31, 1866, to ...ne 30, 1867	47 24
10	January 3, 1867	5,900	...ng.	...ay 3, to ...ne 30, 1867	290 08
					$1,211 43

Total Interest collected, Fiscal Years 1865–6, 1866–7, (Sinking Fund—School Bonds 1861).............. $1,211 43

Of the above amount of Interest $26 50 was due and unpaid July 1, 1865.

NOTES AND INTEREST UNPAID—SINKING FUND SCHOOL BONDS 1861.

6	$350 00	Interest paid to July 2, 1867
9	1,000 00	Interest paid to June 30, 1867
10	5,900 00	Interest paid to June 30, 1867
	$7,250 00	

STATEMENT OF LOANS CONTINUED.—SINKING FUND—FIRE BONDS 1854.

Number of Note.	Date of Note.	Amount of Note.	When paid.	Interest from	Amount of Interest paid.
1	?er 23, 1861	900	?er 10, 1866	?nary 23, 1865, to ?r 10, 1866	$185 00
2	December 31, 1861	3,600	December 16, 1865	May 31, 1865, to ?er 16, 1865	234 00
3	?une 23, 1862	6,600	October 15, 1866	?er 23, 1863, to October 15, 1866	
4	July 3, 1862	4,500	?er 15, 1866	?er 3, 1863, to October 15, 1866	
5	July 7, 1862	6,000	October 15, 1866	?er 7, 1863, to ?er 15, 1866	
6	July 12, 1862	3,600	October 11, 1866	?er 12, ?8, to October 11, 1866	8,955 20
7	September 2, 1862	1,200	December 16, 1865	?er 2, ?8, to December 16, 1865	
8	September 16, 1862	2,100	December 16, 1865	?er 16, 8?3, to December 16, 1865	
9	September 26, 1862	4,800	October 15, 1866	?er 26, 1863, to October 15, 1866	
10	February 18, 1863	3,850	October 15, 1866	December 18, ?63, to ?r 15, 1866	130 80
11	?er 22, 1862	300	June 9, 1866	O?er 22, 1862, to June 9, 1866	516 00
12	?u?ry 2, 1863	2,400	?er 16, 1866	J?nary 2, 1866, to ?er 16, 1866	1,076 25
13	July 2, 1863	5,250	December 20, 1865	?er 2, 1863, to ?er 20, 1865	1,550 00
14	May 7, 1864	7,500	M?h 22, 1866	July 1, 1864, to Mch 22, 1866	1,910 66
15	September 1, 1864	8,000	October 15, 1866	September 1, ?64, to ?er 15, 1866	
16	September 2, 1864	9,100	M ar?h 21, 1866	September 2, 1864, to M?h 21, ?66, ...$1,685	
17	September 3, 1864	14,000	August 19, 1865	Less paid on account of interest on Note 16, previous to July 1, 1865 ...... 490 ?er 3, 1864, to August 19, 1865. $1,194 67 Less Interest on payment on account of principal ... 85 50	1,195 00
18	September 5, 1864	975	July 2, 1866, 8?6,	May 5, 1865, to July 2, 1866, on $650; 1865, to ?er 13, 8?6, on 325	1,109 17
19	December 1, 1864	600	October 11, 1866	July 1, 1865, to October 11, 1866	84 50
20	December 23, 1864	3,000	O ?ber 15, 1866	June 23, 1865, to October 15, 1866	52 79
21	January 3, 1865	2,000	O ?ber 31, 1866	?5, to October 31, 1866	92 00
22	February 28, 1865	5,000	July 3, 1865	February 28, 1865, to July 3, 1865	604 50
23	April 6, 1865	650	August 2, 1865	May 6, 1865, to August 2, 1865	338 60
24	August 30, 1865	49,640	May 16, 1866	?t 30, 1865, to May 16, 1866	208 33 18 63 3,544 12
25	September 6, 1865	1,400	October 31, 1866	September 6, 1865, to October 31, 1866	193 20
					$21,998 75

Carried forward............

STATEMENT OF LOANS CONTINUED.—SINKING FUND—FIRE BONDS 1854—CONCLUDED.

Number of Note.	Date of Note.	When paid.	Amount of Note.	Interest from	Amount of Interest paid.
				Brought forward	$ 298 75
26	September 7, 1865	October 15, 1866	$2,000	1865, to Mar 15, 1866	4 17
27	September 15, 1865	May 9, 1866	18,360	1865, to May 9, 1866	1,193 38
28	Sber 26, 1865	April 4, 1866	5,000	September 26, 1865, to April 4, 1866	81 11
29	Ober 11, 1865	April 4, 1866	2,100	Ober 11, 1865, to April 4, 1866	240 27
30	Ober 21, 1865	May 25, 1866	1,200	Ober 21, 1865, to May 25, 1866	95 08
31	Ober 28, 1865	Ober 15, 1866	5,000	Ober 28, 1865, to May 15, 1866	58 67
32	December 5, 1865	October 15, 1866	2,500	Ober 5, 1865, to October 15, 1866	430 56
33	December 8, 1865	April 20, 1866	12,000	Der 8, 1865, to April 20, 1866	23 19
34	December 20, 1865	May 25, 1866	800	Der 20, 1865, to May 25, 1866	400 00
35	January 28, 1866	October 31, 1866	600	January 28, 1866, to April 20, 1866	26 08
36	March 20, 1866	June 7, 1866	2,835	Mch 20, 1866, to October 31, 1866	44 20
37	Mch 19, 1866	May 3, 1866	11,840	Mch 19, 1866, to June 7, 1866	73 71
38	April 7, 1866	May 25, 1866	16,500	April 7, 1866, to May 3, 1866	77 00
39	April 9, 1866	May 25, 1866	12,000	April 9, 1866, to May 25, 1866	189 75
40	April 24, 1866	May 17, 1866	5,000	April 24, 1866, to May 25, 1866	93 00
41	May 7, 1866	October 15, 1866	3,200	May 7, 1866, to May 25, 1866	22 25
42	May 9, 1866	Ober 15, 1866	10,000	May 9, 1866, to May 17, 1866	6 40
43	May 15, 1866	Mar 15, 1866	13,000	May 15, 1866, to October 15, 1866	46 67
44	May 20, 1866	June 5, 1866	17,000	May 20, 1866, to October 15, 1866	34 30
45	May 21, 1866	October 31, 1866	16,500	May 21, 1866, to Mar 15, 1866	680 00
46	May 27, 1866	October 15, 1866	58,000	May 27, 1866, to June 5, 1866	41 25
47	June 3, 1866	Ober 29, 1866	12,500	June 3, 1866, to Ober 31, 1866	2,385 56
48	June 4, 1866	June 12, 1866	4,740	June 4, 1866, to Ober 15, 1866	458 33
49	June 7, 1866	Ober 9, 1866	2,500	June 7, 1866, to Ober 29, 1866	186 37
50	June 9, 1866	June 12, 1866	3,000	June 9, 1866, to June 12, 1866	2 75
51	June 15, 1866	Ober 9, 1866	58,000	June 15, 1866, to Ober 9, 1866	95 00
52	Ober 31, 1866	June 29, 1867		1867, to June 29, 1867	3,658 03
					$34,105 83

Total Interest collected during fiscal years 1865-6 and 1866-7 (Sinking Fund—Fire Bonds)............

Notes and Interest paid in full. Interest accrued and outstanding July 1,1865, $9,723 83; accrued since July 1, 1865, $24,382.

STATEMENT OF LOANS CONTINUED.—SINKING FUND—BONDS 1855.

Number of Note.	Date of Note.	Amount of Note.	When Paid.	Interest from	Amount of Interest Paid.
1	October 20, 1865	$16,900	April 4, 1866	October 20, 1865, to April 4, 1866	$769 50
2	December 5, 1865	1,000	March 20, 1866	December 5, 1865, to March 20, 1866	35 00
3	August 18, 1866	9,000	December 7, 1866	August 18, 1866, to December 7, 1866	272 50
4	November 11, 1866	22,000	November 30, 1866	November 11, 1866, to November 30, 1866	139 33

Total interest collected, accrued during fiscal years 1865-6 and 1866-7 (Sinking Fund—Bonds 1855)............ $1,216 33

Notes and interest paid in full.

SINKING FUND—BONDS 1863 AND 1864.

Number of Note.	Date of Note.	Amount of Note.	When Paid.	Interest from	Amount of Interest Paid.
1	Mar 12, 1865	$22,300	April 4, 1866	Mar 12, 1865, to April 4, 1866	$1,071 64
2	Mar 20, 1865	20,000	April 4, 1866	October 20, 1865, to April 4, 1866	910 13
3	Mar 8, 1866	2,100	March 20, 1866	March 8, to 20, 1866	8 40
4	May 22, 1866	1,300	Mar 3, 1866	May 22, to 3, 1866	82 77
5	June 1, 1866	700	Mar 3, 1866	June 1, to 3, 1866	42 45
6	August 18, 1866	13,000	Mar 7, 1866	August 18, to 7, 1866	393 61
7	October 28, 1866	21,300	December 7, 1866	October 28, to 7, 1866	230 75
8	Mar 11, 1866	11,000	Nov 30, 1866	30, to 30, 1866	69 67
9	January 26, 1867	675	March 5, 1867	January 26, to Mar 5, 1867	8 50
10	May 9, 1867	5,000	Outstanding.	May 9, to June 9, 1867	41 66

Total interest collected, accrued during fiscal years 1865-6 and 1866-7 (Sinking Fund—Bonds 1863 and 1864)........ $2,859 58

NOTE AND INTEREST UNPAID—SINKING FUND—BONDS 1863 AND 1864.

| No. 10 | .... | $5,000 | .... | Interest from June 9 to 30, 1867............ | $29 16 |

STATEMENT OF STATE AND COUNTY LICENSES ISSUED DURING
THE FISCAL YEAR ENDING JUNE 30, 1867.

		Term.	Value each.	At credit of State of California.	At credit of City County.
3 Merchandise....	1st Class.	3 months	$150 00	$ 225 00	$ 225 00
3 Merchandise....	2d Class.	3 months	112 50	168 75	168 75
26 Merchandise....	3d Class.	3 months	75 00	975 00	975 00
11 Merchandise....	4th Class.	3 months	60 00	330 00	330 00
27 Merchandise....	5th Class.	3 months	45 00	607 50	607 50
91 Merchandise....	6th Class.	3 months	30 00	1,365 00	1,365 00
153 Merchandise....	7th Class.	3 months	22 50	1,721 25	' 1,721 25
348 Merchandise....	8th Class.	3 months	15 00	2,610 00	2,610 00
9th and 10th Classes below.					
4 Bankers........	1st Class.	3 months	300 00	600 00	600 00
13 Bankers........	2d Class.	3 months	180 00	1,170 00	1,170 00
2 Bankers........	3d Class.	3 months	120 00	120 00	120 00
6 Bankers........	4th Class.	3 months	75 00	225 00	225 00
39 Bankers........	5th Class.	3 months	45 00	877 50	877 50
64 Brokers	5th Class.	3 months	15 00	480 00	480 00
68 Brokers	6th Class.	3 months	3 00	102 00	102 00
*41 Pawnbrokers....		3 months	30 00	615 00	615 00
159 Billiard.........	1 Table...	3 months	5 00	397 50	397 50
41 Billiard.........	2 Tables..	3 months	10 00	205 00	205 00
10 Billiard.........	3 Tables..	3 months	15 00	75 00	75 00
12 Billiard.........	4 Tables..	3 months	20 00	120 00	120 00
12 Billiard.........	5 Tables..	3 months	25 00	150 00	150 00
13 Billiard.........	6 Tables..	3 months	30 00	195 00	195 00
7 Bowling........	1 Alley...	3 months	5 00	17 50	17 50
14 Bowling........	2 Alleys ..	3 months	10 00	70 00	70 00
5 Bowling........	4 Alleys ..	3 months	20 00	50 00	50 00
57 Theater.........		1 day....	5 00	142 50	142 50
5 Theater.........		1 month.	100 00	250 00	250 00
8 Theater.........		3 months	200 00	800 00	800 00
3 Theater.		1 year...	600 00	900 00	900 00
1 Bull and Bear Fight........		1 day....	25 00	12 50	12 50
41 Home Insurance		3 months	25 00	512 50	512 50
25 Intellig'ce Office.		3 months	50 00	625 00	625 00
[The above are apportioned ½ to State, ½ to City and County,]					
119 Foreign Insur'nce		3 months	25 00	2,975 00	....
4 Auctioneers.....	1st Class..	3 months	400 00	1,066 66	533 34
5 Auctioneers.....	3d Class..	3 months	200 00	666 67	333 33
8 Auctioneers.....	4th Class..	3 months	125 00	666 66	333 34
7 Auctioneers.....	5th Class..	3 months	100 00	466 67	233 33
71 Auctioneers.....	7th Class..	3 months	25 00	1,183 34	591 66
1,480 Merchandise....	9th Class.	3 months	5 00	....	7,400 00
6,377 Merchandise....	10th Class.	3 months	2 00	....	12,754 00
3,652 Bar.............	3d Class..	3 months	15 00	....	54,780 00
13,035 Licenses.......				$23,739 50	$93,673 50
Collections made by District Attorney (no licenses issued)				30 00	228 00

* Pawnbrokers, by decision of County Court, are declared exempt from State and County License; since which the City has imposed a Municipal License.

	$23,769 50	$93,901 50
		23,769 50
Grand total	....	117,671 00

STATEMENT OF STATE POLL TAX RECEIPTS ISSUED 1866-67.

	State.	General Fund.	School Fund.
1866—9,863 Receipts, $2 each...	$19,726 00		
1867—8,154 Receipts, $2 each...	16,308 00		
	$36,034 00		
Tax Collector's Commission, 15 per cent......	5,405 10		
	$30,628 90	$18,377 34	$12,251 56
1866—2,577 Receipts, $3 each..	$7,731 00		
Tax Collector's Commission, 55 cents each....	1,417 35		
	$6,313 65	2,628 54	1,752 36	$1,932 75
		$21,005 88	$14,003 92	$1,932 75

$2 Receipts (less commissions) amounting to $30,628 90, are apportioned, 60 per cent. to State and 40 per cent. to City and County.

$3 Receipts are apportioned thus: $2 of every Receipt same as $2 Receipts; and the extra dollar, 25 cents to Tax Collector, and 75 cents to School Fund.

STATEMENT OF UNITED STATES LEGAL TENDER NOTES, JUNE 30, 1867.

Amount on hand July 1, 1866, per Report 1865–6........................		$62,290 97
Receipts during the fiscal year 1866-7—		
From Sheriff...................	$338 40	
From Clerk of Chief of Police.....	24 90	
		363 30
Payments during the fiscal year 1866-7 for street repairs................	3,409 05	
Balance on hand June 30, 1867......	59,245 22	
	$62,654 27	$62,654 27

STATEMENT OF SPECIAL FEE FUND.

Amount at credit June 30, 1866......		$2,867 83
Fees received during the fiscal year from City and County officers, viz.—		
Recorder........................	$43,237 25	
County Clerk...................	36,616 95	
Sheriff	16,720 73	
Auditor	2,524 00	
Treasurer	13,118 73	
Tax Collector..................	16,133 30	
Clerk Board of Supervisors.......	854 65	
Clerk Police Court..............	1,740 00	
District Attorney...............	64 00	
		131,009 61
		$133,877 44
Demands paid....................		$45,764 01
Transfer to General Fund—Quarterly balances—		
October 1, 1866..................	$16,502 08	
January 1, 1867................	30,043 90	
April 1, 1867..................	17,100 91	
June 30, 1867..................	21,145 28	
		84,792 17
Amount at credit June 30, 1867, to pay outstanding demands.............		3,321 26
		$133,877 44

STATEMENT OF MUNICIPAL LICENSES ISSUED DURING THE
FISCAL YEAR ENDING JUNE 30, 1867, AT CREDIT OF GEN-
ERAL FUND.

Quarterly Licenses, viz. :		
4 Race Licenses	$75 00	
8 Express Licenses	112 50	
Carried forward........	$187 50	

Brought forward	$187	50
30 Laundry Licenses	114	00
15 Shipping Office Licenses	140	00
23 Runners and Soliciting Agents' Licenses	165	00
32 Street Musicians' Licenses....	265	00
28 Assayers' Licenses .. :	280	00
95 Real Estate and House Brokers Licenses	355	00
53 Powder and Pyrotechnic Licenses	510	00
31 Pawn Brokers' Licenses......	1,085	00
[See page 76.]		
29 Merchandise Peddlers' Licenses	1,225	00
122 Slaughter House Licenses	1,359	65
570 Market Stall Licenses	1,417	50
137 Dance Licenses.............	1,697	50
1,014 Meat Shop and Bakery Licenses	2,190	65
1,085 Hotel, Restaurant, and Lodging House Licenses...........	2,204	75
783 Meat, Fish, and Produce Peddlers' Licenses	8,776	25

4,059 Quarterly Licenses issued on 3,463 blanks, as follows, amounting to.....................	$21,972	80

[Several Licenses, as classified above, being issued on one blank in some cases, the number of blanks issued were not as many as the Licenses.]

777 Licenses, $1 25 each	$971	25
1,005 Licenses, $2 each	2,010	00
485 Licenses, $2 50 each	1,212	50
51 Licenses, $3 each	153	00
7 Licenses, $4 each	28	00
116 Licenses, $5 each	580	00
54 Licenses, $7 50 each	405	00
21 Licenses, $8 each	168	00
359 Licenses, $10 each	3,590	00
8 Licenses, $12 50 each	100	00
Carried forward....................	$9,217	75

Brought forward....................	$9,217 75
58 Licenses, $15 each	870 00
285 Licenses, $20 each	5,700 00
30 Licenses, $25 each	750 00
18 Licenses, $30 each	540 00
31 Licenses, $35 each	1,085 00
17 Licenses, $50 each	850 00
12 Licenses, $75 each	900 00
4 Licenses, $112 50 each	450 00
3 Licenses, each $2 20, $4 20, $4 70, $5 25...	49 05
2 Licenses, each $1 10, $1 50, $1 80, $3 15, $3 50, $3 90, $4 30, $4 55, $4 65.......	57 00
2 Licenses, each $6 25, $7 30, $7 80, $8 25, $12 35, $15 40, $15 75, $19 30, $37 50, $70	399 80
1 License each 65 cents, $1 40, $2 35, $2 45, $2 60, $2 85, $3 05, $3 20, $3 35, $3 60, $3 65, $3 70, $3 75, $3 85, $4 40, $5 20, $6 50, $6 55, $6 80, $6 85, $7 20, $7 65, $7 70, $8 10, $8 30, $8 45, $8 50, $8 60, $8 65, $8 75, $9 25, $9 75	177 65
1 License each $10 25, $10 55, $11 20, $11 40, $11 50, $12, $12 30, $12 75, $12 90, $13 25, $14, $14 20, $14 40, $14 65, $15 15, $15 25, $16 70, $16 90, $17 40, $17 50, $17 60, $17 80, $18 20, $18 65, $18 90, $19 15, $19 50.....................	404 05
1 License each $21 30, $21 50, $23 15, $23 60, $23 75, $24 15, $24 75, $25 65, $26 25, $26 95, $31 40, $32 50, $33 25, $34 30, $72 50, $77 50 ..:..................	522 50
Amount as above	$21,972 80

AT CREDIT OF STREET DEPARTMENT FUND.

Annual Licenses, viz.:

100 Laundry Wagon, Sprinkler, and Hand Cart Licenses.............................	$111 75
Carried forward........	$111 75

Brought forward........	$111	75
129 Drivers' Licenses	129	00
New Numbers for Vehicles, 207 pairs	207	00
146 Coach, Hack, Omnibus, and Coupé Licenses .	821	50
324 Double Wagon and Truck Licenses........	984	75
826 Grocery, Milk, Bakers', and Market Wagon Licenses.............................	1,002	25
1,840 Single Wagon, Truck, Dray, and Cart Licenses	3,016	00
Quarterly Licenses—		
272 Street Railroad Car Licenses..............	3,525	00
3,637 Licenses...............................	$9,797	25

[$7 25 overpaid last year (see Report of 1865-6, page 54), which, deducted from the above amount, leaves $9,790 placed at credit of Street Department Fund, as per Treasurer's Report, page 64.]

The above Licenses were issued on 2,676 blanks of the several amounts below,

12 at 50 cents each........................	6	00
654 at $1..................................	654	00
155 at $1 25..............................	193	75
819 at $1 50..............................	1,228	50
130 at $1 90..............................	247	00
94 at $2..................................	188	00
145 at $2 25..............................	326	25
181 at $2 50..............................	452	50
165 at $3..................................	495	00
10 at $3 25..............................	32	50
42 at $3 75..............................	157	50
53 at $4 50..............................	238	50
85 at $5..................................	425	00
9 at $6..................................	54	00
6 at $6 75..............................	40	50
12 at $7 50..............................	90	00
5 at $9..................................	45	00
18 at $10..................................	180	00
5 at $12..................................	60	00
6 at $12 50..............................	75	00
Carried forward........	$5,189	00

Brought forward....................	$5,189	00
7 at $15.................................	105	00
8 at $275................................	2,200	00
3 each $4, $8, $13 50, $16 50, $212 50.......	763	50
2 each $11, $11 50, $14, $17 50, $18, $20, $24, $30, $112 50..........................	517	00
1 each 50 cents, $5 25, $5 50, $6 25, $9 50, $10 50, $12, $14 50, $15 75, $16, $18 75, $23, $23 50, $25, $25 50, $33, $40, $43 75 $50, $75, $137 50, $225...............	815	75
207 new Numbers.........................	207	00
	$9,797	25

JOSEPH S. PAXSON, TREASURER, IN CASH ACCOUNT WITH AU-
DITOR, FOR STATE MONEY FOR THE FISCAL YEAR ENDING
JUNE 30, 1867.

	Dr.	**Cr.**
Dr.		
To Receipts on account of the State of		
California from Taxes	$848,777 32	
[See Apportionment, page 87.]		
Poll Taxes	21,005 88	
[See Apportionment, page 77.]		
Tax on Premiums of Insurance	17,144 70	
[Items forward, page 84.]		
State and County Licenses........	23,769 50	
[See page 76.]		
Passenger Brokers' Licenses.......	11,185 67	
Stamps........................	65,222 70	
Total Receipts	987,105 77	
To Cash on hand July 1, 1866	57,023 73	
Cr.		
By settlements with Controller of State—		
July 24, 1866..................		$57,023 73
October 20, 1866		296,537 61
November 8, 1866		440,149 48
January 11, 1867..............		129,340 24
April 9, 1867		57,161 27
		$980,212 33
By Cash on hand June 30, 1867		63,917 17
	$1,044,129 50	$1,044,129 50

TAX ON PREMIUMS OF INSURANCE.

FIRE AND MARINE INSURANCE.

Name of Company.	Gross Premiums. Coin.	Tax 2 per cent. Coin.
Ætna..	$32,315 06	$646 30
Arctic	4,126 54	82 52
British and Foreign..........................	28,774 00	575 48
Continental	14,982 00	299 64
Columbian...................................	9,501 00	190 02
Hamburg Bremen	54,424 95	1,088 50
Hartford....................................	23,168 12	463 36
Home	44,991 09	899 82
Imperial....................................	75,209 00	1,504 18
Liverpool and London and Globe...............	87,359 66	1,747 19
Manhattan..................................	27,988 87	559 77
Northern Assurance	8,674 97	173 50
North American..............................	4,252 00	85 04
North British and Mercantile..................	43,270 62	865 41
Pacific Mutual	10,745 00	214 90
Phœnix, of Hartford.........................	83,175 66	1,663 51
Phœnix, of Brooklyn.........................	41,307 33	826 14
Washington.................................	14,854 02	297 08
	$609,119 89	$12,182 36

LIFE INSURANCE.

Name of Company.	Gross Premiums. Value in Coin.	Tax 1 per cent. Coin.
Accidental	$4,526 65	$ 45 26
Brooklyn, $21,127 14 Currency................	14,788 90	147 88
Charter Oak, $29,587 Coin, and $29,377 Currency.	50,150 90	501 50
Connecticut Mutual..........................	26,292 22	262 92
Equitable, $4,200 13 Currency...............	2,982 09	29 83
Germania...................................	73,438 27	734 38
Guardian	17,956 93	179 56
Imperial....................................	2,046 00	20 46
Manhattan, $17,610 88 Coin, and $45,198 18 Currency..........................	49,249 60	492 50
Mutual, $275,040 01 Currency.................	186,656 36	1,866 56
New York, $31,768 47 Currency.	22,237 93	222 37
North America, $5,742 67 Coin, and $29,652 20 Currency........................	26,499 21	264 99
Travelers'..................................	10,501 56	105 01
Universal, $5,185 48 Currency................	3,629 83	36 29
Widows' and Orphans' Benefit, $7,576 26 Currency	5,283 38	52 83
	$496,239 83	$4,962 34

Total Tax on Premiums of Insurance, as per Treasurer's State Account and above Tables, $17,144 70.

STATEMENT OF TAXES 1866–7.

Charles R. Story, Tax Collector, in account with Auditor for Taxes of the Fiscal year 1866-7.

	Assessed value of Property.	Total Tax. $3 10 per $100.
Dr.		
To amount of the Assessment Roll of 1866–7, as transmitted to the Controller of State, September 17 and October 30, 1866—		
Personal Property.............................	$42,387,049 15	
Add error in addition of Roll, found subsequently by Auditor's Annual Examination.........	827,927 28	
		$43,214,976 43	$1,339,664 27
Real Estate.................................	$53,585,421 00	
Duplicate and overpayments on Real Estate....	45,762 00	
[Including Cash over on $19,027 valuation, $589 84.]		
	$53,631,183 00	
Deduct error in addition, found after sending Statement to State Controller..................	100,000 00	53,531,183 00	1,659,466 67
Grand Total.....................	....	$96,746,159 43	$2,999,130 94
Cr.		
PERSONAL PROPERTY.		
By Delinquent, Personal, as follows—		
Mortgages................................	$16,082,975 53	
Shipping.................................	219,853 00	
Other Personal...........................	1,007,562 00	
Total Delinquency carried to New Account.......	....	$17,310,390 53	$536,622 11
By paid on elsewhere (shipping).................	....	487,043 00	15,098 33
By Duplicate and Erroneous Assessments, viz.—		
Mortgages satisfied, canceled, etc..............	$272,205 74	
Shipping....................................	247,665 00	
Other Personal..............................	848,195 00	
		1,368,065 74	42,410 04
By Exemptions authorized by Law—		
Foreign Consuls.............................	$4,400 00	
Incorporated Institutions and Benevolent Societies	48,600 00	
		53,000 00	1,643 00
By amount collected and held under protest......	....	48,928 00	1,516 77
By amount collected and paid into the Treasury..	....	23,947,549 16	742,374 02
		$43,214,976 43	$1,339,664 27
REAL ESTATE.		
By Delinquent, carried to New Account..........		$12,790 00	$396 49
By Erroneous Assessments.......................		43,110 00	1,336 41
By Exemptions authorized by Law, Property of—		
United States.................................	$512,330 00	
State of California............................	1,800 00	
City and County of San Francisco..............	1,125,032 00	
Protestant Churches...........................	409,461 00	
Hebrew Congregations.........................	120,200 00	
Roman Catholic Church	430,054 00	
Benevolent Institutions.......................	368,530 00	
		2,967,407 00	91,989 61
By amount collected and held under protest......		13,000 00	403 00
By amount collected and paid into the Treasury..		50,494,876 00	1,565,341 16
Total Real Estate		53,531,183 00	$1,659,466 67
Total Personal, brought down..............		43,214,976 43	1,339,664 27
Grand Total.......................	....	$96,746,159 43	$2,999,130 94

See Tax Apportionment for statement of Taxes of other years, also of 2½ and 5 per cents collected.

CHARLES R. STORY, TAX COLLECTOR, IN NEW ACCOUNT FOR TAXES OF THE
FISCAL YEAR 1866–67.

	Assessed Value Property.	Total Tax.
To amount of Delinquent Taxes 1866–7—		
Personal Property....................	$17,310,390 53	$536,622 11
Real Estate........................	12,790 00	396 49
	$17,323,180 53	$537,018 60

DELINQUENT TAXES OF THIS AND PREVIOUS YEARS.

Fiscal Year.	Taxes on Mortgages in Litigation.	Other Taxes.	Total.
1866–7...........	$498,572 25	$38,446 35	$537,018 60
1865–6...........	About 395,000 00	27,130 73	422,130 73
1864–5...........	About 365,000 00	35,590 15	400,590 15
1863–4...........	About 283,000 00	91,778 14	374,778 44
1862–3...........	About 330,000 00	81,096 45	411,096 45
1861–2...........	....	....	19,886 51
1860–1...........	....	....	33,536 71
1859–60..........	....	....	38,989 21
1858–9...........	....	....	63,027 50
1857–8...........	....	....	48,849 41
1856–7...........	....	....	148,428 94
			$2,498,332 65

TAXES HELD UNDER PROTEST.

By W. Y. Patch, Taxes 1858–9.................................. $304 08

By J. Hunt, Taxes 1859–60....................................   358 84

By E. H. Washburn, Taxes 1863–4............................   738 67

By Charles R. Story, Taxes 1866–7...........................   1,919 77

$3,321 36

APPORTIONMENT OF TAXES COLLECTED DURING THE FISCAL YEAR 1866-67.

	Total.	State.	General Fund.	Street Light Fund.	Street Department Fund.	School Fund.	Corporation Debt Fund.	Interest Account B'ds 1863 and 1864.	Int'st Tax Acct. S. F. and S. J. R. R. B'ds.	Interest Tax Acct. Pacific R. R. Bonds.	Sinking Fund Bonds 1865.	Sinking Fund B'ds 1863 and 1864.	Loan F'nd Acct. S. F. and S. J. R. R. B'ds.
Taxes collected, per Tax Collector's Account, 1866-7—Real Estate	$1,565,341 16												
Personal	742,374 02												
	$2,307,715 18	$841,199 41	$502,486 35	$111,663 61	$33,499 12	$260,548 54	$286,603 40	$66,998 18	$29,776 93	$63,276 07	$37,221 19	$55,831 81	$18,610 57
2½ per cent. Personal	587 56		587 56										
5 per cent. Personal	5,059 61		5,059 61										
5 per cent. Real Estate	12,077 26	6,038 63	6,038 63										
Taxes 1865-6	1,907 73	703 17	428 01	45 87	61 14	214 00	262 93	61 14	12 92	55 01	18 36	45 88	
5 per cent. Personal	81 25		81 25										
5 per cent. Real Estate	6 49	3 24	3 25										
Taxes 1864-5	5 96	2 50	1 22	15		70	94	35	05			05	
5 per cent. Real Estate	30	15	15										
Taxes 1863-4	38 85	16 65	7 86	1 40		3 70	8 33		92				
5 per cent. Real Estate	1 69	84	85										
5 per cent. Personal	96		96										
Taxes 1862-3	20 79	5 84	5 30	56		2 66	6 43						
5 per cent. Real Estate	1 12	56	56										
Taxes 1861-2	4 87	1 05	1 27	25		60	1 70						
5 per cent. Real Estate	24	12	12										
Taxes 1859-60	3,154 46	597 25	1,113 86*	149 32		348 39	945 64						
5 per cent.	123 34	61 67	61 67										
Taxes 1857-8	53 48	16 28	29 06			8 14							
5 per cent.	2 68	1 34	1 34										
Taxes 1856-7	391 58	119 16	212 79			59 64							
5 per cent.	18 93	9 47	9 46										
	$2,331,263 63	$848,777 32	$516,130 43	$111,861 16	$33,560 26	$261,186 37	$287,829 36	$67,059 67	$29,790 82	$63,331 08	$37,239 55	$55,877 74	$18,610 57

*Including Judgment Fund Tax.

RATE OF TAXATION — 1850–51 TO 1867–68 — PER $100.

Year.	State.	City.	County.													Total
1850–1.	$0 50	$1 00	$0 50	...	...	...	...	...	...	...	...	...	...	...	...	$2 00
1851–2.	0 50	2 45	1 15	...	...	...	...	...	...	...	...	...	...	...	...	4 10
1852–3.	0 30	2 45	1 66$\frac{1}{2}$	...	...	...	...	...	...	...	...	...	...	...	...	4 41$\frac{1}{2}$
1853–4.	0 60	2 00	1 28$\frac{1}{2}$	...	...	...	...	...	...	...	...	...	...	...	...	3 88$\frac{1}{2}$
1854–5.	0 60	2 15	1 10$\frac{1}{2}$	...	...	...	...	...	...	...	...	...	...	...	...	3 85$\frac{1}{2}$
1855–6.	0 70	2 33$\frac{1}{3}$	0 82$\frac{1}{2}$	...	...	...	...	...	...	...	...	...	...	...	...	3 85$\frac{5}{6}$
		General Fund.	Street Light Fund.	Street Department Fund.	School Fund.	Corporation Debt Fund.	Interest Tax Account. S. F. and S J. R. R. Bonds.	Interest Tax Account Bonds 1863 and 1864.	Interest Tax Account Pacific R. R. Bonds	Sinking Fund Bonds 1855.	Sinking Fund Bonds 1858	Sinking Fund Bonds 1863–1864	Sinking Fund S. F. and S. J. R. R. Bonds.	Sinking Fund * Pacific R. R. Bonds.	Judgment Fund.	
1856–7.	0 70	1 25	...	...	$0 35	...	...	...	...	...	...	...	...	...	...	2 30
1857–8.	0 70	1 25	...	...	0 35	...	...	...	...	...	...	...	...	...	...	2 30
1858–9.	0 60	1 25	...	...	0 35	$0 25	...	...	...	...	...	...	...	...	...	2 45
1859–60	0 60	0 65	0 15	...	0 35	0 95	...	...	...	...	...	...	...	...	$0 46$\frac{9}{10}$	3 16$\frac{9}{10}$
1860–1.	0 60	0 75	0 15	...	0 35	1 00	...	...	...	...	...	...	...	...	...	2 85
1861–2.	0 62	0 75	0 15	...	0 35	1 00	...	...	...	...	...	...	...	...	...	2 87
1862–3.	0 77	0 70	0 07$\frac{1}{2}$	...	0 35	0 85	...	...	...	...	...	...	...	...	...	2 74$\frac{1}{2}$
1863–4.	0 90	0 42$\frac{1}{2}$	0 07$\frac{1}{2}$	...	0 20	0 45	$0 05	...	...	...	...	...	...	...	...	2 10
1864–5.	1 25	0 61	0 07$\frac{1}{2}$	...	0 35	0 47	0 02$\frac{1}{2}$	$0 17$\frac{1}{2}$	...	...	...	$0 02$\frac{1}{2}$	...	...	...	2 98
1865–6.	1 15	0 70	0 07$\frac{1}{2}$	$0 10	0 35	0 43	0 02	0 10	$0 08	$0 03	...	0 07$\frac{1}{2}$	...	$0 01	...	3 12
1866–7.	1 13	0 67$\frac{1}{2}$	0 15	0 04$\frac{1}{2}$	0 35	0 38$\frac{1}{2}$	0 04	0 09	0 08$\frac{1}{2}$	0 05	...	0 07$\frac{1}{2}$	$0 02$\frac{1}{2}$	...	...	3 10
1867–8.	1 13	0 60	0 20	0 09	0 35	0 32	0 02	0 07$\frac{1}{2}$	0 04$\frac{1}{2}$	0 04	$0 05$\frac{1}{2}$	0 05	0 02$\frac{1}{2}$	...	...	3 00

* Transferred to Interest Tax Account.

ANNUAL STATEMENT TO MAY 31, 1867, OF THE COMMISSIONERS OF THE FUNDED DEBT OF 1851.

STATEMENT OF RECEIPTS, DISBURSEMENTS, OUTSTANDING LOANS, ETC., OF THE COMMISSIONERS OF THE FUNDED DEBT OF THE CITY OF SAN FRANCISCO, FROM JUNE 1ST, 1866, TO MAY 31ST, 1867, INCLUSIVE.

Balance of Cash on hand, per statement of May 31, 1866....................................	$ 7,180 16
Loans outstanding at that date..................	348,372 40
Stocks taken to account......................	528,993 02
Real Estate taken to account..................	11,639 20

RECEIPTS 1866–67.

City Treasurer, Requisition 1866-67..	$178,990 00	
Interest...........................	103,131 32	
Real Estate......................	9,037 50	
Rent of Lots....................	1,373 35	
Gain on sale of Gas Stock..........	5,900 00	
Gain on sale of Water Stock........	9,000 00	
		$307,432 17
		$1,203,616 95

DISBURSEMENTS.

Interest on Bonds.................	$129,051 60	
Bonds redeemed..................	32,000 00	
Premium on do...................	1,600 00	
Advertising, Notarial and Court Fees, Clerk Hire, etc.................	2,403 25	
Attorneys' Fees..................	2,400 00	
Salaries of Commissioners, including President and Secretary..........	8,850 00	
		$176,304 85

Loans outstanding at this date, to wit—		
On Real Estate.........$100,830 00		
On Stocks and Bonds.... 421,500 00		
Carried forward. $522,330 00		$176,304 85

7

Brought forward. $522,330 00 $176,304 85
Stocks taken to account..   495,635 48
Real Estate taken to acct..   1,158 20
Cash on hand (deposited
   with Parrott & Co)....   8,188 42
             ————$1,027,312 10
             ——————— $1,203,616 95

SCHEDULE OF PROPERTY CONVEYED BY THE COMMISSIONERS OF THE FUNDED
DEBT OF THE CITY OF SAN FRANCISCO, UNDER THE ACTS OF THE LEGIS-
LATURES OF APRIL 14, 1862, AND APRIL 2, 1866.

To whom Conveyed.	Description of Property.	Amount Paid.
Peter Jones..................	Portion Government Reservation Main Street....	$ 52 00
H. P. Coon	Portion South Beach Blocks 14, 22, and 29	108 00
Alexander Crochet.............	Portion 100-vara Lot No. 103...	322 00
V.N.J.Renoult and A.V.A. Préaut	Portion 100-vara Lot No. 103...	372 00
F. Gasné	Portion 100-vara Lot No. 103...	97 00
James and Margaret Mulhare....	Portion 50-vara Lot No. 647....	122 00
Timothy Nailan	Portion 50-vara Lot No. 647....	72 00
Helen Lount..................	For 50-vara Lot No. 1,306......	272 00
A. C. M. Pomier	Part 50-vara Lot No. 1,029	122 00
E. W. Corbett.................	Part 100-vara Lot No. 318......	249 50
E. W. Corbett, Executor	Part 100-vara Lot No. 318......	219 50
Ann Welch	Part 50-vara Lot No. 647.......	72 00
John A. Wills, Wm. A. Quarles, Administ'r, and Michael Kane.	For 100-vara Lot No. 310.......	1,022 00
Mary Henery and Charles O. Miles, her son....................	Part 50-vara Lot No. 647.......	72 00
La Société Francaise de Bienfai-sance Mutuelle..............	For 100-vara Lot No. 308.......	1,422 00
Thomas S. Miller..............	Part 50-vara Lot No. 1,132	137 00
J. W. Brittan	For 50-vara Lot No. 764.......	72 00
Ed. Ford	For Water Lot No. 680.........	1,022 00
A. Wasserman and F. Funcke ...	Part 100-vara Lot No. 340......	112 00
S. S. Wright and C. H. Reynolds	Part South Beach Block No. 20.	44 50
Jno. O. Earle	Part South Beach Block No. 13.	922 00
J. G. Kittle	Part South Beach Block No. 22.	122 00
James Bell....................	Part 100-vara Lot No. 321......	397 00
Spring Valley Water Works	Part Block 37, Western Addition	97 00
H. Pearsons and H. C. Wheeler .	For Water Blocks, W. A.......	854 50
Andrew Duff..................	Part 100-vara Lot No. 319......	42 00
Bridget White.................	Part 100-vara Lot No. 318......	42 00
Dennis White.................	Part 100-vara Lot No. 318......	42 00
Andrew Mullen................	Part 100-vara Lot No. 318......	42 00
Samuel Grosh and T. L. Ruther-ford	Part South Beach Block No. 22.	29 50
J. P. Rynders.................	Part 100. vara Lot No. 322......	397 00
James R. Bolton	Part North Beach Block No. 13.	67 00
		$9,037 50

The amount of Bonds outstanding on the 31st day of
May, 1866, as stated in our report dated June 19th,
1866, was.................................... $1,289,900 00
Redeemed during the past year.................. 32,000 00

Leaving outstanding on the 31st ult.............. $1,257,900 00

The interest on this sum for the year 1867-68 amounts to $125,790,
which, with $50,000 appropriated under the Act as a Sinking Fund
for the redemption of Bonds, makes a total of $175,790 to be pro-
vided for by the City during the current year.

The financial operations of the Board during the past year leave a
net profit to the City, after deducting all expenses, of $105,751 42,
and if there be added thereto the sum of $9,037 50, received under
the Act of the Legislature authorizing the Commissioners to com-
promise with parties in possession of certain lots conveyed to the
Board, the total net gain to the city for the year will be $114,788 92.

The Sinking Fund, on the 31st ultimo, amounted to the sum of
$1,023,359 20, exclusive of the sum of $68,513 43, due from the
City on the requisition of 1856-7. It is made up as follows :

Loans on Real Estate......................... $100,830 00
Loans on Stocks and Bonds.................... 421,500 00
Bonds owned by the Board, to wit—
  313,000 San Francisco City 7 per cents., costing.. 237,284 13
  260,500 San Francisco City 6 per cents., costing.. 153,345 50
  45,000 Santa Clara County 7 per cents., costing.. 31,626 00
  27,000 Spring Valley Water Company 12 per cents.,
    costing................................. 24,790 00
  53,400 United States Seven-Thirties, costing..... 39,925 70
  7,102 Warrants on State Treasury.............. 6,200 00
  3,000 Mississippi Railroad Bonds (P. B. & Co.).. 2,464 15
Real Estate taken to account.................. 1,158 20
Cash on deposit with Parrott & Co.............. 8,188 42

                                     $1,027,312 10
Add accrued Interest on Loans and Investments.... 18,562 10

                                      $1,045,874 20
Less Coupons due............................. 22,515 00

                                      $1,023,359 20

According to the above showing, the Fund amounts to $1,023,-359 20; but if the securities owned by the Board are reckoned at their present market value, the sum of $61,596 52 can be added thereto, making the actual and available Sinking Fund on the 31st ultimo to be $1,087,165 72, within $170,000 of the total sum required to meet the outstanding Bonds becoming due on the 1st of May, 1871.

Appended to the statement of Receipts, Expenditures, etc., accompanying the Report, is also a list of the conveyances made by the Board during the past year, under the Acts of the Legislatures of April 14th, 1862, and April 2d, 1866, embracing the names of the parties to whom the deeds were made, a partial description of the property conveyed, and the price paid therefor.

All of which is respectfully submitted.

Signed,
{
JOHN MIDDLETON,
WM. HOOPER,
WM. M. LENT,
C. M. HITCHCOCK,
C. L. LOW.
}

Office of the Commissioners of the Funded Debt of San Francisco, June 11, 1867.

FUNDED DEBT OF THE CITY AND COUNTY OF SAN FRANCISCO, JUNE 30, 1867.

[The Coupons of Bonds of 1858, 1863, 1864, 1866, and 1867, are receivable for Taxes for the current Fiscal Year.]

	Bonds outstanding.	Annual Interest.	Annual Sinking Fund.
City Bonds of 1851, due May 1, 1871 '(interest 10 per cent. per annum, payable by Commissioners of Funded Debt of 1851, May 1 and November 1)...... [Statutes 1851, page 387.]	$1,257,900 00	$125,790 00	$50,000 00
City Bonds of 1855, due January 1, 1875 (interest 6 per cent. per annum, payable in New York January 1 and July 1)................ [Statutes 1855, page 286, and Ordinance 846, of the Common Council.]	269,500 00	16,170 00	about 32,000 00
City and County Bonds of 1858, due January 1, 1888, (interest 6 per cent. per annum, payable in San Francisco January 1 and July 1)................... [Statutes 1858, page 183.]	1,133,500 00	68,010 00	about 44,000 00
City and County Bonds of 1860 (School), due July 1, 1870 (interest 10 per cent. per annum, payable in New York January 1 and July 1)................... [Statutes 1860, page 101.]	54,500 00	5,450 00	5,000 00
City and County Bonds of 1861 (School), due July 1, 1870 (interest 10 per cent. per annum, payable in New York January 1 and July 1)............................. [Statutes 1861, page 242.]	16,000 00	1,600 00	2,500 00
City and County Bonds of 1862-3 (San Francisco and San Jose Railroad), $30,000 due each July 1, August 1, September 15, November 10, 1877, February 9 and June 1, 1878 ; $17,000 due December 22, 1877 ; $26,500 due April 13, 1878, and $53,500 due September 14, 1878 (interest 7 per cent. per annum, payable in San Francisco)............................. [Statutes 1861, page 198]	277,000 00	19,390 00	about 20,000 00
City and County Bonds of 1863 (Judgment), due October 1, 1883 (interest 7 per cent. per annum, payable in San Francisco April 1 and October 1)............. [Statutes 1862, page 265, and Order 547 of the Board of Supervisors.]	852,266 99	59,658 69	about 40,000 00
City and County Bonds of 1864 (Judgment), due June 1, 1884 (interest 7 per cent. per annum, payable in San Francisco June 1 and December 1)............. [Statutes 1862, page 265, and Order 580 of the Board of Supervisors.]	28,000 00	1,960 00	
City and County Bonds of 1864 (Central Pacific Railroad), due July 1, 1894 (interest 7 per cent. per annum, payable in San Francisco January 1 and July 1) .... [Statutes 1863, page 380, and 1863-4, page 388; Order 582 of the Board of Supervisors.]	400,000 00	28,000 00	commences in 1873
City and County Bonds of 1865 (Western Pacific Railroad),due May 1, 1895 (interest 7 per cent.per annum, payable in San Francisco May 1 and November 1) .. [Statutes 1863, page 380, and 1863-4, page 388, and Order 640 of the Board of Supervisors.]	250,000 00	17,500 00	commences in 1873
City and County Bonds of 1866-7, due April 1, 1881 (interest 7 per cent. per annum, payable in San Francisco April 1 and October 1).................. [Statutes 1866-7, page 302, and Orders Nos. 695 and 768 of the Board of Supervisors.]	210,000 00	14,700 00	15,000 00
Total amount of Bonds outstanding..................	$4,748,666 99		
Amount of annual Interest..............................		$358,228 69	
Amount of annual Sinking Fund			208,500 00
Amount to be provided for from Taxes for Interest and Sinking Funds for Fiscal Year 1866-7			$566,728 69

BONDS REDEEMED DURING THE FISCAL YEAR 1866-7.

City Bonds of 1851	$32,000 00
City and County Bonds (School) of 1860 (at 99½ per cent.)...................................	1,000 00
[See page 20.]	
City and County Bonds (School) of 1861 (at par)...	2,000 00
[See page 20.]	
City and County Bonds (School) of 1866 (at par)...	15,000 00
[See page 20.]	
City Bonds (Fire) of 1854 (at par)	174,500 00
[See page 21]	
City Bonds of 1855 (at 99½ to 99⅞ per cent.).......	36,000 00
[See page 21.]	
City and County Bonds (Judgment) of 1863 and 1864 (at 79½ to 82 per cent.), and balance Certificates ..	65,126 84
[See page 22.]	
City and County Bonds (San Francisco and San José Railroad) of 1862 and 1863 (at 75 to 81¹³⁄₂₀ per cent.)	23,000 00
[See page 23.]	
Total Bonds redeemed....................	$348,626 84

BONDS ISSUED DURING THE FISCAL YEAR 1866-7.

City and County Bonds of 1866-7 (School)........	$150,000 00
[Sold at prices ranging from 81 to 86 per cent]	

EXHIBIT OF THE FUNDED DEBT, WITH ASSETS, JUNE 30, 1867.

Amount of Bonds outstanding, per foregoing statement		$4,748,666 99
Coupons due and not presented for payment, of—		
Bonds of 1851...................	$13,630 00	
Bonds of 1855..................	1,905 00	
Bonds of 1858..................	1,095 00	
Bonds of 1862-3	927 50	
Bonds of 1863-4 (Judgment)......	262 50	
Bonds of 1864-5 (Pacific Railroad).	1,575 00	
		19,395 00
Carried forward....................		$4,768,061 99

Brought forward		$4,768,061 99
Coupons due July 1, 1866, of—			
Bonds of 1858	34,005 00		
Bonds of 1862–3	1,050 00		
Bonds of 1864	14,000 00		
		49,055 00	
			$4,817,116 99
Assets—			
In hands of Fund Commissioners,			
Debt of 1851.................	1,030,588 50		
In hands of New York Agents.....	2,946 78		
In Treasury, etc., at credit of Corporation Debt Fund..............	50,052 73		
Coupon Account—Bonds 1858.....	1,095 00		
Interest Account—Bonds 1863 and 1864........................	5,096 38		
Sinking Fund—School Bonds 1860 (Cash and Loans)..............	18,306 48		
Sinking Fund—School Bonds 1861 (Cash and Loans)..............	7,776 13		
Sinking Fund—Bonds 1855	2,584 67		
Sinking Fund—Bonds 1863 and 1864	5,903 35		
Interest Tax Account—San Francisco and San José Railroad Bonds.	9,512 21		
Loan Fund Account—San Francisco and San José Railroad Bonds....	773 57		
Pacific Railroad Interest Tax Account	26,222 84		
Interest Account—School Bonds 1860 1861, 1866–7.................	1,980 06		
		1,162;838 70	
Net amount of Debt June 30, 1867 ...			$3,654,278 29

Debt reduced during the year, $227,519 46.

STATEMENT OF BONDS ISSUED, REDEEMED, AND OUTSTANDING OF THE ISSUES NAMED BELOW.

Date.	Total Issue.	Redeemed from date of issue to June 30, 1867	Outstanding June 30, 1867.
1851.......................	$1,635,600 00	$377,700 00	$1,257,900 00
1854—Fire..................	200,000 00	200,000 00	....
1854—School...............	60,000 00	60,000 00	....
1855	329,000 00	59,500 00	269,500 00
1858.......................	1,134,500 00	1,000 00	1,133,500 00
1860—School...............	75,000 00	20,500 00	54,500 00
1861—School...............	25,000 00	9,000 00	16,000 00
1862-3—S. F. & S. J. Railroad	300,000 00	23,000 00	277,000 00
1863—Judgment.............	974,385 92	122,118 93	852,266 99
1864—Judgment.............	48,007 91	20,007 91	28,000 00
1864—Central Pacific Railroad	400,000 00	....	400,000 00
1865—Western Pacific Railroad	250,000 00	....	250,000 00
1866-7—School.............	225,000 00	15,000 00	210,000 00
	$5,656,493 83	$907,826 84	$4,748,666 99

RECAPITULATION OF INTEREST COUPONS ON BONDS DUE, PAID, AND OUTSTANDING FROM DATE OF ISSUE OF BONDS TO JUNE 30, 1867.

Bonds of	Total issue of Bonds.	Total Coupons on Bonds to June 30, 1867.	Coupons canceled.	Coupons due and payable to June 30, 1867.	Coupons paid, due to June 30, 1867.	Coupons outstanding, June 30, 1867.
1858	$1,134,500 00	$612,630 00	$ 270 00	$612,360 00	$611,265 00	$1,095 00
1860—School	75,000 00	49,775 00	10,650 00	39,125 00	39,125 00	
1861—School	25,000 00	14,200 00	3,175 00	11,025 00	11,025 00	
1862-3—San Francisco and San José Railroad	300,000 00	87,150 00	1,260 00	85,890 00	84,962 50	927 50
1863-4—Judgment	1,022,393 83	248,710 00	7,735 00	240,975 00	240,712 50	262 50
1864-5—Pacific Railroad	650,000 00	105,000 00	....	105,000 00	103,425 00	1,575 00
1866-7—School	225,000 00	15,750 00	7,000 00	8,750 00	8,750 00	
		$1,133,215 00	$30,090 00	$1,103,125 00	$1,099,265 00	$3,860 00

ESTIMATE OF EXPENDITURES AND REVENUE FOR THE FISCAL
YEAR ENDING JUNE 30, 1868.

EXPENDITURES FROM GENERAL FUND AND FUNDS WHICH ARE PROPERLY SUB-
DIVISIONS OF GENERAL FUND, VIZ: SPECIAL FEE AND POLICE CONTINGENT
FUNDS.

Salaries of City and County Officers, (including extra deputies' salaries,) see recapitulation of City and County Officers' Salaries, page 33	$95,000 00
[Less fees received, as per recapitulation.]	
Salaries of Police Force—4 Captains, $150 each; 1 Clerk, $150, and 79 Officers, $125 each	127,500 00
Office Rent and Stationery for Fire Commissioners..	1,200 00
Salaries Fire Department......................	55,000 00
Running Expenses Fire Department	22,000 00
Purchase of Lots and erection of Engine Houses...	25,000 00
Cisterns and Hydrants...................	10,000 00
Salaries Superintendent, 3 Operators and Repairer Fire Alarm and Police Telegraph, $550 per month	6,600 00
Repairs to Public Buildings...................	12,000 00
Lighting Public Buildings, including Engine Houses	8,000 00
Hospital and Almshouse Supplies, $7,000 per month.	84,000 00
Salaries Visiting Physician and Surgeon, $100 per month each	2,400 00
Almshouse and Hospital Buildings..............	30,000 00
Almshouse and Hospital Furniture...............	20,000 00
Small Pox Hospital Supplies..............	6,000 00
Burials of Indigents and Chemical Analyses.......	2,200 00
Appropriation for "Home of Inebriate"...........	3,000 00
Examining Insane...........................	1,500 00
Sending Insane to Stockton....................	2,000 00
Industrial School Appropriation.................	24,000 00
Industrial School Physician....................	300 00
Industrial School Runaways (pursuit of)...........	300 00
Road Repairs	4,000 00
Road Repairs—special allowance for 1st District....	6,000 00
Enclosing and improving Public Grounds..........	2,000 00
Carried forward........	$550,000 00

Brought forward	$550,000	00
Removal of Dead in Yerba Buena Park to vault....	2,000	00
Registration and Election Expenses..............	10,000	00
Subsistence of Prisoners.......................	15,000	00
Witnesses' Expenses...........................	500	00
District Court Reporters.......................	400	00
Special Counsel—annual allowance..............	5,000	00
Contingent Expenses of Mayor's Office, $150 per month..	1,800	00
Boat Hire and Office Rent for Harbor Master, $75 per month..	900	00
Copying Assessment Roll.......................	2,500	00
Making and Copying Military Roll..............	400	00
Compiling and Publishing Laws and Ordinances....	300	00
Newspapers for Recorder's Office...............	100	00
Celebration of Fourth of July, 1867..............	3,000	00
" Urgent Necessity " allowance, $2,000 per month...	24,000	00
Deficiency in Pound Fee Fund..................	500	00
Appropriation for Police Contingent Fund.........	3,600	00
Assessment for Widening Kearny Street, (less amount advanced).....................................	20,000	00
Stationery for City and County Officers...........	11,000	00
Publishing Delinquent Tax List.................	2,500	00
Deficiencies in Allowances, extra appropriations required, etc., say............................	125,000	00

[For extra Deputies, material Fire Department, Fire Alarm and Police Telegraph, Urgent Necessity, etc., etc.]

Total estimated expenditures General Fund and Subdivisions of do.................	$778,500	00

ESTIMATE OF GENERAL FUND REVENUE.

[Fees received by City and County Officers, deducted from City and County Officers' Salaries in estimate of Expenditures.]

From Taxes Delinquent.......................	$2,000	0
From Poll Taxes..............................	15,000	00
From 5 per cents. on Taxes 1867–68..............	10,000	00
From State and County Licenses................	95,000	00
Carried forward	$122,000	00

Brought forward	$122,000	00
From Municipal Licenses	25,000	00
From Harbor Dues	19,000	00
From Fines in Police Court	28,000	00
From Fines in County Court	5,000	00
From State for Assessment Expenses	8,000	00
From State for advance of Armory Rents	8,800	00
From State for Hospital Dues	2,000	00
From Taxes 1867–8, 60 cents per $100 on $80,000,000 valuation	480,000	00

Total estimated revenue		$697,800	00
Cash on hand June 30, 1867	$132,368 55		
Less demands outstanding at same date	50,700 99		
		81,667	56
		$779,467	56

STREET LIGHT FUND.

Estimated expenditures for lighting streets, repairs to lamps, etc., 12 months, at $13,333⅓ per month		$160,000 00
Taxes 1867-8, 20 cents per $100 on $80,000,000 valuation	$160,000 00	

STREET DEPARTMENT FUND.

Estimated expenditures for repairing and cleaning streets—by Superintendent of Streets and Committee on Streets		$82,000 00
Estimated Revenue—		
Taxes 1867–8, 9 cents per $100 on $80,000,000	$72,000 00	
Licenses on Vehicles	10,000 00	
	$82,000 00	

SCHOOL FUND.

ESTIMATED BY FINANCE COMMITTEE OF BOARD OF EDUCATION.

Estimated expenditures—

Salaries of Teachers	$240,500 00
Salaries of Janitors	13,200 00
Salary of Secretary of Board of Education	1,800 00
Services of Census Marshals	1,500 00
Repairs to School Houses [Includes carpenters' salaries.]	5,500 00
Furniture	14,000 00
Fuel and Light	5,200 00
Water	300 00
Books, Stationery and Advertising	12,500 00
Rents	2,000 00
Incidental Expenses	2,300 00
Insurance	3,000 00
Sinking Fund—School Bonds 1860	5,000 00
Sinking Fund—School Bonds 1861	2,500 00
Sinking Fund—School Bonds 1866–7	15,000 00
Interest School Bonds 1860, 10 per cent. on $54,500	5,450 00
Interest School Bonds 1861, 10 per cent. on $16,000	1,600 00
Interest School Bonds 1866-67, 7 per cent. on $210,000	14,700 00
	$346,050 00

Estimated Revenue—

From Taxes 1867-8, 35 cents per $100 on $80,000,000 valuation	$280,000 00
From Poll Taxes	2,500 00
From Dog Tax	1,000 00
From Rents of Lots	600 00
From Evening Schools	200 00
State Apportionment	60,000 00
	$344,300 00

CORPORATION DEBT FUND.

Estimated Expenditures—

Requisition of Commissioners of Funded Debt of 1851 for Interest	$125,790 00
Requisition of Commissioners of Funded Debt of 1851 for Sinking Fund	50,000 00
Coupons City Bonds 1855, due in New York January 1, 1868, and July 1, 1868, $16,170, with Exchange, say $405	16,575 00
Coupons City and County Bonds of 1858, due in San Francisco July 1, 1867, January and July 1, 1868.	102,015 00
Total estimated Expenditures	$294,380 00

Estimated Revenue—

From Taxes, 32 cents per $100 on $80,000,000 valuation	$256,000 00	
Cash on hand June 30, 1867	50,052 73	
	$306,052 73	

INTEREST ACCOUNT—BONDS 1863 AND 1864.

Estimated Expenditures—

Interest Coupons due and outstanding July 1, 1867	$735 00
Interest Coupons due during the fiscal year 1867-8, say.............	61,600 00
	$62,335 00

Estimated Revenue—

From Taxes, 7½ cents per $100 on $80,000,000..................	$60,000 00	
Cash on hand July 1, 1867	5,096 38	
	$65,096 38	

INTEREST TAX ACCOUNT—SAN FRANCISCO AND SAN JOSE RAILROAD BONDS.

Estimated Expenditures—
Interest Coupons due and unpaid
July 1, 1867 . . . . $927 50
Interest Coupons due during the
fiscal year 1867-8, and July 1,
1868, say 21,500 00
                                                          _____
                                                           $22,427 50

Estimated Revenue—
From Taxes, 2 cents per $100 on
$80,000,000 . . . . $16,000 00
Cash on hand July 1, 1867 . . . .   9,512 21
                                                  _____
                                                  $25,512 21

INTEREST TAX ACCOUNT—PACIFIC RAILROAD BONDS.

Estimated Expenditures—
Interest Coupons due and unpaid
July 1, 1867 . . . . $1,575 00
Interest Coupons due during the
fiscal year 1867-8 and July 1, 1868   59,500 00
                                                          _____
                                                           $61,075 00

Estimated Revenue—
From Taxes, 4½ cents per $100 on
$80,000,000 . . . . $36,000 00
Cash on hand July 1, 1867 . . . .   26,222 84
                                                  _____
                                                  $62,222 84

SINKING FUND—CITY BONDS 1855.

Estimated Expenditures—
Bonds due Jan. 1, 1875, $269,500,
one-eighth of same at par, about.. $33,700 00
[8 Sinking Funds required.]

Estimated Revenue—
From Taxes, 4 cents per $100 on
$80,000,000...................   32,000 00
Cash on hand July 1, 1867..........   2,584 67

                                        $34,584 67

SINKING FUND—CITY AND COUNTY BONDS 1858.

Estimated Expenditures—
Bonds due Jan. 1, 1888, $1,133,500,
$\frac{1}{21}$ of same at an average of 85 per
cent., about $45,900 00
[21 Sinking Funds required.]

Estimated Revenue—
From Taxes, 5½ cents per $100 on
$80,000,000................... $44,000 00

SINKING FUND—CITY AND COUNTY BONDS 1863 AND 1864.

Estimated Expenditures—
Bonds due October 1, 1883 and June
1, 1884, about $880,200, $\frac{1}{17}$ of same
at an average of 90 per cent., about $46,800 00
[17 Sinking Funds required.]

Estimated Revenue—
From Taxes, 5 cents per $100 on
$80,000,000................... $40,000 00
Cash at credit July, 1, 1867........   5,903 35

                                        $45,903 35

SINKING FUND (LOAN FUND ACCOUNT)—SAN FRANCISCO AND SAN JOSE RAIL-
ROAD BONDS.

Estimated Expenditure—
Bonds due in 1877 and 1878, $277,000
$\frac{1}{11}$ of same at an average of 90 per
cent., about.................... $22,600 00
[11 Sinking Funds required.]

Estimated Revenue—
From Taxes, $2\frac{1}{2}$ cents per $100, on
$80,000,000.................... $20,000 00
Cash on hand July 1, 1867..........   773 57

                             $20,773 57

RECAPITULATION OF ESTIMATE OF EXPENDITURES AND REVENUE FOR THE FIS-
CAL YEAR 1867-8.

	Expenditures.	Revenue.
General Fund............................	$778,500 00	$779,467 56
Street Light Fund.......................	160,000 00	160,000 00
Street Department Fund...................	82,000 00	82,000 00
School Fund	346,050 00	344,300 00
Corporation Debt Fund....................	294,380 00	306,052 73
Interest Account—Bonds 1863 and 1864......	62,335 00	65,096 38
Interest Tax Account—San Francisco and San José Railroad Bonds.....................	22,427 50	25,512 21
Interest Tax Account—Pacific Railroad Bonds.	61,075 00	62,222 84
Sinking Fund—City Bonds 1855.............	33,700 00	34,584 67
Sinking Fund—City and County Bonds 1858..	45,900 00	44,000 00
Sinking Fund—City and County Bonds 1863 and 1864................................	46,800 00	45,903 35
Sinking Fund—City and County Bonds 1862-3	22,600 00	20,773 57
	$1,955,767 50	$1,969,913 31

TRANSACTIONS IN CITY LOTS.

PURCHASE OF LOTS, JULY 1, 1856, TO JUNE 30, 1867.

FOR SCHOOL DEPARTMENT.

1857, November 17—50-vara Lot No. 418, on Union, near Montgomery Street..................	$13,000 00
1859, October 3—½ 50-vara Lot No. 121, on Powell, near Clay Street......................	9,175 00
1859, September 19—Lot on Mission, near Center Street, in Block No. 35 (200 feet by 182 feet)	1,350 00
1860, June 27—½ 50-vara Lot No. 159, on Powell, near Jackson Street....................	8,800 00
1860, June 18—Part 50-vara Lot No. 1,320, (97½ by 137$\frac{6}{12}$ feet)............................	2,000 00
1860, September 10—50-vara Lot No. 602, corner of Mason and Washington Streets...........	9,000 00
1862, October 23—50-vara Lot No. 1,023, corner Bush and Taylor Streets.....................	11,800 00
1863, December 4—Part 50-vara Lot northeast corner Powell and Broadway Streets, (69¾ feet by 119$\frac{8}{12}$ feet)............................	8,500 00
1864, July 6—Part 100-vara Lots Nos. 46 and 47, on Tehama Street, 90x175 feet..............	7,500 00
1864, June 13—Lot on Tehama, 297 feet from First Street, 28x75 feet.....................	2,000 00
1864, October 2—Lot on Kentucky, 100 feet south from Napa Street, 50x100 feet...........	200 00
1865, August 23—Lot on East line of Chenery, 200 feet north from Randall Street, 62x175 feet.	550 00
1865, August 23—Lot on Chenery, 50x125 feet, Lot 8, Block 29, Fairmount Tract.............	200 00
1865, November 14—50-vara Lot No. 832..........	210 00
1867, May 8—Lot on Silver, 112 feet from Second, 44x70 feet.............................	4,000 00
1867, May 13—Lot on southwest corner Pine and Larkin Streets, part Western Addition Block No. 14, 200x120 feet....................	5,989 76

SCHOOL LOTS EXCHANGED.

1857, May 4—50-vara Lot 482, on Greenwich Street, obtained for 50-vara Lot 695, corner Stockton and Francisco Streets.

1859, March 19—Lot on Vassar Place, 100x180 feet, obtained for 50-vara Lot No. 732, cor Fremont and Harrison Streets.

1859, April 20—Lot on Eighth Street, 115x275 feet, part 100-vara Lot 274, obtained for 100-vara Lot 258, corner Folsom and Seventh Streets.

1866, June 29—Lot on Broadway, near Powell, $69\frac{1}{4}$x$137\frac{6}{12}$ feet, obtained for part 100-vara Lot 174, corner Fourth and Harrison Streets.

1166, July 17—Lot on Post Street, part 50-vara Lot 581, 70 feet front, obtained for part 100-vara Lot 174, corner Fourth and Harrison Streets.

SCHOOL LOTS SOLD, JULY 1, 1856, TO JUNE 30, 1867.

1863-4—Lot 345, corner California and Mason Streets $13,000 00

1865-6—Lots 11 and 12, Block 15, Fairmount Tract.   400 00

1866-7—Lot 5, Block 289, Western Addition........   500 00

PURCHASE OF LOTS, JULY 1, 1856, TO JUNE 30, 1867.

ALL LOTS EXCEPT SCHOOL LOTS.

1856-7—Tiger Engine Lot, Second Street near Howard

1858-9—Portion 50-vara Lot No. 697, Hospital Lot, (exchanged for 50-vara Lot 482)........... $1,480 00

1862-3—Engine Lot, 22 O'Farrell Street, (with building thereon at time of purchase...........   3,500 00

1862-3—Engine Lot on Dupont, $117\frac{1}{2}$ feet from Green Street, 20x60 feet, (sold 1866-7)...........   2,250 00

1862-3—Engine Lot and House (Monumental, on Brenham Place)......................   16,000 00

1863-4—City Hall addition, Union Hotel building and lot.................................   65,000 00

1863-4—City Hall addition, El Dorado building and lot 42,500 00

1864-5—Engine Lot, Sixth, 115 feet from Folsom, 25x75, part 50-vara Lot 217..............	4,650 00	
1864-5—Engine Lot, Stockton, 27½ feet from Greenwich, 20x97½, part 50-vara Lot 499, (sold 1866-7)................................	2,500 00	
1864-5—Engine Lot, Sutter, 55 feet west from Jones 27½x82½ feet, part 50-vara Lot 1,087, (sold 1866-7)	2,100 00	
1864-5—Engine Lot and House, Bryant, 133 feet from Third, 22x80 feet, part 100-vara Lot No. 84.	2,600 00	
1864-5—Engine Lot, Geary, 67½ feet from Mason, 20x80 feet.............................	2,200 00	
1865-6—Lot and destroying building, to give light to Police Court, in rear of the City Hall......	15,000 00	
1866-7—Engine Lot on Pacific, 137⅚ feet from Jones Street, 23x60 feet, part 50-vara Lot No. 877.	1,200 00	
1866-7—Lot for Almshouse and Pesthouse buildings (80 acres, more or less, of San Miguel Ranch)	30,000 00	

City Slip Lot No. 89 exchanged for 20 feet of City Slip Lot 92.

LOTS SOLD, JULY 1, 1856, TO JUNE 30, 1867.

1864-5—Engine Lot and House No. 1, sold for $9,250, half paid, half unpaid.	
1864-5—Engine Lot and House No. 7, sold for $15,000, all paid	$15,000 00
1864-5—Engine Lot and House No. 10, sold for $5,050, one-fourth paid, but since refunded. Sale canceled.	
1864-5—Engine Lot and House No. 12, sold for $8,500, $50 allowed for mantels, balance paid......	8,450 00
1864-5—Hall of Records lot and building, sold for $11,250, all paid......................	11,250 00
1864-5—City Slip Lots 11 and 12...............	5,100 00
1864-5—City Slip Lot 19, ($3,000 in Bonds of 1863, and $220 in coin.)	
1866-7—City Slip Lot 40, sold for $2,900, compromised on account of defective title, for...........	2,600 00

1866-7—City Slip Lot 91, sold for $1,900; compromised on account of defective title, for.......	1,620 00
1866-7—City Slip Lots 99 and 100, sold for $3,950, compromised on account of defective title, for	3,500 00
1866-7—City Slip Lots 111 and 112, sold for $2,900, compromised on account of defective title, for	1,200 00
1866-7—City Slip Lots 113 and 114, sold for $2,650, compromised on account of defective title, for	1,900 00
1866-7—City Slip Lots 115, 116, and 118, sold for...	3,100 00
1866-7—Engine Lot No. 1, (1½ feet of lot).........	200 00
1866-7—Engine Lot and House No. 3, California Street	27,150 00
1866-7—Engine Lot and House No. 4, Market Street.	16,050 00
1866-7—Engine Lot and House No. 5, sold for $8,000. Allowed for State title, $250.............	7,750 00
1866-7—Hose Lot and House No. 1.............	3,850 00
1866-7—Hook and Ladder Lot and House No. 1.....	8,300 00
1866-7—Engine Lot on Stockton near Greenwich Street	300 00
1866-7—Engine Lot and House on Sutter Street......	2,075 00

Engine House and Lot No. 10, Pacific Street, sold March 11, 1867, for $4,600, unpaid.

CITY SLIP LOTS CONVEYED TO HOLDERS OF JUDGMENTS, IN PART SETTLEMENT OF THE SAME, 1863-4, PER AUDITOR'S REPORT, P. 43.

Nos. 1, 4, 6, 7, 8, 13, 14, 15, 16, 17, 18, 22, 29, 30, 31, 32, 33, 35, 36, 37, 38, 45, 46, 47, 48, 55, 56, 57, 58, 59, 60, 61, 62, 63, 64, 69, 70, 72, 73, 74, 75, 76, 78, 79, 80, 81, 82, 83, 90, 94, 95, 97, 98, 101, 102, 103, 104, 105, 106, 107, 108, 110, 120.

CITY SLIP LOTS SOLD AT AUCTION, BUT DEPOSITS AFTERWARDS WITHDRAWN.

No. 21, for $6,300; No. 39, for $2,100; No. 43, for $4,100; No. 68, for $3,450; No. 92, for $2,300; No. 109, for $1,350.

CITY SLIP LOTS NOT SOLD.

Nos. 21 (lost to the city by decision of Supreme Court, under Statute of Limitations), 85, 86, 87, 88, 121.

INDEX TO STATUTES REGARDING EXPENDITURES, REVENUE, ETC., OBSERVED IN BUSINESS OF THE AUDITOR'S OFFICE.

MEMORANDUM.

The foregoing index affords some idea of the voluminous and complicated laws affecting the financial business of the City and County; many of these statutes are very contradictory, or impose restrictions which are very difficult to comply with, particularly in view of the rapid growth and increasing expenses of the city.

Numerous delicate financial questions have arisen during the business of the year, which need not here be particularized, but in regard to which the Auditor has endeavored to act equitably and impartially, and to extend every accommodation in his power consistent with duty. He regrets having been obliged to refuse numerous bills, to the extent in all of about $25,000, which passed the Board of Supervisors in excess of legal allowances or provisions; such of these as are meritorious will no doubt have the influence of our Legislative Delegation with a view to relief, but the Auditor cannot avoid deprecating the appropriation by the Board of Supervisors of any sums not strictly within the limits allowed by law; it may not always be a sufficient restriction to depend solely upon the Auditor to stop bills which regularly pass the Board.

The foregoing report is necessarily but a condensation of the business of the office. During the year 8,800 demands on the Treasury received the critical examination of the Auditor, and were duly registered and signed; 800 receipts for money paid into the Treasury were registered and countersigned; 13,035 State and County Licenses and 7,696 Municipal Licenses were signed and issued; 20,594 Poll Tax Receipts were issued to Tax Collector and duly accounted for by him; 565 Street Assessments for work done and apportioned on property were received from the Superintendent. of Streets, examined and countersigned; $150,000 of School Bonds with 4,500 Coupons were signed and issued, and various other business transacted. Accounts were kept with the State Controller,

Treasurer, Tax Collector, and License Collector, and duly verified by periodical settlements.

The expenses of the office have been—for Auditor's salary, $4,000 ; salary of one Clerk, $1,800 ; stationery, etc., $255.

Respectfully submitted,

HENRY M. HALE,
Auditor.

TREASURER'S REPORT.

CITY AND COUNTY TREASURY,
San Francisco, July 22, 1867.

To the Honorable the President and Board of Supervisors
Of the City and County of San Francisco—

GENTLEMEN : In accordance with Resolution No. 6,963, of your Honorable Body, I herewith submit my Annual Report for the fiscal year 1866-67, which shows :

The balance at credit of the State of California July 2, 1866.............	$57,023 73
Receipts during the year.............	987,105 77
	$1,044,129 50
Disbursements in settlement with Controller.........................	980,212 33
Balance June 29, 1867..........	$63,917 17

Balance at credit of City and County July 2, 1866....................	$156,754 11	
Receipts during the year............	2,455,293 69	
	$2,612,047 80	
Disbursements.....................	2,340,987 11	
		272,060 69
Balance Cash on hand June 29, 1867..................,.....		$335,977 86

Respectfully submitted by

JOS. S. PAXSON,

Treasurer.

A statement of Treasury Account in detail is included in Auditor's Report, pages 62 to 86.

TAX COLLECTOR'S REPORT.

TAX COLLECTOR'S OFFICE,
San Francisco, June 30th, 1867.

To the Honorable the Board of Supervisors
Of the City and County of San Francisco—

GENTLEMEN: In response to Resolution No. 6,963 of your Honorable Body, I herewith submit my Annual Report for the fiscal year 1866–7, ending with this date.

CHAS. R. STORY,

Tax Collector.

TAX COLLECTOR'S REPORT FOR THE FISCAL YEAR 1866–7, ENDING JUNE 30TH, 1867.

Upon the Assessment Rolls for said fiscal year the assessed valuations of Real Estate and Personal Property appear as are hereinafter shown, to wit:

REAL ESTATE.

	Valuation.	Valuation.
Original Roll	$53,466,896 00	
Supplemental Roll	18,525 00	
Total Real Estate	$53,485,421 00	
Add Duplicate and Overpayments	26,735 00	
Total amount charged by Auditor to Tax Collector on Real Estate Account		$53,512,156 00
Carried forward		$53,512,156 00

	Valuation.	Valuation.
Brought forward.......		$53,512,156 00

PERSONAL PROPERTY.

Original Roll....................$41,770,204 86		
Supplemental Roll............... 1,444,771 57		
Duplicate and Overpayments........ 19,027 00		

Total amount charged by Auditor to Tax Collector on Personal Property Account................   43,234,003 43

Total Real Estate and Personal Property...................... $96,746,159 43

HENRY M. HALE, AUDITOR, IN ACCOUNT WITH TAX COLLECTOR.

Dr.

	Valuation.	Valuation.
REAL ESTATE ACCOUNT for		
Cash paid Treasurer on........		$50,475,849 00
Retained under Protest........		13,000 00
Duplicate and Erroneous Assessments....................		43,110 00
Exemptions from Taxation by Law, on Property of United States....................	$512,330 00	
State of California............	1,800 00	
City and County of San Francisco....................	1,125,032 00	
Asylums, etc................	368,530 00	
Roman Catholic Churches......	430,054 00	
Protestant Churches..........	409,461 00	
Hebrew Congregations........	120,200 00	
Total Exemptions of Real Estate		2,967,407 00
Delinquent on Supplemental Roll....................		12,790 00

Total amount charged by Auditor to Tax Collector on Real Estate Account, as above shown........ $53,512,156 00

	Valuation.	Valuation.
PERSONAL PROPERTY ACCOUNT for		
Cash paid Treasurer on........		$23,966,576 16
Retained under Protest.........		48,928 00
Duplicate and Erroneous Assessment, inclusive of Mortgages Satisfied and Canceled prior to assessment................		1,368,065 74
Exemptions from Taxation by Law, on Property of Asylums, etc......................	$48,600 00	
Foreign Consuls.............	4,400 00	
Total Exemptions of Personal Property...............		1,421,065 74
Property which was found to have been Assessed, and Taxes thereon paid, in other Counties in this State.............		487,043 00
Mortgage Assessments in suspense, awaiting Supreme Court decisions.................		16,082,975 53
Shipping and Water Craft, not to be found.................		219,853 00
Sundry Personal Property Assessed to parties, who (as well as the property assessed) have disappeared, or the parties are now in destitute circumstances.		485,751 00
Delinquent, and presumed to be collectable, a portion already in the hands of the District Attorney for Suit........,.....		521,911 00
Total amount charged by Auditor to Tax Collector on Personal Property Account, as above shown...................		$43,234,003 43

RECAPITULATION AS TO COLLECTIONS.

The Rate of Taxation was $3.10 on each $100 of Valuation, and the Apportionment thereof as follows:

CITY AND COUNTY TAX.

LEVIED BY BOARD OF SUPERVISORS.

	Cents.	
School Fund, (Support of Common Schools)	35	
Street Light Fund (Lighting Streets)	15	
Street Department Fund (City's Street Assessments)	4½	
General Fund (all other current Expenses)	67½	
Total for Current Expenses..		$1 22
Corporation Debt Fund (various Sinking Funds)	38½	
Bonds of 1855 (Sinking Fund)....	5	
City Slip Judgment Bonds (Interest)	9	
City Slip Judgment Bonds (Sinking Fund)...	7½	
Pacific Railroad Interest Tax....	8½	
San Francisco and San Jose Railroad Bonds (Interest)	4	
San Francisco and San Jose Railroad Bonds (Loan Fund).....	2½	
Total for sundry Debts and Interest	75	
Total for City and County.....		$1 97

STATE TAX.

FIXED BY STATUTE.

	Cents.	
General State purposes	30¾	
Interest and Redemption of Bonds of 1857	30	
Interest and Redemption of Bonds of 1860	1¼	
Interest and Redemption of Soldiers' Relief Bonds	4	
Interest and Redemption of Soldiers' Bounty Bonds	12	
Interest and Redemption of Line Officers' Bonds	1	
Support of Common Schools	8	
Interest on Pacific Railroad Bonds	8	
Construction of State Capitol....	10	
Militia Purposes (in lieu of Military Poll Tax)	5	
Insane Asylum Purposes	3	
Total for State Purposes......		$1 13
Total for City and County Purposes		$1 97
Total on each $100 valuation ..		$3 10

	Valuation.	Taxes.
Collections on Real Estate	$50,475,849 00	$1,564,751 32
Collections on Personal Property..	23,966,576 16	742,963 86
Total	$74,442,425 16	$2,307,715 18

CASH PAID INTO THE TREASURY BY THE TAX COLLECTOR DURING THE FISCAL YEAR 1866–7.

For Taxes of 1866–7—Real Estate...	$1,564,751 32
For Taxes of 1866–7—Personal......	742,963 86
For Taxes of 1866-7—Real Estate and Personal—Total..............	$2,307,715 18

5 per cent. on Real Estate, Delinquent.	$12,077 26	
2½ per cent. on Personal, Delinquent..	587 56	
5 per cent. on Personal, Delinquent...	5,059 61	
Total 2½ and 5 per cent. on Real Estate and Personal.................		17,724 43
Total Taxes and Percentages for 1866–7		$2,325,439 61

TAXES OF PRIOR FISCAL YEARS.

Taxes of 1865-6..................	$1,907 73	
Taxes of 1864-5..................	5 96	
Taxes of 1863-4..................	38 85	
Taxes of 1862-3..................	20 79	
Taxes of 1861-2..................	4 87	
Taxes of 1859-60.................	3,154 46	
Taxes of 1857-8..................	53 48	
Taxes of 1856-7..................	391 58	
Total.......................		5,577 72
5 per cent. for said Prior Years		236 30
Sundry Taxes and Percentages collected during 1866-7		$2,331,253 63
State Poll Taxes of 1866 and 1867...		$35,140 35

COMMISSIONS COLLECTED FROM THE STATE AND PAID INTO THE TREASURY.

6 per cent. on $10,000..............	$600 00	
4 per cent. on $10,000..............	400 00	
3 per cent. on $30,000..............	900 00	
2 per cent. on $150,000.............	3,000 00	
1 per cent. on $641,199 41..........	6,411 99	
Tax Collector's Commissions from the State		$11,311 99
Received for 1,066 Tax Sale Certificates, at $2		2,132 00
Received for 72 Tax Deeds, at $4....		292 00
Received for Advertising Delinquent Lists		3,102 00
Sundry Commissions, Extra Fees, etc., paid Treasurer		$16,837 99

EXPENSES OF THE OFFICE.

Tax Collector's Salary	$4,000 00
Deputies' Salaries	6,300 00
Clerks' Salaries	4,050 00
Auctioneer's Salary................	200 00
Advertising, General	888 25
Advertising Delinquent Lists........	2,513 80
Books and Stationery	1,265 00
Total........................	$19,217 05
Deduct Commissions and Fees paid Treasurer	16,837 99
Excess of Expenses over Commissions and Fees paid into Treasury	$2,379 06

San Francisco, June 30, 1867.

CHAS. R. STORY,
Tax Collector.

ASSESSOR'S REPORT.

ASSESSOR'S OFFICE,
San Francisco, August 1, 1867.

To the Honorable the Board of Supervisors
Of the City and County of San Francisco—

GENTLEMEN: In compliance with Resolution No. 6,963, of your Honorable Body, I submit herewith a Report of matters connected with the office of City and County Assessor:

EXPENSES OF THE OFFICE.

Salary of Assessor from July 1, 1866, to July 1, 1867	$4,000 00
Salary of Deputies from July 1, 1866, to July 1, 1867	15,000 00
Books, Maps, Blanks, and Stationery	763 93
Total	$19,763 93
Deduct State's Proportion, $\frac{113}{300}$	7,444 41
City and County's Proportion is	$12,319 52

The Assessment Roll of Personal Property delivered on the first Monday in June last, for the current fiscal year, amounts to $28,556,806 66.

In this Roll was not included "Solvent Debts secured by Mortgage," which alone will amount to at least $18,000,000 00, and will be assessed and returned in a Supplemental Roll. The collection of taxes on this description of Personal Property is still contested, no decision of the Supreme Court of this State having yet been had upon the legality of the assessment of this class of property, the cases heretofore decided by the Courts having been determined upon purely technical grounds.

There is a suit now pending, in the Supreme Court, on appeal, entitled "The People vs. McCreery," in which a decision decisive of the whole question was expected to have been had in July last. Judgment, however, has not yet been rendered therein.

It was in consequence of the pendency of this suit, and the expectation of an early decision, as above stated, that the Assessment of "Solvent Debts secured by Mortgage" was not included in the Assessment Roll of Personal Property, returned on the first Monday in June last.

The Assessor is now engaged in making up a Supplemental Roll, which will include the above class of Personal Property.

The Real Estate Roll is not yet completed. I can, therefore, only give at this time an estimate of the aggregate valuation. It will not vary much from $58,000,000 00.

Enclosed herewith I submit for your approval a copy of my Annual Report to the Surveyor-General of the State. Also, a Supplemental Report of Statistics of the Manufactures and Mechanical Industries of this City and County, which, I request, may be considered by your Honorable Body as an Appendix to this Report.

All of which is respectfully submitted,

WM. R. WHEATON,

Assessor.

REPORT TO THE SURVEYOR GENERAL.

ASSESSOR'S OFFICE,
City and County of San Francisco, Aug. 1, 1867.

Hon. J. F. Houghton,
Surveyor General of the State of California—

SIR : Herewith I hand you supplemental report of statistics of the manufactures and mechanical industries of this city and county, for the year 1866. In making up this report, in conformity with the act of 1866, (requiring information to be collected and reported annually to the Surveyor General of the State,) I have endeavored to return the same in such form as will best give a correct idea of the extent and value of the various products manufactured, and, so far as possible, the quantities of material used. I have also attempted to gather such information as would enable me to estimate and report the condition of manufactures as compared with the previous year, as well as the relative financial prosperity of the manufacturers.

In this, as well as in other inquiries, I have experienced great difficulty, owing to the natural reluctance of manufacturers to give data concerning the prospects or results of their business—the confounding, by many persons, of my office with that of the Assessor of Internal Revenue—and last, though not least, the insufficiency of the law, which requires me to procure the information desired, under a heavy penalty, yet provides no means to enforce a compliance on the part of manufacturers and others engaged in the different branches of trade.

In this connection I would respectfully suggest that you recommend to the next Legislature an amendment to the act above referred to, so that this deficiency of the law may be remedied. The matter of correctness in statistical information concerning the industrial resources of the State, is a most important one, not only for business estimates to our own people, but to encourage immigration from abroad. From a variety of causes not necessary here to mention, a gross ignorance of the resources of California prevails in the Atlantic States as well as in Europe : and in my opinion no more efficient means to furnish proper infoimation in these respects can be had, than an official publication of the variety and extent of those mechanical industries of which this city and county is the great center. Men intuitively reason by comparison; and from the prosperity, variety and extent of our domestic manufactures, the most ignorant can by inference alone form a pretty correct idea of the state of society, and the business advantages that California offers as inducements for the industrious and worthy to settle within her territory. Where the olive, fig, almond, orange and citron grow, men know that the climate must be favorable to physical health; so where manufactures and mechanical industries largely prevail, a moral bond is given for the good order and intellectuality of the people. So far as I could learn from the parties applied to, their manufactures during the year 1866, as a whole, have been more extensive than in preceding years. Their prosperity, in a money point of view, has, as a general thing, been also greater; but in many branches of trade parties complain that competition has been stronger, and profits smaller, than heretofore. No prominent branch of trade, however, has been seriously affected, while many new and important manufactures have been, or are about to be introduced. The most prominent of these is the rolling-mills for copper and iron, the works being reported to be of a capacity sufficient to supply all the manufacturers of those metals upon the Pacific Coast. In addition to the rolling-mills and forge at present being constructed, I am informed that it is contemplated in time to add copper smelting works, for the reduction of low grades of ores; and in case iron ore of a suitable quality, abundance and cheapness can be found to work, an iron furnace will be joined to the establishment.

Another great want of California has been supplied in 1866, by the erection of a linseed oil mill, which has a manufacturing capacity sufficient to supply the entire States and Territories of the Pacific Coast. A new branch of woolen manufactures is also about to be commenced, which will give employment to several hundreds of people, and supply a great want in the manufactures of the State. This is the Pacific Woolen Mills, which will make all varieties of woolen and mixed knit goods used by our people. The mill has been erected, and the machinery set up ready for use, the latter consisting of seven sets of cards, four mules, twenty-seven knitting machines, and sixteen hundred spindles—the whole being driven by a one hundred horse power engine, and estimated to require an annual consumption of eight hundred thousand pounds of wool to keep it constantly employed. Besides this new mill, both the other woolen mills have largely increased their manufacturing capacity by additional buildings and machinery, during the past year. Among other important works erected in 1866, is a dry dock at the Potrero, with a capacity to dock vessels of 1,500 tons register, and a stone dry dock at Hunter's Point, with a capacity to dock any known vessel now afloat, except the Great Eastern and the Dunderberg. The latter dock is expected to be ready for use some time in the latter part of 1867, and when completed, from its size and convenient location, will make the port of San Francisco much resorted to by the larger vessels on the Pacific ocean, when needing important repairs.

The facts connected with manufactures and mechanical industries for 1866, so far as I can learn, indicate a degree of prosperity decidedly encouraging; and I should judge that the statistics of 1867, when taken, will show a healthy increase over those of the preceding year.

The following is a list of manufactures. Where the articles were too small or varied to mention, the value is set down. Only new goods or manufactures are reported.

FLOUR MILLS.   8

Men employed	84
Flour made in 1866, barrels	247,708
Pearl barley, tons	50
Hominy, tons	50
Farina, tons	25
Oat-meal, tons	50
Groats, tons	13
Buckwheat and rye flour, barrels	1,000
Feed barley ground, sacks	25,000
Run of stone	20
Total daily capacity of mills, barrels flour	1,815
Horse power of engines	515

SAW MILLS. 8

Lumber sawed, feet............................	8,950,000
Saws run......................................	38
Men employed.................................	142
Horse power of engines........................	256

SALT MILLS. 5

Men employed.................................	30
Salt ground, (domestic) tons...................	2,400
Salt ground, (foreign) tons....................	1,800
Run of stone..................................	6
Horse power of engines........................	70

RICE MILLS. 2

Men employed.................................	13
Rice cleaned, pounds..........................	7,658,873
Capacity to clean paddy per day...............	70,000
Horse power of engines........................	80

WOOLEN MILLS. 2

Men employed.................................	725
Horse power of engines........................	300
Sets of cards.................................	21
Mules and jacks...............................	28
Looms..	80
Spindles......................................	8,000
Blankets made, pairs..........................	110,000
Broadcloth, cassimeres and tweeds, yards.......	185,000
Flannel.......................................	850,000
Wool used, pounds............................	3,500,000

WADDING MILLS. 1

Men employed.................................	12
Horse power of engine.........................	35
Cotton used, pounds...........................	10,000

10

IRON FOUNDRIES AND BOILER SHOPS.   14

Men employed   1,018
Pig iron used, tons.................................   6,921
Bar iron used, tons.................................   1,448
Sheet and boiler iron used, tons....................   1,027
Rivets of iron used, tons...........................   110

IRON DOOR, SHUTTER AND SAFE SHOPS.   6

Men employed   44
Sheet iron used, tons..............................   151
Bar iron used, tons................................   262

BRASS FOUNDRIES.   4

Men employed   62
Value of manufactures............................ $95,000

LEAD AND SHOT WORKS.   1

Men employed   18
Quantity of lead manufactured, tons................   1,000
Quantity of shot manufactured......................   200
Capacity of works per year, tons...................   4,000

CORDAGE FACTORY.   1

Men employed...................................   47
Horse power of engine............................   150
Hemp manufactured, tons..........................   1,000
Capacity of works per year, tons..................   1,750

WIRE ROPE MANUFACTORY.   1

Men employed...................................   3
Value of manufactures............................ $23,000

SAW TEETH MANUFACTORY.   1

Men employed...................................   9
Value of manufactures............................ $12,500

SAW MANUFACTORY. 1

Men employed... 9.
Value of manufactures, 3 mos........................ 3,000

GLUE MANUFACTORY. 1

Men employed... 10
Glue made, tons...................................... 16
Neatsfoot oil made, gallons.......................... 5,000
Capacity per day for glue, barrels................... 10
Capacity per day for oil, gallons.................... 200

OIL REFINERY. 1

Men employed... 3
Oil refined, gallons................................. 60,000
Capacity of works per day, gallons................... 400

PIANO FORTE MANUFACTORIES. 1

Men employed... 2
Pianos made.. 12
Average value of each instrument..................... $450

ORGAN MANUFACTORIES. 1

Men employed... 2
Organs made.. 2

BELLOWS MANUFACTORIES. 2

Men employed... 5
Bellows made, (mostly blacksmiths').................. 650

STEAM MARBLE SAW WORKS. 1

Men employed... 30
Horse power of engine................................ 15
Saws run, (1 gang)................................... 20

BREWERIES. 17

Men employed... 138
Beer made, barrels................................... 76,602

MALT MANUFACTURERS. 3

Men employed... 8
Grain malted (barley) 100 lb. sacks.................. 29,023

HOSE AND BELTING MANUFACTORIES.   2

Men employed.....................................   12
Hose made, feet...................................   12,000
Hose and belting leather used, sides   2,750
Collar leather used, sides..........................   3,000
Horse collars made, dozen..........................   400

MATCH MANUFACTORIES.   3

Men employed.....................................   14
Matches made, gross..............................   25,000

CUTLERS.   2

Men employed.....................................   6
Value of manufactures............................. $4,800

BOX MANUFACTORIES.   5

Men employed.....................................   62
Lumber used, (pine, fir and spruce) feet.............. 4,000,000
Spanish cedar used, feet...........................   110,000

PETROLEUM REFINERIES.   2

Men employed.....................................   12
Number of stills run..............................   6
Burning oil made, gallons..........................   57,429
Distillery capacity (crude oil, per day) gallons........   2,600

GLASS WORKS.   2

Men employed.....................................   80
Furnaces..   2
Pots..   13
Value of manufactures............................. $80,000
Capacity of works per month....................... $12,000

GLASS CUTTING WORKS.   1

Men employed.....................................   2
Value of manufactures............................. $6,000

MIRROR SILVERING WORKS.   1

Men employed.....................................   4
Silvering tables...................................   3
Value of manufactures............................. $18,000

BILLIARD MANUFACTORIES. 3

Men employed.....................................	12
Tables made.......................................	70
Average value of tables...........................	$480

SOAP MANUFACTORIES. 10

Men employed.....................................	33
Soap made, pounds................................	2,831,419
Capacity of works per month, pounds..............	710,000

BROOM AND WOODEN WARE MANUFACTORIES. 3

Men employed.....................................	86
Brooms made, dozen...............................	17,580
Pails, dozen	6,057
Tubs, nests 4 each.................................)	7,654
Zinc washboards, dozen............................	3,582
Barrel Covers, dozen..............................	459
Peach baskets, dozen..............................	412
Sieves, dozen	161
Powder kegs......................................	60,000

TANNERIES. 5

Men employed.....................................	26
Tan bark used, cords..............................	375
Hides tanned.....................................	2,400
Calf skins tanned, dozen...........................	615
Kip skins tanned, dozen...........................	515
Monthly capacity of works—Hides.................	650
" " " Calf skins, doz.........	300
" . " Kip skins, doz..........	300
Calf skins dressed and finished, doz................	1,200

CHEMICAL WORKS. 2

Men employed.....................................	12
Nitrate of soda used, tons.........................	250
Sulphur consumed, tons...........................	200
Sulphuric and nitric acid made, tons...............	400
Capacity of works per day—Sulphuric acid, tons..	2
" " " Nitric acid, tons.........	1
Sulphate of copper made, tons.....................	120

SUGAR REFINERIES.   3

Men employed.......................................   259
Horse power of engines...........................   225
Raw sugar used, pounds.......................... 22,743,312
Refined sugar made, barrels 230 lbs. each.............   87,630
Syrup made, gallons...............................   570,031
Capacity of works per day, (raw sugar) pounds.......   163,000

Many of the foregoing manufactories have not only a capacity to supply the wants of this State, and the adjoining States and Territories, but also to admit of large exports. The flouring mills have a capacity of over half a million barrels per annum, and during the latter part of the year sent large quantities of flour, via the Isthmus, to New York. There the quality of the flour commanded the highest prices paid, while California wheat was condemned by Eastern millers as being too difficult to grind to make good flour. Many of the iron foundries and boiler shops have capacity sufficient to make the largest castings required, while the largest sized boilers can be made, of as good material and workmanship as can be found in the Atlantic States.

Besides the domestic demand for machinery, etc., the shops and foundries have supplied a large demand from Mexico and other foreign countries. The inauguration of a line of first class steamers to Japan and China promises, when in full operation, to bring large orders to our workshops for machinery which has heretofore been supplied exclusively from Atlantic ports. The glass works which have been established for the manufacture of white glass during 1866, are capable of supplying the entire Pacific Coast with all articles in that line. Our soap works have almost entirely stopped the importation of all but fancy soaps, while the same results have been obtained by the manufacture of brooms and wooden ware, considerable quantities of the former having been exported to foreign ports. The chemical works are of a capacity to supply the entire demand for acids for the refining of the precious metals, and the completion of the Golden City Chemical Works will still further increase this manufacture. These latter works are of most extensive capacity, and promise soon to engage in the manufacture of many chemicals, extracts, etc., which have hitherto been imported. The sugar refineries have a capacity of more than double the requirements of the Pacific States and Territories; and if the importation of melado from the Hawaiian Islands, at comparatively low prices, is successful, they will in all probability become large exporters of refined sugars to other markets now supplied from Europe.

The lead and shot works, and the cordage factory, almost entirely supply the domestic demand. The brass foundries supply about half the demand, while glue and neatsfoot oil are exported to the Atlantic States.

The hose and belting manufacture is largely increasing, and the articles made give entire satisfaction to parties using them. The domestic made matches have completely driven the imported article out from consumption. Two small, yet important manufactures, have been inaugurated during the year, which promise to be of great benefit to our people. One is the manufacture of all kinds of saws from plate steel, and the other the sawing of marble by steam power. Hitherto all marble sawing was done by hand, and was an expensive and tedious process. In fact, the expense of labor was so great that it prevented the opening up of marble quarries in this State, as domestic sawn marble could not compete with that imported from Europe and the Atlantic States, where cheap labor and machinery were used. The present works are limited in capacity to the supplies of block marble to be had; but it is the intention of the owners to import and quarry largely all kinds of marble in the block, when the works will be made more extensive.

A most important manufacture was commenced in December, 1866. This was a type foundry, which, with three machines, employs seven men and thirty boys and girls, the value of the type made averaging at the rate of $20,000 per year. It is the intention of the proprietors to increase the number of machines to six, with proportionate addition of men and children required for the business. The quality of the type made is unexceptionable, and the demand is so large that orders for months ahead have been received.

Respectfully,

WM. R. WHEATON,

Assessor City and County of San Francisco.

STATISTICS, JANUARY 1, 1866, TO JANUARY 1, 1867.

COMPILED FROM THE BOOKS OF THE ASSESSOR OF SAN FRANCISCO COUNTY,
FOR REPORT TO THE SURVEYOR GENERAL.

AGRICULTURAL PRODUCTS.

		Number.
Land inclosed	Acres	18,000
Land cultivated	Acres	2,600
Barley	Acres	245
Barley	Bushels	4,500
Oats	Acres	590
Oats	Bushels	1,400
Buckwheat	Acres	5
Buckwheat	Bushels	125
Peas	Acres	15
Peas	Bushels	150
Beans	Acres	20
Beans	Bushels	300
Potatoes	Acres	1,100
Potatoes	Bushels	45,000
Onions	Acres	20
Onions	Bushels	600
Hay	Acres	200
Hay	Tons	335
Beets	Tons	100
Turnips	Tons	90
Pumpkins & Squashes	Tons	30
Butter	Pounds	1,000
Cheese	Pounds	2,500
Honey	Pounds	75

FRUIT TREES AND VINES.

Apple Trees	1,549
Pear Trees	600
Plum Trees	350
Cherry Trees	200
Nectarine Trees	10
Quince Trees	5
Fig Trees	10
Gooseberry	320
Raspberry	100

	Number.
Strawberry Vines	30,000
Grape Vines	75

LIVE STOCK.

Horses	7,439
Mules	150
Cows	4,048
Calves	87
Beef Cattle	20
Oxen	40
Sheep	11
Hogs	5,625
Chickens	4,652
Turkeys	190
Geese	208
Ducks	1,759
Hives of Bees	8

IMPROVEMENTS.

Grist Mills	8
Steam Power	8
Run of Stone	20
Barrels of Flour made	247,708
Bushels of Corn ground	7,520
Saw Mills	8
Steam Power	8
Lumber sawed, feet	8,950,000
Quartz Mills	1
Woolen Mills	2
Pounds of Wool used	3,500,000
Cotton Mills	1
Pounds of Cotton Used	10,000
Railroads	6
Miles in length	27
Land cultivated in 1867, acres	2,600
Acres of Barley sown in 1867	250

Assessed value of Real Estate, 1866–7, improvements included . . $49,138,027 00
Assessed value of Personal Property $39,264,246 68
Estimated total Population 125,000
Registered Voters, August, 1867 20,672
Poll Tax collected in 1866 by Tax Collector $45,720 00

WM. R. WHEATON,
Assessor San Francisco County.

RECORDER'S REPORT.

HALL OF RECORDS,
San Francisco, August 1st, 1867.

To the Honorable the Board of Supervisors
Of the City and County of San Francisco—

GENTLEMEN: In accordance with the Resolution No. 6,963, of your Honorable Board, passed June 17th, requesting the various City and County Officials to report to you the transactions in their respective departments, I have the honor to submit the following summary of transactions in the Hall of Records:

RECEIPTS.

Fees collected and paid into the Treasury...	$43,237 25

EXPENDITURES.

Recorder's Salary	$4,000 00	
Chief Deputy's Salary	2,100 00	
Second Deputy's Salary	1,800 00	
Porter's Salary	900 00	
Amount paid Clerks for Copying 161,259 folios, at 12 cents	19,351 08	
Books and Stationery	2,184 38	
Newspapers	92 13	
		30,427 59
Surplus		$12,809 66

LIST OF PRINCIPAL BOOKS OF RECORD IN THE RECORDER'S OFFICE.

Deeds	394
Mortgages	210
Releases of Mortgages	39
Powers of Attorney	23
Leases	27
Liens	10
Tax Deeds	15
Covenants	7
Bonds	2
Separate Property of Wife	4
Attachments	8
Lis Pendens	7
Claims of Homesteads	16
Transcripts of Judgments	3
Chattel Mortgages	8
Sheriff's Certificates	8
Miscellaneous, " A " to " T " inclusive	20
Marriage Licenses	7
General Indexes	45
Indexes of Deeds	35
Indexes of Mortgages	11
Attachments, A, B, C, D	4
Deeds of Trust	4
Certified Grants	5
	912

LIST OF INSTRUMENTS RECORDED DURING THE FISCAL YEAR ENDING JUNE 30, 1867.

	1866—July	August	September	October	November	December	1867—January	February	March	April	May	June	Total
Bonds	1	1		3	1	1	3	2	2	1	1		16
Sole Traders	2	4		6	1	5	3	3	1	1		1	27
Tax Deeds	18	9	1	1	5	4	6	3	4	1	2	2	56
Chattel Mortgages	4	4	6	9	5	9	8	8	3	9	1	7	73
Transcripts of Judgments	1	1	3	5	1	2	4	7	2	4	3	6	39
Miscellaneous	5	27	27	19	13	27	29	20	36	18	28	29	278
Assignments of Mortgages	6	15	5	13	11	8	11	16	15	17	11	10	138
Separate Property of Wife	4		3	7	1	5	1		6	4	5	4	40
Tax Certificates	301	32	5	3	3	12	22	25	14	32	17	260	726
Leases, Assignments, and Surrenders	43	44	32	44	23	44	35	32	34	28	45	34	438
Liens	5	8	4	4	7	5	5	3	6	7	2	5	61
Attachments	10	23	81	40	23	11	26	11	16	22	10	28	301
Sheriff's Certificates	13	10	16	9	9	7	6	7	7	9	8	10	111
Lis Pendens	7	9	10	12	11	11	17	24	27	15	22	27	192
Covenants	7	7	7	5	2	6	4	9	4	8	5	7	71
Satisfaction of Mortgages	75	67	40	35	37	48	50	54	70	55	71	45	647
Powers of Attorney, Substitution and Revocation	25	36	33	25	25	27	25	27	34	31	39	23	350
Marriage Licenses	73	114	54	92	106	67	88	105	109	62	77	83	1,030
Declarations and Abandonments of Homesteads	36	28	30	30	24	35	25	25	31	23	38	23	348
MORTGAGES	186	177	151	100	182	174	178	211	193	228	258	176	2,214
DEEDS	501	540	393	517	424	532	588	600	774	780	789	668	7,106

Total, 14,262

I have nothing of importance to add, except to reiterate the recommendation made in my report last year, in regard to obtaining the sanction of the Legislature to create a Sinking Fund for the erection of a Hall of Records, built of materials expressly adapted for the safety of the books and documents deposited therein; an undertaking perfectly feasible, in view of the large surplus now to the credit of this office, to which I call your particular attention, as showing an amount of transactions in Real Estate unprecedented in any former year.

Respectfully submitted,

T. YOUNG,

County Recorder.

COUNTY CLERK'S REPORT.

OFFICE OF THE COUNTY CLERK
OF THE CITY AND COUNTY OF SAN FRANCISCO,
July 31st, 1867.

To the Honorable the Mayor
    and the Board of Supervisors—

GENTLEMEN: In compliance with a Resolution of your Honorable Board, adopted on the seventeenth day of June last, I submit the following Report of the condition of the County Clerk's Office, and of the business transacted in its several departments during the fiscal year ending June 30th, 1867.

      Very respectfully,

WM. LOEWY,
County Clerk.

ORGANIZATION OF THE STATE COURTS OF RECORD IN AND FOR THE CITY AND COUNTY OF SAN FRANCISCO.

District Attorney..................NATHAN PORTER.
City and County Attorney...........H. M. HASTINGS.
County Clerk and *ex officio* Clerk of the
  Courts of Record in and for said
  County.........................WM. LOEWY,
Sheriff............................HENRY L. DAVIS.

FOURTH DISTRICT COURT.

Judge.............................Hon. E. D. SAWYER.
Deputy County Clerk and Minute Clerk.JOHN F. BODEN.
Deputy County Clerk and Register
  Clerk........................·......JAMES E. ASHCOM.
Deputy County Clerk and Assistant
  Register Clerk...................L. J. LEE.
Deputy Sheriff and Bailiff...........S. C. ELLIS.
Court Commissioner................CHAS. HALSEY.
Official Reporter..................GEO. O'DOHERTY.

TWELFTH DISTRICT COURT.

Judge.............................Hon. O. C. PRATT.
Deputy County Clerk and Minute Clerk.L. P. PECK.
Deputy County Clerk and Register
  Clerk ....OCTAVIUS BELL.
Deputy County Clerk and Assistant
  Register Clerk...................J. D. RUGGLES.
Copying Clerk ....H. J. BRADY.
Deputy Sheriff and Bailiff...........B. W. DAVIS.
Court Commissioner................ROBT. C. ROGERS.
Official Reporter..................GEO. O'DOHERTY.

FIFTEENTH DISTRICT COURT.

Judge...........................Hon. SAM'L H. DWINELLE.
Deputy County Clerk and Minute Clerk.ADOLPHUS D. GRIMWOOD.
Deputy County Clerk and Register
  Clerk ....OCTAVIUS BELL.
Deputy County Clerk and Assistant
  Register Clerk...................J. D. RUGGLES.
Copying Clerk....................JOSEPH HOLDEN.
Deputy Sheriff and Bailiff...........JOHN HILL.
Court Commissioner................JOHN L. LOVE.
Official Reporter..................ANDREW J. MARSH.

COUNTY COURT.

Judge............................Hon. SAMUEL COWLES.
Deputy County Clerk and Minute Clerk.WM. HARNEY.
Deputy County Clerk and Register
  Clerk.............................BERT. McNULTY.
Deputy Sheriff and Bailiff............Z. B. ADAMS.

PROBATE COURT.

Judge............................Hon. M. C. BLAKE.
Deputy County Clerk and Minute Clerk.A. J. JEGHERS.
Deputy County Clerk and Assistant
  Probate Clerk....................WM. LEDLIE.
Copying Clerk.....................D BAUM.

FOURTH, TWELFTH, AND FIFTEENTH DISTRICT COURTS.

CAUSES ON FILE IN SAID COURTS JUNE 30, 1867.

In the Fourth District Court (transferred from Court of First Instance) 1,472
In the Fourth District Court (transferred from Superior Court)........ 6,306
In the Fourth District Court....................................... 13,558
In the Twelfth District Court...................................... 13,539
In the Fifteenth District Court.................................... 2,986

Total number of causes on file............................ 37,861

NUMBER OF ACTIONS COMMENCED IN THE DISTRICT COURTS SINCE JULY 1, 1859.

Actions commenced during the year ending June 30, 1860.............. 1,668
Actions commenced during the year ending June 30, 1861............. 1,832
Actions commenced during the year ending June 30, 1862............. 1,884
Actions commenced during the year ending June 30, 1863............. 1,778
Actions commenced during the year ending June 30, 1864............. 1,853
Actions commenced during the year ending June 30, 1865............. 2,348
Actions commenced during the year ending June 30, 1866............. 2,126
Actions commenced during the year ending June 30, 1867............. 2,360

NUMBER OF ACTIONS COMMENCED IN THE DISTRICT COURTS DURING THE YEAR ENDING JUNE 30, 1867, AND THE DISPOSITION MADE OF THEM.

How Disposed of.	4th District Court.	12th District Court.	15th District Court.	Totals.
Discontinued	75	120	135	330
Adjudicated...........................	159	148	298	605
Still Pending	369	414	629	1,412
Transferred..........................		4	9	13
Totals....................	603	686	1,071	2,360.

CHARACTER OF ACTIONS COMMENCED IN THE FOURTH, TWELFTH, AND FIFTEENTH DISTRICT COURTS DURING THE YEAR ENDING JUNE 29TH, 1867.

Character of Actions.	4th District Court.	12th District Court.	15th District Court.	Totals.
For Money............................	305	294	626	1,225
For Ejectment.......................	38	47	39	124
For Recovery of Personal Property......	9	19	29	57
For Foreclosure of Mortgage...........	26	26	33	85
For Enforcement of Lien..............	4	6	2	12
For Injunction	18	18	21	57
For Partition of Real Estate.........	2	2	2	6
To quiet Title against the City..........		5	3	8
To quiet Title against others	23	16	28	67
To compel Conveyance	4	10	6	20
To set aside Conveyance	2	....	6	8
To perpetuate Testimony..............	2	....	1	3
For leave to Sell Real Estate............	2	3	....	5
For leave to Mortgage Real Estate.......	8	1	2	11
For Divorce..........................	56	30	117	203
For Mandamus.......................	2	4	2	8
For Habeas Corpus	15	8	6	29
For leave to act as Sole Trader..........	11	3	14	28
For Submission to Arbitration.........	....	....	1	1
For Violation of Passenger Contract Act. [Passenger Act, I.]	3	11	....	14
To Dissolve Copartnership	1	2	1	4
For Delinquent Taxes.................			4	4
For False Imprisonment..............	1	....	2	3
For Libel.............................	2	3	3	8
For Slander..........................	2	5	16	23
For Malicious Prosecution.............	3	....	2	5
For Breach of Promise of Marriage.....	2	2	1	5
For Personal Injuries.................	8	16	20	44
For Injuries to Property..............	4	8	13	25
For Street Assessments.................	44	118	27	189
Miscellaneous........................	6	29	44	79
Totals	603	686	1,071	2,360

ATTACHMENT SUITS COMMENCED DURING THE YEAR ENDING JUNE 30, 1867.

Fourth District Court.............................. 153

Twelfth District Court............................. 211

Fifteenth District Court........................... 460

Total... 824

JUDGMENTS ENTERED IN THE FOURTH, TWELFTH, AND FIFTEENTH DISTRICT
COURTS DURING THE YEAR ENDING JUNE 30, 1867.

Character of Judgments.	4th District Court.	12th District Court.	15th District Court.	Total.
For Money	138	135	255	528
For Possession of Personal Property.....	2	2	8	12
For Possession of Real Property	25	21	12	58
For Foreclosure of Mortgage............	10	17	15	42
For Partition of Real Estate...........	2	1	....	3
To confirm Partition of Real Estate.....	....	....	....	....
For Cancellation of Mortgages	....	....	....	....
For Foreclosure of Liens..............	10	29	11	50
For granting leave to sell Real Estate....	2	1	....	3
To quiet Title against the City..........	2	....	1	3
To quiet Title against others...........	19	19	18	56
To compel Conveyance.................	1	3	4	8
To compel Execution of Agreement	2	1	....	3
To Dissolve Partnership...............	....	1	....	1
For Cancellation of Deed..............	....	....	....	....
For Divorce..........................	25	20	45	90
For Injunction	....	....	1	1
For Transfer of Personal Property	1	....	....	1
For Nonsuits and Dismissals	45	25	32	102
Miscellaneous	....	6	3	9
Total number of Judgments........	284	281	405	970

AGGREGATE AMOUNTS OF MONEY JUDGMENTS RENDERED IN THE DISTRICT
COURTS DURING THE FISCAL YEAR ENDING JUNE 30, 1867. .

Fourth District Court........................ $597,513 71

Twelfth District Court...... .... 598,510 49

Fifteenth District Court...................... 851,447 32

Total $2,047,471 52

APPEALS TAKEN FROM THE FOURTH, TWELFTH, AND FIFTEENTH DISTRICT COURTS TO THE SUPREME COURT, DURING THE YEAR ENDING JUNE 30, 1867.

Fourth District Court.	70
Twelfth District Court.	54
Fifteenth District Court.	37
Total number of Appeals	161

DISPOSITION MADE IN THE SUPREME COURT DURING THE LAST YEAR OF APPEALS FROM THE FOURTH, TWELFTH, AND FIFTEENTH DISTRICT COURTS.

	4th District Court.	12th District Court.	15th District Court.	Totals.
Judgments affirmed	13	14	6	33
Judgments reversed	11	9	2	22
Appeals dismissed	2	1	3	6
No of Appeals decided	26	24	11	61

CRIMINAL ACTIONS IN THE DISTRICT COURTS DURING THE YEAR ENDING JUNE 30, 1867.

	Indictments Filed and Transferred.	Murder.	Manslaughter.
Fourth District Court	3	2	1
Twelfth District Court	2	2	
Fifteenth District Court	1 Filed. 2 on transfer.	3	

	Convictions.	Acquittals.	Continued.	Appeals.	No Suffered the Penalty of Death
Fourth District Court		2 1 Murder. 1 Manslaughter.	1		
Twelfth District Court		2 Murder.	1	1 Affirmed.	1
Fifteenth District Court		2 Murder.	1		

NATURALIZATION OF FOREIGNERS.

Number of Declarations of Intention made during the year ending June 30th, 1867	383
Number of Certificates of Citizenship issued	749

DECLARATIONS OF INTENTION.

The Nationalities of Foreigners who made Declarations of Intention are as follows:

Great Britain	222
Germany	105
Denmark	12
France	10
Norway and Sweden	9
Russia	6
Austria	4
Italy	4
Holland	3
Portugal	2
Switzerland	2
Belgium	1
Mexico	1
Costa Rica	1
Chile	1
	383

CERTIFICATES OF NATURALIZATION

Issued in the Fourth, Twelfth, and Fifteenth District Courts, and Nationalities of Naturalized Citizens:

Great Britain—Ireland	497
Germany	175
Denmark	18
Norway and Sweden	14
France	14
Russia	10
Switzerland	7
Austria	6
Italy	2
Belgium	1
Holland	1
Chile	2
Peru	1
Portugal	1
	749

COUNTY COURT.

(CIVIL.)

Increase of causes during the year ending June 30th, 1867.......................................	790
Whole number of causes on File..................	6,305
Of these 790 causes were :	

On Appeal from Justice's Court.............	515	
Transferred from other Courts..............	2	
Original Actions and Proceedings...........	273	
		790

CHARACTER OF ORIGINAL ACTIONS AND PROCEEDINGS.

Insolvency	177
Dissolution of Incorporations.........................	3
Habeas Corpus..	4
Forcible Entry and Unlawful Holding Over...............	89
Total	273

CHARACTER OF JUDGMENTS ENTERED.

For Money	218
For Possession of Property...........................	68
For Discharge in Insolvency	107
For Dismissal of Actions..............................	93
For Dismissal of Appeals.............................	49
Total	535

APPEALS.

During the last fiscal year five Appeals were taken from the County Court to the Supreme Court, in civil cases. Three of these Appeals are still pending. In one of them the Judgment of the County Court was affirmed, and in one reversed.

INCORPORATIONS.

Number of Certificates of Incorporation filed within
the fiscal year ending June 30th, 1867 115
Whole number of Certificates of Incorporation on file
in the office of the County Court............ 3,763
The character of the Incorporations who filed Certifi-
cates during the last year, is as follows :
Gold, Silver, and Copper Mining Incorporations.   31
Petroleum..................................   3
Quicksilver................................   3
Commercial.................................   28
Homestead..................................   15
Insurance   1
Religious..................................   7
Benevolent.................................   5
Scientific and Educational.................   1
Masonic and Odd Fellows....................   1
Order of Druids............................   1
Cemetery...................................   4
Track Laying...............................   1
Wood.......................................   1
Water......................................   2
Social and Literary........................   3
Steam Navigation...........................   1
Canal......................................   1
Chemical Works.............................   1
Photographic...............................   1
Sugar Refinery.............................   1
Telegraph   1
Dry Dock...................................   2
                                            ——— 115

INSANE.

Number of Persons committed during the past year to the
Insane Asylum, from this city....................,. 128
Whole number of commitments on record since October,
1858.. 907
Number of Insane committed during the year ending June
30th, 1864.................................... 90

Number of Insane committed during the year ending June
30th, 1865..   116
Number of Insane committed during the year ending June
30th, 1866..   100
Number of Insane committed during the year ending June
30th, 1867..   134

CORONER'S INQUESTS.

Number of Inquests filed during the last fiscal year........   98
Whole number of Inquests on file.....................   867

ATTORNEYS' OATHS.

Number of Attorneys' Oaths filed during the last fiscal year.   15

MARRIAGE LICENSES,

Issued during the fiscal year ending June 30th, 1867 :

July, 1866..	128
August, 1866......................................	83
September, 1866...................................	119
October, 1866.....................................	149
November, 1866....................................	146
December, 1866....................................	129
January, 1867.....................................	142
February, 1867....................................	142
March, 1867.......................................	121
April, 1867.......................................	124
May, 1867...	140
June, 1867..	115
Total.....................................	1,538

Fifty-four Licenses were issued to minors, with the consent of
their parents or guardians. Of this number seven Licenses were
issued to males (under 21 years) and 47 Licenses to females (under
18 years.)

Number of Marriage Licenses issued :

During the year ending June 30th, 1864..............   1,376
During the year ending June 30th, 1865..............   1,417
During the year ending June 30th, 1866..............   1,348
During the year ending June 30th, 1867..............   1,538

COUNTY COURT (CRIMINAL).

INDICTMENTS FILED DURING THE LAST FISCAL YEAR		DISPOSITION OF INDICTMENTS, AND OF THE DEFENDANTS THEREIN.					
Nature of the Crimes charged in said Indictments.	Number of Indictments.	Defendants found guilty.	Defendants not tried.	Indictments Dismissed.	Defendants Discharged.	Defendants who forfeited Bail.	Indictments transferred to Dist. Courts.
Assault with deadly weapon, to commit bodily injury	20	8	5	1	4	2	
Assault with intent to murder	4	2		1	1	1	
Assault and Battery	6	5		1	1		
Arson	6	4	1	5	1		
Burglary	37	21	9				
Bigamy	1		1				
Conspiracy	6	4		2			
Embezzlement	3	2	1				
Extortion	2		1	2			
Forgery	10	2					
Grand Larceny	60	32	9	7	12		
Gambling	24	8	10	3	3		
Housebreaking in the day time	11	6	2	1	2		
Incest	2	1		1			
Libel	1						
Murder	3						3
Manslaughter	2						2
Misdemeanor	11	2	4	5			
Mayhem	2		1	1			
Nuisance	4	1	2	1			
Obtaining Money by false pretenses	6	2	1	3			
Petit Larceny	10	7	2	1			
Perjury	2		2				
Resisting an officer	2		1	1			
Robbery	12	7	3	2			
Totals	247	114	60	41	24	3	5

COUNTY COURT.

[CRIMINAL.]

Number of Indictments filed :

During the year ending June 30th, 1860	147
During the year ending June 30th, 1861	
During the year ending June 30th, 1862	482
During the year ending June 30th, 1863	213
During the year ending June 30th, 1864	164
During the year ending June 30th, 1865	222
During the year ending June 30th, 1866	198
During the year ending June 30th, 1867	247

APPEALS.

Eleven Appeals were taken to the Supreme Court in criminal cases. In seven of these the judgment of the County Court was affirmed; in two reversed, and two are still pending.

FINES.

The aggregate amount of fines inflicted by the County Court during the year ending June 30th, 1867, was $3,075, which was paid into the County treasury.

APPEAL FROM THE POLICE COURT.

Number of Appeals from the Police Court during the year, were		32
Of these are—		
Undetermined	15	
Judgments reversed	3	
Dismissed	14	
		32

PROBATE COURT.

Whole number of Estates	2,614
Estates upon which proceedings were commenced during the year ending June 30th, 1867	328

These may be classified as follows :

Applications for Probate of Wills............	93
Applications for Letters of Administration upon Intestate Estates.......................	159
Applications for Letters of Guardianship (minors)	70
Applications for Letters of Guardianship (insane)	6

          328

Applications were granted and Letters issued as follows:

Letters Testamentary......................	62
Letters of Administration, with the Will annexed.	17
Letters of Administration....................	124
Special Letters of Administration.............	26
Letters of Guardianship (minors).............	57
Letters of Guardianship (insane).............	4

Applications still pending; no Letters issued and no fees paid :

For Letters Testamentary....................	14
For Letters of Administration...............	35
For Letters of Guardianship (minors).........	13
For Letters of Guardianship (insane)..........	2

VALUE OF ESTATES.

The Value of the Estates, upon which Letters were issued during the last fiscal year, is............	$2,127,000 00
Testate................................	1,221,000 00
Intestate..............................	906,000 00

NON-PAYMENT OF FEES.

Number of Estates in which there was no property...	2

NUMBER OF ESTATES IN WHICH PROCEEDINGS WERE COMMENCED DURING EACH FISCAL YEAR SINCE JULY 1st, 1859.

During the year ending June 30th, 1860.................	87
During the year ending June 30th, 1861.................	107
During the year ending June 30th, 1862.................	148
During the year ending June 30th, 1863.................	172

During the year ending June 30th, 1864.................. 234
During the year ending June 30th, 1865.................. 214
During the year ending June 30th, 1866.................. 255
During the year ending June 30th, 1867.................. 328

RECORDS IN THE COUNTY CLERK'S OFFICE ON THE FIRST DAY
OF JULY, 1867.

RECORDS OF ALCALDE GEARY.

Register, Nos. 1, 2 (Geary) 2
General Index...................................... 1

COURT OF FIRST INSTANCE.

Register, Nos. 1, 2.................................... 2
General Index...................................... 1
Records, A, B, C 3
Plaintiffs' Index.................................... 1
General Index to Judgments........................... 1
Criminal Record.................................... 1
General Index to Book A (Miscellaneous)................ 1
General Index to Book B 1
Record of Dismissed and Discontinued Cases............. 1

SUPERIOR COURT.

[Transferred to the Fourth District Court.]

Registers of Actions, 1, 2, 3, 4, 5, 6, 7, 8, 9, 10 10
Judgment Books, A, B, C, D, E 5
Minute Books, A, B, C, D, E, F 6
Docket No. 1....................................... 1

FOURTH DISTRICT COURT.

General Index (Plaintiffs'), A, B 2
General Index (Defendants'), A 1
Registers of Actions, A, B, C, D, E, F, G, H, I, J, K, L.... 12
Judgment Records, A, B, C, D, E, F, G................. 7

Dockets, A, B, C, D 4
Minute Books, A, B, C, D, E, F, G, H 8
Register of Criminal Causes, A 1
Execution Book, A 1

TWELFTH DISTRICT COURT.

Indices (Plaintiffs'), A, B, C 3
Index (Defendants'), A 1
Registers of Actions, A to L 12
Minutes of Court, A to F 6
Judgment Records, A to F 6
Judgment Dockets, A to E 5
Execution Book, A 1

FIFTEENTH DISTRICT COURT.

Index (Plaintiffs') 1
Index (Defendants') 1
Registers of Actions, A, B, C, D 4
Minutes of Court, A, B 2
Judgment Record, A 1
Judgment Docket, A, B 2
Execution Book, A 1

BOOKS OF NATURALIZATION.

Minutes of Naturalization (Fourth District Court), A, B 2
Minutes of Naturalization (Twelfth District Court), A 1
Minutes of Naturalization (Fifteenth District Court), A 1
Declarations of Intention, A, B, C, D, E, F 6
Certificates of Citizenship, A, B, C, D, E, F, G, H, I, J, K.. 9

[C, F, I, J, K, belong exclusively to the Fourth; G, to the Twelfth; and H, to the Fifteenth District Court.]

General Index to Declarations of Intention, A 1
General Index to Certificates of Citizenship, A 1

MISCELLANEOUS BOOKS IN THE COUNTY CLERK'S OFFICE.

Record of School Land Warrants 1
Record of Deposits of Money in Court 1
Record of Filing of Delinquent Tax Lists 1
Record of Official Bonds 1
Great Register of Citizens, 2 volumes 2
Duplicate Report of Kearny Street Commissioners 1

COUNTY COURT.

Execution Book, A.................................... 1
G^en^eral Index of Actions (Civil), A...................... 1
Registers of Civil Actions, 1, 2, 3 3
Register of Criminal Actions, 1 1
Minutes of Court (County), 1, 2, 3, 4, 5, 6 6
Judgment Dockets, A, B.............................. 2
Minutes of Court of Sessions, 1, 2, 3, 4................. 4
Register of Court of Sessions......................... 1
Record of Bonds..................................... 1
Records of Incorporations, 1, 2....................... 2
Index of Incorporations............................... 1
Index of Insolvents 1
Index of Protests to Street Grades 1
Index of Oaths of Allegiance.......................... 1
Index of Ordnance Stores, Receipts by Militia Companies... 1
Index of Indentured Apprentices....................... 1
Index of Coroner's Inquests 1
Index of Marriage Licenses (males).................... 1
Index of Marriage Licenses (females) 1
Applications for Marriage Licenses, 1, 2, 3, 4 4
Commitments to Insane Asylum....................... 6
Final Report of Kearny Street Commissioners, 1 volume 1

PROBATE COURT.

Succession, A 1
Succession, B 1
Journal Probate Court................................ 1
Minutes entitled "Record Probate Court," 2 to 10.......... 9
Minutes entitled "Minutes Probate Court," 11 to 16........ 6
Letters of Administration, 1, 2....................... 2
Letters Testamentary................................. 1
Letters of Guardianship.............................. 1
Bonds.. 3
Records of Wills, 1, 2, 3, 4, 5........................ 5
Registers of Wills, 1, 2, 3, 4......................... 4
General Index, A..................................... 1

RECEIPTS OF FEES DURING THE YEAR ENDING JUNE 30, 1867.

PAID INTO THE SPECIAL FEE FUND.

Months.	4th District Court.	12th District Court.	15th District Court.	County Court.	Probate Court.	Totals.
July, 1866	$1,190 65	$510 75	$687 75	$616 50	$ 74 50	$3,080 15
August, 1866	1,154 05	456 25	956 15	576 00	212 00	3,354 45
Sept., 1866	896 80	490 50	1,114 00	621 50	182 50	3,305 30
October,1866	633 00	558 25	1,159 50	745 75	356 75	3,453 25
Nov., 1866	528 00	531 75	769 50	670 75	300 00	2,800 00
Dec., 1866	564 50	495 20	665 00	719 25	299 70	2,743 65
January,1867	548 75	681 00	815 75	709 85	249 00	3,004 35
Feb., 1867	434 45	445 75	876 75	679 25	414 50	2,850 70
March, 1867	645 00	636 25	800 75	613 50	244·00	2,939 50
April, 1867	592 25	719 50	777 75	598 00	346 00	3,033 50
May, 1867	510 25	748 25	651 00	538 50	290 10	2,738 10
June, 1867	513 50	587 00	875 50	497 75	858 75	3,332 50
	$8,211 20	$6,860 45	$10,149 40	$7,586 60	$3,827 80	$36,635 45

NOTE.—The Receipts in the County Court include $3,076 for 1,538 Marriage Licenses.

EXPENDITURES DURING THE YEAR ENDING JUNE 30, 1867.

Salaries of County Clerk and eleven Deputies................ $25,475 00
Copyists.. 3,079 40
Stationery and Records for Offices and Courts................ 2,476 99

     Total... $31,031 39

♦ RECAPITULATION.

Total Receipts.. $36,635 45
Total Expenditures 31,031 39

     Receipts over Expenditures............................ $5,585 56

COURT TAXES AND APPEAL FEES.

The following amounts were paid to the District Judges during the last Fiscal Year, resulting from a tax of $3, collected by the Clerk on the filing of each suit and of each Notice of Appeal.

To the Judge of the Fourth District Court............ $1,902 00
To the Judge of the Twelfth District Court 2,127 00
To the Judge of the Fifteenth District Court ,........ 3,279 00

     $7,308 00

FINES.

Amount of Fines inflicted by the County Court and paid
into the Police Fund during the Fiscal Year ending
June 30, 1867.............................. $3,075 00

DEPOSITS IN COURT.

	Coin.	Legal Tender Notes.
Amount on deposit in Court July 1, 1866 (deposited by the County Clerk with the County Treasurer)..................	$4,469 56	$2,492 95
Deposited July 1, 1866, to June 30, 1867 ..	35,652 04	15,285 85
	40,121 60	17,778 80
Amount withdrawn during the last Fiscal Year by order of Court	31,711 63	16,605 35
Amount remaining on deposit July 1, 1867 .	$8,410 97	$1,175 45

TABLE OF RECEIPTS OF FEES AND OF EXPENDITURES IN THE COUNTY CLERK'S
OFFICE FROM JULY 1, 1859, TO JUNE 30, 1867.

	Fees received.	Expenditures.	Balance of Receipts over Expenditures.
Fiscal Year ending June 30, 1860..........	$21,684 30	$23,749 92	
Fiscal Year ending June 30, 1861..........	23,073 43	23,185 35	
Fiscal Year ending June 30, 1862..........	23,291 72	22,020 90	$ 270 82
Fiscal Year ending June 30, 1863..........	22,786 84	22,542 85	243 99
Fiscal Year ending June 30, 1864..........	28,815 80	24,353 23	4,462 57
Fiscal Year ending June 30, 1865..........	33,201 30	28,813 96	4,387 34
Fiscal Year ending June 30, 1866..........	31,829 70	30,842 90	986 80
Fiscal Year ending June 30, 1867..........	36,635 45	31,031 39	5,585 56

REGISTRATION OF CITIZENS.

During the last year, the additional duties imposed upon this
office, in connection with the Registration of citizens, have very
seriously interfered with the business of the Clerk's Office of the
District Courts. The office, though inadequate in space even to its
legitimate purposes, has been thronged day after day with citizens
desiring to be registered, or seeking information in regard to the
Registry Law. The immensity of the work done in carrying out
this Law may be conceived from the fact that the arrangement in
alphabetical order of a copy of the "Great Register," for publication, has occupied two persons, day and night, from September, 1866,

to March, 1867, and the printing and proof reading, which commenced in January last, was not completed until the present month.

Even the daily correspondence addressed to me upon the subject of the Registry Law, and the applications from all parts of the State for cancellation and for Certificates of Registration, have grown to such an extent, that one Clerk would be fully occupied to attend alone to this branch of the Registration duties.

There can be no question as to the necessity of relieving the County Clerk's Office in this County of this overwhelming burthen, and to transfer it to a new department, exclusively devoted to Registration.

As only a very limited number of copies of the "Great Register" has been published, I desire to include in this Report some statistics which I prepared for that publication, and which it may be useful to circulate among our citizens:

Number of citizens registered up to July 1, 1867.......... 16,550

Number of citizens registered up to August 3, 1867........ 20,108

Number of cancellations up to July 1, 1867.............. 278

NATIVITY OF CITIZENS REGISTERED IN THE GREAT REGISTER, TO JULY 1, 1867.

NATIVES OF THE UNITED STATES.

Maine.................	1,040	Arkansas...............	2
New Hampshire.........	396	Kansas.................	6
Vermont...............	351	Maryland	267
Massachusetts	1,711	District of Columbia.....	29
Connecticut	315	Virginia	194
Rhode Island...........	190	Kentucky	127
New York..............	2,686	Tennessee..............	55
New Jersey............	284	North Carolina.........	27
Pennsylvania...........	761	South Carolina.........	47
Delaware	37	Georgia................	26
Ohio	372	Florida.................	5
Wisconsin..............	18	Alabama................	26
Indiana	82	Louisiana..............	100
Illinois	104	Mississippi.............	19
Iowa..................	11	Texas,.................	9
Missouri,..............	82	Born at Sea............	6
California.............	6		

Total number...9,441

FOREIGN BORN.

England and Scotland....	770	Hungary...............	7
Ireland................	3,579	Greece................	3
France................	108	British-American Colonies	152
Germany and Switzerland.	2,056	Spanish-America........	17
Scandinavia and Denmark	170	Mexico	1
Holland...............	17	West Indies...........	10
Belgium	11	East Indies...........	6
Spain.................	1	Australia.............	28
Portugal..............	14	China.................	2
Italy.................	21	Sandwich Islands.......	2
Russia and Poland.......	136		

Total number.................................. 7,109

FIFTEENTH DISTRICT COURT.

It will be seen by the Table of "Organization of the Courts" in the first part of this Report, that the Office of the Fifteenth District Court is still in the same unfortunate situation, in which it was left by the oversight of the Legislature of 1864. The Fifteenth District Court having been created during that session, without any provision being made for Clerks, and a supplemental bill, which passed both Houses during the session of 1866, having failed to receive the approval of the Executive, the business of that Court has for more than three years past been discharged by the Clerks of the Twelfth District Court. This state of things has been as oppressive to the office as it is unjust to the public and to the Court, whose business cannot receive the prompt and exclusive attention it requires.

All of which is respectfully submitted.

WM. LOEWY,
County Clerk.

REPORT OF THE CHIEF OF POLICE.

POLICE OFFICE,
San Francisco, August 1, 1867.

To the Honorable the Board of Supervisors

Of the City and County of San Francisco—

GENTLEMEN: In accordance with Resolution No. 6,963 of your Honorable Board, the following Report of the operations of the Police Department for the fiscal year ending June 30th, 1867, is respectfully submitted:

Schedule "A"—showing the number of arrests made by the Police during the year.

Schedule "B"—an exhibit of the amount of property reported as stolen and lost, and the amount recovered by the Police during the year.

Schedule "C"—an exhibit of money and cash value of articles passed through the hands of the Police during each month—having been taken for the most part from persons inebriated, and otherwise unable to care for themselves at the time of their arrest, and temporarily in the possession of the Chief of Police.

Schedule "D"—showing the number of witnesses subpoenaed for the Police Judge's Court; nuisances on private property abated; street obstruction notices served; and lost children restored to their parents or guardians by the Police, for the year ending June 30th, 1867.

12

Schedule " E "—an exhibit of cash received from Sheriffs of other counties; masters of vessels, and others, for the keeping of prisoners in the City Prison, during the year ending June 30th, 1867.

Schedule " F "—a list of unclaimed money and property; also, of articles lost and stolen, in the possession of the Chief of Police, to June 30th, 1867.

STRENGTH OF THE FORCE.

The number of Officers employed and paid by the city is four Captains of Police and eighty Policemen.

HARBOR POLICE STATION.

The Harbor Police Station is situated on Davis near Pacific street, and has communication by telegraph with the Central Office at the City Hall. Nine officers are detailed for duty as Harbor Police. For some time past one of the Harbor Police has been detailed to board all deep water ships on their arrival, in order to preserve the peace and prevent confusion among solicitors for boarding houses, and others, who frequently interfere with the crew in bringing the vessel to anchor. This arrangement is beneficial to the shipping interest, while it does not interfere with any legitimate business.

THE MISSION STATION.

The Mission Station is situated near the corner of Valencia and Center streets, about two miles from the Central Office, with which it has telegraphic communication. Three officers are detailed for duty at this station and vicinity.

FOURTH STREET STATION.

The Fourth Street Station is located at the corner of Fourth and Harrison streets, one mile from the Central Office; the Policemen, five in number, on duty in the neighborhood, report themselves at stated times through the telegraph instrument in this station.

HAYES PARK STATION.

The Hayes Park Station is located near the corner of Hayes and Laguna streets, one and one half miles from the Central Office, and two officers patroling that neighborhood report through the instrument in that station, at regular intervals.

JONES STREET STATION.

The Jones Street Station is situated near the corner of Pacific and Jones streets, and is used by two officers patroling that neighborhood, to report at stated hours. This station is distant half a mile from the Central Office.

There is also an instrument connected with the Police Telegraph in use at the Chief's house, which, with the instrument in the Central Office, makes a total of seven Police Telegraph instruments in frequent use.

The three Police Telegraph stations last named were erected somewhat in advance of the actual wants of the city, but their cost was small, and they already serve a useful purpose. Undoubtedly, as the city increases in size, and the Police force is enlarged, it will become necessary to attach a squad of officers to each of these stations.

The officers have promptly performed their duties, and on many occasions, the knowledge which the older officers have acquired in the detection of crime, has in a marked degree contributed to the successful administration of justice.

P. CROWLEY,

Chief of Police.

SCHEDULE A.

NUMBER OF ARRESTS MADE BY THE POLICE FOR THE YEAR ENDING JUNE 30, 1867.

July, 1866	767
August, 1866	818
September, 1866	757
October, 1866	800
November, 1866	849
December, 1866	909
Jannary, 1867	1,060
February, 1867	687
March, 1867	870
April, 1867	802
May, 1867	839
June, 1867	738
Total	9,896

CLASSIFICATION OF ARRESTS MADE BY THE POLICE OF THE CITY AND COUNTY OF SAN FRANCISCO FOR THE YEAR ENDING JUNE 30, 1867.

Abduction	2
Aiding a Prisoner to Escape	1
Arson	11
Assault	37
Assault and Battery	1,297
Assault with a Deadly Weapon	84
Assault with Intent to Commit Rape	6
Assault with Intent to Kill	8
Attempt at Bribery	4
Attempt to Commit Arson	1
Attempt to Commit Burglary	8
Attempt to Commit Robbery	3
Attempt to commit Larceny	3
Bench Warrants	71
Bigamy	2
Burglary	93
Carried forward	1,631

Brought forward	1,631
Carrying concealed Weapons	67
Common Drunkards	42
Common Prostitute	1
Conspiracy to Cheat and Defraud	18
Defrauding United States Revenue	3
Desertion	178
Drunk	3,532
Embezzlement	7
Escape from Industrial School	20
Escape from Prison	10
Escape from St. Mary's College	2
Escape from Stockton Insane Asylum	1
Exhibiting a Deadly Weapon	9
Extortion	2
False Imprisonment	2
Felony	16
Forgery	19
For the Industrial School	85
Grand Larceny	190
Indecent Exposure of Person	5
Incest	1
Insane	167
Kidnapping	2
Libel	2
Lodgers and Persons for Safe Keeping	773
Malicious Mischief	152
Manslaughter	1
Mayhem	6
Misdemeanor	340
Misdemeanor by Gambling	14
Misdemeanor by Violating City Orders	1,603
Murder	8
Mutiny	1
Obtaining Money and Goods by False Pretences	28
On Writ of Habeas Corpus	1
Peddling without a License	34
Perjury	11
Carried forward	8,984

Brought forward	8,984
Petit Larceny	450
Rape	1
Receiving Stolen Goods	3
Resisting an Officer	10
Riot	28
Robbery	44
Rout	1
State Prisoners, en route	133
Surrendered by Bondsmen	2
Suspicion of Arson	2
Suspicion of Burglary	6
Suspicion of Felony	1
Suspicion of Larceny	67
Suspicion of Murder	2
Suspicion of Robbery	2
Swindling	2
Threats	44
Vagrancy	57
Witnesses detained in Prison	57
Total	9,896

SCHEDULE B.

AMOUNT OF PROPERTY REPORTED STOLEN AND LOST, AND AMOUNT RECOV-
ERED BY THE POLICE FOR THE YEAR ENDING JUNE 30, 1867.

Months.	Property Stolen.	Property Lost.	Amount Recovered
July, 1866	$3,311 00	$2,250 00	$ 741 00
August, 1866	1,744 00	495 00	9,023 00
September, 1866	2,227 00	270 00	· 4,794 00
October, 1866	4,669 00	5 00	1,478 00
November, 1866	4,575 00	915 00	3,434 00
December, 1866	4,708 00	235 00	3,356 00
January, 1867	4,004 00	399 00	2,047 00
February, 1867	2,835 00	10 00	2,550 00
March, 1867	2,984 00	850 00	965 00
April, 1867	2,146 00	478 00	1,648 00
May, 1867	6,463 00	112 00	2,556 00
June, 1867	1,566 00	1,505 00	1,045 00
	$41,232 00	$7,524 00	33,637 00

Amount of Property stolen at other places, not in this County,
and recovered by the Police, or through their agency, during
the year 24,800 00

$58,437 00

SCHEDULE C. ˙ ·

MONEY AND MONEY VALUE OF ARTICLES PASSED THROUGH HANDS OF POLICE,
HAVING BEEN TAKEN FROM PERSONS INEBRIATED, AND OTHERWISE UNA-
BLE TO CARE FOR THEMSELVES AT THE TIME OF THEIR ARREST, AND
TEMPORARILY IN THE POSSESSION OF THE CHIEF OF POLICE, FOR THE
YEAR ENDING JUNE 30, 1867.

July,	1866	$4,500 22
August,	1866	15,792 75
September,	1866	10,029 01
October,	1866	6,151 10
November,	1866	9,032 25
December,	1866	9,904 40
January,	1867	7,094 40
February,	1867	6,709 35

Carried forward $69,213 48

Brought forward	....	$69,213	48
March,	1867.	....	5,523	30
April,	1867.	....	6,594	40
May,	1867.	....	8,394	50
June,	1867.	....	4,743	90

$94,469 58

SCHEDULE D.

NUMBER OF WITNESSES SUBPENAED FOR THE POLICE JUDGE'S COURT—NUIS-
ANCES ON PRIVATE PROPERTY ABATED—STREET OBSTRUCTION NOTICES—
AND LOST CHILDREN RESTORED TO THEIR PARENTS OR GUARDIANS, BY
THE POLICE, FOR THE YEAR ENDING JUNE 30, 1867.

Month.	Witnesses Sub-penaed.	Street Obstruc-tion Notices.	Nuisances Abat-ed.	Restored Lost Children.
July, 1866	424	47	31	47
August, 1866	407	36	23	39
September, 1866	379	30	19	24
October, 1866	351	33	19	19
November, 1866	401	27	12	21
December, 1866	338	25	5	7
January, 1867	312	23	4	16
February, 1867	391	33	9	30
March, 1867	398	57	17	38
April, 1867	440	51	19	32
May, 1867	410	48	23	58
June, 1867	404	96	20	29
	4,655	506	201	360

SCHEDULE E.

CASH RECEIVED FROM SHERIFFS OF OTHER COUNTIES, MASTERS OF VESSELS, AND OTHERS, FOR THE KEEPING OF PRISONERS IN THE CITY PRISON, FOR THE YEAR ENDING JUNE 30, 1867.

1866.

Aug.	4.	From French ship "Orixa"	$24 00
	11.	From French ship "Harriet"	8 00
	13.	From Hanoverian brig "Carl"	39 00
Sept.	9.	From Hamburgh ship "A. H. Willie"	31 00
	10.	From Sheriff A. Jones, of Santa Cruz County ..	1 00
	18.	From Deputy Sheriff E. Groat, of Napa County.	2 00
	18.	From Sheriff Sneden, of Mono County	1 00
	20.	From Sheriff Adams, of Santa Clara County....	2 00
Oct.	4.	From Sheriff Bourland, of Tuolumne County ...	1 00
	4.	From Under Sheriff Cotter, of Calaveras County	5 00
	10.	From Under Sheriff Groat, of Napa County	1 00
	10.	From Sheriff Cosgrove, of Amador County.....	1 00
	17.	From Sheriff Griffiths, of El Dorado County....	2 00
	17.	From French ship "Jean Pierre"	50 00
	22.	From Deputy Sheriff J. S. Haines, of Santa Clara County	1 00
	22.	From Sheriff Poole, of Placer County	2 00
	26.	From Sheriff Cooper, of Colusa County	1 00
Nov.	1.	From Sheriff Griffith, of El Dorado County.....	2 00
	6.	From Sheriff Sexton, of Placer County	1 00
	16.	From Sheriff Adams, of Santa Clara County....	1 00
	27.	From Sheriff E. F. Boyle, of Sacramento County	2 00
	27.	From Sheriff Day, of Butte County	2 00
	28.	From bark "Massachusetts"	6 00
	28.	From Under Sheriff G. A. Swain, of Contra Costa County	3 00
Dec.	4.	From ship "Aurora"	8 00
	17.	From bark "Harrison," P. H. Cooley, Master ..	4 00
	18.	From Sheriff Ellis, of Napa County	1 00
	20.	From bark "Alpha"	2 00
	20.	From Sheriff I. Y. Lees, of Monterey County ...	2 00

Carried forward......................$206 00

Brought forward $206 00

1867.

Jan.	2.	From Sheriff Cosner, of Amador County	2 00
	9.	From Deputy Sheriff A. B. Asher, of Sierra County	1 00
	9.	From Sheriff G. R. Lees, of Monterey County ..	1 00
	10.	From Deputy Sheriff H. B. Mitchell, of Colusa County	1 00
	11.	From Sheriff Peck, of Calaveras County	1 00
	18.	From French ship " Tropique "	29 00
Feb.	19.	From Deputy Sheriff Len Harris, of Sacramento County	2 00
	28.	From Sheriff N. Breen, of Merced County......	1 00
March	1.	From ship " Emma "......................	7 00
	6.	From Sheriff R. Cosner, of Amador County	2 00
	17.	From Deputy Sheriff Len Harris, of San Mateo County	2 00
	21.	From Deputy Sheriff Whitlock, of Sacramento County	1 00
	27.	From French bark " Polimina "	10 00
	30.	From Sheriff G. P. Bullock, of Yolo County.....	1 00
	31.	From Sheriff Griffith, of El Dorado County.....	1 00
April	2.	From Sheriff A. W. Poole, of Placer County....	5 00
	9.	From Under Sheriff J. Johnson, of Placer County	2 00
	15.	From Sheriff O. Root, of Santa Cruz County....	1 00
	17.	From Sheriff Friend, of Sutter County.........	1 00
	21.	From Under Sheriff Hall, of Santa Clara County	2 00
	26.	From Deputy Sheriff W. M. Muffley, of El Dorado County	2 00
May	1.	From Under Sheriff R. B. Hall, of Santa lara County	1 00
	2.	From Sheriff T. M. Brown, of Klamath County .	2 00
	8.	From Sheriff Glassen, of Contra Costa County..	1 00
	10.	From Sheriff Wm. Minis, of Yolo County	1 00
	31.	From Sheriff W. B. Ross, of Kern County	1 00
June	6.	From Sheriff T. W. Lathrop, of San Mateo County	1 00

Carried forward........................$288 00

Brought forward $288 00

18. From Deputy Sheriff John Burke, of Amador
County 1 00
27. From Sheriff W. F. Colton, of Calaveras County 3 00

Total $292 00

SCHEDULE F.

LOST, STOLEN, AND UNCLAIMED PROPERTY IN THE POSSESSION OF THE CHIEF
OF POLICE TO JUNE 30, 1867.

LOT A.

No. 1. Three dollars coin, Thomas Wilson, Jannary 1, 1867.

2. Twenty-five cents and purse, Garibaldi, Jannary 1, 1867.

3. One and $\frac{50}{100}$ dollars, Jane Doe Spanish, January 2, 1867.

4. Fifty cents, John Kelly, January 4, 1867.

5. Fifteen and $\frac{35}{100}$ dollars, purse, and key, George Mellen, January 5, 1867.

6. Thirty-five cents, Harry Love, January 7, 1867.

7. Fifty cents and two knives, John Porter, January 9, 1867.

8. Ninety cents, Frank Williams, January 11, 1867.

9. One and $\frac{30}{100}$ dollars, Mary Ann Smith, January 14, 1867.

10. One and $\frac{5}{100}$ dollars, Fred. Marble, January 14, 1867.

11. Four dollars, Joseph Drennan, Jannary 16, 1867.

12. One and $\frac{50}{100}$ dollars, Harry Knapps, January 18, 1867.

13. Fifty cents, Margaret Brown, Jannary 21, 1867.

14. Twenty-five cents and knife, John Feeney, January 22, 1867.

15. Eighty-five cents, Richard Keegan, January 24, 1867.

16. Ten cents and knife, William Jones, January 28, 1867.

17. One gold and quartz specimen, James Keely, January 28, 1867.

18. Twelve and $\frac{55}{100}$ dollars and key, Henry Burns, January 29, 1867.

19. One five dollar United States Legal Tender Note, Mrs. Smith, January 31, 1867.

20. Twenty-seven pocket knives, two pairs of compasses, and one rule, miscellaneous.

21. Fifty cents and purse, Pat Duffy, February 4, 1867.

22. Fifty cents, Jesns Monos, February 6, 1867.

23. Two dollars and key, Frank Husard, February 9, 1867.

24. Two dollars and purse, Albert Leman, February 10, 1867.

25. Twenty-five cents, Stephen Sullivan, February 17, 1867.

26. Sixty cents, Thomas Donn, February 22, 1867.

27. Seventy-five cents and pocket knife, John Petty, February 22, 1867.

28. Forty cents, two knives, and key, John Kingston, February 26, 1867.

29. Fifty cents, Thomas H. Burton, February 26, 1867.

30. Five and $\frac{75}{100}$ dollars, purse, and knife, John O'Connell, February 26, 1867.

31. Fifty cents, James Butcher, February 27, 1867.

32. Seventy-five cents, James Craney, February 28, 1867.

33. Twenty-seven pocket knives, one razor, and two keys, miscellaneous.

34. Thirty-five cents, spectacles, and pocket knife, John Fulton, March 1, 1867.

35. Thirty cents, neck tie, memorandum book, two keys, and pocket knife, Patrick Sparks, March 2, 1867.

36. One and $\frac{5}{100}$ dollars, coin, and purse, Thomas Donovan.

37. Twenty cents and pocket knife, Richard Rumbold, March 6, 1867.

38. Eighty-five cents, purse, and knife, B. Martin, March 11, 1867.

39. One gold brooch containing picture, Catherine Smith, March 12, 1867.

40. One breastpin and pocket knife, Ed. Maguire, March 14, 1867.

41. Thirty-five cents, Michael Redding, March 16, 1867.

42. Fifty cents and pocket knife, Henry Meyer, March 19, 1867.

43. Seventy-five cents, two knives, and key, Samuel Morrison, March 19, 1867.

44. Forty cents, papers, knife, and key, John C. Kennedy, March 20, 1867.

45. Fifty cents, Joseph Trusty, March 23, 1867.
46. One and $\frac{20}{100}$ dollars, Joseph Mattison, March 24, 1867.
47. Three and $\frac{55}{100}$ dollars, key, and meal ticket, Pitkins, March 26, 1867.
48. One dollar and key, Frank Donnelly, March 30, 1867.
49. Twenty pocket knives and one key, miscellaneous.
50. Twenty-five cents and knife, John McLoughlin, April 1, 1857.
51. Sixty-seven cents, purse, and knife, Nicholas Gasten, April 5, 1867.
· 52. Twenty-five cents, and pocket knife, Manuel Gavalli, April 5, 1867.
53. Ten cents and purse, Patrick Seeley, April 7, 1867.
54. Sixty cents, John Brower, April 11, 1867.
55. Eighty cents, Peter Sweeney, April 15, 1867.
56. Three and $\frac{55}{100}$ dollars, Peter Johnson, April 20, 1867.
57. Sixty cents, Henry Armstrong, April 20, 1867.
58. Seventy-five cents, Kanaka, April 20, 1867.
59. Two and $\frac{10}{100}$ dollars, purse, and knife, Wm. Moore, April 21, 1867.
60. Fifty cents and key, John Devlin, April 21, 1867.
61. One and $\frac{30}{100}$ dollars and knife, Chas. O'Neil, April 23, 1867.
62. Twenty-three pocket knives, miscellaneous.
63. Twenty-five cents and pocket knife, Peter Rollins, May 1, 1867.
64. Five and $\frac{40}{100}$ dollars, purse, and knife, John Culnan, May 3, 1867.
65. One and $\frac{60}{100}$ dollars, Mary Kingsbury, May 7, 1867.
66. Ten cents, John Brown, May 11, 1867.
67. Thirty-five cents, William Montgomery, May 14, 1867.
68. Four and $\frac{15}{100}$ dollars and pocket knife, Mose Alvin, May 14, 1867.
69. Ten cents and pocket knife, Anderson, May 15, 1867.
70. Ten cents, Timothy Collins, May 25, 1867.
71. Forty-five cents, Vallandigham Snyder, May 26, 1867.
72. One and $\frac{40}{100}$ dollars and knife, Delio, May 29, 1867.
73. Eleven pocket knives, miscellaneous.

74. One and $\frac{95}{100}$ dollars and five franc piece, B. Duffy, June 3, 1867.

75. One and $\frac{40}{100}$ dollars coin, thirteen cents fractional currency, nine copper coins, key, and knife, Wm. F. Munay, June 5, 1867.

76. Twenty cents, Bernard McCann, June 6, 1867.

77. One and $\frac{95}{100}$ dollars, G. Goldberg, June 11, 1867.

78. Fifty cents, George Wilson, June 11, 1867.

79. Ninety-five cents and purse, Peter Olsen, June 12, 1867.

80. One dollar, Hugh Heaney, June 15, 1867.

81. Forty cents, William Wilson, June 17, 1867.

82. One and $\frac{20}{100}$ dollars, one certificate of deposit of eighty dollars, by John Donnelly, in favor of Mr. Rider, dated May 30, 1867, one gold specimen breastpin, one open face English lever silver watch, " No. 1208, Wm. Gardner, Manchester," with silver guardchain attached, bunch of keys, and purse, James Ryder, June 26, 1867.

83. Fifteen pocket knives, and one key, miscellaneous.

JEWELRY, ETC., FOUND AND UNCLAIMED.

84. One brown velvet purse, steel chain and clasp, with four gold tassels, from a Chinaman, on suspicion of having been stolen, January 3, 1867.

85. One plain gold cross, found by Officer Brant in Car 19, Fourth Street, February 14, 1867.

86. One pair gold glove buttons and chain, found on Stockton Street, near Market, by Officer Cullen, March 4, 1867.

87. One gold chatelaine pin, pearl and jet setting, found by Owen McCoy, on Montgomery Street, near Clay, March 22, 1867.

88. One purse, containing pawn ticket for gold watch and chain, $50, loaned by Hyman to Webb, dated March 23, 1866, found by Wm. Joy and delivered to officer Watkin, March 26, 1867.

89. One pair plain gold sleeve buttons, found in Fourteenth District Court room by A. J. Green, March 29, 1867.

90. One gold sleeve button, form of a bow knot, setting three small pearls, found by George Hill, April 19, 1867.

91. One lady's gold hunting case watch, No. 13177, Ducommun Freres, cylinder, with guard chain and slide attached, found by Local Officer Woodruff, in ruins of fire corner Jackson and Kearny Streets, June 25, 1867.

92. One lava brooch and two gold pencil cases, Evidence vs. William Lear—recovered by officer Sproul, March 17, 1866—identified by Mrs. Clarke.

93. One pair gold sleeve-buttons, marked "F. J. L.," Evidence vs. Ah Yin, January 22, 1867.

94. One lady's gold buckle, marked "Union," with belt, taken from boys by John Jordan, January 26, 1867.

95. One pair white stone cluster ear-rings, taken from Taaffe, by Local Officer Woodruff, February 8, 1867.

96. Three certificates—Nos. 22, 23, and 24—twenty-five shares Richmond Gold and Silver Mining Company, issued to John Priely, June 10, 1863 ; also, three certificates Gibraltar Gold and Silver Mining Company—Nos. 38, 39, and 40—twenty-five shares, to John Priely, August 11, 1863, found in the street, February 9, 1867, Officer Greer.

97. One New York State Warrant—appointment of Martin J. Bell Second Lieutenant Second Cavalry New York Volunteers, dated November 12, 1864 ; also, army discharge of Martin J. Bell, First Lieutenant, Captain Charles F. Millards, Company I, Second New York Cavalry Volunteers, dated June 5, 1865, found in the street by Manuella Voz, May 9, 1867.

98. One pair round gold sleeve buttons, black enameled chasing, single pearl center setting, and one woolen knit hood, red and black, brought from the Cosmopolitan Hotel fire, by Officer Rose, April 23, 1867.

99. One silver mustard spoon, marked in German text "F. T. C.," and one silver cruet top, from Cosmopolitan Hotel fire.

100. One large microscope and case, from Cosmopolitan Hotel fire, by Capt. Douglass, April 23, 1867.

Lot B.

No. 1. Four cotton sheets and one table-cloth, taken from Ah Gee, by Officer Rose, January 2, 1867.

2. One box brass weights, found in basement of City Hall, by Officer McWilliams, January 3, 1867.

3. One pair ribbed cassimere pants, one black silk sack, one fur victorine, and one blue blanket, found under culvert, Valencia and Twenty-second streets, by Officer Young, January 19, 1867.

4. One piece bed-ticking, Evidence vs. George Davis, Chief Crowley and Officer McCormick, January 31, 1867.

5. One brown fur tippet, found by Local Officer Dillon, on Sixth street, March 11, 1867.

6. One brown fur cape, found by citizen P. H. Morrissey, corner Fifth and Tehama streets, March 22, 1867.

7. One willow basket containing eleven papers and two "1-℔" baskets tea, thrown away by a Chinese tea peddler to escape arrest, Local Officer Wm. A. Cook, April 12, 1867.

8. One black beaver overcoat, black plush facings, white sleeve-lining, marked "J. S. & Co., custom-made," with white linen handkerchief, red border, brought from the Cosmopolitan Hotel fire, by Officer Hoyt, April 23, 1867.

9. One brown beaver frock coat, velvet collar, red sleeve-lining, with two pairs kid gloves, from Cosmopolitan Hotel fire, by Capt. Lees and Gannon, April 25, 1867.

10. One bronze cigar stand, from Cosmopolitan Hotel fire, by B. Gardiner, Jr., April 26, 1867.

11. One pair dungaree overalls and three pairs cotton socks, found by Officer Fogarty, April 30, 1867.

12. One blue cloth vest, from Cosmopolitan Hotel fire, by Dr. J. M. McNulty, May 8, 1867.

13. One white cotton sheet, Evidence vs. Ah Ham, by Officer Rose, May 15, 1867.

14. One grey Mission horse blanket, with straps, Evidence vs. James Welch, May 30 1867.

15. One pig lead, Evidence vs. Ah Fee, by Officer Smith and Woodruff, January 28, 1867.

16. Eight pieces iron castings and seven grain sacks, Evidence vs. Ah How, by Officer Rose, May 20, 1867.

17. One white blanket, two women's nightgowns, one calico

sack, one white shirt, one woolen shirt, four towels, two handkerchiefs, one cloth sack, one fur cape, one checked woolen shawl, one brown apron, one yard figured poplin, one napkin, and one velvet vest, from possession of Ah Ho and Ah Sing, Pike street, by Local Officer Davis, March 19, 1867; also, one smoothing plane, one hatchet, two dirk-knives, two chisels, two files, one pair shoemakers' pincers, one single-barrel pistol, two razors, one dozen teaspoons, three pairs scissors, bunch of keys, one padlock, one lot of brass buttons, and one gilt gas turner, from Ah Ho and Ah Sing, by Local Officer Davis, March 19, 1867.

18. One soldiers' overcoat, two black frock coats, one pair black pants, one cloth vest, three pairs women's hose, marked " B," five pairs woolen socks, two pairs cotton socks, five handkerchiefs, four towels, three infants' under garments, one check woolen overshirt, one knit undershirt, two woolen scarfs, two scarlet silk poplin waists, and muslin remnants, and lot of pamphlets, brought in by Officer Moses Davis, from room of Ah Ho and Ah Sing, Pike street, between Clay and Sacramento, March 19, 1867.

REPORT

CITY AND COUNTY ATTORNEY.

OFFICE OF THE CITY AND COUNTY ATTORNEY, }
San Francisco, July 29, 1867. }

To the Honorable the Board of Supervisors
Of the City and County of San Francisco—

GENTLEMEN : In compliance with Resolution No. 6,963, I hereby submit the following statement in regard to the City and County litigation since the date of the last report relative thereto by my predecessor, John H. Saunders, Esq., 1st of August, 1866.

PART FIRST.

ACTIONS BEGUN SINCE THE DATE OF THE LAST REPORT.

John Center,		12th District Court.
Plaintiff,		
vs.		No. 12,929.
The City and County of San Francisco.		Clark & Carpentier,
Defendant,		*Attorneys for Plaintiff.*

Action to quiet title to portions of Blocks 33, 42, 49. *First—* Northwest corner Center and Folsom streets, 220 feet on Folsom by 245 feet on Center street. *Second—*Southeast corner Center and Folsom streets, 300 feet on Center by 260 on Folsom. *Third—*

Southwest corner Folsom and Center, 369 feet on Center by 520 feet on Folsom. ' Mission Addition. Suit begun on the 14th September, 1866. Answer of City filed on October 5th, 1866. Afterwards the case was referred to Court Commissioner and tried; judgment in favor of plaintiff, and findings to that effect filed and served on the 12th of December, 1866.

Daniel R. Bedell and Peter V. Dorland, Plaintiff, *vs.* R. S. Thompson and the City and County o San Francisco, et al. Defendant.	4th District Court. No. 12,951. G. W. Tyler, *Plaintiffs' Attorney.*

Action to obtain partition of the land known upon Hoadley's Map of 1853 as the Hill Tract. Suit begun September 22d, 1866. Answer of City filed October 12th, 1866. This case is not yet ready for trial; there are so many defendants that up to the last term of Court they had not all been served with process.

City and County of San Francisco, Plaintiff, *vs.* Isaac Blythe and Manuel Venina, Defendant.	4th District Court. No. 13,101. James Mee, *Attorney for Defendants.*

Action of ejectment for City Slip Lot No. 91, begun on September 24th, 1866; was brought on for trial at the February Term of the Court, 1867, and judgment rendered in favor of the City; possession of the lot was recovered under the judgment.

People ex rel. Cornelius Mooney, | 12th District Court.
              Plaintiff, | No. 13,028.
                    | Felton & Hittel,
          vs. | *Attorneys for Plaintiff.*
  The Board of Supervisors, | Wilson & Crittenden with City
             Defendant. | Attorney,   *For Defendant.*

Application for a mandamus to compel the Board of Supervisors to declare certain persons elected Constables. Action began October 16th, 1866. On November 9th, 1866, case argued and judgment in favor of the city. The case has since been appealed to the Supreme Court and there argued. It awaits the decision of the Court.

———

James Robbins, | 15th District Court.
             Plaintiff, |
                    | No. 2,358.
         vs. |
                    | Haight & Pierson,
The Omnibus Railroad Company, | *Defendants' Attorneys.*
             Defendant. |

Action brought to determine whether the liability rests on the City or on the Railroad Companies to pave that portion of the street which lies outside of that upon which the horses attached to the cars travel. In other words to determine the meaning of the words " track " and " space between the rails," used in the Statute. Action begun November 16th, 1866. The case was heard before the District Court; judgment in favor of the City; appeal to the Supreme Court taken by Railroad Company; case argued at January term, 1867, and decision reversed; Supreme Court holding City liable.

James Robbins,
                    Plaintiff, | 15th District Court.

        vs. | No. 2,357.

The North Beach and Mission | Crane & Boyd,
    Railroad Company, | *Attorneys for Defendant.*
                    Defendant.

Same case as to question as preceding, begun at same time. Demurrer sustained to complaint.

Thos. W. Mulford,
                    Plaintiff, | 15th District Court.

        vs. | No. 2,409.

The City and County of San | Thomas A. Brown,
    Francisco, | *Attorney for Plaintiff.*
                    Defendant.

Action to quiet title to land commencing at northeast corner of Mission and Brown (now Twelfth) streets; lot 150 by 170. Complaint served on December 10th, 1866; answer filed and served January 8th, 1867. Case stands ready for trial.

William Martin,
                    Plaintiff, | 4th District Court.

        vs. | No. 13,291.

The Board of Supervisors of the
    City and County of San | Tevis, Jarboe & Cobb,
    Francisco, | *Plaintiff's Attorneys.*
                    Defendants.

Certiorari to inquire if Board of Supervisors have a right to allow San Jose Railroad Company the use of portions of sidewalks and streets of City and County. Writ sued out and served January 18th, 1867. Case was argued and decision rendered in favor of the City. Order dismissing proceedings entered April 13th, 1887.

John Perry, Jr., and Daniel S. | 12th District Court.
    Turner, *Trustees of Lone*
        Mountain Cemetery,   No. 13,190.
                    Plaintiffs, | John W. Dwinelle,
        vs.
                                    Plaintiffs' Attorney;
The Board of Supervisors of the
    City and County of San Fran- | Felton & Hittell, with City
    cisco,   Attorney,
                    Defendants. | *For Defendants.*

This suit brought to restrain the Board of Supervisors from passing an Ordinance prohibiting further interments in said Cemetery.
The issue was joined March 14th, 1867. The equity branch of the
case has been heard and determined in favor of the defendants. In
the answer of defendants a cross action for possession of the land
claimed as a Cemetery has been set up, and this ejectment suit is
now on the calender, No. 199, of the 12th District Court, and will
be heard as soon as reached. The equity branch is to be appealed
to the Supreme Court.

Jesse B. Hart,
                    Plaintiff, | 12th District Court.
        vs.
                                   No. 13,167.
Louis Ritter and City and Coun-
    ty of San Francisco,   Plaintiff,
                    Defendants. | *Attorney in Person.*

Action to recover out of the Argenti judgment $39,500, and to en-
force a lien thoreon for that amount. The action does not concern
the City except as to whom this portion of that judgment shall be
paid.
On the final settlement, if the controversy be not adjusted between the parties, the City can interplead, or pay the money into
court, or submit to an injunction. Action was begun on June 11,
1867.

Elizabeth Douglass,
                        Plaintiff, | 15th District Court.

              vs. | No. 2,855.

Robert Murdock, The City and | T. R. Wise,
  County of San Francisco, et al. | *Plaintiff's Attorney.*
                     Defendants. |

Action to quiet title to City Slip Lot No. 43, corner of Commercial and Drumm Streets. Suit began sixteenth of May, 1867. Answer filed twentieth of June, 1867, and case ready for trial.

The Spring Valley Water Works | 15th District Court.
                        Plaintiff, |

              vs. | No. 2,825.

The City and County of San | Eugene Lies,
  Francisco, | *Plaintiff's Attorney.*
                     Defendants. |

Suit to determine the right of the City to water for the purpose of irrigating Plaza, and as to what particular purpose or purposes the water must be applied in order that the City may obtain the same free of charge.

Action began May 4, 1867; answer filed June 14, 1867; case ready for trial. Since the above was written the case has been tried, argued, and submitted.

Edward Rondell,
                        Plaintiff, | 4th District Court.
              vs. |

                                     | No. 13,354.
North San Francisco Homestead |
  and Railroad Association, The | Cutter & Washington,
  City and County of San Fran- | *Plaintiff's Attorneys.*
  cisco, et al., |
                     Defendants. |

Action to quiet title to land bounded by Fillmore, Steiner, Chestnut, and Scott Streets, and the shores of the Bay of San Francisco.

Action began March 1, 1867 ; answer filed April 10, 1867.   Case
ready for trial so far as concerns the City, but will await the action
of defendants joined with her.

E. E. White,

Plaintiff,   4th District Court.

vs.   No. 13,476.

Board of Education and City and   Burnett & Burnett,
County of San Francisco,   *Plaintiff's Attorneys.*
Defendants.

Action in ejectment to recover a portion of the Tehama Street
School Lot.   The portion sought to be recovered out of the Lot is 28
feet by 75.

Suit began on May 7, 1867 ; answer filed June 11, 1867, and case
ready for trial.

Michael Greany,

Plaintiff,   4th District Court.

vs.   No. 13,505.

Daniel Callaghan, The City and   C. H. Parker,
and County of San Francisco,   *Plaintiff's Attorney.*
et al.,
Defendants.

Suit to enforce a lien for Street Assessments for $768, on lot of
land lying between Mason Street and West Mission Street, south of
Powell and North of Ridley Streets, claimed by City as a Public
Square.

Action began May 30, 1867 ; demurrer filed July 10, 1867 ; whole
question to be tested by the demurrer.

Joseph Frank,
                    Plaintiff,   15th District Court.

        vs.   No. 2,959.

The City and County of San   George & Carey,
  Francisco,   Plaintiff's Attorneys.
                    Defendant.

Action to quiet title to Lot corner of Commercial and Drumm Streets ; Lot 38$_{12}^{4}$ feet by 59$_{12}^{6}$ feet.
Action began on June 19, 1867 ; answer filed July 5, 1867.

———————

E. V. Sutter,
                    Plaintiff,   12th District Court.

                                  No. 13,398.
        vs.
                                  E. A. Lawrence & J. McM. Shaf-
The City and County of San   ter,
  Francisco,   Plaintiff's Attorneys.
                    Defendant.

Action for the partition of lands, commencing at a point on the southeast side of Folsom Street, 275 feet south of Sixth Street, thence running southerly on Folsom Street 275 feet ; thence, at right angles southeasterly, 550 feet, etc.

Action began May 3, 1867. No answer has been filed in this case, but a motion to strike out the greater portion of the complaint has been made and argued ; the same is now awaiting decision of the Court. If the motion is granted it will dispose of the whole case. The motion has just been granted.

——— · ———

George McKinstry,
                    Plaintiff,

        vs.   No. 13,411.

The City and County of San   E. A. Lawrence and J. McM.
  Francisco,   Shafter,
                    Defendant.   Attorneys for Plaintiff.

Action the same as the last—for the same land, and same course taken with it.

PART SECOND.

ACTION HAD IN CASES AT ISSUE PRIOR TO DATE OF LAST REPORT, AUGUST 1,
1866.

City and County of San Francisco,
     Plaintiff,
      vs.
Jonathan Hunt,
     Defendant.

12th District Court.

No. 8,339.

J. B. Felton,
    Defendant's Attorney.

This case has been tried, and judgment obtained in favor of the
City on the ninth of April, 1867, for the sum of $3,277 80, The
amount of the judgment in gold coin was paid to me on that day, and
by me on same day paid into the City Treasury.

D. W. Perley,
     Plaintiff,
      vs.
F. A. Hassey and the City and
County of San Francisco et al.,
     Defendants.

12th District Court.

No. 10,376.

Hall McAllister,
    Plaintiff's Attorney.

The plaintiff has dismissed his action as against the City.

The People, etc., ex rel. Jonathan Hunt,
     Plaintiff,
      vs.
The Board of Supervisors of the
City and County of San Francisco,
     Defendant.

12th District Court.

No. 8,638.

Whitcomb, Pringle & Felton,
    Attorneys for Plaintiff.

This case was brought by plaintiff to compel, by mandamus, the auditing of a claim of $561 89, commission and salary said to be due plaintiff as Tax Collector.

Cause was argued, and at the last term of Court judgment was rendered in favor of the City.

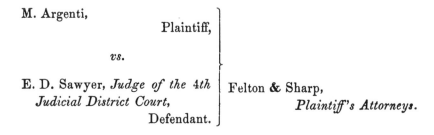

Felix Argenti,	4th District Court.
Plaintiff,	
vs.	No. 3,455.
The City of San Francisco,	Felton & Sharp,
Defendant.	Plaintiff's Attorneys.

At the date of the last report of Mr. Saunders this case had been reargued before the Supreme Court upon petition for rehearing. Since then the Supreme Court has rendered judgment against the City and in favor of the plaintiff.

A part of the same case is that of

M. Argenti,	
Plaintiff,	
vs.	
E. D. Sawyer, *Judge of the 4th Judicial District Court*,	Felton & Sharp,
Defendant.	Plaintiff's Attorneys.

The plaintiff claimed under the decision of the Supreme Court *twenty thousand dollars* more than the City thought her entitled to. The Judge of the Fourth District Court, supporting the views taken, refused to enter judgment for such excess. A mandamus was obtained, and the cause argued at the April Term of the Supreme Court. Judgment as to this excess was rendered in favor of the City by that Court. The whole judgment was then entered in the Fourth District Court, and amounts to $174,000.

D. W. Perley,
     Plaintiff, 12th District Court.

   vs.   No. 11,108.

The City and County of San Hall McAllister,
Francisco,   *Plaintiff's Attorney.*
     Defendant.

This action has been dismissed by the plaintiff.

———

D. P. Belknap, *Administrator, etc.*
of the estate of D. C. Brode- 12th District Court.
rick, deceased,
     Plaintiff, No. 7,470.

   vs.   William Loewy,
        Plaintiff's Attorney.
Charles Whitney, et al.,
     Defendant.

D. P. Belknap, *Administrator, etc.*
     Plaintiff, 12th District Court.

   vs.   No. 6,639.

H. W. Byington, et al., Wm. Loewy,
     Defendant. *Plaintiff's Attorney.*

These two cases are fully noticed by the former City Attorney, John H. Saunders, Esq., in his report of 1866, page 144, last Municipal Reports. The cases had at that time just been appealed to the Supreme Court. Since then both cases have been argued, briefs filed, and cases submitted, and they are awaiting the decision of that tribunal.

Mary Polack,
     Plaintiff,

    vs.

Isaac E. Davis, et al.,
     Defendant.

4th District Court.

No. 11,491.

Jarboe,
    Plaintiff's Attorney.

Dwinelle with City Attorney.

Motion for new trial in this case, pending at date of last report, has since been dismissed. (See Municipal Reports of 1866, pages 148 and 146.)

———

Edward Tompkins,
     Plaintiff,

    vs.

The City and County of San
  Francisco,
     Defendant.

4th District Court.

No. 11,794.

Plaintiff in person.

The plaintiff in this case made a motion for new trial. The same was submitted on briefs. A new trial has been denied.

———

City and County of San Francisco,
     Plaintiff,

    vs.

A. Calderwood,
     Defendant.

4th District Court.

No. 12,160.

Defendant in person.

Judgment had been obtained for the City in this case at date of last report, the case being one of ejectment for City Slip Lot No. 21, southwest corner of Clay and Drumm Streets, and the cause had been appealed to the Supreme Court. Argument was had, briefs filed, and the judgment of the Court below was reversed at the January Term, 1867. A petition for rehearing has since been denied.

Edmond Brooks,
        Plaintiff,
     vs.
W. T. Douglass et al.,
        Defendant.

12th District Court. .

No. 12,262.

D. Rogers,
     Plaintiff's Attorney.

This case, at date of last report, had been tried and decree entered for the plaintiff. Defendant appealed to Supreme Court, decision was rendered at April Term, 1867, affirming judgment below. Rehearing · denied at July Term, 1867.

B. S. Brooks,
        Plaintiff,
     vs.
The City and County of San Francisco and The Commissioners of Funded Debt,
        Defendant.

15th District Court.

No. 1,509.

Plaintiff in person.

Action to quiet title to Fifty-vara Lot No. 934, northwest corner of Bay and Hyde Streets.

Commenced January 11, 1866 ; answer of City filed January 27. Case tried by the Court and decree for plaintiff in December, 1866.

Simon Lazard,
        Plaintiff.
     vs.
The City and County of San Francisco,
        Defendant.

12th District Court.

No.

Clark & Carpentier,
     Attorneys for Plaintiff.

Action to queit title to Mission Block No. 33. Decree for plaintiff. Findings filed December 12, 1866.

Donald McLennan,
                    Plaintiff,   12th District Court.

          vs.   No.

The City and County of San   Clark & Carpentier,
    Francisco,   *Attorneys for Plaintiff.*
                    Defendant.

Action to quiet title to Mission Block No. 48. Decree for plaintiff. Findings filed December 12, 1866.

Jacob Browning,
                    Plaintiff,   12th District Court.

          vs.   No.

The City and County of San   Haight & Pierson,
    Francisco,   *Plaintiff's Attorneys.*
                    Defendant.

Action to quiet title to Fifty-vara Lot No. 948. This case, at date of last report, was not ready for trial. It has since been settled by the plaintiffs purchasing the City's interest.

The City and County of San
    Francisco,
                    Plaintiff,   No.

          vs.
                                   Sewall,
Martin Fulde et al.,   *Plaintiff's Attorney.*
                    Defendants.

Action of ejectment for City Slip Lot No. 43, southwest corner o Commercial and Drumm Streets. Case has been tried while this Report was in press. Judgment obtained in favor of the City.

PART THIRD.

At the date of Mr. Saunders' last report (in Municipal Reports for 1866, page 168) the case known as the " Pueblo Case " was about to be appealed to the Supreme Court of the United States.   It has since been before that tribunal and decided in favor of the City.

Two other cases in the Supreme Court within the past year, to wit, De Haro vs. United States, and O'Neil vs. Fitzpatrick, in which special counsel had been retained in Washington, have been decided at the last term of that Court in accordance with the interests of the City.

The Kearny Street cases have all been disposed of by the late de cision of the Supreme Court of the State.   The determination is favorable to the City, the Supreme Court having affirmed the decision of the County Court.

Respectfully,

HORACE M. HASTINGS,

City and County Attorney.

REPORT

BOARD OF FIRE COMMISSIONERS.

FIRE COMMISSIONERS' OFFICE, }
San Francisco, August 1st, 1867. }

To the Honorable Board of Supervisors—

GENTLEMEN : In compliance with the request of your Honorable Body, in Resolution No. 6,963, adopted June 18th, 1867, the Board of Fire Commissioners herewith submit their report, showing the organization, operation, expenditures, and condition of the Fire Department of the City and County of San Francisco for the fiscal year ending June 30th, 1867.

Under provisions of the law to establish a Paid Fire Department, approved March 2d, 1866, and of amendatory Act approved April 2d, 1866, the Board of Fire Commissioners was duly organized, two Commissioners having been elected by the people, one appointed by the Board of Supervisors, and two appointed by the Board of Fire Underwriters, to wit :

Benjamin H. Freeman and John V. McElwee, by the electors of San Francisco, September 5th, 1866 ; Jacob S. Dimon, appointed by the Board of Supervisors, September 10th, 1866 ; Erastus N. Torrey and John C. Merrill, appointed by the Board of Underwriters, September 14th, 1866.

The term of office fixed is five years, one Commissioner to retire yearly, the classification for their respective terms to be determined by lot.

14

The Board thus constituted, held a first and preliminary meeting on the 22d of September, at which John C. Merrill was chosen temporary President, and Jacob S. Dimon temporary Secretary. The ballot for classification was had, resulting as follows : E. N. Torrey drawing term of five years, John C. Merrill drawing term of four years, Benjamin H. Freeman drawing term of three years, John V. McElwee drawing term of two years, Jacob S. Dimon drawing term of one year.

A second meeting was held on the 29th of September, when the Board permanently organized by appointing Benjamin H. Freeman, President, and John P. Jourden, Clerk.

The contemplated force and composition of the Department, with other particulars relating thereto, are shown in sections four and six of Act approved March 2d, 1866. See Statutes 1865–66, pages 193 and 194, Consolidation Act, published 1866, to wit :

SECTION 4. The Fire Department of the City and County of San Francisco shall, when organized under this Act, consist of a Chief Engineer, two Assistant Engineers, one Corporation Yard Keeper, six (6) Steam Fire Engine Companies—to consist each of one Foreman, one Engineer, one Driver, one Fireman, and eight extra men ; two Hook and Ladder Companies—to consist each of one Foreman, one Driver, one Tillerman, and twelve (12) extra men ; and three Hose Companies—to consist each of one Foreman, one Driver, one Steward, and six (6) extra men. Each Steam Fire Engine Company shall have one steam fire engine, one hose reel, with one thousand (1,000) feet of hose, and not more than four (4) horses. Each Hook and Ladder Company shall have one truck, with hooks and ladders and necessary appurtenances, and two horses. Each Hose Company to have one hose reel, with one thousand (1,000) feet of hose, and one horse. But the said Board of Supervisors shall have power to increase or diminish the number of Fire Companies, as the public safety of the City and County may require, and to purchase the necessary steam engines and apparatus therefor, and to organize such volunteer companies for outside districts of said City and County as they may see fit ; provided, such volunteer companies shall be subject to the provisions of this Act ; but none of the members thereof, except the steward for each of such volunteer companies, shall receive any salary.

SEC. 6. The salaries of the officers and men comprising the said Fire Department shall not exceed the following sums, payable monthly : To the Chief Engineer, two hundred and fifty dollars ($250) per month ; to each Assistant Engineer, one hundred dollars ($100) per month ; to each Foreman, thirty ($30) per month ; to each Engineman, eighty dollars ($80) per month ; to each Driver, sixty dollars ($60) per month ; to each Fireman, fifty dollars ($50) per month ; to each Tillerman, fifty dollars ($50) per month ; to each steward, fifty dollars ($50) per month ; to each extra man, twenty dollars ($20) per month ; to the Corporation Yard Keeper, fifty dollars ($50) per month. All the paid members of the Fire Department, except the Foremen and extra men, shall give their undivided attention to their respective duties. The Foremen and extra men shall perform such duties as may be prescribed from time to time by the Board of Fire Commissioners. The terms of office of the Chief Engineer and Assistant Engineers are for two years, unless removed by the Board, for some cause ; that of subordinate officers, during good behavior ; the Clerk, during pleasure of Commissioners, by whom regulations are to be adopted for the government and regulation of the Department. Appointments for Chief Engineer and Assistant Engineers to be confirmed by the Board of Supervisors.

At a third meeting of the Fire Commissioners, held on the sixth day of October, the following appointments were made, and on the eighth day of the same month confirmed by the Board of Supervisors, to wit :

> F. E. R. WHITNEY............ *Chief Engineer.*
> H. W. BURCKES.............. 1st *Assistant Engineer.*
> CHAS. H. ACKERSON........ 2d *Assistant Engineer.*

On the 5th day of March, 1866, a certified copy of the Act, having been received by the Board of Supervisors, the subject was referred to a special committee, composed of E. N. Torrey, A. H. Titcomb, G. W. Bell, A. J. Shrader, and W. H. Phelps.

This special committee took the matter immediately in hand, and by telegraph, in the month of April thereafter, through Mr. Chas. Main, who gratuitously acted as their agent, purchased of the Amoskeag Manufacturing Company, of Manchester, New Hampshire, four (4) steam fire engines of their patent, one of the first and three of the second class, and one hose reel, for the sum of $17,655 34, in gold coin of the United States ; terms—all complete, freight paid, delivered in San Francisco.

The terms of the contract were complied with ; all the engines and the hose reel were received in contract time, and ready for service.

On the 16th day of July, 1866, the Board of Supervisors appointed a special committee to purchase horses for the Department, consisting of Chas. H. Stanyan, I. Rowell and A. J. Shrader; who purchased twenty-seven horses, prior to the time when this Act was to take effect.

Its organization thus being completed, the Department went into active operation on the first Monday in December, 1866, since which time its workings have been repeatedly tested, and are believed to have met with the approval of the public.

The Department at present consists of six (6) Steam Fire Engines, eleven (11) Horse Hose Reels, two (2) Hook and Ladder Trucks, thirty (30) Horses, with the various equipments and appurtenances.

The number of Members to which it is entitled by the Act organizing a Paid Fire Department, and Order No. 743 of the Board of Supervisors, is 148, exclusive of the Board of Engineers, divided as follows: Six Enginemen, six Firemen, thirteen Drivers, five Stewards, two Tillermen, one Corporation Yard Keeper, who are permanently employed, and 115 members who do fire duty only when alarmed. These, together with four men employed by the Board of Supervisors in the Corporation Yard, one Superintendent of Steamers, Assistant Superintendent, Hydrantman, and Drayman, constitute the entire force of the Fire Department.

Referring to the Report of the Chief Engineer, herewith accompanying, for details of transactions for seven months ending June 30th, 1867,

We are respectfully,

ERASTUS N. TORREY,
JOHN C. MERRILL,
BENJAMIN H. FREEMAN,
JOHN V. McELWEE,
JACOB S. DIMON,
Board of Fire Commissioners.

REPORT OF THE CHIEF ENGINEER

OF THE

SAN FRANCISCO FIRE DEPARTMENT

To the Honorable Board of Fire Commissioners—

GENTLEMEN: In compliance with the request of your Honorable Body, I have the honor to submit the following Report for the portion of the fiscal year which closed June 30th, 1867, being seven months since the organization of the Paid Fire Department.

Following is a detailed account of Expenditures, List of Members, their names, ages, and residence, the apparatus and property owned by the city and under its control, the total number of cisterns and hydrants, their location, the number of cisterns and hydrants where a supply of water can be obtained in case of fire; the number of fires and alarms; the losses by fire, amount of insurance injured or destroyed, together with such other information relating to the Department as may be of interest to your Honorable Board and the citizens generally.

In changing from the old to the new system, so far as deemed practicable the members of the Paid Department have been selected from the Volunteer Department, as experienced Firemen. Of course, many of them were of undisciplined habits and imbued with home prejudices, and even yet, with some, prejudices have not been entirely overcome : but few instances have occurred, however, where the exercise of strict and stern discipline has been necessary to bring them to the duty required.

I am proud that in so short a time the Department has so far surmounted the old prejudices and opposition, and become a pride and a safeguard to our citizens. I do not claim that the department is perfect in all its operations, but I do claim that under all of the circumstances, and in the same period of time from its organization, no Fire Department ever excelled it, and that it has more than met the expectations of its most sanguine friends ; and there is every reason to believe it will continue to merit the support and approval of our citizens.

It is a source of much pleasure to acknowledge the harmonious action of the whole Department, and their zealous devotion to the interest of the citizens, for which I return the thanks of the Board of Engineers. We also gratefully recognize the valuable aid of the Police force ; and to the efficient Fire Marshal the Board tender their thanks for his cordial support ; and to the Honorable Board of Fire Commissioners I am happy to say, that upon proper representation your assistance and co-operation has always been promptly and cheerfully rendered, so far as you could act in strict accordance with your duties, as the law has been construed; and I take pleasure in availing myself of this opportunity to acknowledge the uniform courtesy with which I have been officially treated by each and every gentleman of your Honorable Body, in all matters pertaining to my duties as an officer.

FORCE, CONDITION OF THE DEPARTMENT, AND RECOMMENDATIONS.

The present force of the Department comprises a Chief Engineer, two Assistant Engineers, and 153 men; which includes Steamer Engineers, Drivers, Firemen, Stewards, Tillermen, Officers of Companies, and Superintendent and Assistant Superintendent of Steamers, Corporation Yard Keeper, Hydrantman, and Drayman.

The apparatus consists of six (6) Steamers, and Horse Hose Cart Tenders, two (2) Hook and Ladder Trucks, three (3) two-wheeled Hose Carts, and two (2) four-wheeled Hose Carriages.

Five of the Steamers were built by the Amoskeag Manufacturing Company, of Manchester, N. H., the other was built by Lee & Larned, of New York.

My experience with the Amoskeag Engines, since their introduction here, and the information gained in regard to steamers of other build, has convinced me that they are a superior Engine, and I deem that the Committee merits praise for their selection. They are not only a reliable, efficient, and durable Engine, but they are economical—but a trifling amount has been expended on them for repairs, notwithstanding the great number of times they have been in service, and the rough and uneven streets they have had to run over. They are of two classes : First Class—Double Engine, 4-inch pump, 8-inch cylinder, 12-inch stroke; weight, without supplies, about 7,000 pounds, and is run by Company No. 1. Second Class—Single Engines, U tank, 4¾-inch pump, 8-inch cylinder, 12-inch stroke ; weight, without supplies, 5,000 pounds, and are now run by Nos. 2, 3, 4, 5, 6. The two-wheeled hose carts or tenders now in use are of the Amoskeag pattern, built by Casebolt & Co., of this city, and are entitled to the highest recommendations, possessing, as they do, every requisite for efficiency for level cities ; but for a city like San Francisco, where nine times out of ten they have to ascend a hill, they cannot be used advantageously, or with safety to any single horse. Their weight, with 600 feet of hose and the necessary fuel, is 2,500 pounds.

At your request, Mr. Hayes, Superintendent of Steamers, constructed a new style of four-wheeled horse hose carriage, but it has not yet been sufficiently tested for me to speak definitely as to its merits, but I am thus far favorably inclined towards its adoption— only, I think the rims of the wheels are deficient in strength.

I would here call your attention to the large increase of residences and buildings for manufacturing purposes at the Mission and in the vicinity. In former reports to your Board I recommended the building in that locality of four cisterns, to hold 100,000 gallons of water each. I am satisfied that your Honorable Body will do all in your power to carry out this recommendation, but its importance demands that it should be done without delay. In view of the exigency of the case, I further recommend that a steamer be placed in charge of Hose Company No. 5, at the Mission, to be known as Steamer No. 7, and that Hook and Ladder Truck known as Independent No. 3, be placed in the yard of Hose Company No. 5, and a temporary shed erected over it to protect it from the weather, to be used by that Company in case of a fire in their locality.

This distant portion of the city will then be well protected, which, from their isolated condition, they cannot otherwise be. I also recommend that the Horse Hose Reel of Hose Company No. 5, with all its appurtenances, be located in Hayes Valley, and retain the same number.

The two Hook and Ladder Trucks have been in constant service since 1853, and are now becoming dilapidated, so much so that they are almost constantly in the repair shop. .

I urge the building of one new Truck, this year, with all the necessary improvements. This will give us a spare Truck, in case of accident to one of the others.

It is requisite that there should be one other Assistant Engineer, whose residence and business should be in the 11th or 12th District, and, excepting a large fire should occur in the more populous part of the city, should be required to do duty only in those Districts. Often times as much damage is done by water as by fire, and often a threat-cuing fire may be checked or subdued by a single stream of water, by judicious management at the outset; but it is impossible for either of the present Assistants, living as they are at great distance from those districts, to meet this urgent need. I offer the above as a recommendation, and urge its adoption.

I have before stated to you, that for the welfare of the city, and the necessary protection of property from fires, an increase of men to the present force of the Department is an actual necessity. You are aware that by the Rules of the Department, none but those having a legitimate calling can become members; many of the men are so situated in their business that to leave it to attend a fire in the day-time, they are liable to be discharged by their employers; in some cases this has been done. The pay as fireman is so meagre that rather than risk a discharge from employment, they prefer to neglect their duty as firemen; consequently we often have not sufficient force to manage a line of hose at a fire of any magnitude. For ordinary occasions, the force is sufficient; but for fires on some of the hills, or in three or four story buildings, which I think in the future will be of more frequent occurrence, it is totally inadequate. I again recommend that this increase be made, and also, that (excepting the Chief Engineer) the pay of all the officers, members, engineers, firemen, and drivers, be increased so that the best men may be obtained for the various positions, and they should then be required to do patrol duty in their several districts, which would give better security from fire as well as to life and property.

HOSE.

The statistics will show the amount and condition of the Hose belonging to the city, and its distribution to the various Companies. The amount of reliable hose in the possession of the Department is only 7,500 feet; the remainder has been in service of the Volunteer Department at least eight years.

Imagine, gentlemen, a large fire raging—and it is as likely here as in any other city—when everything would depend on the quantity and strength of Hose ; and suppose this old Hose attached to any of the Steamers or Hydrants connected with 6-inch mains in the lower section of the city, how long, think you, could it be relied upon ? Should it be necessary to elevate it to the third story of a building, not one length in ten would stand the pressure ; and the most disastrous result might occur thereby.

These facts have been before presented to your Honorable Board, though, perhaps, not in so strong a light as now, for I was aware that the state of the city's finances was such that your endeavors with the Board of Supervisors for an appropriation for new Hose would be of no avail. Although your hands in this respect have been tied, your appeal has been heard, and citizens, upon examination, have become convinced of the importance of supplying this deficiency, and made aware of the danger in delay. As an instance : a worthy and appreciative citizen generously provided the Department with 2,500 feet of good, serviceable Hose, which has been constantly in service, and with which, by judicious management, we have been enabled to subdue threatening fires, but which, with rotten Hose, would doubtless have proven disastrous.

Although this 2,500 feet has been a great relief, yet it is but a trifle of what is needed. With these facts before you, it appears to me that the only course to pursue is to order for every foot of old Hose one of new, or at least 10,000 feet, of *pure oak-tanned leather ;* the leather to be not less than twenty pounds to the side ; half the quantity to be single-riveted, and the other double-riveted ; all to be finished with loops and rings, and not less than sixty pounds weight to each fifty feet, exclusive of the couplings. The couplings the same as now used by this Department ; the tail bands and tail pieces to be two inches in width and length respectively, and to be secured by three rivets. Said Hose to be warranted to stand a pressure of not less than 200 pounds to the square inch.

I earnestly trust that we may speedily be supplied with this Hose, whether it be California or Eastern, so that it comes up to the above standard.

HORSES.

There are thirty (30) horses owned by the city; twenty-seven are in good condition and in the service of the Fire Department. The other three have been reported, from time to time, as unserviceable. From the nature of their complaint, they are of no earthly use but for labor on a farm. There they would perform the duty required as well as the best. I deem it a great mistake that your Honorable Board have not the power to sell or exchange Horses as they become disabled, which they are liable to do at any fire. We are constantly in want of one or two extra Horses, and we have been obliged to place out of service a Steamer which has sound Horses, so as to give them to Companies in combustible localities, whose Horses have become disabled.

It would be economy to at once remove the three Horses above mentioned. The Horses alluded to were worthless when turned over to the Department. They consume as much and require the same care as the other Horses, without rendering any service in return, and are, therefore, only a pecuniary burden to the Department. I again recommend their disposal, and others purchased in their stead.

FIRES.

The past seven months have been remarkable for numerous fires, not only here, but throughout the United States. There have been here 159 fires, and, singularly, up to this date, not one false alarm has been struck. The suspicious circumstances attending many of these leave little doubt that most of them were incendiarism. Fire Marshal Durkee, in the pursuit of his official investigations, estimates the number of incendiary fires during the past seven months to be forty-four; the loss by the same, $477,376.

I would ask, is this not a fearful showing for a city as prosperous as San Francisco claims to be; or perhaps I should say, evil. The remedy, I believe, to a great extent, lies with our Insurance Companics; I allude to the too hasty adjustment of losses by fire, and the issuing of Policies for the amount of the apparent value of the property, especially where the hand of the incendiary is so often plainly visible; should they not pause, I ask, before adjusting such claims? In former reports I have called your attention to this subject, and I now trust that through your Honorable Board the Insurance Companies may be prevailed upon to aid in preventing incendiarism, instead of encouraging its increase, by their liberality in issuing Policies and paying claims.

This should receive your serious consideration.

HYDRANTS.

I have visited every portion of the City to learn where Hydrants are placed and where they are needed. In this Report is a list of the localities where I think extra Hydrants should be placed, and which, if the proper sized pipes are laid, I believe will give, so far as water is concerned, protection to all but the most isolated points. But I am told by those in authority that the Water Company have not the required sized pipes on hand, but they have been ordered from the East, and are occasionally arriving, and that in due time all the requirements will be met.

I asked of the Water Company why it was that in many localities three inch pipe had been laid and Hydrants attached? They answered that the property owners were cognizant of the size, but requiring water for domestic purposes, they urged the laying of these only for those uses; but after the pipes were laid the parties would petition the Board of Supervisors for Hydrants, and their petitions were granted without the Supervisors knowing the size of the pipes to which the Hydrants were to connect.

This would have been the case with most of the fifty-seven petitioners who, within the last seven months were granted the same privilege, only there were no Hydrants on hand.

There are Hydrants now located and attached to three and four inch pipes in localities where there is a valuable amount of property; these are deceivers to the Firemen, for they are not expected to know the size of every main that is laid, or whether every Hydrant they see will furnish a supply of water. It frequently occurs in these districts that, for instance, a Hose Company attaches to a Hydrant and leads into a fire, and on the start does good service; but a Steamer arrives and attaches to another Hydrant connected with the same pipe ; the water is then taken from the first, leaving the Hosemen in a dangerous position, and a retreat is the only resort, which, to a Fireman, is humiliating ; besides, the steamer cannot get more than half a supply—the fire which at first was checked again renews its ravages, until other positions are taken. The cry is then raised that the fire was not properly managed ; or if it is acknowledged that the supply of water is deficient, the Department or the Chief is to blame ; when really at the time I know not the cause, nor am I consulted in regard to the kind of pipes to be laid.

I am not particularly desirous of imposing on myself more labor or duties than is now incumbent upon me ; but I do think that not a Hydrant should be set unless by the sanction of the Chief Engineer, or some one who is interested in putting out fires.

Why I have been thus lengthy in this matter of Hydrants and water pipes is, that I have before called your attention to it, and for the reasons : first, its urgent necessity ; secondly, that the citizens when they complain, which they have just cause to do, the blame may rest where it properly belongs, and not be charged to any want of attention or dereliction of duty on my part as a public officer.

C I S T E R N S.

Your attention has been called before to the leaky condition of nearly all of the Cisterns. If they are to be repaired at all, I really hope that it will be done at once, and in such a manner that it will not be necessary, as heretofore, to have the work done over again every year. I also asked that four new Cisterns be built in the sections of the city between Sixteenth and Twenty-fourth streets, and I designated the points where they should be located.

That portion of the city is entirely destitute of water for fire purposes, and should a fire occur there, it would be very destructive·

I also recommended the building of two others on Telegraph Hill, as near the top as the Steamers can be drawn, for the protection of this increasing neighborhood ; and one at the junction of Harrison and Sêcond streets ; one at the junction of Fourth and Folsom, Stockton and Ellis, Taylor and Market streets ; the last two, located as they would be, in a central part of the city, are especially important, for should a break occur in the main pipe, or the water be shut off, as is frequently the case, the Department would have to go blocks, or perhaps to the bay, to obtain a supply of water.

If these facts are apparent to you, the matter should receive your immediate attention.

FIRE ALARM TELEGRAPH.

The Fire Alarm Telegraph has proven a complete success, and convinced the most skeptical of its great benefits.

The faithfulness and vigilance of the Superintendent and opera tives are demonstrated by the fact that but one miss has occurred from any cause, and not one false alarm struck since the new organization has been in operation.

The advantages over the old system of striking the hell are now generally recognized.

There are eighty-four Alarm Boxes now located in the city, and it is easy for any citizen, if he will take the trouble to do so, to inform himself of the location of the Box in his neighborhood, and I deem it important that every one should know where to go to give an alarm.

By turning on an alarm from a Box it is instantly communicated to each Engine, Hose, and Hook and Ladder House throughout the city, and to the citizens by the striking of four splendid bells, located at different points of the city.

The rapid growth of some localities has made it necessary to have more Boxes, and they have been placed in the following localities, and the number continued without regard to other numbers or localities, viz :

Box 81, Franklin and Hayes streets.
Box 82, Pioneer Woolen Mills, Black Point.
Box 83, Brannan and Eighth streets.   .
Box 84, San José Railroad Depot.
Box 85, Pacific Mail Steamship Company's new wharf.

I would recommend the erection of at least twenty additional Boxes, and that as soon as may be, all the boxes and numbers be re-arranged in this wise, viz : No. 1 to 19 inclusive be located in one District ; No. 2 to 29, in another ; No. 3 to 39 in another ; and so on to the highest number. By this arrangement the Department need not wait for the last stroke, but can start immediately at the pause, because they will know that all Boxes beginning with and including certain numbers are located in certain Districts ; for instance, if an alarm was struck from Box 39, they would start at the pause after three, because all the threes on from three to thirty-nine inclusive are located together.

You will perceive that under the present system considerable time is lost in counting the whole round of the bell before starting; besides, the Drivers are liable to miss a count in the higher numbers, and the time consumed before the mistake would be discovered, especially to the Company nearest to the Box from which the alarm is sounded, would be important.

The Fire Alarm Telegraph was placed in working order by contract; but now we have an energetic Superintendent, whose duty it is to make all necessary improvements and alterations that may present themselves.

I deem the above an improvement, and hope it will meet with your approval, and that it will be soon carried into effect.

NEW HOUSES.

All the Houses and Lots now occupied by the Department are too valuable for the purposes for which they are used. They are mostly located on the busiest thoroughfares, which, in my opinion, should not be; besides, in most cases the Houses are inconvenient in every respect. I would recommend that they be sold, and lots obtained in suitable localities, and good, substantial, one-story brick buildings be erected thereon, with the necessary improvements within, so as to make as near as possible a home for the members who are required to devote their whole time to the service of the Department. The size of lots should not be less than 30 feet front by 137 feet in depth.

Those that should receive your immediate attention are Hose Company, No. 1, on Jackson street, and Hose No. 2, on Folsom street; both are in a dilapidated and leaky condition, and unhealthy for the Men and Horses.

In the construction of Houses for Hose Companies, facilities should be provided the same as in Engine Houses, that is—size, conveniences, and plenty of stable accommodations, so that should the interest of the city at any time demand it, these Houses can be occupied by Steam Engine Companies without extra expense for alterations.

COST OF MAINTAINING THE FIRE DEPARTMENT.

The amount directly from the City Treasury is more, and the expense necessarily will continue to be greater, under the present system than under the old, but to the tax-payers individually, only a little more than half as much. The reasons why are well known to all who have assisted in sustaining the Volunteer Organizations.

At the time I was appointed Chief Engineer, and before the Department went into service, I found that the greater portion of the appropriations, which were set apart for the Department, was nearly consumed in the purchase of apparatus, etc., and no provisions made for other necessary requirements, and I became convinced that it would be impossible to carry on the Department for the year with the desired efficiency, without a further appropriation.

I am satisfied, from conversation with the originators of the paid system, that they could not, or did not, foresee the additions and appendages that would naturally follow, and be indispensable necessaries. For instance: Two extra Companies were needed, which have been organized by order of the Board of Supervisors; one located at the Mission, the other at No. 10's House, on Stockton street. The Horses, Harness, Blankets, Hose Reels, etc., etc., had to be purchased; then the pay of the members of said Companies; besides, no provisions were made or thought of for Superintendent and Assistant of Steamers, Hydrant and Drayman; neither for the purchase of tools for the Corporation Yard, the purchase of cots and beds; and numerous other items were overlooked, which were urgent necessities. All of which, in the aggregate, amount to so large a sum that to-day we are running the Department on the means provided by a few citizens, to whom all honor and credit is due.

During the short time the Department has been in service, I have often seen the great importance of having the several parts of each and every Engine duplicated, so that, in the event of a deficiency, loss, or injury to any part, it could be at once replaced.

I earnestly hope that soon we may be enabled to establish a proper repair shop at the Corporation Yard, and furnished with the required tools for doing this and all other work needed by the Department; for, in my opinion, the work would be done better, and more substantial and economical to the city, in the end.

CORPORATION YARD.

In another portion of this report I alluded to the advantages and economy in establishing in the Corporation Yard a repair shop, where all the repair for the Department can be done. In some cases repairs have been made by the men in the Yard, but in most instances the work has to be done outside. I am convinced that with the necessary tools and practical machinist, blacksmith, and wheelwright, the necessary labor can be performed to much better satisfaction, and you will find it a great saving to the finances of the city.

The Corporation Yard is a substantial and commodious brick building, just suited to all the requirements.

In connection with the Yard are the stables for the relief and sick horses, and both of these departments, I am pleased to say, are properly attended to. There is stored in the building nearly all of the apparatus of the Volunteer Department. I would suggest that the proper parties take some action in regard to the disposing of said property. I frequently have had inquiries made, by parties in the interior, in regard to their condition, price, etc., but am unable to give them a satisfactory answer as to price and terms. It seems to me that the sooner they are disposed of the better.

I would make one more recommendation—that gas be introduced into the building, and one jet allowed to be burned during the night, and a substantial sleeping room fitted up for the Drayman, so that he may sleep on the premises, to answer any call that may be made in the night for horses, hose, and apparatus, which is likely to be needed at almost any large fire.

POLICE AT FIRES.

The Police have rendered valuable assistance to the Department, in giving alarms, and in various ways ; but the force has not been sufficient at most fires to prevent interference with the duties of the Firemen, by the great number of spectators that crowd around. In some instances I have been compelled (although loth to do so) to order a stream of water on the crowd to give the Firemen a chance to operate. Let it be borne in mind that the force of the Department is small, and that it is discouraging to the men to be obstructed in their duties by outsiders. The presence of twenty or thirty Policemen at a fire would greatly aid in the efficient working of the Department.

CARDS.

I will here direct your attention to another recommendation—that a sufficient number of Cards be ordered printed, designating the location of Cisterns and Hydrants, to be furnished each Engine, Hose, and Hook and Ladder House, and public office.

I will here close this Report, trusting that the next Legislature will more clearly define the duties of your Honorable Board. As the law is now construed by some, you are merely entitled to hold office as Fire Commissioners, without the power to act as such.

This construction of the law can never work beneficially to the city, nor to the welfare of the Fire Department. Some one body must have supreme control, or the time will soon come when trouble will arise which will greatly impair the efficiency of the Department. I am informed by those who were instrumental in the passage of the Bill creating the Paid Fire Department, that it was understood and intended that the whole control of the Department should be in the hands of a Board of Commissioners.

In my opinion, it should be so. I have no complaint to make, however, for I have never come in contact with any other power assuming the supervision of the Fire Department ; but as I have said, unless the Legislature decides who shall control, I fear the Department will lose its efficiency, and the citizens the necessary protection.

The recommendations and suggestions herein made, even though they should not in every respect meet your views, I trust will receive your due consideration.

All of which I respectfully submit.

15

SAN FRANCISCO ENGINE COMPANY NO. 1.

HOUSE ON THE SOUTH SIDE OF JACKSON STREET, BETWEEN KEARNY AND
MONTGOMERY.

ROLL.

Name.	Position.	Occupation.	Age.	Residence.
W. O. T. Smith, ..	Foreman	Clerk.............	26	
Sam. Rainey, Jr...	Engineman ...	....	28	Engine House.
N. E. Waters......	Driver........	....	29	Engine House.
John Day.........	Fireman	....	26	Engine House.
J. Augustus.......	Asst. Foreman.	Painter..........	30	Engine House.
H. Hazeltine, Jr...	Clerk.........	Steward	29	
J. B. Butler.......	Extraman.....	Janitor	39	Engine House.
W. H. Godfrey....	Extraman.....	Porter...........	21	Engine House.
Wm. Smith.......	Extraman.....	Frame Maker	31	118 Fifth Street.
Theodore Brown ..	Extraman.....	Stevedore........	25	Engine House.
W. Brewer........	Extraman.....	Stevedore........	26	Engine House.
O. S. Baker.......	Extraman.....	Stevedore........	28	Engine House.

The Engineman, Fireman, and Driver are permanently employed.
These, together with the Foreman and eight Hosemen, who do duty
only when alarmed, constitute the entire company.

This Engine was built by the Amoskeag Manufacturing Company,
at Manchester, New Hampshire.

The pump is driven by two vertical reciprocating steam cylinders,
$7\frac{3}{4}$ inches diameter and $9\frac{1}{2}$ inches stroke, that are connected directly
with the shaft of the pump. The pump is a rotary, and is the most
generally approved pump of that description known to the public.
At a fair rate of speed it will discharge 600 gallons per minute.

A tender, to carry fuel and a water tank for the supply of the
boiler, make a part of the machine. The tender will carry fuel
enough for two hours' consumption, and the water tank will contain
60 gallons.

This Company was organized December 3d, 1866; from which
time they have had charge of this Engine.

The weight of this Engine, with three men, is about 8,500 pounds.

The House of this Company is in fair condition.

This Company have in charge 500 feet of Hose, in good condition.

The Hose Reel is two-wheeled; of the Amoskeag build; in fair
order.

The returns show that this Company have rolled to 111 alarms;
at work 25 times; number of hours' duty performed, 38.

INVENTORY OF PROPERTY IN POSSESSION OF THIS COMPANY.

One extra length of rubber suction, in bad order.
Three horses.
One double harness.
One single harness.
One full set of tools for Engine.
One feed box.
Four lanterns.
Three horse blankets.
Two whips.
Five hydrant wrenches.
Six hose spanners and belts.
Two blunderbusses.
Fifty feet of $\frac{3}{4}$-inch rubber hose and pipe.
One hose washer.
One stable broom.
One pitchfork.

One shovel.
One currycomb.
Two coarse brushes.
One chamois.
One sponge.
Two buckets.
Two wash bowls.
Three cots (useless).
Three mattresses (straw).
Three pillows.
One cylinder stove.
One kettle.
Four spittoons.
One jackscrew.
Four chairs.
One table.
One double and single block and fall.

SAN FRANCISCO STEAM ENGINE COMPANY No. 2.

HOUSE ON THE NORTH SIDE OF BUSH, BETWEEN KEARNY AND DUPONT STREETS.

ROLL.

Name.	Position.	Occupation.	Age.	Residence.
Jer. J. Kelley	Foreman	Clerk.............	28	Engine House.
Ira H. Chapman ..	Engineman ...	....	35	Engine House.
Peter Collins......	Driver........	....	33	Engine House.
C. E. Franz.......	Fireman	....	28	Engine House.
S. Davis..........	Asst. Foreman.	Bricklayer	..	Engine House.
Thomas Sands	Extraman.....	Stevedore........	22	Engine House.
B. C. Donnellan ..	Extraman.....	Carpenter........	43	Engine House.
P. O'Reilly	Extraman.....	Bricklayer	34	
P. S. Slockinger...	Extraman.....	Blacksmith	24	Engine House.
W. B. Fleming....	Extraman.....	Plasterer ·........	22	Engine House.
James Clashy	Extraman.....	Painter..........	27	Engine House.
George Post	Extraman.....	Butcher	27	Engine House.

The Engineman, Fireman, and Driver are permanently employed. These, together with the Foreman and eight Hosemen, who do duty only in case of fire, constitute the entire Company.

This Company was organized and took charge of their present Engine on the 3d day of December, 1866.

It has one steam cylinder, 8½ inches in diameter, and one double-acting vertical plunger pump, of 4⅜ inches in diamer and 12-inch stroke At a fair working speed, her manufacturers, the Amoskeag Manufacturing Company, claim that she can discharge 400 gallons per minute. The weight of this Engine, including the permanent members of the Company, is sixty-five hundred pounds.   .

This Company have in charge 550 feet of 2½-inch Leather Hose; in good condition. Also, one two-wheeled Horse Hose Reel, of the New York style; in fair order.

The House of this Company is in fair condition.

The returns of the Clerk of this Company show that since the 3d day of December, 1866, the Engine has rolled to 110 alarms, and worked at 35 fires; number of hours at work, 49⅓.

INVENTORY OF PROPERTY IN POSSESSION OF THIS COMPANY.

One extra length of rubber suction.
Three horses.
One double harness.
One single harness.
One full set of tools for Engine.
One feed box.
Four lanterns.
Three horse blankets.
Two whips.
Five hydrant wrenches.
Six hose spanners and belts.
Two blunderbusses.
Sixty-five feet of ¾-inch rubber hose and pipe.
Three buckets.

One jackscrew.
Two wash bowls.
One stable broom.
One pitchfork.
One shovel.
One currycomb.
Two coarse brushes.
One chamois and sponge.
One hose washer.
Three cots (useless).
Three mattresses and pillows.
Four chairs.
One cylinder stove.
Four iron spittoons.
One table.

SAN FRANCISCO ENGINE No. 3.

HOUSE ON THE SOUTH SIDE OF SUTTER, NEAR JONES STREET.

R O L L.

Name.	Position.	Occupation.	Age.	Residence.
M. E. Fitz Gibbon.	Foreman	Contractor	38	Jones St. cor. Pine.
John Keefe,.......	Engineman ...	....	..	Engine House.
Ed. O'Neil, ...	Driver.......	....	24	Engine House.
L. Stivers, ...	Fireman	....	40	Engine House.
John Carroll, ...	Asst. Foreman.	Painter..........	36	Engine House.
Geo. W. Pierce, ...	Clerk.........	Drayman	32	Cor. Jones & Geary.
Dan. Wiles,.......	Extraman....	Roofer	37	Cor. Jones & Geary.
E. F. Maynard, ...	Extraman.....	Housemover	35	Mason, near Geary.
J. McKiernan, ...	Extraman....	Carpenter........	27	Hyde, cor. Larkin.
C. E. Deuisenbury,	Extraman....	Roofer	27	Corner of Dupont and Harlem Place.
Wm. McDermott, .	Extraman.....	Cigar Dealer	..	Minna St. near 2d.
Benj. Blake, ...	Extraman.....	Clerk.............	..	

The Engineman, Fireman and Driver are permanently employed. These, together with the Foreman and eight Hosemen, who do duty only when alarmed, constitute the entire Company.

This Company was organized and took charge of their present Engine on the 3d day of December, 1866.

It is of the Amoskeag build, second class, and has one steam cylinder 8½ inches in diameter, and one double acting vertical plunger pump of 4¾ inches in diameter, and 12-inch stroke. At a fair working speed she will discharge 400 gallons of water per minute. The weight of the Engine, and three men, is about 6,500 pounds.

This Company have in charge 650 feet of 2½-inch leather Hose, in good condition. Also, one two-wheeled Horse Hose Reel, of the New York style, in fair order.

The House of this Company is in good order.

The monthly reports of the Clerk of this Company show that since the 3d of December, 1866, the Engine has rolled to 107 alarms, worked at 13 fires, for the period of 26 5-6 hours.

INVENTORY OF PROPERTY IN POSSESSION OF THIS COMPANY.

Three horses.
One double harness.
One single harness.

One extra length of rubber suction, for hydrants.
One set of tools for Engine.

Two hydrant wrenches.

Six hose spanners and belts.

Two blunderbusses.

Three horse blankets.

Two whips.

Sixty feet of ¾-inch rubber hose and pipe.

One feed box.

Three buckets.

Two oil cans.

Four lanterns.

Four cots (worthless).

Four mattresses and pillows.

One jackscrew.

Two wash bowls.

One shovel.

One ax.

One stable broom.

One pitchfork.

Two coarse brushes.

One currycomb.

One hose washer.

Four iron spittoons.

One "May Queen" stove and fixtures.

Four chairs.

One table.

SAN FRANCISCO ENGINE NO. 4.

HOUSE ON THE NORTH SIDE OF SECOND, BETWEEN HOWARD AND NATOMA STREETS.

ROLL.

Name.	Position.	Occupation.	Age.	Residence.
J. E. Mitchell, ...	Foreman	Cigar Dealer	38	Engine House.
J. S. Jones,.......	Engineman ...	....	30	Engine House.
Jas. Swanton,....	Driver........	....	38	Engine House.
H. E. Scott, ...	Fireman......	....	30	Engine House.
Frank Clapp, ...	Asst. Foreman.	Wagon Maker.....	23	534 Howard Street.
G. W. Emmons,...	Clerk.........	Trunk Maker	21	Engine House.
J. Tickner, ...	Extraman.....	Painter..........	29	564½ Howard St.
J. Miller, ...	Extraman.....	Trunk Maker	..	Engine House.
J. E. Bailey,......	Extraman.....	Bricklayer	34	3 Hubbard Street.
Jno. Romer, ...	Extraman.....	Stage Machinist...	21	Engine House.
J. S. Kane, ...	Extraman.....	Sail Maker........	34	Stevenson & 1st St.
W. T. Ballars, ...	Extraman.....	Sash and Blind Maker............	29	627 Howard Street.

The Engineman, Fireman, and Driver are permanently employed. These, together with the Foreman and eight Hosemen, who do duty only when alarmed, constitute the entire Company.

This Company was organized December 3d, 1866, from which time they have been doing duty with their present Engine, a second class Amoskeag build, which has one steam cylinder 8½ inches in diameter, and one double-acting vertical plunger pump, 4¾ inches in diameter and 12-inch stroke. At a fair working speed, her manufacturers, the Amoskeag Manufacturing Company, claim that she can discharge 400 gallons of water per minute. The weight of the Engine, including the permanent members, is about 6,500 pounds.

This Company have in charge about 600 feet of Hose, in good condition. Also, one two-wheeled Horse Hose Reel, of the New York style, built by Casebolt, of this city, in fair order.

The House of this Company is in fair condition.

The returns of the Clerk show the amount of duty performed by this Company, from December 3d, 1866, to June 30th, 1867, to have been as follows: Whole number of alarms at which apparatus has been called out, 114; whole number of fires at which apparatus was in service, 33; whole number of hours' duty performed by the Hosemen, 49⅓.

INVENTORY OF PROPERTY IN POSSESSION OF THIS COMPANY.

One extra length of rubber suction, for hydrants (in bad order).
One set of tools for Engine.
Three fine horses.
One double harness.
One single harness.
Three horse blankets.
Six hydrant wrenches.
Six hose spanners and belts.
Two blunderbusses.
Two whips.
One feed box.
Three buckets.
Two oil cans.
Four lanterns.
One jackscrew.

Fifty feet of rubber hose, ¾-inch, and pipe.
Two wash bowls.
Four iron spittoons.
One hose washer.
One sponge, chamois, and curry-comb.
Two brushes.
Two cots (worthless).
Two mattresses and pillows.
Four chairs.
One table.
One cylinder stove.
One kettle.
One stable broom.
One shovel.
One pitchfork.

SAN FRANCISCO ENGINE No. 5.

HOUSE ON THE WEST SIDE OF STOCKTON STREET, BETWEEN PACIFIC AND
BROADWAY.

ROLL.

Name.	Position.	Occupation.	Age.	Residence.
J. E. Ross, ...	Foreman	Drayman	26	Engine House.
H. Colvin, ...	Engineman . . .	. . . .	37	Engine House.
Silas Lander, ...	Driver	. . . .	22	Engine House.
W. S. Downs, ...	Fireman	. . . .	29	Engine House.
Jno. Mahoney, ...	Asst. Foreman.	Gas Fitter	26	Vallejo & Kearny.
Alf. Dennoe, ...	Clerk	Clerk	26	123 Jessie Street.
T. Langan, ...	Extraman	Soda Water	35	Stockton Street.
Steph. Bunner, ...	Extraman	Porter	23	St. Mary Street.
Geo. Kennard, ...	Extraman	Drayman	37	St. Mary Street.
D. Sullivan, ...	Extraman	Coppersmith	25	Kearny & Vallejo.
Jas. Grady, ...	Extraman	Clerk	25	St. Mary Street.
Jas. Dodd, ...	Extraman	Teamster	29	Engine House.

The Engineman, Fireman and Driver are permanently employed.
These, together with the Foreman and eight Hosemen, who do duty
only when alarmed, constitute the entire Company.

This Company was organized on the 3d day of December, 1866,
and took charge of the small Button Steam Engine, formerly used
by California Engine Company No. 4, of the Volunteer Department,
and did duty with her till the 5th day of January, 1867, when
they received the new, second class, Amoskeag Steam Engine, with
which they do duty. It has one steam cylinder, $8\frac{1}{2}$ inches in
diameter, and one double-acting vertical plunger pump, $4\frac{3}{8}$ inches in
diameter and 12-inch stroke. At a fair working speed, she will discharge 400 gallons of water per minute.

The weight of this Engine, and the three permanent men belonging to the Company, is about 6,500 pounds.

The Company have in charge about 750 feet of Hose, New York
standard, in good order. Also, a two-wheeled Horse Hose Reel,
built in this city, by Casebolt & Co., in fair order. The House of
this Company is in fair condition.

The returns of the Clerk of this Company show the amount of
duty performed from December 3d, 1866, to June 30th, 1867, to
have been as follows: Number of times apparatus has been called
out, 108; number of times apparatus has been at work, 24; number
of hours apparatus has been at work, 27 7-12.

INVENTORY OF PROPERTY IN POSSESSION OF THIS COMPANY.

One extra length of rubber suction for hydrants.
One set of tools for Engine.
Three horses.
One double harness.
One single harness.
Four hydrant wrenches.
Nine hose spanners.
Six hose spanner belts.
Two blunderbusses.
Two whips.
Three horse blankets.
One feed box.
Two buckets.
Fifty feet of $\frac{3}{4}$-inch rubber hose and pipe.
Two oil cans.

Four lanterns.
One jackscrew.
Two wash bowls.
Four iron spittoons.'
One hose washer.
One sponge and chamois:
One cylinder stove.
One kettle.
One stable broom.
One pitchfork.
One shovel.
One currycomb.
Two coarse brushes.
Three cots (worthless).
Three mattresses and pillows.
Four chairs.
One table.

SAN FRANCISCO ENGINE NO. 6.

HOUSE ON THE EAST SIDE OF SIXTH STREET, SOUTH OF FOLSOM.

ROLL. •

Name.	Position.	Occupation.	Age.	Residence.
Adam Smith	Foreman '.	Carpenter	27	24 Natoma Street.
Wm. Simpson	Engineman		31	Engine House.
R. Tennent	Driver		22	Engine House.
J. P. Wyckoff	Fireman		35	Engine House.
James Riley	Asst. Foreman.	Stevedore	25	633 California St.
Chris. Cox	Clerk	Caulker	28	Engine House.
John Conway	Extraman	Painter	22	Engine House.
John Murphy	Extraman	Cooper	23	Engine House.
T. Donnecliff	Extraman	Drayman	30	Engine House.
T. Sawyer	Extraman	Porter	40	935 Mission Street.
E. C. Sparhawk	Extraman	Currier	28	Engine House.
W. Cremmens	Extraman	Blacksmith	26	Mission Street.

The Engineman, Fireman, and Driver are permanently employed. These, together with the Foreman and eight Hosemen, who do duty only when alarmed, constitute the entire Company.

This Company was organized December 3d, 1866, when they took charge of No. 12's (of the Volunteer Department) old Steam Engine, and did duty with it till Feb. 13th, 1867, when they took charge of their present Engine, which was built by Lee & Larned, of the Novelty Iron Works, of New York. It has a water cylinder, 5 inches in diameter, and 8½-inch stroke, and a 9-inch steam cylinder, and will discharge 400 gallons of water per minute, when in good order. The Company did service with her up to the time of the Cosmopolitan Hotel fire, when she strained her pump ; since which time she has been undergoing repairs.

This Company have also in charge a two-wheeled Horse Hose Reel, of the New York style, built by Casebolt & Co., of this city, in fair order. Also, 600 feet of 2½-inch leather Hose, in good order. The House of this Company is in good condition.

The returns of the Clerk of this Company state the amount of duty performed from December 3d, 1866, to June 30th, 1867, to have been as follows : Whole number of alarms attended, 110 ; whole number of fires at work, 18 ; whole number of hours at work, 26½.

INVENTORY OF PROPERTY IN POSSESSION OF THIS COMPANY.

Three horses.
One double harness.
One single harness.
Three horse blankets.
One extra length of rubber suction, in bad order.
One set of tools for Engine.
Four hydrant wrenches.
Six hose spanners and belts.
Two blunderbusses.
Two whips.
One feed box.
Two buckets.
Fifty feet ¾-inch rubber hose and pipe.
Two oil cans.

Four lanterns.
One jackscrew.
Two wash bowls.
Four iron spittoons.
One hose washer.
One cylinder stove.
One stable broom.
One pitchfork.
One currycomb.
One shovel.
Two coarse brushes.
Three cots (worthless).
Three mattresses and pillows.
Four chairs.
One table.

SAN FRANCISCO HOSE COMPANY NO. 1.

HOUSE ON THE NORTH SIDE OF JACKSON, BETWEEN FRONT AND DAVIS STREETS.

ROLL.

Name.	Position.	Occupation.	Age.	Residence.
W. G. Olwell......	Foreman	Salesman.........	33	1612 Stockton St.
John Riley........	Driver........	....	26	Hose House.
James Dyer.......	Steward	....	23	Hose House.
J. H. T. Smith....	Asst. Foreman.	Janitor...........	25	Hose House.
Richard Cox	Extraman.....	Cork Cutter.......	22	Hose House.
John J. Sheay.....	Extraman.....	Pressman.........	23	Hose House.
George Burr	Extraman.....	Stevedore.........	28	Hose House.
J. Bain...........	Extraman.....	Iron Door and Shutter Maker.......	24	Hose House.
J. Cosgrove	Extraman.....	Stevedore.........	29	Hose House.

The Driver and Steward are permanently employed; these, together with the Foreman and six extra men, who do duty only when alarmed, constitute the entire Company.

This Company was organized December 3d, 1866, and have in charge a two-wheeled Horse Hose Reel, of the New York style, built by Casebolt & Co., of this city.

This Company have in charge 750 feet of 2½-inch leather Hose, New York standard, all of which is in fair condition.

The returns of this Company state the amount of duty performed from the date of its organization to June 30th, 1867, to have been as follows: Whole number of alarms attended, 110; whole number of times at work, 29; whole number of hours at work, 48¼.

The House of this Company is in bad condition.

INVENTORY OF PROPERTY IN POSSESSION OF THIS COMPANY.

One horse.
One single harness.
One horse blanket.
One whip.
One feed box.
Two lanterns.
Two buckets.
Two blunderbusses.
Fifty feet of ¾-inch rubber hose and pipe.
Two hydrant wrenches.
Six hose spanners and belts.
Two oil cans.
One jackscrew.

Two wash bowls.
Four iron spittoons.
Two hose washers.
One cylinder stove.
One stable broom.
One pitchfork.
One shovel.
One currycomb.
Two coarse brushes.
Two cots (worthless).
Two mattresses and pillows.
Four chairs.
One table.

SAN FRANCISCO HOSE COMPANY NO. 2,

HOUSE ON FOLSOM STREET, EAST OF BEALE.

ROLL.

Name.	Position.	Occupation.	Age.	Residence.
William H. Spencer	Foreman			
Frank Coyle	Driver			Hose House.
Ed. Cain	Steward		28	Hose House.
H. Ryder	Asst. Foreman.	Shoe Maker	25	Hose House.
Corn. Haggarthy	Extraman	Stevedore	29	Hose House.
W. C. Ashman	Extraman	Stevedore	23	Hose House.
J. Gillerlan	Extraman	Painter	21	Hose House.
G. W. Bartlett	Extraman	Blacksmith	22	Hose House.
P. Linahan	Extraman	Stevedore	28	Hose House.

The Driver and Steward are permanently employed; these, together with the Foreman and six Hosemen, who do duty only when alarmed, constitute the entire Company.

This Company was organized December 3d, 1866, and have in charge a two wheeled Horse Hose Reel, of the New York style, built by Casebolt & Co., of this City.

This Company have in charge 750 feet of 2½ inch leather Hose, New York Standard, in good condition.

The House of this Company is in good condition.

The returns of the Clerk of this Company show the amount of duty performed from December 3d, 1866, to June 30th, 1867, to have been as follows: Number of alarms attended, 110; number of fires at work, 24; number of hours at work, 33⅓.

INVENTORY OF PROPERTY IN POSSESSION OF THIS COMPANY.

One horse.

One single harness.

One horse blanket.

One whip.

One feed box.

Two lanterns.

Two buckets.

50 feet ¾-inch rubber hose and pipe.

Four hydrant wrenches.

Six hose spanners.

Six hose spanner belts.

Two blunderbusses.

Two oil cans.

One jackscrew.

Four iron spittoons.

Two wash bowls.

One hose washer.

One cylinder stove.

One stable broom.

One pitchfork.

One shovel.

One curry comb.

Two coarse brushes.

Two cots (worthless).

Two mattresses.

Two pillows.

Four chairs.

One table.

SAN FRANCISCO HOSE COMPANY NO. 3.

HOUSE ON THE NORTH SIDE OF PACIFIC, WEST OF JONES STREET.

ROLL.

Name.	Position.	Occupation.	Age.	Residence.
Hubert D. Claffey .	Foreman	Carpenter	29	Pacific near Hyde.
G. W. Amos........	Driver........	....	23	Hose House.
C. Wilber	Steward	....	25	Hose House.
H. Kingsley.......	Asst. Foreman.	Clerk.............	..	Hose House.
J. W. Kentzell	Clerk.........	Gas Fitter	23	Hose House.
J. C. Wilber	Extraman.....	Butcher	22	Hose House.
L. Varney	Extraman.....	Painter...........	35	Washington & Dupont.
J. H. Ross........	Extraman.....	Clerk.............	22	Hose House.
H. Wills..........	Extraman....	Ship Joiner	21	Hose House.

The Driver and Steward are permanently employed; these, together with the Foreman and six Hosemen, who do duty only when alarmed, constitute the entire Company.

This Company was organized December 3d, 1866, and have charge of a two-wheeled Horse Hose Reel, New York style, in fair order, built by Messrs. Casebolt & Co., of this city.

The Company have in charge 750 feet of 2½-inch leather hose, New York standard, in fair condition. The House is in good condition.

The returns of the Clerk of this Company show the amount of duty performed since December 3d, 1866, to June 30th, 1867, to have been as follows : Number of alarms attended, 108; number of fires at work, 13 ; number of hours at work, 23¾.

INVENTORY OF PROPERTY IN POSSESSION OF THIS COMPANY.

One horse.
One single harness.
One blanket.
One whip.
Two lanterns.
Four hydrant wrenches.
Six hose spanners and belts.
Two blunderbusses.
Two oil cans.
One jackscrew.
Two wash bowls.
Four iron spittoons.

One hose washer.
One cylinder stove.
One stable broom.
One shovel.
One pitchfork.
One currycomb.
Two coarse brushes.
Two cots (worthless).
Two mattresses and pillows.
Four chairs.
One table.

SAN FRANCISCO HOSE COMPANY NO. 4. •

HOUSE ON STOCKTON, NORTH OF GREENWICH STREET.

R O L L.

Name.	Position.	Occupation.	Age.	Residence.
Ber. Wolff	Foreman	Fruit Dealer	34	1,501 Stockton St.
M. Brady	Driver		23	Hose House.
C. Armstrong	Steward		50	Hose House.
Ed. Furley	Asst. Foreman.	Gold Beater	22	Hose House.
James Rodgers	Clerk	Baker	23	522 Union Street.
G. Maxwell	Extraman	Gas Fitter	23	Vallejo, bet. Stockton and Dupont.
B. Whitehead	Extraman	Grainer	21	612 Vallejo Street.
G. Hogan	Extraman	Butcher	21	Union Place.
John Kennedy	Extraman	Bar Tender	22	Hose House.

The Driver and Steward are permantly employed; these, together with the Foreman and six Hosemen, who do duty only when alarmed, constitute the entire Company.

This Company was organized December 3d, 1866, in accordance with Order No. 743, of the Board of Supervisors, and did duty with a Hand Hose Reel up to the 4th of May, 1867, when the Carriage of Liberty Hose of the Volunteer Department, having been rebuilt so as to be drawn by a horse, was placed in their charge, with a Horse. This Carriage was built in New York.

This Company have in charge 700 feet of 2½-inch leather Hose, New York standard, in fair order.

The returns of the Clerk of this Company state the amount of duty performed from December 3d, 1866, to June 30th, 1867, to have been as follows: Whole number of alarms attended, 110; whole number of times at work, 13; whole number of hours at work, $13\frac{1}{12}$.

INVENTORY OF PROPERTY IN POSSESSION OF THIS COMPANY.

One horse.
One single Dutch harness.
One horse blanket.
Three hydrant wrenches.
Six hose spanners and belts.
Two lanterns.
Two blunderbusses. .

Two oil cans.
One jackscrew.
Two wash bowls.
Four iron spittoons.
One hose washer.
One cylinder stove.
Two cots (worthless).

Two mattresses and pillows.
Four chairs.
One table.
One shovel.
One pitchfork.
One stable broom.

One currycomb.
Two coarse brushes.
Two buckets.
Fifty feet ¾-inch rubber hose and
pipe.

SAN FRANCISCO HOSE COMPANY NO. 5.

HOUSE ON SIXTEENTH BETWEEN GUERRERO AND VALENCIA STREETS.

ROLL.

Name.	Position.	Occupation.	Age.	Residence.
J. V. Denniston...	Foreman	Real Estate	38	Corbett & 17th Sts.
Thomas Kearney ..	Driver.........	....	27	Hose House.
Jer. Crowley	Steward	....	23	Hose House.
Wm. H. Shear	Asst. Foreman.	Blacksmith	22	16th and Mission.
John Crowley.....	Clerk.........	Butcher	34	16th near Valencia.
W. H. Mason	Extraman.....	Carpenter.........	37	Dolores, bet. 16th and 17th Sts.
P. Fitzsimmons ...	Extraman.....	Stone Cutter	34	Harriet, bet. 15th and 16th Sts.
Ed. Daley	Extraman.....	Butcher	30	16th near Valencia.
Samuel Shear.....	Extraman.....	Blacksmith	21	16th and Mission.

The Driver and Steward are permanently employed; these, together with the Foreman and six Hosemen, who do duty only when alarmed, constitute the entire Company.

This Company was organized December 3d, 1866, in accordance with Order No. 743, of the Board of Supervisors, and have in charge a four-wheeled Hose Carriage, in good order.

They also have in charge 750 feet of leather Hose, in fair condition. The House is in good order.

The returns of the Clerk of this Company state the amount of duty performed from December 3d, 1866, to June 30th, 1867, to have been as follows : Whole number of alarms attended, 102; whole number of fires at work, 4 ; whole numbers of hours at work, 14.

INVENTORY OF PROPERTY IN POSSESSION OF THIS COMPANY.

One horse.
One single harness.
One horse blanket.
One whip.
One feed box.
Two lanterns.
Two buckets.
Fifty feet ¾-inch rubber hose and pipe.
Four hydrant wrenches.
Six hose spanners and belts.
Two blunderbusses.
Two oil cans.
One jackscrew.

Two wash bowls.
Four iron spittoons.
One hose washer.
One cylinder stove.
One stable broom.
One shovel.
One pitchfork.
One currycomb.
Two coarse brushes.
Two cots (worthless).
Two mattresses and pillows.
Four chairs.
One table.

SAN FRANCISCO HOOK AND LADDER COMPANY NO. 1.

HOUSE ON THE NORTH SIDE OF O'FARRELL STREET, WEST OF DUPONT.

ROLL.

Name.	Position.	Occupation.	Age.	Residence.
Fred. Roskamp ...	Foreman	Grocery Dealer....	34	Cor. Jessie and 4th.
Samuel Ratcliff....	Driver.........	....	33	Truck House.
H. Roskamp	Tillerman....	....	24	Truck House.
D. J. Slicer	Asst. Foreman.	Bricklayer	28	Truck House.
W. S. Carrol	Clerk.........	Butcher	23	585 Market Street.
J. Connolly	Extraman.....	Laborer	34	Truck House.
L. Marks	Extraman.....	Plumber..........	30	Cor. Jessie and 4th.
P. Fitzpatrick.....	Extraman.....	Bricklayer	24	Dupont & Jackson.
M. Haley	Extraman.....	Butcher	22	Truck House.
M. Mullins........	Extraman.....	Laborer	24	Truck House.
W. Herring	Extraman.....	Butcher	21	Truck House.
H. Crawford	Extraman.....	Butcher	22	Truck House.
John McGee	Extraman.....	Blacksmith	22	Truck House.
W. Keeler	Extraman.....	Butcher	22	Market, bet. 3d and 4th.
H. St. Clair.......	Extraman.....	Porter	26	Truck House.

The Driver and Tillerman are permanently employed; these, together with the Foreman and twelve extra men, who do duty only when alarmed, constitute the entire Company.

This Company was organized and took charge of their present Truck December 3d, 1866.

The Truck was built by J. L. Berry, of this city, with the usual complement of Hooks, Ladders, etc.

The following is the return of duty performed by this Company from December 3d, 1866, to June 30th, 1867.

Whole number of alarms attended, 104 ; whole number of fires at work, 40 ; whole number of hours at work, 65¾.

INVENTORY OF PROPERTY IN POSSESSION OF THIS COMPANY.

Two horses.
One double harness.
Two horse blankets.
One whip.
One feed box.
Two buckets.
Two oil cans.
Fifty feet of ¾-inch rubber hose and pipe.
Three lanterns.
One jackscrew.
Two wash bowls.

Four iron spittoons.
One cylinder stove.
One stable broom.
One pitchfork.
One shovel.
One currycomb.
Two coarse brushes.
Two cots (worthless).
Two mattresses and pillows.
One table.
Four chairs.

SAN FRANCISCO HOOK AND LADDER COMPANY NO. 2.

HOUSE ON THE SOUTH SIDE OF BROADWAY, BETWEEN DUPONT AND STOCKTON STREETS.

ROLL.

Name.	Position.	Occupation.	Age.	Residence.
A. Bourgeoise	Foreman	Carriage Maker	38	630 Broadway.
J. O. Bayard	Driver		36	Truck House.
M. Phillipe	Tillerman		35	Truck House.
E. Tappaine	Asst. Foreman.	Wine Dealer	37	716 Green Street.
F. Garnier	Clerk	Marketman	36	Sansome & Pacific.
J. Gillett	Extraman	Basket Maker	49	1,428 Stockton.
A. Brerson	Extraman	Carpet Dealer	44	720 Washington.
E. Herteman	Extraman	Bar Keeper	37	417 Kearny.
J. Maisson	Extraman	Bar Keeper	38	611 Pacific.
P. Gibbon	Extraman	Barber	29	1,006 Dupont.
H. Ducrochet	Extraman	Laborer	43	814 Sacramento.
O. Leroux	Extraman	Laborer	36	621 Pacific.
P. Quintal	Extraman	Painter	21	520 Broadway.
S. Mistre	Extraman	Tinsmith	38	837 Dupont.
L. Mortier	Extraman	Restaurant Keeper.	28	620 Pacific.

The Driver and Tillerman are permanently employed; these, to gether with the Foreman and twelve extra men, who do duty only when alarmed, constitute the entire Company.

This Company was organized and took charge of their present apparatus on the 3d of December, 1866.

The Truck was built by J. L. Berry, of this city, which, with the usual number of Hooks, Ladders, Axes, Ropes, and Battering Ram, are in good order. The House of this Company is also in good order.

The following is the return of duty performed by this Company from December 3d, 1866, to June 30th, 1867: Whole number of alarms attended, 103; whole number of fires at work, 23; whole number of hours at work, $52\frac{1}{12}$.

INVENTORY OF PROPERTY IN POSSESSION OF THIS COMPANY.

Two horses.
One double harness.
Two horse blankets.
One whip.
One fuel box.
Two buckets.
Fifty feet $\frac{3}{4}$-inch rubber hose and pipe.
Two oil cans.
Four lanterns.
One cylinder stove.

One stable broom.
One pitchfork.
One shovel.
One currycomb.
Two coarse brushes.
Two cots (worthless).
Two mattresses and pillows.
Four chairs.
One table.
Four iron spittoons.
Two wash bowls.

CORPORATION YARD.

LOCATED ON SACRAMENTO STREET, EAST OF DRUMM.

House, one-story brick, in good order. Stable in Yard for four horses.

INVENTORY OF PROPERTY.

One complete set of tools.
Eight thousand one hundred and fifty feet of hose.

One thousand ft. condemned hose.
Three hundred and eighty seamless brass tubes.

Four barrels neatsfoot oil.
Fifteen gallons lard oil.
Ten gallons coal oil.
Five gallons benzine.
Five boxes castile soap.

Five gross matches.
Three horses (sick).
Two single sets harness.
One dray.
One set of stable utensils.

LIST OF HYDRANTS.

[All the Hydrants in this list are in good order, except as otherwise noted.]

1. Southwest corner of Broadway and Front.
2. Southeast corner of Broadway and Battery.
3. Southwest corner of Broadway and Sansome.
4. Southeast corner of Broadway and Montgomery.
5. Northwest corner of Broadway and Kearny.
6. Northwest corner of Broadway and Dupont.
7. Southwest corner of Broadway and Stockton.
8. Southwest corner of Broadway and Powell.
9. Northeast corner of Broadway and Mason, on Broadway.
10. Northeast corner of Broadway and Mason, on Mason.
11. North side of Broadway, between Front and Davis.
12. Broadway, at California Steam Navigation Company's Yard; private.
13. Southeast corner of Broadway and Polk.
14. Southwest corner of Bush and Battery.
15. Northwest corner of Bush and Sansome.
16. Northeast corner of Bush and Montgomery.
17. Southwest corner of Bush and Montgomery.
18. Southwest corner of Bush and Kearny.
19. North side of Bush, at Engine Company No. 2's House.
20. Northeast corner of Bush and Dupont.
21. Northwest corner of Bush and Dupont.
22. Northwest corner of Bush and Stockton.
23. Northeast corner of Bush and Powell.
24. Northwest corner of Bush and Powell.
25. Northwest corner of Bush and Mason.
26. Northwest corner of Bush and Taylor.
27. Northwest corner of Bush and Hyde.

28. Southeast corner of Bush and Taylor.
29. Northwest corner of Bush and Jones.
30. Northeast corner of Bush and Jones.
31. Southeast corner of Bush and Leavenworth.
32. Northwest corner of Bush and Leavenworth.
33. Northwest corner of Bush and Larkin.
34. Northwest corner of Bush and Franklin.
35. Northwest corner of Bush and Laguna.
36. Northwest corner of Bryant and Rincon Place.   3 inch pipe.
37. Northwest corner of Bryant and Second.
38. North side of Bryant between Second and Third.
39. Southeast corner of Bryant and Third.
40. North side of Bryant between Third and Fourth.
41. North side of Bryant opposite Ritch.
42. Northeast corner of Bryant and Fourth.
43. Northeast corner of Bryant and Fifth.
44. Northeast corner of Bryant and Park Avenue.
45. Northeast corner of Bryant and Garden.
46. Northwest corner of Brannan and Second.
47. Northeast corner of Brannan and Third.
48. Northeast corner of Brannan and Center Place.
49. Northeast corner of Brannan and Fourth.
50. Northeast corner of Brannan and Fifth.
51. Northeast corner of Brannan and Sixth.
52. North side of Brannan between Sixth and Seventh.
53. Northeast corner of Brannan and Seventh.
54. North side of Brannan between Seventh and Eighth.
55. Northwest corner of Brannan and Eighth.
56. Northeast corner of Brannan and Ninth.
57. Northeast corner of Brannan and Noe.
58. Southwest corner of Commercial and Dupont.
59. Southeast corner of Commercial and Kearny.
60. Southwest corner of Commercial and Montgomery.
61. Southwest corner of Commercial and Sansome.
62. Southeast corner of Commercial and Battery.
63. Northwest corner of Commercial and Battery.
64. Southwest corner of Commercial and Front.
65. Northwest corner of Clay and East.
66. Northwest corner of Clay and Davis.

67. Northeast corner of Clay and Front.
68. Northeast corner of Clay and Battery.
69. South side of Clay east of Montgomery.
70. Southwest corner of Clay and Stockton.
71. Southeast corner of Clay and Powell.
72. Southwest corner of Clay and Powell on Powell.
73. Southeast corner of Clay and Mason.
74. Northeast corner of Clay and Mason.
75. Northwest corner of Clay and Taylor.
76. Southeast corner of Clay and Taylor.
77. Northwest corner of California and Drumm.
78. Southwest corner of California and Davis.
79. Southeast corner of California and Front.
80. Southeast corner of California and Battery.
81. Southeast corner of California and Sansome.
82. Southwest corner of California and Montgomery.
83. Southwest corner of California and Dupont.
84. Southeast corner of California and Stockton.
85. Northeast corner of California and Powell.
86. Northwest corner of California and Powell.
87. Southeast corner of California and Taylor.
88. Southeast corner of California and Leavenworth.
89. Southeast corner of California and Larkin.
90. Southeast corner of California and Gough.
91. North side of Chestnut between Powell and Mason.
92. Southwest corner of Chestnut and Stockton.
93. Southeast corner of Chestnut and Mason.
94. Southeast corner of Chestnut and Leavenworth ; poor.
95. Southwest corner of Clementina and First.
96. South side of Clementina between First and Second.
97. North side of Clementina between First and Second.
98. Southeast corner of Clementina and Second ; bad.
99. Southeast corner of Clementina and Third.
100. North side of Clementina between Third and Fourth.
101. Northwest corner of Clementina and Fifth.
102. North side of Clementina between Fifth and Sixth.
103. Northeast corner of Clary and Fourth.
104. North side of Clary between Fourth and Fifth.
105. North side of Clary between Fifth and Sixth.

106.   East side of Ritch opposite Clary.
107.   East side of Dupont between Pacific and Jackson.
108.   Northwest corner of Ellis and Stockton.
109.   Northeast corner of Ellis and Powell.
110.   North side of Ellis between Powell and Mason.
111.   Northwest corner of Ellis and Mason.
112.   Northeast corner of Ellis and Taylor.
113.   Northeast corner of Ellis and Hyde.
114.   Northeast corner of Ellis and Jones.
115.   Northwest corner of Ellis and Franklin.
116.   Northeast corner of Ellis and Larkin.
117.   Northwest corner of Eddy and Leavenworth.
118.   Southwest corner of Eddy and Powell.
119.   Southwest corner of Eddy and Mason.
120.   Northeast corner of Eddy and Hyde.
121.   Northwest corner of Everett and Third.
122.   Southeast corner of Everett and Fourth.
123.   Southeast corner of Essex Place and Essex Street ; bad.
124.   Southwest corner of Francisco and Dupont ; bad.
125.   Northwest corner of Francisco and Powell.
126.   Southwest corner of Francisco and Stockton.
127.   Southwest corner of Filbert and Battery.
128.   Southwest corner of Filbert and Dupont ; bad.
129.   Northeast corner of Filbert and Stockton.
130.   Northeast corner of Filbert and Powell.
131.   Southwest corner of Filbert and Mason.
132.   Northeast corner of Filbert and Mason.
133.   Southwest corner of Filbert and Hyde ; bad.
134.   Southwest corner of Filbert and Jones ; bad.
135.   East side of Fremont between Howard and Folsom.
136.   East side of Fremont between Howard and Mission.
137.   East side of Fremont between Market and Mission ; bad.
138.   Northwest corner of Folsom and Stewart ; bad.
139.   Northeast corner of Folsom and Main.
140.   Northeast corner of Folsom and Beale.
141.   Northwest corner of Folsom and Fremont.
142.   Northeast corner of Folsom and First.
143.   Northwest corner of Folsom and First.
144.   Northwest corner of Folsom and Second.

145. North side of Folsom between Second and Third.
146. Northeast corner of Folsom and Third.
147. North side of Folsom between Third and Fourth.
148. Northwest corner of Folsom and Fourth.
149. Southwest corner of Folsom and Fourth.
150. North side of Folsom between Fourth and Fifth.
151. Northeast corner of Folsom and Fifth.
152. North side of Folsom between Fifth and Sixth.
153. Northwest corner of Folsom and Sixth.
154. Southeast corner of Folsom and Sixth.
155. Northwest corner of Folsom and Rausch.
156. Northwest corner of Folsom and Eighth.
157. Northeast corner of Folsom and Ninth.
158. Northwest corner of Folsom and Eleventh.
159. East side of Folsom opposite Mission Woolen Mills.
164. Five Hydrants at Mission Woolen Mills; private.
165. Southwest corner of Greenwich and Dupont; bad.
166. Northwest corner of Greenwich and Stockton.
167. Northeast corner of Greenwich and Powell.
168. Southeast corner of Greenwich and Mason.
169. Northeast corner of Greenwich and Jansen.
170. Northeast corner of Greenwich and Jones; bad.
171. Northwest corner of Green and Kearny; bad.
172. Southeast corner of Green and Dupont.
173. Southeast corner of Green and Stockton.
174. Southwest corner of Green and Powell.
175. Northwest corner of Green and Mason.
176. Northwest corner of Green and Calhoun; bad.
177. Northwest corner of Green and Montgomery.
178. Northwest corner of Green and Hyde.
179. Northwest corner of Geary and Kearny.
180. Northeast corner of Geary and Dupont.
181. Northwest corner of Geary and Stockton.
182. Southwest corner of Geary and Powell.
183. South side of Geary between Powell and Mason.
184. Northwest corner of Geary and Mason.
185. Northwest corner of Geary and Taylor.
186. Northeast corner of Geary and Jones.
187. Southeast corner of Geary and Hyde.

188. South side of Guy Place near First ; bad.
189. Northeast corner of Grove and Laguna.
190. Southeast corner of Harrison and Main; bad.
191. Northeast corner of Harrison and Beale ; bad.
192. Northeast corner of Harrison and Fremont ; bad.
193. Southwest corner of Harrison and First ; bad.
194. Northeast corner of Harrison and Essex ; bad.
195. Southwest corner of Harrison and Second; bad.
196. Southwest corner of Harrison and Stanley Place; bad.
197. Northwest corner of Harrison and Third.
198. North side of Harrison between Third and Fourth.
199. Southwest corner of Harrison and Fourth.
200. North side of Harrison between Fourth and Fifth.
201. Northeast corner of Harrison and Fifth.
202. North side of Harrison between Fifth and Sixth.
203. Southeast corner of Harrison and Sixth.
204. Northwest corner of Harrison and Seventh.
205. Corner of Harrison and Garden.
206. Northeast corner of Howard and Fremont.
207. Southwest corner of Howard and First.
208. North side of Howard between First and Second.
209. Southwest corner of Howard and Second.
210. South side of Howard between Second and Third.
211. Northwest corner of Howard and Third.
212. Union Hall, Howard between Third and Fourth ; private.
213. North side of Howard between Third and Fourth.
214. Northwest corner of Howard and Fourth.
215. South side of Howard near Fifth, in Gas Company's yard;
        private.
216. Southeast corner of Howard and Sixth.
217. Southeast corner of Howard and Seventh.
218. Southeast corner of Howard and Eighth.
219. Southeast corner of Howard and Langton.
220. Southeast corner of Howard and Russ.
221. Southeast corner of Howard and Rausch.
222. Northeast corner of Howard and Twelfth.
223. Northeast corner of Howard and Thirteenth.
224. Northeast corner of Howard and Sixteenth.
225. Northeast corner of Hayes and Laguna.

226. Northwest corner of Hayes and Octavia.
227. Northwest corner of Hayes and Gough.
228. Northwest corner of Hayes and Franklin.
229. Northwest corner of Hayes and Van Ness Avenue.
230. Northwest corner of Hayes and Polk.
231. Northwest corner of Jackson and Drumm.
232. Northwest corner of Jackson and Davis.
233. Northwest corner of Jackson and Front.
234. Northwest corner of Jackson and Battery.
235. Northeast corner of Jackson and Sansome.
236. Northeast corner of Jackson and Montgomery.
237. Southwest corner of Jackson and Montgomery.
238. South side of Jackson in front of No. 1 Engine House.
239. Southwest corner of Jackson and Kearny.
240. Southeast corner of Jackson and Dupont.
241. Northwest corner of Jackson and Dupont.
242. Northwest corner of Jackson and Stockton.
243. Southeast corner of Jackson and Powell.
244. Southwest corner of Jackson and Powell.
245. Northwest corner of Jackson and Virginia.
246. Northeast corner of Jackson and Mason.
247. Northwest corner of Jackson and Mason.
248. Southeast corner of Jackson and Mason.
249. Northeast corner of Jackson and Taylor.
250. Southwest corner of Jackson and Taylor.
251. Southwest corner of Jackson west of Kearny.
252. Southwest corner of Jessie and First.
253. Northwest corner of Jessie and Ecker.
254. Northeast corner of Jessie and Annie.
255. Northwest corner of Jessie and Fourth.
256. North side of Jessie between Third and Fourth; bad.
257. North side of Jessie between Fourth and Fifth.
258. North side of Jessie between Fifth and Sixth.
259. West side of Kearny between Pine and California.
260. West side of Kearny between Sacramento and California.
261. South side of King near Second.
262. North side of King near Third; private.
263. Northwest corner of Lombard and Kearny; bad.
264. Southwest corner of Lombard and Dupont; bad.

265. Southwest corner of Lombard and Stockton.
266. Southwest corner of Lombard and Powell.
267. Southwest corner of Lombard and Mason.
268. Northeast corner of Lombard and Taylor.
269. Northeast corner of Lombard and Jones; bad.
270. Southeast corner of Louisa and Fourth.
271. Northeast corner of Louisa and Fourth.
272. Southeast corner of Laurel Place and Essex; bad.
273. Northeast corner of Laundry Alley and Ritch.
274. Southeast corner of Market and Beale; bad.
275. Southeast corner of Market and Fremont; bad.
276. Southwest corner of Market and First.
277. North side of Market between Sansome and Battery.
278. South side of Market between First and Second.
279. South side of Market between Second and Third.
280. Southwest corner of Market and Third.
281. Corner of Market and Brooks.
282. South side of Market between Third and Fourth.
283. Southwest corner of Market and Fourth.
284. Northwest corner of Market and Taylor.
285. Southeast corner of Market and Fifth.
286. Southeast corner of Market and 11th.
287. Southwest corner of Mission and Stewart; bad.
288. Southwest corner of Mission and Spear.
289. Southwest corner of Mission and Main.
290. Southwest corner of Mission and Beale.
291. Northeast corner of Mission and Beale.
292. Southwest corner of Mission and Fremont.
293. Northeast corner of Mission and Fremont.
294. Northwest corner of Mission and First.
295. Southwest corner of Mission and First.
296. North side of Mission between First and Second.
297. Northwest corner of Mission and Second.
298. North side of Mission between Second and Third.
299. Northeast corner of Mission and Fourth.
300. North side of Mission between Fourth and Fifth.
301. Southeast corner of Mission and Fifth.
302. North side of Mission between Fifth and Sixth.
303. Southeast corner of Mission and Sixth.

304. Southeast corner of Mission and Seventh.
305. Northeast corner of Mission and Ninth.
306. Northeast corner of Mission and Eleventh.
307. Southeast corner of Mission and Twelfth.
308. Northwest corner of Mission and Sixteenth.
309. Northwest corner of Mission and Ridley.
310. Northwest corner of Minna and First.
311. Southeast corner of Minna and Second.
312. North side of Minna between First and Second.
313. North side of Minna between First and Second. .
314. South side of Minna between Second and Third; small pipe.
315. Northwest corner of Minna and Third.
316. Southwest corner of Minna and Fourth.
317. South side of Minna between Fourth and Fifth.
318. Southwest corner of Minna and Seventh.
319. Northwest corner of McAllister and Fillmore.
320. Northwest corner of McAllister and Buchanan.
321. Southwest corner of Natoma and First.
322. North side of Natoma between First and Second.
323. Northeast corner of Natoma and Jane.
324. Northwest corner of Natoma and Fifth.
325. Northwest corner of O'Farrell and Dupont.
326. Northwest corner of O'Farrell and Stockton.
327. Northeast corner of O'Farrell and Mason.
328. Northeast corner of O'Farrell and Jones.
329. Northeast corner of O'Farrell and Leavenworth.
330. Northeast corner of O'Farrell and Hyde.
331. Northeast corner of O'Farrell and Larkin.
332. Northeast corner of O'Farrell and Franklin.
333. Northwest corner of Oak and Buchanan.
334. East side of Park Avenue between Harrison and Bryant.
335. Northwest corner of Pacific and Davis.
336. Northwest corner of Pacific and Front.
337. Northwest corner of Pacific and Battery.
338. Northwest corner of Pacific on Battery.
339. Southeast corner of Pacific and Sansome.
340. Northeast corner of Pacific and Montgomery.
341. Southwest corner of Pacific and Montgomery.
342. North side of Pacific east of Kearny.

343. Northwest corner of Pacific and Dupont.
344. North side of Pacific between Dupont and Stockton.
345. Southwest corner of Pacific and Powell.
346. Northeast corner of Pacific and Mason.
347. Northeast corner of Pacific and Taylor.
348. Southwest corner of Pacific and Taylor.
349. Northwest corner of Pacific and Jones.
350. Southwest corner of Pacific and Jones.
351. Northwest corner of Pacific and Leavenworth.
352. Northwest corner of Pacific and Hyde.
353. Northeast corner of Pacific and Larkin.
354. Northeast corner of Pacific and Polk.
355. North side of Pacific opposite Virginia.
356. Southeast corner of Pine and Front.
357. Southeast corner of Pine and Battery.
358. Southwest corner of Pine and Sansome.
359. Southwest corner of Pine and Montgomery.
360. North side of Pine east of Montgomery.
361. Southwest corner of Pine and Kearny.
362. Southeast corner of Pine and Dupont, on Pine.
363. Southeast corner of Pine and Dupont, on Dupont.
364. Northeast corner of Pine and Stockton.
365. Northwest corner of Pine and Powell.
366. Northwest corner of Pine and Jones.
367. Southwest corner of Pine and Mason.
368. Southeast corner of Pine and Larkin.
369. Northwest corner of Pine and Polk.
370. Northwest corner of Post and Montgomery.
371. Southwest corner of Post and Montgomery.
372. Northwest corner of Post and Kearny.
373. Northwest corner of Post and Mason.
374. Southwest corner of Post and Taylor.
375. Southeast corner of Post and William.
376. Southeast corner of Post and Jones.
377. Southwest corner of Post and Leavenworth.
378. Northeast corner of Post and Hyde.
379. Northeast corner of Post and Powell.
380. North side of Perry between First and Second ; bad.
381. North side of Perry between Second and Third.

382. Southeast corner of Perry and Fourth.
383. South side of Perry between Fourth and Fifth.
384. Northeast corner of Perry and Fifth.
385. West side of Potrero Avenue, south of Brannan Bridge.
386. Southeast corner of Richmond and Battery.
387. Southwest corner of Sacramento and Drumm ; bad.
388. Southwest corner of Sacramento and Market.
389. Southwest corner of Sacramento and Davis ; bad.
390. Southwest corner of Sacramento and Front; bad.
391. Northwest corner of Sacramento and Front ; bad.
392. Northeast corner of Sacramento and Battery ; bad.
393. Southwest corner of Sacramento and Sansome ; bad.
394. Northeast corner of Sacramento and Sansome ; bad.
395. Northeast corner of Sacramento and Leidesdorff; bad.
396. South side of Sacramento, in front of What Cheer House; private ; bad.
397. Southeast corner of Sacramento and Kearny.
398. Southwest corner of Sacramento and Dupont.
399. South side of Sacramento, opposite Waverly Place.
400. Southwest corner of Sacramento and Stockton.
401. Southwest corner of Sacramento and Powell.
402. Northwest corner of Sacramento and Taylor.
403. Southeast corner of Sacramento and Taylor.
404. Southwest corner of Sacramento and Jones ; bad.
405. Southeast corner of Sacramento and Leavenworth.
406. Southeast corner of Sacramento and Larkin.
407. Northwest corner of Sutter and Sansome.
408. Southwest corner of Sutter and Montgomery.
409. Northwest corner of Sutter and Montgomery.
410. Southwest corner of Sutter and Kearny.
411. South side of Sutter between Dupont and Kearny.
412. Northeast corner of Sutter and Dupont.
413. Northwest corner of Sutter and Stockton.
414. Southwest corner of Sutter and Stockton.
415. Northwest corner of Sutter and Mason.
416. Northwest corner of Sutter and Taylor.
417. Northeast corner of Sutter and Taylor.
418. South side of Sutter in front of Engine No. 3.
419. Southeast corner of Sutter and Larkin.

420. Southwest corner of St. Mark's Place and Dupont.
421. Southwest corner of Stevenson and First.
422. Northeast corner of Stevenson and Second.
423. Northwest corner of Stevenson and Third.
424. Northeast corner of Stevenson and Seventh ; bad.
425. South side of Shipley between Fourth and Fifth.
426. Southeast corner of Shipley and Fifth.
427. Southeast corner of Shipley and Sixth.
428. Southwest corner of Silver and Second.
429. Southwest corner of Silver and Third.
430. North side of Silver between Third and Fourth.
431. Northeast corner of Sixteenth and Dolores.
432. Northwest corner of Sixteenth and Guerrero.
433. Northwest corner of Sixteenth and Valencia.
434. North side of Sixteenth between Guerrero and Dolores.
435. North side of Sixteenth, in front of house of Hose No. 5.
436. Northwest corner of Sixteenth and First Avenue.
437. Northwest corner of Sixteenth and Potrero Avenue.
438. Northwest corner of Seventeenth and Guerrero.
439. Northeast corner of Seventeenth and Valencia.
440. Northeast corner of Seventeenth and Dolores.
441. Northwest corner of Seventeenth and Second Avenue.
442. East side of Sixth between Folsom and Harrison.
443. South side of South Park Avenue between Second and Third.
444. Southeast corner of Turk and Taylor.
445. Southeast corner of Turk and Jones ; bad.
446. Southeast corner of Turk and Leavenworth.
447. Northeast corner of Turk and Larkin.
448. Northeast corner of Turk and Hyde.
449. Northwest corner of Tehama and First.
450. North side of Tehama between First and Second.
451. South side of Tehama between First and Second.
452. Southeast corner of Tehama and Second.
453. North side of Tehama between Third and Fourth.
454. Northwest corner of Tehama and Fifth.
455. Northeast corner of Tehama and Sixth.
456. Southeast corner of Townsend and Third.
457. Southeast corner of Townsend and Crook's Alley.

458. Southwest corner of Union and Montgomery; bad.
459. Southwest corner of Union and Kearny; fair.
460. Southwest corner of Union and Dupont.
461. Northeast corner of Union and Dupont.
462. Southwest corner of Union and Stockton.
463. Southeast corner of Union and Stockton.
464. Southeast corner of Union and Stockton.
465. Southeast corner of Union and Powell.
466. Southwest corner of Union and Mason.
467. Southeast corner of Union and Jones.
468. Northwest corner of Union and Hyde.
469. Southeast corner of Union and Larkin.
470. Vallejo Street Wharf; private.
471. Southwest corner of Vallejo and Front.
472. Southwest corner of Vallejo and Battery.
473. Northwest corner of Vallejo and Kearny.
474. Southwest corner of Vallejo and Dupont.
475. Northeast corner of Vallejo and Montgomery.
476. Southwest corner of Vallejo and Stockton.
477. Southwest corner of Vallejo and Powell.
478. Southeast corner of Vallejo and Mason.
479. Northwest corner of Vallejo and Hyde.
480. Southeast corner of Washington and Drumm.
481. Southeast corner of Washington and Davis.
482. Southeast corner of Washington and Front.
483. Southeast corner of Washington and Battery.
484. Northwest corner of Washington and Sansome.
485. Southeast corner of Washington and Sansome.
486. Southeast corner of Washington and Montgomery.
487. Southwest corner of Washington and Kearny.
488. Southwest corner of Washington and Brenham Place.
489. Northwest corner of Washington and Dupont.
490. Southwest corner of Washington and Stockton.
491. Southwest corner of Washington and Powell.
492. Southeast corner of Washington and Mason.
493. Southeast corner of Washington and Mason, on Mason.
494. Southwest corner of Washington and Taylor.
495. Northeast corner of Washington and Leavenworth; suction.
496. Northeast corner of Washington and Larkin.

497. Northeast corner of Washington and Polk.
498. Corporation Yard; poor.
503. Five at the Pioneer Woolen Mills at Black Point; private.
506. Three at the Pacific Mail Steamship Company's new wharf.

Total number of Hydrants set, 506.

CISTERNS.

The following is the number and condition of Fire Cisterns :

Built of	Location.	Capacity.	Remarks.
Brick,	Powell corner Filbert	20,000,	arched, in good order.
Brick,	Powell corner Green	30,000,	arched, in bad order.
Brick,	Powell corner Broadway	30,000,	in good order.
Brick,	Powell corner Pacific	30,000,	in bad order.
Brick,	Powell corner Jackson	30,000,	in good order.
Brick,	Powell corner Washington	30,000,	in good order.
Brick,	Powell corner Bush	60,000,	in bad order.
Brick,	Stockton corner Union	30,000,	arched, in good order.
Cement,	Stockton corner Green	21,000,	arched, in bad order.
Brick,	Stockton corner Vallejo	20,000,	arched, in good order.
Brick,	Stockton corner Broadway	20,000,	arched, in good order.
Brick,	Stockton corner Pacific	25,000,	arched, in good order.
Brick,	Stockton corner Washington	20,000,	arched, in good order.
Brick,	Stockton corner Clay	20,000,	arched, in good order.
Brick,	Dupont corner Union	20,000,	arched, in bad order.
Brick,	Dupont corner Green	32,000,	arched, in good order.
Brick,	Dupont corner Vallejo	30,000,	arched, in good order.
Brick,	Dupont corner Broadway	35,000,	arched, in good order.
Brick,	Dupont corner Pacific	31,000,	arched, in good order.
Brick,	Dupont corner Jackson	25,000,	arched, in good order.
Brick,	Dupont corner Washington	25,000,	arched, in bad order.
Brick,	Dupont corner Clay	15,000,	arched, in good order.
Brick,	Dupont corner California	30,000,	arched, in good order.

Carried forward..........658,000

Built of   Location.   Capacity.   Remarks:

Brought forward.......... 658,000

Brick, Dupont corner Bush ....29,000, arched, in good order.

Brick, Kearny corner Pacific........30,000, arched, in bad order.

Brick, Kearny corner Merchant......30,000, arched, in good order.

Brick, Kearny corner Sacramento....30,000, arched, in good order.

Brick, Kearny corner California .....20,000, arched, in good order.

Brick, Kearny corner Bush ....27,000, arched, in good order.

Brick, Kearny corner Post..........30,000, arched, in bad order.

Brick, Montgomery corner Pacific....30,000, arched, in good order.

Brick, Montgomery corner Washington 30,000, wooden cover, in good
order.

Brick, Montgomery corner Commercial 32,000, arched, in good order.

Brick, Montgomery corner California .32,000, arched, in good order.

Brick, Montgomery corner Bush .....25,000, in good order.

Brick, Sansome corner Pacific.......25,000, in good order.

Brick, Sansome corner Bush ....30,000, in bad order.

Brick, Battery corner Bush ....30,000, in good order.

Wood, First corner Jessie ....25,000, useless.

Brick, First corner Folsom..........29,000, arched, in good order.

Brick, Third corner Mission ....30,000, in good order.

Brick, Second corner Folsom........51,000, arched, in good order.

Brick, Stevenson corner Ecker ......27,000, in good order.

Brick, Broadway corner Ohio ....40,000, in good order.

Brick, Taylor corner Clay ....45,000, arched, in good order.

Brick, Powell corner Ellis (filled by a
spring) ....25,000, arched, in good order.

Brick, Sixteenth corner Mission .....27,000, arched, in bad order.

Brick, Sixteenth corner Dolores .....42,000, arched, in good order.

Brick, Davis corner California ......40,000, arched, in good order.

Brick, Fremont corner Mission ......40,000, arched, in good order.

Total number of gallons....1,480,000

LIST OF HYDRANTS RECOMMENDED FOR LOCATION.

Market and Stewart.

Market and Main.

Market, north side, at the junction
of Bush.

17

Market and Brady.
Market and Van Ness Avenue.
Market, south side, between Fourth
  and Fifth.
Market and Ninth.
Mission and Third.
Mission bet. Third and Fourth.
Mission and Eighth.
Mission and Fifteenth.
Mission and Fourteenth.
Mission and Erie.
Stevenson and Fourth.
Stevenson and Fifth.
Stevenson and Sixth.
Howard and Beale.
Howard and Fifth.
Howard bet. Fourth and Fifth.
Howard and Ninth.
Howard and Fifteenth.
Howard and Fourteenth.
Minna and Sixth.
Minna and Eighth.
Tehama and Fourth.
Welch and Fourth.
Folsom and Seventh.
Folsom opposite Essex.
Folsom and Russ.
Folsom and Fifteenth.
Folsom and Fourteenth.
Folsom and Thirteenth.
Folsom and Twelfth.
Harrison and Hawthorne.
Harrison and Eighth.
Bryant and Stanley Place.
Bryant and Sixth.
Bryant and Seventh.
Bryant and Eighth.
Valencia and Ridley.
Valencia and Fifteenth.

Oak and Franklin.
Oak and Gough.
Oak and Laguna.
Buchanan and Hayes.
Buchanan and Turk.
Buchanan and Sutter.
Fulton and Laguna.
Fulton and Gough.
Fulton and Franklin.
McAllister and Laguna.
McAllister and Steiner.
Grove and Franklin.
Turk and Franklin.
Turk and Fillmore.
Bush and Devisadero.
Bush and Steiner.
Bush and Franklin.
Bush and Buchanan.
Bush and Van Ness Avenue.
Post and Buchanan.
Post and Laguna.
Post and Octavia.
Post and Gough.
Post and Franklin.
Post and Van Ness Avenue.
Post and Polk.
Post and Larkin.
Sutter and Polk.
Bush and Polk.
Austin and Polk.
California and Polk.
Sacramento and Polk.
Clay and Polk.
Ellis and Polk.
Larkin and Jackson.
Ellis and Van Ness Avenue.
Sutter and Hyde.
California and Hyde.
Sacramento and Hyde.

Clay and Hyde.
Washington and Hyde.
Jackson and Hyde.
Jackson and Leavenworth.
Clay and Leavenworth.
Sutter and Leavenworth.
Geary and Leavenworth.
Eddy and Jones.
Eddy and Taylor.
Jones and Clay.
Jones and Washington.
Jones and Jackson.
Taylor and Broadway.
Taylor and O'Farrell.
Powell and O'Farrell.
Stockton and St. Mark's Place.
Stockton and Post.
Powell and Sutter.
Mason and California.
Mason and Sacramento.
Mason and John.
Sacramento and Prospect Place.
Stockton and Pacific.
Clay and Dupont.
Kearny and California.
Kearny and Clay.
Kearny and Merchant.
Kearny and Pacific.
Montgomery and Sacramento.
Sansome and Clay.
Battery and Merchant.

Front and California.
Front and Clay.
Davis and Oregon.
Davis and Broadway.
Davis and Commercial.
Davis and Vallejo.
Drumm and California.
Drumm and Clay.
Drumm and Clark.
Drumm and Pacific.
Battery and Green.
Battery and Union.
Broadway and Ohio.
Kearny and Chestnut.
Dupont and Chestnut.
Powell and Chestnut.
Taylor and Chestnut.
Jones and Chestnut.
Hyde and Chestnut.
Francisco and Mason.
Francisco and Taylor.
Filbert and Larkin.
Green and Larkin.
Vallejo and Larkin.
Broadway and Larkin.
Broadway and Hyde.
Broadway and Leavenworth.
Filbert and Taylor.
Greenwich and Taylor.
Union and Taylor.
Hinckley and Dupont.

FIRE APPARATUS AT STATIONARY POINTS.

There is apparatus located at the following points, for the more immediate protection of the neighborhood, and without organized companies :

One Hand Hose Reel, with 700 feet Hose, at the Central Railroad stables, on Brannan street, between Eighth and Ninth.

Two Hand Hose Reels, with 350 feet Hose each, in Hayes Valley, on Grove street, between Laguna and Octavia.

One Hand Hose Reel, with 450 feet of Hose, at San Francisco and Pacific Sugar Refinery, on the corner of Eighth and Brannan streets.

Three hundred feet of Hose in charge of P. Finnegan, on Ellis street, between Powell and Mason streets.

Two hundred and fifty feet of Hose in charge of H. Koster, corner of Crook and Townsend streets.

Two hundred and fifty feet of Hose at the corner of Vallejo and Montgomery streets.

One hundred feet of Hose at the South Park Livery Stables.

One Hand Engine, Reel, and four hundred feet of Hose on the Potrero.

Accompanying the above is the needful supply of Blunderbusses, Spanners, and Hydrant Wrenches.

I have also placed Battering Rams at the following points:

Corner of Richmond and Battery streets; corner of Richmond and Front streets; corner Merchant and Front streets.

REVIEW OF THE AMOUNT OF HOSE IN THE DEPARTMENT.

	Feet.	Feet.
Engine No. 1	500	
Engine No. 2	550	
Engine No. 3	650	
Engine No. 4	600	
Engine No. 5	750	
Engine No. 6	600	
Hose No. 1	750	
Hose No. 2	750	
Hose No. 3	750	
Hose No. 4	700	
Hose No. 5	750	

Carried forward..........................   7,350

Brought forward   7,350
Hayes Valley   700
Central Railroad Company's stable   700
Potrero   400
Crook and Townsend streets   250
Finnegan's stables   300
San Francisco and Pacific Sugar Refinery   450
Telegraph Hill   250
South Park stables   100
Corporation Yard 8,150
                                              ———— 11,300

    Total   18,650

Of which amount 10,650 feet is unreliable.

There is also in the Corporation Yard about 1,000 feet of condemned Hose.

TABULAR VIEW OF THE DUTY PERFORMED BY THE SEVERAL COMPANIES FROM DECEMBER 3, 1866, TO JUNE 30, 1867.

	Alarms attended.	Times in service.	Hours in service.
San Francisco Engine, No. 1	111	25	39
San Francisco Engine, No. 2	110	35	49½
San Francisco Engine, No. 3 ..:.................	107	13	26 5-6
San Francisco Engine, No. 4	114	33	49⅓
San Francisco Engine, No. 5	108	24	27 7-12
San Francisco Engine, No. 6	110	18	26½
San Francisco Hose, No. 1	110	29	48¼
San Francisco Hose, No. 2	110	24	33⅓
San Francisco Hose, No. 3 .....:..............	108	13	23¾
San Francisco Hose, No. 4	110	13	13 1-12
San Francisco Hose, No. 5	102	4	14
San Francisco Hook and Ladder, No. 1..........	104	40	65¾
San Francisco Hook and Ladder, No. 2..........	103	33	52 1-12

PAY ROLL OF THE FIRE DEPARTMENT.

1 Chief Engineer, $3,000 per year $3,000
2 Assistant Engineers, each $1,200 per year   2,400

    Carried forward .... $ 5,400

Brought forward.	$ 5,400
1 Secretary, $1,200 per year.......................	1,200
1 Superintendent of Engines, $1,800 per year........	1,800
1 Assistant Superintendent of Engines, $1,800 per year	1,800
1 Corporation Yard Keeper. $600 per year...........	600
6 Enginemen, each $960 per year...................	5,760
13 Drivers, each $720 per year......................	9,360
6 Firemen, each $600 per year.....................	3,600
5 Stewards, each $600 per year....................	3,000
2 Tillermen, each $600 per year...................	1,200
1 Drayman, $900 per year........................	900
1 Hydrantman, $900 per year.....................	900
13 Foremen, each $360 per year.:...................	4,680
102 Extramen, each $240 per year...................	24,480
	$64,680

CONSTRUCTION FUND.

For Engines Nos. 1, 2, 3, and 4.......	$16,407 67	
For Freight on same...............	1,247 67	
For 27 Horses, and $464 50 commis-		
sions.......................	10,154 50	
For Independence Truck.............	750 00	
For 8 Hose Reels, (of Casebolt).......	3,205 00	
For 709 feet of California Hose, at $1 60		
per foot.....................	1,134 40	
For Harness and Stable Utensils......	2,079 42	
		$34,978 66

OUTSTANDING.

For 3 Horses.....................	$1,300 00	
For Engine No. 5, and 8 lengths Rub-		
ber Suction...................	3,898 50	
For Freight on Engine No. 5.........	309 88	
For 2,527 feet of California Hose..:...	3,649 59	
		9,157 88
Total.............................		$44,136 54

Appropriation, $35,000.

RUNNING EXPENSES.

For Repairs......................	$6,115 67	
For Hose......................	8,261 34	
For Horse Feed..................	2,400 79	
For Fuel.........................	956 10	
For Horse Shoeing................	513 50	
For Hardware....................	2,218 23	
For Oils, etc....................	1,199 97	
For Sundries....................	2,284 82	
For Salaries not provided for in Salary Fund......................	2,667 85	
		$26,618 27

Appropriation, $22,000. Outstanding, $4,618 27.

SALARIES.

Salary of—

Chief Engineer, December 1st, 1866, to June 30th, 1867, seven months, at $250 per month........	$1,750 00
Two Assistant Engineers, December 1st, 1866, to June 30th, 1867, seven months, at $100 per month	1,400 00
Clerk, October 1st, 1866, to June 30th, 1867, nine months, at $100 per month..................	900 00
Corporation Yard Keeper, December 1st, 1866, to June 30th, 1867, seven months, at $50 per month.	350 00
Enginemen of six Steam Engines, to June 30th, 1867, at $80 per month.........................	3,959 13
Drivers of six Engines, three Hose Carriages, and two Trucks, to June 30th, 1867, at $60 per month..	5,121 35
Firemen of six Steam Engines, to June 30th, 1867, at $50 per month........................	2,547 78
Stewards of three Hose Companies, to June 30th, 1867, at $50 per month.....................	1,065 00
Tillermen of two Trucks, to June 30th, 1867, at $50 per month................................	700 00

Carried forward..............................$17,793 26

Brought forward............................	$17,793	26
Foremen of six Engine, three Hose, and two Truck		
Companies, to June 30th, 1867, at $30 per month	2,310	00
Extramen of six Engine Companies, eight men each,		
to June 30th, 1867, at $20 per month..........	6,720	00
Extramen of three Hose Companies, six men each, to		
June 30th, 1867, at $20 per month............	2,508	00
Extramen of two Truck Companies, twelve men each,		
to June 30th, 1867, at $20 per month..........	3,360	00
Man taking charge of Horses, September 19, 1866, to		
December 3d, 1866, at $60 per month.........	149	02
Outstanding—		
Salary of Hose Companies 4 and 5, December 3d,		
1866, to June 30th, 1867....................	3,340	00

[Organized by the Board of Supervisors, but no provision made for in Salary Fund.]

$36,180 28

PURCHASE OF LOTS, ERECTION AND REMOVAL OF ENGINE HOUSES, ETC.

Dr.

Lot on north line of Pacific street, 137½ feet from Jones,		
23 x 60, part of 50-vara lot 877..............	$1,200	00
Deposit of E. Walter, one-fourth payment of Engine		
House and Lot No. 10, refunded (title defective)..	1,262	50
Purchase of title to same........................	250	00
Building Brick Engine House and Warehouse at Cor-		
poration Yard, Sacramento street, between Drumm		
and East streets............................	13,865	95
Bell Tower and Glass in Engine House No. 9, belonging		
to Company................................	315	00
Commission on Sale of Engine Houses and Lots—		
Engine House and Lot No. 3, 1 per cent. on $27,150,		
United States Tax, $\frac{1}{10}$.................$298 65		
Engine House and Lot No. 4, 1 per cent. on		
$16,050............................ 160 50		

Carried forward........................$459 15 $16,893 45

Brought forward..................$459 15 $16,893 45

Engine House and Lot No. 5, 1 per cent. on
$8,000 .... 80 00

Hose House and Lot No. 1, 1 per cent. on
$3,850 .... 38 50

Hook and Ladder House and Lot No. 1, 1 per
cent. on $8,300..................... 83 00

            660 65

Placing Building purchased of Eureka Hose Company
on Lot on Pacific street, near Jones (described
above) 260 00

Cleaning Engines preparatory to sale............... 200 00

House purchased of Rincon House Company......... 850 00

  Total.................................$18,864 10

Cr.

Amount at credit of account June 30th, 1865......... $5,921 78

Receipts from sale of Engine House and Lot No. 12
(part payment).......................... 6,325 00

Receipts from Engine Houses and Lots, 1866–67, viz—

Engine House and Lot No. 3...........$27,150 00

Eighteen inches of Engine Lot No. 1..... 200 00

Engine House and Lot No. 4............ 16,050 00

Hook and Ladder House and Lot No 1... 8,300 00

Engine House and Lot No. 5............ 7,750 00

Hose House and Lot No. 1.............. 3,850 00

Engine Lot on Stockton, near Greenwich.. 300 00

House and Lot on Sutter street.......... 2,075 00

           65,675 00

Sale of Engine No. 7........................... 1,090 00

  Total $79,011 78

Less amount paid out............................. 18,864 10

  Balance to credit of Fund....................... $60,147 68

FIRES, FIRE ALARMS, AND LOSSES, DECEMBER 3D, 1866, TO JUNE
30TH, 1867.

Total number of Alarms..........................	159
Hall Bell Alarms.............................	111
Still Alarms.................................	48
Fires	158
False Alarms................................	0
Alarm turned in by one of the operators by accident..	1

CAUSES.

Incendiary....................................	44
Accidental....................................	17
Carelessness	28
Spontaneous combustion.......................	5
Defective stove pipes and flues................	30
Sparks from locomotive........................	2
Gas lights....................................	3
Gas meter....................................	1
Hot ashes....................................	4
Explosion of kerosene stoves...................	2
Rekindling	2
Bonfire......................................	1
Tar pot......................................	1
Unknown.....................................	18
	—— 158

LOSSES.

Month.	Total loss.	Paid on Insurance.	Am't of Insurance.
December, 1866, 27 days.............	$43,560 00	$35,956 00	$202,200 00
January, 1867....................	3,336 00	2,896 00	24,300 00
February, 1867....................	72,215 00	47,360 00	97,850 00
March, 1867....................	26,005 63	19,270 63	87,800 00
April, 1867....................	212,445 00	112,121 74	221,825 00
May, 1867.	104,345 00	90,359 00	194,300 00
June, 1867....................	15,469 60	11,058 75	56,050 00
Totals....................	$477,376 23	$319,022 12	$884,325 00

FIRE ALARM AND POLICE TELEGRAPH REPORT.

OFFICE OF FIRE ALARM AND POLICE TELEGRAPH, }
July 29th, 1867. }

To the Honorable the Board of Supervisors
Of the City and County of San Francisco—

GENTLEMEN : In compliance with Resolution No. 6,963, of your Honorable Body, I herewith submit my second annual report of the condition and workings of the Fire Alarm and Police Telegraph, for the fiscal year ending June 30th, 1867.

All the machinery of the Fire Alarm and Police Telegraph has worked with remarkable regularity during the year. All the apparatus connected with this Department is under the care and control of the Superintendent of Fire Alarms and a Standing Committee of the Board of Supervisors—Messrs. Torrey, Phelps, and Reynolds. A constant watch is kept at the Central Office, City Hall, night and day, by the operators. Each operator serves two alternate terms of four hours each, as Principal, and the same as Assistant Operator, so that sixteen hours' service out of every twenty-four is required from each operator. No operator is permitted to sleep during his watch. Each operator is accountable to the Superintendent for any omissions or mistakes that may occur at the Central Office during his hours of duty.

An accurate account is kept of the time of giving each alarm, and the station from which it originates.

The meridian bells, five bells and eighteen gongs at their various locations at Engine Houses and other localities, are struck from the Fire Alarm Office, at noon, every day, (Sunday excepted). No arrangement has ever been made for securing strictly accurate time. Some time ago, Mr. Thomas Tennent submitted a proposition to the Board for furnishing standard time to the city. As our means of communicating time are far ahead of any other in the city, I would recommend that some arrangement be made to furnish correct time for the city.

EXTENSIONS.

Four new Signal Boxes have been erected during the year, located as follows : No. 82, at Pioneer Woolen Mills, Black Point ; No. 83, corner of Eighth and Brannan streets ;. No. 84, San José Railroad Depot, corner of Valencia and Market streets ; No. 85, Pacific Mail Steamship Company's wharf, corner of First and Brannan streets. Two first-class bronze Bells, weighing about 2,000 pounds each, have been purchased from Henry N. Hooper & Co., of Boston, Mass., and erected, one on the House of Engine Company No. 6, on Sixth street, near Folsom, (to replace a broken one); the other on the House of Engine Company No. 4, on Second street, near Howard. A new Bell Tower has been erected for the Bell on No. 4 Engine House. A small Bell, weighing 248 pounds, has been placed on the House of Engine Company No. 3, on Sutter street. The Bell on the House formerly occupied by Washington Hose Company, on Dupont street, has been removed to the House of Engine No. 5, on Stockton street, near Broadway.

New and powerful striking apparatus has been purchased and erected for the Bell on the City Hall. The striking apparatus previously used on the Hall Bell is now in use for striking the Bell on Second street.

Gongs have been placed in all the Engine, Hose, and Hook and Ladder Houses, except those having Bells. Gongs have also been placed in the houses of the Chief Engineer and Assistants, Corporation Yard, Fire Commissioners' office, and the Superintendent of Steamers. Two of the insurance offices are also furnished with Gongs, supplied at their own expense.

In accordance with the recommendation of the Chief Engineer of the Fire Department, the Signal Boxes have all been painted so as to make them more conspicuous. Those located on dark-colored buildings have been painted white, with red lettering ; those on light-colored buildings are painted red, with white lettering. A more general distribution of keys to the Signal Boxes has been made. Greater economy has been practiced in the battery power, so that the cost has been reduced one-half since last year.

From July 1st, 1866, to June 30th, 1867, there were 198 alarms given by means of the Telegraph. Of this number 158 were actual fires ; the balance were as follows : second alarms, 9 : general alarm, 1 ; chimneys, 17 ; re-kindled, 3 ; falling walls, 4 ; false, 6. Of this number 105 were for the first half of the year, against 93 for the last half. The monthly average for the year has been 16½. The highest number of alarms given during any month was 23, in October last. The smallest number was given in January, when only 10 occurred. The days of the week on which alarms were given are as follows : Sunday, 25 ; Monday, 26 ; Tuesday, 30; Wednesday, 35; Thursday, 25 ; Friday, 21 ; Saturday, 36. The greatest number of alarms have occurred on Saturday ; the least on Friday. The hours of the day when alarms have been most frequent are from 1 to 3 A. M., while from 7 to 11 A. M., has been most free. The boxes from which the largest number of alarms have been struck are Nos. 8, 19, 32 and 62. Out of 70 Signal Boxes, alarms have been received from all but 17. With the exception of the above named, the alarms have been pretty generally distributed among the remaining boxes. Alarms have been received from all but three of the boxes originally put up.

The Police Telegraph is in daily use, and is working satisfactorily ; seven instruments out of the ten are in use.

The Signal Boxes are all tested once in every two weeks. The striking machinery of the Bells is carefully examined every few days, so that it is scarcely possible for any serious derangement of the apparatus to occur.

Keys to the Signal Boxes are in the hands of the Police, and are also left in grocery stores and dwellings, most convenient to the boxes. The instructions to key holders are the same as heretofore, viz : Upon the discovery of or positive information of a fire near your Signal Box, turn the crank slowly and steadily twenty-five or thirty times ; then wait a few moments, and if you hear no ticking in the box, or alarm on the large bells, turn again : if you still hear no alarm, go to the nearest box and give the alarm from that. 1st. Never touch the crank except to give an alarm ; 2d. Never signal for a fire seen at a distance ; 3d. Be sure your box is locked before leaving it ; 4th. Give an alarm for no cause whatever other than an actual fire ; 5th. Do not give an alarm for a burning chimney ; 6th. Touch no part of the box but the crank. Upon a second alarm being struck for the same fire, it will be considered a general alarm. Second alarms will be turned in only by the Chief Engineer or his Assistants. Alarms are transmitted to the Central Office from the Signal Boxes by turning the crank. Alarms are usually struck in thirty seconds from the time the crank is turned. Property owners and tenants are requested to inform themselves of the location of all the boxes near their property; also, of the places where keys are kept. Upon the breaking out of a fire, see that the alarm is promptly and correctly given. Complaints concerning the workings of the Fire Alarm Telegraph, irregular striking of the bells or gongs, broken wires, etc., should in all cases be made at the Fire Alarm Telegraph Office, City Hall.

The boxes are located as follows :

FIRE ALARM SIGNAL STATIONS.

1—Corner Stockton and Francisco streets.
2—Corner Mason and Lombard streets.
3—Corner Stockton and Greenwich streets.
4—Corner Sansome and Greenwich streets.
5—Corner Battery and Union streets.
6—Corner Jones and Filbert streets.
7—Corner Union and Hyde streets.
8—Corner Powell and Union streets.
9—Corner Dupont and Green streets.
12—Corner California and Kearny streets.
13—Corner Front street and Broadway.
14—Corner Stockton street and Broadway.
15—Corner Leavenworth and Pacific streets.
16—Corner Mason and Pacific streets.
17—Corner Kearny and Pacific streets.
18—Corner Sansome and Jackson streets.
19—Corner Davis and Washington streets.
21—City Hall
23—Corner Taylor and Clay streets.
24—Corner Powell and Clay streets.
25—Corner Dupont and Clay streets.
26—Corner Battery and Clay streets.
27—Corner Montgomery and Commercial.
28—Corner Leavenworth and Sacramento.
29—Corner Stockton and California streets.
31—California street, near Sansome.
32—Corner Drumm and California streets.
34—Corner Mason and Pine streets.
35—Corner Hyde and Bush streets.
36—Engine House No. 2, Bush street.
37—Market street, near Battery.
38—Corner Montgomery and Sutter streets.
39—Corner Stockton and Sutter streets.
41—Engine House No. 3, Sutter street.
42—Corner Geary and Mason streets.

43—H. and L. No. 1, O'Farrell, near Dupont.
45—Corner Hyde and O'Farrell streets.
46—Corner Jones and Turk streets.
47—Corner Market and Powell streets.
48—Corner Kearny and Geary streets.
49—Corner Mission and Steuart streets.
51—Corner Folsom and Spear streets.
52—Corner Mission and Fremont streets.
53—Corner Folsom and First streets.
54—Engine House No. 4, Second street.
56—Corner Harrison and Second streets.
57—Corner Brannan and Second streets.
58—Corner Townsend and Third streets.
59—Corner Bryant and Third streets.
61—Corner Howard and Third streets.
62—Corner Fourth and Mission streets.
63—Corner Harrison and Fourth streets.
64—Corner Howard and Fifth streets.
65—Corner Mission and Sixth streets.
67—Engine House No. 6, Sixth street.
68—Corner Harrison and Seventh streets.
69—Corner Howard and Eighth streets.
71—Corner Mission and Eleventh streets.
72—Corner Mission and Thirteenth streets.
73—Corner Folsom and Sixteenth streets.
74—Hose House No. 5, Sixteenth street.
75—Corner Kearny and Union streets.
76—Corner Montgomery and Green streets.
78—Corner Folsom and Eleventh streets.
79—Corner Polk and Broadway streets.
81—Corner Hayes and Franklin, Hayes Valley
82—Pioneer Woolen Mills, North Beach.
83—Corner Eighth and Brannan streets.
84—Corner Market and Valencia streets.
85—Mail Co.'s Wharf, First and Brannan.

All persons interfering with, or maliciously injuring the Telegraph apparatus, or giving false alarms through the Signal Boxes, are made liable to heavy penalties. It is also provided that when found necessary for any person or persons to remove, interfere with, or disturb any portion of the Telegraph lines, for removal of buildings, or other cause, due notice must be given to the Superintendent, or in his absence, to the operator on duty at the City Hall, between the hours of six o'clock, A. M., and twelve o'clock, M., stating the locality at which, and the manner it may be necessary to disturb, interfere with, or remove the wire.

Since the introduction of the Paid Fire Department, false alarms have almost entirely ceased, having had but one maliciously false alarm since the new Department came into existence. The officers and members of the Paid Fire Department have interested themselves to make its workings as effective as possible. No effort will be spared by those having it in charge to make it work in entire harmony with the new Department, and to the satisfaction of the public.

The expenditures of this Department have been as follows:

Repairs and Extensions................................	$545 95
Batteries	195 43
Tools	22 50
Printing Cards......................................	38 00
Cartage	47 00
One Striking Machine (Currency, $1,000,) Coin.........	759 60
Freight on Striking Apparatus from Boston.............	51 70
Bell for Engine House No. 3..........................	156 40
Placing Bell on Engine House No. 3..................	31 65
Moving Bell from Washington Hose House to Stockton street	190 00
Two Bells and Fixtures, (Currency, $1,955 50,) Coin....	1,496 75
Freight on same from Boston.........................	181 73
Five Magnets and Switches..........................	62 08
Building Bell Tower on Engine House No. 4...........	835 00
Hanging two Bells on Sixth street and Second street.....	134 63
Total......................................	$4,748 42

This exhausts the appropriation of six thousand dollars allowed for two years. The excess of expenditures for the past year is owing to the purchase of the new bells and new striking apparatus. I would recommend that authority be obtained from the next Legislature for an annual expenditure of three thousand dollars for repairs and extensions.

I would recommend the purchase and erection of more Signal Boxes, as soon as authority for the expenditure can be obtained.

Various improvements and alterations have been made in the apparatus, until it has been brought as near perfection as possible.

Respectfully submitted,

M. GREENWOOD,

Superintendent Fire Alarm and Police Telegraph.

REPORT

CITY AND COUNTY SURVEYOR.

CITY AND COUNTY SURVEYOR'S OFFICE, }
San Francisco, July 2, 1867. }

To the Honorable the Board of Supervisors
 Of the City and County of San Francisco—

GENTLEMEN :   In compliance with Resolution No. 6,963, of your Board, I submit the following Report :

The number of surveys made by this office from the 1st of July, 1866, to the 30th of June, 1867, was six hundred and seventy-five.

During the same time I have made out six hundred and thirteen certificates for street work and other work under my charge.

Respectfully submitted,

GEO. C. POTTER,

City and County Surveyor.

18

CORONER'S REPORT.

OFFICE OF THE CORONER,
San Francisco, July 1, 1867·

To the Honorable the Board of Supervisors

Of the City and County of San Francisco—

GENTLEMEN : In conformity with Resolution 6,963, of your Board, I respectfully submit the following Report of the number of dead that came under my supervision as Coroner, from July 1, 1866, to June 30, 1867.

Also, the number and character of Inquests and Autopsies held by me during the same period.

Expenditures charged to the City during the year by Coroner, for Stationery $25 00

SUICIDES.

1866—July	3	1867—January	1
August	1	February	3
September	1	March	3
October	3	April	3
November	2	May	1
December	0	June	4

Total 25

SUICIDES COMMITTED IN THE FOLLOWING MANNER.

Drowning 1

Fracture of the skull 1

Carried forward 2

Brought forward............................ 2
Gun shot 1
Hanging 2
Knife cuts, throat.. 1
Laudanum 1
Morphine 6
Opium 2
Pistol shots....................................... 3
Razor cuts, throat................................ 1
Strychnia 6
                                                  ——
In all, as above.................................. 25
                                                  ══

ACCIDENTAL DEATHS.

1866—July	6	1867—January	6
August	12	February	6
September	4	March	4
October	15	April	6
November	6	May	8
December	14	June	4

Total................................... 91
                                         ══

ACCIDENTAL DEATHS CAUSED IN THE FOLLOWING MANNER.

Burned.. 11
Bursting of grindstone............................ 1
Crushed by machinery, foundry..................... 3
Crushed by lumber 2
Crushed by wagon.................................. 1
Crushed by bank of earth.......................... 3
Crushed by boat................................... 1
Crushed by chain locker, schooner Milton Badger... 1
Caught in fly wheel............................... 1
                                                  ——
Carried forward................................. 24

Brought forward....................................	24
Drowning	28
Explosion of steam drum, steamer Julia...................	11
Falling from yard arm of ship	1
Falling of building on Summer Street.....................	8
Falling from buildings..................................	4
Falling from cart	1
Falling from truck......................................	1
Falling down stairs	2
Falling on sidewalk.....................................	1
Laudanum by mistake...................................	1
Pistol shots, accidental	2
Run over by railroad cars, San José......................	3
Run over by railroad car, North Beach and Mission.........	1
Run over by railroad sprinkler..........................	1
Run over by truck......................................	1
Thrown from wagon.....................................	1
In all, as above.................................	91

SUDDEN DEATHS FROM OTHER CAUSES.

1866—July...............	1	1867—January...........	1
August.............	4	February..........	2
September'..........	2	March	1
October	0	April	1
November	0	May	1
December	1	June..............	0

Total...	14
Murders......................................	2
Infanticide ..:...............................	10
Stillborn	2
In all, as above................................	14

OTHER CAUSES OF DEATH.

Brain—Apoplexy of....................................	11
Congestion of...................................	7
Effusion of.....................................	2
Heart—Organic disease of	3
Aneurism ascending aorta of.....................	4
Aneurism abdominal aorta of.....................	4
Aneurism arch aorta of..........................	2
Valvular disease of.............................	3
Dropsy of......................................	2
Rupture of left oracle of........................	1
Pericarditis...	1
Lungs—Apoplexy of.................................	3
Congestion of.................................	4
Hemorrhage of................................	6
Phthisis Pulmonalis.................................	6
Pneumonia	4
Hydrothorax..	1
Convulsions..	5
Fatty degeneration of liver	1
Enteritis...	2
Diarrhea	1
Dysentery	1
Mania a potu.......................................	3
In all, as above................................	77

WHOLE NUMBER OF CASES DURING THE YEAR.

Inquests..	77
Autopsies	90
Cases in which neither Inquests or Autopsies were held......	40
Total...	207
Cases in which both Inquests and Autopsies were held	29

NATIVITIES AND AGES.

UNITED STATES.		FOREIGNERS.	
California	23	England	12
Maine	7	Ireland	30
New Hampshire	2	Scotland	6
Vermont	1	France	11
Massachusetts	7	Spain	2
Connecticut	2	Portugal	3
New York	15	Italy	3
Pennsylvania	3	Switzerland	2
Delaware	1	Austria	1
Maryland	2	Germany	20
Ohio	1	Prussia	5
Louisiana	2	Russia	1
Indiana	1	Norway	1
	—	Sweden	4
United States	67	Denmark	3
Foreigners	133	Bavaria	2
Unknown	7	China	11
		Manila	1
Total	207	Sandwich Islands	1
		Central America	2
Under 1 year	15	Western Islands	2
From 1 to 10	8	Gibraltar	1
From 10 to 20	6	South America	1
From 20 to 30	38	Mexico	3
From 30 to 40	60	Canada	2
From 40 to 50	42	Nova Scotia	1
From 50 to 60	21	St. Johns, N. B	1
From 60 and over	10	Victoria	1
Unknown	7		
Total	207	Foreigners	133

STEPHEN R. HARRIS, M.D.,

Coroner.

HARBOR MASTER'S REPORT.

HARBOR MASTER'S OFFICE, }
San Francisco, July 31, 1867. }

To the Honorable the Board of Supervisors
 Of the City and County of San Francisco—

GENTLEMEN : In compliance with your directions, I have the honor of submitting the Harbor Master's Report for the fiscal year ending June 30th, 1867.

During the year three wharves have been rebuilt and a new front constructed from Market to Clay streets.

The completion of the Pacific Mail Company's wharf is a great improvement to that portion of the city and harbor, and, together with the cribbing adjoining, afford a good protection to the shipping from the heavy southerly gales that frequently prevail during the winter months.

The wharfage at present is ample, but constant dredging is necessary to keep sufficient depth of water in the slips for the accommodation of the larger vessels.

The tabular statement annexed shows an increase of twenty-seven vessels from Eastern ports, and a decrease of thirty-eight from Foreign ports, as computed with last year. Thirty whaling vessels arrived, which are exempt from harbor dues. The fishing trade seems to be rapidly increasing. Fourteen vessels, 1,607 tons, arrived this year, against seven vessels, 524 tons, last year; and a still larger number may be expected the ensuing year. Twenty schooners, amounting to 1,408 tons, and twelve barges, amounting to 1,429 tons, have been built this year.

Harbor dues to the amount of $19,035 35 have been collected,˙ and paid over to the City and County Treasurer.

Respectfully submitted,

MARCUS HARLOE,

Harbor Master.

VESSELS IN THE COASTING AND BAY TRADE.

37	Steamers	18,355 tons.
3	Ships	1,969 tons.
32	Barks	12,669 tons.
20	Brigs	4,383 tons.
227	Schooners	10,123 tons.
83	Sloops	1,793 tons.
402		49,292 tons.

VESSELS ARRIVED FROM FOREIGN AND EASTERN PORTS IN THE YEAR ENDING JUNE 30, 1867.

WHENCE.	STEAMERS		SHIPS		BARKS		BRIGS		SCHOONERS		TOTAL	
	No.	Tons.	No.	Tons.	No.	Tons.	No.	Tons.	No.	Tons.	No.	Tons.
Eastern States	5	5,998	89	102,455	7	5,818	1	200	3	476	105	114,947
Australia and New Zealand			15	10,776	42	19,704	5	1,395	1	143	63	32,018
Brazil					5	1,338	4	818			9	2,156
Central America	49	122,875			2	527			2	181	53	123,583
Chili					2	890	1	262	1	134	4	1,286
China	2	8,019	20	17,129	10	4,249	3	764			35	30,161
East Indies			6	4,857	10	3,911					16	8,768
France			3	1,930	8	3,696					11	5,626
Germany			1	588	6	2,103					7	2,691
Great Britain			21	16,205	18	9,187					39	25,392
Japan			4	3,780	4	1,432	4	1,050	2	297	14	6,559
Mexico	13	17,342			15	3,913	14	2,441	19	1,989	61	25,685
Peru			1	944	1	295	1	453	1	130	4	1,822
Russian America and Amoor River			7	5,021	5	1,143	2	434			14	6,598
Sandwich and Society Islands	1	238			32	11,258	7	1,436	16	2,117	56	14,948
British Columbia and Vancouver Island	19	11,707	9	7,378	5	1,858	2	477	1	164	36	21,584
Spain					2	674					2	674
Fishermen					1	290	5	694	8	523	14	1,607
	89	166,179	176	171,063	175	72,286	49	10,424	54	6,153	543	426,105

[Whalers, 30 vessels, 8,305 tons.]

HEALTH OFFICER'S REPORT.

To the Honorable the President and Board of Supervisors
Of the City and County of San Francisco,

GENTLEMEN : I have the honor of submitting to you my Report of the affairs of this Bureau for the fiscal year ending June, 1867.

Although the Mortuary Statistics are as correct as it is possible to make them from our present sources of information, it is much to be regretted that they are not more comprehensive, as statistical tables for reference in future years, but which is owing to the want of the registration of births, in this office.

The infant mortality for the past year is unquestionably very large, notwithstanding the hygienic measures used to better the sanitary condition of the city. This is a matter of great importance to the future welfare of our State, and to which I will allude in its proper place in this Report.

It should be a source of gratification to the community to know, that owing to our invigorating climate, the death record will compare favorably with any city in the Union, of comparative population, notwithstanding the well-known fact that San Francisco is the City of Refuge for the halt, the lame, and the blind of the Pacific coast. In this connection, I would remark, that it is more easy to satisfy mankind of the value of any other branch of statistics than that which relates to the number that die annually, their ages, sex, occupation, condition, and nativity, and the causes which produce such deaths; the consequence is that the facts remain uncollected or unrecorded—hence, while everybody seems busy enough, in our practical, money making State, in running after information regarding the fluctuations of stocks and matters relating to mineral discoveries—investigations having for their object sanitary improvement are either lost sight of, or are pursued in a slower manner than those which relate to real estate, the life of man being considered of less importance than commercial interests.

In the absence of official data, we have to be guided by the "City Directory" for 1867, which is allowed to be the most correct means of information in the State. The Directory rates the population of the city at one hundred and thirty-five thousand; and if we continue the same ratio of increase per annum for the next six years, San Francisco will rate as the tenth city, in the order of population, in the Union. Who would have dreamed of this seventeen years ago, when canvas tents were the rule and frame buildings the exception on the peninsula of Yerba Buena? But the canvas has disappeared, and the houses of wood have given place to those of brick and stone, and structures have been built that would do credit to any of our Eastern cities, and all this has been accomplished in less than two decades.

The following table will show the number of deaths for the year ending June 30th, 1867:

SUMMARY OF DEATHS.

Caucasian	2,322
Mongolian	161
African	38
Total	2,522

Males	1,669
Females	853
Total	2,522

Adults	1,398
Minors	1,124
Total	2,522

Table 1 will give the number and cause of death, the Ward in which the death occurred; also, deaths in Public Institutions, casualties, suicides, with their age and sex.

TAB

INTERMENTS IN THE CITY OF SAN

Cause of Death.	Total	Under 1 year	Betw'n 1 & 2	Betw'n 2 & 5	Bet. 5 & 10.	Bet. 10 & 15.	Bet. 15 & 20.	Bet. 20 & 30.	Bet. 30 & 40.	Bet. 40 & 50.	Bet. 50 & 60.	Bet. 60 & 70.	Bet. 70 & 80.	Bet. 80 & 90.	Bet. 90 & 100.	Unknown
Ateleclasis Pulmonum	3	3														
Asthma	5									1		1	2	1		
Amputation of arm	1									1						
Atrophia	19	15	1				1			2						
Anemia	12	6	1	1		1				1	2					
Asphyxia	7	7														
Apoplexy	37							1	3	8	13	6	5	1		
Abscess	1									1						
Abscess pulmonary	3								1	2						
Abscess of liver	5									2	3					
Abscess lumbar	3								1	2						
Abscess internal	1										1					
Angina	2			2												
·Angina pectoris	2			1							1					
Ascitis	1										1					
Aphtha	2	2														
Aneurism of aorta	36								4	15	10	4	2	1		
Aneurism of the heart	4									2		1	1			
Aneurism of int. iliac	1								1							
Bronchitis	21	11	3	3	1					2			1			
Bright's disease	9		2	2						3		1		1		
Child birth	2								1		1					
Convulsions	15			2	2			2	5	3			1			
Convulsions infantile	125	92	19	14												
Convulsions puerperal	2								2							
Congestion of brain	46	3	6	3	1				12	6	10	4	1			
Congestion of lungs	44	17	3	2	3	3			4	2	6	3	1			
Cholera morbus	7	1			1						1	3	1			
Cholera infantum	54	38	12	4												
Croup	37	5	8	16	7	1										
Cirrhosis	4	1								1		1	1			
Cancer (not defined)	8								2	2		3		1		
Cancer of uterus	6								1	2	2		1			
Cancer of liver	1									1						
Cancer of stomach	15								1	3	3	6	2			
Cancer of ovary	1											1				
Cancer of breast	2									1			1			
Cancer on face	1										1					
Cancer of mouth	1		1													
Congestive chills	4	2		1					1							
Carditis	6									4	1		1			
Caries of vertebra	2								2							
Coxalgia	7		3		1				3							
Cyanosis	10	10														
Cachexia	1			1												
Concussion of brain	1								1							
Colic spasmodic	1											1				
Colic bilious	1										1					
Dislocation of spine	1								1							
Debility general	105	18	2	4				2	14	23	30	9	3			
Drowning	32			1	1	2	1	4	10	5	4					4
Dropsy	39		2						9	9	12	4	2	1		
Droysy ovarian	1										1					
Diphtheria	90	12	12	39	20	5	1	1								
Diarrhea	23	11	2	1					2	4	3					
Dysentery	29	10	6						1	8	1	1	2			
Dentition	26	17	6	3												
Disease of heart	68	1		1	4	2	2	5	18	12	12	8	3			
Carried forward	993	282	89	101	41	14	8	80	149	126	66	33	10			4

L E I.

FRANCISCO, FOR THE YEAR ENDING JUNE 30, 1867.

Male	Female	Caucasian	Mongolian	African	1st Ward	2d Ward	3d Ward	4th Ward	5th Ward	6th Ward	7th Ward	8th Ward	9th Ward	10th Ward	11th Ward	12th Ward	Public Institutions	Casualties	Suicides
3		3				1							1		1				
2	3	5							1				1	1		2			
1		1																	
12	7	18	1		1	1		4					5	2	3	1		2	
4	8	12					3	1		2		1	1					4	
5	2	7			1	1			1			1		1	2				
28	9	32	4	1	3	2			7		4	1	2	3	4	2	3	6	
1		1												1					
3		3																3	
3	2	5				1			1		1			1				1	
3		3																3	
1		1											1						
2		2											1		1				
1	1	2				1					1								
1		1													1				
1	1	2															2		
34	2	33	1	2	1		3	5	1	3	1	3		3			1	15	
4		4												1				3	
1		1																1	
11	10	21			3	3	1	2			2	3	1	4	2				
8	1	9				2				1			2	2			2		
2		2												1				1	
12	3	15				8		2			2	1	1					1	
68	57	122	1	2	8	19	1	10	5	2	10	17	3	25	18	2	5		
2		2										2							
37	9	40	6		3	2	2	8	1	4	2	6		7	3		8		
31	13	39	5		1	5		6	3	3	4	5	2	5	4	1	5		
7		7				2						2	1	1	1				
35	19	54			2	9		6	1	1	5	6	2	16	6				
23	14	36	1		1	6		3		3	2	6	3	10	2		1		
3		4															1	3	
3	5	8				1		1			1			3			1	1	
6		6				1		1			1				1	1	1		
1		1															1		
9	6	14	1		1			2	1	2		1		1	1	2	4		
1		1						1											
2		1	1					1					1						
1		1			1														
1		1						1				1							
2	2	4				1					1	1		1		1			
5	1	6				1					1	1		1		1	2		
2		2															2		
4	3	7				1		1			1	2		1		1			
7	3	10			1		1	1			1			2	1	1	2		
1		1												1					
1		1									1								
1		1			1														
	1	1																	1
75	30	47	57	1	6	9	2	25	4	13	13	5	3	13	5	3	4	1	
32		32																	32
27	12	32	6	1	5	1		5	1	4	2	1	1	5	1		13		
	1	1												1					
45	45	90			6	11		5	1		8	11	8	18	17	4	1		
17	6	23			2	3		1		1	3	6	3	1	3				
19	10	27	1	1		2		2			2	1	8	4	9				
13	13	26			1	4		3		1		1	3	4	4	3	2		
49	19	64	1	3	4	9	1	2	3	3	7	3	2	10	1	2	21		
659	334	896	36	11	55	107	12	103	25	36	68	92	42	164	82	32	132	33	

TABLE

Cause of Death.	Total.	Ages.														
		Under 1 year	Betw'n 1 & 2	Betw'n 2 & 5	Bet. 5 & 10	Bet. 10 & 15	Bet. 15 & 20	Bet. 20 & 30	Bet. 30 & 40	Bet. 40 & 50	Bet. 50 & 60	Bet. 60 & 70	Bet. 70 & 80	Bet. 80 & 90	Bet. 90 & 100	Unknown
Brought forward	993	282	89	101	41	14	8	80	149	126	66	33	10			4
Disease of ovary	1									1	1					
Disease of aortic valves	1								1							
Disease of mitral valves	4								1	1	2					
Disease of spine	2							1				1				
Disease of uterus	2							1		1						
Disease of prostate gland	2									1	1					
Delirium tremens	6								2	3	1					
Dyspepsia	1	1														
Dothenteritis	1									1						
Diabetes	2									2						
Deficient organization	1	1														
Effusion on brain	12	3	1	1	2				2	1	1		1			
Enteritis	74	26	8	7	2			1	10	6	4	6	3	1		
Erysipelas	13	6					1	2	1	1	2					
Epilepsy	5			1					3		1					
Empyema	7								5	1	1					
Embolia	3	1							1		1					
Effects of morphine	1								1							
Endocarditis	5		1						3	1						
Effects of intemperance	1								1							
Enlargement of heart	1								1							
Enlargement of spleen	1	1														
Exposure	1	1														
Fever, remittent	6	1	1						1	2			1			
Fever, intermittent	3							1	1	1						
Fever, continued	6	1	1			1		2			1					
Fever, nervous	4								1	1	2					
Fever, puerperal	12						1	4	6	1						
Fever, scarlet	29	4	3	8	14											
Fever, typhus	23	2			4	2	3	3	5	4						
Fever, typhoid	66		1	6	6	2	7	22	10	10		2				
Fever, bilious	5								1	2	2					
Fever, gastric	2	1								1						
Fever, Panama	1															
Fever, congestive	5			1			1		1	1	1					
Fatty degeneration of liver	1								1							
Fracture of skull	8			2			1	1		2	1	1				
Fracture of neck	2									1	1					
Fracture of spine	5				1					2	1	1				
Gangrene	12	1	1		2				1		3	1	3			
Gastritis	12	5						2	3		1		1			
Gastromalacia	1	1														
Gunshot wound	1									1						
Hemorrhage (cause not stated)	4	1								1	2					
Hemorrhage of lungs	17								3	8	3	2		1		
Hemorrhage uterine	5									4	1					
Hepatitis	34		1				1	1	14	10	2	5				
Hoematemesis	1								1							
Hydrocephalus	48	26	12	7	1	1	1									
Hysteria	1															
Hysteritis	1								1							
Hernia	1										1					
Hydrocele	2									1		1				
Hypertrophy of heart	9						1		3	1	1	2	1			
Hydrothorax	8		1	2				3	1		1					
Hemiplegia	1								1							
Hanging (sentence of Court)	2								1	1						
Injuries, inhaling gas	1											1				
Injuries, railroad sprinkler	1							1								
Injuries, swallowing a button	1	1														
Carried forward	1479	366	120	136	73	21	26	160	237	191	89	54	15			4

I---Continued.

Male	Female	Caucasian	Mongolian	African	1st Ward	2d Ward	3d Ward	4th Ward	5th Ward	6th Ward	7th Ward	8th Ward	9th Ward	10th Ward	11th Ward	12th Ward	Public Institutions	Casualties	Suicides
695	334	896	36	11	55	107	12	103	25	36	68	92	42	164	82	32	132	33	..
....	1	1	....	....	....	....	....	....	....	....	1	....	....	....	....	....	....	....	..
1	....	1	....	....	....	....	....	....	....	....	....	....	....	....	....	....	1	....	..
4	....	3	....	1	....	....	....	....	....	....	....	....	....	....	....	....	4	....	..
2	....	2	....	....	....	....	....	....	....	1	....	....	....	....	....	....	1	....	..
....	2	2	....	....	....	....	....	....	....	....	....	....	....	....	....	....	....	....	..
2	....	2	....	....	....	1	....	....	....	1	....	....	....	1	....	....	1	....	..
6	....	6	....	....	....	....	1	....	....	....	....	....	....	1	....	....	4	....	..
....	1	1	....	....	....	....	....	....	....	....	....	....	1	....	....	....	....	....	..
1	....	1	....	....	....	....	1	....	....	....	....	....	....	....	....	....	....	....	..
2	....	2	....	....	....	....	....	....	....	....	....	....	....	....	....	....	2	....	..
....	1	1	....	....	....	....	....	....	....	....	....	....	....	1	....	....	....	....	..
11	1	12	....	....	....	1	3	....	....	....	....	1	1	4	....	....	2	....	..
43	31	69	5	....	....	6	7	1	6	5	5	7	8	9	7	4	4	....	..
8	5	13	....	....	....	1	1	....	....	....	1	1	1	3	1	1	3	....	..
2	3	5	....	....	....	....	....	....	....	1	....	....	....	3	....	....	1	....	..
7	....	7	....	....	....	....	....	....	1	....	....	....	....	....	....	....	6	....	..
1	2	3	....	....	....	....	....	....	....	....	1	....	1	....	....	....	1	....	..
1	....	1	....	....	....	....	....	....	....	....	....	....	....	....	....	....	1	....	..
2	3	5	....	....	....	....	....	....	....	....	....	....	....	1	....	....	4	....	..
....	1	1	....	....	....	....	....	....	....	....	....	....	....	....	....	....	1	....	..
....	1	1	....	....	....	....	....	....	....	....	....	....	....	1	....	....	....	....	..
1	....	1	....	....	....	1	....	....	....	....	....	....	....	....	....	....	....	....	..
1	....	1	....	....	....	....	....	....	....	....	....	....	....	....	....	....	....	1	..
2	4	6	....	....	....	1	....	....	....	1	1	....	....	2	....	....	1	....	..
2	1	3	....	....	....	....	....	....	....	1	....	....	....	1	....	....	1	....	..
3	3	5	1	....	....	....	1	3	....	1	....	....	1	....	....	....	....	1	..
....	4	4	....	....	1	....	....	....	....	....	....	....	....	2	....	....	1	....	..
....	12	12	....	....	....	2	3	....	....	....	1	1	1	2	1	1	....	....	..
15	14	29	....	....	....	2	6	1	1	1	2	2	4	1	4	5	....	....	..
17	6	21	1	1	....	3	1	....	4	1	....	....	2	1	3	1	1	6	..
41	25	62	4	....	....	3	2	3	3	6	4	8	5	6	7	3	16	....	..
4	....	4	1	....	....	....	1	1	1	....	....	....	1	....	....	....	1	....	..
2	....	2	....	....	....	....	....	....	....	1	....	....	1	1	....	....	....	....	..
1	....	1	....	....	....	....	....	....	....	1	....	....	....	....	....	....	....	....	..
4	....	3	1	1	1	....	3	....	....	1	....	....	....	....	....	....	....	....	..
1	....	1	....	....	....	....	....	....	....	....	....	....	....	1	....	....	....	....	..
6	2	8	....	....	....	....	....	....	....	....	....	....	....	....	....	....	....	8	..
2	....	1	....	1	....	....	....	....	....	....	....	....	....	....	....	....	....	2	..
5	....	5	....	....	....	....	....	....	....	....	....	....	....	....	....	....	....	....	5
10	2	12	....	....	....	....	1	....	....	1	....	....	....	1	3	....	6	....	..
4	8	12	....	....	....	....	1	....	....	....	1	....	2	2	4	2	1	....	..
1	....	1	....	....	....	....	1	....	....	....	....	....	....	....	....	....	....	....	..
1	....	1	....	....	....	....	....	....	....	....	....	....	....	....	....	....	....	....	1
2	2	4	....	....	....	....	....	....	....	....	1	....	....	2	1	....	....	....	..
12	5	14	2	1	1	1	2	4	....	....	....	....	1	1	3	....	4	....	..
....	5	5	....	....	....	1	2	....	....	1	....	....	....	....	1	....	....	....	..
25	9	34	....	....	....	1	2	1	1	....	2	2	1	3	4	2	15	....	..
....	1	1	....	....	....	....	....	....	....	....	....	1	....	....	....	....	....	....	..
23	25	48	....	....	....	3	4	....	1	1	3	1	8	4	14	5	2	2	..
....	1	1	....	....	....	1	....	....	....	....	....	....	....	1	....	....	....	....	..
....	1	1	....	....	....	....	....	....	....	....	....	....	....	....	....	....	....	....	..
....	1	1	....	....	....	1	....	....	....	....	....	....	....	....	....	....	....	....	..
2	....	1	1	....	....	....	....	....	....	....	....	....	1	....	....	1	....	6	..
2	7	9	....	....	....	1	1	....	....	....	....	....	....	1	....	....	6	....	..
4	4	8	....	....	....	....	1	....	....	1	....	....	1	1	1	....	3	....	..
....	1	1	....	....	....	....	....	....	....	....	....	....	....	....	....	1	....	....	..
2	....	1	1	....	....	....	....	....	....	....	....	....	....	....	....	....	....	2	..
1	....	1	....	....	....	....	....	....	....	....	....	....	....	....	....	....	....	1	..
1	....	1	....	....	....	....	....	....	....	....	....	....	....	....	....	....	....	1	..
1	....	1	....	....	....	....	....	....	....	....	....	....	....	....	....	....	....	1	1
949	532	1362	53	16	80	147	25	141	40	62	90	132	72	246	120	45	231	55	..

TABLE

Cause of Death.	Total	Under 1 year	Betw'n 1 & 2	Betw'n 2 & 5	Bet. 5 & 10	Bet. 10 & 15	Bet. 15 & 20	Bet. 20 & 30	Bet. 30 & 40	Bet. 40 & 50	Bet. 50 & 60	Bet. 60 & 70	Bet. 70 & 80	Bet. 80 & 90	Bet. 90 & 100	Unknown
Brought forward	1479	366	120	136	73	21	26	160	237	191	89	54	15			4
Injuries, falling of lumber	1															1
Injuries from fall	5				1			2		1		1				
Injuries from burns	13	1		4	1		1	2	2							2
Injuries, run over by steam cars	2											1	1			
Injuries, run over by horse cars	1					1										
Injuries, run over by wagon	1										1					
Injuries, caving of earth	4				1					3						
Injuries from scalding	4	1	1	2												
Injuries from machinery	3				1			1				1				
Injuries, internal	1				1											
Injuries from knife wound	2									2						
Injuries of spine	2									2						
Injuries of head	1										1					
Injuries, bursting of steam drum	11								2	8	1					
Injuries, explosion of lamp	1								1							
Injuries, falling of building	8								3	5						
Inanition	23	17	3		1					1	1					
Infanticide	1	1														
Intussusception	3	1							1	1						
Inflammation of lungs	147	35	17	14	5	5		18	18	20	8	5	1			1
Inflammation of brain	30	9	3	4	3	1		1	5	3	1					
Inflammation of bladder	1											1				
Jaundice	2									2						
Leprosy	1											1				
Laryngitis	6		1					2			2	1				
Malformation	1	1														
Meningitis	71	22	18	13	5	3	1	3	1	2	1		1	1		
Marasmus	53	40	7	2						1	2	1				
Mania a potu	2									2						
Metrorrhagia	1									1						
Myelitis	1	1														
Nephritis	3					1				2						
Obstipation	1									1						
Old age	10												3	3	3	1
Ossification of valves of heart	1												1			
Occlusion of bowels	1	1														
Organic disease of stomach	1									1						
Ovaritis	1									1						
Pistol shot	2											1	1			
Premature birth	33	33														
Pericarditis	9	2					2		1	1	2	1				
Paralysis	36			1						5	15	5	4	5	1	
Phthisis	324	1	2	3	2	2	14	106	109	54	21	9				1
Peritonitis	25	2	2			1		7	5	5	2			1		
Pyemia	14			1		1		1	5	5	1					
Pneumothorax	2									2						
Phlegmatia dolens	1									1						
Pleurisy	3								1		1		1			
Phlebitis	2									2						
Rupture of blood vessel	2									1		1				
Rheumatism	2										1	1				
Rachitis	2		1				1									
Rubeola	7	2	1	4												
Suicide	29									9	11	7	2			
Syphilis	33	1							2	13	10	5	2			
Scrofula	10	2		1					2	2	3					
Softening of brain	23	1		2	1			1		7	4	6	1			
Sphacelus	1								1							
Scurvy	4	1		1							1	1				
Strangulated hernia	1										1					
Carried forward	2465	541	177	188	96	38	48	344	467	316	145	81	22	5	1	9

I---Continued.

Male	Female	Caucasian	Mongolian	African	1st Ward	2d Ward	3d Ward	4th Ward	5th Ward	6th Ward	7th Ward	8th Ward	9th Ward	10th Ward	11th Ward	12th Ward	Public Institutions	Casualties	Suicides
949	532	1362	101	18	80	147	25	131	40	72	90	132	72	236	130	45	223	55	
1		1																1	
4	1	5																5	
8	5	13																13	
2		2																2	
1		1																1	
1		1																1	
3	1	3	1															4	
4		4																4	
3		3																3	
1		1																1	
2		2																2	
2		1	1															2	
1		1																1	
11		11																11	
1		1																1	
8		8																8	
12	11	21	2		2	2		4			1	2		5	5	2			
	1	1																1	
1	2	3					1			1				1					
99	48	124	21	2	15	14	4	23	2	4	11	11	7	22	8	4	22		
24	6	28	1	1	1	4	4				1	2	3	5	3	1	6		
1		1													1		1		
1	1	2				1												1	
1		1																1	
5	1	6				1								2			3		
	1	1														1			
49	22	71			4	10	1	4	1	3	5	9	7	18	5		4		
36	17	53			2	2		3		2	3	7	2	11	6	5	10		
1	1	2												1			1		
	1	1							1										
2	1	3									1	1					1		
	1	1							1					1					
4	6	10				1		1				1		2	2		3		
	1	1													1				
	1	1														1			
1		1					1												
	1	1														1			
2		2																2	
20	13	33			2	2		3		2	1	6		8	5		4		
7	2	9				2						1		1	2		3		
31	5	31	3	2	4	3	1			2	3	1	1	2	1		18		
218	106	308	4	12	21	23	15	17	4	6	11	21	14	52	18	6	116		
13	12	25			2	1		1	1	1	1	1	2	2	3	2	8		
11	3	13	1		1			1				1		3			8		
2		1	1							1					1				
	1	1												1					
1	2	3				1				1							1		
	2	2						1											
2		2			1			1											
2		2				1						1							
1	1	2			1									1					
2	5	7	2					1			2		1	1	1	1			
29		27	2																29
23	10	15	18		2	4		9		3		1		1			13		
6	4	6	3	1	2	2		3		1	1						3		
21	2	21		2	1	1		3	1	1		1	1	2	2	1	9		
1		1			1														
2	2	4										1		1	1		1		
1		1													1				
1634	833	227	159	38	142	217	53	208	49	101	132	195	111	379	196	70	469	118	29

19

TABLE

Cause of Death.	Total	Under 1 year	Betw'n 1 & 2	Betw'n 2 & 5	Bet. 5 & 10.	Bet. 10 & 15.	Bet. 15 & 20.	Bet. 20 & 30.	Bet. 30 & 40.	Bet. 40 & 50.	Bet. 50 & 60.	Bet. 60 & 70.	Bet. 70 & 80.	Bet. 80 & 90.	Bet. 90 & 100	Unknown
Brought forward	2467	541	177	188	96	38	48	344	457	315	145	81	22	5	1	9
Stomatitis	1	1														
Septaemia	1									1						
Tabes dorsalis	1											1				
Tabes mesenterica	7	5		1	1											
Tetanus	6	1		1				1	1	2						
Tumor abdominal	3									3						
Tumor ovarian	2									1	1					
Tumor on brain	1									1						
Tumor uterine	1									1						
Trismus nascentium	1	1														
Ulceration of stomach	2										1		1			
Uremia	1										1					
Variola	4				2	1					1					
Variola confluent	2								1	1						
Whooping cough	22	11	10	1												
Total	2522	560	187	193	98	38	48	346	462	324	147	82	22	5	1	9

TABLE II.

AGES OF DECEDENTS IN THE DIFFERENT MONTHS.

Ages.	Total	1866.						1867.					
		July	August	September	October	November	December	January	February	March	April	May	June
Under 1 year of age	560	51	49	41	35	36	44	44	53	51	25	56	69
From 1 to 2 years of age	187	20	14	12	17	19	10	30	18	10	13	14	10
From 2 to 5 years of age	193	14	12	15	27	16	20	19	16	13	16	15	10
From 5 to 10 years of age	98	8	10	6	12	12	12	4	8	6	6	7	7
From 10 to 15 years of age	38	5	3	2	4	5	3	6	1	4	2	2	1
From 15 to 20 years of age	48	7	5	2	4	6	2	4	6	3	5	2	2
From 20 to 30 years of age	346	23	29	28	30	33	32	37	19	40	23	22	30
From 30 to 40 years of age	462	36	48	28	56	29	45	29	38	41	38	39	35
From 40 to 50 years of age	324	31	24	33	32	31	31	33	15	23	27	24	20
From 50 to 60 years of age	147	11	18	12	12	12	14	12	12	12	12	12	8
From 60 to 70 years of age	82	5	6	7	7	10	3	7	9	5	6	12	5
From 70 to 80 years of age	22	1	1		2	1	3	1	4	2	1	3	3
From 80 to 90 years of age	5					1				2	2		
From 90 to 100 years of age	1	1											
Age unknown	9	1					4		2				1
Total	2522	214	219	186	239	210	223	226	201	219	176	208	201

I---Concluded.

Male	Female	Caucasian	Mongolian	African	1st Ward	2d Ward	3d Ward	4th Ward	5th Ward	6th Ward	7th Ward	8th Ward	9th Ward	10th Ward	11th Ward	12th Ward	Public Institutions	Casualties	Suicides
1634	833	2270	159	38	142	217	53	208	49	101	132	195	111	379	196	70	469	118	29
1		1										1							
1		1													1				
1		1													1				
2	5	7			2	2						1	1	1					
5	1	6									3			1	1		1		
3		3			1				1					1					
	2	2							1				1						
1		1																1	
	1	1																1	
	1	1							1									1	
2		2									1							1	
	1	1																1	
4		2	2															4	
1	1	2													1				
14	8	22			1	4	3	2		1	2	4	1	3		1			
1669	853	2323	161	38	146	223	56	213	49	103	138	200	114	385	199	71	478	118	29

TABLE III.

SEX, RACE, AND NATIONALITY OF DECEASED PERSONS.

Sex, Race, and Nativity.	Total	1866.						1867.					
		July	August	September	October	November	December	January	February	March	April	May	June
SEX.													
Male	1669	146	135	131	170	137	142	157	127	147	122	135	120
Female	853	68	84	55	69	73	81	69	74	72	54	73	81
Total	2522	214	219	186	239	210	223	226	201	219	176	208	201
RACE.													
Caucasian	2323	194	198	165	222	202	207	207	190	199	163	192	184
Mongolian	161	15	18	18	12	2	13	15	9	18	11	14	16
African	38	5	3	3	5	6	3	4	2	2	2	2	1
Total	2522	214	219	186	239	210	223	226	201	219	176	208	201
NATIVITIES.													
United States	1487	135	122	110	133	126	123	139	129	125	99	119	127
Foreigners	1028	78	97	76	106	84	100	85	70	93	77	89	73
Unknown	7	1						2	2	1			1
Total	2522	214	219	186	239	210	223	226	201	219	176	208	201

TABLE IV.

NATIVITIES OF DECEDENTS.

	Total	1866.						1867.					
		July	August	September	October	November	December	January	February	March	April	May	June
UNITED STATES.													
California	1023	99	84	73	87	77	86	100	92	89	51	91	88
Missouri	9	1	....	....	2	4	....	1	....	....	....	....	1
Massachusetts	89	6	8	7	12	11	5	9	9	5	7	5	5
Pennsylvania	31	4	3	....	2	1	5	1	1	2	5	1	6
New York	129	8	12	12	11	11	16	9	10	11	12	8	9
Maine	30	2	4	....	3	4	....	4	2	5	1	4	1
Kentucky	14	1	2	....	1	....	1	2	1	....	2	3	1
Ohio	19	2	....	2	3	....	2	2	....	1	4	1	2
New Jersey	6	1	....	2	....	....	....	1	1	....	1	....	....
Michigan	7	1	....	1	1	....	1	....	1	1	1	....	....
Vermont	11	2	....	2	1	1	....	....	....	....	3	....	2
Delaware	4	1	....	....	....	1	....	....	1	....	....	1	....
Iowa	4	1	....	1	1	....	....	....	1	....	....	....	....
Louisiana	7	1	1	....	....	1	....	....	2	1	....	....	1
Connecticut	11	1	1	....	....	1	1	3	1	1	1	1	....
Indiana	4	1	....	1	1	....	....	1	....	....	....	....	....
Mississippi	1	1	....	....	....	....	....	....	....	....	....	....	....
Maryland	17	2	....	4	2	2	1	....	2	1	....	1	2
Nevada	7	....	1	2	....	3	....	....	....	1	....	....	....
Illinois	7	....	2	1	1	2	....	1	....	....	....	....	....
New Hampshire	13	....	1	....	....	1	2	3	1	3	....	1	1
Virginia	10	....	1	....	1	1	1	....	2	2	1	....	1
Minnesota	1	....	1	....	....	....	....	....	....	....	....	....	....
South Carolina	1	....	1	....	....	....	....	....	....	....	....	....	....
District of Columbia	4	....	....	1	....	1	....	....	....	1	....	1	....
Washington Territory	4	....	....	1	....	....	1	....	....	....	1	....	1
Rhode Island	7	....	....	....	1	1	1	....	1	1	....	1	1
Wisconsin	3	....	....	....	....	1	....	1	....	1	....	....	....
Oregon	4	....	....	....	1	1	....	1	....	....	....	....	1
Florida	2	....	....	....	1	....	....	....	....	....	....	....	1
Tennessee	4	....	....	....	....	....	1	....	1	....	....	2	....
Idaho Territory	1	....	....	....	....	....	1	....	....	....	....	....	....
Georgia	1	....	....	....	....	....	....	....	....	....	....	....	1
Arizona	1	....	....	....	....	....	....	....	....	....	....	....	1
Colorado	1	....	....	....	....	....	....	....	....	....	....	....	1
Total	1487	135	122	110	133	126	123	139	129	125	99	119	127

TABLE IV---Concluded.

FOREIGNERS.

	Total	1866.						1867.					
		July	August	September	October	November	December	January	February	March	April	May	June
FOREIGNERS.													
England	80	10	12	5	13	6	6	6	2	4	6	6	4
Ireland	330	20	28	26	26	22	35	30	27	33	28	34	21
Scotland	27	2	....	2	4	4	4	2	1	5	1	2	....
British Provinces	33	1	4	2	3	3	3	7	3	2	2	1	2
France	75	6	4	4	7	6	6	4	10	5	5	10	8
Germany	138	9	10	10	13	12	13	12	11	11	9	8	14
Denmark	15	1	1	2	2	1	3	2	1	....	....	2	....
Sweden	17	3	2	2	....	1	....	2	2	1	1	2	1
Italy	21	4	4	....	1	6	....	2	....	....	....	4	....
Spain	3	2	....	....	....	1	....	....	....	....	....	....	....
Hanover	3	3	....	....	....	....	....	....	....	....	....	....	....
China	163	14	14	17	19	9	14	13	9	19	11	9	15
Sandwich Islands	5	2	1	....	....	1	1	....	....	....	....	....	....
Chili	8	1	1	1	1	1	1	....	....	1	....	1	....
Portugal	12	....	3	2	2	2	....	....	1	1	1	1	1
Mexico	33	....	2	3	3	5	3	1	1	4	5	4	4
Holland	3	....	1	....	....	....	1	....	....	....	1	....	....
Western Islands	5	....	1	1	1	....	....	....	....	1	1	....	....
Switzerland	16	....	....	2	2	1	1	1	2	3	2	2	1
Russia	3	....	....	....	2	....	....	1	....	....	....	....	....
Norway	8	....	....	1	1	1	2	....	....	....	2	....	1
Hamburg	1	....	....	....	1	....	....	....	....	....	....	....	....
Cape de Verde Islands	2	....	....	....	1	....	....	....	....	....	1	....	....
Fejee Islands	1	....	....	....	1	....	....	....	....	....	....	....	....
Peru	2	....	....	....	....	1	....	1	....	....	....	....	....
Belgium	1	....	....	....	....	1	....	....	....	....	....	....	....
Central America	5	....	....	....	....	....	3	....	2	....	....	....	....
Brazil	2	....	....	....	....	....	1	....	....	....	....	....	1
Africa	1	....	....	....	....	....	1	....	....	....	....	....	....
Hayti	1	....	....	....	....	....	....	....	1	....	....	....	....
Poland	1	....	....	....	....	....	....	....	....	1	....	....	....
Bavaria	1	....	....	....	....	....	....	....	....	1	....	....	....
Russian America	1	....	....	....	....	....	....	....	....	....	1	....	....
West Indies	1	....	....	....	....	....	....	....	....	....	1	....	....
Austria	10	....	3	....	3	....	2	1	....	....	....	1	....
Unknown	7	1	....	....	....	....	....	2	2	1	....	....	1
Total Foreigners	1035	79	97	76	106	84	100	87	72	94	77	89	74
Total United States	1487	135	122	100	133	126	123	139	129	125	99	119	127
General Total	2522	214	219	186	239	210	223	226	201	219	176	208	201

TABLE V.

MONTHLY DISTRIBUTION OF MORTALITY.

Wards, Hospitals, Casualties, and Suicides.	Total.	1866.						1867.					
		July......	August. ...	September. ...	October. ...	November	December	January .	February	March ...	April ...	May ...	June ....
First Ward.................	146	11	8	6	13	12	23	14	12	14	14	9	10
Second Ward...............	223	31	15	12	18	22	27	15	12	13	20	18	20
Third Ward	56	1	7	4	3	6	7	9	4	7	3	4	1
Fourth Ward	213	23	23	21	20	11	11	19	18	20	11	18	18
Fifth Ward.................	49	3	3	3	3	7	7	9	4	4	5	....	1
Sixth Ward.................	103	2	4	10	8	12	11	12	13	9	5	5	12
Seventh Ward..............	135	9	14	7	14	14	14	20	12	5	2	20	7
Eighth Ward	200	22	16	17	18	17	15	14	17	14	8	23	19
Ninth Ward	114	9	12	7	12	12	12	6	5	12	12	7	8
Tenth Ward................	385	32	28	29	42	30	30	36	34	41	30	29	24
Eleventh Ward	199	12	16	14	18	14	15	20	16	15	18	17	24
Twelfth Ward	71	5	8	7	6	5	5	7	5	4	7	6	6
Public Institutions	478	41	50	41	40	38	32	32	39	54	31	40	40
Casualties	118	8	13	7	20	8	14	10	8	5	7	10	8
Suicides	29	5	2	1	4	2	....	1	2	4	3	2	3
Total..................	2522	214	219	186	239	210	223	226	201	219	176	208	201

TABLE VI.

LOCALITIES OF DEATH FOR EACH MONTH.

Localities.	Total.....	1866.						1867.					
		July......	August. ...	September. ...	October. ...	November	December	January .	February	March ...	April ...	May ...	June ....
Died in the City Wards	1907	162	161	138	177	164	173	175	157	168	133	153	146
City and County Hospital....	229	21	21	17	23	16	19	22	14	21	16	22	17
United States Marine Hospital	24	2	3	1	1	....	5	3	....	1	4	1	3
St. Mary's Hospital..........	94	9	13	9	5	10	3	6	10	7	6	4	12
French Hospital.............	39	3	2	3	3	3	2	3	4	2	3	5	6
German Hospital	37	4	5	4	3	4	3	3	3	3	1	4	....
Fort Alcatraces Hospital.....	1	....	....	1	....	....	....	....	....	....	....	....	....
Home for the Inebriate	3	....	1	1	....	....	....	1	....	....	....	....	....
Roman Catholic Asylums....	36	....	....	4	1	3	1	2	2	8	3	7	5
Protestant Asylums..........	3	....	....	....	....	....	1	....	1	....	....	....	1
County Jail (execution of sentence).....................	2	1	....	1	....	....	....	....	....	....	....	....	....
Casualties	118	7	11	6	22	8	16	10	8	5	7	10	8
Suicides	29	5	2	1	4	2	....	1	2	4	3	2	3
Total..................	2522	214	219	186	239	210	223	226	201	219	176	208	201

RECAPITULATION.

Total number of deaths from July, 1866, to June, 1867.   2,522
    White.. 2,323
    Black.......................................   38
    Copper.....................................   161
                          Total   2,522

Adults 1,398
Minors..................................... 1,124

                          Total   2,522
Deduct—Premature births, 30 ; cyanosis, 11..........   41
    Old age, 10 ; casualties, all classes, 118.......   128
    Suicides, various, 29 ; execution of sentence, 2.   31
                                   ——   200

Leaving deaths from registered diseases................... 2,322

In addition to the above there were still-born.......... 211
Country interment.............................. 152

Admitting the population of the city, for the fiscal year ending June 30th, 1867, to be one hundred and thirty-five thousand, and the recorded deaths from diseases two thousand three hundred and twenty-two, we find the following per centage of deaths per annum, viz : one and five-sevenths ($1\frac{5}{7}$).

Mortality per day, $6\frac{1}{3}$; mortality per month, $193\frac{1}{2}$; mortality per year, 2,322. Or, per diem, one in 20,925; per month, one in $697\frac{1}{2}$; per year, one in $58\frac{1}{4}$.

STILLBORN INFANTS.

Stillbirths each month	Total	1866.						1867.					
		July	August	September	October	November	December	January	February	March	April	May	June
Stillbirths each month.......	211	21	13	16	18	16	13	11	17	24	21	19	22

The large number of interments under this head should awaken the most profound concern and deepest regret on the part of the married community, yet its chief cause is a subject of too great delicacy to admit, with propriety, of public discussion in an official report like this; it is, however, a subject of vital importance to the well-being of society, and one which should be thoroughly understood by all parents who do, or do not desire issue.

MORTALITY OF INFANTS UNDER TWO YEARS OF AGE.

This large army of innocence, beauty, and promise swept down by the inexorable hand of death, ere life had scarce begun, and with them all the bright hopes and fond anticipations of parental ambition, is not without causes, which in many instances might be removed or materially mitigated. Our climate, the whole year round, is undoubtedly as healthy as that of any city in the world, but it needs to be properly understood, and its sudden changes guarded against with appropriate clothing. Adults make no mistake in this particular; ladies and gentlemen take their morning exercise in light, summer goods, while if their walk or ride is prolonged or deferred to past meridian, winter clothing, furs, shawls, capes, cloaks, and overcoats, are in requisition. But not so with these little victims of fashion. It is nothing uncommon to see the father, dressed in flannel underclothing from neck to heels, heavy cloth pants, vest, coat, and overcoat, taking his children out for an *airing*, dressed in the hight of fashion—with plaids and panties which have suffered fashion's amputation above the knee, and leaving the lower extremities unprotected save by light cotton hose and cloth gaiters. These little loved ones, look very pretty, but by being thus foolishly exposed to colds, coughs, and their concomitant results—diptheria or croup—they often, despite the doctor's skill, become a silent monitor to the parent of the wrong done them. Improper diet, both as to quality and quantity, is another fruitful source of disease and death among children. Swill milk has had its share in this work of infant mortality, but thanks to a discerning press and public opinion, *not the law*, a marked improvement has been wrought in this article in the babies' bill of fare during the past year; but there is still room for further improvement. Mothers cannot be too watchful as to the purity of the source of the milk upon which their children feed. Again, overcrowding the brain, trying to make a little man or woman out of a baby, kills numbers every year, who would, if left

to the pure and simple dictates of nature, grow to be healthy men
and women; but this unnatural parental pride to see the children
precocious and smart, this stuffing of the stomach and brain with
food and ideas fit only for maturer years, together with fashionable
exposure, go far to roll up this infant mortality which it is our painful duty to record.

PHTHISIS PULMONALIS.

Of this disease there are three hundred and twenty-four (324)
cases reported for the year. This apparently large number of consumptives would naturally convey the impression that our climate is
exceedingly favorable to the development of pulmonary diseases, but
a more intimate acquaintance with all the facts in the premises would
materially modify that opinion.

As will be seen by a reference to the tables, a very large percentage
of the cases reported are from public institutions, who, with a
majority of the balance, bring the disease with them, more or less
matured, and really only come here to die. While we do not claim
that San Francisco is a sanitarium for consumptives, we feel safe in
the assertion (after a practice of eighteen (18) years in this city)
that very few idiopathic cases of tuberculosis occur in San Francisco. Of aneurisms we have forty-one (41) cases; of heart disease
sixty-eight (68) cases. This is a large percentage of the deaths reported; but when we consider that these cases are the result of exposure, severe labor, and working in water, as is the case with our
mining population, we cease to wonder at the figures.

The number of casualties is unusually large, one hundred and
eighteen (118); this increase may be attributed to the falling of the
Summer Street House, the accident on board the steamer "Julia,"
and the great number of deaths from burns, during the year.

The roll of suicides is also in excess—twenty-nine (29); disap-
pointed hopes have been the prevailing cause. Alas! for poor
humanity, that cannot look stern necessity in the face, but must
needs fly to the ills it knows not of.

We may congratulate ourselves upon the sobriety of the city
during the past year; out of a population of one hundred and
thirty-five thousand, there were but eight (8) deaths from "King
Alcohol." This speaks volumes in favor of the habits of our people,

and tends to show that notwithstanding the great temptation to indulge in strong drinks, they are law-abiding, moral, and sober.

VACCINATION.

The number of vaccinations in this office during the last four
months have been very great, viz: one hundred and eighty (180).
This is, no doubt, owing to the Ordinance of the Board of Supervisors, giving publicity to its prophylatic importance, together with
the fact that free vaccination, with pure virus, in all cases, could be
had at this office, for all applicants.

The spread of epidemic small pox is only prevented by universal
vaccination and re-vaccination, together with the most rigid sanitary
measures in regard to the seclusion of those who are attacked, in
special hospitals, provided by a generous and cautious public. Availing ourselves of the means at our command for its prevention, the
spread and mortality of this loathsome disease would always be cir-
cumscribed in its extent, and limited to a very small number.

An open question for professional debate in regard to the possibil-
ity of conveying other diseases by vaccination than the prophylatic
discovered by the *immortal Jenner*, has never been lost sight of.
None other than the purest matter, from young and healthy children,
whose parentage and pedigree are known and approved, is used
by the incumbent of this office.

Leaving the abstract theory of the duality of disease being contained in, and propagated from, one and the same vesicle, to be
settled by the professional metaphysician, we take no chances for
those who apply here for vaccination.

The number of children whose health is such as to merit the approval of virus obtained from their vaccination is comparatively
small, hence good virus is always scarce. While we have always
promptly and cheerfully furnished virus to all physicians from the
country who have applied at this office, and that free of charge, we
yet deem it a matter of vital importance for all physicians to keep a
supply of fresh, pure matter, whenever and wherever it can be obtained.

SMALL POX.

The number of cases of this much dreaded disease reported at this office during the last five months, was thirty. This comparatively small amount of mortality, which will be seen by reference to the statistical tables (especially small when it is considered that some of the cases were in "articulo mortis" when reported here), is due to the careful and prompt manner of their removal to the hospital, and the unremitting attention and skill of the hospital physician, Dr. Wm. T. Garwood.

Section 4, Chapter 3, General Orders, Board of Supervisors, ordains as follows:

No person shall construct or maintain upon his premises, or premises under his control, any privy or privy vault, without connecting the same with the street sewer in such a manner that it shall be effectually drained and purified.

The system of connecting cesspools and privies with the public sewers is one of the most reprehensible allowed by law. It throws into our sewers a flow of undiluted liquid of the most fœtid character, rendering them in fact immense cesspools, filled with human ordure. Nothing more prejudicial to public health or offensive to the senses could well be devised, than the discharge of thousands of privy vaults into the street sewers. If such is the fact in our Atlantic cities (as experience has fully demonstrated in every instance, and the order has been rescinded), then it is most emphatically true in regard to San Francisco, where we have no rains for three-fourths of the year.

Should cholera break out in epidemic form in our city, the connecting of privy vaults with the public sewers would do more to spread it far and wide, than all other causes; unrestrained by any sanitary measures whatever. I would, therefore, respectfully ask your Honorable Board, for the reasons above stated, to rescind the Order.

Since my administration of the affairs of this office, there have been five hundred and thirty-one complaints of nuisance reported; of this number, one hundred and thirteen were, upon examination, found groundless; the balance, four hundred and eighteen, were abated. And I would here say, that San Francisco, cosmopolitan in its character, and made up of every grade of humanity from every clime, has proved to be a law-abiding city; for, without coercion, threats, or arrests, the people have cheerfully responded to requests or orders of the attachés of this office, and have complied with the requirements of the law.

I would ask your Honorable Board to take such steps as in your wisdom you may think fit, to have a law passed by the next Legislature, to make the property of non-residents responsible for infractions of the Health Laws of this city; great hardship and much sickness is caused by the lack of power on the part of the Health Officer to abate nuisance when the owner of the property complained of is absent from the State; hence, vacant lots owned by them are frequently covered with pools of stagnant water, and are generally made the dumping ground for filth of all sorts by the surrounding neighborhood; and yet, for want of legislation, this office is powerless to remedy the evil.

The proper location of the slaughter houses or abattoirs for the city, is, and has been, a vexed question. In a sanitary as well as a commercial point of view, this matter is one of vital importance to the public. The unfitness of the present location of the slaughter houses is apparent to the most casual observer; situated as they are, on the sluggish waters of Mission creek, it requires two or three tides to carry the offal to the bay, where a great portion of it drifts in on our irregular water front, putrifying in the sun, and sending up its pestilential gases, poisoning the atmosphere of our city, and causing disease wherever it abounds.

I would respectfully suggest to your Honorable Body, that the most important sanitary point in connection with this subject, is the providing for the present and future population of this great and growing city, *healthy butchers' meat;* to secure this great desideratum, healthy animals to be slaughtered, the proper and careful driving to the abattoirs, proper rest, food, and drink after driving, the most approved and humane mode of slaughtering, dressing, and cooling before sending to market for sale, low temperature, pure air, close proximity to the city, accessibility, cheapness, both for driving stock and transporting their food, as well as cheap and ready transit from the abattoirs to the city markets, all are important points for your consideration.

I cannot too earnestly recommend to your Honorable Body the sanitary and commercial importance of a proper location for the slaughter houses, with a view to securing all the above named points, together with proper drainage, and such improved manner of construction as shall be thought proper. This will go far to settle this long vexed question to the satisfaction of the public, and in justice to that respectable and industrious class of our fellow-citizens, the butchers.

In conclusion, we may congratulate ourselves that our death record shows a much smaller amount of mortality than any other American city, and that, under circumstances infinitely less favorable, this is due to the salubrity of our climate, the abundance of food, the absence of poverty, the skill and attention of our numerous physicians, and the blessings of an all-bountiful Providence, for which we should be truly and fervently thankful.

I. ROWELL, M. D.,

Health Officer.

HOSPITAL REPORT.

CITY AND COUNTY HOSPITAL,
SAN FRANCISCO, July 1st, 1867.

To the Honorable the Board of Supervisors
Of the City and County of San Francisco—

GENTLEMEN :   I have the honor to present the annual report of the Hospital from July 1st, 1866, to June 30th, 1867, inclusive.

Patients in Hospital, July 1st, 1866   315
Patients admitted 1,429

To be accounted for   1,744

Patients discharged cured 1,051
Patients discharged by request   162
Patients died   240
                                  —— 1,453
Patients remaining July 1st, 1867   291

Average number of patients . . . .   307$\frac{2}{3}$
Outside treatments   5,284
Children born—Girls   13
             Boys   9
                                     ——   22

Respectfully submitted.

WM. T. GARWOOD, M. D.,
Resident Physician.

NATIVES OF THE UNITED STATES.

Maine	21	Louisiana	5
New Hampshire	9	Ohio	24
Vermont	10	Indiana	1
Massachusetts	63	Illinois	7
Connecticut	6	Iowa	1
Rhode Island	5	Michigan	3
New York	120	Missouri	11
New Jersey	11	Kentucky	11
Pennsylvania	33	Tennessee	3
Delaware	2	Arkansas	2
Maryland	15	California	18
District of Columbia	1	Idaho	1
Virginia	11	Russian-America	1
North Carolina	3		
Florida	2		
Mississippi	3	Total	403

FOREIGNERS.

Africa	1	Ireland	454
Austria	2	Isle of Man	1
Australia	2	Jamaica	1
Azores	5	Lower California	1
Bavaria	2	Manila	1
Belgium	2	Mexico	24
Brazil	1	Norway	12
Canada East	14	Nova Scotia	5
Canada West	1	New Brunswick	1
Cape de Verde	6	New Granada	2
Calcutta	1	Peru	2
Caledonia	2	Poland	2
Chili	12	Portugal	13
China	19	Porto Cabello	1
Denmark	20	Porto Rico	1
Ecuador	1	Prussia	59
East Indies	3	Russia	1
England	81	Sandwich Islands	4
France	80	Spain	5
Finland	5	San Salvador	1
Germany	52	Sweden	24
Hanover	4	Switzerland	8
Holland	12	Scotland	36
Italy	11	Tahiti	1
Island of Guernsey	1	Wales	8
Island of Madeira	1		
Island of Santiago	1		
Islands, Western	16	Total	1,026

TABLE I.

CAUSES OF DEATH.

Diseases:	1866.						1867.						Total ......
	July......	August ...	September ...	October ...	November ...	December ...	January ...	February ...	March	April	May...	June	
Abscess of chest............	....	....	...	1	....	....	....	....	....	....	....	....	1
Abscess lumbar.............	....	....	1	....	....	....	....	....	....	....	....	....	1
Abscess psoas	....	....	....	....	....	1	....	....	....	....	....	....	1
Anemia	1	....	....	....	....	....	1	....	....	....	....	....	2
Aneurism of aorta...........	....	....	2	....	....	....	....	1	....	1	..	....	4
Aneurism of aorta abdominal	....	....	....	....	....	....	....	....	....	....	1	....	1
Aneurism of aorta arch.....	....	....	....	....	....	1	....	....	1	....	....	....	2
Aneurism of aorta descending	....	....	....	....	....	....	2	....	....	....	....	....	2
Aneurism of illiac artery....	....	....	....	1	....	....	....	....	....	....	....	....	1
Apoplexy cerebral	....	....	....	....	1	1	....	....	....	....	....	....	2
Aorta, rupture of...........	....	1	....	....	....	....	....	1	....	....	....	....	2
Aorta, atheroma of	....	....	....	1	....	....	....	....	....	....	....	....	1
Brain, disease of	....	....	....	1	....	....	....	....	1	....	....	....	2
Brain, inflammation of.....	....	....	....	....	....	....	....	....	1	....	....	....	1
Brain, softening of	....	2	1	....	....	1	1	....	....	1	....	1	7
Bowels, inflammation of....	....	1	....	....	....	....	....	....	....	....	....	....	1
Cancer of stomach..........	....	....	....	....	....	....	....	2	....	....	....	....	2
Cancer of uterus...........	....	....	....	....	....	....	....	....	....	....	1	....	1
Consumption, pulmonary....	8	5	...	6	3	4	7	3	9	4	2	4	55
Carditis	1	....	....	....	....	....	....	....	....	....	....	1	2
Cirrhosis	1	....	....	....	2	....	....	....	....	....	....	....	3
Cystitis chronic	....	....	....	....	....	1	....	....	....	....	....	....	1
Convulsions	....	....	....	....	....	....	....	1	....	....	....	....	1
Diabetis....................	....	....	....	....	....	....	....	....	1	....	1	....	2
Debility, nervous...........	....	....	....	....	....	....	....	....	....	1	....	....	1
Diarrhea, chronic...........	2	1	....	....	....	....	....	....	....	....	....	....	3
Dropsy.....................	1	1	....	....	....	....	....	....	....	....	....	....	2
*Dysentery.................	1	1	....	....	....	....	....	....	....	....	....	....	2
Dysentery, chronic	....	....	....	....	....	1	....	....	....	1	....	....	2
Effusion of brain	....	....	....	....	....	....	....	....	....	1	....	....	1
Empyema...................	....	....	....	....	....	....	1	1	1	1	....	....	4
Endocarditis	....	....	....	....	....	....	....	....	1	....	....	....	1
Epilepsy	....	....	....	....	....	1	....	....	....	....	....	....	1
Erysipelas.................	....	....	....	....	....	....	....	....	....	1	....	....	1
Fracture of ankle and delirium tremens................	....	....	....	....	....	....	....	1	....	....	....	....	1
Fracture of femur & humerus	....	....	....	....	....	....	....	1	....	....	....	....	1
Fever, typhoid	....	1	....	1	1	2	2	....	....	....	....	....	7
Fever, typhus..............	....	....	....	1	....	....	....	....	....	....	....	1	2
Gangrene	1	....	....	....	....	....	....	....	....	....	....	....	1
Gastritis	....	....	....	1	....	....	....	....	....	....	....	....	1
Heart, disease of	....	....	....	....	....	....	1	....	1	....	....	....	2
Heart, disease of mitral valves	....	....	....	2	....	2	....	....	....	1	....	....	5
Heart, valvular disease of....	....	1	1	....	1	1	....	....	....	1	1	....	6
Heart, dilatation of.........	....	....	....	1	....	....	....	....	....	....	....	....	1
Heart, hypertrophy of	....	....	....	....	....	1	2	1	....	....	....	....	4
Hydrothorax	....	....	1	....	....	....	....	....	....	1	....	....	2
Injuries received by car	....	1	....	....	....	....	....	....	....	....	....	....	1
Injuries received by fall	....	....	1	....	....	....	....	....	....	....	....	....	1
Kidneys, disease of.........	....	....	....	....	....	....	....	....	....	1	....	....	1
Laryngitis	....	....	....	1	....	....	....	....	....	....	....	....	1
Liver, disease of	2	2	....	1	1	1	1	1	....	....	....	1	10
Liver, hypertrophy of	....	....	....	....	....	....	1	....	....	....	....	....	1
Liver, atrophy of, chronic ...	....	....	....	....	....	....	....	....	....	....	....	1	1
Lungs, congestion of	....	....	....	....	1	....	....	....	....	....	....	....	1
Lungs, gangrene of.........	1	....	....	....	....	....	....	....	....	....	....	....	1
Mania a potu...............	....	....	1	....	....	....	....	....	....	....	....	1	2
Marasmus..................	....	1	....	....	....	....	....	....	....	....	....	....	1
Carried forward	19	18	8	18	10	18	19	13	15	11	10	11	170

TABLE I---Concluded.

Cause of Death.	1866.						1867.						Total
	July	August	September	October	November	December	January	February	March	April	May	June	
Brought forward	19	18	8	18	10	18	19	13	15	11	10	11	170
Old age	....	....	....	1	....	....	....	....	....	....	....	....	1
Operation, ununited fracture	....	....	....	....	....	....	....	....	....	....	....	1	1
Paralysis	....	1	1	1	1	2	1	1	1	....	4	2	15
Pericarditis	....	....	....	....	....	....	....	....	....	....	2	....	2
Pneumonia	....	....	1	....	1	....	1	....	....	1	1	1	6
Pneumonia, chronic	....	....	1	....	....	....	....	....	....	1	....	....	2
Pneumonia, pleuro	....	....	....	1	....	1	1	....	....	....	....	....	3
Premature birth	....	....	....	....	....	....	....	1	....	....	....	....	1
Prostate glands, disease of	....	....	....	....	....	....	....	....	....	1	....	....	1
Pulmonary abscess	1	....	....	....	....	....	....	....	....	....	....	....	1
Pyemia	....	1	1	2	1	1	1	....	....	....	....	....	7
Scrofula	1	....	....	....	....	....	....	....	....	....	....	....	1
Stomach, ulceration of	....	....	1	....	....	....	....	....	....	....	....	....	1
Spine, disease of	....	....	....	....	....	....	....	....	....	....	1	....	1
Spine, fracture of	1	....	....	1	....	1	....	....	....	....	....	....	3
Spine, necrosis of	....	....	....	....	....	....	....	1	....	....	....	....	1
Syphilis, tertiary	....	3	1	2	1	1	1	1	....	....	1	....	11
Tumor, encephaloid	....	....	1	....	....	....	....	....	....	....	....	....	1
Uremia	....	1	....	....	....	....	....	....	....	....	....	....	1
Uterus, fibroid tumor of	....	....	....	....	....	....	....	....	....	1	....	....	1
Variola	....	....	....	....	....	....	....	....	....	1	1	2	4
Variola, confluent	....	....	....	....	....	....	....	....	1	1	....	....	2
Wound of chest, knife	....	1	....	....	....	....	....	....	....	....	....	....	1
Unknown, Coroner's cases	....	....	....	1	....	....	....	....	1	....	2	....	4
Total	22	25	15	27	14	24	24	17	18	17	22	17	242

NOTE.—Three of the above, infants, are not entered upon the register.

TABLE II.

DISEASES OF PATIENTS.

Diseases.	1866.						1867.						Total
	July	August	September	October	November	December	January	February	March	April	May	June	
Abscess of back	....	....	....	....	....	....	....	....	....	1	....	....	1
Abscess of breast	....	....	....	1	....	....	....	....	....	....	....	....	1
Abscess of chest	....	1	....	....	....	....	....	....	....	....	....	....	1
Abscess of foot	....	....	....	....	....	....	....	1	1	....	....	....	2
Abscess of hand	....	....	....	....	1	....	....	1	....	....	....	....	2
Abscess of nares	....	....	....	....	....	1	1	....	1	2	....	....	5
Abscess of perineum	....	....	....	....	....	....	....	1	....	....	....	....	1
Abscess of thigh	....	....	1	....	....	....	....	....	....	....	....	....	1
Amaurosis	....	....	....	....	....	1	....	....	....	....	....	....	1
Aneurism of aorta	1	1	1	....	....	1	....	....	1	1	....	1	7
Aneurism of aorta abdominal	....	....	....	....	1	....	....	....	3	....	....	....	4
Aneurism of femoral artery	1	....	....	....	....	....	....	....	....	....	....	....	1
Aneurism of popliteal artery	1	....	....	....	....	....	....	....	....	....	....	....	1
Carried forward	3	2	2	1	2	3	1	2	4	7	....	1	28

20

TABLE II--- Continued.

Diseases.	1866.						1867.						Total
	July	August	September	October	November	December	January	February	March	April	May	June	
Brought forward	3	2	2	1	2	3	1	2	4	7	....	1	28
Amputation, result of		2								1			3
Anchylosis of knee joint										1			1
Ankle, injury by car												1	1
Ankle, sprain of			1	1							1	1	4
Ankle, ulcer of		3	1										4
Arthritis, rheumatic					1								1
Apoplexy				1	1					1			3
Asthma					2		1						3
Bite, Dog			1				1						2
Bladder, disease of								1					1
Blind	2	1	1					2		3		1	10
Brain, concussion of					1								1
Brain, congestion of						1							1
Brain, effusion of											1		1
Brain, softening of		1	1	2					1	1		1	7
Bronchitis	1	2	1	5	1		4	2		1	3	2	22
Bubo			2	1	1	2						1	7
Burn of hand and arm											1		1
Burn of hand and chest									1				1
Burn of scalp and hand								1					1
Cancer of stomach	1			1		1							3
Cancer of tongue		1											1
Cancer of uterus											1		1
Carditis	1						1					1	3
Carditis rheumatic								1					1
Cataract					1								1
Cirrhosis	1											1	2
Contraction, masseter muscle								1					1
Contraction of finger								1	1				2
Contusion of ankle		1			1			1	1	1			5
Contusion of arm					1				1				2
Contusion of back										1			1
Contusion of body	1	1	1		1				1	3	1		9
Contusion of face	1		1	3			1		1		1	1	9
Contusion of foot	1				2					1			4
Contusion of hand											1		1
Contusion of head			1		2								3
Contusion of hip	1					1				1		1	4
Contusion of knee			1	1	1				1				4
Contusion of leg	1						1	1					3
Contusion of shoulder		1	1	1							1		4
Congestive chill					1								1
Conjunctivitis					2	2		1		2			7
Conjunctivitis granula										1			1
Cornea, ulceration of		1											1
Cornitis												1	1
Cripple				2	1		2						5
Debility general	3	2				1		2	3	1		1	13
Debility nervous				1	1				1				3
Debility from fever	3			2	1			1			1		8
Debility from intemperance	1												1
Deformed foot, from burn											1		1
Delirium tremens		2	1		1	2	2		2		2	2	14
Destitution	1	3	2	4		4	1	3	2	4	1	2	27
Diabetes							1		1				3
Diarrhea	1			2	1		1						5
Diarrhea, chronic					1		1	2	1		2		7
Dislocation of humerus						1							1
Dislocation of knee		1											1
Dislocation of scapula	1												1
Carried forward	23	24	18	28	28	18	20	20	22	30	16	21	268

TABLE II---Continued.

Diseases.	1866.						1867.						Total
	July	August	September	October	November	December	January	February	March	April	May	June	
Brought forward	23	24	18	28	28	18	20	20	22	30	16	21	268
Dislocation of thigh and fracture of humerus	....	1	....	....	....	....	....	....	....	....	....	....	1
Dropsy	3	....	....	3	2	3	....	....	1	1	....	....	13
Dysentery	....	1	1	1	1	1	....	....	....	1	2	....	8
Dysentery, chronic	....	....	....	....	....	1	1	....	....	....	....	....	2
Dyspepsia	....	....	....	....	....	....	....	....	2	1	....	....	3
Endocarditis	....	....	....	....	....	....	....	1	....	....	....	1	2
Epilepsy	5	1	3	1	4	3	2	1	1	....	....	2	23
Epistaxis	....	....	....	....	....	....	....	....	....	....	1	....	1
Erythema	....	....	1	....	....	....	....	....	....	....	....	....	1
Erysipelas of face	1	....	....	1	....	....	2	....	2	2	1	1	10
Erysipelas of foot	....	....	....	....	....	....	....	....	1	....	....	....	1
Fever, continued	....	....	1	....	2	....	....	....	....	....	....	....	3
Fever, intermittent	12	15	7	16	14	5	5	2	6	10	3	9	104
Fever, remittent	1	1	1	1	3	2	....	1	....	1	2	....	13
Fever, typhoid	....	2	....	1	2	2	....	....	....	....	....	1	8
Fever, result of	....	....	....	1	....	....	1	....	....	....	....	....	2
Fistula of anus	....	1	2	....	....	....	3	1	....	1	....	....	8
Fistula of groin	....	....	....	....	1	....	....	....	....	....	....	....	1
Fistula of perineum	....	....	....	....	....	....	....	....	....	....	1	....	1
Fistula of urethra	....	....	1	....	....	1	1	....	....	1	....	1	5
Foot, injury of	....	....	....	1	....	....	....	....	....	....	....	....	1
Foot, injury by frostbite	....	....	1	....	....	....	....	....	....	1	....	....	2
Foot, ulcer of	....	1	....	....	....	....	....	....	....	....	....	....	1
Fracture of ankle	....	....	....	....	....	....	....	....	1	....	....	....	1
Fracture of clavicle	1	1	1	....	....	....	....	....	....	....	....	....	3
Fracture of femur	....	2	....	....	....	....	....	....	....	....	1	....	3
Fracture of femur, both	....	1	1	....	....	....	....	....	....	....	....	....	2
Fracture of femur & humerus	....	....	....	....	....	....	....	....	1	....	....	....	1
Fracture of fibula	....	....	....	....	....	1	....	....	....	....	....	....	1
Fracture of patella	....	....	1	....	....	....	....	....	....	....	....	....	1
Fracture of rib	....	....	....	....	....	1	....	1	....	....	....	....	2
Fracture of skull	....	....	....	....	....	1	....	....	....	....	....	....	1
Fracture of tibia	....	....	1	....	....	1	1	1	....	....	....	....	4
Fracture of tibia and fibula	....	....	....	1	....	2	....	....	....	....	1	1	5
Fracture of ulna	....	....	....	....	....	1	1	....	....	....	....	....	2
Fracture, result of	....	....	1	....	1	1	....	1	1	....	1	1	7
Fracture, ununited	....	....	2	....	....	....	....	....	....	....	....	....	2
Gangrene of penis	....	1	....	....	....	....	....	....	....	....	....	....	1
Gastritis	....	....	....	1	1	....	....	....	....	....	....	....	2
Glands, disease of prostate	....	....	....	....	....	....	....	....	1	....	....	....	1
Glaucoma	2	....	....	....	....	....	....	....	....	....	....	....	2
Gonorrhea	1	....	....	....	....	....	....	....	....	....	....	....	1
Gout, rheumatic	....	....	....	....	....	....	....	....	1	....	....	....	1
Groin, ulcer of	....	....	....	....	....	1	....	....	....	....	....	....	1
Hœmatemesis	....	....	....	....	1	....	....	....	....	....	....	....	1
Hœmoptisis	....	....	1	....	....	....	....	....	....	....	2	1	4
Hœmorrhoids	....	....	....	....	....	....	....	....	....	1	....	....	1
Heart, disease of	1	....	2	....	1	....	....	....	....	....	....	....	4
Heart, aortic valvular disease	....	1	2	....	1	1	1	1	....	....	1	....	8
Heart, mitral valvular disease	1	....	2	1	....	2	....	1	1	2	....	....	10
Heart, hypertrophy of	....	1	3	3	....	1	3	2	....	....	....	....	13
Hip, disease of	....	....	....	....	....	....	....	....	....	....	1	....	1
Hydrocele	....	....	....	....	....	....	....	....	....	....	....	1	1
Hydrothorax	....	....	1	....	1	1	....	....	1	1	....	....	5
Hypochondriasis	....	....	1	....	....	....	....	....	....	....	....	....	1
Idiocy	....	....	....	....	....	....	....	....	1	....	....	....	1
Inguinal glands, disease of	....	....	....	1	....	....	....	....	....	....	....	....	1
Influenza	....	....	....	....	1	....	....	....	....	....	....	....	1
Injury of hip	....	....	....	....	....	....	1	....	....	....	....	....	1
Injuries of spine	....	1	....	....	1	....	....	....	....	....	....	....	2
Carried forward	51	55	55	61	65	50	42	37	39	53	33	40	581

TABLE II---Continued.

Diseases.	1866.						1867.						Total.
	July.	August.	September.	October.	November.	December.	January.	February.	March.	April.	May.	June.	
Brought forward	51	55	55	61	65	50	42	37	39	53	33	40	581
Insanity		1		1		2	1			2	1		8
Insanity, syphilitic				1									1
Intemperance, result of	1	1	4	1	3	1	1	1	2	2	2	5	24
Intersusception of bowels									1				1
Iretis									1		2		3
Iretis syphilitic			1										1
Jaundice			1							1			2
Kidneys, disease of									2				2
Lachrymal duct, obstruction				1									1
Laryngitis				1									1
Leg, ulceration of	4	7	1	2	5	5	4	5	3	8	3	6	53
Leg, ulcer of, varicose		2	1		1	1		1		1			7
Leg, varicose veins of						1							1
Lepra					1								1
Liver, disease of	1				1	2	2			2			8
Liver, inflammation of					1			2					3
Lungs, solidification of									1		1		2
Masturbation, effects of	1										1	1	3
Menorrhagia		1										1	2
Miscarriage, effects of											1		1
Moribund											1		1
Necrosis of ankle joint				1		1			1				3
Necrosis of femur		1	1										2
Necrosis of humerus				1							1		2
Necrosis of metatarsal bones	1	1		1			1	1			1	2	8
Necrosis of phalanges		1											1
Necrosis of tibia			1										1
Neuralgia		1		1	1	1	1	2			1		8
Neuralgia syphilitic				1	1	1				2		2	7
Nose, loss of right ulœ					1								1
Old age										1		1	2
Ophthalmia						2					1		3
Ophthalmia gonorrheal							1						1
Ophthalmia purulent					1								1
Ophthalmia syphilitic		1	1				1						3
Orchitis			2			2		1	4	1			10
Orchitis syphilitic									1				1
Paralysis	5	7	6	6	5	6	4	2	4	7	13	9	74
Paralysis of tongue					1		1			1			3
Paronychia	1									2			3
Pericarditis							1			1			2
Peritonitis											1	1	2
Phthisis pulmonalis	2	6	4	9	7	9	4	9	5	4	7	7	73
Pleurisy				4		1			1				7
Pneumonia	1		1	1		1		1		1	1	1	8
Pneumonia, chronic			1	1			2	1	1	1			7
Pneumonia, double					1								1
Pneumonia, pleuro			1	2		1							4
Poisoned by toxicodendron	1	1							1		1	1	6
Pregnant	1		2	4	3	1	2	3	4	2	3	2	27
Psoriasis			1										1
Rectum, ulceration of				1						1			2
Rheumatism	9	6	10	8	16	13	13	8	14	8	8	12	125
Rheumatism, acute							1						1
Rheumatism, chronic	1												1
Rheumatism, gonorrheal									1				1
Rheumatism, inflammatory		1	1		1	2	1	2	2	2		1	13
Rheumatism, syphilitic	3	2	5	3	1	3		2	5	4	3	4	35
Roseola												1	1
Salivation					1		1						2
Scabies	1	1								1			3
Carried forward	84	96	100	113	117	106	84	81	93	106	84	99	1163

TABLE II---Concluded.

Diseases.	1866. July	August	September	October	November	December	1867. January	February	March	April	May	June	Total
Brought forward	84	96	100	113	117	106	84	81	93	106	84	99	1163
Scrotum, inflammation of....	....	....	1	....	....	....	....	....	....	....	....	....	1
Scrotum, ulcer of...........	....	....	....	1	....	....	....	....	....	....	....	....	1
Spermatic chord, enlargement	....	....	....	....	....	....	....	....	....	....	1	....	1
Spine, disease of	....	....	....	1	....	....	....	....	....	....	....	....	1
Spine, injury of	1	....	....	....	....	1	....	....	....	....	....	....	2
Sprain of knee	....	....	....	....	....	....	....	....	1	....	....	....	1
Sprain of wrist............	....	....	....	....	....	....	....	....	2	1	....	....	3
Sprain of back and ankle....	....	....	....	....	....	1	....	....	....	....	....	....	1
Stricture..................	1	2	3	2	3	....	2	2	1	....	1	1	18
Suicide, attempted.........	....	....	1	....	..	1	....	1	2	....	....	....	4
Sygnovitis of knee joint.....	....	1	....	....	1	....	....	....	....	....	....	....	2
Syphilis..................	5	5	2	6	9	....	1	3	3	4	1	3	42
Syphilis, secondary..........	5	14	6	6	10	9	9	6	8	10	4	5	92
Syphilis, tertiary............	4	1	3	....	2	4	....	1	2	1	3	....	21
Tape worm.................	....	....	....	....	....	....	....	....	....	....	....	1	1
Testes, enlargement of......	....	1	....	....	....	....	....	....	....	....	....	....	1
Testes, scrofulus diseas of...	....	....	....	....	....	....	....	....	....	1	..	....	1
Throat, ulceration of.........	....	1	....	....	2	1	....	....	....	....	1	....	5
Tumor, encephaloid.........	....	1	....	....	....	....	....	....	....	....	....	....	1
Tumor of uterus fibroid.....	....	....	....	....	....	....	.·.	....	1	....	....	....	1
Urine, non-retention of......	....	..	1	....	....	....	....	....	....	....	.·.	.·.	1
Variola....................	....	1	....	....	....	....	1	1	5	7	6	4	25
Variola, confluent...........	....	....	....	....	....	....	....	....	2	....	....	....	2
Vesical calculi........... ..	....	1	....	....	....	....	....	....	....	....	....	1	2
Wound of abdomen, knife...	....	....	....	....	1	....	....	....	....	....	....	....	1
Wound of ankle.............	....	....	....	....	....	....	....	....	1	....	....	....	1
Wound of arm, shot.........	1	....	....	....	....	....	....	....	....	1	....	....	2
Wound of back, shot........	....	....	....	....	....	....	....	....	1	....	....	....	1
Wound of breast, knife......	..	..	....	....	....	....	....	1	....	....	....	....	1
Wound of chest, knife.......	1	1	....	....	....	....	....	....	....	....	....	....	2
Wound of circumflex illiac artery.................	....	....	....	1	...,	....	....	....	....	....	....	....	1
Wound of face..............	....	....	....	....	....	....	....	2	....	....	....	....	2
Wound of face, knife........	....	....	....	....	....	....	....	....	....	....	....	1	1
Wound of foot, ax..........	....	....	....	1	....	....	....	....	....	....	....	....	1
Wound of hand, ax..........	....	1	....	....	....	....	....	....	....	1	1	....	3
Wound of head and throat, knife.................	....	1	....	....	...	1	....	....	....	....	....	....	2
Wound of head, shot........	....	....	....	....	....	....	....	....	....	....	....	1	1
Wound of head, knife.......	....	....	....	....	....	....	....	1	....	....	....	....	1
Wound of head.............	....	....	....	....	....	....	....	2	....	....	....	....	2
Wound of knee, knife........	1	....	....	....	....	....	....	....	....	....	....	....	1
Wound of knee, shot	....	1	....	....	....	....	....	....	....	....	....	....	1
Wound of knee, ax	....	....	1	....	....	....	....	....	....	....	....	....	1
Wound of leg, knife........	1	....	....	....	....	1	....	....	....	....	....	....	2
Wound of thigh, shot........	....	....	....	....	....	1	....	....	....	....	....	....	1
Wound of scalp, knife.......	....	....	....	....	....	....	....	....	2	2	....	....	4
Womb, disease of............	....	....	1	....	1	....	....	....	....	....	....	....	2
Womb, inflammation of......	....	....	....	....	....	....	....	....	....	....	1	....	1
Womb, ulceration of.........	....	....	....	....	....	....	....	....	....	....	.·.	1	1
Total.................	104	128	119	131	146	125	97	101	124	134	103	117	1429

REPORT

OF THE

INDUSTRIAL SCHOOL DEPARTMENT.

Office of the Industrial School Department, ⎱
August 1st, 1867. ⎰

To the Honorable the Board of Supervisors
Of the City and County of San Francisco—

Gentlemen : Responding to Resolution No. 6,963, passed by your Honorable Body, June 17th, 1867, I respectfully present for your consideration the report of the President of this Department to the Board of Managers, together with that of the Auditor.

Your obedient servant,

JAS. S. THOMSON,

Secretary Industrial School Department.

PRESIDENT'S REPORT.

To the Board of Managers
Of the Industrial School Department—

Gentlemen : In conformity to the request of your Honorable Board, I submit the following report of the Industrial School Department for the fiscal year 1866–7 :

Since the opening of the institution, May 3d, 1859, there have been committed as follows, viz :

Boys. 501
Girls. 129
——— 630

Of this number there have been recommitted—
Boys. 26
Girl.. 1
——— 27

Making the whole number of commitments since May
3d, 1859—
Boys. 527
Girls. 130
——— 657

Remaining in the institution June 6th, 1866. 153
Committed during the year ending June 6th, 1867—
Boys. 89
Girls. 11
——— 100

Recaptured—
Boys. 9
Returned—who had been absent on leave—
Boys. 41
Girls. 18
——— 59

Returned—who had been indentured—
Boys. 4

To be accounted for. 325

Absent on leave—
Boys. 49
Girls. 14
——— 63

Carried forward. 63

Brought forward   63

Indentured—

    Boys.   5

    Girl.   1

                                 ——   6

Discharged—

    Boys.   37

    Girls.   21

                                 ——   58

Escaped—

    Boys.   8

Deceased—

    Boys.   2

                                 ——   137

Remaining in the institution June 6th, 1877—

    Boys. 168

    Girls. 20

                                 ——   188

                                     ——   325

NATIVITY.

Maine	1	England	1
Massachusetts.	12	Scotland.	2
Connecticut.	1	Australia.	2
New York.	23	Canada	2
New Jersey.	2		
Pennsylvania.	2	Great Britain and Dependencies	7
Maryland	1		
Louisiana.	3		
Texas.	1	Italy.	1
Michigan.	1	Austria.	1
Wisconsin.	2	Germany. .:	1
Missouri	3	Mexico.	6
Iowa.	1	Central America.	1
Minnesota.	1	China.	1
California.	28		

Total from United States.... 82   Total Foreigners. 18

Total 100

AGES.

6 years old	1	13 years old	9
7 years old	1	14 years old	14
8 years old	8	15 years old	12
9 years old	6	16 years old	8
10 years old	11	17 years old	5
11 years old	13		
12 years old	12	Total	100

CAUSES OF COMMITMENT.

Leading an idle and dissolute life	71
Leading an idle life	8
Leading an idle life, and being addicted to pilfering	1
Malicious mischief	1
Grand larceny	2
Petit larceny	14
Burglary	2
Forgery	1
Total	100

BY WHOM COMMITTED.

Police Judge	78
Police Judge's Court	16
County Court	5
Surrendered by guardian	1
Total	100

TABLE I.

SHOWING THE NUMBER OF COMMITMENTS FOR EACH MONTH DURING THE
PAST YEAR, AND PREVIOUSLY.

MONTHS.	PAST YEAR.		PREVIOUSLY.		TOTAL.
	Boys.	Girls.	Boys.	Girls.	
June, 1866	7	4	36	10	57
July	11	1	42	20	74
August	7	0	33	8	48
September	10	0	36	10	56
October	14	0	36	4	54
November	6	0	43	8	57
December	5	2	21	8	36
January, 1867	8	0	44	8	60
February	4	2	32	2	40
March	8	1	33	5	47
April	2	1	39	12	54
May	7	0	43	24	74
Totals	89	11	438	119	657

TABLE II.

SHOWING THE NUMBER OF DISCHARGES FOR EACH MONTH DURING THE PAST
YEAR, AND PREVIOUSLY.

MONTHS.	PAST YEAR.		PREVIOUSLY.		TOTAL.
	Boys.	Girls.	Boys.	Girls.	
June, 1866	6	3	7	2	18
July	2	3	3	6	14
August	1	2	8	6	17
September	1	2	7	1	11
October	4	0	13	1	18
November	5	2	5	0	12
December	6	1	12	4	23
January, 1867	3	0	16	1	20
February	2	1	9	0	12
March	4	0	9	1	14
April	2	2	11	2	17
May	1	5	20	5	31
Totals	37	21	120	29	207

TABLE III.

SHOWING THE NUMBER OF PERMITS OF ABSENCE GRANTED FOR EACH MONTH
DURING THE PAST YEAR, AND PREVIOUSLY.

Months.	Past Year.		Previously.		Total.
	Boys.	Girls.	Boys	Girls.	
June, 1866	5	2	31	10	48
July	8	2	59	26	95
August	2	1	31	7	41
September	2	1	30	9	42
October	8	2	15	8	33
November	5	0	34	6	45
December	4	0	45	7	56
January, 1867	1	1	27	8	37
February	2	1	37	12	52
March	2	2	40	4	48
April	6	1	37	5	49
May	4	1	41	32	78
Totals	49	14	427	134	624

TABLE IV.

SHOWING THE NUMBER OF INDENTURES FOR EACH MONTH DURING THE PAST
YEAR, AND PREVIOUSLY.

Months.	Past Year.		Previously.		Total.
	Boys.	Girls.	Boys.	Girls.	
June, 1866	2	1	2	3	8
July	1	0	3	1	5
August	0	0	4	3	7
September	0	0	4	2	6
October	0	0	6	0	6
November	0	0	2	2	4
December	0	0	4	1	5
January, 1867	0	0	2	1	3
February	0	0	1	1	2
March	1	0	3	4	8
April	0	0	4	0	4
May	1	0	4	2	7
Totals	5	1	39	20	65

TABLE V.

SHOWING THE NUMBER OF ESCAPES FOR EACH MONTH DURING THE PAST
YEAR, AND PREVIOUSLY.

MONTHS.	PAST YEAR.		PREVIOUSLY.		TOTAL.
	Boys.	Girls.	Boys.	Girls.	
June, 1866	0	0	23	0	23
July	0	0	11	0	11
August	5	0	14	3	22
September	10	0	15	1	26
October	4	0	8	1	13
November	0	0	10	2	12
December	1	0	4	3	8
January, 1867	5	0	14	1	20
February	0	0	14	0	14
March	5	0	27	0	32
April	9	0	11	0	20
May	0	0	31	0	31
Totals	39	0	182	11	232

TABLE VI.

SHOWING THE NUMBER OF DEATHS FOR EACH MONTH DURING THE PAST
YEAR, AND PREVIOUSLY.

MONTHS.	PAST YEAR.		PREVIOUSLY.		TOTAL.
	Boys.	Girls.	Boys.	Girls.	
June, 1866	0	0	0	0	0
July	0	0	0	0	0
August	1	0	0	0	1
September	0	0	1	0	1
October	0	0	1	0	1
November	0	0	1	0	1
December	0	0	1	0	1
January, 1867	0	0	0	0	0
February	0	0	0	0	0
March	0	0	0	0	0
April	0	0	0	0	0
May	1	0	2	0	3
Totals	2	0	6	0	8

T A B L E V I I .

SHOWING THE DISPOSAL AND EMPLOYMENT OF THOSE WHO LEFT DURING THE
PAST YEAR, AND PREVIOUSLY.

DISPOSITION.	PAST YEAR.		PREVIOUSLY.		TOTAL.
	Boys.	Girls.	Boys.	Girls.	
Discharged—					
Delivered to friends..........	22	8	101	21	152
Attained their majority.......	13	12	5	10	40
Sent to Deaf, Dumb, and Blind Asylum...................	0	0	1	0	1
Sent to Prot. Orphan Asylum.	0	0	4	0	4
Sent to the "Home".........	2	1	0	0	3
Absent on leave—					
With relatives...............	32	5	107	50	194
Placed at housewifery........	0	5	0	24	29
With farmers................	3	0	26	0	29
With carpenters.............	1	0	2	0	3
With undertaker.............	0	0	1	0	1
With wire-workers...........	0	0	3	0	3
With merchants.............	3	0	3	0	6
With milliner...............	0	0	0	1	1
With dress-maker...........	0	1	0	0	1
With file-cutter.............	0	0	1	0	1
With tinsmith..............	0	0	1	0	1
With expressman...........	0	0	1	0	1
With glass-blower	0	0	1	0	1
With plasterers.............	0	0	2	0	2
With cooper................	0	0	1	0	1
With butchers..............	0	0	2	0	2
With iron-worker...........	0	0	1	0	1
With marble-cutter.........	0	0	1	0	1
With plumbers.............	0	0	2	0	2
With shoemakers...........	0	0	2	0	2
With baker	0	0	1	0	1
With physician.............	1	0	0	0	1
With woodenware manufact'rs	2	0	0	0	2
With steamboatman	1	0	0	0	1
With fruit dealer	1	0	0	0	1
With metal roofer..........	1	0	0	0	1
With collector.............	1	0	0	0	1
With hotel keeper	1	0	0	0	1
With druggist..............	1	0	0	0	1
As errand boys	0	0	2	0	2
At sea (merchant service).....	1	0	16	0	17
At sea (whaling service)......	0	0	15	0	15
At sea (naval service)........	0	0	31	0	31
In United States army.......	0	0	10	0	10
Removed to City and County Hospital................	0	0	1	0	1
Carried forward.........	86	32	344	106	568

TABLE VII—Concluded.

DISPOSITION.	PAST YEAR.		PREVIOUSLY.		TOTAL.
	Boys.	Girls.	Boys.	Girls.	
Brought forward........	86	32	344	106	568
Removed to Magdalen Asylum	0	3	0	3	6
Indentured—					
To farmers................	5	0	26	0	31
To dairyman...............	0	0	1	0	1
To brewer.................	0	0	1	0	1
To surveyor...............	0	0	1	0	1
To tailor.................	0	0	1	0	1
To tinsmith...............	0	0	1	0	1
To broker.................	0	0	1	0	1
To barber.................	0	0	1	0	1
To machinist..............	0	0	1	0	1
To carpenter..............	0	0	1	0	1
To engineer...............	0	0	1	0	1
Placed at housewifery......	0	1	0	18	19
Escaped...................	8	0	39	0	47
Deceased..................	2	0	6	0	8
Totals..............	101	36	425	127	689

TABLE VIII.

SHOWING THE AGES OF THOSE COMMITTED DURING THE PAST YEAR, AND PREVIOUSLY.

AGES.	PAST YEAR.		PREVIOUSLY.		TOTAL.
	Boys.	Girls.	Boys.	Girls.	
Less than one year...........	0	0	0	1	1
Three years old..............	0	0	3	1	4
Four years old...............	0	0	3	3	6
Five years old.....	0	0	7	3	10
Six years old................	1	0	15	7	23
Seven years old..............	0	1	11	2	14
Eight years old..............	7	1	28	4	40
Nine years old...............	6	0	26	10	42
Ten years old................	11	0	35	10	56
Eleven years old.............	13	0	31	10	54
Twelve years old.............	10	2	52	5	69
Thirteen years old...........	8	1	52	5	66
Fourteen years old..........	11	3	60	12	86
Fifteen years old.............	10	2	45	17	74
Sixteen years old	7	1	34	19	61
Seventeen years old...........	5	0	26	10	41
Eighteen years old...........	0	0	9	0	9
Unknown....................	0	0	1	0	1
Totals................	89	11	438	119	657

TABLE IX.

SHOWING THE NATIVITY OF THOSE COMMITTED DURING THE PAST YEAR, AND PREVIOUSLY.

NATIVITY.	Past Year.		Previously.		Total.
	Boys.	Girls.	Boys.	Girls.	
Alabama	0	0	2	0	2
California	26	2	89	17	134
Connecticut	1	0	2	1	4
Delaware	0	0	1	0	1
Georgia	0	0	2	0	2
Illinois	0	0	4	0	4
Indiana	0	0	1	0	1
Iowa	1	0	1	1	3
Kentucky	0	0	1	0	1
Louisiana	3	0	21	2	26
Maine	1	0	4	2	7
Maryland	1	0	4	1	6
Massachusetts	11	1	42	10	64
Michigan	1	0	1	1	3
Minnesota	1	0	0	0	1
Mississippi	0	0	5	0	5
Missouri	3	0	3	1	7
New Hampshire	0	0	1	0	1
New Jersey	2	0	8	2	12
New York	20	3	90	18	131
Ohio	0	0	4	2	6
Oregon	0	0	2	1	3
Pennsylvania	1	1	17	3	22
Rhode Island	0	0	2	0	2
South Carolina	0	0	3	0	3
Tennessee	0	0	5	0	5
Texas	1	0	2	1	4
Vermont	0	0	1	0	1
Virginia	0	0	3	0	3
Wisconsin	2	0	2	0	4
District of Columbia	0	0		0	1
Territories	0	0	4	1	5
Natives	75	7	328	64	474
Australia	2	1	0	21	6	29
Austria	1	0	0	0	
Belgium	0	8	0	1	1
British Guiana	0	1	0	1	0
Canada	1	0		2	8
Central America	1	0		0	2
Chili	0	1	0	5	5
China	1	0	0	7	31	39
England	1	0	0	14	2	17
Carried forward	82	0	8	382	105	577

TABLE IX—Continued.

NATIVITY.	PAST YEAR.		PREVIOUSLY.		TOTAL.
	Boys.	Girls.	Boys.	Girls.	
Brought forward	82	8	382	105	577
France	0	0	3	4	7
Germany	0	1	10	2	13
Ireland	0	0	11	3	14
Italy	1	0	6	1	8
Jamaica	0	0	1	0	1
Macquarie Islands	0	0	1	0	1
Mexico	4	2	14	2	22
Newfoundland	0	0	1	0	1
New Granada	0	0	2	0	2
Peru	0	0	1	0	1
Poland	0	0	1	0	1
Prussia	0	0	1	0	1
Scotland	2	0	2	1	5
Switzerland	0	0	0	1	1
Turkey	0	0	1	0	1
Vancouver Island	0	0	1	0	1
Foreigners	14	4	110	55	183
Totals	89	11	438	119	657

TABLE X.

SHOWING THE CAUSES OF COMMITMENT OF THOSE RECEIVED DURING THE
PAST YEAR, AND PREVIOUSLY.

CAUSE OF COMMITMENT.	PAST YEAR.		PREVIOUSLY.		TOTAL.
	Boys.	Girls.	Boys.	Girls.	
Leading an idle life	8	0	33	12	53
Leading an idle life, and addicted to pilfering	1	0	0	0	1
Leading an idle and dissolute life	60	11	312	96	479
Leading an idle, criminal, and dissolute life	0	0	0	1	1
Dissolute and untruthful	0	0	0	1	1
Manifesting vicious tendencies	0	0	0	1	1
Burglary	2	0	1	0	3
Forgery	1	0	1	0	2
Arson in second degree	0	0	1	0	1
Grand larceny	2	0	5	0	7
Petit larceny	14	0	70	3	87
Attempt to commit grand larceny	0	0	1	0	1
Attempt to commit petit larceny	0	0	3	0	3
Malicious mischief	1	0	0	0	1
Misdemeanor	0	0	4	0	4
Assault and battery	0	0	1	0	1
Vagrancy	0	0	4	0	4
For protection	0	0	3	4	7
Totals	89	11	439	118	657

T A B L E   X I.

SHOWING THE DOMESTIC CONDITION OF THOSE COMMITTED DURING THE
PAST YEAR, AND PREVIOUSLY.

DOMESTIC CONDITION.	PAST YEAR.		PREVIOUSLY.		TOTAL:
	Boys.	Girls.	Boys.	Girls.	
Lost father....................	25	7	124	17	173
Lost mother...................	7	0	58	10	75
Lost both parents.............	16	3	43	15	77
Parents living................	28	1	155	53	237
Parents living, but separated...	13	0	55	19	87
Unknown.....................	0	0	6	2	8
Totals................	89	11	441	116	657
Deserted by father............	0	0	42	13	55
Deserted by mother...........	2	1	8	1	12
Deserted by both parents......	3	0	6	2	11
Father intemperate...........	0	0	7	5	12
Mother intemperate...........	1	1	19	14	35
Have stepfathers	7	1	21	4	33
Have stepmothers	1	0	2	5	8
Father insane.................	0	0	2	1	3
Mother insane....	0	0	7	2	9

T A B L E   X I I.

SHOWING HOW LONG THOSE WHO WERE DISCHARGED, INDENTURED, ESCAPED,
AND DIED, HAD BEEN IN THE INSTITUTION.

TIME.	PAST YEAR.		PREVIOUSLY.		TOTAL,
	Boys.	Girls.	Boys.	Girls.	
One month or less............	2	0	17	9	28
Two months	1	0	8	4	13
Three months....	0	0	9	3	12
Four months.................	3	0	10	0	13
Five months.......	0	0	11	0	11
Six months	4	1	12	1	18
Seven months................	1	0	7	0	8
Eight months	1	0	3	2	6
Nine months.................	1	0	6	1	8
Ten months..................	1	1	7	3	12
Eleven months...............	0	0	3	1	4
Twelve months...............	1	0	3	5	9
Thirteen months	1	0	6	3	10
Fourteen months.............	2	0	10	0	12
Fifteen months...............	0	4	7	1	12
Sixteen months...............	1	0	9	2	12
Seventeen months............	0	0	5	1	6
Carried forward........	19	6	132	36	194

21

TABLE XII—Concluded.

Time.	Past Year.		Previously.		Total.
	Boys.	Girls.	Boys.	Girls.	
Brought forward...........	19	6	132	36	194
Eighteen months............ ...	0	2	4	1	7
Nineteen months......	0	0	4	0	4
Twenty months................	0	1	0	0	1
Twenty-one months............	0	0	3	1	4
Twenty-two months...........*	0	0	2	0	2
Twenty-three months.......,....	0	0	4	0	4
Twenty-four months..........	0	5	4	5	14
Twenty-five months...........	1	0	3	0	4
Twenty-six months............	0	0	2	1	3
Twenty-seven months.........	1	0	2	1	4
Twenty-eight months..........	0	1	3	0	4
Twenty-nine months..........	0	0	3	0	3
Thirty months	1	0	1	0	2
Thirty-one months............	0	1	3	0	4
Thirty-two months............	1	0	3	0	4
Thirty-three months...........	0	0	3	0	3
Thirty-four months...........	1	2	2	1	6
Thirty-five months............	2	1	1	0	4
Thirty-six months............	0	1	1	1	3
Thirty-seven months..........	0	0	1	0	1
Thirty-eight months..........	1	0	1	0	2
Thirty-nine months...........	1	0	2	0	3
Forty months.................	2	0	2	0	4
Forty-one months.............	0	1	0	0	1
Forty-two months.............	2	0	0	0	2
Forty-four months............	1	0	1	0	2
Forty-five months............	1	0	1	0	2
Forty-six months.............	0	0	1	0	1
Forty-seven months...........	1	0	0	0	1
Forty -eight months...........	2	0	2	0	4
Fifty months.................	2	0	2	0	4
Fifty one months..	1	0	1	0	2
Fifty five months....	1	0	0	0	1
Fifty-six months..........	1	0	0	0	1
Fifty-seven months...........	2	0	1	0	3
Sixty months.................	1	0	2	0	3
Sixty-one months.............	1	1	0	0	2
Sixty-two months.............	0	0	1	0	1
Sixty-three months	1	0	0	0	1
Sixty-four months............	0	0	1	0	1
Sixty-six months	1	0	0	0	1
Sixty-seven months...........	1	0	1	0	2
Ninety months...............	1	0	0	0	1
Ninety-one months...........	1	0	0	0	1
Ninety-two months...........	1	0	0	0	1
Totals....................	52	22	201	47	322

TABLE XIII.

SHOWING THE WEEKLY REPORT OF THE NUMBER OF CHILDREN IN THE IN-
STITUTION, WITH THE AVERAGE NUMBER FOR THE FISCAL YEAR ENDING
JUNE 6, 1867.

Date.	Boys.	Girls.	Total.	Date.	Boys.	Girls.	Total.
June 7, 1866....	128	25	153	December 13, 1866....	161	25	186
June 14, ...	136	27	163	December 20, ...	154	24	178
June 21, ...	142	28	170	December 27, ...	155	24	179
June 28, ...	144	29	173	January 3, 1867....	155	24	179
July 5, ...	143	29	172	January 10, ...	159	23	182
July 12, ...	148	29	177	January 17, ...	159	23	182
July 19, ...	146	28	174	January 24, ...	160	23	183
July 26, ...	147	28	175	January 31, ...	161	23	184
August 2, ...	147	28	175	February 7, ...	162	24	186
August 9, ...	150	28	178	February 14, ...	166	24	190
August 16, ...	148	28	176	February 21, ...	165	24	189
August 23, ...	151	28	179	February 28, ...	164	24	188
August 30, ...	146	28	174	March 7, ...	164	23	187
September 6, ...	149	28	177	March 14, ...	165	23	188
September 13, ...	148	27	175	March 21,·	166	24	190
September 20, ...	151	27	178	March 28, ...	167	24	191
September 27, ...	153	27	180	April 4, ...	164	22	186
October 4, ...	151	27	178	April 11, ...	166	22	188
October 11, ...	155	25	180	April 18, ...	157	21	178
October 18, ...	156	24	180	April 25, ...	163	22	185
October 25, ...	156	24	180	May 2, ...	164	21	185
November 1, ...	155	24	179	May 9, ...	166	21	187
November 8, ...	155	24	179	May 16, ...	166	21	187
November 15, ...	157	24	181	May 23, ...	167	20	187
November 22, ...	158	24	182	May 30, ...	167	20	187
November 29, ...	160	23	183	June 6, ...	168	20	188
December 6, ...	160	25	185				

Yearly average................................180⅔

OBSERVATIONS AND SUGGESTIONS.

Our greatest want is suitable employment for the inmates. The success of the shoe shop warrants the supposition that other trades could
be made beneficial and profitable. It needs no argument to prove that
steady and well directed employment, out of school hours, is essential
to the development of a perfect system of reform. To that end additional buildings will be required. A new wing, extending west from
the south end of the present building, would best answer the requirements, and would afford room for a separate dormitory for the larger
boys, and for a boys' hospital, both of which are much needed.

The boys' playroom is too small, and unless some arrangements can be perfected for a separate room for the smaller boys, it should be enlarged.

Boys from sixteen to twenty years of age, hardened in crime as some of them are, coming here from the seaport towns of the British Isles, and from the larger cities of the Eastern States—sailors and soldiers, who have treasured up all the bad and rejected the good with which experience has made them acquainted, are hopeless subjects for reform until long continued and firm discipline has made them realize that it is their interest to behave themselves. There should be some place for such boys. I am glad to say their number is very few; yet one boy of this class is capable of poisoning the minds of hundreds comparatively innocent. And I would ask, is it right that such boys, I mean the majority of the school, should be contaminated by a few so steeped in crime. These few boys should have a place where there can be more restraint exercised, without curtailing the privileges now enjoyed by the majority. Not the close confinement of the cells, but separate and distinct employment, and separate sleeping departments. With new buildings this should be provided for.

With the greatest economy the institution is showing a great deficiency, growing larger every month, and we must have aid from some quarter before any further improvements can be made.

The fence inclosing the yard is old and unsubstantial. A new one will soon be required, and it should be more suitable to the purpose for which it is intended.

The present condition of the school is encouraging; order and system prevails in all departments. Cases in which any severity of punishment is required rarely occur, and are confined to a small number. The majority of the inmates are improving day by day. They are interested in their books, and are making commendable progress in their studies. There are, of course, exceptions; but that is to be expected. Captain Morrill is at the head of the school department, carrying out to the letter the orders of Colonel Wood, the Superintendent. I will venture to say that no man can make Capt. Morrill's place good; too much cannot be said in his praise; he is always at his post, doing his duty faithfully. I do not speak of this in any way but from the truest feelings, and to do justice to one of the best men who is in the Industrial School Department.

Of the large number to whom leave of absence has been granted during the past year, a few have returned to the school. This is a matter that requires the serious attention of the Board of Managers. The fact that any boys or girls, taken from the School with the endorsement of the Board, are, after a few months' trial, returned as unmanageable, argues a serious fault somewhere; and each case so returned is an argument (and used as such) against the School. Is there care enough exercised in the matter? Does it not sometimes happen that these children are placed with people who think more of their *labor* than their welfare? Are they not sometimes taken too soon from the School? As a rule the boy who begins to reform begins to study, and after being once interested in his books, his conduct improves. Is it advisable, is it just to remove him where his studies are necessarily interrupted, for the purpose of giving him a temporary leave? With those children who go with their parents, and continue at school, the case is different. Reformation is a plant of slow growth, as bad conduct is usually the result of long continued evil associations. So to eradicate bad and inculcate good principles requires time as well as effort. Boys here are *required* to conform to the outward show of goodness, and it frequently happens that very bad boys receive for a limited time excellent per centages for good conduct in School. The argument is, that if held to that course long enough good conduct will become habitual. This is our only hope of effecting any permanent good with boys whose lives have always tended towards the bad. It is evident that discharges and leaves of absence ought to be granted with great care, and never because of the importunities of parents or friends.

There are a great many boys who have left this School completely reformed, and have become ornaments to society, who may to-day bless God for the Industrial School which has placed their feet in the right paths. Many of these boys I see from week to week with bright and happy faces. I saw one boy last week who was reformed at our School. He showed me his bank book that had hundreds of dollars to his credit. Certainly we should all feel greatly encouraged in this great work in which we are all engaged. It is all a labor of love. No more humane work could engage our time than rescuing these youths from crime, degradation, and ruin.

I cannot close this report without making most honorable mention of Col. Wood, our present efficient Superintendent. He has labored most faithfully in the discharge of his duty. His post is not an easy one to fill, yet it has been filled with marked ability. The Industrial School speaks volumes in his praise. With his excellent wife as Matron, it gives a home influence to the whole School. The refining influence of Miss Hutchinson upon the girls has worked the greatest reformation in many of them. The Board cannot appreciate too highly her services.

In conclusion, I would say that the Superintendent, teachers, and other officers seem to have the good of the School at heart, and are laboring harmoniously together for the greatest good.

WM. G. BADGER,

President.

ANNUAL REPORT OF THE AUDITOR, JUNE, 1867.

OFFICE OF THE INDUSTRIAL SCHOOL DEPARTMENT, }
San Francisco, August 1st, 1867.   }

To the Honorable the Board of Supervisors
    Of the City and County of San Francisco—

GENTLEMEN: I beg leave to submit the following Report of the receipts into, and demands on the Treasury, for the year ending June 6th, 1867 :

RECEIPTS IN TREASURY.

Cash on hand June 7th, 1866.............			$676 35
Received from City and County Treasury, amount appropriation of $2,000 per month for twelve months, as authorized by Act approved March 20th, 1866............	$24,000 00		
Received from Bank of California, balance of appropriation of $14,000, made by the State....................$2,000 00			
Less interest............ 8 34			
	1,991 66		
Received for labor of boys...............	106 50		
		26,098 16	
Total receipts....................			$26,774 51

DEMANDS ON THE TREASURY.

Groceries and provisions.......................... $6,712 51
Clothing...   796 48
Furniture..   1,791 20
Improvements and repairs.........................   1,235 62
Farm...   2,421 94
Shoe shop..   183 07
Printing and advertising..........................   188 60
Books and stationery.............................   109 13
Fuel and lights..................................   1,358 40
Salaries... 10,012 67
Miscellaneous....................................   1,803 69

Total demands audited.......................$26,613 31
Cash on hand June 7th, 1867.................   161 20

$26,774 51

Respectfully submitted,

JAS. S. THOMSON,

Sec'y and ex officio Auditor Ind. Sch. Dept.

OFFICERS OF THE INDUSTRIAL SCHOOL DEPARTMENT.

PRESIDENT, 1867–8,

WILLIAM G. BADGER.

VICE PRESIDENT, 1867–8,

JÁCOB DEETH.

MANAGERS, 1867–8,

WILLIAM H. L. BARNES,   BENJAMIN D. DEAN, M.D.,
EDWARD BOSQUI,   LEONARD W. KENNEDY,
HENRY L. DAVIS,   MORITZ MAYBLUM.

MANAGERS, 1867–9.

CHARLES D. CARTER,   JAMES R. KELLY,
HENRY A. COBB,   EDWARD MARTIN,
ALFRED F. DURNEY,   RICHARD O'NEILL.

APPOINTED FROM BOARD OF SUPERVISORS,

WILLIAM S. PHELPS,   MONROE ASHBURY, EDWARD FLAHERTY.

TREASURER,

JOHN ARCHBALD.

SECRETARY,

JAMES S. THOMSON.

OFFICERS AND EMPLOYEES OF THE INDUSTRIAL SCHOOL.

SUPERINTENDENT,

JOSEPH WOOD.

PRINCIPAL TEACHER AND DEPUTY SUPERINTENDENT,

JOSEPH C. MORRILL.

MATRON,

MRS. R. A. WOOD.

First Assistant Teacher...............WILLIAM D. WALKER.

Second Assistant Teacher.............JOHN C. SHIPLEY.

Farmer.............................OSCAR TRAVER.

Assistant Farmer...................DAVIDSON WALLER.

Carpenter.........................'. LABAN PATRIQUIN.

Nurse and Seamstress ....MRS. RUTH THORNTON.

Teacher of Girls....................MISS JANE HUTCHINSON.

Janitor............................WILLIAM HASTY.

Watchman..........................JAMES P. STILL.

Foreman of Shoe Shop...............HENRY HARBOURNE.

Laundryman........................ALSON COOK.

Cook..............................MRS. ADA F. COOK.

Physician.........................BENJAMIN D. DEAN.

ADDRESS OF WILLIAM G. BADGER, PRESIDENT OF THE INDUSTRIAL SCHOOL
DEPARTMENT, AT THE CELEBRATION OF THE EIGHTH ANNIVERSARY OF
THE INSTITUTION, MAY 18TH, 1867.

Another revolving year has convened us to celebrate the eighth anniversary
of this Institution, and as this may be the last occasion on which I shall have
the privilege to address you as the President of the Industrial School Department, I beg leave to say, in all sincerity, that among all the public enterprises
in which I have been engaged, none has addressed itself to my sympathies
with greater effect, or awakened in my heart more pleasant memories, than this
Institution.

It is not only our duty, but our high privilege, to foster and encourage public
charities of all kinds; but a man of proper instincts can have no higher or
nobler aim in life, than to aid, in whatever way he can, to rescue from vice
and crime poor, feeble, unprotected children.

Industrial schools for the reformation of juvenile offenders are the offspring
of modern civilization. In the olden time an idle, dissolute boy or girl was
either left to follow without restraint the broad road to ruin, or was subjected
to brutal and degrading punishment. The punishment for trivial offenses was
confinement in jails and station houses, amid thieves and felons; and for graver
offenses they were incarcerated in State Prisons, amongst murderers, burglars
and robbers. In all the whole machinery of society nothing was more horrible
than this exposure of children of tender age to the degrading and brutalizing
influences of such associations as those. In the light of modern civilization
we look back upon those things with utter amazement and inexpressible
horror. We can scarcely realize how it was that men, wise law-makers, intelligent and humane, could have failed to perceive that this mode of punishment, instead of suppressing vice and crime, tended only to foster and develop
them. It degraded and brutalized the youth of the country, and speedily
hardened its victims into thorough ruffians and irredeemable criminals. They
entered the prisons comparatively innocent of any deliberate crime, but they
came out of them with all the wicked arts and practical skill of the most
adroit thieves, and without any incentive to reformation. Youthful innocence
had no longer any charms for those who had thus grown prematurely old in
vice; and they entered upon life with no accomplishments except those of the
skillful felon, and with no hope in the future except to evade the demands of
justice. But finally a new light dawned upon the minds of the law-makers.
It occurred to some noble minds that instead of punishing children in this
brutal manner for trivial offenses, it would be far better to snatch them away
from evil associations, and by considerate kindness, gentle admonition, and
parental care, win them from vicious courses, whilst their intellects were ex-
panded by education and habits of industry were inculcated. The establishment
of such institutions as this was the happy result of this heaven-born idea ; and
thousands of respectable and prosperous men and women, who have been thus
rescued from vice and crime, do this day attest their gratitude to the founders
of such institutions as this.

No city in the world needs such an institution as much as San Francisco, where the temptations to vice are great, and where many hundreds of young children are annually cast upon our shores, bereft of home influences, practically abandoned by their parents, and turned into the streets as vagabonds and outcasts.

The humble part which I have taken in building up and fostering this institution will always be a source of profound gratification to me, and if I have been instrumental in rescuing but one helpless outcast child from vice and crime, I shall feel I have not lived in vain.

And now I wish to address to you, my young friends, the pupils of the school, a few words on parting. My intercourse with you has been most agreeable, and I shall not cease to feel a profound interest in your future welfare. I shall watch over your future career with a parental solicitude, and I hope to see you, a few years hence, grown up to be honorable and respected men and women, getting high positions in society, and earning a living in the various walks of life by honest industry, and, above all, thorough integrity and truthfulness. I beg you to remember that there is but one course to success in life, and that is constant industry and perfect honesty of conduct. Avoid idleness and evil associates as you would fly from a pestilence. When you leave this school, if troubles should beset you, seek advice from the managers of this institution, who will at all times be your friends ; but in whatever circumstances you are placed, scorn to do a dishonest act. Suffer any privation and want, sooner than tarnish your good name and offend your conscience by dishonorable conduct. Act upon these principles, and your success in life is certain. You will increase daily in the esteem and confidence of your acquaintances, and in your future lives you will pour out grateful thanks to God, that He has blessed you with kind friends who have snatched you away from temptation and vice, and guided your youthful feet into the paths of peace and honor.

I bid you all a most affectionate farewell, and invoke the blessings of divine Providence on each one of you.

LICENSE COLLECTOR'S REPORT.

OFFICE OF THE COLLECTOR OF LICENSES, {
San Francisco, July 20, 1867.

To the Honorable the Board of Supervisors
Of the City and County of San Francisco—

GENTLEMEN : In compliance with Resolution No. 6,963, passed by your Honorable Body June 18, 1867, I respectfully submit the following Report of Quarterly and Annual Municipal Licenses sold during the Fiscal Year ending June 30, 1867.

Very respectfully,

E. P. BUCKLEY,

Collector of Licenses.

GENERAL FUND.

Quarterly Licenses.

4 Races	$75 00
8 Expresses	112 50
30 Laundries	114 00
15 Shipping Offices	140 00
23 Runners and Soliciting Agents	165 00
32 Street Musicians	265 00
28 Assayers	280 00
95 Real Estate and House Brokers	355 00
Carried forward	$1,506 50

Brought forward.	$1,506 50
53 Powder and Pyrotechnics	510 00
31 Pawnbrokers....................	1,085 00
29 Merchandise Peddlers	1,225 00
122 Slaughter Houses	1,359 65
570 Market Stalls..................	1,417 50
137 Dances	1,697 50
1,014 Meat Shops and Bakeries	2,190 65
1,085 Hotels, Restaurants, and Lodging Houses	2,204 75
783 Meat, Fish, and Produce Peddlers..	8,776 25

$21,972 80

4,059

STREET DEPARTMENT FUND.

Annual Licenses.

100 Laundry Wagons, Sprinklers, and Handcarts	111 75
129 Licensed Drivers................	129 00
207 Pair of new Numbers, for Vehicles..	207 00
146 Coaches, Hacks, Omnibuses, and Coupés	821 50
324 Double Wagons and Trucks	984 75
826 Grocery, Milk, Baker, and Market Wagons....................	1,002 25
1,840 Single Wagons, Trucks, Drays, and Carts	3,016 00
272 Street Railroad Cars (paid quarterly)	3,525 00

9,797 25

3,844

Total amount $31,770 05

PUBLIC ADMINISTRATOR'S REPORT.

OFFICE OF THE PUBLIC ADMINISTRATOR, }
San Francisco July 1, 1867. }

To the Honorable the President and Board of Supervisors
Of the City and County of San Francisco,

GENTLEMEN :   Herewith I submit a Report of my operations as
Public Administrator, showing the names of all estates administered
by me, the value of property belonging thereto, and the amount of
expenditures, from the commencement of my term of office to and including June 30, 1867.

Respectfully Yours,

WM. A. QUARLES, ,

Public Administrator.

ESTATES ADMINISTERED UPON.

Estate of William Shanahan.
   Letters of Administration issued December 22, 1866.
   Total value of Estate...... .... $617 00
   Expenditures by Administrator 304 76

Estate of John Thomas.
   Letters of Administration issued January 7, 1867.
   Total value of Estate......................... $250 00
   Expenditures by Administrator 25 00

Estate of George C. Petersen.
   Letters of Administration issued January 19, 1867.
   Total value of Estate.......................... $345 02
   Expenditures by Administrator 138 40

Estate of James McKnight.
   Letters of Administration issued January 15, 1867.
   Total value of Estate.......................... $22 00
   Expenditures 22 00

Estate of Samuel H. Parker.
   Letters of Administration issued January 8, 1867.
   Total value of Estate, real and personal..........$24,152 76
   Expenditures by Administrator.................. 2,810 60

Estate of Ellen O'Connell.
   Letters of Administration issued January 19, 1867.
   Total value of Estate.......................... $622 26
   Expenditures by Administrator 424 00

Estate of George Fitzgerald.
   Letters of Administration issued February 9, 1867.
   Total value of Estate.......................... $609 28
   Expenditures by Administrator 296 50

Estate of O. W. Heurlin.
   Administration commenced January 19, 1867.
   Total value of Estate.......................... $188 30
   Expenditures by Administrator 89 00

Estate of Noah Ripley.
Letters of Administration issued February 8, 1867.
Total value of Estate.......................... $3,000 00
Expenditures 50 00
The property of this Estate has not come to the possession of the
Administrator.

Estate of William Johnson.
Letters of Administration issued February 9, 1867.
Total value of Estate.......................... $230 00
Expenditures by Administrator.................. 125 56

Estate of Henry Mollenhauer.
Letters of Administration issued February 12, 1867.
Total value of Estate remaining not ascertained.
Expenditures by Administrator.................. $154 12
Only partial Administration is had of this Estate for the purpose
of closing the same. Administration at request of widow.

Estate of Hiram Hurlbut.
Partial Administration for the purpose of distributing the Estate.
Total value of Estate in legal tenders............. $4,800 00
Expenditures by Administrator.................. 117 00

Estate of James E. Reas.
Letters of Administration issued February 26, 1867.
Total value of Estate.......................... $250 00
Expenditures by Administrator.................. 40 00

Estate of George H. Riddell.
Letters of Administration issued February 26, 1867.
Total value of Estate.......................... $5,010 50
Expenditures by Administrator.................. 542 20

Estate of Caroline Huebner.
Letters of Administration issued February 26, 1867.
Total value of Estate.......................... $1,348 12
Expenditures by Administrator 157 00

Estate of Michael McGinnity.
Letters of Administration issued March 12, 1867.
Total value of Estate.......................... $5,489 62
Expenditures by Administrator 505 00

Estate of Wm. J. Dodge.
Letters of Administration issued March 16, 1867.
No property or money received by Administrator.
Expenditures by Administrator $2 00

Estate of J. L. McLean.
Administration commenced March 14, 1867.
Total value of Estate.......................... $192 35
Expenditures by Administrator 117 00

Estate of Charles Mitchell.
Letters of Administration issued April 10, 1867.
Total value of Estate.......................... $1,957 53
Expenditures by Administrator 791 53

Estate of Henry S. Magraw.
Letters of Administration issued March 14, 1867.
No property received.
Expenditures by Administrator $25 00

Estate of Ludwig Igel.
  Letters of Administration issued April 10, 1867.
    Total value of Estate............................ $1,238 50
    Expenditures by Administrator 196 25

Estate of Anthony Gifford.
  Letters of Administration issued April 10, 1867.
  No property received.
    Expenditures by Administrator $13 50

Estate of B. A. Holgel.
  Letters of Administration issued April 11, 1867.
    Total value of Estate.......................... $83 98
    Expenditures by Administrator.................. 83 98

Estate of Patrick Donohoe.
  Letters of Administration issued April 10, 1867.
    Total value of Estate.......................... $283 79
    Expenditures by Administrator 70 21

Estate of Charles E. Rowan.
  Letters of Administration issued April 18, 1867.
    Total value of Estate.......................... $243 00
    Expenditures by Administrator 41 00

Estate of Thomas R. Hope.
  Letters of Administration issued May 6, 1867.
  Value of Estate not ascertained.
    Expenditures by Administrator $15 50

22

Estate of Henry C. Cornish.
Letters of Administration issued May 13, 1867.
Total value of Estate........................... $461 75
Expenditures by Administrator 218 50

———

Estate of Peter Longworth.
Letters of Administration issued May 6, 1867.
Total value of Estate........................... $5,093 00
Expenditures by Administrator.................. 415 00

———

Estate of B. W. Hathaway:
Letters issued June 3, 1867.
Total value of Estate........................... $1,333 78
Expenditures by Administrator 788 80

———

Estate of H. Gariety.
Administration commenced June 13, 1867.
Total value of Estate........................... $54 00
Expenditures by Administrator 10 00

All of which is respectfully submitted.

WM. A. QUARLES,

Public Administrator.

POUND MASTER'S REPORT.

POUND MASTER'S OFFICE,
San Francisco, July 31st, 1867.

To the Honorable the Board of Supervisors
Of the City and County of San Francisco—

GENTLEMEN : In compliance with Resolution No. 6,963, I herewith submit to you the following statements of the Public Pound, from July 1st, 1866, to June 30th, 1867 :

July, 1866.	$24 00
August.	22 00
September	18 00
October.	44 00
November.	27 00
December.	39 00
Jannary, 1867.	26 00
February.	22 00
March.	39 00
April.	48 00
May.	158 00
June.	23 00

Total receipts from July 1, 1866, to June 30, 1867... $490 00

REPORT OF THE DOG POUND.

I herewith submit to you the report of the Dog Pound, from July 1st, 1866, to June 30th, 1867.

MONTHS.	Impounded.	Redeemed.	Killed.	Cash Received.
July, 1866:	192	15	177	$ 75 00
August	399	21	378	105 00
September	240	15	225	75 00
October	403	23	380	115 00
November	337	24	313	120 00
December	204	12	192	60 00
January, 1867	344	17	327	85 00
February	287	15	272	75 00
March	393	31	362	155 00
April	287	23	264	115 00
May	251	22	229	110 00
June	238	. 20	218	100 00
Totals	3,575	238	3,337	$1,190 00

JOHN SHORT, JR.,

Pound Keeper.

REPORT

OF THE

SUPERINTENDENT OF PUBLIC SCHOOLS.

Office of Superintendent of Public Schools, ⎫
San Francisco, October 15th, 1867. ⎭

To the Honorable the Board of Supervisors
Of the City and County of San Francisco—

Gentlemen :—In obedience to law and custom, I herewith submit for the information of your Honorable Body and the public generally, the Annual Report of the Public School Department of San Francisco for the fiscal year 1866–7. This report also represents the eighteenth year since the inauguration of free schools on the Pacific Coast. It gives me pleasure to say, that no similar period in the history of our city schools has witnessed a greater degree of general prosperity than has the past year. During no period has so much been done, as during the past and preceding years, to increase the accommodations of the School Department of San Francisco, and to extend the benefits of our common school system. This will at once be apparent on examination of the following table.

...NGS ERECTED BY THE BOARD OF EDUCATION, FROM JULY 1, 1865, TO JULY 24, 1867.

Location	Materials used	Date of Contract	Architect	Character of Building	No. of Classes	Gr'm	Pr'm	Contract price of Building	Cost per class-room	Cost per seat
		1865								
...y Addition... Grove street, bet. Larkin and Polk	Wood	July 13	Wm. Craine	Primary	2		120	$2,590	$1,290 00	$21 61
...eet... Pine, bet. Scott and Devisadero	Wood	Aug. 2	Wm. Craine	Primary	1		75	1,863		24 82
...mount... Corner of Cheney and Randall sts	Wood	Aug. 4	Wm. Craine	Primary	1		75	1,944		25 80
Spring Valley Broadway, bet. Polk and Larkin	Wood	Sept. 30	S. C. Bugbee	Grammar	4	240		7,800	1,950 00	32 50
		1866								
Market Street Primary Corner of Fifth and Market	Wood	May 29	S. C. Bugbee	Primary	12		720	5,744	478 66	7 97
Tehama Tehama, bet. First and Second	Brick	June 30	S. C. Bugbee	Primary	17		1020	25,850	1,520 58	25 33

PUBLIC SCHOOL BUILDINGS ERECTED BY THE BOARD OF EDUCATION, FROM JULY 1, 1866, TO JULY 24, 1867.

Location	Materials used	Date of Contract	Architect	Character of Building	No. of Classes	Gr'm	Pr'm	Contract price of Building	Cost per class-room	Cost per seat
Synagogue Broadway, bet. Powell and Mason	Brick	Aug. 31	Wm. Patton	Primary	12		720	12,910	1,075 83	17 93
Spring alley Addition Broadway, bet. Polk and Larkin	Wood	Oct. 15	S. C. Bugbee & Son	Primary	4		240	4,975	1,243 75	20 71
Filbert st. Filbert, bet. Jones and ...	Wood	Oct. 26	Wm. Patton	Bay...	11		660	16,000	1,500 00	25 00
Union Alteration Union, bet. Kearny and Dupont	Brick	Dec. 3	Wm. ...e	Bar...	2	120		1,811	905 50	15 08
		1867								
Post street (Cohn Building) Post, bet. ...	Brick	Jan. 10	Patton	Gram. & Prim.	15	360	540	13,227	881 80	14 70
...er Building Shotwell, bet. 22d and 23d	Wood	Mar. 26	Bee & Son	Gam. & Prim.	8	240	240	8,000	1,000 00	16 66
Fifth St. Building ...th, bet. Harrison and Bryant	Wood	April 8	S. C. Bugbee & Son	Primary	8		480	8,000	1,000 00	16 66
Pine and Larkin streets SW. ...ner of Pine and Larkin	Wood	April 9	S. C. Bugbee & Son	Primary	8		480	8,000	1,000 00	16 66
Filbert and Kearny NW. ...er of Filbert and Kearny	Wood	April 25	S. C. Bugbee & Son	Primary	8		480	8,000	1,000 00	16 66
State Normal School Addition ...et, bet. Fourth and Fifth	Wood	Mar. 14	S. C. Bugbee & Son	Primary	4		240	2,700	675 00	11 25
West End ...r, bet. Scott and Devisadero	Wood	July 22	S. C. Bugbee & Son	Primary	1		75	1,585		21 13
Tyler street	Wood	Jly 24	S. C. Bugbee & Son	Primary	4		240	4,370	1,092 00	18 30
					122	960	6405	$135,868		

Total number of classrooms provided in new buildings, 122; total number of seats, 7,365, at a total cost of $135,868, exclusive of valuation of Post street Synagogue Buildings, purchased by the Board of Education, and afterwards enlarged and improved; also exclusive of extras. These forenamed items added would increase the total cost of above buildings to about $158,398, and increase the cost per seat to about $21 37.

* Erected from the current School Fund.   † Full capacity, without reference to the present number of pupils.

The economy displayed by the Board of Education in the erection of school buildings, during the past year and a half, must receive the unqualified approbation of all who have desired to see the greatest practical good secured to the greatest possible number of our children and youth, by the judicious application of the funds placed at their disposal.

One hundred and fifty-eight thousand three hundred and ninety-eight dollars ($158,398) have provided comfortable and very respectable accommodations for seven thousand three hundred and sixty-five pupils, being a greater number than the total number of pupils accommodated in all the school houses erected by the Board of Education from the organization of the Public Schools, in 1849–50, to the commencement of the improvements embraced in this report; and which, though for the most part economical buildings, had cost the city over $300,000. The wisdom of procuring the recent issue of bonds, for the purpose of placing our schools in buildings belonging to the city, instead of continuing to rent therefor extemporized school houses and detached class-rooms, inconvenient and unsuitable, requiring constant alterations and repairs, will be apparent upon a very slight examination of the subject. Soon after the organization of the schools, at the commencement of last school and fiscal year (1865–66), the School Department was renting 43 class-rooms, and paying therefor monthly $1,350 and within these rented rooms there were 2,720 pupils, or about one-third of all the scholars in the Department. Subsequently, at different periods, as demands arose, we were compelled to organize some thirty additional classes. Had we continued to rent rooms for these seventy or more classes, and in this way meet the increasing demands on the Department for school accommodations, our rents and repairs would now amount to not less than $36,000 per annum—a sum equal to more than two per cent. per month on the building disbursements of our Board, which have secured to the city the superior accommodations now enjoyed by nearly all our schools. Our rents, which, near the beginning of last year, were, as stated, $1,350 monthly, will soon nearly cease. Our actual saving, by the erection of new buildings, during the past thirteen months, amounts to about $6,000; but the saving of money and other immense benefits resulting from our improvements (which benefits can only be duly appreciated by those familiar with the circumstances of the Department heretofore and at present), will be experienced hereafter.

The general condition of the city schools is such as should give great satisfaction to their patrons and to those who labor in and for them, as well as to those who are taxed for their support.

It may be safely asserted, that at no period in the history of our city have the Public Schools exhibited a higher degree of efficiency, or enjoyed more popular favor and confidence ; nor has there ever been manifested in the community at large a more lively interest in the cause of public education, and in the integrity, welfare and permanence of our school system. Never before have the Public Schools received so generally the patronage of all classes of the community, especially that of the more intelligent of our citizens ; and the business of our Department, the conduct of the Board of Education in the management of its affairs, the character of school officers and that of teachers, the condition and efficiency of the schools, and the merits of our public school system, never before received so much attention from the press and from citizens. And, although criticism has sometimes lacked intelligence and candor, we should not and do not complain, for we regard all as auspicious of good results ; for such criticisms, though ungenerous and sometimes unjust, serve to increase the watchfulness and fidelity of those who have charge of our schools, and thus tend to insure the success and integrity of our free school system itself.

It may with truth be said that our schools have become popularized—have become the institutions of the people, in which every class of society is represented, and every interest subserved ; in which all justly feel that they have a direct and vital interest. This is a most gratifying condition of public sentiment—this general interest and good will for our schools which we everywhere remark. To help to call into existence the active sympathy of our people, with and for. our Public Schools, has been to accomplish a great and noble work ; a work of primary importance and of the most vital consequence to the future welfare of the schools, and of the city itself; and for this, at least for most that has been accomplished which reflects so much credit upon the Department and upon our city, we are chiefly indebted to an intelligent, conscientious and ever vigilant corps. of teachers, male and female. In this respect, never has a city been more fortunate than ours, from the organization of our schools to the present time, and during no previous year in our history more fortunate than during the past. Our teachers from abroad have generally been found well educated and competent, and devoted to their profession. Those more recently employed, who have been educated in our own schools—in our High Schools and Normal School—have proved zealous, industrious and faithful; those from the Normal School especially ambitious and successful. In charge of such a corps of teachers, Public Schools can but be successful. They are sure of meeting with just appreciation of patrons and citizens generally; certain of enjoying that generous approval, liberal support and popular favor which will render them ornaments to the city, a blessing to our present society, and a boon of incalculable value to the moral welfare and intelligence, and also the material interests of that vast multitude which a few brief years hence will constitute the society of San Francisco. It remains for the future laborers in our good cause to foster this important interest and advance our Department to still better results and higher achievements. As a means to this end, the community should be kept constantly informed of the actual condition of our schools; of their improvement and general progress; of their present necessities and prospective wants. Few of our people, however intelligent and well informed in relation to the general affairs of the city, fully comprehend the present magnitude of our Public School Department, or appreciate the interests which it involves and the duties it imposes upon its patrons, the friends of education, and the people at large. The rapid growth of the city during the past eighteen years of its Americanized history is scarcely realized by those who have been its constant residents; but when comprehended, though faintly, is justly regarded with wonder; but the rapid increase of our Public School children, especially during the past few years, is even more astonishing. Eighteen years ago the present month (October) I arrived in this city and commenced to form the nucleus of our present School Department.* Then, a few warehouses, scattered along a

---

* The following notice I then addressed to the people of San Francisco, announcing the object with which I came to California:

TO THE CITIZENS OF SAN FRANCISCO.

The subscriber proposes to establish in San Francisco a Free Public School.

In order that the school may be free to all who may be disposed to avail themselves of its privileges, it is proposed to admit free of tuition all who may apply; no other compensation being required at present than what the friends of the school and the public generally may be disposed to contribute.

It is also proposed, until better arrangements can be made, that the school consist of

narrow beach, a score or two of diminutive and hastily constructed dwellings, and a hundred or two improvised tents, clustering in the background and dotting the various hill-sides, constituted *San Francisco*. Within its undefined, uncertain limits, there were no schools and but few children. Creditable to the then little town, and fortunate for my purpose, there were churches, in one of which, a little board and cloth building, was soon gathered a public school, having on the first day of its organization three pupils.

---

children and youth of both sexes and of the different ages that usually attend primary and more advanced schools, and that the course of study include those English branches taught in the Public Schools of New England.

The Baptist Chapel, situated on Washington Street, has been generously tendered, and a sufficient sum guaranteed to conveniently fit the same for the uses of the proposed school.

The school will commence on Wednesday the 26th inst.

Before leaving the States, the subscriber procured, at an expense of much time and pains, an ample supply of the most approved school books, with which those pupils who wish can be supplied at the school room.

The subscriber is permitted to refer to Mr. F. P. Fitts, Mr. Wm. W. Gallaer, Mr. Wm. Hooper, and the Rev. Mr. Wheeler.

The names of the Trustees will appear in a subsequent number of this paper.

J. C. PELTON.

On the day announced, I organized the proposed school with three pupils, sustaining it chiefly with my own means until March following, when the action of the City Council, embraced in the resolution following, temporarily relieved me from its support :

In meeting of Ayuntamiento, March 29th, 1850, it was, on motion of Mr. Green,

Resolved, That from the first day of April, A. D. 1850, John C. Pelton, and Mrs. Pelton his wife, be employed as teachers for the Public School in the Baptist Church, which has been offered to the Council free of charge, and that the average number of scholars shall not exceed one hundred ; and that they shall be entitled to a monthly salary, during the pleasure of the Council, of five hundred dollars per month, payable each and every month.

The school became now permanently organized, and provided for by the following action of the city, April 8, 1850 :

AN ORDINANCE FOR THE REGULATION AND SUPPORT OF COMMON SCHOOLS.

1st. Be it ordained by the Common Council of San Francisco, That from and after the passage of this Act, it shall be the duty of J. C. Pelton, who has been employed by the Council as a public teacher, to open a school in the Baptist Chapel.

2d. Said school shall be opened from half-past 8 A. M. to 12 M., and from 2 P. M. until 5 P. M., and shall continue open from Monday until Friday at 5 o'clock P. M.

3d. The number of scholars shall not exceed the number of one hundred ; and no scholar shall be admitted under the age of four, or over the age of sixteen.

4th. All persons desirous of having their children instructed in said school shall first obtain an order from the Chairman of the Committee on Education, and all children obtaining said order shall be instructed in said school free of charge.

5th. It shall be the duty of said Pelton to report to the Council on the first of each and every month the number of scholars and the progress of said school.

H. C. MURRAY.
F. TILFORD.

Contrast with the above the city of San Francisco and its circumstances of to-day—how changed the picture. San Francisco has become one of the prominent cities of the world; a great vital center, from which no region of earth seems remote, or is not reached by its pulsating life. Stretched far and wide, over an area of several leagues, spread out through broad valleys and clustered upon her seven hills, she is an object of wonder; most remarkable in her growth and history, and probably already more important to the civilization and interests of mankind than is now that great city which was once the proud mistress of the world. In our busy streets throng the jostling multitudes of every clime, Israelite, Christian and Pagan; at every step we meet the representatives of every nation and of every shade of civilization, custom, and taste. And we have here, too, our representative institutions, commercial, literary, social, benevolent, and religious; and second in importance to none of these, we have our thirty-six Public Schools, with their thirteen thousand three hundred and seventy-five pupils. These, better than all things else, and more truly, represent the public spirit and intelligence of our community; and thus, these argue most favorably for the future character of our people and the permanence of our prosperity.

How much of encouragement to all friends of true progress do we find in the present magnitude of our School Department, and the efficient condition of our Public Schools; how much to stimulate to renewed exertion and bolder effort in behalf of popular education of a still higher standard! But the limits of a report like this are intended more especially to embrace financial and miscellaneous statistics, exhibiting the condition and cost of the schools, and the practical details of our Department. The annexed statistical tables and financial memoranda will, I trust, also be read and examined with interest.

The following tabular exhibit shows a great deal in a very small space, and if carefully examined gives a good idea of what now constitutes the

PUBLIC SCHOOL DEPARTMENT OF SAN FRANCISCO.

GENERAL STATISTICS OF PUBLIC SCHOOLS OF SAN FRANCISCO, AS ORGANIZED NOV. 1, 1867.

Name and Character.	Location of Schools.	Character of Building.	Cost of Building.	Ownership ..	When erected	Size of Lot.	Size of Building exclusive of the wings.	No. of Stories.......	No. of Rooms	No. of pupils in attendance	No. Teachers	Cost of Instruction per pupil, mon'ly
HIGH SCHOOLS.												
Boys' High School..........	Powell, near Clay..................	Brick & Wood	$14,487 00	City...	1860	69¾x127½	32 x 88	2	5	78	4	$8 12
Girls' High School..........	Corner of Bush and Stockton........	Brick	11,300 00	City...	1854	137½x137½	30 x 70	2	4	116	5	5 02
San Francisco Latin School.	Corner of Second and Bryant........	Wood	....	Rented	.....	....	....	....	3	42	2	5 35
TRAINING SCHOOLS.												
Normal Training Schools ...	Market, near Fifth.................	Wood	12,499 00	City...	.....	100 x190	50 x 50 } 50 x 70 }	2	6	264	3	98
City Training School	Corner of Bush and Stockton........	Wood	....	City...	§1867	....	....	2	6	204	4	1 06
GRAMMAR SCHOOLS.												
*Lincoln	Fifth, near Market.................	Brick	93,940 00	City...	1865	190 x175	63½x141½	3	19	1026	19	1 45
*Denman	Corner of Bush and Taylor..........	Brick	52,864 35	City...	1864	137½x137½	61 x 98⅓	3	15	779	15	1 49
*Union	Union, near Montgomery	Brick	33,321 00	City...	1854	137½x137½	46 x 99	2	11	448	10	1 94
*Rincon	Vassar Place, Harrison near Second .	Wood	10,566 00	City...	1861	100 x180	50 x 50	3	10	605	11	1 40
Washington	Corner of Mason and Washington ...	Wood	17,117 00	City...	1861	137½x137½	62½x 81¼	2	7	380	8	1 95
*Mission..................	Mission, bet. Fifteenth and Sixt'nth.	Wood	11,383 00	City...	1860	200 x182	61⅔x 62¼	2	7	484	9	1 57
*Spring Valley	Broadway, bet. Larkin and Polk.....	Wood	13,423 00	City...	1866	137½x137½ Including Prmy	60 x 86	2	8	593	10	1 29
South Cosmopolitan	Post, bet. Dupont and Stockton.....	Brick	†12,000 00	City...	1866	68¾x122½	36 x 70	2	8	405	8	1 64
*Shotwell	Shotwell, bet. 22d and 23d	Wood	8,000 00	City...	1867	122½x122½	50 x 76	2	8	324	7	1 53
*North Cosmopolitan.......	Filbert, near Jones	Wood	16,500 00	City...	1867	100 x120	49 x 71	3	11	639	12	1 35
PRIMARY SCHOOLS.												
Tehama	Tehama, near First................	Brick	27,910 00	City...	1866	90 x175 } 28 x 75 }	52 x 75	2	17	1041	17	1 10
Lincoln	Corner of Fifth and Market.........	Wood	6,000 00	City...	1866	....	58¼x170-7	1	12	817	13	1 13
Broadway	Broadway, bet. Powell and Mason...	Brick	‡12,000 00	City...	1866	65-2x137½	....	3	12	613	12	1 26
Cosmopolitan (includi'grented rooms on St. Marks Pl.)	Post. bet. Dupont and Stockton.....	Brick	8,043 00	City...	1866	....	57 x 37	2	12	682	12	1 11
Fourth Street	Corner of Fourth and Harrison......	Wood	5,190 00	City...	1863	80 x125	30 x 72	2	10	616	11	1 23
Eighth Street..............	Eighth, bet. Harrison and Bryant ...	Wood	8,000 00	City...	1867	115 x275	50 x 76	2	8	435	8	1 12
Filbert and Kearny	Northwest corner Filbert and Kearny	Wood	8,000 00	City...	1867	137½x137½	50 x 76	2	8	551	7	88
Pine and Larkin............	Southwest corner of Pine and Larkin	Wood	8,000 00	City...	1867	200 x120	50 x 76	2	8	437	7	1 11

School	Location	Material	Cost	Owned	Built	Size of lot	Size of building			No.		Rate
Powell Street	Powell, bet. Washington and Jackson	Wood	3,185 00	City...	1851	68¾x137½	27 x 80½	2	8	493	8	1 08
Hayes Valley	Grove, bet. Larkin and Polk	Wood	6,808 00	City...	1862	137½x120	55½x 61½	1	4	272	5	1 17
Tyler Street	Tyler, bet. Pierce and Scott	Wood	4,370 00	‡	1867	100 x137½	50 x 70	1	4	45	1	1 55
Bryant Street	Bryant, near Third	Wood		Rented...					4	235	4	1 10
San Bruno	San Bruno Road, near Toll Gate	Wood	3,517 00	City...	1864	100 x200	29½x 46	1	1	77	1	97
Fairmount	Fairmount Tract	Wood	2,698 00	City...	1865	150 x125	29½x 46	1	1	30	1	2 33
West End	Near Six Mile House	Wood	1,585 00	City...	1867	80 x168 / 82 x150	35 x 24	1	1	32	1	2 34
Potrero	Corner of Kentucky and Napa	Wood	2,180 15	City...	1865	200 x100	29½x 46	1	1	85	2	1 47
Pine	Pine, near Scott	Wood	2,167 84	City...	1865	137½x137½	29½x 46	1	1	74	2	1 70
Ocean House	Near Ocean House	Wood		Rented						21	1	3 43
Drumm Street	Corner of Drumm and Sacramento	Wood		Rented						120	2	-1 08
Colored School	Broadway, bet. Powell and Mason	Wood	4,435 00	§	1861	69¾x 91½	30¼x 75½	1	1	117	2	1 43
||Hyde Street	Corner of Hyde and Bush	Wood	3,700 00	City...	1857	97½x137½	37 x 97	1	4			

EVENING SCHOOLS.

Corner of Fifth and Market streets (Lincoln Building), two classes										132	2	83
Post street, between Dupont and Stockton (Cosmopolitan Building), one class (foreign)										40	1	25
Broadway, between Powell and Mason (Broadway Primary Building), one class										60	1	83
Corner of Bush and Stockton (Girls' High School Building), one class (female)										30	1	66
Broadway, near Powell, one class (colored)										271	1	85

* Including Primary Department.

† For new improvement of old building, and erection of a new Primary, and exclusive of cost of ground and old building. Present valuation of ground and improvements, $35,000.

‡ Alteration and improvement of old building, and exclusive of cost of lot and old building. Present valuation of ground and improvements, $35,000.

§ Established.

|| Vacant at present.

FINANCIAL.

SCHOOL FUND OF 1866-7—RECEIPTS.

1866—For the first quarter of the fiscal year....... $78,343 30
For the second quarter of the fiscal year.....   169,434 64
For the third quarter of the fiscal year.......   66,045 71
For the fourth quarter of the fiscal year......   6,983 92

Total............................... $320,807 57

DEMANDS UPON THE SCHOOL FUND OF 1866-7.

	First Quarter.	Second Quarter.	Third Quarter.	Fourth Quarter.	TOTAL.
Salaries of Teachers	$52,510 05	$53,353 78	$52,610 67	$51,400 25	$209,874 75
Salaries of Janitors.	4,027 83	4,031 00	3,600 95	3,125 40	14,785 18
Marshals and Insurance..........	750 00	308 88	164 76	75 55	1,299 19
Clerks.............	450 00	450 00	450 00	450 00	1,800 00
Carpenters........	690 85	750 00	750 00	750 00	2,940 85
Lights.............	182 19	214 51	318 87	197 50	913 07
Water.............	81 00	64 00	68 00	69 20	282 20
Furniture.........	1,500 00	1,748 27	3,340 29	474 62	7,301 01
Books and Supplies	1,800 00	1,032 94	1,857 17	162 45	5,476 90
Rents.............	3,906 83	3,760 00	1,952 33	1,414 50	11,033 66
Fuel..............	46 90	1,586 93	1,974 64	51 75	3,660 22
Repairs...........	1,285 57	3,099 42	2,728 26	821 98	7,073 06
Incidentals.......	1,040 00	255 83	504 50	415 00	2,215 33
Imp'ment of Streets	1,199 78	1,391 68	693 63	152 94	3,438 03
Improvem't of Lots	593 35	2,856 71	27 50	470 00	3,947 56
Removal of Legal Incumbrance...	2,250 00	300 00	....	....	2,550 00
Legal Services....	....	....	....	20 00	20 00
Totals......	$72,314 35	$75,203 95	$71,041 57	$60,051 14	$278,611 01

Total demands audited on the School Fund of 1866–7,
less demand of Lemon & Co., for $67 50, canceled $278,543 51
Demands not yet audited.......................   1,000 00
Transfers to Sinking and Interest Funds...........   40,515 37

Total disbursements from the School Fund of 1866–7 $320 058 88

RECAPITULATION.

SCHOOL FUND 1866-7, FOR THE CURRENT SCHOOL YEAR COMMENCING JUNE 30TH, 1866, AND ENDING JUNE 30TH, 1867.

Total receipts into School Fund 1866-67............ $320,807 57

Total disbursements............................ 320,058 88

Balance on hand in School Fund, June 30th, after
    payment of all demands..................... $748 69

PROOF.

Cash on hand, per report of Auditor, June 30, 1867.. $20,990 77

Outstanding audited demands........... $19,241 98

Demands not yet audited.............. 1,000 00

                                                 20,241 98

Balance cash on hand, after payment of demands
    as above............................. $748 69

SPECIAL BUILDING FUND.

STATEMENT OF PROCEEDS OF SCHOOL BONDS AUTHORIZED BY ACT OF MARCH 17TH, 1866.

[Amount of Bonds authorized, $275,000.]

The proceeds from the sale of these Bonds have been as follows :

1866.

June 23.   From sale of 45 Bonds at 81 cents.$36,450 00

June 23.   From sale of 30 Bonds at 82 cents. 24,600 00

                                      $61,050 00

July 31.   From sale of 20 Bonds at 81⅖ cents.$16,325 00

July 31.   From sale of 15 Bonds at 82⅚ cents. 12,393 75

July 31.   From sale of 15 Bonds at 84 cents.. 12,600 00

1867.   41,318 75

Jan. 23.   From sale of 50 Bonds at 83½ cents........ 41,750 00

April.   From sale of 10 Bonds at 86 cents......... 8,600 00

April.   From sale of 40 Bonds at 85¼ cents........ 34,012 50

       Interest on 50 Bonds from January 14th, date
       of bid, to February 18th, date of delivery.. 284 13

Total proceeds of Bonds up to June 30th, 1867. $230,015 38

STATEMENT OF DISBURSEMENT OF PROCEEDS OF SCHOOL BONDS AUTHORIZED
BY ACT OF MARCH 17TH, 1867.

Appropriated for deficiency of 1865–66.....$76,324 55
Appropriated for building expenses of 1865–6   6,138 00
                        —————— $82,454 55
Expended for the erection of school buildings and purchase of school lots from July 1st, 1866, to June 30th,
1867, as follows :

Buildings—

    For Tehama Street, near Second.......$28,324 52
    For Filbert Street, near Jones.......... 17,010 00
    For Broadway Street, near Mason....... 12,470 00
    For Broadway Street, near Polk......... 5,623 24
    For Post Street, near Stockton.......... 16,095 79
    For Eighth Street, near Bryant (part
      payment)....................... 6,185 00
    For Shotwell Street, near Twenty-fourth
      (part payment).................. 6,005 00
    For Union Street, near Montgomery..... 2,370 00
    For Normal School, corner Fifth and
      Market Streets (part payment)...... 1,000 00
    For West End Plans................ 18 00
    For services of architect, $5\frac{1}{10}$ months at $150.
      and one month at $100............ 865 00
                        —————— 95,966 55

Lots—

    Balance on exchange of a portion of School
      Lot 174 for property on Broadway,
      near Mason Street............... 420 00
    For purchase of lot on corner of Pine and
      Larkin Streets, 200 feet on Pine by
      120 feet on Larkin Street.......... 5,989 76
    For purchase of lot on Silver Street, adjoin-
      ing Rincon Lot, 44 feet by 70 feet... 4,000 00
                        —————— 10,409 76

Total demands audited upon proceeds of above Bonds.$188,830 86

RECAPITULATION OF STATEMENT OF SCHOOL BONDS AUTHORIZED BY ACT OF
MARCH 17TH, 1867.

Total proceeds of Bonds up to June 30,
1867 .... $187,015 38
Total demands audited upon proceeds of
said Bonds up to June 30, 1867 .... $188,830 86
Outstanding audited demands June 30,
1867 .... 5,018 00
Cash on hand June 30, 1867 ....   3,202 52
                                      _____   _____
                                      $192,033 38 $192,033 38
                                      ===========   ===========

Fifty Bonds, of $1,000 each, are yet to be issued, from the pro-
ceeds of which, at 86 cents, may be realized $43,000.

SUPPLEMENTARY STATEMENT OF SCHOOL BONDS OF 1866-7, UP TO SEPTEMBER
30TH, 1867.

To cash on hand June 30th, 1867 ....$ 3,202 52
Probable receipts from sale of remaining 50
Bonds, at 86 cents 43,000 00
Outstanding audited demands June 30, 1867 $ 5,018 00
Demands audited since June 30, 1867. ....   25,037 50
Balance due on Eighth Street building 1,000 00
Balance due on Pine and Larkin Street
building 2,000 00
Balance due on Filbert and Kearny Street
building 2,000 00
Balance due on Tyler Street building 1,870 00
Contract price of West End building 1,585 00
Purchase of lots on Silver Street 2,500 00
Extra work on Shotwell Street building ...   631 70
Planking Filbert Street School yard 500 00
Grading Pine and Larkin Street lot 312 50
Purchase of Filbert Street lot 760 00
Balance 2,987 82
                                      _____   _____
                                      $46,202 52 $46,202 52
                                      ===========   ===========

23

Note.—In this connection it may be appropriate to give a statement of School Bonds heretofore issued.

TOTAL ISSUES SINCE THE ORGANIZATION OF THE PUBLIC SCHOOL DEPARTMENT (1849).

Date of Issues.	Amount Issued.	Amount Redeemed.	Amount Outstanding	Rate of Interest	Annual Interest.	Annual Sinking Fund
1854	$60,000	$60,000				
1860	75,000	20,500	$54,500	10 per cent	$5,450	$5,000
1861	25,000	9,000	16,000	10 per cent	1,600	2,500
1866-7	225,000	15,000	210,000	7 per cent	14,700	15,000
	$385,000	$104,500	$280,500		$21,750	$22,500

I beg to call attention to the foregoing table and the facts it discloses. It will be seen that the present funded debt of the School Department amounts to $280,500. The interest ($21,750) and the annual Sinking Fund ($22,500), apportioned for the redemption of the above Bonds, now annually amounts to $43,250, and this large sum is deducted from our current School Fund—a heavy draft from a fund already inadequate.

SUMMARY OF STATISTICS OF THE PUBLIC SCHOOLS.

The number of Public Schools in our city (October 1st) is 36. Three High (one English for boys, one English for girls, and one Latin for boys fitting for college); nine Grammar (two for girls exclusively, one for boys exclusively, and six in which the sexes occupy the same buildings); twenty-four Primaries (in which are both boys and girls).

Increase of classes for the year....................   57
In the Grammar Schools, 23; in the Primary Schools, 34.

Increase in classes in two years, to wit: since June 30, 1865......................................   98
In High Schools, 4; Grammar, 40; Primary, 54.

ATTENDANCE OF PUPILS.

Whole number of days which the schools were in session during the year......................   210
The present enrollment of pupils in the Public Schools is   *13,517
Increase in the total enrollment since June 30, 1865   6,386
Per cent. of increase in the total enrollment since June 30, 1865. :............................   .89$\frac{4}{10}$

*There are enrolled in the evening schools 315 scholars, making a total enrollment of 13,832.

The average number belonging to all the schools has been   10,846
High, 240 ; Grammar and Primary, 10,242.

Increase for the year......................... 2,152

Whole number of days' attendance during the year.... 2,098,921

Whole number of days' absence.................... 132,775

Per cent. of absence on attendance................. $.06_{10}^{3}$

Whole number of tardinesses..................... 62,461

Per cent. of tardiness on attendance................ $.02_{10}^{9}$

The average daily attendance has been.............. 10,177
High, 235 ; Grammar and Primary, 9,633.

Increase for the year......................... 2,046

The average per centage of attendance, in all the schools,
on the average number belonging, has been....... $.93_{10}^{7}$
High, .97 8-10 ; Grammar and Primary, .94 2-10.

CENSUS RETURNS.

The number of white children in the city between five
and fifteen years of age, July, 1867, was......... 20,088
In the First District, 1,220; Second, 2,231; Third, 171 ; Fourth, 1,622 ; Fifth,
263 ; Sixth, 1,001; Seventh, 1,405 ; Eighth, 2,698 ; Ninth, 1,562 ; Tenth,
3,606 ; Eleventh, 2,564 ; Twelfth, 1,743.

Number of negro children between five and fifteen years
of age...................................... 165

Total number of census children between five and fifteen
years of age............................... 20,253

Number of Mongolian children under fifteen years of age   179

Total number between five and fifteen.......... 20,432

SCHOOL ACCOMMODATIONS.

Supplied since July 1st, 1865, in new buildings—

Class-rooms...:............................... 122

Seats... 7,365

Grammar seats................................. 960

Primary seats................................. 6,405

Increase for the year—

Class-rooms 84

Grammar seats................................. 600

Primary seats................................. 4,380

Number of seats in rooms now rented, all Primary.. 340

Decrease during the year, all Primary 2,660
Total number of rooms supplied, both in buildings be-
longing to the city and in rented buildings 240
High, 12 ; Grammar, 104 ; Primary, 124.
Total increase during the past year 52
Total increase during the past two years, to wit, since
June 30, 1865 96

TEACHERS IN THE PUBLIC SCHOOLS.

The number of teachers employed, Sept. 30, 1867 253
Male 33
Female 220
Increase for the year 47
Increase in two years, since June 30, 1865 115
Number of teachers in the High Schools 11
Male 6
Female 5
Number of teachers in the Grammar Schools 97
Male 16
Female 81
Number of teachers in the Primary Schools 135
Male 2
Female 133
Number of teachers in the Evening Schools 6
Male 5
Female 1
Number of special teachers (male) 4

TOTAL CURRENT ANNUAL EXPENSES—(MISCELLANEOUS).

Aggregate of expenditures, including salaries, fuel, care
of fires and school rooms, books and stationery, etc.. .$320,058 88
Increase for the year 43,951 41
Increase in two years, to wit, since June 30, 1865. 85,014 89
Grand total of expenses for the year ending June 30,
1867, including buildings and purchase of lots 508,889 74

COST OF TUITION.

The amount paid for tuition (teachers' salaries) during
the year, has been $209,736 92
Including special teachers and substitutes.
Increase for the year 26,201 84
Increase in two years, to wit, since June 30, 1865. . 75,037 84

For the High Schools............................ 19,799 88
Excluding special teachers and substitutes.
Increase for the year......................:....... 2,100 00
Increase for two years, to wit, since June 30, 1865.. 7,599 95
For the Grammar Schools......................... 75,269 76
Excluding special teachers and substitutes.
Increase during the year.................... 1,240 20
Increase in two years, to wit, since June 30, 1865... 20,193 96
For the Primary Schools........................ 100,569 96
Excluding special teachers and substitutes.
Increase for the year........................ 26,662 20
Increase in two years, to wit, since June 30, 1865... 44,942 52
For the teachers of penmanship and drawing......... 2,675 00
Decreased during the past year.
For the teachers of music....................... 3,650 00
Slight decrease during the year.

*TOTAL COST OF EDUCATION.

Average cost of each scholar in all the schools, for tuition,
per year.................................... $19 34
For salaries only, calculated on the average number belonging.
Average cost of each scholar in the High Schools, per year, 82 49
Average cost of each scholar in the Grammar and Primary
Schools, per year............................ 17 17
Decrease for the year, per pupil.................... 1 75
Average cost of each scholar in our Public Schools....... 29 50
Including the whole expenses as above, excepting for erection of buildings
and purchase of lots.
Decrease for the year, per pupil.................... 2 26
Resulting from the erection of schoolhouses, and the consequent saving of
the payment of rents from the current fund.

SCHOOL FUNDS.

Current School Fund............................$320,807 57
Increase for the year........................ 28,587 04
Received from State School Fund.................. 55,641 50
Increase for the year...................... 12,597 95
Increase for two years, to wit, since June 30, 1865. 15,206 42

* The following apt remarks I find in one of the Eastern reports : "The subject of comparative statistics is one of general interest and importance ; but, unfortunately, there is no common basis upon which we may arrive at exact results, in comparing one city with another. One gives the cost per pupil based on instruction only ; another on cost of tuition and incidental expenses ; while still another includes all of the foregoing, and six per cent. on all school property. Again, some find the cost per scholar, reckoning on the entire register, and others from the average attendance."

Total receipts into this Fund from the sale of School
Bonds, to Sept. 30th, 1867...................... $187,015 38
Expenditures to be credited to this Fund up to Septem-
ber 30, 1867, for contracts effected............... 227,027 56

The following statement shows the total receipts into the current
School Fund during the past year 1866-67.

The monthly receipts of 1866-67 have been as follows:

For July, 1866............................... $21,846 77
  August.................................... 42,515 37
  September................................. 13,981 16
  October................................... 133,497 25
  November.................................. 19,975 26
  December.................................. 15,962 13
  January, 1867.............................   8,937 32
  February.................................. 56,465 07
  March.....................................   643 32
  April.....................................   586 87
  May.......................................   5,099 68
  June......................................   1,297 37

      Total................................. $320,807 57

GENERAL REMARKS.

The foregoing statistics suggest a few general observations. It
will be observed that the aggregate number of Public Schools, as
shown in the first paragraph of the " Summary of Statistics," is
less than the number given in former reports. This, however, by no
means indicates diminution, but results from the transfer of detached
and isolated classes from rented rooms (where each has heretofore
been reckoned as a school) to the new buildings erected by the Department during the past year. In these new locations they have

been reorganized and permanently consolidated into large schools, as
in the case of the Tehama Street Primary, which is composed of the
classes which were formerly known as the Stevenson Street, Mission
and Second Street, and Natoma Street schools.

THE INCREASE OF CLASSES.

The increase of 57 classes during the past year, or 98 since
June 30, 1865, and the increase of pupils from 9,980 to 12,362,
during the year just closed, or since June 30, 1865, to date, the increase from 7,131 to 13,517, and the increase in the number of
teachers employed during the above periods (in one year 57, and in
two years 115), clearly indicate the rapid growth of our School Department, and the increase of the population of the city; not that
the latter corresponds entirely or very nearly with the former. This
is not the case; for it will be observed that the total enrollment of
pupils at the present date (October) is $.89^4_{10}$ per cent. greater than at
the close of the school year ending June 30, 1865, a period of less
than two and a half years; while the increase in the total population
of the city has been as follows: Total population of 1864,
112,700; of 1865, 119,100; of 1866, 125,400, and of 1867,
132,000. The average increase for the last three years being $.05^3_{10}$
per cent. per annum. The increase in the total annual enrollment of
pupils being an average of $.23$ per cent. per annum greater than
the increase in the total population of the city.

It would at least appear from the foregoing statistics that a much
greater proportion of the children of the city attend public schools
at the present time than formerly. The following statistics are interesting in this connection:

PUBLIC AND PRIVATE SCHOOL ATTENDANCE.

	Total attendance in the Public Schools.	School Children of the City between 4 and 18 years of age.	Per cent. of the number attending Public Schools upon the total census of School Children.	Number of Pupils attending Private Schools.	Per cent of Pupils attending Private Schools on number attending the Public Schools.
1864	....	18,748	.48 4-10	4,823	.53 1-10
1865	8,000	20,581	.38 8-10	5,450	.68 1-10
1866	10,153	*17,369	.58 4-10	4,403	.43 3-10
1867	13,385	*20,253	.66 8-10	4,165	.31 1-10

* Between 5 and 15 years of age.

It will be observed that the per centage of pupils in attendance in the public schools on the total number embraced in the census returns has steadily increased, and during the last two years from $.38_{10}^{8}$ to $.66_{10}^{8}$, while the per cent. of children in private schools on the number of those attending public schools has decreased as rapidly, particularly during the last two years, to wit: decrease last year from $.68_{10}^{1}$ to $.43_{10}^{3}$, and for the year just closed from $.43_{10}^{3}$ to $.31_{10}^{1}$, or in the two years past from $.68_{10}^{1}$ to $.31_{10}^{1}$, more than 100 per cent. in the two years.

I have in former reports frequently called the attention of the public to the very rapid growth of our School Department, and especially to the disproportionate increase of public school children, as compared with the population of the city, and more especially as compared with the taxable property of the city, (which latter is the important consideration in this connection); yet I feel that I should again urge these highly interesting and suggestive facts upon the Honorable Board of Supervisors, and again commend them to the friends of our Department and to the public; for as our schools become so excellent, and find so much favor with all classes of the community, and increase so rapidly, it is obvious that there should also be a corresponding increase in the funds raised for their support. We have not heretofore been thus favored.

THE FUNDS.

The current school fund for 1865–66 was $292,220 53, an increase of $1,578 75, or .05 per cent. on that of the preceding year; while the increase of scholars attending public schools during that year was 2,153, equal to .27 per cent.

The school fund for 1866–67, the year just closed, was $320,807 57, an increase of $28,587 04, or $.09_{10}^{4}$ per cent. on the fund of the preceding year; the increase of our pupils for this year was 3,232, or equal to $.31_{10}^{8}$ per cent. It requires no farther argument to explain the embarrassments which have frequently attended the School Department. To keep the schools open the whole of the past year, justly afford the facilities of education to *all* applying, pay our teachers undiminished salaries through the entire year, and meet all the miscellaneous and inevitably large expenditures of our Department, has required good financiering—the most rigid economy ; and these have been exercised, whatever may, from political or personal motives, sometimes have been ungenerously said or written to the contrary. I can scarcely conceive how public trusts could have been more regarded, the public interest more faithfully subserved, and its funds more judiciously applied than has been done by the Board of Education during the past two years. In the management of its affairs, economy, sometimes almost amounting to parsimony, has been the constant rule. Except for the relief afforded by the building fund granted by the last Legislature, (a large amount, though inadequate to our wants), the schools could not have been thus sustained through the year. A large *deficiency* at the close of each year, or the suspension of the schools for a considerable portion of each year, would otherwise have been unavoidable. The rents saved by the erection of new buildings have given important aid.

But our building fund, so essential heretofore, and indispensable hereafter, is now exhausted, and yet the demand upon us for more room is unceasing. Applications for admission to schools are made in large numbers daily, in almost every portion of the city. In the southern and central districts especially, the class-rooms are already crowded to excess, and still they come; and the teachers, in anxiety, almost in consternation, are vainly asking for more room, more seats for pupils, and more assistance to instruct them. From the census returns* it will be seen that there are 20,088 white children between the ages of five and fifteen years, who are entitled to admission into the public schools, and to the enjoyment of the common benefits of the school fund; and besides these the special school law of this city entitles all youth between the ages of fifteen and eighteen years to the same educational facilities as are provided for those between five and fifteen. Of this latter class there are probably five to eight hundred. There are also 165 negro and 169 mongolian children in this city between five and fifteen years of age, who, in justice, and with due regard to good policy as well as law, should be provided for. How the means, to the necessary amount, are to be procured to meet the increased demands upon the School Department for enlarged facilities, and the employment of a large number of additional teachers, is a question yet to be solved, and one which should be at once considered.

The following financial statistics must concern the members of the Board of Education for the ensuing year, and my successor elect, the executive officer of the Department:

---

* It will be interesting to those who have pleasure in watching the growth of the city, to examine attentively the comparative census statistics found in the appendix.

ESTIMATE OF THE PROBABLE RECEIPTS AND DISBURSEMENTS FOR THE FISCAL
YEAR 1867-68, AS PER REPORT OF FINANCE COMMITTEE OF 1867.

Estimated revenue from taxes, as per estimate of the
    Auditor...................................$280,000 00
Estimated poll taxes.............................. 2,500 00
Estimated dog taxes.......................... ... 1,000 00
Estimated rent of school property................. 600 00
Estimated evening schools...................... . 200 00
State Apportionment, estimate of State Superintendent. 60,000 00

DISBURSEMENTS, AS PER ESTIMATE OF THE FINANCE COMMITTEE
OF THE BOARD OF EDUCATION.

For salaries of teachers................$240,552 00
For salaries of janitors................ 13,200 00
For salary of Secretary, fixed.......... 1,800 00
For salaries of carpenters, estimated.... 2,500 00
Rents, estimated...................... 2,000 00
Insurance, estimated.................. 3,000 00
Lights, estimated..................... 1,200 00
Water, estimated..................... 300 00
Books, supplies, advertising and printing,
  estimated 11,000 00
Fuel, estimated...................... 4,000 00
Incidentals, estimated................. 2,300 00
Furniture, estimated.................. 14,000 00
Repairs, estimated.................... 3,000 00
Transfer to Interest and Sinking Funds,
  fixed 42,500 00
District Library Fund, say............. 1,500 00
Census Marshals..................... 1,448 00

$344,300 00 $344,300 00

THE FIRST QUARTER'S ACTUAL RECEIPTS AND DISBURSEMENTS, FOR THE
PRESENT FISCAL YEAR, 1867-68.

Receipts.. $83,690 34
Disbursements................................... 81,456 25

The foregoing shows the receipts and disbursements of the School Department for the *first* quarter of the present fiscal year (1867–68,) and the estimates of the Finance Committee for the *whole* year. The agreement of the disbursements with the estimates is as near as could reasonably be expected. With reference to street improvements, the Committee had no data upon which to base their calculations; this item was therefore omitted. It is believed that the estimates, as a whole, will at the end of the year be found to have been very carefully considered, and as nearly correct as such calculations can be expected to be. It is my opinion that the amount estimated for teachers' salaries is somewhat too low; the demands upon the Board for a constantly increasing number of teachers has not, I think, been entirely appreciated even by our committee.

It is gratifying to note that the cost of instruction of pupils has decreased considerably in the last year, to-wit: Average cost of each scholar in all the schools, for tuition (for salaries only), calculated on the *average number belonging*, from $21.09 to $19.34. But this decrease in the cost of instruction should mislead none in regard to the rapid increase of the total expenses of the Department; for as elsewhere clearly shown, the *increase* of school pupils has been much more rapid than the decrease in the cost of instruction. It is also gratifying to note, from the expenses of the past two years, as well as from the above estimates, that the ordinary expenses of the Department, teachers' salaries and wages of other employés, expenses of furniture and repairs, books, supplies, etc., can, with strict economy, and without lessening the efficiency of the schools, be brought within the amount of the *current fund*. All other expenditures of our Department, for rents, building and other permanent improvements, interest on school bonds heretefore issued, and the sinking funds for the redemption of said bonds, should be provided for from sources independent of the current fund raised by taxation and State apportionment.

The great and indispensable necessity of the Public School Department of this city is a

SPECIAL BUILDING FUND.

It has become customary to apply the term " Special Building Fund " to the moneys secured from the sale of the school bonds issued under the authority of an act of the last Legislature; and this title suggests a fund which should be as independent, regularly provided and permanent as any other pertaining to the city government. It should be annually raised, and so much as required be set apart and devoted exclusively to the erection of schoolhouses.

If from a regular building tax more should be raised in any one year than required for building purposes for and during that particular year, it could be placed at interest by competent authority, and called in when wanted; or otherwise devoted to the redemption of bonds outstanding. The last issue of school bonds having been already devoted to building schoolhouses and the payment of the outstanding indebtedness of the School Department when they were authorized, issue of Bonds or other means for meeting the increasing wants of the School Department must be devised by the next Legislature, or serious embarrassment will soon overtake the schools and those who conduct them. The regular increase in the population of the city, warns us that the building of schoolhouses is a work which can scarcely be suspended.

These schools for the peoples' children, the nurseries of morality and intelligence, must be kept perpetually increasing, in every valley and on every hillside of our rapidly spreading city.

The history of the School Department since its organization, or rather an examination into its financial history, proves conclusively that the school tax has never been fixed at a rate sufficient to raise a current fund for the efficient support of the schools, and for the building of schoolhouses also. The ordinary current tax, as now provided, will as elsewhere stated, with the exercise of great economy, support the schools, and that is all it will do. Subtract the smallest amount from the ordinary current fund for other than current disbursements for the support of schools, and to that extent they will be embarrassed or temporarily closed, or else a deficiency will be created.

Public schoolhouses, like other public buildings, should be erected without encroaching upon the school fund, either directly by special appropriations therefrom, or indirectly, as heretofore, by issuing bonds, *the interest upon which and the sinking fund for their annual payment has to be set apart from said school fund.* It may be noted here, that the grading of school lots and improvements of streets about all school lots and schoolhouses, have with strange absurdity always been paid from the school fund. Considering the large annual amount of these improvements in a new and rapidly growing city like ours—and remembering, too, the very large sum that has now annually to be set apart from our current fund to meet the *interest* on the school bonds heretofore issued and now outstanding, and the amount annually to be set aside for a *sinking fund* for the redemption of the bonds at maturity, all taken from the current fund which has been raised for the support of the schools — few, I imagine, understanding these facts, will wonder that we are so frequently embarrassed, and that school bonds affording a temporary relief are so often called for.

MISCELLANEOUS SUGGESTIONS AND RECOMMENDATIONS.

SCHOOLHOUSES AND INCREASED ACCOMMODATIONS.

Notwithstanding the large number of new schoolhouses erected during the past eighteen months (mostly for Primary Schools,) the supply is yet by no means equal to the demands of the Department. During the coming year the Grammar and High Schools require early attention; the necessary means should be secured, and the following buildings at once erected. These improvements are now pressing wants of the Department.

1st. BOYS' HIGH SCHOOL.—The necessary lots, corner of Clay and Powell Streets, adjoining the one recently purchased by the Department, should be secured and a building erected, for the farther and better accommodation of the Boys' High School, which is already crowded. The proposed addition should also furnish accommodations for the Latin School, which is at present inconveniently located in a rented building at South Park ; rent, $50 per month.

2d. GIRLS' HIGH SCHOOL.—A suitable building should be erected for the Girls' High School, and the Training School now connected with the High School. These schools are at present compelled to occupy four detached buildings, and a fifth will soon be required. The inconvenience of this arrangement, especially in bad weather, and the necessity for an improvement in their external condition is too apparent to require discussion.

3d. THE COSMOPOLITAN SCHOOLS, POST STREET.—The Cosmopolitan Grammar School, in the old building, has seven classes with sufficient pupils for eight. When the next examination of the fifth grade in the Cosmopolitan Primary occurs, two other classes will be added to the Grammar Department, making ten, without considering any to be formed by new applicants, which it will be safe to calculate as equal to one additional at the end of the next term. Where are they to be placed? The Grammar building is already more than filled, and the Primary School has now eleven classes, though the building contains but six class rooms. At the end of next term, if new applicants are to be admitted, this number will doubtless be increased to fourteen or fifteen classes. In both schools, then, at the end of the next term, there will be twenty-two and probably twenty-five classes. But both buildings have only fifteen class rooms. It will therefore be seen that additional accommodation for these schools is an absolute necessity. I would urge the erection of a building for the Grammar School of twelve or more class rooms, and the surrender of both the present buildings to the exclusive use of the Primary classes, which by the end of the next term will fill both to repletion.

4th. COSMOPOLITAN SCHOOL, FILBERT STREET. — This school, though organized but three months since, with six classes, now has twelve, and all more or less crowded. The old building on Greenwich Street, recently vacated, should at once be repaired or rebuilt for the reception of new applicants to the above school, and to form a branch of it. The building contains four rooms not very unsuitable for use; two are good. There are also two basement rooms, quite habitable in good weather. The lower grades could here be well and comfortably provided for. This would allow the new building to be used by the higher grades of the school, and soon by the Grammar Department exclusively.

5th. THE RINCON GRAMMAR SCHOOL.—A suitable building for this school was one of the very first which the present Board determined to erect. Owing to the difficulty of procuring an eligible lot upon which to build, nothing has yet been accomplished but the purchase of ground partially sufficient for the proposed building. The crowded condition of the Primary Schools in the Rincon District, and in the southern portion of the city generally, should receive the earliest attention possible. In this district we are occupying an engine house on Bryant Street, from which we may be compelled at any moment to remove. Erect a new building for the Grammar School, and the old building will then afford room for the Bryant Street School, and also for the isolated classes at present on Silver Street. In these schools there are now already organized six classes ; two others will probably be formed before the proposed building can be erected, and these, with the six now organized, will fill the building now occupied by the Rincon Grammar School.

6th. SCHOOLHOUSE ON NEW OCEAN HOUSE ROAD.—Another small house should be erected for the accommodation of residents on the new Ocean House road, far beyond the toll-gate, and yet too far this side of the Ocean House School to be accommodated by it. The wants of this neighborhood have already been too long neglected.

7th. A PRIMARY ON THE PRESIDIO ROAD.—A building of perhaps four class rooms, should be erected on Fillmore near Greenwich Street. The old Spring Valley Schoolhouse is too far from the central part of the district to suitably accommodate the larger portion of the residents and parents. The old Spring Valley Schoolhouse should be at once repaired.

8th. COLORED SCHOOL—NEW LOCATION.—A new location and new building should be secured for the Colored School, in some more central portion of the city. One Colored School will for several years be sufficient for the whole city ; but it is quite evident that it should be so located as to be available for those requiring its advantages. The present location is unsuitable ; besides, its proximity to the Broadway Primary is found objectionable.

9th. A CHINESE SCHOOLHOUSE.—The Chinese School, elsewhere spoken of, should be provided with a suitable building in some central location. I suggest the vicinity of Sacramento and Powell Streets.

10th. THE MISSION GRAMMAR SCHOOL building should be enlarged by the addition of four class rooms. This improvement was once decided upon.

In this connection I offer another suggestion, that the Board of Education be relieved of the burdensome responsibility of

BUILDING SCHOOLHOUSES

I propose this for two reasons :

1st. The Board of Education has enough to attend to in the prop-

er care and supervision of the schools, and in the efficient management of the varied interests of the Department, exclusive of the
erection of schoolhouses.

2d. The building of schoolhouses entails duties and responsibilities
which do not harmonize with the other and more legitimate responsibilities connected with the proper conducting and management of the
schools. The amount of business necessarily involved in the erection of school buildings is very great, and requires a corresponding
amount of time and attention from Directors. This time, subtracted
from that which is necessary for the suitable care and supervision of
the schools, results in their great loss, if not in absolute neglect, as
is sometimes apparent. And farther, I beg to suggest that the building of schoolhouses has frequently been observed to attract to and
into the Board of Education elements and influences which, to say
the least, have been unnecessary and inappropriate to the care of the
schools, and often exceedingly unfavorable to their welfare. The
contracts for labor and building material, and claims of rival
architects, have heretofore often been a source of serious mischief to
the School Department, and consequently the schools themselves.
In this connection I respectfully again call attention to the unnecessary *engagement of carpenters* as regular employés of the Board. I
believe this to be the most expensive plan which could be adopted
to secure the work absolutely necessary to be done. When furniture
is required, or fences are to be erected, yards planked, or other work
performed, I believe it would be found much more economical and
every way more satisfactory to let such work out to competition, to
be done under contract, or otherwise when regular contracts would be
undesirable or impracticable. I do not wish to charge that there has
ever been intentional extravagance in the purchase of materials, or
in repairs and other work performed, or that there has been carelessness or waste of time ; but I do think there has often been in many
respects a lack of true economy in this carpenters' department.
Whatever the Board requires it can obtain with facility and more
economy, otherwise than by the constant employment of a regular
force of carpenters and other mechanics.

SALARIES.

Heretofore when embarrassments have overtaken our department—
almost always in consequence of the disbursements from the school

fund, of some extraordinary character, for buildings, street improvements, etc., which rightly considered have no relation to the regular support of schools—it has sometimes occurred to our Board and others, in their search for opportunities of retrenchments, that the teachers' salaries might without injustice be slightly reduced from the present rates, at least so far as several grades are concerned; but this fact should be borne in mind, that no proposition for a general reduction of salaries has ever been discussed or entertained in the Board of Education, since my connection with the department. No one I am confident, now connected with the department believes that the gross amount paid to teachers can scarcely, if at all, be reduced; in fact, as others are employed without diminution of rates, it must be increased. I have on several occasions, unfortunately for myself, perhaps, brought the subject of salaries before the Board of Education, believing as I still do that our present schedule is not wise or just in its rates, not sufficiently discriminating in favor of known ability, experience, and well proved success. It is not just to those who have identified themselves with our department and made teaching their profession from year to year; but the subject has no sooner been brought before the Board, than a general apprehension has been awakened that the salaries of teachers were to be reduced. Then have commenced the general criticisms of the press and of the people; the cry of injustice, parsimony, meanness, etc.; personal appeals and intercession with the members of the Board; and thus needed and just action has been defeated. On such occasions we are at once assured that the salaries of our lady teachers are too low, entirely unremunerative, a mere pittance, and that the salaries paid to the gentlemen are excessive, almost profligate in liberality. What has at any time given this sudden nervous fear of a general reduction, I am at a loss to imagine, for neither myself, nor to my knowledge has any member of the Board ever advocated such action, (a policy which all who are well informed upon the subject concede to be uncalled for, if not unjust and injurious), false accusations to the contrary. I once prepared a graduated schedule of salaries for circulation among the teachers of the department (it was never before the Board), and it was generally approved. I would again call attention to the propriety of a more discriminating, and to the older teachers a more generous schedule of salaries, and urge its early consideration and action. Our present schedule is entirely behind the times; it scarcely dis-

24

criminates at all in favor of knowledge, success and professional experience—that which in every other known profession is strictly regarded and reasonably rewarded. To assist in the better understanding of this subject I beg to call attention and commend for careful examination the following

SCHEDULE OF TEACHERS' SALARIES,

	Per month.	Per annum.
Principal of Boys' High School	$208 33	$2,500 00
Teacher of Mathematics in Boys' High School	175 00	2,100 00
Teacher of Modern Languages in Boys' High School	150 00	1,800 00
Teacher of Belles-Lettres	100 00	1,200 00
Principal of Girls' High School	208 33	2,500 00
Assistants in Girls' High School	100 00	1,200 00
Principal of Latin School	208 33	2,500 00
Assistant in Latin School	150 00	1,800 00
Principal of Grammar School	175 00	2,100 00
Sub-Master in Grammar School	125 00	1,500 00
Male Assistant in Grammar School	100 00	1,200 00
Head Assistant in Grammar School	83 33	1,000 00
Head Assistant in Primary School	72 50	870 00
Special Grammar Assistant in Grammar School	80 00	960 00
Assistant in Second Class of Grammar School	75 00	900 00
Assistant in Grammar School	67 50	810 00
Principal of Primary School of twelve Classes	115 00	1,380 00
Principal of Primary School of six Classes	100 00	.1,200 00
Principal of Primary School of four Classes	85 00	1,020 00
Principal of Outside School of two or more Classes	75 00	900 00
Principal of Outside School of one Class	70 00	840 00
Principal of Colored School	100 00	1,200 00
Principal of Chinese School	80 00	960 00
Assistants	67 50	810 00
Teacher of Music	150 00	1,800 00
Teacher of Penmanship and Drawing	150 00	1,800 00
Probationery Teacher, 1st six months, $300	50 00	} 630 00
Probationery Teacher, 2d six months, $330	55 00	

Let the above rates be examined as compared in the following

TABLE OF COMPARATIVE SALARIES.

City	Boys' High School			Girls' High School		Boys' Grammar School								Girls' Grammar School				Primary School					Teacher of Music	Teacher of Drawing
	Principal	Assist. Male	Assist. Female	Principal	Assistant	Principal	Sub Master	Head Assistant	2d Assistant	3d Assistant	Assist. 1st yr.	Assist. 2d yr.	Assist. 3d yr.	Principal	1st Assistant	2d Assistant	3d Assistant	Principal	Head Assistant	Assist. 1st yr.	Assist. 2d yr.	Assist. 3d yr.		
New York	4000	2500 to 3000				2000 to 3000	1000 to 1800				500 to 800			900 to 1200	‡600 to 900		300 to 600	600 to 1000	500 to 800			250 to 500		
*Boston	3500	2000 .o2500	3500			†2500	2000	700			450	500	550							450	500	550		
*Chicago	2500	2000	1000			†2000		1000			550	650	700							550	650	700		
Philadelphia	2250	1500 & 1800		1800	600	1500		450	380	340	300	300	300	750	450	380	340	400	340	300	300	300		
Baltimore	2200	1800		2200	700	1600		$1100 ‖800	550		500			1000	700	500	500	700		500			2000	
*Cincinnati	2200	1760	660			†1900		1300			700	700	700										1500	900
*St. Louis	2700	1500	1200	‖1200	1020	†1700		1000			550	600	650										1800	
New Orleans	2000	1700				†1500		1000	660	600	600			1200	800	660	600						1500	
Lowell	2000	1500	500			1500		400			350	375	400	750				900 to 1200		350	375	400	1800	1500
San Francisco	2500	1800	1200	2500	1200	2100	1500	1000	960	810	630	810	810	2100	1000	960	810		870	630	810	810	1800	1800

In most of the above cities an increase of salaries has been urged from year to year. The present rates are generally regarded as quite inadequate to the labor performed, and to the responsibility attending the position of teachers, and to the almost universal increase in the cost of living.

* Boys' and Girls' High School combined. † Grammar and Primary Schools combined. ‡ Vice Principal. § Male. ‖ Female.

COMPARATIVE SALARY STATISICS.

Let the above table be carefully examined, It will be seen that our rates of salaries for female teachers are as a rule not more than they should with justice be paid—they are not over generous; but compared with the most liberal rates of any other city in the Eastern States, or perhaps in the world, they appear *extremely* liberal. I would also call attention to the rates of salaries paid to our female teachers as compared with those received by our male teachers. And for the credit of our Department and our city and State I invite attention to the proportion which these salaries of male and female teachers bear to each other in our Deparment. Let those interested compare the proportion they bear to each other with that exhibited between the salaries of male and female teachers in Eastern cities. This comparison must satisfy all that in California the services of our lady teachers are somewhat suitably appreciated and rewarded. This cannot with the same truth be said in reference to the annual compensation which our Board awards to the gentlemen whom it employs, They are not as well paid as they would be in New York or in other Eastern Cities. These gentlemen of ability and enterprize who consent to ignore the more lucrative occupations—those professions and fields of labor in which ordinary success is attended with much greater rewards and higher distinctions—should be more liberally compensated than at present. In what other profession in our city would a man of good ability and fair industry be satisfied with $2,100 per annum? and yet what profession requires better talents, more varied learning and constant reading and study, or a greater amount of industry and constant labor (and that too of the most wearing and wasting character), than that of the faithful teacher.

OF PUBLIC SCHOOLS.

THE GRAMMAR SCHOOLS.

These schools are, as is often expressed, the people's colleges. In these the mass of our children obtain their main culture, reach the end of their school career, complete the course commenced in the Primary Schools, and finish their education. However incomplete this course ; however unfinished that great work which *should* commence in the earliest moments of life, and continue till its last sun sets ; *here,* for the most part, books are closed and school tasks are laid aside. However unpractical and superficial their knowledge; however careless and inapt their preparation for life ; they leave school, and with what they have and what they are, they become our citizens—to adorn society ; to add to its intelligence, its enterprise, its industrial and intrinsic wealth ; or else become unproductive elements in its turbid mass, the burdens, not the blessings, of the State.

How important, then, that the Grammar Schools have that character which shall best fit them to supply the necessary, and the best possible training and educational development for our boys and girls. Have they that character at the present time ? Good, or excellent as they are ; complete as seems to be their organization and course of study ; faithful and zealous as are our teachers, and good as is the instruction given, are they still just what they ought to be, considering the objects which they should subserve ? From my observations I am compelled to say that they are not. Much yet remains to make them just what they may and should be made.

I will briefly suggest that the course of study in the Grammar Schools is not sufficiently practical. There is too much mere abstract teaching; too much of text-book routine work. Perpetually memorizing that which is abstract and incomprehensible is simply mere time-killing, intellect-suffocating and stifling, mind dwarfing—little or nothing more. I have seen these results, and am not mistaken. I do not much blame teachers; they teach as they are required to teach and as they have been taught. They "bring up their pupils " in the prescribed manner ; they "take the classes through " the prescribed pages and chapters of the prescribed and inexorable text-book—and they do all in schedule time. What fault, then, can be charged upon teachers ? Their classes pass the examinations ; they spell, they " say their tables," they "*analyze* " and "*parse,*" they go glibly through with and correctly apply the rules of grammar. They solve their questions in arithmetic, explain the almost unexplainable rules, formulas and principles of fractions and duodecimals, per centages, and the roots. And in history they give you the longest catalogues of battles and sieges, attacks and repulses, of marches and counter marches of armies in this campaign and that. In geography they are ready with exceeding volubility to give the names and localities of common and of unheard of towns, and rivers, and mountains, small or great, important or otherwise, all the same. Yet I am presumptuous and radical enough to say that our boys and girls are not as well *educated* as they should be in our Grammar Schools. , There is a want of wholesome *culture*, a want of a suitable *practical* preparation for the ordinary vocations of an intelligent society, and for the successful discharge of its common duties.

Hours upon hours, days upon days, months upon months, and I might say years upon years, are wasted upon matter which has no real value except in "passing examinations"—upon abstractions which are meaningless, and which are at once gone and forever dead when the textbook is finally closed. This need not be so, and *should* not be so. With so much that is real, practical and useful to be learned, there is no necessity or propriety, or to the pupil justice, in this waste of the golden moments and opportunities of childhood and youth.

Examine the questions (in the appendix) upon which pupils of our Grammar Schools are examined for graduation. What do they call for? Is it that kind of knowledge that will in future life be most useful to them? and which they might have learned in the six, seven, or eight years' Grammar School course?

I submit these queries to thoughtful educators and an intelligent public.

PRIMARY SCHOOLS.

In the Primary Schools there exists to some extent the same fault as noted in the Grammar Schools. But here we expect to meet with much to be memorized. The minds of young children are prepared for this work. Much time must and should be consumed in spelling—in the endless repetition of and drill upon spelling lessons. Here the troublesome arithmetical tables must be learned—not those tables found in most of the higher arithmetics, of compound numbers, many of which are obsolete and useless, seen and learned no where except in the books—but those which must be memorized, and with most economy of time, in childhood.

In the Primary School, almost entirely, should correct habits of reading be formed, and this requires some drilling. Other exercises in the Primaries require more or less of memorizing, though the *practical* should constantly and as much as possible be interwoven, at every step, in everything learned. Children learn by appeals to their senses, their eyes especially, much more naturally and hence better than by appeals to their understandings. In all our schools, I think, there is far too much abstract arithmetic; it is made too prominent in the course. (It has occurred to me that they would be appropriately called "arithmetic schools.") More essential benefit would result to the small children, if a portion of the time now consumed in constant repetition of abstract facts were employed in counting beans or playing marbles—in dealing with something in the natural and tangible world, with which they might associate some correct ideas. With the universe of nature overhead, and on all sides, upon which the opening, ever eager, and curious eyes of children are constantly directed with interest and delight—in the world where there is so much that is real, useful, and beautiful to be learned by children, it seems strange that they should be so generally insulted with husks from text-books; their God-given senses practically disregarded, their instincts stultified with the dry, tasteless, senseless, and useless lessons and recitations (often ill adapted and undigested), while a living, intelligent, communicative human being is associating with them as their *teacher*.

But while I call attention to this evil, or what seems to me to be such, I am aware, as elsewhere remarked, that while teachers are bound by the strict requirements of our manual, they will to a large degree confine themselves to the text-book lessons, in accordance with which their classes are to be examined. Not many teachers will exert themselves beyond this. Should an earnest, intelligent teacher take a class over work that is not specified in the "Manual," no matter how interesting or instructive, what credit does he or she receive for it? One of our teachers has repeatedly taught her classes the beautiful classification and arrangement of Natural History, after she had thoroughly drilled them to pass the required examination. Yet what award did she win otherwise than the pleasure of imparting knowledge that was loved and appreciated by her pupils? Therefore, I say, we cannot expect teachers to exert themselves beyond what they are asked to do, and the present form of teaching and examining should be at once changed.

In my report to the Board of Education, I shall endeavor to point out *special* defects in our present system and methods of instruction, and in the text-books now in use, and shall attempt to suggest required and practicable improvements. To that Board the recommendations which I have to make in this connection will be more properly addressed.

SCHOOLS HAVING SPECIAL OBJECTS.

We have a city of a very mixed character, composed of people of various nationalities, religious opinions, customs, and other peculiarities ; I might perhaps add that it has its prejudices, also.

It is well that a school system may be flexible, for here it must bend somewhat to meet the wants and gratify the various tastes and sentiments of a people like ours. If it did not do this, it would fail, for large minorities of citizens, representing the sentiments and wishes of particular classes of the community, will not long cheerfully come forward with their liberal contributions to the public fund, unless they have some direct interest and participation in the institutions supported, and in the benefits they afford. Otherwise murmurings and discontent will surely follow, and sooner or later, a question of time merely, absolute and open opposition will be raised. At first, this opposition may be insignificant, may be disregarded ; but at length it becomes formidable, and then endangers the very existence of the system opposed. Not perceiving, or seeing yet not heeding these facts, has caused much trouble in other States and communities in our own country in regard to common schools.

Let us not wreck our system in this State, or in this city, by failing to avoid the rock on which others have foundered ; and we have been already sufficiently forewarned. Let us take heed, that our system be generous in its provisions, liberal in its organization, and complete in its adaptability ; adjusting itself to our people as they are, meeting the demands of San Franciscans, whether they be or be not the same as exist in Boston, Chicago, New York, or elsewhere. With these views, while I of course give primary importance to the elementary or primary schools of our Department, I have not overlooked the wishes of those citizens who have desired the advantages of our schools of *special* character—those which meet special but really existing wants of citizens.

At the commencement of my term of office there were only 7,131 pupils in all the public schools, and in the various private schools there were at that time 5,450 pupils. I had studied the question enough to understand that no good system of schools could long be maintained with so large a proportion of our citizens giving their interest, sympathy, and support to private institutions.

As before remarked, I give paramount importance and chief consideration to the essential features of the old-fashioned and ever honored school system of New England, and the older States, and regard the primary and lower grades of schools as worthy of and entitled to our first and chief attention. This consideration has governed our Department for the past two years most essentially. Of the $135,868 devoted to the erection of new school buildings, $126,257, or more than nine-tenths, have been expended on primary schools. For this class of pupils accommodations have been secured for 6,405 pupils, while for those of higher classes or grades only 960 seats have been provided. Still, on the importance of Primary schools I would not build up and force an argument against higher and not less important branches and parts of our system, and thus *needlessly* cripple those schools, which are an ornament to our Department, which constitute its brightest and most attractive features. In short, I would not excise the head to give greater vitality to the body. Hence I have urged, and do still, the support of the High Schools, and the Latin school at least as a part of our High School system. I am in favor of a generous and efficient support of our whole system, as it now is, and of improving and enlarging upon it, as the future change of our great and growing city shall require.

I would suggest another generous feature as a modification of our present excellent system: If the people of any certain district, or the patrons of any school, desire the privilege of using school-rooms, before or after the close of school, and the completion of ordinary studies, for special studies of any desirable or useful kind, religious or industrial—the teachers, of course, to be employed and paid by those who enjoy their services—let such privilege be granted. No harm, but much good may thus be gained by pupils, and for the system.

THE CITY TRAINING SCHOOLS.

Our Training School for Teachers, in connection with the Girls' High School, now under the able management of Mrs. A. E. Du Bois, I regard as one of the most important branches of our department; its future influence upon, and benefits to other schools can scarcely be overestimated. I feel great pleasure in its organization, in its present success and future prospects. Established only three months since, with one class, it now numbers six classes with forty pupils in each. The city employs one Principal and one Assistant; the other teachers are drafted weekly from the Normal Class of the Girls' High School. Except for this Training School, these young ladies of the graduating class would soon be elected teachers of the Department, and be placed in charge of schools and classes, without experience in teaching or discipline. We know the result of inexperience in the class room, and we know also the value of even a brief experience in the Training School, from the success of those who have been elected during the past few years from the State Normal School. The first few months, with most of those young teachers elected immediately upon leaving school, are of little value to pupils placed in their charge. Weeks at least, and months more probably, are consumed by them in learning how to go to work; meanwhile the valuable time of the children is lost — perhaps more than lost, for children in school are either doing well or ill — are never idle; and unfortunately it is customary to elect teachers of inexperience to classes of small children. The Training School rectifies all these mistakes. Hereafter when teachers are elected from this class, the Board of Education will have full knowledge of what has been their success as teachers, not merely as scholars. It will be known that they have received the necessary instruction and experience to enable them at once to enter upon the successful discharge of their duties as teachers.

In this connection I would suggest regulations to the effect that before any persons shall be eligible as teachers to have full charge of classes in any Primary or Grammar School, they shall have taught in the Training School of the city or State, or as a *substitute* in other schools, an amount of time equal to at least three months. Those now applying should avail themselves of this regulation. The influence of the Training Schools would then soon be felt throughout our Department.

THE COSMOPOLITAN SCHOOLS.

These schools of recent establishment are designed to afford the facilities for acquiring the modern languages—German, French, and Spanish — in connection with the ordinary English course. As elsewhere stated, it has been conceived that the object of our Public School system, its true policy and leading idea, is to meet all reasonable educational demands. A few years since a great number of our citizens, native as well as foreign, were compelled to patronize private institutions, with their less perfect classification, and less thorough instruction, for the sake of the modern languages, which by the more observing and thoughtful of our people are considered of greater importance in the ordinary vocations and positions of society than much, very much else included in the English course, especially in our advanced High School course. And there were many of our best citizens who were unable to meet the expense of private tuition for their children; and yet they were unwilling to permit their sons and daughters to grow up to maturity, and remain forever ignorant of their mother tongue.

Some two years since, to meet this public demand, I recommended the establishment of a single class, now grown to be the Cosmopolitan Schools of this city. This system, though by no means unique, and confined to this city, is here perhaps better organized, and on a more liberal and comprehensive basis, than elsewhere. The plan is European; Germany has multitudes of schools where the French and English are recognized as we recognize the German, French, and Spanish. There are many such schools in the Eastern States.

This system, though at first opposed here, as it had been elsewhere when first proposed and adopted, and before its merits and practicability had been tested, is now exceedingly popular in the community, and enjoys a very intelligent and excellent patronage. Most of its former opponents are now its advocates — some its warmest supporters. These schools now can stand upon their own recognized and admitted merits. I predict that they will more than justify all that has been claimed in their behalf. That I am not alone in this, I will here insert the intelligent approval recently given to the cosmopolitan system by some of our popular teachers, and other intelligent schoolmen.

DEPARTMENT OF PUBLIC INSTRUCTION, }
San Francisco, August 23d, 1867. }

JOHN C. PELTON,

    Superintendent of Public Schools,

        City and County of San Francisco—

DEAR SIR :—In answer to your request desiring me to state my opinion concerning the organization, value, and efficiency of the Cosmopolitan School, I take pleasure in replying that, from your first organization of the school, I favored the plan, and never had any doubts as to its ultimate success and popularity. I recently visited the school since its reorganization, and was gratified to find that it exceeded my most sanguine expectations in respect to order, classification, and evident progress.

I fully concur with the philosophical and scholarly reports of the gentlemen appointed to conduct the examinations at the close of the last term.

The school meets a great want of the people. If children are to learn the modern languages at all, they should begin in the primary departments. I am confident that after three years' instruction it. will be found that the pupils, while acquiring a knowledge of French, or German, or Spanish, will have made equal progress in the ordinary common school studies with those in other schools, who have been occupied exclusively in studying. the English language.

It is not strange that so marked an innovation on the old system of education should have excited some doubts as to its success, and some hostility to its progress; but the school having demonstrated, to a considerable extent, its own value, has now become a part of our practical system of public instruction, which few desire to dispense with, and which all thinkers and scholars will cherish and protect.

It has been urged that this school was established in contravention to certain sections of the Revised School Law. I see no force in the objection; I know of no section of the law which, by any construction or misconstruction, can be tortured into hostility to schools conducted on this plan. The whole spirit of the law is in favor of it, for the object of the public school system is to give the children of the people such a practical education as the spirit of the age requires, and such as the citizens, gathered from all nationalities, may demand.

        Very respectfully,

            JOHN SWETT,

            Sup't Public Instruction.

James Denman, Esq., Superintendent of Public Schools elect, in a recently published letter, says :

I pledge myself, as Superintendent of Public Schools, to use my best endeavors to extend the sphere of usefulness of the Cosmopolitan Schools, to perfect their organization and secure their success.

Ira G. Hoitt, Principal of the Lincoln Grammar School, also, in a letter recently addressed to the public, says:

I think the Cosmopolitan School meets the wants of a large portion of our population.

Mr. Hoitt furthermore says that in case of his election (being then a candidate for the Superintendency) "I shall do all in my power to promote their welfare."

The report of the Committee on Examination of the Cosmopolitan Schools contains the following in relation to the present character and the general merits of the Cosmopolitan Schools and the "Cosmopolitan system":

FROM REPORT OF FRENCH COMMITTEE ON EXAMINATION.

*   *   *   *   *   *   *   *   *   *

We give the most unqualified approbation to the fundamental idea of the Cosmopolitan School—the simultaneous instruction of youth in three modern languages, in their elementary and grammatical branches. Among most of the civilized nations it was [once] generally conceded that this kind of instruction presented the insurmountable difficulty of producing in young minds a confusion of words and ideas. Like many other theories long accepted as true, this has been proved to be unfounded. It has been demonstrated to us not only that this confusion is not to be feared, but that an entirely opposite and favorable effect is produced by this method of instruction. The differences existing in the genius of the different languages seem to establish in the minds of the children fixed points, precious guides for the memory, which prevent its straying. To whatever cause this effect may be due, it was made manifest to us in the most convincing manner. Among the hundreds of children, of every age, whom we questioned, or heard questioned, not one mingled together in his reply words belonging to different languages. We insist strongly upon this point, because we consider it the very basis of the special instruction given in the Cosmopolitan Schools. If this basis had been unsound we should have regarded it as our duty to advise the closing of the school, or its transformation into separate schools for English, French, and German. But we repeat that the contrary has been proved to us; and consequently this school is an *advance* upon the advances already made.

We consider it an excellent rule which brings the children under the care of American, German, and French teachers, in succession; for it has long been known that a good pronunciation in any language is only to be acquired under a master to whom that language is native. In this respect, also, the Cosmopolitan School is fortunate; all the teachers speak well at least two languages, and some understand three. We should recommend that, so far as possible, an identity of method be applied to the explanations and demonstrations made to the classes; not that we observed any positive defect in this matter, but the point is important.

＊   ＊   ＊   ＊   ＊   ＊   ＊   ＊   ＊   ＊

We would call attention, in the first place, to the eminent value of the Cosmopolitan Schools as a place of preparation for pupils destined for the High School. The great familiarity with English, French, and German, acquired almost without pains by the pupils of the Cosmopolitan Schools, gives them great advantages for the active pursuits of commerce, of the law, of chemistry, of every branch of business life in which it is advantageous to know more than one tongue; and in which one is it not advantageous? Such is the activity of the human mind to-day, so many and so great are the discoveries in every branch of knowledge constantly being made, that it is not possible to dispense with the knowledge of several languages; is it not better if two or three can be learned at once, and equally well, that they should be learned?

We remark that, while there are children of several nations in the Cosmopolitan Schools, *the greatest advantages of the instruction there given fall to the lot of those whose native language is English.*

The reason of this is plain. The children of foreign parents, living in a city so decidedly American, have facilities supplied them in the very lives of every day, for the acquisition of the English language; while the English-speaking children, surrounded in their daily life by their native language, fail of such resources for acquiring foreign tongues. To these children the Cosmopolitan Schools are peculiarly valuable; and we have found upon classification, that the Americans, with their practical good sense, have availed themselves of the school.

We found the proportion of the scholars of the different nations to be: Americans, 50 per cent.; Germans, 30 per cent.; French, 20 per cent.

The Pacific Coast is rich in minerals, beyond example; and these riches lay upon us as obligations to develop them wisely.

We leave to the good sense of the Board to decide whether a young man competent to read and study in their original languages the works of the great European masters of scientific research, is better fitted to do good service to the State than one who must depend upon one single language.

Satisfied as we are of the grand results already achieved by the Cosmopolitan Schools, we would most strongly urge the establishment of similar schools in various parts of the city; and more especially towards North Beach. In that portion of San Francisco the population is largely European; the school facilities are not all that could be desired, and the necessity of education is strongly felt by the people.

A Cosmopolitan School in that part of the city would have the greatest effect upon the future status of the population; *thousands of children who might otherwise remain essentially alien, would become Americanized by contact with American children, and by learning easily and thoroughly the English language.* The singular freedom of our life has already this influence; but the slow and partial assimilation to our ways of thought and life might be greatly accelerated by the association of our children with those of the Europeans not yet thoroughly at home in San Francisco.

As a measure of economy, the establishment of these schools especially recommends itself to the public. It is proved, by actual experiment, that the creative energy of these schools, and an admirable simultaneity of progress in the various classes, are combined in the institution we are contemplating; and the public is surely interested to know at how small a cost so great advantages are obtained. An institution at once so useful, so catholic, so humanizing in its influences upon thousands of young and growing natures, is an invaluable boon to the people; and in the development of this — the crowning glory of her admirable system of Public Schools — San Francisco will lay yet more broadly the sure foundations of a lasting civilization. Gratitude is due to those enlightened men who have conceived and carried out a design so beneficent. They have felt, no doubt, in their full force, the profound words of Goethe: "He who knows but his own language does not even know that." The men of every land and of every tongue — exiles from their own homes — find a refuge and a country in America; and in America, more than elsewhere, the word *Cosmopolitan* should have peculiar meaning. It is here that the children of men draw near to one another. Let every barrier between them be broken down !

Respectfully submitted,

TH. THIELE,
JACQUES T. RAY,
F. A. FIRMIN,
G. C. HURLBUT,
E. COHN, D.D.

French Committee on Examination of Cosmopolitan School.

FROM REPORT OF EXAMINERS OF GERMAN DEPARTMENT.

*　　*　　*　　*　　*　　*　　* .　　*　　*　　*

The impression, therefore, which the examination has made upon us is the more favorable, as, during a period of eighteen months, fifteen classes, in which so large a number of children were instructed, have been formed into two consistent and harmonious institutions — the Grammar and the Primary Schools. We are free to confess that heretofore we were no admirers of the principle which is the basis of the Cosmopolitan Schools. We questioned seriously whether the time could be found to instruct children of a public school in three languages, without neglecting very necessary branches of instruction.

These doubts did not originate in mere speculations, but in the experiences of our own education — with regard to several members of this committee — in no superficial acquaintance with school and school-systems. We remembered how many years we had spent in the higher schools in studying "living" languages, which, as we were afterwards obliged to acknowledge, failed in ourselves to show any signs of life.

But now, having seen and examined the practical working of the Cosmopolitan School, we cannot but recognize the superiority of its mode of teaching languages over very many of European schools; and we consider that institution no longer a doubtful experiment, but a reality highly creditable to those who labored to produce it, and full of rich results to the children.

As to the examination in French, which was limited to children *not* of French extraction, we desire to state, that in reading, grammar, and conversation, the various classes exhibited a considerable amount of knowledge. The children answered questions with readiness, and their pronunciation was very good. We beg leave to express the hope that the teacher may, as far as practicable, converse with the children in German and French, for we regard the constant communication in the language being taught as the main element of the success of the Cosmopolitan Schools.

From the examination in German, children of German parents were excluded. We were surprised when the teacher spoke to the children in German, and our surprise became greater when we saw that the children not only understood all the teacher said, but readily responded in the same language. In the elements of grammar considerable progress has been made. After taking active part in the examination, the Committee could not but acknowledge that the results obtained by the teacher were highly satisfactory.

Our expectations have been greatly exceeded, and we cheerfully admit the success of the principle on which the Cosmopolitan Schools have been conducted. Though there are of course deficiencies, and though the work is by no means completed, yet the foundation is well and firmly laid. May those who have so manfully, and in face of most serious obstacles, labored to build up that excellent institution, continue to receive the public esteem and recognition.

All of which is respectfully submitted,

F. HANSEN, D.D.,
E. COHN, D.D.,
LEO ELOESSER,
WM. LOEWY,
Committee on Examination of the German Department of the
Cosmopolitan School.

REPORT OF DR. J. ECKMAN, AND OTHERS.

To the Committee on Ancient and Modern Languages—

GENTLEMEN:—Having been charged, during your absence, to watch carefully and conscientiously over the examination of the Cosmopolitan School, we declare ourselves perfectly and astonishingly satisfied with the result of the instruction in German reading, spelling, translating, writing, arithmetic, and grammar. It is our sincere conviction that teachers as well as pupils have fulfilled their duty to the best of their ability. The institution itself is not only a benefit, but also a necessity both to the German and to the whole population of our city, and is highly calculated to direct the current of immigration, more than ever before, to California. We confess that only on few occasions it was possible for us to distinguish, in reading or answering questions, the American child from the child of German parents — only the name of the child called for would speak for it — but this token did not prove good during the examination of Miss Graf's class, for the pupils of either the first or second divisions pronounced the German without the least foreign accent. So our presumption of their nativity would only remain presumption. The questions presented were always carefully and accurately answered, and we ascertained, by altering and changing the questions, that the pupils were not previously drilled for the examination. If this school could be more carefully graded, and if, in the higher classes, more time could be devoted to mathematics, and elementary geometry· be introduced, and the school allowed to remain under the direction of its present faithful and efficient Principals, and the Hon. Superintendent, Mr. Pelton, by whom this system was founded, we may heartily express our well-founded hope that this school will develop into one of the best of our department, of the State, or even of the United States — become an honor to the community, and even to every citizen.

M. MENDHEIM,
A. SOLOMON,
DR. JULIUS ECKMAN.

In a recent letter, received from J. L. Pickard, Superintendent of Public Schools of Chicago, that officer says :

Instruction is given in French and German in our High Schools, and in German in one of our District (Grammar and Primary) Schools. German will be introduced during the ensuing year *in several of our Grammar Schools.*

He further says that all instruction in the modern languages themselves is given in the use of the languages, *i. e.*, they are made the medium of communication between teachers and. pupils so far as they can be.

In the recently published reports of the Chicago schools, it appears that the introduction of the German into the public schools, is with them a recent experiment. Upon the subject of German the Superintendent says :

The experiment of introducing German as a study in our District Schools *has proved a success.* It was feared that this innovation upon our system might seriously affect the scholarship of those pupils who should take German as an additional study.

In two particulars we were peculiarly fortunate in trying this experiment. 1st. In the course of study marked out ; and, 2d. In the selection of teachers.

The course of study recognizes the duty of the city to furnish an English education to all her children, and to make this the paramount object of school work, in that it permits no pupil to study German until he shall have passed through two grades of the course in which a thorough knowledge of simple reading is attained. Throughout the course, the German is kept two grades behind the English studies. Only reading, writing, spelling, and grammar are taught by the German teacher, and only enough of the grammar to make pupils accurate speakers of the language. *The conversation of the recitation room is conducted entirely in the German language.* The majority of the pupils pursuing

German in the school in which the experiment has been tried, are of American or Irish parentage.

The results are hardly developed enough to warrant positive assertions as to the effect of its introduction upon the general scholarship of the pupils. This, however, may be safely asserted, that no unfavorable result has as yet transpired. While I am not prepared to speak definitely as to its effect upon *general scholarship*, I am prepared to say that the knowledge gained of the German has been quite remarkable. The advancement of the German classes has been very rapid. No one can doubt the importance of a knowledge of the German to our pupils. But aside from its utility to one who every day meets in all the business walks more or less of the German element of our population, I must say that a knowledge of the structure of the German language will add greatly to the facility with which we use our own. Any one who will observe carefully, will see that Germans seldom misunderstand each other. It is very rarely the case that a question, or a statement made, needs repetition. Their language has a peculiar adaptation to all shades of thought. Our own language has words enough for the expression of all thought, words too that may be easily understood, while many words have been incorporated into it that are comprehended only by classical scholars. One skilled in the use of German will almost unconsciously choose the former class of English words, which certainly are the most forcible and for this reason the most valuable.

The Cincinnati Reports, speaking of the German-English schools, says : ꙮ

The fact developed in the monthly reports of the Superintendent, that about one-half of the pupils in the District Schools are pursuing the study of German, will be received by many with no little surprise, especially as comparatively very few children of English parentage are included in the number. In the two highest grades, instruction in the German language is attended with an expense additional to what would be otherwise incurred. In the lower grades, it is attended with no increased expense, inasmuch as the German teacher occupies a place which would otherwise have to be filled by an English teacher. In other words, in the German-English Schools of Grades C, D, E, and F, only one-half the number of English teachers are employed which would have to be employed if German were not taught.

From Superintendent L. Hastings, of Cincinnati, Ohio, we learn that German is taught in nine Grammar schools in Cincinnati, having 1,200 pupils ; in the Cincinnati High Schools, French and German. Superintendent Hastings further says that in fourteen of the eighteen Primary Schools the children spend, in the four lower grades, one-half of each day with the German, in reading, spelling, and writing the German language.

A letter from the Superintendent of Oswego, says that French and German are taught in the schools of that city.

S. S. Randall, Superintendent of Public Schools of New York City, in a letter recently received, says:

The German and French languages only are taught in our] Public Schools.

Superintendent John N. McJilton, of Baltimore, says:

The modern languages taught in our Central High Schools are German, French, and Spanish.

Superintendent Francis Berg, of the St. Louis School Department, says :

Instruction in French and German is given in the High School, and in German in seven District (Grammar) Schools, to which two more will be added during the present year.

Mr. Berg says that the plan of having ordinary recitations in the modern languages studied as a means of more rapid advancement and greater perfection, has been taken into consideration in St. Louis, and may at no distant time be partially carried into operation.

Superintendent E. A. Hubbard, of the Springfield, Mass., Schools, says :

French and German are taught in the Public Schools of this city.

The Rev. Dr. Bellows, in a recent letter on educational topics, (published in the *Liberal Christian,*) speaks of the incorporation of the study of modern languages into our Public School system, as one of its bright features—full of promise of more general and more liberal culture.

I learn by reports and from correspondence with Eastern and Western School Departments generally, that the introduction of the modern languages, the German and French particularly, in the Public Schools of large cities, is becoming the general rule—their omission the exception.

As practical illustrations of what children can do in the acquisition of French and German in the Cosmopolitan Schools, *in addition to the ordinary English studies*, which conform entirely to the course pursued in other Grammar and Primary Schools, I give examples in the appendix.

THE LATIN SCHOOL.

I trust the prosperity of this school will not longer be disturbed by opposition from any quarter. I believe that its objects and merits have not heretofore been and are not now fully understood. In the

English High School, as formerly organized, there were found many boys and young men who were fitting for college. They had passed through our Grammar Schools, or elsewhere fitted for the High School; and being under age and pupils by law, were still at school enjoying their legal and equitable rights. But it was found that the prescribed course of study in the High School, (including an extensive course in the higher mathematics, the sciences, modern languages, and English literature,) required an unnecessary amount of study, and more time for a preparation for college, than could reasonably be given by these pupils, many being already sixteen or seventeen years of age. This kind of preparatory course, very properly embraced in a schedule of studies for our High School, comprised various branches which these pupils would be pursuing all along through their entire college course. So that to go through the High School and through the necessary classical course, and then through college, was like doubling a task, and, what is far worse, the unnecessary consuming of nearly double the needful amount of time. This was seen to be a serious embarrassment. Hence the Latin or Classical Department of the High School was detached from the English Department, with seeming advantage to both, and organized separately, to enable those who wished to apply themselves directly to a course which would prepare them as rapidly as possible for entering college. It should be noted that the Latin School has thus relieved our Department from the expense of one or two years' tuition of those Latin School pupils who have already graduated and are in college, and who, except for the establishment of the school in question, would probably have remained at least much longer as pupils in our Department. In the same manner this branch of our school system will, if properly and economically conducted, continue to reduce rather than to add to our expenses; that is to say, if boys are anywhere in our public schools to be prepared for a college course, the Latin School is the place for them.

The present cost per pupil for instruction in this school is less than the cost per pupil in either of the other High Schools, viz :: $5.35 per month. In the Boys' English High School, $8.12 per month; in the Girls' High School, $5.02 per month.

It has frequently been objected to the Latin and other High Schools, that they were supported more especially for the accommodation of wealthy and highly favored citizens. A greater mistake could not be committed.   And to correct this false notion, I have collected the following statistics :

VARIOUS OCCUPATIONS OF THE PARENTS AND GUARDIANS OF PUPILS.

IN THE LATIN SCHOOL.

Merchants	5	Lumber Dealer	1
Bookseller	1	Tailors	2
Manufacturer	1	Contractor	1
Undertakers	2	Clergymen	2
Hairdresser	1	Brick-mason	1
Compositor	1	President of Insurance Company	1
Book-keepers	3	Broker	1
Milkmen	1	Photographer	1
Editor	1	Pawn Broker	1
Carpenters	3	Wine Grower	1
Saddler	1	Collector	1
Surveyors	2	Butcher	1
Assayer	1		

BOYS' HIGH SCHOOL.

Surveyor	1	Baker	1
Manufacturers	5	Weigher	1
Engaged in Mining	2	Teamster	1
Brokers	3	Clerk	1
Commissioner	1	Real Estate Agents	2
Secretary	1	Smith	1
Capitalists	2	Salesman	1
Tax Collector	1	Lumber Dealer	1
Recorder	1	Ship Master	1
Merchants	7	Grocer	1
Architect	1	Upholsterer	1
Farmers	5	Clergyman	1
Notary Public	1	Waiter	1
Lawyer	1	Ship Chandler	1
Bookkeepers	3	Drayman	1
Street Grader	1	Laborer	1
Carpenters	12	Furniture Dealer	1
Contractor	1	Livery Stable Keeper	1
Physician	1	Brewer	1
Storekeeper	1	Coopers	2

GIRLS' HIGH SCHOOL.

Shipmasters	3	Milkman	1
Drayman	1	Pork Packer	1
Upholsterer	1	Police Officer	1
Merchants	10	Contractors	3
Clerks	5	Real Estate Agents	2
Carpenters	8	Manufacturers	4
Hotel-keepers	2	Auctioneer	1
Architect	1.	Bookkeepers	3
Engaged in Mining	2	Machinists	2
Painters	2	Laborer	1
Property Holder	1	Carriagemaker	1
Miller	1	Expressman	1
Farmers	2	Revenue Adjuster	1
Cooper	1	Milliner	1
Bricklayers	2	Agents	3
Brickmaker	1	Shoemaker	1
Musicians	2	Tinsmith	1
Surveyor	1	Lawyers	2
Coal Dealer	1	Patternmakers	2
Liquor Dealer	1	Teacher	1
Physicians	2		

RECAPITULATION OF THE ABOVE PATRONS OF THE HIGH SCHOOLS.

Agents, 3; architect, 1; assayer, 1; auctioneer, 1; baker, 1; blacksmith, 1; book-keepers, 9; book-seller, 1; brewer, 1; brick-layers, 3; brickmaker, 1; brokers, 4; butcher, 1; carpenters, 23; carriage-maker, 1; clergymen, 3; clerks, 7; coal-dealer, 1; collector, 1; commission merchant, 1; compositor, 1; contractors, 5; draymen, 2; editor, 1; engaged in mining, 2; expressman, 1; farmers, 7; furniture-dealer, 1; grocer, 1; hair-dresser, 1; hotel-keepers, 2; laborers, 2; lawyers, 3; liquor-dealer, 1; livery stable keeper, 1; lumber-dealers, 2; machinists, 2; manufacturers, 10; merchants, 22; milliner, 1; miller, 1; musicians, 2; notary public, 1; painters, 2; pattern-makers, 2; pawnbroker, 1; photographer, 1; police officer; 1; pork packer, 1; president insurance company, 1; property holder, 1; real estate agents, 3; recorder, 1; revenue officer, 1; saddler, 1; secretary, 1; shipmasters, 3; salesman, 1; store-keeper, 1; shoemaker, 1; street contractor, 1; surveyors, 4; tailors, 2; tax collector, 1; teacher, 1; teamster, 1; tinsmith, 1; undertakers, 1; upholsterer, 1; waiter, 1; weigher, 1; wine grower, 1.

Carpenters head the list, and other industrial pursuits are well represented. Very few of the *wealthy* are found among the above patrons.

A CHINESE SCHOOL.

From the census returns we find that there are 179 Chinese children in this city, under fifteen years of age. Of these only thirty-seven are attending school. None are in public schools, such being excluded from all except the Colored School, which they will not attend. They are provided with no school for their special accommodation. Here we have a striking instance of taxation without representation; a principle and practice which we are accustomed to condemn as wrong. The Chinese, it is estimated, pay about one twentieth of our total taxation, this year amounting to about $120,000, and of this amount $14,000 goes to make up our school fund. Should not at least the very small portion of this sum necessary for that purpose, be devoted to the support of a school especially for the Chinese children now seen in groups upon many of our streets? Would not police and moral considerations, as well as those of justice, urge this same measure? There are many of our citizens, too, who, in view of our probable future relations with the East, desire and intend to give their sons a knowledge of the Chinese language. A department of the proposed school might, if properly organized under the instruction of teachers familiar with the English and Chinese languages, supply this opportunity to such as desire it, at no increased expense to the Department.

A COMMERCIAL CLASS,

Our Public Schools, as elsewhere urged in this report, should supply every reasonable educational necessity of the community.

It has been observed that a great number of boys who graduate from the Grammar Schools stop here in their educational career, at least so far as the schools are concerned. In fact, not a large proportion of those who go through the Primary Schools ever fully complete even the Grammar School course. It is a circumstance to be deeply 'regretted. But when boys get through with the Grammar Schools, they in too many cases go directly to business, or at least desire to do so, but generally find themselves unprepared. They have not had just that kind of education which fits them for general business pursuits—for the active and practical vocations of life. Most that is practical and useful, that which meets the demands of every day life, has yet to be learned by them. This is a matter of common remark, and to my mind plainly argues that there is something not quite sufficient in the present system; at least something incomplete, and which should be improved.

The practicable remedy which suggests itself has recently and frequently been adverted to in the educational journal of this State and in the city press, to-wit : the formation of a Commercial Class, to supplement the Grammar School course. This is another completing feature of our noble free school system which may be supplied at once. The expense of this branch of our Department would be inconsiderable, especially when compared with its benefits. The students in this school would not be occupying seats required otherwise, and an evening class would probably meet the present demand, and perhaps be sufficient for some time to come.

The course of study for this class should be short and entirely practical. Bookkeeping, drawing, business forms, correspondence, writing, and commercial arithmetic, should form its prominent and essential features.

The proposed class could perhaps be formed in the Boys' High School. It might or might not become a part of that institution. I would advise its early organization. The present is a suitable season, and the favorable period when young men have long, evenings at their disposal, which could not be more usefully or profitably employed than in study and a better preparation for the future active and practical duties of life.

It may be found desirable to make the Commercial Class a permanent branch, the "business college" of our Department; but I hope at no distant day to see all the Grammar Schools so constituted and conducted, with such a practical and general course of study, and so practically instructed, as to render quite unnecessary anything farther or additional for fitting boys for the duties of life awaiting them as they close their school books, and leave their class room to enter the factory or shop, store or counting room.

OBJECT OF PUBLIC SCHOOLS.

What objects are public schools designed to subserve, and what accomplish? What should be their scope? Whom should they accommodate?

These are questions frequently asked, often discussed, but are in San Francisco not so clearly understood and as well settled as they should be. A definite comprehension of these questions is of the very greatest importance, for they at once define the practical workings of the schools and determine the results to follow from all our labor. Is it enough that the education of the State to its children be restricted to the simple English elements, or is it a wiser political economy to elevate all to the highest attainable standard—the highest standard possible and practicable.

I think it may be safely affirmed that a system of public schools, to be enduring and to be useful in the highest degree, to be an ornament, pride and blessing in a community, should be of a very complete and high character, so wisely constituted as to subserve the interests and obtain the confidence of all; the cordial good will and the patronage of all; not of the poor and middle classes merely, but of all, rich and poor equally, and alike. Such a patronage and such a support, is a sure guarantee of the success of a public school system. It is its triumph, ensuring brilliant and glorious results in rich and enduring fruits of intelligence, industry, virtue and thrift. The school system to reach those conditions should be studied carefully, and be wisely adapted to our peculiar wants.

LEGISLATION REQUIRED.

As elsewhere suggested (in connection with remarks on Building Fund), our School Department should receive the early attention of the next Legislature. I will suggest a few important measures, which should be carefully and generously acted upon.

SCHOOL LANDS.

It seems to be popularly understood that the city yet possesses a large amount of public lands subject to its future disposition. It is to be hoped that a much more liberal appropriation of lots will hereafter be made for Public School sites, than was formerly made from city lands by the early Commissioners of 1851, and by those under the Van Ness Ordinance in 1855-56. And it would seem a most wise and beneficent policy, also, to appropriate a very liberal portion of whatever lands the city may still retain subject to its disposition, to a fund for the erection of schoolhouses to meet the future wants of the Public School Department, as the rapid growth of our great city may develop and add to them.

The fund created by the future disposition of these lands might also be made to lighten the annual drafts upon the current school fund, and reduce the rate of school taxes. A considerable quantity of lands now of little value, worth but a few thousand dollars, will in a few years, judging from the growth of the city, and the rapid and universal advance of real estate within its limits, be valued by millions. It is easy to perceive how judicious legislation at the present time, may in the rapidly approaching future be such an inestimable blessing to the coming generations of this city, as to cause its authors to be remembered with everlasting gratitude.

SURPLUS SINKING FUNDS.

As another measure for the benefit of our school funds, I would respectfully suggest the transfer thereto, during the ensuing three or four years, of the surplus moneys which may be collected for the redemption of the Funded Debt of 1851. It is understood that there may be a large amount collected which will not be required for that purpose; the moneys already accumulated being quite or nearly sufficient for the liquidation of the debt at maturity.

The proposed action at the next session of the Legislature will, it is thought by those well informed, place nearly $500,000 in our inadequate school fund ; a very important, and, if so appropriated, a very essential and opportune relief. The beneficial effects of such a measure would be felt for generations to come. This money, appropriated from year to year to the building of schoolhouses, would leave the *Current Fund* unembarrassed for the legitimate support of the schools. The resources here suggested might not be available for the erection of those buildings now needed, and others that will be required during the ensuing season ; but the necessary arrangements for buildings now wanted could probably be effected in anticipation of the proposed resources, when once *secured* by the necessary legislation.

ELECTION OF SCHOOL OFFICERS.

I believe San Francisco is the only city in our country which elects her School Superintendent and all other school officers by popular vote at a general election ; the only city which thus inevitably and at once throws her schools into the political arena, amid elements generally turbulent and unmanageable. *Elections by the people are popular, and justly so ; but I think observation and experience suggest a better method for the election of persons to take charge of our schools—those who *should* possess special qualifications and fitness for the offices they are to fill. We need not go far back, nor look long into the history of our city elections, to see the inexpediency if not the mischief of the present practice. It is the popular remark, that political influences should find no place or toleration in the judicial and educational departments of the city or State. It is said that such influences are as inappropriately mingled with these interests as they would be with the sacred rites and administrations of the church ; yet, by the present system of nominating and electing, the results so deprecated by all true men become as inevitable as they are harmful. We are sometimes belittled, and our educational interests humiliated if not degraded, by political tests forced in the mouths of candidates like gags in the half consenting jaws of animals. Partizan platforms are formed, and school officers, whose duties bear as close relationship to their creeds as to the politics of the moon, are forced upon them. Questions of reconstruction and tide lands, negro suffrage and national taxation, Chinese suffrage, toleration or expulsion —become important questions, overtowering and subordinating all others. But views on educational questions, how insignificant are they ! How little it matters what the claims of candidates are on educational grounds ! They may even despise public schools in their hearts, and it matters little ; these sentiments are permitted to be entertained, if candidates only be politically pliable, and sound in party faith and antecedents.

In other cities, in our own State as well as elsewhere, the election of school officers is carefully made as inaccessible to party management and political influences as possible. Special *school* elections are called for the choice of school officers, and these local elections are generally quite free from partizan intrigues and influences ; hence, those most directly interested in matters of public education succeed, with little difficulty, in electing competent and suitable persons for the important and sacred trusts which are to be reposed in their hands. How sadly different are the results which generally attend the nominations of a political convention, composed of and conducted by professional politicians (as they are usually everywhere), and followed by a general political canvass.

The Board of Education in many cities is elected by the Board of Aldermen or Board of Supervisors ;• sometimes, and better still, as in some cities, by the Mayor and his counselors. The Superintendent is generally elected, or appointed by the Board of Education for a term of from four to six years. Any system, I believe, is better than that now in vogue in this city.

ENLARGEMENT AND REORGANIZATION OF THE BOARD OF EDUCATION.

No one acquainted with the present organization and general business of the School Department of San Francisco, and familiar with the varied nature of its responsibilities and the endless details of its affairs, can fail to see the necessity of an enlargement and reorganization of the Board of Education, and a different assignment of its duties. No one, I think, can attend a sitting of our Board, and listen to its proceedings for a single evening, without receiving this impression.

Any disbursement of moneys, no matter how trifling, or how urgent the necessity, must, to comply with the rules, come first before the whole Board for its approval, then be referred to a standing committee, then be reported upon, then ordered, then disbursed, and so on. The slightest matter of discipline in one of the schools, the most unimportant regulation as well as the gravest, is liable and by the rules may have to pass before and receive grave consideration in the full open public meeting. Every application of a teacher throughout the year must be presented to the open Board, and the names of every person applying, male or female, have also to be brought before the public eye. Their personal merits or demerits, their qualifications or the lack of them, may thus at any time be dragged before the community for its edification—matter for comment and general remark. This is unique; and in this respect our Department is, so far as I am informed, unlike that of any other city in the world. It might do for a small town or country village, but is not suitable for San Francisco.

As a remedy, we should have either three or five paid Commissioners of Education, of intelligence and integrity, to manage our schools —each being appointed to the *special* duties of some particular department of the system, and all acting together in the more important concerns requiring their united discretion and wisdom; or else a much larger number of members elected to our Board of Education, with large sub-committees or Trustees, empowered to act promptly and finally in all matters of minor importance in the different schools and districts. Three Directors, elected from each District, should form local or District Trustees; this would be a suitable number, and an appropriate organization for the Board of Education of San Francisco. By this means the special wants or convenience of the various schools and their patrons could with greater facility be consulted and provided for, as in New York and other large cities. •

The following will exhibit the number and constitution of the Boards of Education which have the management of educational matters in other cities :

CINCINNATI.—A " Board of Trustees and Visitors," consisting of *thirty-six* members—two from each ward—from which Boards of Local District Trustees are organized; also a Union Board on the Cincinnati High Schools.

LOWELL.—The " School Committee " consists of the Mayor of the City, the President of the Common Council, and *twelve* members— two from each ward.

BROOKLYN. — The "Board of Education" consists of *twenty-three* members.

PHILADELPHIA.—The " Board of Controllers of Public Schools " consists of *twenty-six* members, one from each section—the city being divided into twenty-six sections.

BALTIMORE.—The " Board of Commissioners of Public Schools" consists of *twenty* members—one from each ward.

NEW YORK.—The " Central Board of Trustees" consists of *forty-four* members—two from each ward ; in addition to which there is in each ward a Board of Trustees consisting of *eight* members ; also, two Commissioners and Inspectors. The School Boards, in all, number —— members.

TRUANT LAW.

I will call attention to the subject of truancy. Among boys, in every large city, there is a greater or less disposition to truancy. It is a great evil, and is everywhere more and more complained of, till prevented, or at least checked, by stringent laws, with corresponding school regulations. In San Francisco, parental discipline is often found to be exceedingly inefficient, and the disposition to break away from its wholesome restraints is very common, especially so among boys of parents who from various circumstances are prevented from giving that constant attention and personal supervision to their children which is so necessary everywhere, but especially in large cities like ours, where bad examples are common, and temptations varied and numerous. The remedy of this evil to which attention is called, is a judicious truant law. Such laws are now enacted and enforced in almost every country in Europe—in all that are advancing in educational improvements—and are found in several of the States of our own country. There are many large cities in the United States whose educational systems embrace a judicious Truant Law—more or less rigorous in its provisions, as circumstances require. Why should not San Francisco ere this have had the benefit of such statutes? No city needs such a law more. Why should the carelessness, disciplinary weakness, or cupidity of parents and guardians be left to poison the community with the insufferable presence of hundreds of ignorant and vicious truant boys? Many such are now seen in this city, growing up in loaferism, and from their poisoned tastes and ignorance are, or soon will be, fit for nothing and for no place except the jail and prison.

The community cheerfully submits to self-imposed taxation; a liberal school fund is raised; schools with room for all are supported, are thrown open and free to all. The expense of the schools is met, and is not lessened a farthing by the hundreds of cases (this year 505) of truancy which annually occur with so much damage to future society. Has not the State in *loco parentis* a just right to seek a remedy for this growing evil. And is she not, from all considerations, bound to apply it when found. As elsewhere stated, this question should be practically answered in the affirmative. In those States where the right is assumed of compelling attendance, no person is allowed to employ a boy or girl who cannot show that he or she has attended school during at least six months of the twelve preceding months. This, or a similar provision, should form a part of the truant law in this State, applicable at least to this city.

DUTIES OF THE SUPERINTENDENT.

I beg to call attention to the duties of the Superintendent of Public Schools, and to embrace this opportunity of recommending that either by some regulation of the Board of Education, or revision of the School Law, the present duties of that office be limited and better defined.

I speak of the duties of that position, not as they are now defined by law or in the manual of the Board, but as they have been assigned or outlined by custom, and confirmed by practice. That officer, to fulfill the present duties of his position and meet public expectations, has probably more to do, more *different* matters to give his attention to, than has the President of the United States, or any other officer known. He is· expected to be always in his office and accessible to everybody upon every conceivable and inconceivable business or errand, whether important or unimportant; and yet he feels the momentary necessity of being somewhere else, and is constantly expected in every school in every portion of the city. He feels that to be Superintendent of Schools in fact, he must visit them, to encourage and advise with teachers, observe their discipline, study their methods of instruction, and suggest modifications and improvements. Let one consider this latter work alone in a School Department covering an area of eight or ten square miles, numbering 37 schools, 253 teachers, with nearly 14,000 pupils, and he will see enough to do. Yet herein is the important work of the Superintendent, which he should not be compelled to neglect, and cannot omit without feeling that his work is at least partially undone. But as the office of the Superintendent is the *omnium gatherum* of the School Department, he must attend to, or at least attempt to assist in attending to every interest of the schools, financial and educational. He is *ex officio* a member of the Board and of two or three of the most important Committees, and virtually connected with them all. He must be informed as to the position and merits and success of every teacher; he must attend the meeting of the City and State Boards of Examination of Teachers, and see to the issuing of certificates; he should be equally well informed with regard to the claims and merits of those who are seeking positions in the schools. He must examine, approve, and endorse every bill—numbering monthly three hundred and fifty to four hundred.

He is expected to be informed as to the wants of every portion of the city, in regard to school accommodations and necessary repairs on school houses and premises. He is expected to know when and where furniture and supplies are wanted, of what kind and amount. He must know where the school lots are, and see that they are kept secure from intrusion. He must see that the janitors perform their duties faithfully, and give satisfaction to the teachers. He must attend the meetings of the Board of Education, and meetings of most of the committees, and always be at hand to advise in regard to anything and everything pertaining to the business of the Department. He must be aware of the delinquencies of teachers, of pupils, and patrons, and in the latter cases he has often to consume an indefinite amount of time in listening to confused and conflicting statements and complaints, from which the right of the case is often difficult and sometimes impossible to unravel. He must attend to supplying books to the indigent, and grant transfers, first learning the necessity. He must, in short, listen to everybody's wants and everybody's complaints; accommodate all; displease none; cater to caprices; combat, yet often succumb to prejudices; defy opposition, yet sometimes yield to it; be everywhere; do everything and know everything; or else he is a very negligent, unfaithful, unkind, unjust, and short-coming Superintendent.

To be just and faithful, a Superintendent must be self-abnegating entirely. He must expect to be the object of complaint and abuse while he is in office, but may comfort himself with the assurance of being relieved from his unpleasant position, with its varied duties and liabilities, as soon as election day arrives.

There is not only a necessity that the Superintendent be relieved of much that he has now devolving upon him, and that he be aided by subordinate assistants; but to secure his greater independence from political influences and intrigues, and thus enhance his usefulness, he should be elected by the Board of Education or by the Board of Supervisors, or perhaps, jointly by both Boards, and for a much longer term than two years, as at present; and his removal should be safely guarded—possible only for good cause, first shown.

ASSISTANT SUPERINTENDENT.

In a preceding paragraph I have hinted at the necessity of an Assistant Superintendent. I would here do more—I would urge the creation of that office. Unless the Superintendent be relieved of most of those general business duties which he has now to perform, he of necessity must leave undone the more legitimate and appropriate duties of his office, to-wit: the visiting of schools, advising with teachers and pupils, suggesting and illustrating improved methods of instruction, examining and promoting pupils, attending to the interior and special care of schools. This is the important work of the Superintendent; and in our department the proper and sufficient discharge of this duty cannot—simply cannot—be performed by any one man, however competent and skillful. A suitable or even a reasonable care and supervision of the schools requires at least two persons. Each of these would find sufficient and important work to occupy every moment of his time, and employ his best skill and talents.

THE FUTURE.

Let the aid suggested in the foregoing pages be seasonably extended to the San Francisco School Department, and its future will be most encouraging.

It must be profoundly gratifying to the friends of education—and not to such alone, but to all who look hopefully forward to the future permanent prosperity of our city, to contemplate her superior educational advantages. Her system of Public Schools, having been planted here when the city itself was but a dream of the future, has taken deep root in the confidence and affections of her people. Her schools already enjoy the sympathy and favor of her best citizens; they have been nurtured in her adversity and advanced in her prosperity, till they have become her pride and boast—an ornament alike creditable to our intelligence and patriotism. Indeed, our schools have become a moral power which few would dispense with, cripple, or retard—which none with impunity can assail. It is freely admitted by those well informed, that they may already

26

safely challenge comparison with those of any city in the world—at least in the completeness of the system, its liberal features, affording as it does, the most ample and thorough educational facilities to every child within its limits. The physical and intellectual character of our pupils; the intelligence, faithfulness and professional ambition of our teachers; and, what is most important, the intelligence and proverbial liberality of our people—are auspicious of a glorious future for our Public Schools. Let all friends of liberty, and human progress, extend their patronage and co-operative support, and strive to open wide the schoolhouse doors, that the schools may scatter their blessings, making the people wiser, better, and happier.

Respectfully submitted.

J. C. PELTON,

Superintendent Public Schools.

APPENDIX.

BOARD OF EDUCATION OF THE CITY AND COUNTY OF SAN
FRANCISCO, FOR 1866–67.

PRESIDENT......JOSEPH W. WINANS.

MEMBERS.

1st District—E. H. COE, North Point of Battery Street, (Flint's
Warehouse.)
2d District—H. T. GRAVES, 412 Clay Street.
3d District—Dr. W. F. HALE, 520 Kearny Street.
4th District—JOS. W. WINANS, 604 Merchant Street.
5th District—DR. W. AYER, 408 Kearny Street.
6th District—A. C. NICHOLS, 316 Washington Street.
7th District—*IRA P. RANKIN, First Street, between Mission
and Howard.
8th District—G. C. HICKOX, N. E. corner Montgomery and Sacramento Streets.
9th District—A. W. SCOTT, S. W. corner Stewart and Folsom
Streets.
10th District—S. C. BUGBEE, 73 and 74 Montgomery Block.
11th District—P. B..CORNWALL, foot of Jackson Street.
12th District—†J. A. ROGERS, N. E. corner Polk and Pacific Sts.

SUPERINTENDENT OF PUBLIC SCHOOLS, JOHN C. PELTON, office
No. 22 City Hall; residence, northwest corner Polk and Pine.

SECRETARY...............DANIEL LUNT, 22 City Hall.
ASSISTANT SECRETARY.....GEORGE BEANSTON, 22 City Hall.
COPYIST.................RICHARD OTT, 22 City Hall.
MESSENGER...............JAMES DUFFY, 22 City Hall.

---

* Vice Wm. G. Badger, resigned.
† Vice Austin Wiley, resigned. Mr. Wiley filled the vacancy caused by the resignation of
Mr. Chas. M. Plum.

STANDING COMMITTEES.

On Nominations—Messrs. Scott, Cornwall, Hickox, President and
Superintendent.
On Rules—Rankin, Coe, Cornwall.
On Classification—Ayer, Graves, Scott.
On High and Normal Schools—Hale, Bugbee, Rankin.
On Ancient and Modern Languages—Cornwall, Nichols, Hale.
On Special Teachers—Coe, Ayer, Scott.
On Text Books—Nichols, Hale, Rankin.
On Accommodations—President, Superintendent, Graves, Cornwall,
Hickox.
On Schoolhouses—Bugbee, Graves, Rogers.
On Evening Schools—Coe, Bugbee, Ayer.
On Furniture—Graves, Rogers, Hale.
On Salaries—Hickox, Bugbee, Nichols.
On Finance—Nichols, Ayer, Hickox.
On Teachers' Institute—Rankin, Hale, Bugbee.
On Printing—Rogers, Cornwall, Scott.
On Grammar Schools—Graves, Ayer, Hale, Scott, Cornwall, Bugbee.
On Primary Schools—Rogers, Coe, Rankin, Hickox, Nichols, Scott.

MEMBERS-ELECT OF THE BOARD OF EDUCATION.

The following named gentlemen were elected at the municipal
election on the fourth of September last, and will take their seats on
the second of December next :

2d District—THOS. HOLT.   8th District—R. P. HAMMOND.
4th District—H. A. COBB.   10th District—A. K. HAWKINS.
6th District—Jos. W. WINANS.   12th District—J. A. ROGERS.
7th District—Jos. A. DONOHOE.

JAMES DENMAN, Superintendent of Public Schools.

THE PUBLIC SCHOOLS OF SAN FRANCISCO,

As Organized September 30, 1867.

—

BOYS' HIGH SCHOOL.

Location..................................Corner of Clay and Powell Streets.

Name of Teacher.	Position Occupied.	Grade of Class.	No. in Class.	Monthly Salary of Teacher.
Theodore Bradley	Principal........................	....	78	$208 33
Thomas C. Leonard.......	Teacher of Mathematics.......	....	......	175 00
John M. Sibley...........	Assistant Teacher...............	....	......	150 00
Mrs. C. L. Atwood.........	Teacher of Belles Lettres.......	....	......	100 00

Number of Teachers, 4; number of pupils, 78; amount of salaries, $633 33; cost of instruction for each pupil, $8 12 per month; $97 44 per annum.

GIRLS' HIGH SCHOOL.

Location............................Corner of Bush and Stockton Streets.

Ellis H. Holmes	Principal........................	....	116	$208 33
Miss S. S. Barr...........	Assistant.......................	....	......	90 00
Miss M. McKenzie.........	Assistant.......................	....	......	90 00
Mrs. S. R. Beals..........	Assistant.......................	....	......	100 00
Mad. V. Brisac	Teacher of Modern Languages..	....	......	100 00

Number of Teachers, 5; number of pupils, 116; amount of salaries, $588 33; cost of instruction for each pupil, $5 02 per month; $60 24 per annum.

CITY TRAINING SCHOOL.

Location..................................Corner Bush and Stockton Streets.

Mrs. A. E. Du Bois........	Principal......................	9th and 10th....	204	$100 00
Miss H. M. Gates.........	Assistant......................	9th and 10th....	......	67 50
Miss A. L. Gray..........	Probationary Teacher, 2d grade.	9th and 10th....	......	50 00

Number of Teachers, 3; number of pupils, 204; amount of salaries, $217 50; cost of instruction for each pupil, $1 06 per month; $12 72 per annum.

SAN FRANCISCO LATIN SCHOOL.

Location..................................Corner of Second and Bryant Streets.

Wm. K. Rowell*	Principal......................	....	42	$175 00
A. L. Mann.............	Assistant......................	....	......	150 00

* Vice George W. Bunnell, resigned

Number of Teachers, 2; number of pupils, 42; amount of salaries, $225; cost of instruction for each pupil, $5 35 per month; $64 20 per annum.

LINCOLN DISTRICT.

LINCOLN GRAMMAR SCHOOL.

Location..Fifth, near Market Street.

N ime of Teacher.	Position Occupied.	Grade of Class.	No. in Class.	Monthly Salary of Teacher.
Ira G. Hoitt...............	Principal......................	1st.............	......	$175 00
Miss E. A. Cleveland......	Head Assistant...................	1st.............	63	83 33
T. W. J. Holbrook.........	Sub-Master.....................	2d.............	61	125 00
Philip Prior...............	Sub-Master.....................	2d.............	64	125 00
Miss P. M. Stowell.........	Assistant......................	3d.............	56	67 50
Miss L. B. Jewett.........	Assistant......................	3d.............	55	67 50
Miss M. J. Ritchie.........	Assistant......................	3d.............	57	67 50
Miss E. A. Shaw...........	Assistant......................	3d.............	61	67 50
Miss A. M. Manning.......	Special Grammar Assistant.....	4th.............	55	80 00
Miss E. F. Eaton	Assistant......................	4th.............	51	67 50
Miss C. L. Smith...........	Assistant......................	4th.............	57	67 50
Mrs. E. M. Ludlum........	Assistant......................	4th.............	45	67 50
Miss L. S. Swain	Assistant......................	4th.............	52	67 50
Miss M. T. Kimball........	Assistant......................	4th.............	54	67 50
Mrs. E. H. B. Varney......	Assistant......................	4th.............	54	67 50
Miss M. J. Hall............	Assistant......................	5th.............	62	67 50
Miss Jennie Forbes........	Assistant......................	5th.............	62	67 50
Miss B. Comstock	Assistant......................	5th.............	60	67 50
Miss Ellen Casebolt........	Probationary Teacher, 1st grade.	5th.............	57	55 00

Number of Teachers, 19; number of pupils, 1,026; amount of salaries, $1,520.83; cost of instruction for each pupil, $1 48 per month; $17 76 per annum.

NORMAL TRAINING SCHOOL.

Location..Market Street, near Fifth.

Mrs. C. H. Stout...........	Principal......................	....	264	$100 00
Mrs. P. C. Cook...........	Assistant......................	....	......	90 00
Miss Mary Heydenfeldt....	Assistant......................	....	......	67 50

Number of Teachers, 3; number of pupils, 264; amount of salaries, $257 50; cost of instruction for each pupil, 98 cents per month; $11 76 per annum.

FOURTH STREET PRIMARY SCHOOL.

Location....................................Corner Fourth and Clary Streets.

Mrs. L. A. Morgan.........	Principal......................	5th.............	......	$100 00
Miss Mary Stincen.........	Head Assistant................	5th.............	48	72 50
Miss S. Davis...............	Assistant......................	5th.............	43	67 50
Miss E. Cushing...........	Assistant......................	6th.............	63	67 50
Miss A. Gibbons...........	Assistant....	6th.............	55	67 50
Miss C. Comstock.........	Assistant......................	7th.............	65	67 50
Miss G. Garrison..........	Assistant......................	7th.............	43	67 50
Mrs. R. F. Ingraham.......	Assistant......................	8th.............	71	67 50
Miss Hattie J. Estabrook...	Probationary Teacher, 2d grade.	8th.............	73	50 00
Miss T. J. Carter..........	Assistant......................	9th.............	70	67 50
Miss A. Jourdan.........	Assistant......................	10th.............	85	67 50

Number of Teachers, 11; number of pupils, 616; amount of salaries, $762 50; cost of instruction for each pupil, $1 23 per month; $14 86 per annum.

LINCOLN PRIMARY SCHOOL.

Location............................... .. ...Corner Fifth and Market Streets.

Name of Teacher.	Position Occupied.	Grade of Class.	No. in Class.	Monthly Salary of Teacher.
Miss Kate Sullivan	Principal.........................	....	......	$115 00
Miss C. L. Hunt...	Head Assistant.................	5th............	66	72 50
Miss Filena T. Sherman...	Assistant.......................	5th	67	67 50
Miss M. A. Salisbury......	Assistant.......................	6th	65	67 50
Miss J. M. Hurley	Assistant......	6th	64	67 50
Miss H. S. Arey............	Assistant.......................	7th	63	67 50
Miss L. A. Clegg..........	Assistant.......................	8th...	56	67 50
Miss E. Holmes..........	Assistant.......................	8th	64	67 50
Miss M. Jordan..........	Assistant.......................	8th	64	67 50
Miss N. Littlefield........	Assistant.......................	9th	61	67 50
Miss M. George..........	Assistant.......................	9th	69	67 50
Miss B. Molloy...........	Assistant.......................	10th	88	67 50
Miss R. B. Childs.........	Assistant.......................	10th	90	67 50

Number of Teachers, 13 ; number of pupils, 817 ; amount of salaries, $930 ; cost of instruction for each pupil, $1 13 per month ; $13 56 per annum.

RINCON DISTRICT.

RINCON GRAMMAR SCHOOL.

Location.......Vassar Place, Harrison Street, between Second and Third Streets.

Ebenezer Knowlton	Principal.........................	....	......	$175 00
Miss H. Thompson........	Head Assistant.................	1st	52	83 33
Miss H. M. Clarke........	First Assistant.................	2d	59	75 00
Miss S. M. Scotchler......	Assistant.......................	3d	54	67 50
Miss M. E. Stowell........	Special Grammar Assistant.....	3d	61	80 00
Miss A. M. Dore..........	Assistant........................	4th	69	67 50
Miss M. A. E. Phillips.....	Assistant.......................	4th	63	67 50
Miss L. B. Easton..........	Assistant.......................	5th	87	67 50
Miss Margaret Wade.......	Assistant.......................	5th	63	67 50
Miss M. S. Moulthrop	Probationary Teacher, 2d grade.	6th	62	50 00
Miss A. C. Robertson......	Probationary Teacher, 2d grade.	7th	35	50 00

Number of Teachers, 11 ; number of pupils, 605 ; amount of Salaries, $850 83 ; cost of instruction for each pupil, $1 40 per month ; $16 80 per annum.

TEHAMA PRIMARY SCHOOL.

Location...Tehama, near First Street.

Mrs. E. A. Wood..........	Principal.........................	......	......	$100 00
Miss Jennie Smith........	Head Assistant.................	5th	64	72 50
Miss E. White.............	Assistant.......................	5th	52	67 50
Miss Mary J. Pascoe.......	Assistant.......................	5th	48	67 50
Miss S. S. Knapp........	Assistant.......................	6th	55	67 50
Miss Mary Smith..........	Assistant.......................	6th	64	67 50
Miss F. A. E. Nichols.....	Assistant.......................	7th and 8th	73	67 50
Miss Mary Guinness.......	Assistant.......................	7th	51	67 50
Mrs. S. N. Joseph.........	Assistant.......................	7th	64	67 50
Miss Hattie Lyons........	Assistant.......................	8th	59	67 50
Miss Helen A. Grant.......	Assistant.......................	8th	61	67 50
Mrs. E. N. C. Huntington..	Assistant.......................	9th	66	67 50
Mrs. L. W. D. Wallace.....	Assistant.......................	9th	61	67 50
Miss A. S. Ross............	Assistant.......................	10th	88	67 50
Miss Julia A. Hutton......	Probationary Teacher, 1st grade.	10th	80	55 00
Miss Lizzie A. Morgan.....	Assistant........................	10th	78	67 50
Miss Ellen Gallagher.......	Probationary Teacher, 2d grade.	10th	77	50 00

Number of Teachers, 17 ; number of pupils, 1,041 ; amount of salaries, $1,155 ; cost of instruction for each pupil, $1 10 per month ; $13 20 per annum.

BRYANT STREET PRIMARY SCHOOL.

Location...Bryant Street, near Third.

Name of Teacher.	Position Occupied.	Grade of Class.	No. in Class.	Monthly Salary of Teacher.
Miss E. G. Smith..........	Principal........................	10th............	130	$85 00
Mrs. R. J. Cochrane........	Assistant........................	9th.............	47	67 50
Miss A. S. Cameron..	Assistant........................	8th.............	58	67 50
Miss Sarah Porter.........	Probationary Teacher, 2d grade.	10th.............	......	50 00

Number of Teachers, 4; number of pupils, 235; amount of salaries, $270; cost of instruction for each pupil, $1 10 per month; $13 20 per annum

DRUMM STREET PRIMARY SCHOOL.

Location.............................Corner of Drumm and Sacramento Streets.

Miss A. M. Murphy......	Principal........................	7th and 8th....	120	$75 00
Miss S. B. Cooke.........	Probationary Teacher, 2d grade.	9th and 10th..	.....	55 00

Number of Teachers, 2; number of pupils, 120; amount of salaries, $130; cost of instruction for each pupil, $1 08 per month; $12 96 per annum.

FRANKLIN DISTRICT.

—

DENMAN GRAMMAR SCHOOL.

Location.......................................Corner Bush and Taylor Streets.

James Denman............	Principal................ }	1st and 2d..... {	47	$175 00
Mrs. E. M. Baumgardner ..	Head Assistant.......... }		.....	83 33
Miss C. M. Pattie..........	Assistant, Teaching 2d Class....	2d...............	52	75 00
Miss N. Doud.............	Assistant, Teaching 2d Class....	2d...............	53	75 00
Miss Alice Kenney.........	Assistant........................	3d...............	59	67 50
Miss A. C. Bowen.........	Assistant........................	3d...............	52	67 50
Miss Jessie Smith.........	Assistant........................	3d...............	53	67 50
Mrs. E. P. Bradley........	Assistant........................	4th.............	57	67 50
Miss C. C. Bowen.........	Assistant........................	4th.............	55	67 50
Miss Annie Holmes........	Assistant........................	4th.............	56	67 50
Miss M. J. Little.........	Assistant........................	5th.............	63	67 50
Mrs. L. A. Clapp..........	Special Grammar Assistant.....	5th.............	53	80 00
Miss A. Flint.............	Assistant........................	5th and 6th.....	61	67 50
Miss L. Gummer..........	Assistant........................	6th.............	56	67 50
Miss Jennie Armstrong....	Assistant........................	6th.............	62	67 50

Number of Teachers, 15; number of pupils, 779; amount of salaries, $1,163 33; cost of instruction for each pupil, $1 49 per month; $17 88 per annum.

HYDE STREET PRIMARY SCHOOL.

Location..Corner Bush and Hyde Streets.

Miss Hannah Cooke........	Principal........................	5th and 6th....	47	$85 00
Miss A. B. Chalmers.......	Assistant........................	7th.............	56	67 50
Miss D. Hyman............	Assistant........................	8th.............	58	67 50
Miss K. Bonnell...........	Assistant........................	8th.............	69	67 50

Number of Teachers, 4; number of pupils, 230; amount of salaries, $287 50; cost of instruction for each pupil, $1 12 per month; $13 44 per annum.

PINE STREET PRIMARY SCHOOL.

Location..Pine Street, near Scott.

Name of Teacher.	Position Occupied.	Grade of Class.	No. in Class	Monthly Salary of Teacher.
Miss L. A. Prichard........	Principal......................	4th, 5th, 6th, 7th,	74	$75 00
Miss Abbie F. Sprague.....	Probationary Teacher, 2d grade.	8th, 9th, 10th...	......	50 00

Number of Teachers, 2; number of pupils, 74; amount of salaries, $125; cost of instruction for each pupil, $1 70 per month ; $20 40 per annum.

GEARY AND HYDE STREET SCHOOL.

Location..Corner Geary and Hyde Streets.

Miss L. A. Humphreys...	Principal...............	9th and 10th....	64	$75 00
Miss F. M. Benjamin....	Assistant...............	10th............	67	67 50

Number of Teachers, 2; number of pupils, 131; amount of salaries, $142 50 ; cost of instruction for each pupil, $1 08 per month; $12 96 per annum.

POLK STREET PRIMARY SCHOOL.

Miss M. E. Perkins......	Probationary Teacher, 1st grade.	10th.........	76	$55 00

Cost of instruction for each pupil, 72 cents per month; $8 64 per annum.

UNION DISTRICT.

UNION GRAMMAR SCHOOL.

Location......................Union Street, between Montgomery and Kearny.

Thos. S. Myrick..........	Principal......................	1st............	49	$175 00
J. D. Littlefield............	Sub-Master....................	2d.............	51	125 00
Miss Susie Carey..........	Head Assistant................		......	83 33
Mrs. M. Kincaid...........	Assistant.....................	3d.............	41	67 50
Miss S. S. Sherman........	Assistant.....................	3d.............	45	67 50
Miss A. F. Aldrich.........	Special Grammar Assistant.....	4th............	58	80 00
Miss E. M. Tibbey.........	Assistant.....................	4th............	46	67 50
Miss C. A. Cummings......	Assistant.....................	5th............	49	67 50
Miss S. H. Thayer.........	Assistant.....................	6th............	54	67 50
Miss E. White.............	Assistant.....................	6th............	55	67 50

Number of Teachers, 10 ; number of pupils, 448; amount of salaries, $868 33 ; cost of instruction for each pupil, $1 94 per month ; $23 28 per annum.

UNION PRIMARY SCHOOL.

Location.............................Corner Montgomery and Union Streets.

Mrs. A. Griffith...........	Principal......................	6th............	51	$100 00
Miss L. Solomon..........	Assistant.....................	7th............	63	67 50
Miss A. V. Lunt..........	Assistant.....................	8th............	68	67 50
Miss Anna Younger........	Assistant.....................	9th............	68	67 50
Miss Ellen G. Grant.......	Assistant.....................	10th...........	65	67 50
Miss Mary H. Estabrook...	Assistant.....................	10th...........	66	67 50
Miss Victoria Schaap......	Probationary Teacher, 1st grade.	10th...........	85	55 00

Number of Teachers, 7; number of pupils, 466; amount of salaries, $492 50 ; cost of instruction for each pupil, $1 05 per month ; $12 60 per annum.

WASHINGTON DISTRICT.

WASHINGTON GRAMMAR SCHOOL.

Location.............................Corner Washington and Mason Streets.

Name of Teacher.	Position Occupied.	Grade of Class.	No in Class.	Monthly Salary of Teacher.
James Stratton..............	Principal........................	1st.............	52	$175 00
Mrs. L. G. Deetken........	Head Assistant.................	....	......	83 33
H. E. McBride..............	Sub-Master.....................	2d..............	50	125 00
Miss Jean Parker..........	Assistant teaching 2d class......	2d..............	49	75 00
Miss D. S. Prescott........	Special Grammar Assistant.....	3d..............	54	80 00
Miss S. J. White...........	Assistant.......................	3d..............	54	67 50
Miss H. Satterlee..........	Assistant.......................	4th.............	63	67 50
Miss S. A. Jessup..........	Assistant.......................	4th.............	58	67 50

Number of Teachers, 8; number of pupils, 380; amount of salaries, $740 83; cost of instruction for each pupil, $1 95 per month; $23 40 per annum.

POWELL STREET PRIMARY SCHOOL.

Location......................Powell Street, between Washington and Jackson.

Miss Carrie V. Benjamin...	Principal........................	5th.............	55	$100 00
Miss Selia W. Burwell.....	Assistant........................	5th.............	58	67 50
Miss Anna Giles..........	Probationary Teacher, 2d grade.	5th.............	63	50 00
Miss Mary E. Morgan......	Assistant........................	6th.............	56	67 50
Miss S. E. Thurton........	Assistant........................	6th.............	65	67 50
Mrs. E. S, Forester........	Assistant........................	7th.............	64	67 50
Miss M. E. Tucker.........	Assistant........................	8th and 9th.....	66	67 50
Miss Alice Allen..........	Probationary Teacher, 2d grade.	10th............	66	50 00

Number of Teachers, 8; number of pupils, 493; amount of Salaries, $537 50; cost of instruction for each pupil, $1 08 per month; $12 96 per annum.

BROADWAY PRIMARY SCHOOL.

Location......................Broadway Street, between Powell and Mason.

Mrs. W. R. Duane.........	Principal........................	5th.............	49	$100 00
Mrs. M. W. Phelps.........	Head Assistant.................	5th.............	......	72 50
Miss E. Overend...........	Assistant.......................	5th.............	41	67 50
Miss A. E. Hucks..........	Assistant.......................	6th.............	55	67 50
Miss N. S. Baldwin........	Assistant.......................	7th.............	61	67 50
Miss Fannie Howe.........	Probationary Teacher, 2d grade.	8th.............	60	50 00
Miss Grace Wright.........	Probationary Teacher, 2d grade.	9th.............	62	50 00
Mrs. B. M. Hurlbut........	Assistant.......................	9th.............	60	67 50
Miss Mary A. Lloyd........	Assistant.......................	9th.............	40	67 50
Miss E. G. Morse..........	Probationary Teacher, 2d grade.	10th............	73	50 00
Miss Mary A. Haswell	Probationary Teacher, 2d grade.	10th............	57	50 00
Miss Mary Solomon........	Assistant.......................	10th............	55	67 50

Number of Teachers, 12; number of pupils, 613; amount of salaries, $777 50; cost of instruction for each pupil, $1 26 per month; $15 12 per annum.

MISSION DISTRICT.

MISSION GRAMMAR SCHOOL.

Location..............Mission Street, between Fifteenth and Sixteenth Streets.

Name of Teacher.	Position Occupied.	Grade of Class.	No in Class.	Monthly Salary of Teacher.
E. D. Humphrey...........	Principal....................	1st and 2d.....	56	$175 00
Mrs. F. E. Reynolds.......	Head Assistant...............		.....	83 33
J. H. Sumner..............	Assistant....................	3d and 4th......	66	100 00
Miss S. Barker............	Assistant....................	4th.............	62	67 50
Mrs. J. H. Sumner.........	Assistant....................	5th.............	60	67 50
Miss A. A. Rowe...........	Assistant....................	7th and 8th.....	63	67 50
Miss A. M. Lane...........	Assistant....................	6th.............	56	67 50
Miss A. Ciprico...........	Assistant....................	9th.............	62	67 50
Miss Maria O'Connor......	Assistant....................	10th........ ...	59	67 50

Number of Teachers, 9 ; number of pupils, 484 ; amount of salaries, $763 33 ; cost of instruction for each pupil, $1 57 per month ; $18 84 per annum.

SHOTWELL STREET GRAMMAR SCHOOL.

Location.........Shotwell Street, between Twenty-second and Twenty-third Streets.

Silas A. White............	Principal....................	2d and 3d.......	46	$125 00
Miss Mary J. Bragg........	Assistant....................	4th.............	48	67 50
Miss Annie A. Hill........	Special Assistant............		.....	72 50
Miss Mary J. Morgan......	Assistant....................	5th.............	59	67 50
Miss Bessie Hallowell......	Assistant....................	7th and 8th.....	68	67 50
Miss Hattie L. Wool.......	Probationary Teacher, 2d grade.	10th...........	60	50 00
Miss A. J. Hall......... ..	Probationary Teacher, 2d grade.	6th and 9th.....	43	50 00

Number of Teachers, 7 ; number of pupils, 324 ; amount of salaries, $500 ; cost of instruction for each pupil, $1 53 per month ; $18 36 per annum.

EIGHTH STREET PRIMARY SCHOOL.

Location.............................Eighth Street, between Harrison and Bryant.

Miss A. E. Slavan.........	Principal....................	5th.............	46	$100 00
Miss M. A. Humphreys....	Assistant....................	6th.............	49	67 50
Miss S. E. Frissell........	Assistant....................	7th.............	58	67 50
Miss Grace Chalmers......	Probationary Teacher, 2d grade.	7th and 8th.....	52	50 00
Miss S. E. Johnson........	Probationary Teacher, 2d grade.	8th and 9th.....	53	50 00
Miss Maggie Bevans.......	Probationary Teacher, 2d grade.	10th............	60	50 00
Miss M. Brady............	Probationary Teacher, 1st grade.	10th............	56	55 00
Miss Carrie Watson.... ...	Probationary Teacher, 2d grade.	10th............	61	50 00

Number of Teachers, 8 ; number of pupils, 435 ; amount of salaries, $490 ; cost of instruction for each pupil, $1 12 per month ; $13 44 per annum.

HAYES VALLEY SCHOOL.

Location.............................Grove Street, between Larkin and Polk.

Miss L. J. Mastick........	Principal....................	5th.............	67	$85 00
Miss H. P. Burr	Pupil Assistant..............		......	50 00
Miss J. E. Gunn..........	Assistant....................	6th and 7th.....	58	67 50
Miss F. A. Stowell........	Assistant....................	8th and 9th.....	71	67 50
Miss K. A. O'Brien........	Probationary Teacher, 2d grade.	10th............	76	50 00

Number of Teachers, 5 ; number of pupils, 272 ; amount of salaries, $320 ; cost of instruction for each pupil, $1 17 per month ; $14 04 per annum.

STEINER STREET PRIMARY SCHOOL.

Location.......................................Steiner Street, near Turk Street.

Name of Teacher.	Position Occupied.	Grade of Class.	No. in Class.	Monthly Salary of Teacher.
Miss S. H. Whitney.......	Principal....................	{ 5th, 6th, 7th, 8th, 9th, and 10th. }	} 45	$70 00

Cost of instruction for each pupil, $1 55 per month; $18 60 per annum.

FAIRMOUNT SCHOOL.

Location...Fairmount Tract.

Mrs. T. J. Nevins........	Principal....................	Mixed..........	30	$70 00

Cost of instruction for each pupil, $2 33 per month; $27 96 per annum.

SAN BRUNO SCHOOL.

Location.....................................San Bruno Road, near Toll Gate.

Miss Jennie Sheldon.....	Principal..................	{ 4th, 5th, 6th, 8th, and 10th. }	} 77	$75 00

Cost of instruction for each pupil, 97 cents per month; $11 64 per annum.

POTRERO SCHOOL.

Location.................................Corner Kentucky and Napa Streets.

Miss A. S. Jewett........	Principal......................	4th and 10th...	85	$75 00
Miss Sarah Anderson....	Probationary Teacher, 2d grade	....	......	50 00

Number of Teachers, 2 ; number of pupils, 85 ; amount of salaries, $1 25 ; cost of instruction for each pupil, $1 47 per month; $17 64 per annum.

WEST END SCHOOL.

Location.................... ....Near Six-Mile House.

Robert Desty...........	Principal......-.............	{ 4th, 5th, 7th, 8th, and 10th. }	} 33	$75 00

Cost of instruction for each pupil, $2 27 per month; $27 24 per annum.

OCEAN HOUSE SCHOOL.

Location...Near Ocean House.

Mrs. M. McGilvray.....	....	{ 2d, 3d, 6th, 8th, and 10th. }	} 21	$70 00

Cost of instruction for each pupil, $3 43 per month; $41 16 per annum.

SPRING VALLEY DISTRICT.

SPRING VALLEY GRAMMAR SCHOOL.

Location..........................Broadway, between Larkin and Polk Streets.

Name of Teacher.	Position Occupied.	Grade of Class.	No. in Class.	Monthly Salary of Teacher.
L. D. Allen................	Principal........................	1st............	12	$175 00
Miss Carrie Field..........	Head Assistant.................	2d..............	57	83 33
Miss Frances Simon.......	Assistant.......................	3d and 4th......	55	67 50
Miss Mary Murphy........	Assistant.......................	5th............	58	67 50
Miss P. A. Fink...........	Special Grammar Assistant.....	5th and 6th.....	59	80 00
Mrs. Therese Sullivan	Assistant.......................	7th and 8th.....	66	67 50
Miss J. V. Barkley........	Assistant.......................	8th and 9th.....	75	67 50
Miss Esther Goldsmith....	Probationary Teacher, 2d grade.	10th...........	64	50 00
Miss Annie Kelly..........	Assistant.......................	8th and 9th.....	92	67 50
Miss Mattie B..Cooke......	Probationary Teacher, 2d grade.	10th...........	54	50 00

Number of Teachers, 10; number of pupils, 593; amount of salaries, $765 83; cost of instruction for each pupil, $1 29 per month; $15 48 per annum.

NORTH COSMOPOLITAN SCHOOL.

Location...Filbert, near Jones Street.

Miss Kate Kennedy........	Principal........................			$100 00
Miss F. Mitchell...........	Head Assistant.................	3d.............	47	83 33
Mrs. U. Rendsburg........	Special Assistant..............	4th............	46	83 33
Miss C. Ehlin.., ...	Assistant.......................	5th............	56	67 50
Miss A. Chalmers..........	Assistant.......................	5th............	53	67 50
Miss A. Wells..............	Probationary Teacher, 2d grade.	5th............	59	50 00
Mde. B. Chapuis..........	Assistant.......................	6th............	69	67 50
A. Solomon................	Assistant.......................	7th............	50	67 50
Miss F. Soule..............	Assistant.......................	8th............	67	67 50
Miss A. Campbell..........	Assistant.......................	9th............	65	67 50
Miss R. Levison...........	Assistant.......................	10th...........	63	67 50
Mrs. L. M. Covington......	Assistant.......................	10th...........	64	67 50

Number of Teachers, 12; number of pupils, 639; amount of salaries, $856 66; cost of instruction for each pupil, $1 35 per month; $16 20 per annum.

COLORED SCHOOL.

Location.......................Broadway, between Powell and Mason Streets.

Mrs. Georgia Washburn.	Principal....................	3d, 5th, and 6th.	54	$100 00
Mrs. H. F. Byers	Assistant....................	7th,8th,9th,10th	63	67 50

Number of Teachers, 2; number of pupils, 117.; amount of salaries, $167 50; cost of instruction for each pupil, $1 43 per month; $16 96 per annum.

SOUTH COSMOPOLITAN GRAMMAR SCHOOL.

Location....................Post Street, between Dupont and Stockton Streets.

H. N. Bolander............	Principal......................	2d.............	63	$175 00
Miss L. T. Fowler.........	Head Assistant.................	....	......	83 38
Miss Sarrh Gunn..........	Special Grammar Assistant......	3d.............	67	80 00
C. Morell.................	Sub-Master....................	4th....	57	125 00
A. Dulon.................	Assistant.....................	4th............	50	67 50
Mrs. A. H. Hamill.........	Assistant.....................	4th............	44	67 50
Mad. Dejarlais............	Assistant.....................	5th............	63	67 50
Mrs. E. Foster............	Assistant.....................	5th............	61	67 50

Number of Teachers, 8; number of pupils, 405; amount of salaries, $733 33; cost of instruction for each pupil, $1 80 per month; $22 60 per annum.

SOUTH COSMOPOLITAN PRIMARY SCHOOL.

Location..........................Post Street, between Dupont and Stockton.

Name of Teacher.	Position Occupied.	Grade of Class.	No. in Class.	Monthly Salary of Teacher.
Miss M. Graf.............	Principal......................	5th............	55	$100 00
Miss E. Roeben...........	Pupil Assistant.................	....	......	50 00
Miss Grace Smith.........	Probationary Teacher, 2d grade.	5th and 6th.....	51	50 00
Miss Julia Haehnlen.......	Assistant......................	6th............	59	67 50
Miss Virginie Coulon......	Assistant......................	6th and 7th.....	64	67 50
Miss Lizzie York..........	Assistant......................	7th............	83	67 50
Miss E. Siegemann........	Assistant......................	8th............	57	67 50
Miss C. E. Campbell.......	Assistant......................	8th............	66	67 50
Mrs. K. McLaughlin.......	Assistant......................	8th and 9th.....	67	67 50
Miss Sarah Miller.........	Probationary Teacher, 1st grade.	9th............	69	55 00
Miss E. Dames............	Probationary Teacher, 2d grade.	10th............	56	50 00
Mrs. Josephine Clifford....	Probationary Teacher, 2d grade.	10th............	55	50 00

Number of Teachers, 12; number of pupils, 682; amount of salaries, $760; cost of instruction for each pupil, $1 11 per month; $13 32 per annum.

EVENING SCHOOLS.

R. K. Marriner............	Principal.......................	....	74	$60 00
Robert Desty.............	Assistant......................	....	58	50 00
F. J. Leonard.............	Assistant......................	....	60	50 00
W. W. Theobalds..........	Teacher Foreign Evening School	....	40	50 00
J. B. Sanderson..........	Teacher Colored Evening School	....	27	50 00
Miss E. Pitts.............	Teacher Female Evening School	....	30	50 00

Number of Teachers, 6; number of pupils, 289; amount of salaries, $310; cost of instruction for each pupil, $1 08 per month; $12 96 per annum.

SPECIAL TEACHERS.

Fr. Seregni...............	Teacher of Drawing...........	....	......	$150 00
H. Burgess...............	Teacher of Drawing...........	....	......	150 00
F. K. Mitchell............	Teacher of Music.............	....	......	150 00
A. J. Griswold............	Teacher of Music.............	....	......	150 00

TEACHERS ELECTED DURING THE YEAR.

Name.   To what School.

Miss M. F. George.....Spring Valley Primary; now in Market St. Primary.

Miss M. Guinness.....Stevenson Street Primary; now in Tehama St. Primary.

Mr. S. A White........West End School; now in Shotwell Street School.

Mr. H. N. Bolander ...Cosmopolitan Grammar School.

Mr. Choy Cum Chew..Chinese School (not in existence now).

Miss S. E. Miller......Cosmopolitan School.

Miss S. D. Carey......Cosmopolitan School; now in Union Gram. School.

Miss M. J. Ritchie.....Lincoln School.

Miss M. E. Perkins....Polk and Austin Street School.

Miss L. Solomon......Union Primary School.
Miss E. White........Union Grammar School.
Miss Julia A. Hutton..Tehama Street Primary.
Miss Mary Hart.......Eighth Street Primary (left).
Miss B. Comstock.....Potrero School; now in Lincoln School.
Mr. J. M. Sibley......Boys' High School.
Mr. A. Dulon..........Cosmopolitan School.
Miss C. E. Campbell...Cosmopolitan School.
Mrs. K. McLaughlin...Cosmopolitan School.
Mrs. E. Varney.......Lincoln School.
Miss L. A. Morgan....Tehama Street Primary.
Miss Victoria Schaap..Union Primary School.
Miss A. H. Giles......Powell Street Primary.
Miss M. B. Cook......Spring Valley Primary,
Miss G. A. Garrison....Fourth Street Primary.
Mrs. T. J. Nevins......Fairmount School.
Mrs. A. H. Hamill.....South Cosmopolitan School.
Miss F. H. Whitney....Steiner Street School.
Miss M. J. Hall.......Lincoln School.
Miss E. M. Casebolt...Lincoln School.
Miss J. A. Forbes......Lincoln School.
Mrs. Therese Sullivan..Spring Valley Grammar School.
Miss Grace Smith.....Cosmopolitan Primary School.
Miss E. Roeben.......Cosmopolitan Primary School.
Miss E. Dames........Cosmopolitan Primary School.
Miss Mary A. Lloyd...Broadway Primary.
Miss S. B. Cook.......Drumm Street Primary.
Miss M. J. Morgan....Shotwell Street.
Miss E. A. Cleveland..Lincoln Grammar School.
Mrs. E. P. Bradley....Denman School.
Miss F. Howe.........Broadway Primary School.
Miss Grace Wright.....Broadway Primary School.
Miss Bertha Chapuis...North Cosmopolitan School.
Miss R. Levison.......North Cosmopolitan School.
Miss A. S. Gray.......City Training School.
Miss Kate O'Brien.....Hayes Valley School.
Miss Carrie Watson....Eighth Street Primary School.
Miss Grace Chalmers..Eighth Street Primary School.
Miss A. J. Hall.......Shotwell Street School.
Miss H. S. Wooll......Shotwell Street School.
Miss A. C. Allen.......Powell Street Primary.
Mrs. M. Kincaid.......Union Grammar.
Miss E. F. Webber ....Spring Valley School (resigned).
Miss S. H. Thayer.....Union Grammar School.
Mrs. C. R. Beals......Girls' High School.
Mrs. R. F. Ingraham..Fourth Street School.
Miss Mary Heydenfeldt.Fourth Street School; now in State Training School.

Miss M. J. Armstrong. . Denman School.
Miss J. Morse . . . . Broadway Street Primary.
Miss M. A. Haswell. . . . Powell Street Primary; now in Broadway Primary.
Miss E. Goldsmith . . . . Spring Valley School.
Miss Mary Stincen. . . . . Shotwell Street School; now in Fourth Street Primary.
Mr. Robert Desty . . . . . . West End School.
Miss H. Featherly . . . . . Filbert Street School.
Miss A. Wells . . . . Filbert Street School.
Miss Maggie Bevans . . . Filbert Street School; now in Eighth Street Primary.
Miss H. Burr. . . . . Filbert Street School; now in Hayes Valley School.
Miss A. C. Robertson. . Silver Street Shool.
Miss S. E. Anderson . . . Silver Street School; now in Potrero School.
Miss S. Jessup . . . . Broadway Primary.
Miss S. E. Porter. . . . . . Broadway Primary; now in Bryant Street Primary.
Mrs. A. E. Du Bois. . . . City Training School.
Mr. F. Seregni . . . . Teacher of Drawing.
Mr. H. Burgess. . . . . . . Teacher of Drawing.
Mr. A. J. Griswold . . . . Teacher of Music.
Mr. F. K. Mitchell . . . . Teacher of Music.
Mr. R. K. Marriner. . . . Evening School.
Mr. W. W. Theobalds. . Evening School.
Mr. Robert Desty . . . . . Evening School.
Mr. F. J. Leonard . . . . . Evening School.
Mr. J. B. Sanderson . . . Evening School.
Miss Emily Pitts . . . . . . Evening School.

DIED.

*Mrs. E. C. Burt . . . . . . Tehama School.

TEACHERS RESIGNED DURING THE YEAR.

Name.	From what School.
Miss M. E. Very	Powell Street Primary.
Miss H. A. Hanecke	Spring Valley School.
Miss Julia Clayton	Mission Grammar School.

* At a meeting of the Board of Education, held June 4th, 1867, Mr. Rankin presented the following resolution, a just tribute to the memory of the deceased :

Resolved, That the Board of Education has heard with unfeigned grief of the death of Mrs. Elizabeth C. Burt, late Principal of the Tehama Street School. For a period of thirteen years she was connected with the School Department of this city, and during that time her capacity to govern and at the same time to impart instruction was frequently brought to attention. Her amiability was fully recognized by her assistant teachers, her scholars, and officers and members of the Department, of which she was one of its brightest ornaments. She united with many lady-like qualities, which endeared her to a large circle of devoted friends, eminent ability for discharging the responsible and honorable duties of teacher. The Board offers to the members of the bereaved family their deep sympathy and condolence.

On motion, the resolution was unanimously adopted, ordered to be spread upon the minutes and a certified copy of the same transmitted to the family of the late Mrs. E. C. Burt.

Miss Jennie Drummond.................,.........Union Grammar School.
Miss L. B. Hitchings....................Lincoln School.
Miss F. E. Cheney......................Washington Grammar School.
Miss L. M. Drummond.................Union Primary School.
Mr. S. D. Simonds......................Colored School.
Miss M. F. Austin.......................Girls' High School.
Mrs. H. L. Weaver....................,......Washington Grammar School.
Mrs. B. Marks..........................Spring Valley Grammar School.
Miss L. E. Field........................Denman School.
Miss F. E. Bennett......................Cosmopolitan Primary.
Miss M. A. Krauth.....................Broadway School.
Miss M. E. Cheney ....Washington School.
Miss F. Holmes........................Broadway School.
Miss E. F. Webber.....................Spring Valley School.
Miss M. L. Bodwell....................·.Girls' High School.
Mr. Geo. W. Bunnell...................Latin School.
Mrs. M. L. Swett......................Model School.
Miss N. M. Chadbourn.................Denman School.
Miss F. Lynch. ......,.................Rincon School.
Miss A. Van Reynegom.................Spring Valley School.

NOTES ON RESIGNATIONS.

During the past year, several of our most useful and excellent teachers have found it desirable, for their own advantage, or necessary from other circumstances, to dissolve their connection with our Department.

I trust it may not be thought invidious if I refer in kindly terms to the efficient services of several in the foregoing list.

Mr. Geo. Woodbury Bunnell arrived in this country, from New Hampshire, when fourteen years of age. He soon became connected as a pupil with one of our city Public Schools, in which he distinguished himself as a close student and fine scholar. He afterwards (but for a short period) attended the High School. Soon after he was an assistant with James Denman, Esq., in one of the early Grammar Schools; whence he was elected to the Greenwich Street School; thence transferred to the Hyde Street School; thence to the Principalship of the Spring Valley Grammar School, which position he resigned to prepare himself for a competitive examination for the Classical Department, then to be established in connection with the High School. Being successful in the examination, he was elected to that Professorship in 1865; this Department subsequently becoming the Latin School, and Mr. Bunnell its Principal. He retained this position till his resignation, in consequence of ill health, July 16, 1867.

27

Mr. Bunnell may with great propriety be called a self-made man. His persevering efforts in self-education have been alike creditable and remarkable. His resignation from the Public School Department of this city is to be regretted. May the school which he did so much to establish and render creditable to the city and State, long remain a monument to his ripe scholarship and persevering industry.

Miss Mary L. Bodwell arrived in this city, from Buffalo, N. Y., in December, 1863, immediately passed a very superior examination, and was elected to the State Normal School, where remaining a few months, she was elected to the Girls' High School. Here her earnest and persevering industry gained for her the confidence of her Principal and associate teachers, and the affectionate regards of her pupils. After retaining the position some three years, she resigned to assume other duties and more agreeable relations of life.

It was with deep regret that the Board of Education accepted the resignation of Miss Minnie Austin, resigning in consequence of failing health. She had occupied her position in the Girls' High School to the great satisfaction of the faculty and the Board for several years, gaining for herself the kind regards and tender sympathy of all who enjoyed her acquaintance.

Several others, after faithful and appreciated services, have also resigned their positions in Grammar and Primary Schools, to occupy others, which it is presumed will be found happier, more permanent, and more remunerative.

STATISTICS OF THE SEVERAL PUBLIC SCHOOLS,

SHOWING THE NUMBER OF DAYS' ATTENDANCE, THE AVERAGE NUMBER BELONG-
ING, NUMBER OF ABSENCES, NUMBER OF INSTANCES OF TARDINESS, PER
CENT. OF ABSENCE ON ATTENDANCE, PER CENT. OF TARDINESS ON ATTEND-
ANCE, AND NUMBER OF INSTANCES OF TRUANCY.

BOYS' HIGH SCHOOL.

	1866.					1867.					
	July	August	September	October	November	January	February	March	April	May 10th.	May 31st.
Whole No. days' attendance	1,736	1,810	1,769	1,704	1,623	1,450	1,535	1,363	1,367	1,162	914
Average No. belonging........	91	91	89	86	81	81	77	72	68	61	61
No. of absences..	10	10	14	16	5	9	5	13	8	8	1
No. of instances of tardiness....	4	2	3	......	......	......	......	......	......	......	......
Per cent. absence on attendance .	.005	.005	.007	.009	.003	.006	.003	.009	.005	.006	.001
Per cent. tardiness on attendance .	.002	.001	.001	......	......	......	......	......	......	......	......
No. instances of truancy	......	......	......	......	......	......	......	......	......	......	......

GIRLS' HIGH SCHOOL.

Whole No. days' attendance	2,167	2,241	2,169	2,103	2,083	1,703	1,841	1,738	1,899	1,648	1,103
Average No. belonging........	115	114	112	108	106	97	94	94	96	93	93
No. of absences..	25	40	79	53	35	44	49	51	31	28	23
No. of instances of tardiness....	4	10	4	3	12	15	8	9	13	6	3
Per cent. absence on attendance .	.011	.017	.036	.025	.016	.025	.025	.029	.016	.016	.020
Per cent. tardiness on attendance .	.001	.004	.001	.001	.005	.008	.004	.005	.006	.003	.002
No. of instances of truancy.....	......	......	......	......	......	......	......	......	......	......	......

SAN FRANCISCO LATIN SCHOOL.

Whole No. days' attendance	1,288	1,359	1,244	1,235	1,192	1,145	1,102	1,103	1,044	855	740
Average No. belonging........	70	70	65	64	62	59	57	56	53	52	52
No. of absences..	42	44	59	52	41	40	39	27	19	48	35
No. of instances of tardiness....	33	21	49	45	53	44	31	23	38	35	27
Per cent. absence on attendance .	.032	.032	.047	.042	.034	.034	.035	.024	.017	.056	.047
Per cent. tardiness on attendance .	.025	.015	.039	.036	.044	.038	.028	.020	.036	.040	.036
No. of instances of truancy.....	......	......	......	......	......	......	......	......	......	1	......

LINCOLN GRAMMAR SCHOOL.

	1866.					1867.					
	July	August	September	October	November	January	February	March	April	May 10th	May 31st
Whole No. days' attendance	17,794	19,029	18,214	18,327	18,224	15,504	18,620	17,350	17,605	17,208	12,689
Average No. belonging	926	982	959	960	950	956	965	955	927	942	879
No. of absences	605	623	975	904	781	671	798	835	793	785	534
No. of instances of tardiness	512	566	507	500	473	497	315	284	224	127	150
Per cent. absence on attendance	.033	.032	.052	.049	.042	.043	.042	.048	.045	.045	.042
Per cent. tardiness on attendance	.028	.029	.036	.027	.025	.038	.016	.016	.012	.007	.011
No. of instances of truancy			12	6	9	1	25	6	10	7	

DENMAN GRAMMAR SCHOOL.

	July	August	September	October	November	January	February	March	April	May 10th	May 31st
Whole No. days' attendance	13,382	13,927	13,520	13,819	13,111	11,893	12,233	12,514	13,538	11,449	9,161
Average No. belonging	725	719	716	724	688	689	694	705	703	667	642
No. of absences	392	453	814	521	662	512	726	911	527	545	347
No. of instances of tardiness	322	216	206	135	217	174	226	154	168	146	86
Per cent. absence on attendance	.029	.033	.060	.038	.050	.046	.059	.073	.039	.049	.038
Per cent. tardiness on attendance	.024	.016	.016	.009	.016	.015	.019	.012	.012	.013	.009
No. of instances of truancy											

RINCON GRAMMAR SCHOOL.

	July	August	September	October	November	January	February	March	April	May 10th	May 31st
Whole No. days' attendance	11,111	9,431	7,998	8,133	8,900	7,858	9,122	8,401	4,948	7,647	5,731
Average No. belonging	488	492	477	477	463	454	471	461	468	427	422
No. of absences	268	415	490	421	392	297	303	390	366	399	224
No. of instances of tardiness	251	288	273	204	213	199	181	110	109	104	110
Per cent. absence on attendance	.024	.044	.061	.052	.044	.038	.033	.046	.074	.052	.040
Per cent. tardiness on attendance	.022	.030	.034	.025	.024	.026	.020	.013	.022	.014	.020
No. of instances of truancy										1	

UNION GRAMMAR SCHOOL.

	1866.					1867.					
	July.	August.	September	October.	November	January.	February.	March.	April.	May 10th.	May 31st.
Whole No. days' attendance	9,418	10,013	8,932	9,407	9,612	6,796	9,304	8,856	8,609	7,861	6,653
Average No. belonging.......	518	522	532	501	508	515	489	482	468	418	342
No. of absences..	429	438	708	621	550	304	478	788	464	512	198
No. of instances of tardiness....	320	313	252	292	279	169	206	220	179	179	87
Per cent. absence on attendance .	.046	.044	.080	.066	.057	.045	.051	.089	.054	.065	.030
Per cent.tardiness on attendance .	.034	.030	.027	.030	.028	.025	.022	.026	.020	.023	.013
No. of instances of truancy.....	16	11	1	.....	8	2	9	7	......	6	3

WASHINGTON GRAMMAR SCHOOL.

Whole No. days' attendance	7,077	7,403	7,166	9,182	9,311	6,076	6,772	6,223	6,711	5,662	4,715
Average No. belonging.......	385	386	382	478	481	352	352	351	350	333	334
No. of absences..	245	267	413	367	445	285	310	456	300	349	143
No. of instances of tardiness....	171	146	141	204	185	184	179	126	133	229	118
Per cent. absence on attendance .	.035	.036	.057	.040	.047	.046	.046	.073	.044	.062	.030
Per cent.tardiness on attendance .	.024	.020	.020	.022	.020	.030	.026	.020	.020	.040	.025
No. of instances of truancy.....	.....	.....	2	1	.....	1	.....	.....	.....	.....	.....

MISSION GRAMMAR SCHOOL.

Whole No. days' attendance	7,996	8,198	8,137	7,786	7,513	6,717	7,066	7,041	7,964	6,666	5,938
Average No. belonging.......	441	444	435	415	398	391	387	414	416	400	410
No. of absences..	615	678	594	525	656	427	478	730	333	532	242
No. of instances of tardiness....	389	497	417	416	449	410	309	319	333	404	310
Per cent. absence on attendance .	.078	.083	.073	.067	.087	.063	.067	.100	.042	.080	.040
Per cent.tardiness on attendance .	.049	.060	.050	.053	.060	.059	.043	.045	.042	.060	.052
No. of instances of truancy.....	.....	2	3	4	1	1	2	2	.....	.....	.....

SPRING VALLEY GRAMMAR SCHOOL.

	1866.					1867.					
	July	August	September	October	November	January	February	March	April	May 10th.	May 31st.
Whole No. days' attendance	8,234	8,941	8,477	8,380	8,076	7,288	7,854	7,929	10,132	8,648	5,478
Average No. belonging.......	455	471	451	443	437	432	424	433	531	510	515
No. of absences..	416	525	555	513	631	440	635	694	541	623	473
No. of instances of tardiness....	394	544	395	412	384	452	479	547	506	565	443
Per cent. absence on attendance .	.050	.059	.065	.061	.078	.060	.082	.087	.053	.072	.086
Per cent. tardiness on attendance .	.048	.060	.044	.049	.047	.062	.061	.069	.050	.065	.080
No. of instances of truancy.....	3	......	......	4	1	2	1	......	1	4	3

COSMOPOLITAN GRAMMAR SCHOOL.

	July	August	September	October	November	January	February	March	April	May 10th.	May 31st.
Whole No. days' attendance	......	.....	......	......	......	......	6,220	6,010	6,121	5,268	4,462
Average No. belonging.......	......	.....	......	......	......	......	338	330	321	315	311
No. of absences..	......	......	......	......	......	......	542	581	294	412	208
No. of instances of tardiness....	......	......	......	......	......	......	72	147	190	236	138
Per cent. absence on attendance .	......	......	......	......	......	......	.087	.096	.048	.078	.047
Per cent. tardiness on attendance .	......	.....	......	......	......	......	.011	.024	.031	.045	.031
No. of instances of truancy.....	......	......	......	......	......	......	3	3	1	1	......

COSMOPOLITAN PRIMARY SCHOOL.

	July	August	September	October	November	January	February	March	April	May 10th.	May 31st.
Whole No. days' attendance	8,339	9,773	9,263	11,133	11,947	9,748	7,976	8,210	9,991	9,164	7,381
Average No. belonging.......	460	521	556	572	636	515	475	510	527	530	536
No. of absences..	232	699	924	693	714	510	543	807	544	709	656
No. of instances of tardiness....	218	237	317	218	170	182	292	258	267	248	117
Per cent. absence on attendance .	.028	.071	.099	.062	.060	.052	.068	.097	.054	.077	.089
Per cent. tardiness on attendance .	.026	.024	.034	.019	.014	.019	.037	.031	.027	.027	.016
No. of instances of truancy.....	......	......	......	1	1	......	1	4	3	2	3

UNION PRIMARY SCHOOL.

	1866.					1867.					
	July.	August.	September.	October.	November.	January.	February.	March.	April.	May 10th.	May 31st.
Whole No. days' attendance	6,149	7,223	8,503	7,382	7,239	6,939	7,604	7,609	8,533	7,403	6,212
Average No. belonging........	355	375	397	389	383	402	397	427	448	436	431
No. of absences..	429	438	450	405	426	302	335	517	434	449	257
No. of instances of tardiness....	320	313	169	223	230	189	188	223	193	190	159
Per cent. absence on attendance .	.070	.060	.053	.055	.059	.045	.044	.068	.051	.071	.041
Per cent. tardiness on attendance .	.052	.044	.020	.030	.032	.028	.024	.029	.023	.026	.025
No. of instances of truancy.....		2		1			1	2	5	2	

GREENWICH STREET PRIMARY SCHOOL.

	1866.					1867.					
Whole No. days' attendance	5,480	6,133	6,039	5,795	5,506	3,623	5,272	4,942	4,825	4,484	4,010
Average No. belonging........	305	320	313	308	298	275	282	285	276	268	275
No. of absences..	323	268	349	384	461	343	379	483	307	336	160
No. of instances of tardiness....	208	209	240	217	248	189	303	229	168	113	118
Per cent. absence on attendance .	.060	.044	.057	.066	.084	.095	.072	.098	.064	.075	.040
Per cent. tardiness on attendance .	.038	.034	.040	.036	.045	.052	.057	.046	.035	.025	.029
No. of instances of truancy.....	6	6	2	1	7		4	4	4	5	1

FOURTH STREET PRIMARY SCHOOL.

	1866.					1867.					
Whole No. days' attendance	9,577	10,802	10,802	10,8C8	10,584	9,935	11,662	10,675	11,485	10,034	8,250
Average No. belonging........	551	568	574	588	562	583	627	606	610	603	571
No. of absences..	378	577	787	711	826	470	802	1,074	755	843	569
No. of instances of tardiness....	253	326	306	377	251	215	270	332	360	363	242
Per cent. absence on attendance .	.039	.053	.073	.065	.078	.047	.068	.105	.065	.084	.068
Per cent. tardiness on attendance .	.026	.030	.028	.034	.023	.021	.023	.031	.031	.036	.029
No. of instances of truancy.....		6	2	3	2		3		1	3	3

POWELL STREET PRIMARY SCHOOL.

	1866.					1867.					
	July...	August...	September	October...	November	January ..	February	March...	April....	May 10th.	May 31st..
Whole No. days' attendance ...	8,271	7,014	9,136	9,147	8,877	8,139	9,198	8,410	8,956	7,480	6,323
Average No. belonging........	444	463	476	480	471	468	486	469	465	443	438
No. of absences..	236	374	480	486	577	404	490	474	438	585	244
No. of instances of tardiness....	235	192	114	204	247	147	212	93	106	103	64
Per cent. absence on attendance .	.028	.053	.052	.052	.065	.049	.053	.056	.048	.078	.038
Per cent.tardiness on attendance .	.028	.027	.012	.022	.027	.018	.023	.011	.011	.013	.010
No. of instances of truancy.....	......	5	......	5	......	......	......	1	2	1	......

HYDE STREET PRIMARY SCHOOL.

Whole No. days' attendance	4,209	4,527	4,338	4,425	4,145	3,773	3,995	3,937	4,276	3,677	3,118
Average No. belonging........	230	238	232	236	223	213	213	222	225	211	203
No. of absences..	234	245	300	298	319	242	296	392	227	277	177
No. of instances of tardiness....	127	73	115	68	77	67	83	66	51	47	57
Per cent. absence on attendance .	.055	.054	.069	.068	.076	.064	.074	.099	.053	.075	.056
Per cent.tardiness on attendance .	.030	.016	.026	.015	.016	.017	.020	.016	.011	.012	.018
No. of instances of truancy.....	......	......	......	1	3	......	......	......	2	......	......

MARKET STREET PRIMARY SCHOOL.

Whole No. days' attendance	12,740	13,814	13,740	14,566	14,012	12,488	14,230	13,379	14,639	12,266	9,984
Average No. belonging........	690	727	737	782	753	747	765	772	778	741	711
No. of absences..	406	659	1,013	1,069	1,081	862	1,025	1,284	838	1,085	722
No. of instances of tardiness....	349	473	361	429	386	358	498	325	373	320	204
Per cent. absence on attendance .	.031	.047	.073	.076	.077	.068	.072	.095	.057	.088	.072
Per cent, tardiness on attendance .	.027	.036	.026	.029	.027	.028	.034	.024	.025	.026	.020
No. of instances of truancy.....	......	......	......	......	......	......	......	......	7	......	......

BROADWAY STREET PRIMARY SCHOOL.

	1866.					1867.					
	July	August	September	October	November	January	February	March	April	May 10th	May 31st
Whole No. days' attendance	7,190	7,468	8,305	8,511	7,430	7,005	9,192	9,370	9,922	8,593	8,002
Average No. belonging	394	398	446	450	405	573	490	543	536	517	565
No. of absences	313	490	609	493	667	454	624	958	801	632	482
No. of instances of tardiness	343	397	305	367	299	215	510	399	310	309	205
Per cent. absence on attendance	.043	.035	.073	.057	.088	.064	.067	.102	.080	.073	.060
Per cent. tardiness on attendance	.047	.053	.036	.043	.040	.030	.055	.042	.031	.036	.025
No. of instances of truancy			12	10	6		3	3	4	6	3

EIGHTH STREET PRIMARY SCHOOL.

	July	August	September	October	November	January	February	March	April	May 10th	May 31st
Whole No. days' attendance	5,343	6,051	6,246	6,050	6,365	5,650	6,394	6,024	6,707	5,184	4,518
Average No. belonging	292	320	325	314	329	323	339	337	350	320	314
No. of absences	206	233	258	229	231	181	395	374	300	545	201
No. of instances of tardiness	218	207	187	178	152	110	182	143	164	124	130
Per cent. absence on attendance	.036	.038	.041	.037	.036	.032	.060	.060	.044	.151	.044
Per cent. tardiness on attendance	.040	.034	.028	.029	.023	.019	.028	.023	.024	.023	.028
No. of instances of truancy		3		3		1					

HAYES VALLEY PRIMARY SCHOOL.

	July	August	September	October	November	January	February	March	April	May 10th	May 31st
Whole No. days' attendance	3,970	4,337	4,293	4,638	4,435	4,258	4,631	4,649	4,975	4,796	3,981
Average No. belonging	217	226	222	247	242	245	250	268	261	284	275
No. of absences	150	231	211	296	299	197	366	340	252	311	147
No. of instances of tardiness	208	183	148	222	180	176	298	227	141	209	183
Per cent. absence on attendance	.040	.053	.049	.063	.067	.043	.079	.073	.050	.064	.037
Per cent. tardiness on attendance	.052	.042	.034	.047	.040	.041	.064	.048	.028	.043	.045
No. of instances of truancy		1	1	4	3		1	3		2	

TEHAMA PRIMARY SCHOOL.

	1866.					1867.					
	July	August	September	October	November	January	February	March	April	May 10th	May 31st
Whole No. days' attendance						4,433	17,647	17,828	19,978	16,587	13,027
Average No. belonging........						897	1,027	995	1,044	1,039	932
No. of absences..						52	885	1,172	839	1,318	885
No. of instances of tardiness....						44	424	499	364	437	239
Per cent. absence on attendance .						.011	.050	.065	.041	.079	.067
Per cent.tardiness on attendance .						.010	.024	.025	.018	.026	.017
No. of instances of truancy.....							25	8	5	7	3

NORMAL TRAINING SCHOOL.

Whole No. days' attendance	4,158	4,368	4,317	4,175	4,159	3,789	4,169	3,682	3,966	3,310	2,926
Average No. belonging........	214	228	230	221	222	217	222	213	209	196	202
No. of absences..	132	194	277	237	276	113	270	361	210	221	104
No. of instances of tardiness....	125	140	126	154	178	120	140	133	164	108	201
Per cent. absence on attendance	.051	.044	.032	.056	.066	.029	.064	.096	.052	.066	.035
Per cent.tardiness on attendance .	.030	.032	.029	.036	.042	.030	.033	.036	.041	.032	.068
No. of instances of truancy.....			1		1			2	2	2	

COLORED SCHOOL, BROADWAY STREET.

Whole No. day's attendance	1,125	1,457	1,369	1,435	1,332	1,126	1,434	1,576	1,722	1,618	1,351
Average No. belonging........	65	80	78	81	79	74	78	98	97	96	98
No. of absences..	157	163	195	185	243	183	118	253	217	135	118
No. of instances of tardiness....	212	259	166	235	196	162	202	220	183	202	104
Per cent. absence on attendance .	.130	.112	.142	.128	.183	.161	.082	.160	.125	.083	.087
Per cent.tardiness on attendance .	.188	.177	.121	.156	.146	.143	.140	.133	.106	.125	.076
No. of instances of truancy.....						6	2				

COMPARATIVE SCHOOL STATISTICS, EMBRACING THE YEARS FROM 1849-50 TO 1866-7,

SHOWING THE NUMBER AND THE INCREASE IN THE NUMBER OF TEACHERS, THE NUMBER AND INCREASE IN THE NUMBER OF CHILDREN IN THE PUBLIC SCHOOLS, THE NUMBER AND THE INCREASE IN THE NUMBER OF CHILDREN BETWEEN FOUR AND EIGHTEEN YEARS OF AGE, THE NUMBER AND PER CENT. OF INCREASE IN NUMBER OF CHILDREN ATTENDING PRIVATE SCHOOLS, ANNUAL CURRENT SCHOOL FUND AND PER CENT. OF INCREASE, ANNUAL ASSESSMENT ROLL, RATE OF CURRENT SCHOOL PROPERTY TAX, ANNUAL APPORTIONMENT OF STATE SCHOOL FUND, ETC., ETC.

Year	Total no. of teachers employed	Increase	Total no. of children attending Public Schools	Increase	No. of children bet. 4 and 18 years reported by Census Marshal	Increase	Total no. children attending Private Schools	Per ct. Private on Public	Annual Current School Fund	Increase	Per ct. of Increase	Total Assessment Roll	Per ct. of Increase	Rate School Tax — State	City	Total	Per ct. School Tax on total State Tax	State Apportionment	Per ct. of increase	State Apportionment per pupil
1849-50	2		150		500															
1850-1	4	2	325	175	1,500	1,000						$21,621,214								
1851-2	15	11	600	275	2,132	632			$23,125 00			14,016,903	.35		.23	.23				
1852-3	16	4	1,200	600	2,730	598			35,040 00	$11,915 00	.51	18,481,737	.31		.28	.28				
1853-4	19	3	1,350	150	3,268	538			159,249 00	124,209 00	354	28,900,150	.57		.28	.28	.05			$2 72
1854-5	29	10	2,200	850	4,531	1,263			136,580 00	*22,669 00	*.14	34,762,827	.20		.43½	.43½	.07	$18,125 00		3 12
1855-6	61	32	3,370	1,170	4,751	220			125,064 00	*11,516 00	*.08	32,076,572	*.08		.35	.35	.162	12,913 00	*.28	3 68
§1856-7	60	*1	2,821	*549	4,751		2,777	.419	92,955 00	*32,109 00	*.25	30,368,254	*.03		.35	.35	.152	12,780 00	.01	2 69
1857-8	67	7	‡5,273	2,452	6,375	1,624	3,139	.382	104,808 00	11,853 00	.12	35,397,176	.16		.35	.35	.142	8,061 00	*.38	1 49
1858-9	75	8	‡6,201	928	7,767	1,392	4,552	.556	134,731 00	29,923 00	.28	30,725,950	*.13		.35	.35	.107	11,092 00	*.45	1 78
1859-60	68	*7	‡6,108	*93	9,025	1,258	4,823	.531	156,407 00	21,676 00	.16	30,019,222	*.02		.35	.35	.122	13,048 00	*.12	1 66
1860-1	73	5	‡6,617	509	13,316	4,291	5,450	.681	168,855 00	12,448 00	.01	35,967,499	.19		.35	.35	.121	12,725 00	*.02	1 40
1861-2	82	9	‡8,204	1,587	13,358	43	4,403	.433	134,567 00	*24,288 00	*.14	41,845,119	.17		‖.20	‖.20	.127	14,780 00	.16	1 10
1862-3	94	8	‡8,177	*27	16,208	2,850	4,165	.311	178,929 00	44,362 00	.32	66,531,208	.59		.35	.35	.095	26,192 00	.77	2 02
1863-4	108	14	‡9,075	898	18,748	2,540			228,411 00	49,482 00	.27	77,129,066	.16		.35	.35	.117	27,912 00	.07	1 69
1864-5	138	30	8,000	*1,075	20,081	1,833			265,706 76	37,295 76	.16	80,736,165	.045		.35	.35	.112	36,371 00	.30	1 96
1865-6	206	88	10,153	2,153	17,369	*3,212			289,392 01	23,686 25	.08	88,266,457	.09	.05	.35	.40	.126	40,435 08	.11	1 38
†1866-7	253	47	13,385	3,232	20,263	2,884			320,807 57	31,415 56	.10	96,981,436	.085	.08	.35	.43	.14	55,641 00	.37	3 19

* Decrease.   † The number of Pupils and Teachers in this year are from reports of August, 1867.

‡ These figures show the total number of pupils that were enrolled during the respective years, and not the average per month, as are shown by the other figures. Were the monthly transfers deducted the actual number of pupils in the Department could be seen.   § The Ward Schools were this year withdrawn from the Public School Department.

‖ Twenty cents tax levied this year in consequence of the special appropriation of $60,000 from the General Fund.

SCHOOL CENSUS, REPORTED JULY, 1867.

District	No. of children bet. 6 and 15 years of age not attending school (White)	No. of children bet. 6 and 15 years of age attending Private Schools (White)	No. of children bet. 6 and 15 years of age attending Public Schools (White)	No. of children between 5 and 6 years of age (White)	Number of children under 5 years of age (White)	Number of negro children between 5 and 15 years of age — Total	Girls	Boys	Number of white children between 5 and 15 years of age — Total	Girls	Boys
1st District	165	249	701	105	956	2	2	...	1,220	610	610
2d District	206	548	1,221	266	1,559	29	9	20	2,231	1,129	1,102
3d District	39	25	86	23	160	...	...	...	173	90	83
4th District	228	332	902	160	1,005	51	30	21	1,622	790	832
5th District	36	80	125	22	180	3	2	1	263	132	131
6th District	90	171	627	113	588	28	18	10	1,001	539	462
7th District	212	310	758	125	1,037	7	4	3	1,405	686	719
8th District	402	529	1,538	229	2,014	9	4	5	2,698	1,369	1,329
9th District	259	348	883	72	1,305	9	5	4	1,562	777	785
10th District	316	759	2,027	308	2,582	9	6	3	3,410	1,704	1,706
11th District	131	628	1,430	244	1,959	1	1	...	2,433	1,254	1,179
12th District	197	196	954	94	1,112	20	6	14	1,441	730	711
Totals	2,281	4,165	11,252	1,761	14,457	165	86	79	19,459	9,810	9,649
10th District—Roman Catholic Orphan Asylum									196	196	
11th District—...en Asylum									15	15	
11th District—Def, Dnb, and Bld Asylum									5	2	3
11th District—Industrial School									111	12	99
12th District—St. Boniface Asylum									9	5	4
12th District—Protestant Orphan Asylum									179	76	103
12th District—Ladies' Protection and Relief Home									114	62	52
Grand totals	2,281	4,165	11,252	1,761	14,457	165	86	79	20,088	10,178	9,910

NOTE.—The number of Mongolian children under 15 years is 179, 37 of whom attend school.

COMPARATIVE CENSUS STATISTICS, FROM 1861 TO 1867.

	1861	1862	1863	1864	1865	1866	1867
Number of blind children between 4 and 18 years of age	6	22	29	25	24	42 (Between 5 and 21)	.....
Number of deaf and dumb children between 4 and 18 years of age	10	32	32	28	45	36 (Between 5 and 21)	.....
Number of Negro children between 4 and 18 years of age	219	192	234	269	191	146 (Between 5 and 15)	165
Number of Mongolian children between 4 and 18 years of age	65	181	117	434	279	68 (Under 15)	179
Number of Indian children between 4 and 18 years of age	.....	.....	.....	55	59	.....	.....
Number of children between 6 and 18 years of age not attending any school	.....	1,989	.....	2,653	3,565	3,746 (Between 5 and 15)	2,281
Total number of children reported as attending Private Schools	2,115	3,139	4,552	4,823	5,450	4,403 (Between 5 and 15)	4,165
Total number of children reported as attending Public Schools	.....	4,604	5,155	6,561	7,805	9,621	11,974
Number of children between 4 and 6 years of age attending private schools	.....	.....	.....	454	604	.....	.....
Number of children between 4 and 6 years of age	.....	.....	3,172	3,747	3,995	1,761 (Between 5 and 6)	.....
Number of white children under 21, born in California	8,890	13,282	14,655	18,321	21,123	.....	.....
Number of white children between 18 and 21 years of age	.....	898	952	1,157	1,291	.....	.....
Number of white children under 4 years of age	6,740	9,059	9,744	10,974	11,413	13,238 (Under 5)	14,457
Total number of white children between 4 and 18 years of age	8,669	13,358	16,208	18,748	20,581	17,223 (Between 5 and 15)	20,088
Number of girls between 4 and 18 years of age	7,859 (Under 18)	.....	.....	9,475	10,577	8,721 (Between 5 and 15)	10,178
Number of boys between 4 and 18 years of age	7,541 (Under 18)	.....	.....	9,273	10,004	8,502 (Between 5 and 15)	9,910
Number of applicants for school accommodation	.....	.....	.....	.....	1,142	.....	.....

SUMMARY OF MONTHLY REPORTS OF TEACHERS FOR THE YEAR 1865-6, COMMENCING JULY 1, 1865, AND ENDING JUNE 30, 1866.

Months	Whole number of days' attendance	Whole number of days' absence	Whole number of tardinesses	Per cent. of tardiness	Whole number of boys enrolled on Register	Whole number of girls enrolled on Register	Total number enrolled	Average number belonging	Average daily attendance	Percentage of attendance on average No. belonging	Number of Pupils entered	Number left	Number transferred	Number registered for admission	No. of days absent	Number of times tardy	Time lost by tardiness (h. m.)	Time lost by absence during school hours (h. m.)	No. of visits to parents, made by teachers	Number of visits made by School Directors	Number of visits made by Superintendent	Number of school visits made by other persons
July 28, 1865	126,450	4,633	3,680	.036	3,690	4,262	7,952	7,065.5	6,816.6	.964	3,779	1,683	324	233	38	67	10–58	7	234	268	194	900
Aug. 28, 1865	154,970	6,874	4,730	.044	4,494	4,335	8,829	8,114.8	7,736.8	.953	940	600	69	231	66	106	11–8	3–25	261	242	91	1,850
Sept. 29, 1865	160,790	9,085	4,422	.056	5,369	4,657	10,026	9,000.1	8,518.8	.946	1,962	734	317	210	60	174	8–32	4–50	392	181	89	1,171
Oct. 27, 1865	169,983	10,797	4,282	.063	5,285	4,562	9,847	8,871.3	8,330.7	.939	1,009	740	211	268	31	111	13–40	11–55	340	272	116	1,088
Nov. 24, 1865	163,944	13,691	4,155	.083	5,106	4,398	9,504	8,685.9	7,939.6	.914	598	691	98	202	69	136	15–28	33–10	319	369	232	1,001
Jan. 5, 1866	139,018	9,504	3,486	.068	5,100	4,494	9,594	8,642.6	8,071.5	.933	657	607	156	268	36	90	11–31	12–20	293	149	87	1,084
Feb. 2, 1866	163,094	14,590	4,457	.089	5,280	4,663	9,943	8,681.9	7,974.0	.918	1,741	902	317	237	55	142	19–42	7–55	220	93	15	916
March 2, 1866	162,981	11,464	4,559	.070	5,452	4,565	10,017	8,934.7	8,240.9	.930	794	582	132	162	68	190	19–32	14–5	281	182	69	1,264
April 6, 1866	171,265	12,580	4,607	.072	5,352	4,638	9,990	8,988.7	8,507.6	.913	740	701	91	274	71	127	14–57	22–25	287	136	6	943
May 4, 1866	166,414	10,930	4,301	.065	5,419	4,734	10,153	9,376.0	8,829.2	.940	1,032	632	73	48	117	94	10–20	9	291	172	191	1,444
May 31, 1866	165,707	11,540	4,204	.069	5,297	4,683	9,980	9,273.8	8,083.7	.936	779	844	37	44	66	88	9–32	10–20	301	261	39	2,246
Aggregate for the year	1,744,625	115,688	46,973	.....	55,844	49,991	105,835	95,635.3	89,449.4	.....	14,031	8,716	1,825	2,177	677	1,325	145–20	136–45	3,219	2,325	1,129	13,907
Monthly Average	158,602	10,517	4,270	.066	5,077	4,544	9,621	8,694.1	8,131.7	.935	1,275	792	165	197	61	120	13–12	12–25	292	211	102	1,264

BY OF MONTHLY REPORTS OF TEACHERS FOR THE YEAR 1866–7, COMMENCING JULY 1, 1866, AND ENDING JUNE 30, 1867.

RECORD OF VISITS													
Number of school visits made by other persons	1,197	1,390	1,443	1,368	1,270	2,205	1,215	1,045	1,245	3,526	2,557	18,461	1,678
Number of visits made by Superintendent	147	113	147	184	174	122	119	138	129	65	134	1,472	133
Number of visits made by School Directors	257	141	155	108	146	176	281	229	195	96	143	1,957	177
Number of visits to parents made by teachers	243	331	393	340	409	356	234	323	408	247	203	3,487	317
ATTENDANCE OF TEACHERS AT SCHOOL													
Time lost by absence during school hours (h. m.)	4–10	15–58	21–6	19–35	24–5	5–58	15–15	16–55	12–21	20–40	9	166–42	15–9
Time lost by tardiness (h. m.)	17–8	26–11	29	18–18	26–30	17–39	26–24	37–19	29–13	23–53	17–17	272–24	24–45
Number of times tardy	126	176	183	190	209	144	216	206	241	177	124	1,992	181
Number of days absent	89	51½	88	96½	93½	83	92½	104½	105	54½	55½	913	83
Total number of instances of truancy		75	56	44	57	17	86	43	52	54	21	505	45
Total number promotions		124	35	65	23	2,367	69	29	31	16	1,846	4,605	418
Total number expelled		3	6	5	7	2	3	4	4	5	4	43	3
Number registered for admission	79	51	79	92	88	32	102	49	155	197	183	1,107	100
Number transferred	612	148	185	105	106	282	230	152	105	91	63	2,079	189
Number left	839	570	815	690	769	931	971	792	757	754	656	8,644	776
Number of pupils entered	4,287	880	1,031	863	702	1,206	1,460	804	944	445	494	13,116	1,192
Per centage of attendance on average No. belonging	.953	.950	.934	.934	.933	.944	.930	.920	.946	.923	.949		.938
Average daily attendance	9,851.8	10,154.3	10,031.6	10,184.5	9,918.0	10,875.3	10,261.6	10,227.8	10,660.1	9,886.2	9,901.5	111,952.9	10,177.5
Average number belonging	10,330.4	10,679.9	10,729.4	10,900.9	10,626.2	11,507.5	11,026.9	11,105.8	11,267.2	10,707.4	10,427.7	119,309.3	10,846.3
Total number enrolled	11,552	11,584	11,917	11,831	11,785	13,322	12,376	12,205	12,362	11,595	11,190	131,719	11,974
Whole number of girls enrolled on Register	5,450	5,384	5,532	5,469	5,452	6,143	5,737	5,643	5,733	5,504	5,314	61,361	5,578
Whole number of boys enrolled on Register	6,102	6,200	6,385	6,362	6,333	7,179	6,639	6,562	6,629	6,091	5,876	70,358	6,396
Whole number of tardinesses	6,130	6,964	5,782	6,248	5,920	5,250	6,348	5,522	5,162	5,358	3,777	62,461	5,670
Per cent. of absence on attendance	.043	.051	.069	.066	.075	.060	.064	.082	.056	.068	.052		.063
Whole number of days' absence	8,261	10,399	13,933	13,425	14,350	10,517	13,220	16,179	12,127	12,551	7,807	132,775	12,070
Whole number of days' attendance	190,128	201,170	199,356	202,474	189,786	173,183	203,990	195,566	213,418	182,045	147,805	2,098,921	190,811
	66	66	66	66	66	67	67	67	67	67	67	or :–v–:	67

FORMER MEMBERS OF THE BOARD OF EDUCATION OF SAN FRANCISCO.

FROM THE YEAR 1856 TO 1857-8.

Names of Members from 1851 to 1856.	DISTRICTS.	1856-7.	1857-8.
C. J. Brenham........ C. L. Ross............	First District.........	R. W. Fishbourne	R. O'Neil.
Joseph F. Atwell ..... John Wilson	Second District.......	J. C. Mitchell	A. S. Edwards.
Henry E. Lincoln..... S. R. Harris	Third District........	William Sherman.....	Wm. Sherman.
N. Holland.........:... W. H. Bovee	Fourth District.......	William Hooper	S. B. Stoddard.
R. K. Waller.......... C. O. West	Fifth District	W. W. Estabrook	A. Tandler.
W. H. Talmage....... H. J. Wells	Sixth District	J. Hunt	C. L. Taylor.
J. K. Rose............ C. K. Garrison........	Seventh District......	Wm. Pearson.........	Wm. Pearson.
S. P. Webb........... J. B. Moore	Eighth District.......	E. B. Goddard........	E. B. Goddard.
F. Billings .... J. P. June............	Ninth District........	P. M. Randall	J. O. Eldridge.
W. A. Piper .... J. P. Buckley.........	Tenth District	George M. Blake......	C. C. Knowles.
J. S. Benson.......... R. S. Tibbetts........	Eleventh District.....	George Seger	E. Judson.
F. C. Ewer .... Elisha Cook .... James Van Ness......	Twelfth District......	L. P. Sage............	J. S. Dungan.
T. J. Nevins, Superintendent and Secretary, 1852 and 1853. W. H. O'Grady, Superintendent, 1853 and 1854.		J. C. Pelton, Superintendent and Sec'y. W. H. O'Grady, Superintendent and Sec'y. E. A. Theller, Sup't. B. Macy, Secretary.	J. C. Pelton, Superintendent and Sec'y. H. P. Janes, Superintendent and Sec'y.

FROM THE YEAR 1858-9 TO 1861-2.

Districts.	1858-9.	1859-60.	1860-1.	1861-2.
First District	R. O'Neil	R. O'Neil	E. Donnelly	E. Daly.
Second District	J. H. Mer	J. H. Mr	J. H. Widber	J. H. Widber.
Third District	I. B. Dy	William M. Hixon	H. D. Ellerhorst	H. D. Ellerhorst.
Fourth District	William Bartling	William Bartling	William Bartling	William Bartling.
Fifth District	John H. Brewer	John H. Brewer	G. W. Beers	A. L. My.
Sixth District	H. R. Janes	H. R. Janes	H. R. Janes	James Bowman.
Seventh District	William Pearson	William Pearson	William Pearson	William Pearson.
Eighth District	George Cofran	George Cofran	Eris Bke	George rh.
Ninth District	J. O. Fldridge	J. O. Fldridge	W. L. Palmer	W. L. Mr.
Tenth District	C. C. Knowles	C. C. Knowles	C. C. Knowles	C. C. Knowles.
Eleventh Dist.	E. Judson	E. Judson	M. La	M. Lynch.
Twelfth Dist.	J. S. Dungan	J. S. Dungan, S	J. S. Dungan, Superintendent	Joseph M. Wd.
	H. P. Janes, Superintendent	Jas. Denman, Superintendent	Jas. Denman, Superintendent	Jas. Denman, Superintendent.
	Sael Barkley, Secretary	James Pen, Secretary	James Pearson, Secretary	James Pearson, Secretary.

FROM THE YEAR 1862-3 TO 1866-7.

Districts.	1862-3.	1863-4.	1864-5.	1865-6.	1866-7.
First District	L. B. Mastick	L. B. Mastick	L. B. Mastick	L. B. Mastick	E. H. Coe.
Second District	J. H. Mr	John F. Pope	J hen F. Pope	H. T. Graves	H. T. 1 de.
Third Dist.	J. W. Dodge	J. W. Dodge	Washington Ayer	Washington Ayer	William F. Hale.
Fourth Dist.	Wm Bartling	George B. Hitchcock	George B. Hitchcock	J seph W. Winans	Joseph W. Ms.
Fifth District	Lafayette Story	Lafayette Story	W. A. Gr	W. A. Grover	Washington Ayer.
Sixth Dist.	James Bowman	twin Inis	Giles H. Gray	A. C. Nichols	A. C. Ms.
Seventh District	Wm G. Badger	William G. Bger	William G. Badger	Wm G. Badger	Ira P. Rn.
Eighth Dist.	George Cofran	E. D. Sawyer	J. I. N. Shepard	George C. Hickox	George C. Hickox.
Ninth District	W. L. Palmer	J. N. Risdon	S. B. Rson	S. B. Thompson	A. W. Scott.
Tenth District	C. C. Knowles	J. H. Mr	M. Lynch	S. C. Bugbee	S. C. Bugbee.
Eleventh Dist.	M. Lynch	M. Lynch	M. Lynch	M. Lynch	P. B. Cornwall.
Twelfth Dist.	Joseph M. Wood	Daniel uht	Abner Doble	Charles M. Plum	Astin My.
	George Tait, Super't	George Tait, Super't	George Tait, Super't	John C. Pelton, Super't	John C. Pelton, Super't.
	D. H. Whittemore, Sec'y	D. H. Whittemore, Sec'y	l del uht, Secretary	Daniel uht, Secretary	del uht, Secretary.

28

INVENTORY OF SCHOOL FURNITURE, AUGUST 30, 1867.

Name of School	Pupils' Desks, single and double	Class Tables & Desks	Chairs	Settees	Benches	Pianos	Clocks	Swinging Blackboards	Cupboards	Chart Racks	Map Stands	Closets	Book Cases	Cabinets	Rubbers	Stoves	Numeral Frames	Globes	Cost
Boys' High	95	3	19	47			3	1					2	1		3			$1,089 60
Girls' High	179	4	16	17		1		1	1		3			1		4		1	1,683 00
Latin	73	4	7	10			2				1			1		2			852 40
Lincoln Grammar	1019	22	51	87	186	1	19	1	1	4	16	1	2			4			8,962 30
Denman Grammar	766	14	39	100	152	2	14	1		6	11		3						6,880 40
Rincon Grammar	464	15	33	6	1	2	7		2	1	3					9			3,495 10
Union Grammar	420	9	21	2	43		8			4	2		1		132	9		2	3,361 80
Washington Gram'r	354	8	20		55	2	7	1					1	7	46	8		1	2,988 40
Spring Valley Gram.	326	11	20	37	8	2	8			3						10			2,608 20
Mission Grammar	295	9	14		55	1	7	1			2			1		8			712 00
Shotwell Grammar	84	4	14		39											1			816 80
Cosmopolitan Gram.	477	12	19	7	57	1	11		1					1					3,185 50
Tehama Primary	398	18	47	75	108	1	16			7	9	2			260	16			4,131 60
Lincoln Primary	205	12	27	8	104	2	12				4	3	5		183	12	4		2,124 20
North Cosmopolitan Primary	281	9	15		61		4				1			3	97		2		2,424 30
Broadway Primary	91	13	27	1	134		12		2	1					242	12	2		1,547 50
Powell St. Primary	294	9	26		33		7	1		2	2	2		1		8	1		2,216 70
Eighth St. Primary	234	9	15		63		5		1		4					6			2,110 20
Fourth St. Primary	123	12	41		83		10					1				10			1,495 70
Union Primary		7	16		129		7				1			1	38	5			690 80
Hayes Valley Prim'y	117	4	8		36		3	2		2	2					4			1,102 80
Steiner St. Primary	14	1	3		10		1												107 00
Bryant St. Primary	2	1	5		54		3								15	2	2		708 50
Hyde and Bush Sts. Primary	120	4	12		53	1	4	1		1	1	1		1	45	4	1		1,235 60
Hyde und Geary Sts. Primary		2	4		35		2								3	2			195 70
Model and Normal	238	15	45	21	29	1	8	1		9		3		5	108	8	2		2,691 60
Fairmount	24	1	4		12		1				1					1			216 00
Ocean House	8	1	2		8											1			68 00
West End	12	1	2		8		1									1			112 50
San Bruno	24	1	2		11				1		1					1			252 50
Potrero	36	1	3		16		1				1					1	1		361 00
Silver Street		1	3		36											1			136 50
Drumm Street	21	1	2		12		1				1					1			179 50
Polk and Austin Sts.		1	3		17		1			1						1			115 00
Pine Street	30	1	3		8		1			1				1	22	1	1		258 20
St. Mark's Place		2	2		27										6		1		120 50
City Training		4	6		35										24				188 20
Colored	76	2	14		13		2	1				2				2			653 00
Totals	6903	248	610	418	1711	17	189	12	8	43	62	19	15	23	1221	157	17	4	62,078 60
Carpenter's Shop and contents..																			1,000 00
Total amount..																			$63,078 60

P. S. The value of the above furniture is taken at cost price, deduct 5 per cent, for wear and usage, and the present value of School Furniture will be about $60,000.

REAL ESTATE OF THE SAN FRANCISCO SCHOOL DEPARTMENT.

LOTS DEEDED BY COMMISSIONERS OF FUNDED DEBT.

Fifty vara lot No. 301, corner of Bush and Stockton Streets.

Fifty vara lot No. 462, corner of Kearny and Filbert Streets.

Fifty vara lot No. 663, corner of Vallejo and Taylor Streets.

One hundred vara lot No. 128, corner of Market and Fifth Streets.

Lot on Fourth Street, 80 feet by 125 feet, portion of one hundred vara No. 174, corner of Harrison and Fourth Streets.

LOTS OBTAINED BY EXCHANGE.

Fifty vara lot No. 482, on Greenwich Street, received in exchange for fifty vara lot No. 695, corner of Stockton and Francisco Streets.

Inner portion of one hundred vara lot No. 76, fronting on Vassar Place, Harrison Street, near Second Street (100 x 180 feet,) obtained in exchange for fifty vara lot No. 732, corner of Fremont and Harrison Streets.

Part of one hundred vara lot No. 274, 115 feet on Eighth Street by 275 feet deep, received in exchange for one hundred vara lot No. 258, corner of Folsom and Seventh Streets.

Part of fifty vara lot No. 157, on Broadway near Powell Street (69¼ x 137½ feet,) received in exchange for portion of one hundred vara lot No. 174, corner of Fourth and Harrison Streets.

Part of fifty vara lot No. 581, 70 feet on Post Street, between Dupont and Stockton Streets; received in exchange for portion of one hundred vara lot No. 174, corner of Fourth and Harrison Streets.

Lot 100 feet on Tyler Street, by 137½ feet deep, between Pierce and Scott Streets, for lot No. 2, block 431, Western Addition.

LOTS OBTAINED BY PURCHASE.

Fifty vara lot No. 418, on Union, near Montgomery Street.

One half of fifty vara lot No. 121, on Powell near Clay Street.

Lot on Mission Street, 200 by 182, in block 35.

Part of fifty vara lot No. 1320, 97½ feet on Bush Street by 137½ feet on Hyde Street.

One half of fifty vara lot No. 159, on Powell near Jackson street.

Fifty vara No. 602, corner of Mason and Washington Streets.

Fifty vara No. 1023, corner of Bush and Taylor Streets.

Lot on Broadway Street, 39¾ by 91⅜ feet; portion of fifty vara lot on the northeast corner of Powell and Broadway Streets.

Lot on Tehama Street, 28 by 75 feet, commencing at the southerly line of Tehama Street, at a point distant 297 feet westerly from the southwest corner of First and Tehama Streets.

Lot on Tehama Street, 90 by 75 feet, numbered on the official map of the city of San Francisco as lots Nos. 46 and 47 of the one hundred vara lot survey.

Lot on Kentucky Street, 50 by 100 feet, commencing at a point on the westerly line of Kentucky Street, distant one hundred feet southerly from the southwest corner of Kentucky and Napa Streets.

Lot on Chenery Street, 62 by 125 feet, commencing at a point on the east line of Chenery Street, distant northerly 200 feet from the northerly corner of Randel and Chenery Streets.

Also, lot on the San Jose Railroad, 62 by 175 feet, commencing at a point on the westerly line of the San Jose Railroad, distant 183 feet northerly from the northwest corner of Randall Street and the San Jose Railroad.

Lot on Chenery Street, 50 by 125 feet, being known as Lot No. 8, in Block 29, as laid down upon the map of the Fairmount Tract, San Miguel Ranch.

Lot on Silver Street, 44 by 70 feet, commencing at a point on the northwesterly line of Silver Street, distant 112 feet from the northwesterly corner of Silver and Second Streets.

Lot on the corner of Pine and Larkin Streets, 200 by 120 feet, portion of Block 14, Western Addition.

Lot on Clay Street, near Powell, 26½ by 75 feet, adjoining Boys' High School lot on the north.

Lot on Silver Street, 24 by 80 feet, with house and improvements; purchased of S. King.

Lot on Silver Street, 20 by 80 feet, with house and improvements; purchased of M. Kelsy.

Lot on Silver Street, 25 by 75, purchased of Mr. O'Connelly.

LOTS OBTAINED BY DONATION.

Nos. 13, 14, 15, 16, 26, 27, and 28, in Block No. 85, Potrero Nuevo.   Donated by Geo. Treat; value $1,500.

No. 4, in Block No. 23, Bernal Ranch, West End Map, six miles out, County Road.   Donated by Harvey S. Brown; value $1,400.

Lot on the southwest corner of Kentucky and Napa Streets, 100 by 100 feet, Potrero. Donated by Robert Dyson, J. W. Raymond, J. Ward, Samuel Gilmore, Jas. L. Riddle, and C. G. Eaton; value, $2,800.

Lots 247, 248, 249, 250, 251, 252, 253, Precita Valley' Lands, on Adams St., near Eve St., 50 by 132 feet. Donated by Vitus Wackenreuder; value $500.

Lot on Vermont Street, 120 by 200 feet, being a portion of Block No. 127, Potrero Nuevo. Donated by Nathan Porter and E. D. Sawyer; value $1,000.

Lot on Bernal Ranch, 80 by 180 feet, designated on West End Map No. 2, as Lot No. 4, Block 27. Donated by Nathan Porter; value $1,000.

Lot on Filbert Street, between Taylor and Jones, 100 feet front, portion of fifty-vara No. 446; donated to School Department by the Board of Supervisors; value $10,000.

Lot on Shotwell Street, 122½ by 122½ feet, between Twenty-second and Twenty-third Streets. Donated by John Center; value $8,000.

Lot on Montana Street, 200 by 125 feet, known as Lot No. 4, Block W, upon a certain map marked "Map of Lands of the Railroad Homestead Association. Donated by Association; value $1,000.

LOTS OBTAINED BY VAN NESS ORDINANCE.

In Mission Blocks—
    Fifty vara lot in Block No. 8.
    Fifty vara lot in Block No. 21.
    Fifty vara lot in Block No. 34.
    Fifty vara lot in Block No. 61.
    Fifty vara lot in Block No. 93.
    Fifty vara lot in Block No. 104.

In Western Addition—
    Fifty vara lot No. 2, in Block No. 3.
    Fifty vara lot No. 6, in Block No. 14.
    Fifty vara lot No. 5, in Block No. 21.
    Fifty vara lot No. 5, in Block No. 29.
    Fifty vara lot No. 2, in Block No. 62.
    Fifty vara lot No. 5, in Block No. 111.
    Fifty vara lot No. 5, in Block No. 117.
    Fifty vara lot No. 5, in Block No. 123.
    Fifty vara lot No. 2, in Block No. 136.
    Fifty vara lot No. 2, in Block No. 158.

Fifty vara lot No. 5, in Block No. 281.
Fifty vara lot No. 5, in Block No. 289.
Fifty vara lot No. 2, in Block No. 318.
Fifty vara lot No. 2, in Block No. 325.
Fifty vara lot No, 6, in Block No. 374.
Fifty vara lot No. 2, in Block No. 419.
Fifty vara lot No. 2, in Block No. 460.
Fifty vara lot No. 2, in Block No. 565.

In Potrero Nuevo—
Lot in Block No. 39, 100 by 200 feet.
Lot in Block No. 46, 100 by 200 feet.
Lot in Block No. 163, 100 by 200 feet.

VALUATION OF SCHOOL PROPERTY.

	Value of Improvements.	Value of Lot.	Total.
Lincoln School lot and building	$100,000	$175,000	$275,000
Boys' High School lot and building	15,000	15,000	30,000
Girls' High School lot and building	10,000	30,000	40,000
Denman School lot and building...............	50,000	35,000	85,000
Union School lot and building	15,000	10,000	25,000
Rincon School lot and building...............	10,000	20,000	30,000
Washington School lot and building...........	15,000	15,000	30,000
Spring Valley School lot and building..........	13,000	12,000	25,000
North Cosmopolitan School lot and building	12,000	13,000	25,000
South Cosmopolitan School lot and building....	17,000	18,000	35,000
Mission School lot and building	10,000	20,000	30,000
Shotwell Street School lot and building.........	8,000	8,000	16,000
Powell Street School lot and building	3,000	12,000	15,000
Fourth and Clary Street School lot and building.	5,000	15,000	20,000
Bush and Hyde Street School lot and building ..	3,000	9,000	12,000
Tehama School lot and building	28,000	12,000	40,000
Hayes Valley School lot and building...........	7,000	8,000	15,000
Eighth Street School lot and building	8,000	12,000	20,000
San Bruno School lot and building............	3,500	1,500	5,000
Fairmount School lot and building.............	2,700	1,300	4,000
Potrero School lot and building...............	2,200	2,800	5,000
Pine Street School lot and building...........	2,200	3,800	6,000
Broadway School lot and building	12,000	23,000	35,000
Colored School lot and building	4,500	5,500	10,000
Filbert and Kearny School lot and building	8,000	7,000	15,000
Greenwich Street School lot and building.:.....	3,000	7,000	10,000
Tyler Street School lot and building...........	4,370	630	5,000
Pine and Larkin School lot and building	8,000	7,000	15,000
West End School lot and building.............	1,600	1,400	3,000
Lot, corner of Vallejo and Taylor streets.......	....	....	6,000
Forty lots in the suburbs, at $4,000 each.......	....	....	160,000
Total....................................			$1,057,000

SHERIFF'S REPORT.

OFFICE OF THE SHERIFF OF THE
CITY AND COUNTY OF SAN FRANCISCO. ⎱

To the Honorable the Board of Supervisors
of the City and County of San Francisco—

GENTLEMEN :—In compliance with Resolution No. 6,963 of your Honorable Board, I submit the following Report for the fiscal year ending June 30th, 1867.

RECEIPTS.

Paid into the Treasury from July 1st, 1866, to June 30th, 1867, inclusive, as per monthly statements filed with the Auditor................................. $16,720 73

DISBURSEMENTS.

Books, Stationery and Printing.................... $304 00
Transportation of 111 Insane, exclusive of bills of the California Steam Navigation Company.......... 457 50

Total................................. $761 50

COUNTY JAIL.

PRISON STATISTICS OF THE COUNTY JAIL FOR THE FISCAL YEAR ENDING
JUNE 30TH, 1867.

Prisoners in Jail July 1st, 1866......................		118
Received for Murder.................................		3
"	Attempt to commit Murder.................	8
"	Manslaughter	3
"	Mayhem	3
"	Arson...................................	3
"	Assault with deadly weapon................	12
"	Burglary.................................	49
"	Riot.....................................	10
"	Incest	1
"	Grand Larceny...........................	62
"	Threats..................................	1
"	Forgery..................................	7
"	Felony...................................	15
"	Conspiracy	9
"	Robbery	15
"	Malicious Mischief........................	11
"	Obtaining Money falsely...................	4
"	Embezzlement	3
"	Insane...................................	4
"	Assault and Battery.......................	89
"	Petit Larceny.............................	167
"	Misdemeanor and Vagrants.................	208
"	Safe Keeping.............................	100
"	The Industrial School.....................	70
"	Assault	6
"	Contempt of Court........................	4
"	Libel....................................	1
"	Civil Suits	7
	Total	993

Males, 930; Females, 63.

DISPOSED OF AS FOLLOWS:

Executed...	2
Conveyed to the Insane Asylum.........................	4
Delivered to Sheriffs of other Counties..................	16
Transported to State Prison..........................	66
Legally discharged, and expiration of sentence............	778
Escaped from Jail Yard.................................	2
Number remaining in Jail July 1st, 1867................	125
Total..............................	993

NUMBER OF PRISONERS UNDISPOSED OF.

CRIMES.—Murder......................................	3
Assault to commit Murder....................	1
Burglary	10
Grand Larceny.............................	5
Threats.....................................	1
Forgery	2
Robbery.....................................	5
Obtaining Money falsely......................	2
Assault and Battery..........................	4
Petit Larceny.................................	67
Misdemeanors and Vagrancy..................	15
Safe Keeping.................................	10
Total..............................	125

Males, 118 ; Females, 7.

The most important matter in connection with the County Jail, and which I think should receive your earnest consideration, is the establishment of a workhouse or some system of labor, whereby a large class of the persons now sentenced for various offenses to imprisonment in the County Jail, could be dealt with in a manner more profitable both to themselves and the public ; besides, more effectual as a measure for the prevention of crime.

Of the number confined in the Jail, amounting much of the time to more than one hundred and fifty, probably three fourths of them are under sentence; many of them for terms of from one to six months, and in some cases for a longer period. These, with the exception of such as are employed in necessary labor about the jail, lie in their cells during their confinement, frequently half a dozen occupying the same cell, with nothing to do but to eat, sleep, read such literature suited to their tastes as they can procure, and indulge in such conversation as would be looked for under the circumstances. Such associations and habits cannot but be corrupting to all, and especially to young men, novices in crime, who have been convicted of some light offense, and in default of the fine imposed, have been sent here for punishment, where they meet with a class of men wholly abandoned to vice and immorality, and learn from them enticing secrets of crime. Besides, such a mode of life begets habits of idleness, and tends to debilitate the prisoners in body, so that when released they are neither as able or have the inclination to labor, as they would have were they employed during their confinement.

Again, there are a class of petty thieves, who, too lazy to work, depend upon the Jail for an asylum. Many of them, when the winter season draws nigh, will commit thefts for no other object or purpose than to be committed to the jail for the inclement season; for there they get enough to eat and a bed to sleep on, and are more contented and apparently enjoy life more, than do many honest men who have their liberty and are compelled to earn their own bread by honest labor. The record shows many such cases as the above having occurred every year during my connection with the shrievalty.

If the punishment was made more onerous for this class, they would probably come to the conclusion that it is better and more profitable to themselves to work where they could realize something for their labor, than to do so solely for the public.

As to the best system or plan for the accomplishment of the object desired, I will not here suggest; but hope that your Honorable Board will agitate the matter, and take such action in the premises and obtain such legislation, as I think its importance requires.

Respectfully submitted.

HENRY L. DAVIS,
Sheriff.

San Francisco, August 1, 1867.

REPORT

OF THE

SUPERINTENDENT OF PUBLIC STREETS

HIGHWAYS AND SQUARES.

SAN FRANCISCO, August 12th, 1867.

To the Honorable Board of Supervisors—

GENTLEMEN:— I herewith submit my Annual Report of the amount and cost of street work completed during the year ending July 1st, 1867, and the location of the same; together with a summary of the cost of all street work done during each year, from July 1st, 1856, to July 1st, 1867, and the length of all the sewers.

It is well known to the members of your Honorable Body that the cleaning of the sewers, streets, and street crossings is now being done, by your direction, under my supervision, by men, horses and carts hired for that purpose by the day; the former method of doing this work by contract having proved a failure. I would recommend that, as a matter of economy, your Board obtain an act from the Legislature, authorizing the purchase of horses and carts by the city, and the hiring of men by the month.

Respectfully submitted.

GEO. COFRAN,

Superintendent of Public Streets, Highways and Squares.

GRADING.

Date	Streets	Streets Between	Cubic Yards	amt.	Remarks.
September 1st, 1866	Sixth	Mission to Howard	12,218	$2,314 93	
September 22d	Clementina	Fifth to Ninth	1,604	301 20	
September 22d	Howard	Eighteenth to Nineteenth	10,411	2,909 62	
October 3d	Guerrero	Sixteenth to Seventeenth	2,237	456 26	
October 1st	Sutter	Buchanan to Fillmore	9,368	2,538 28	
September 3d	Dupont	First to Union	1,120	708 40	
October 4th	McAllister	Larkin to Fillmore	77,928	23,832 40	
October 6th	Elizabeth	275 feet south of Folsom	116	64 40	
October 6th	Tenth	Mission to Howard	49,736	9,511 44	
October 6th	Zoe	Bryant to Brannan	6,253	1,781 82	
October 12th	Eleventh	Folsom to Harrison	11,164	1,017 95	
	Union	Franklin to Gough	10,166	2,983 47	
July 14th	Fell	Van Ness to Franklin	3,445	821 11	
July 23d	Crossing	Dupont and Greenwich	368	379 52	
July 19th	Pine	Steiner to Pierce	17,942	4,595 24	
July 28th	Crossing	Pine and Steiner	288	143 28	
July 28th	Crossing	Pine and Pierce	656	256 30	
July 28th	Crossing	Pine and Fillmore	559	248 97	
July 31st	Fillmore	Pine to Sacramento	9,526	2,342 21	
July 31st	Crossing	Pine and Sacramento	2,310	573 15	
July 31st	Crossing	Sutter and Powell	48	65 27	
August 4th	Sixteenth	Guerrero to Dolores	3,444	1,094 80	
August 22d	Crossing	O'Farrell and Van Ness	7,179	2,402 67	
August 30th	Sacramento	Stockton to Powell	9,868	1,988 67	
July 31st	Crossing	Fillmore and California	1,709	431 91	
August 29th	Fell	Eighth to	2,590	469 00	
August 29th	Crossing	Fell and Gough	113	53 86	
August 29th	Crossing	Fell and Octavia	759	183 10	
August 29th	Crossing	Polk and Polk	5,399	2,466 80	
July 1st	Polk	Polk and Fell	1,817	403 00	
July 19th	Seventeenth	Mission to Valencia	3,823	800 08	

Date				
July 19th	Sevent enth	Valencia to Dol...	8,309	1,551 75
July 24th	...le	Union to ...sh	6,052	3,434 95
July 24th	Crossing	Fillmore and Filbert	295	90 67
July 30th	Grove	...th to Franklin	1,536	332 08
July 30th	Grove	...th to Oct ...	1,537	332 26
July 30th	Grove	Polk to Van Ness Avenue	5,172	986 56
August 1st	Grove	Van Ness to Franklin	3,198	631 24
August 1st	...do	Van Ness and Grove	1,672	332 76
August 1st	Crossing	Grove and Polk	999	211 62
August 18th	Crossing	...ve and Gough	236	75 80
August 18th	Third	Bryant to Brannan	2,774	012 63
August 22d	Grove	...cia to Laguna	1,277	229 86
August 25th	Crossing	...ch and Fillmore	1,959	1,108 25
...ber 4th	Crossing	Union and ...le	296	142 30
September 4th	Crossing	Hyde and Sutter	147	86 52
September 4th	Crossing	Ellis and Buchanan	439	92 19
...tember 4th	Crossing	Ellis and Laguna	803	144 54
September 4th	Ellis	Ellis and ...	1,758	527 40
September 4th	Crossing	Laguna to Buchanan	7.902	1,501 38
September 15th	Crossing	...th and Howard ...no	2,689	779 79
Spt...ber 15th	...do	Mason and ...	1,240	471 25
September 28th	...le	Polk to Larkin	5,941	1,123 98
October 3d	Greenwich	Powell to Mason	5,064	1,587 51
Oct ber 3d	Crossing	Fulton to Grove	2,411	1,181 39
Oct ber 6th	Howard	...ne to Steiner	3,324	1,353 61
Oct ber 8th	Crossing	Fillmore and Fell...	566	277 30
...ber 17th	Howard	Twentieth to	9,377	2,773 93
...ber 17th	Crossing	Nineteenth and Howard	559	173 35
...ber 17th	...al	Nineteenth to Twentieth	10,411	28 80
February 2d	Second Avenue	Howard and ...	1,673	435 12
November 3d	Fillmore	...rd to Fourth ...	21,764	7,132 90
...ber 29th	...th	Seventeenth to	2,509	199 22
...ber 29th		Pine to Bush	1,292	325 92
		Sacramento to ...ly	1,221	1,153 53
		Carried forward	380,566	$102,361 47

GRADING. — CONTINUED.

Date.	Streets.	Streets Between.	Cubic Yards.	amt.	Remarks.
		Brought ...	380,566	$ 161 47	
	Crossing...	... and Drumm...	1,732	555 79	
December 11th...	...	... to J ...	1,727	57 16	
January 23d...	...	... to ...	177	10 40	
	Fillmore...	Sixteenth ...	337	56 77	
October 16th...	...	Post to ... Sutter...	2,314	50 68	
... 16th...	...	... to ...	177	76 08	
... 9...	...	... to ...	1,843	43 06	
... 18th...	...	Bush ...	2,155	36 30	
... 26th...	...	... to ...	943	25 21	
... 2d...	Fourth...	... to ...	3,882	1,906 93	
November ...	...	Filbert ...	37,119	844 54	
... 2...	...	... nd ...	2,363	78 87	
... 22d...	Ivy Avenue...	... to Laguna...	2,736	65 56	
... 22d...	... Avenue...	... to ...	810	208 50	
... 19th...	...	...	11,109	31 38	
... 8...	Van N ...	...	689	33 41	
December 26th...	...	... to ...	14,737	3,334 58	
... 24th...	...	... ad Van N ...	6,534	49 46	
... 26th...	...	... and Clay...	6,516	46 96	
January 26th...	...	... ad ...	2,140	53 20	
... 16th...	...	...	423	29 70	
... 25th...	...	Bush to Sutter...	840	39 35	
... 3l...	...	Broadway to Pacific...	393	24 64	
... 8th...	Battery...	Union to ...	5,968	69 30	
... 8th...	...	... ad Hyde...	120	47 60	
... 27th...	Sixteenth...	... to ...	3,088	39 44	
...	...	... to ...	12,348	2,417 98	
December ...	...	... to Sixteenth...	38,050	93 25	
December 6th...	...	... to ...	7,259	23 17	
... 14th...	...	... to Vallejo...	9,383	40 07	

Date	Street	Location		
?er 28th	Gough	Post to O'Farrell	24,304	3,203 26
December 28th	Crossing	Geary and Gough	2,976	396 34
January 3d	Crossing	Turk and Polk	1,817	323 85
January 3d	Crossing	Turk and Van Ness	1,712	418 32
January 4th	Fern ?ne	Polk to Van Ness	3,963	629 23
January 19th	Mission	Fifteenth to Sixteenth	8,926	2,010 32
February 28th	Sacramento	Jones to Leavenworth	743	258 50
March 7th	Brannan	Third to Fourth	9,546	2,0? 07
March 19th	Crossing	?in and Leavenworth	504	150 57
M?h 25th	Sixth	275 feet s?h of Brannan	3,946	565 0
March 26th	Devisadero	Sutter to Post	968	?7 80
March 26th	Devisadero	Post to ?ry ?	1,301	247 75
March 26th	Devisadero	Geary to O'Farrell	2,480	437 0
March 26th	Howard	?th to Twenty-first	2,750	853 25
M?h 26th	Crossing	Howard and ?y-first	2,073	550 85
March 31st	Brannan	Second to Third	15,160	5,302 80
June 22d	Crossing	Harrison ?d S?ar	1,217	1,239 43
June 22d	Spear	Harrison to Folsom	20,639	15,332 36
June 24th	Eddy	Hyde to Larkin	6,824	2,298 17
June 24th	Crossing	Geary a?d Polk	1,322	188 58
June 8th	Jones	Eddy to Ellis	2,417	795 52
June 13th	Laguna	Sutter to Post	1,614	211 68
June 13th	Laguna	Post to ?ry	1,773	236 84
February 7th	Crossing	Lombard and Fillmore	576	349 90
February 26th	Sacramento	Mason to Taylor	2,997	442 21
February 20th	Pine	Larkin to Polk	8,345	2,097 12
March 20th	Ma?	Eighth to Ninth	1,086	320 24
M?h 22d	Fillmore	Sacramento to ? ?c	21,507	5,223 74
M?h 2d	Clay	Jones to Leavenworth	39,921	27,196 12
April 17th	Crossing	Pacific and Fillmore	387	?70 59
March 17th	Crossing	Jackson and Hyde	617	274 11
M?h 22d	Turk	Leavenworth to Hyde	3,025	914 30
March 21st	Fillmore	Lombard to Greenwich	7,194	2,030 95
March ?h	Crossing	Sacramento and Mason	1,793	1,556 65
Carried forward			764,901	$220,138 24

GRADING. — CONCLUDED.

Date	Streets	Streets Between	Cubic Yards	Amount	Remarks
		Brought forward	764,901	$220,138 24	
April 15th	Geary	Larkin to Polk	20,775	6,907 35	
April 15th	Crossing	Larkin to ...	13,493	727 75	
April 15th	Crossing	Fulton and Webster	162	80 52	
April 15th	Crossing	Fulton and Fillmore	1,646	540 56	
April 30th	...	...et to Mission	78,728	14,814 10	
April 30th	Crossing	Geary and Devisadero	1,160	301 05	
May 1st	Sutter	Laguna to Bu...	9,490	1,429 15	
May 22d	Van Ness	Hayes to Fell	3,857	555 66	
May 3d	Crossing	Sutter and Laguna	1,359	236 95	
May 8th	Hyde	... to Broadway	8,086	2,848 67	
May 9th	Broadway	Polk to Van Ness	9,328	2,524 54	
May 9th	Crossing	Gough and O'Farrell	10,387	2,888 02	
May 10th	Polk	Broadway to Pacific	2,237	1,97 13	
May 20th	Fell	Octavia to Laguna	5,434	1,019 72	
May 23d	California	Polk to Franklin	32,845	7,330 50	
May 23d	Crossing	Sutter and ...	469	99 26	
June 4th	Howard	...th to	0,220	1,66 10	
June 24th	Crossing	Hayes and Steiner	1,338	635 35	
June 25th	Filbert	Filbert and Fillmore	5,248	1,304 16	
June 28th		...er to Fillmore	2,241	592 41	
June 29th	King	Geary and Laguna	779	260 60	
April 19th	King	Hyde and Green	637	198 87	
	Fulton	Buchanan to Fillmore	20,729	6,214 45	
	Van Ness	Bush to ...	39,025	6,129 04	
May 3d	Crossing	...ry and Van Ness	1,279	251 82	
May 7th	Franklin	Ellis to ...Fk	17,607	5,358 69	
May 7th	Crossing	Eddy and Franklin	1,292	42 99	
May 13th		Hayes to Grove	861	24 34	
May 11th	Van Ness	Hayes to ...	6,526	845 68	
May 22d	Min	Mission to Folsom	71,890	24,582 20	

Date	Streets	Streets Between		Cost	
May 22d	Crossing	Main and Howard	7,527	2,867	22
May 22d	Freelon	Fourth to Zoe	2,451	1,028	49
May 29th	?dia	Eight ?h to ?ith	831	324	09
May 29th	Valencia	Seventeenth to Eighteenth	289	34	18
May 29th	Crossing	Eighteenth and ?a	1,512	544	32
June 13th	Fourteenth	Howard to Mission	896	258	31
June 13th	Van Ness	Turk to Eddy	16,864	2,154	25
June 17th	Seventeenth	Dolores to Sanchez	7,958	2,487	00
June 27th	Seventeenth	Sanchez to Castro	9,739	2,822	91
June 29th	Lafayette	?a to Union	161	106	75
Totals			1,191,257	$327,333	38

MACADAMIZING.

Date	Streets	Streets Between	Square Feet	Cost	Remarks.
August 8th	Ninth	Howard to Folsom	22,917	$2,989 77	and curb.
August 8th	Crossing	Ninth ?ite Tehama	1,180	161 00	ard urb.
August 8th	Crossing	Ninth opposite Clementina	1,180	161 0	and curb.
August 17th	?dia	?et to Fourteenth	48,230	4,118 95	ard ?eb.
August 17th	Crossing	?ia ?d Herman	4,364	481 59	and curb.
August 17th	Crossing	Valencia and Ridley	4,514	495 49	ard ?b.
S?er 29th	?h Ness	Oak to Fell	22,275	2,211 37	and ?b.
?er 30th	Guerrero	Sixteenth to Seventeenth	23,140	1,368 80	
?r 30th	Fell	Franklin to Van Ness	14,909	1,184 77	and curb.
?er 1st	Sutter	Buchanan to Fillmore	31,969	2,067 66	
?ly 11th	?er	Larkin to ?ie	141,680	8,808 80	
July 7th	Ninth	Mission to Howard	23,696	1,935 26	and curb.
J?y 7th	Crossing	Ninth ?ite Minna	1,199	97 87	and curb.
July 17th	Ninth	?t to Mission	23,807	2,360 50	and curb.
July 17th	Crossing	Ninth opposite Jessie	1,025	99 08	and curb.
		Carried forward	366,085	$28,541 91	

29

MACADAMIZING. — CONTINUED.

Date.	Streets.	Streets Between.	Square Feet.	Cost.	Remarks.
February 15th	Sixteenth	...to to Dolores	366,085	$28,541 91	
...t 29th	Fell	Gough to Octavia	19,693	1,359 64	And curbs.
August 29th	Crossing	Fell nd Gough	15,984	1,255 56	And curbs.
July 7th	Crossing	Fell nd ...	4,020	294 00	And curbs.
July 7th	Crossing	Bush and Gough	4,020	292 0	And curbs.
July 7th	Crossing	Bush and ...in	4,020	416 78	
July 20th	Seventeenth	...a to Dolores	38,080	416 78	
July 30th	Grove	Franklin to ...h	15,984	2,094 40	
July 30th	Grove	...a to Gough	15,984	1,080 64	
July 30th	Grove	Polk to Van Ness	14,908	1,097 64	Ad ...bs.
...st 1st	Crossing	...e and Polk	4,020	1,175 50	Ad ...s.
August 1st	Grove	Grove nd Van Ness	7,566	391 65	And ...bs.
August 1st	Grove	Polk to Van Ness	14,880	568 22	And ...bs.
August 2d	Seventeenth	Van to Valencia	19,040	1,092 48	And ...bs.
August 6th	Crossing	...e and ...gh	4,020	1,324 80	And ...bs.
...th	Grove	Grove and Octavia	4,020	261 50	And ...s.
August 28th	...e	Octavia to Laguna	15,984	264 30	And curbs.
September 4th	Crossing	Ellis and Buchanan	4,020	0 32	And ...bs.
S...er 4th	Ellis	Buchanan to Webster	15,984	393 70	And ...s.
S...er 4th	Crossing	Ellis and Laguna	4,020	1,316 19	And ...bs.
...ber 4th	Ellis	Ellis nd ...a	4,020	421 80	And rbs.
September 4th	Ellis	...a to Buchanan	15,984	424 10	And ...s.
September 10th	Crossing	Ellis and ...r	4,020	1,436 50	Ad ...bs.
September 22d	Grove	Larkin to Polk	15,984	362 40	And curbs.
...er 3d	...lle	Fulton to ...e	9,978	1,182 31	Ad ...s.
...er 6th	Crossing	...e and Fell	4,020	935 98	Ad curbs.
...r 6th	...lle	Hayes to Fell	18,906	49 76	Ad ...s.
...er 6th	Crossing	Fillmore nd Hayes	4,726	2,001 17	Ad bs.
January 23d	Crossing	Howard nd Seventh	4,400	545 83	And curbs.
...er 3d	Second Ave	...th to Seventeenth	1600	433 60	And curbs.
				956 30	Ad rbs.

Date	Location				
Gr 29th	...re	10, 56	740	14	And curbs.
November	...g	7,673	628	44	And curbs.
...er 8th	...t	10, 22	592	88	And curbs.
January 1th	Crossing	3, 86	308	95	
...y 1th	...g	36	308	95	
Mar 8th	Sixteenth	9, 063	1,292	72	And curbs.
My 23d	...g	4,501	358	81	And curbs.
My 11th	Crossing	3, 86	308	95	
January 11th	...er and Mn Ness	7,274	567	55	
Gr 6	...e	10, 56	70	14	Ad curbs.
Gr 16th	Crossing	40	302	82	Ad curbs.
Gr 6th	...h to ...r	10, 66	740	14	Ad bs.
Gr 18th	...r ...d Bush	620	97	60	
Gr 29th	Pine to Sacramento	20, 92	1,740	50	Ad bs.
Gl er 29th	Sacramento ...d ...ne	909	391	07	Ad bs.
Gl or 29	...d	420	321	84	Ad bs.
	Crossing	27,300	62	50	Ad bs. & c'bs.
Gr 10th	...d and ...th	4, 94	69	88	Ad bs.
Gr 10th	Crossing	437	896	45	Ad bs.
Gr 22d	Ivy Avenue	27,300	1,630	70	{ Ad bs. nd bs.
Gr 19th	...d	22,275	1,501	10	
December 26th	Vn N ss	10,656	540	76	
December 25th	Mn	51,170	3,756	91	
Gr 24th	Mt	27,307	2, 04	11	Ad bs.
Gr 28th	...h to Sixteenth	15,600	1, 66	80	
Gr 4h	Bt Avenue	19,375	1,491	41	
Gr 6th	Mn to	3,419	230	78	
Gr 10th	Gk nd Mt	7,490	545	77	And curbs.
Gr 10th	Gk nd Mt	1,587	173	07	And curbs.
Mar 0th	Gk nd Mt	481	38	89	And curbs.
Gr 10th	Be nd Mt	7,831	583	38	
Gr 6	...in	27,300	1,887	60	
Hy 9h	Mn ...	22,960	786	70	And curbs.
Mry 25th	Mt	20,685	50	82	And curbs.
Hay 9th	Mt				
Carried forward		1,136,347	$85,396	8	

MACADAMIZING.—CONTINUED.

Date.	Streets.	Streets Between.	Square Feet.	Cost.	Remarks.
January 25th	Crossing	Market opposite Tenth	1,136,347	$85,396 89	
January 25th	Crossing	Mt, Polk, and Fell	3,757	279 97	
January 30th	Crossing	Market, ...h, and Haight	10,269	771 14	And curbs.
March 6th	Mission	...h to Thirteenth	13,845	973 50	
Mch 6th	Mission	Opposite Twelfth	42,738	3,205 35	And curbs.
January 19th	Crossing	California and Leavenworth	5,001	406 45	
March 28th	Crossing	Howard and Eighteenth	4,996	498 05	And curbs.
March 29th	Mason	Clay to Sacramento	4,574	298 60	
June 12th	Harrison	Eleventh to ...h	11,100	573 70	
June 8th	Sutter	Scott to Devisadero	10,487	1,087 26	And curbs.
Ju n8th	Crossing	Sutter and Devisadero	28,359	2,164 63	And ubs.
June 8th	Crossing	Geary and Devisadero	5,671	411 81	And curbs.
February 13th	Vallejo	Battery to Front	5,671	376 80	And curbs.
March 20th	Minna	Eighth to Ninth	12,650	932 47	And ubs.
Mh 25th	Fillmore	Sacramento to Pacific	11,550	1,756 22	And curbs.
March 28th	Crossing	Sanchez and Seventeenth	39,583	3,294 15	
March 28th	Crossing	Noe and Seventeenth	4,446	270 90	
April 17th	Crossing	...e and Jackson	4,446	275 90	
April 17th	Crossing	Fillmore and Pacific	4,020	339 42	
April 17th	Crossing	Fillmore and Clay	4,020	340 50	
April 17th	Crossing	Fillmore and Washington	4,020	312 84	
April 19th	Bush	Hyde to Leavenworth	4,020	312 84	
April 19th	Crossing	Lombard and Fillmore	15,984	1,447 24	
April 19th	Van Ness	Hayes to Fell	4,020	270 45	
May 15th	Crossing	Pine and ...	19,440	1,298 77	
May 24th	Crossing	Sutter and Buchanan	4,020	329 15	
May 30th	Crossing	...ry and O'Farrell	4,020	344 00	
April 24th	Howard	Eighteenth to ...h	22,550	1,839 00	Sidew'ks & c'bs.
April 24th	Crossing	Nineteenth and Howard	27,300	1,473 85	Curbs.
April 25th	Crossing	...a and Fourteenth	4,574	275 80	Corners.
	Crossing		1,591	232 21	

Date	Streets	Streets Between	Lineal Feet	Cost	Remarks
April 27th	Sacramento	Mason to Taylor	11,020	798 30	And curb.
M'y 13th	Octavia	Hayes to Gle	11,462	975 55	And curb.
May 16th	Van Ness	Hayes to fove	19,440	1,550 35	And curb.
May 25th	Howard	Twenty-First to Twenty-Second	27,300	1,892 22	And curb.
May 29th	Valencia	Eighteenth to Nineteenth	1,613	256 30	
May 29th	Mia	Seventeenth to Eighteenth	1,613	112 71	
May 29th	Crossing	Valencia and Eighteenth	3,454	307 0	
June 6th	Crossing	Howard and Twentieth	4,574	294 80	And curbs.
June 5th	Crossing	Howard and Twenty-First	4,574	294 80	And curbs.
		Totals	1,560,119	$117,271 89	

BRICK SEWERS.

Date	Streets	Streets Between	Lineal Feet	Cost	Remarks
August 31st	Vn Ness	Fell to Oak	275	$2,543 85	
far 24th	Green	Kearny to Dupont	412.6	2,100 85	
July 10th	Crossing	Greenwich opposite am Place	34.3	297 60	
July 31st	Crossing	Pine and ar	137.6	1,485 60	
July 19th	Mission	Fifth to Sixth	550	3,724 10	
July 26th	Taylor	Bush to Pine	278	1,892 32	
August 15th	Ross	Washington to Jackson	200	1,022 61	
August 11th	Crossing	Washington te Ross	24.6	130 39	
August 15th	Cards Alley		230.6	1,310 72	
August 23d	Crossing	Geary and ar	103	1,501 44	
September 1st	Taylor	O'Farrell to Ellis	275	1,871 85	
September 1st	Crossing	Taylor and Ellis	103	1,536 07	
August 31st	Crossing	Mason opposite Valparaiso	34	197 50	
July 7th	Crossing	Second opposite Minna	41.3	339 61	
July 10th	ath	at to Mission	550	4,868 85	
July 10th	Market	Oak to Eleventh	33.10	328 18	
July 13th	Cl ana	First to Second	825	5,52 050	
		Carried forward	4,107.4	$30,672 04	

BRICK SEWERS. — CONCLUDED.

Date.	Streets.	Streets Between.	Lineal Feet.	Cost.	Remarks.
		Brought forward	4,107.4	$30,672 04	
15th	First	Opposite Minna	41.3	$263 58	
August 28th	Belden	Pine to Bush	275	1,910 10	
..st 21st	Crossing	First and Harrison	165	1,920 80	And corners.
August 24th	Powell	Pine to Bush	275	1,380 10	
August 25th	Crossing	Eleventh and Mission	123.9	2,247 16	And corners.
August 28th	Post	Mason to Taylor	412.6	3,023 85	
August 28th	Market	Oak and Van Ness	253.2	3,183 78	And corners.
September 4th	Oak	Van Ness to Franklin	769.6	1,333 41	And cors.
September 4th	Crossing	Van Ness and Fell	193.9	2,864 66	And corners.
October 9th	Crossing	Clay and Mason	93.4	1,462 32	And corners.
November 23d	Sixth	Mission and Howard	550	3,648 35	
December 8th	Brannan	Fourth to Third	825	5,152 50	
February 4th	Sixth	Market to Mission	550	3,613 10	
December 4th	Kearny	Sutter to Post	275	1,811 98	
December 4th	Crossing	Sutter and Kearny	34.4	227 12	
December 1st	Crossing	Post and Kearny	34.4	227 12	
February 6th	Crossing	Post and Taylor	103.2	1,569 44	And corners.
February 6th	Crossing	Mission and Sixth	82.6	1,364 90	And corners.
December 26th	Battery	Union to Pine	275	1,912 10	
December 27th	Dupont	Sacramento to California	275	1,893 6?	
December 27th	Crossing	O'Farrell and Jones	103.2	1,524 63	
16th	Fourth	Market to Mission	550	3,746 00	
..th	Eddy	Powell to Jones	412.6	3,317 72	
October 24th	Pine	Front to Market	333	2,459 70	
October 25th	Mission	Third to Fourth	825	5,221 35	
October 29th	Virginia	Washington to Jackson	275	1,391 50	
..r 31st	Van Ness	Hayes to Fell	275	2,484 55	
..er 9th	Van Ness	Hayes to Oak	275	2,324 60	
..er 30th	Ritch	Brannan to Townsend	550	3,613 60	
December 4th	Dupont	Filbert to Union	275	1,729 75	

Date	Street	Location		Amount	
December 4th	Crossing	Van Ness and Grove	193.6	2,899 28	
December 31st	Mason	Geary to O'Farrell	275	1,863 60	
December 7th	Kearny	Bush to Sutter	275	1,781 10	
December 7th	Crossing	Kearny and Bush	52	333 40	
January 7th	Crossing	Kearny and Sutter	34.4	224 12	
January 16th	Crossing	Hayes ad Van Ness	193.9	2,950 28	
January 29th	Mason	Sutter to Post	275	1,876 10	
February 6th	Lombard	Stockton to Powell	416.6	2,928 98	
February 18th	Lafayette	Union to Green	275	1,566 85	
February 8th	Green	Opposite Lafayette	34.4	193 03	
February 18th	Green	Opposite Sonoma	34.4	207 16	
February 20	Crossing	Pacific and Leavenworth	117.9	1,572 79	
March 4th	Townsend	Third to Crook	426	2,918 72	
March 19th	Pacific	Jones to Leavenworth	412.6	2,730 60	
March 13th	Post	...or to Jones	412.6	3,131 72	Corners.
March 12th	Crossing	Third and Townsend	......	333 60	
March 13th	Ellis	...or to Jones	412.6	2,734 25	
May 7th	Mason	Broadway to ...	275	1,911 35	
May 18th	Crossing	Townsend ...	41.3	290 62	
April 4th	Crossing	Post and Jones	103.8	1,628 01	
April 8th	Mason	Post to Geary	275	1,843 75	
April 11th	Sansome	...nt to Washington	162.3	1,133 70	
April 1	Crossing	Jackson and Sansome	......	95 76	Corners.
April 27th	Crossing	Ellis ad Jones	103.2	1,450 17	
May 3d	Crossing	Townsend and Ritch	41.3	275 52	Corners.
May 11th	Lafayette	Jackson and ...on	......	731 75	
May 10th	Fifteenth	Union to ...	275	1,534 50	
May 11th	Crossing	...n to Howard	559	3,627 50	
May 15th	Silver	Fifteenth and Mission	114.6	1,535 13	
May 25th	Crossing	Third to Second	827	4,395 70	
May 25th	Merchant	Silver and Third	41.3	231 97	
June 4th	Sansome	Montgomery to ...	412.6	2,812 75	
June 4th	Howard	Opposite Merchant	34.5	222 75	
June 4th		Fifteenth to Sixteenth	520	2,444 00	
Totals			21,203.10	$156,745 92	

REDWOOD SEWERS.

Date	Streets	Streets Between	Lineal Feet	Cost	Remarks
July 21st	...	Fifth to Sixth	825	$4,076 45	
July 21st	Crossing	Fifth	41.3	202 33	
...er 6th	...g	Fourth ...d Harrison	123.9	582 30	
...er 6th	...th	...n to ...om	550	2,424 60	
September 21st	Washington	...is to ...m	275	1,475 10	
September 21st	Washington	...is to ...t	275	1,426 22	
September 21st	Crossing	...	68.9	401 76	
September 21st	Crossing	... and ...	68.9	468 66	
...er 3d	Louisa	550 feet east of Fourth	540	1,844 81	
...er 3d	Crossing	Fourth	41	138 93	
...er 3d	Crossing	...a and ...	10	33 88	
August 9th	Fourth	...n to Perry	160	782 60	
...er 0th	Fourth ...	...l to ...	276	960 04	
December 29th	Crossing	...c to Broadway	275	1,033 35	
December 29th	...th	...th and	110	486 60	
...er 9th	...n	...	310	1,353 99	
...er 9th	Crossing	Spear to Stewart	82.6	390 85	
N ...er 9th	...r	...n and Spear	275	953 10	
N ...er 9th	Crossing	...ay to Washington	24.6	83 45	
November 9th	Freelon	Clay ...	295	90 44	
...er 9th	Valparaiso	275 feet west of ...th	412.6	1,385 48	
N ...ber 23d	Crossing	...n to Taylor	103	376 32	
N ...ber 23d	Jones	Jones and ...	275	952 85	
November 1?th	Fourteenth	...h to ...	550	1,750 85	
...er 17th	Mission	...d to ...	275	1,342 60	
N ...er 22d	Broadway	...n to Spear	148.9	533 82	
N ...er 2?th	Freelon	..., west	440	1,368 60	
February 6th	Fourth	Fourth to Zoe	41.3	123 72	
N ...ber 8th	Jones	...te	275	965 85	
N ...ber 8th	Fourth	...l to ...	518	2,465 60	
January 26th	Crossing	...h to Brannan	82.6	399 42	

Date	Streets				Feet	$ ¢	Corners.
January 20th	...ing	r ...th and ...			82.6	384 42	
...ary 20th	Crossing	...th and Guerrero			82.6	378 13	
March 4th	...	Fourth and ...			123.9	558 87	
March 4th	Crossing	...th to ...s.			399	1,858 60	Corners.
June 25th	Crossing	...th and Seventh			......	245 60	
June 25th	Sixth	...m to ...in			550	2,822 35	
June 5th	...	...m to ...he Bay			371.4	1,523 25	
June ...th	Crossing	...al to Drumm			68.9	467 68	
June 6th	...lk	...th of ...d			275	769 75	
...ry 7th	...n	Beale to ...Mn			275	922 50	
...ary 11th	Crossing	...Mn and Mn			82.6	276 75	
May 7th	Broadway	...e to ...th			265	91 75	
May 7th	Crossing	...lbert and ...ary			68.2	367 35	
April 6th	...y	Hyde to Larkin			414	1,517 35	
April 24th	...	...s to ...th			412.6	1,188 00	
April 29th	Market	Spear to ...he Bay			150	642 75	
June ...0th	Fifteenth	...d to ...t			550	1,926 75	
	Crossing	...al and ...de			68.9	423 78	
February 16th	...ing	...ay and H...e			151.3	588 00	
Totals					12,137.6	$49,578 20	

PLANKING.

Date	Streets.	Streets Between.	Feet.	$ ¢	Remarks.
...er 6th	...ing	Fourth and Harrison	16,138	$ 587 83	
...er 6th	Fourth	Harrison to Folsom	46,426	1,572 22	
...er ...th	Crossing	Fourth opposite Clara	5,954	259 20	Corners.
...er ...th	Crossing	Fourth opposite Louisa	4,395	177 20	Corners.
September 22d	...na	Eighth to Ninth	43,083	2,186 34	
...ember 29th	Mar	Hyde to Larkin	58,678	1,867 61	
Carried forward			174,674	$6,650 40	

PLANKING. — CONTINUED.

Date.	Streets.	Streets Between.	Feet.	$	Remarks.
		Brought forward	174,674	$40 40	
Oct ber 6th		275 feet south of Folsom	10,862	38 18	
Oct ber 5th	Cards Alley		9,871	30 15	
...er 9th	O'Farrell	Mason to Taylor	58,750	2,031 41	
July 6th	Crossing	Fourth and Bryant	16,138	574 81	
July 30th	...g	Turk and Hyde	10,763	555 67	
July 3...	Crossing	Turk and Larkin	10,763	539 01	
...st 3d	Turk	Van Ness to Polk	33,984	2,434 30	
August 17th	Crossing	Sansome and Pacific	10,065	395 61	
July 7th	...a	First to Second	64,211	2,103 70	
July ...	Ma	...rd to Fourth	58,375	5,006 44	
...er 6th	Crossing	Larkin and McAllister	14,447	630 69	
August 7th	...s	O'Farrell to Ellis	37,125	43 02	Corners.
...	Turk	Hyde to Larkin	37,517	31 98	
August 11th	...g	Fourth and Perry	6,826	360 57	
Agust 16th	...a	First to Second	62,665	2,241 60	
Agt 16th	...er	Hyde to Leavenworth	56,477	30 28	
...st 16th	...h	Bryant to Harrison	54,977	1,957 95	
...er 13th	Berry	Dupont to Mary	2,375	39 68	
...er 26th	Drumm	Sacramento to Clay	41,591	1,520 00	
September 28th	Belden	Pine to Bush	11,644	42 50	Corners.
...er 6th	...g	McAllister and Leavenworth	12,130	572 42	
...er 6th	Crossing	McAllister opposite Hyde	12,130	57 10	
...er 10th	...h	Bryant to Branan	68,992	2,663 87	
...	Eddy	Washington and Davis	9,789	46 08	
November 3d	Crossing	Powell to ...n	59,194	2,007 91	
...er 3d	Crossing	Turk and Polk	10,843	52 75	
January 6th	...g	Turk and Van Ness	20,821	89 69	
...er ...h	...g	Washington to Jackson	15,460	57 07	
...er ...h	Hayward	Eighth and Howard	16,021	69 29	
		Folsom to Louisa	7,160	22 67	

Date	Street	Location			And corners.
January 5th	Washington	Front to Davis	25,681	401 96	
November 3d	Crossing	Fifth and Bryant	20,015	844 89	
October 27th	Crossing	Washington and Drumm	11,069	495 45	
November 2d	Turk	Larkin to Polk	36,300	1,410 32	
...er 12th		Bush to Sutter	39,123	1,325 65	
December 5th	Bryant	Third to Fourth	125,165	4,176 75	
December 5th	Bryant	Mrd to Fourth	8.913	294 13	
December 5th	Fourth	Brannan to nd	81,885	4,485 90	
December 5th	Fourth	Bnn to Townsend	7,413	337 95	
December 26th	Everett	Third to Fourth	26,449	882 31	
December 28th	Pacific	Hyde to Larkin	42,370	1,463 14	
January 8th	Crossing	Kin and Stewart	41,367	807 51	
My 14th	Crossing	Fourth and Brannan	9,B24	842 77	
January 21st	Pacific	Leavenworth to Hyde	44,440	1,557 56	
March 11th	Crossing	Pacific and Leavenworth	10,705	377 47	
March 19th	Pacific	Jones to Leavenworth	43,894	1,540 70	
April 20th	Crossing	Jones and Pacific	10,705	566 80	
Mah 4th	Crossing	Folsom and Seventh	15,736	588 17	
April 17th	Ritch	Bryant to Brannan	41,158	1,445 97	
April 17th	Ash	Fourth to Zoe	34,687	1,209 95	
April 25th	Fifth	Harrison to the Pay	89,654	3,176 80	
May 4th	Howard	Seventh to Eighth	87,037	3,115 45	
March 30th	Crossing	Drumm and Jackson	11,098	514 14	
April 25th	Crossing	Folsom and Spear	27,828	1,125 90	
April 25th	Folsom	Spar to Stewart	60,241	2,086 93	
April 25th	Mason	Sutter to Post	37,718	1,336 25	
April 29th	Crossing	Pacific and Larkin	15,025	670 45	
May 20th	Beale	Harrison to Folsom	87,450	2,933 98	
June 10th	Beale	Harrison to Bryant	87,808	3,007 42	
March 16th	Turk	Leavenworth to Hyde	36,712	1,288 30	
June 6th	Crossing	Turk and Jones	10,825	524 21	
June 6th	Crossing	Turk and Leavenworth	10,825	524 21	
June 25th	Crossing	Folsom and Fifth	16,009	855 05	
April 5th	Crossing	Post and Taylor	14,431	506 30	
Carried forward.			2,296,210	$87,036 54	

PLANKING.—CONCLUDED.

Date.	Streets.	Streets Between.	Feet.	Cost.	Remarks.
		Brought forward	2,296,210	$87,036 54	
April 8th	Mission	Main to Spear	43,725	1,491 67	
April 8th	Crossing	Mission and Spear	19,906	812 64	
April 10th	Mission	Spear to Stewart	43,725	1,442 92	
April 20th	Na	Fifth to Sixth	64,211	2,249 90	
April 27th	Crossing	Oy and Mason	10,705	430 86	
April 27th	Crossing	Post and Mason	14,431	506 40	
May 7th	Chestnut	Powell to Stockton	58,469	1,985 61	
June 25th	Crossing	Leavenworth and Jackson	10,378	515 60	
June 29th	Lafayette	Green to Union	12,333	425 12	
		Totals	2,574,083	$96,897 26	

PAVING.

Date.	Streets.	Streets Between.	Square Feet. Cobblestone.	Square Feet. Nicolson.	Cost.	Remarks.
September 3d	Crossing	Mason and Chestnut	3,404		$918 08	
September 6th	Clay	Front to Battery	9,006		563 90	
October 11th	Crossing	Front and Vallejo	3,441		1,895 35	
July 10th	Crossing	Market opposite Fourth	2,096		572 60	
July 18th	Crossing	Stockton and Geary	2,044		106 97	
July 28th	Crossing	Broadway and Battery	2,588		216 49	
July 27th	Crossing	Front and Pacific	2,374		807 16	
August 2d	Front	Broadway to Vallejo	11,579		3,857 99	
August 22d	Crossing	Broadway and Front	3,931		1,493 56	
August 22d	Bartlett	Jackson to Pacific	3,738		1,143 56	
17th	Greenwich	Powell to Mason		11,180	,086 33	In gold.

Date	Street	Description			Amount	Remarks
December 5th	Broadway	Powell to Stockton	12,272	......	2,728 00	In gold.
December 24th	Third	Brannan to Bryant	......	16,633	5,084 49	In gold.
December 24th	Crossing	Third and Brannan	9,962	3,384	961 20	
December 21st	Jackson	Montgomery to Sansome	......	6,600	2,983 84	
November 17th	Mason	Greenwich to Lombard	......	6,600	1,931 60	In gold.
December 11th	Jones Alley	Washington to Jackson	......	3,781	1,094 92	In gold.
January 26th	Crossing	Stockton and Green	2,499	......	110 45	Repairs.
...ary 23d	Leidesdorff	Sacramento to ...ia	......	3,966	1,168 24	In gold.
November 5th	Crossing	Leidesdorff opposite Halleck	......	329	94 48	In gold.
November 5th	Crossing	Greenwich and Mason	......	3,203	925 42	In gold.
...er 24th	Crossing	Bush and Leavenworth	......	4,020	1,148 10	In gold.
December 19th	Battery	Union to Filbert	......	10,887	3,116 08	In gold.
February 20th	Fourth	Market to Mission	10,263	......	2,562 54	In gold.
February 20th	Fourth	Opposite Jessie	1,405	......	344 22	Old and new.
February 20th	Fourth	Opposite Stevenson	821	......	201 14	In gold.
...er 23d	Broadway	Front to Battery	12,237	......	3,322 81	
January 14th	Pine	Montgomery to Kearney	......	16,013	4,566 74	In gold.
...ry 25th	Market	First to Second	24,987	......	3,397 72	
February 5th	...n	Lombard to ...n	10,911	......	1,908 60	In gold.
February 7th	Washington	Powell to ...n	6,600	......	3,251 63	
February 2?	Dupont	Union to Filbert	......	12,062	1,891 60	
March 7th	Jackson	Powell to Mason	......	......	3,437 86	In gold.
March 1th	Stockton	Vallejo to Green	5,711	......	481 40	
M...h 25th	Crossing	Kearny and Union	2,150	......	607 37	
May 16th	Sacramento	Montgomery to Kearny	11,804	......	2,069 96	Old and new.
May 28th	Crossing	...y and Front	2,609	......	430 98	
February 14th	Dupont	Sacramento to California	......	6,600	1924 60	In gold.
May 3d	Jackson	Battery to Front	7,448	......	642 40	Old and new.
April 3d	Third	...n to Townsend	......	16,363	6,311 69	In currency.
April 3d	Crossing	Third and Townsend	......	4,866	1,373 75	In currency.
April 17th	Third	Townsend to King	......	8,675	3,331 50	In currency.
April 17th	Powell	Greenwich to Lombard	......	6,187	2,425 00	In currency.
April 24th	Powell	Greenwich to Filbert	......	4,790	1,882 95	In currency.
April 30th	Waverly Place	Clay to ...n	......	5,798	2,260 49	In currency.
		Carried forward	165,883	151,938	$84,635 76	

PAVING.—CONCLUDED.

Date.	Streets.	Streets Between.	Square Feet. Cobblestone.	Square Feet. Nicolson.	Cost.	Remarks.
		Brought forward	165,883	151,938	4,835 96	In currency.
May 3d	Powell	Chestnut to Francisco		6,187	2,208 81	In currency.
May 6th	Crossing	Jackson and Mason		2,997	1,155 11	In currency.
May 22d	Crossing	Powell and Lombard		6,187	2,426 81	In currency.
May 22d	Brannan	Third to Fourth		38,084	4,182 81	In currency.
June 17th	Crossing	Jackson and Powell		2,965	1,862 45	& or's in cur'cy.
June 21st	Sacramento	Kearny to Dupont		11,281	4,382 03	In ey.
June 25th	Sansome	Pacific to Broadway		10,695	4,152 85	In currency.
June 27th	Crossing	Folsom and Beale		5,672	2,188 11	In currency.
Totals			165,883	236,005	$117,594 74	

SIDEWALKS.

Date.	Streets.	Streets Between.	Front Feet.	Cost.	Remarks.
August 8th	Ninth	Howard to Folsom	1,030	$803 40	
Aust 15th	Market	Eighth to Ninth	1,020	2,399 60	
September 6th	Clay	Front to Battery	431.4	388 20	
September 12th	Crossing	Fourth and Bryant		217 60	Corners.
September 6th	Fourth	Harrison to Folsom	825	835 00	
September 15th	Market	Eleventh to Potter	915.4	1,755 89	
October 3d	Grove	Polk to Van Ness	768	1,233 04	
October 3d	Grove	Larkin to Polk	825	1,321 30	
Mar 3d	Fell	Franklin to Van Ness	769.6	1,046 80	
July 5th	Pine	Powell to Mason		751 72	
July 11th	Crossing	Dupont and Greenwich	412.6	304 60	Corners.

Date	Street		Amount	Cost	Notes
February 15th	Sixteenth	Guerrero to Dolores	1,029.3	1,698 26	
July 6th	Bryant	Fourth to Fifth	1,650	2,889 10	
July 7th	Tehama	First to Second	1,435	996 15	
August 2d	Front	Broadway to Vallejo	550	1, DO 00	
...st 7th	Jones	O'Farrell to Ellis	550	711 60	
August 9th	Turk	Hyde to Larkin	825	1,212 75	Old and new.
August 16th	N...tna	First to Second	1,283	880 15	
...st 16th	McAllister	Hyde to Leavenworth	825	957 00	
August 25th	Hyde	Bush to Sutter	522.6	821 90	
August 27th	...ove	Gough to ... ia	825	1,274 60	
August 27th	Crossing	Grove and Octavia		161 96	Corners.
August 27th	Grove	Gough to ... lin	825	1,134 35	
August 27th	Crossing	...e and Gough		128 00	Corners.
September 13th	Fourth	Harrison to Bryant	995	443 59	
September 13th	Berry	Dupont to Mary	455	385 02	
September 21st	Leavenworth	Sutter to Bush	137.6	234 47	
September 26th	Drumm	Sacramento to Clay	478	143 40	
September 27th	Franklin	Fell to Oak	540	892 58	Corners.
September 27th	Franklin	Hayes to Fell	540	993 58	Corners.
September 27th	Hayes	Franklin to Gough	445	646 40	
September 28th	Belden	Pine to Bush	435	226 20	
September 28th	...lia	Market to Fourteenth	2,635.5	4,766 46	
September 28th	Crossing	Valencia and Ridley		131 00	Corners.
September 28th	Crossing	...ia and Herman		131 00	Corners.
...er 3d	Fillmore	Grove to Fulton	515	517 00	
...er 10th	Fourth	Bryant to Brannan	990.6	297 15	
November 3d	Market	Potter to Valencia	1,335.6	2,708 21	Old.
November 17th	Greenwich	Mason to Powell	312.6	12 50	Old and new.
...ry 23d	Eddy	Mason to Powell	771	525 25	
January 23d	Taylor	Greenwich to Powell	436.7	774 13	
December 11th	Jones Alley	Washington to Jackson	439.6	263 70	
...ary 16th	Virginia	Washington to Jackson	550	311 30	
January 16th	Haywood	Folsom to Louisa	230.9	87 69	
February 10th	Francisco	Powell to Mason	569.1	940 06	
		Carried forward.	30,127.9	$40,453 66	

S I D E W A L K S. — CONCLUDED.

Date	Streets	Streets Between	Front Feet	Cost	Remarks
		Brought forward	30,127.9	$40,553 66	
January 5th	Washington	Front to Davis	104	237 47	
January 23d	Leidesdorff	Sacramento to California	423	203 03	
Mh tH	Valencia	Sixteenth to Seventeenth	810	952 15	
November 10th	Leavenworth	Ellis to Eddy	308	507 52	
December 26th	Battery	Union to Filbert	513	723 43	
January 24th	Sixteenth	Howard to Mn	490	716 45	
February 20th	Fourth	Market to Mission	965	1,395 60	
October 24th	Bush	Leavenworth to Hyde	412.6	641 35	
er 2d	Turk	Larkin to Polk	825	1,179 75	Old and new.
November 13th	Taylor	Bh to Sutter	550	619 56	
December 26th	Bryant	Mrd to Fourth	1,426	2,253 08	
December 5th	Everett	Mrd to Fourth	1,266	745 87	
aUry 21st	Pacific	Hyde to Larkin	784.6	730 84	
January 21st	Pacific	Leavenworth to Hyde	825	828 16	
January 22d	Mason	Clay to Sacramento	435	741 95	
January 25th	Market	First to Second	1,004	1,445 40	
February 5th	Mason	Lombard to Chestnut	423	148 05	
February a	Washington	Powell to Stockton	505	383 88	
February 27th	Dupont	Union to Filbert	550	737 00	
February 28th	Sacramento	Jones to Leavenworth	787.6	944 62	
Mh 6th	Jackson	ll to Mason	636.6	671 05	
Mh 6th	Stockton	Vallejo to Green	465.8	512 84	
March 1th	Pacific	Jones to Leavenworth	825	533 77	
Mh 23d	Leavenworth	Geary to O'Farrell	550	567 33	
April 20th	Crossing	Jones and Pacific		379 60	Corners.
Mh 28th	Valencia	Nineteenth to Twentieth	848	1,247 07	
Mh 28th	Crossing	Valencia and Twentieth		119 62	Corners.
April 17th	Ritch	Bryant to Brannan	1,050	918 57	
April 17th	Welch	Fourth to Zoe	880	632 28	
April 17th	Fifth	Harrison to the Bay	927.6	1,623 12	

Date	Street	Location			
May 16th	Sacramento	Montgomery to Ke nay	466.3	1,305 38	
May 20th	Howard	Seventh to Eighth	56.5	102 55	
Mh 28th	Valencia	...ty-first to ...d	1,040	1,599 52	
April 9th	M...	Seventh to Eighth	1,357	1,110 81	
April 25th	Folsom	Spear to Stewart	239	233 60	
April 25th	...a	Sutter to Post	412.6	550 24	Corners.
May 20th	Beale	Folsom to Harrison	623.4	124 66	
June 10th	Beale	Harrison to Bryant	1,100	2,085 75	
February 12th	Mason	Chestnut to Francisco	351	555 55	
February 7th	Seventeenth	...ro to Dolores	983	1,474 94	
March 16th	Turk	Leavenworth to Hyde	825	1,237 50	
Mrh 28th	Valencia	Twentieth to Twenty-first	1,040	1,578 72	
April 25th	Seventeenth	Mission to Valencia	789	1,166 29	
May 13th	Jackson	Battery to Front	550	544 50	
April 3d	Third	Branman to ...d	784	1,342 14	
April 3d	Seventeenth	Guerrero to Valencia	738.6	1,341 81	
Aril 18th	Mission	Main to Spear	374.10	674 70	
April 10th	Mission	Stewart to Spear	550	967 75	
April 15th	Brannan	Third to Fourth	1,505	1,937 42	
April 13th	Mission	Fremont to Beale	501	934 55	
April 17th	Third	Townsend to King	550	1,060 75	
April 20th	Natoma	Fifth to Sixth	1,557.6	00	
April 19th	Powell	Greenwich to Filbert	502.4	529 36	
April 27th	Sacramento	Mason to Taylor	760	722 00	
April 30th	Waverly	Gly to Washington	550	688 42	
April 27th	Crossing	Howard and Sixteenth		162 25	Corners.
May 4th	Crossing	Fourth and Perry		63 50	Corners.
May 4th	Crossing	Fourth and Shipley		63 50	Corners.
May 4th	Crossing	Fourth and Freelon		63 50	Corners.
May 30th	Powell	Chestnut to Francisco	550	260 15	
May 22d	Powell	Lombard to Chestnut	505	554 42	
...he 21st	Sacramento	Kearny to ...t	262	307 85	
June 29th	Lafayette	Green to Union	485.6	269 50	
		Total	69,725.1	$90,154 65	

30

CROSSWALKS AND CURBS.

Date	Streets	Streets Between	Crosswalks	Curbs	Cost	Remarks
September 3d.	Crossing	Mason and Chestnut	462.3		832 05	Corners.
September 3d.	Crossing	Mason and Chestnut			821 60	
September 6th.	Clay	Front to Battery		275.8	509 99	
October 11th.	Crossing	Front and Vallejo	634.8		1,269 33	
July 10th.	Crossing	Market, opp. Fourth	305		506 30	
July 18th.	Crossing	Stockton and Geary	324.8		395 70	
July 28th.	Crossing	Broadway and Battery	550		859 00	
July 9th.	Crossing	Front and Pacific	419.9		863 15	
August 2d.	Front	Broadway to Vallejo		550	990 00	
August 22d.	Crossing	Front and Broadway	695.10		1,431 50	Corners of small streets.
...er 6th.	Bartlett	Jackson to Pacific		550	1,115 60	
...er 17th.	Greenwich	Powell to Mason		782.6	1,435 60	
December 3d.	Broadway	Stockton to Powell		711.11	1,278 33	
December 3d.	Crossing	Third and Branman	540		918 00	
December 21st.	Jackson	Montgomery to Sansome	36		57 60	
December 21st.	Jackson	Montgomery to Sansome		483	923 25	
...er 17th.	Mason	Greenwich to Lombard		552.10	956 40	
December 11th.	Jones Alley	Washington to Jackson		440	792 00	
January 26th.	Crossing	...n and Green	287.5	133	993 04	
...ly 23d.	Leidesdorff	California to Sacramento		309	549 00	
December 26th.	Battery	Union to Filbert		513	897 75	
February 20th.	Fourth	Market to Mission		965	1,717 70	
February 20th.	Fourth	Opposite Jessie	172.2		291 74	
February 20th.	Fourth	Opposite Jessie	186.4		315 96	
February 20th.	Fourth	Opposite Jessie	94.2		160 70	
January 1..th	Pine	Montgomery to Kearny		508.6	889 39	
January 25th.	Market	First to Second		686.8	1,304 75	
February 5th.	Mason	...d to Chestnut		550	906 60	
February 7th.	Washington	Powell to St ...	66.6	661	1,244 23	

Date.	Street.	Streets Between.	Piles.	Caps.	Cost.	Remarks.
February 27th	Dupont	Union to Filbert		550	979 00	
Mch 7th	Jackson	Powell to Mason		825.10	1,323 33	
May 16th	Stockton	Vallejo to Green		530	965 40	
May 2?h	Crossing	Kearny and Union	279.7		510 45	
May 16th	Sacramento	Montgomery to Kearny	12.8	121.5	244 57	
June 13th	Crossing	?na and Second	265.8		521 11	
February 14th	Dupont	Sacramento to California		551	887 70	
May 3d	Jackson	Battery to Front		550	1,031 10	
April 3d	Third	Brannan to		1,059	1,948 56	
April 3d	Crossing	Third and Townsend	605		1,034 10	Corners.
April 15th	Brannan	Third to Fourth		1,535	3,180 60	
April 17th	Third	Townsend to King		550	1,012 00	
April 17th	Powell	Greenwich to Lombard		550	1,012 00	
May 28th	Crossing	Clay and Front	358.2		1,032 74	
February 13th	Vallejo	Battery to Front		282	507 60	
April 17th	Powell	Greenwich to Filbert		550	1,064 10	
April 3d	Waverly Place	Clay to Washington		550	970 75	
May 3d	Powell	Chestnut to Francisco		550	990 00	
May 3d	Powell	Lombard to Chestnut		550	973 50	
June 21st	Sacramento	Ke ray to Dupont		665.5	1,097 93	
June 25th	Sansome	Broadway to Pacific		552	910 80	
Totals			6,296.10	19,193.9	$47,423 60	

PILES AND CAPS.

Date.	Street.	Streets Between.	Piles.	Caps.	Cost.	Remarks.
January 8th	Crossing	Mission and Stewart	418	28	$884 08	

RECAPITULATION.

FROM JULY 1, 1866, TO JUNE 30, 1867.

Work	Measurement	Amount	Cost.
Grading	Cubic yards	1,191,257	$327,333 39
Paving	Square feet { Cobblestone Nicolson	165,883 236,005	117,594 74
Brick Sewers	Lineal feet	21,303.10	156,745 92
Planking	One thousand feet	2,574,083	96,897 26
Sidewalks	Front feet	69,725.1	90,154 65
Curbs	Lineal feet	19,193.9	47,423 60
Crosswalks	Lineal feet	6,296.10	
Macadamizing	Square feet	1,560,119	117,271 89
Piles		28	884 08
Caps	Lineal feet	418	
Redwood Sewers	Lineal feet	12,137.6	49,578 20
Total Cost			$1,003,883 73

SUMMARY OF COST OF WORK DONE FOR EACH YEAR, FROM JULY 1, 1856, TO JULY 1, 1867.

	1856-7.	1857-8.	1858-9.	1859-60.	1860-1.	1861-2.	1862-3.	1863-4.	1864-5.	1865-6.	1866-7.
Grading	......	$3,556	$7,732	$41,593	$200,815	$226,788	$141,759	$209,114	$319,519 84	$404,539 71	$327,333 39
Planking	$45,303	39,242	25,901	68,452	27,036	39,248	61,329	59,545	65,531 12	81,145 99	96,897 26
Paving	2,138	......	5,754	30,802	26,278	20,542	42,089	79,537	166,933 81	117,763 99	117,594 74
Macadamizing	......	......	......	1,853	4,718	1,436	43,188	12,261	44,582 59	89,491 53	117,271 89
Sidewalks	......	......	54	5,475	6,388	16,251	30,801	49,588	125,307 98	81,061 69	90,154 65
Brick Sewers	......	......	4,883	22,633	30,830	61,915	116,709	173,389	287,200 29	203,920 82	156,745 92
Redwood Sewers	......	......	670	3,398	1,897	4,881	21,640	27,975	29,060 60	39,068 04	49,578 20
Curbs and Crosswalks	......	......	195	7,088	9,572	7,778	18,217	49,350	104,064 79	56,345 93	47,423 60
Piles and Caps	......	......	1,070	23,010	634	2,607	12,133	1,664	14,856 25	16,226 48	894 08
Bulkhead	......	......	......	......	......	......	......	......	2,200 00	......	......
	$47,433	$42,798	$46,259	$204,304	$308,168	$381,446	$487,865	$662,423	$1,159,257 27	$1,089,564 18	$1,003,883 73

Total length of Sewers constructed, from July 1,
 1856, to July 1, 1866, feet 132,042.2
Constructed from July 1, 1866, to July 1, 1867 ...   33,441.2

               165,483.4

The entire cost of Street work, from July 1, 1856,
 to July 1, 1866, ... $4,429,403 45
Cost from July 1, 1866, to July 1, 1867.........   1,003,883 73

            $5,434,287 18

APPENDIX

TO

THE MUNICIPAL REPORTS

OF 1866-67.

———————

THE SEVENTEENTH FISCAL YEAR of the incorporated Municipal Government of San Francisco closed on the 30th day of June, 1867; the first organization of the City and County Government, under Act of the State Legislature approved April 13th, 1850, having been made on the 6th day of May of the latter year.

In accordance with provisions of the Consolidation Act of 1856, the reports of the various officers of the municipality, as rendered to the Board of Supervisors at the close of the year, are presented in the foregoing pages. These reports refer exclusively to local affairs, and are intended to give a full exhibit of the *financial transactions*, *operations* and *general condition* of the different departments during and at the end of the year 1866-67; also, to furnish a history of City and County matters in that time, for comparison with preceding and reference to in after years.

In the year the progress of the City and County has been great, both in population and wealth. Real estate has appreciated in a much greater ratio, perhaps, than the Assessment Roll denotes. Many improvements of high architectural beauty, and of more than an usual costly character, have been completed. The city limits have been largely extended by the erection of very many private dwellings in its southern and western sections, or in the so called Potrero Nuevo, Mission, and Western Additions; a large number of streets in those localities have been opened, graded, sidewalks and crosswalks laid, sewers constructed, etc., until it can be confidently asserted that in no previous year has the solid growth of San Francisco equaled that of the last.

Throughout the State business in general has prospered, the harvests were fruitful, and the earth yielded prolifically of its mineral wealth. The unusually large export of grain and other domestic produce to European and Atlantic ports has formed a prominent feature of the year, and both at home and abroad attracted particular attention; as well as presenting the anomaly of the young State which seventeen years before imported nine tenths of her breadstuffs, and in whose markets but fifteen years ago flour by cargo brought forty dollars per barrel, now exporting to distant markets, and under the burden of heavy freights, thousands of tons of wheat, barley and flour, as the surplus of her agricultural products for a single year—and a large portion of this sent either by steamers via Panama or sailing vessels around Cape Horn, to a market within fifteen hundred miles transit from the heretofore believed to be greatest grain-producing region of the earth.

In other respects the year will be a memorable one in the history of San Francisco and the State. The inauguration of the Pacific Mail Company's line of steamships to China and Japan, combined with the rapid building of the Atlantic and Pacific lines of railroad; the acquisition of the recent Russian possessions at the north, presenting there a new field for commercial enterprize and for development of the mercantile marine of the country; the re-opening of the coast trade with Mexican ports, as well as the now demonstrated to become large trade from the successful navigation of the Colorado River into the very heart of the continent;— all seem to portend large accessions to the population of the Pacific States with each coming year, and a corresponding increase in commercial importance.

California, Oregon, Nevada, and Washington Territory, with Arizona, Utah, Montana and Colorado Territories, have ample room each for millions of inhabitants, and will have them in the course of time, as emigration shall flow steadily and understandingly—when the emigrant shall come with full confidence that he will be protected in the enjoyment of all the rights of civil and religious liberty guaranteed by the Constitution and Laws of the United States. Much has been done and is doing to point out the way and promote the influx of population, yet it is probable that not until the completion of the great inter-oceanic railroad will the anticipated results begin to be prominently developed. Perhaps that time will mark the commencement of an era, in the progress and culmination of which, and from the varied revolutions of trade, San Francisco may become the equal of any commercial city in the world.

Following this brief reference to the present and prospective, there will be found in the succeeding pages and several tables an exposition of the receipts and expenditures of the Municipal Government since its organization.

THE REVENUE.

A full statement of the receipts of the year is presented in the account of the Treasurer, included in the Auditor's Report, pages 62 to 86. The succeeding table will show from what sources revenue was derived, as well as present a comparison with receipts of the five preceding years.

REVENUE.

Source.	Fiscal Year 1861–62.	Fiscal Year 1862–3.	Fiscal Year 1863–4.	Fiscal Year 1864–5.	Fiscal Year 1865–6	Fiscal Year 1866–7.
Taxes...........	$857,482 40	$982,304 79	$683,600 23	$1,098,195 00	$1,361,876 26	$1,482,476 31
Licenses........	132,278 11	160,686 79	129,409 13	117,173 00	118,052 50	125,664 30
Fees............	95,071 85	101,628 53	107,628 57	117,086 00	116,977 86	132,158 11
Fines of Courts.	28,252 05	34,428 20	32,750 35	44,751 00	41,970 56	30,421 75
Harbor Dues....	16,913 05	18,127 05	20,297 25	21,242 00	20,136 85	19,035 30
Rents...........	11,187 41	9,789 00	2,725 72	1,313 00	1,225 50	1,170 75
Sale of Sch'l B'ds	11,960 00	....	....	....	61,050 00	125,965 38
Poll Taxes......	3,033 00	18,852 43	17,434 80	18,975 00	15,384 99	15,936 67
Interest on Loans	6,976 62	3,680 08	15,152 26	13,605 00	26,335 66	17,923 86
Sales of City Property	....	....	....	41,235 00	9,970 00	81,185 00
Sundries.......	596 10	5,184 47	1,761 05	9,513 00	1,891 40	4,569 00
	$1,163,750 59	$1,334,681 34	$1,010,759 36	$1,483,088 00	$1,774,871 58	$2,036,506 43
Collected for the State of Cal'a..	303,526 02	520,960 47	685,712 66	952,579 00	944,812 35	987,105 77
Totals........	$1,467,276 61	$1,855,641 81	$1,696,472 02	$2,435,667 00	$2,719,683 93	$3,023,612 20

The above is exclusive of receipts from the State of California for School Apportionment, Hospital Dues and Assessment Expenses; which in 1865 were, respectively, $43,043 55, $2,533 05, $6,403 05; and in 1866–7, $55,641 60, $2,533 05, $8,424 00; also of loans from Sinking Funds repaid, and moneys received from the State for Armory rents advanced from the city treasury.

ASSESSMENTS.

The Real Estate and Personal Property Assessment Rolls, since 1850–51, were returned as follows:

Fiscal Years.	Real Estate.	Improvements.	Personal Property.	Total Annual Amount.
1850–1	$16,849,054	⎫ Included in Personal. ⎬	$4,772,160	$21,621,214
1851–2	11,141,463		2,875,440	14,016,903
1852–3	15,676,356	⎭	2,805,381	18,481,737
1853–4	17,889,850	$6,158,300	4,852,000	28,900,150
1854–5	19,765,285	9,159,935	5,837,607	34,762,827
1855–6	18,607,800	8,394,925	5,073,847	32,076,572
1856–7	17,827,617	8,345,667	4,194,970	30,368,254
1857–8	15,576,545	7,394,296	11,426,335	35,397,176
1858–9	13,554,565	5,946,585	11,224,800	30,725,950
1859–60	14,172,235	6,523,985	9,323,002	30,019,222
1860–1	25,148,885	⎰ Included in Real Estate Mortgages. ⎱	10,818,614	35,967,499
1861–2	31,871,897		9,973,222	41,845,119
1862–3	36,975,250	13,900,208	15,655,750	66,531,208
1863–4	43,116,538	14,634,381	19,378,147	77,129,066
1864–5	47,292,903	11,621,662	21,822,000	80,736,165
1865–6	49,138,027	*...........	39,264,247	88,402,274
1866–7	53,485,421	....	43,214,976	96,700,397
1867–8	57,882,113	....	51,154,613	109,036,726

The original Assessment Roll of Real Estate was $57,880,468 00

The supplemental Assessment Roll of Real Estate was....... 1,645 00

Making....................................... $57,882,113 00

The original Assessment Roll of Personal Estate was................................ $28,556,806 00

Carried forward................... $28,556,806 00 $57,882,113 00

Brought forward.................... $28,556,806 00 $57,882,113 00

The supplemental Assessment Roll of Person-
al Estate was........................   22,597,807 22

Total Personal Estate 51,154,613 22

Grand total Real and Personal Estate................. $109,036,726 22

The Personal Roll is constituted as follows:

Mortgages... $23,857,404 99
Shipping...   2,584,170 00
Other Personal... 24,713,038 23

Total $51,154,613 22

Note.—Assessments upon improvements are included in Real Estate, and Mortgages in Personal Property Roll ;
the average amount of the latter for five years past being about $12,000,000.

The Supplemental Roll returned by the Assessor on the 26th of October, is included in the total footing for the
year, for particulars of which see detailed statement above.

RATES OF TAXATION.

Fiscal Years.	For State.	For City.	For County.	Annual Rates.
1850–1	...... $0 50......	.... $1 00	.... $0 50	.... $2 00
1851–2	...... 0 50......	.... 2 45	.... 1 15	.... 4 10
1852–3	...... 0 30......	.... 2 45	.... 1 66½	.... 4 41½
1853–4	...... 0 60......	.... 2 00	.... 1 28½	.... 3 88½
1854–5	...... 0 60......	.... 2 15	.... 1 10½	.... 3 85½
1855–6	...... 0 70......	.... 2 33⅓	.... 0 82½	.... 3 85 5-6
1856–7	...... 0 70......	.... 1 60		.... 2 30
1857–8	...... 0 70......	.... 1 60	The City and County	.... 2 30
1858–9	...... 0 60......	.... 1 85	Consolidated.	.... 2 45
1859–60	...... 0 60......	.... 2 56 9-10 ...		.... 3 16 9-10
1860–1	...... 0 60......	.... 2 25	War Tax.	.... 2 85
1861–2	...... 0 62......	.... 2 25		.... 2 87
1862–3	...... 0 62......	.... 1 97½	.... 0 15	.... 2 74½
1863–4	...... 0 90......	.... 1 20	....	.... 2 10
1864–5	...... 1 25......	.... 1 63	....	.... 2 98
1865–6	...... 1 15......	.... 1 97	....	.... 3 12
1866–7	...... 1 13......	.... 1 97	....	.... 3 10
1867–8	...... 1 13......	.... 1 87	....	.... 3 00

For the funds to which particularly apportioned in the last year, see Audit-
or's Report, page 87.

EXPENDITURES.

From August, 1849, to May 8, 1850 .... $ 649,859 82
From May 8, 1850, to June 30, 1851...................................   1,813,447 00
In Fiscal Year 1851–2...   456,332 00
In Fiscal Year 1852–3...   1,009,029 00
In Fiscal Year 1853–4...   1,831,825 00
In Fiscal Year 1854–5...   2,646,190 00

Carried forward,... $8,406,682 82

Brought forward...	$8,406,682 82
In Fiscal Year 1855–6...	856,120 00
In Fiscal Year 1856–7...	353,292 00
In Fiscal Year 1857–8...	366,427 00
In Fiscal Year 1858–9...	480,895 00
In Fiscal Year 1859–60...	745,014 00
In Fiscal Year 1860–1...	579,131 00
In Fiscal Year 1861–2...	591,656 00
In Fiscal Year 1862–3...	700,364 00
In Fiscal Year 1863–4...	785,894 53
In Fiscal Year 1864–5...	915,325 48
In Fiscal Year 1865–6...	1,085,941 96
In Fiscal Year 1866–7...	1,315,294 31
Total...	$17,182,038 10

It should be observed that the above figures for the last eleven years give the gross current expenses, exclusive of the large sums paid in liquidation of the bonded debts and for permanent improvements, but which, for uniformity in making comparisons, include the expenses of Fee Officers, State Schools apportionment, etc., as shown in the succeeding table of

RECEIPTS OF THE LAST FOUR YEARS.

Fiscal Year.	Fees of Officers.	State, for School purposes.	State Assessment Expenses.	State, for Hospital Dues.	Total.
1863–4	$107,629	$23,918	$5,445	....	$136,992
1864–5	117,086	40,435	6,875	$6,744	171,140
1865–6	116,977	43,044	6,453	2,533	169,007
1866–7	132,158	55,642	8,424	2,533	198,757
Totals....	$473,850	$163,039	$27,197	$11,810	$675,896

Making proper allowance for the receipts as above, and further deductions as shown in the detailed statement in Report of the Auditor, pages 59 and 60, the expenditures proper, foot up $939,285 05, or $22,351 more than in the preceding year.

The aggregate Municipal Expenditure of the year has been necessarily increased by appropriations for special purposes—as the purchase of land for the erection of an Alms House and Small Pox Hospital buildings ; the purchase of Steam Fire Engines and apparatus incident to the establishment of a Paid Fire Department; the settlement of the Camanche claim; the increased number of street lamps erected, with the cleaning of street sewers, etc., consequent to the extension of the city limits. Still, the rate of taxation has been reduced, and property valuations not materially advanced. The large payment to the State, nearly one million dollars, has absorbed within a fraction of one third of the entire revenue, and it will be remarked that since the year 1861–2 the amount of tax levied for State purposes has more than trebled, while for City and County purposes it has been increased in a much less proportion; San Francisco now contributing more than two-fifths of the entire State revenue.

The aggregate of yearly payments to the State is shown in the following table, also sources whence revenue has been derived.

PAYMENTS TO STATE.

Fiscal Years.	Property Taxes.	Poll Taxes.	Licenses.	Stamps, etc.	Total.
1850-1	$95,879	$ 2,220	$38,904	....	$137,003
1851-2	78,675	2,180	21,665	....	102,520
1852-3	61,218	11,833	20,532	....	93,583
1853-4	188,659	3,828	17,852	....	210,339
1854-5	179,617	3,800	108,479	....	291,896
1855-6	168,588	....	11,431	....	180,019
1856-7	119,572	4,907	22,480	....	146,959
1857-8	224,359	3,640	54,323	$39,751	322,073
1858-9	181,471	2,325	28,456	94,216	306,468
1859-60	192,198	1,826	33,000	90,409	317,433
1860-1	200,574	4,325	32,418	39,964	277,281
1861-2	239,561	8,075	27,653	28,237	303,526
1862-3	390,655	48,229	24,619	57,457	520,960
1863-4	506,171	68,740	45,421	65,380	685,712
1864-5	790,809	64,748	26,039	70,983	952,579
1865-6	794,977	40,626	29,425	79,784	944,812
1866-7	848,777	21,006	34,956	82,368	987,107
Totals....	$5,261,760	$292,308	$577,653	$648,549	$6,780,270

The State Revenue from all sources for the Fiscal Year ending November 30,
1866, amounted to $3,841,717.

THE SPECIAL FEE FUND

Was created by enactment of the State Legislature in 1858-9, but then made
applicable to a few offices only. In the year 1861, under the so-called "Fee
and Salary Bill," the requirements were enlarged so as to include all fee-re-
ceiving officers, with exception of the Assessor, then collecting poll taxes, but
in 1863 transferred to the Tax Collector. Under the Acts referred to, the
receipts and expenditures of all offices included in the provisions of the enactment are given in the two following tables.

First, from 1858 to 1861:

RECEIPTS.

Date.	From the Sheriff.	From County Clerk.	From County Recorder.	Total.
May 1 to June 30, 1858....................	$ 1,468 70	$ 4,277 65	$ 3,440 44	$ 9,186 79
July 1, 1858, to June 30, 1859.............	11,750 71	20,894 38	19,794 89	52,439 98
July 1, 1859, to June 30, 1860.............	9,668 14	21,321 20	24,267 50	55,256 84
July 1, 1860, to June 30, 1861.............	9,906 21	43,420 50	34,352 95	67,679 66
Totals...........................	$32,793 76	$89,913 72	$81,855 78	$184,563 27

SALARIES AND EXPENSES.

May, 1858, to June 1, 1859................	$33,355 60	$30,045 14	$19,348 14	$87,748 88
Blank Books and Stationery..............	415 00	731 10	1,197 75	2,343 85
July 1, 1859, to June 30, 1860.............	25,899 96	23,166 58	18,323 72	67,390 26
Blank Books and Stationery..............	194 00	1,031 75	1,059 75	2,285 50
July 1, 1860, to June 30, 1861.............	25,474 96	22,399 92	27,650 67	75,525 55
Blank Books and Stationery.............	200 12	785 35	1,572 37	2,557 84
Totals...........................	$85,539 64	$78,159 84	$69,352 40	$237,851 88

FROM 1861 TO 1867.—RECEIPTS.

Offices.	1861-2.	1862-3.	1863-4.	1864-5.	1865-6.	1866-7.	Total.
Recorder's Office	$34,605 00	$33,653 75	$34,534 25	$302 00	$37,348 50	$43,237 25	$221,000 75
County Clerk's Office	22,553 72	22,637 84	28,676 40	33,618 80	31,829 70	36,616 05	175,933 41
Sheriff's Office	11,287 54	9,877 86	11,095 49	11,038 72	13,022 55	16,720 73	73,042 89
Auditor	4,700 95	5,945 80	3,980 00	2,488 16	2,472 50	2,624 00	22,201 41
Treasurer	554 10	11,891 05	12,538 14	12,843 29	12,517 44	19,118 73	72,462 84
Ex	9,317 05	14,542 88	13,053 29	1,020 55	16,141 72	16,183 30	85,817 79
Clerk of Board of Supervisors	359 25	375 75	658 50	87 00	983 35	864 65	3,892 10
Clerk of Police Court	1,337 75	898 50	1,020 00	762 00	1,764 00	1,740 00	7,360 75
District Attorney	116 00	1,110 00		555 00	1,402 10	64 00	4,267 10
Prosecuting Attorney					2 50		2 50
Totals	$93,921 45	$100,913 48	$106,027 57	$116,575 12	$116,484 36	$131,009 61	$605,831 04

SALARIES AND EXPENSES.

Offices.	1861-2.	1862-3.	1863-4.	1864-5.	1865-6.	1866-7.	Total.
Recorder's Office	$26,792 50	$24,984 65	$33,358 25	$36 00	$28,092 24	$30,427 59	$172,831 23
County Clerk's Office	22,029 80	22,542 85	24,430 28	20,314 00	30,842 90	31,031 39	4,891 22
Sheriff's Office	376 82	28,292 87	28,729 36	30,575 00	32,546 62	31,987 10	183,247 67
Auditor	5,143 04	5,369 06	6,733 70	6,049 00	5,865 85	6,055 45	33,807 60
Treasurer	7,718 39	7,000 26	7,985 02	9,716 00	10,037 75	10,044 30	5,421 71
Ex	16,042 16	15,605 07	1,802 43	17,789 00	18,646 18	19,217 05	103,001 89
Clerk of Board of Supervisors	2,789 86	2,538 12	2,009 07	4,204 00	4,447 24	5,461 75	2,240 04
Clerk of Police Court	2,705 63	2,645 42	2,601 25	2,633 00	2,772 12	1,879 71	16,097 18
Prosecuting Attorney	4,959 25	5,364 52	1,126 50	7,230 00	8,206 35	6,642 00	39,528 62
					3,025 00	8,000 00	6,025 00
This	$119,358 35	$114,883 41	$129,225 86	$136,286 00	$144,492 25	$143,664 34	$790,892 21

On the preceding page (461) are exhibited the totals of receipts and expenditures of all the offices included in the Fee and Salary Bill of 1861; showing also how nearly self-sustaining the different offices have been.

The credit balance carried to the General Fund from Special Fee Fund in the year was $84,792 17.

INDEBTEDNESS OF THE CITY AND COUNTY OF SAN FRANCISCO FOR BONDS OUTSTANDING JUNE 30, 1867.

Issued in	For City and School Purposes.	Payable in	Annual Rates.	Annual Sinking Fund.	In circulation.
1851	City..................................	1871	10 per cent.	$50,000	$1,257,900
1855	City..................................	1875	6 per cent.	32,000	269,500
1858	City and County....................	1888	6 per cent.	44,000	1,133,500
1860	School	1870	10 per cent.	5,000	54,500
1861	School	1870	10 per cent.	2,500	127,000
1862	San Francisco and San Jose Railroad Company	1877	7 per cent.		16,000
1863	San Francisco and San Jose Railroad Company	1878	7 per cent.	20,000	150,000
1863	City Slip	1883	7 per cent.		852,267
1864	City Slip	1884	7 per cent.	40,000	28,000
1864	Central Pacific Railroad Company...	1894	7 per cent.	Commences	400,000
1865	Western Pacific Railroad Company..	1895	7 per cent.	1873	250,000
1866	School	1881	7 per cent.	15,000	210,000
	Total...				$4,748,667

In the report of the Auditor, pages 93 to 96, a detailed statement is presented of Bonds issued and Bonds redeemed during the year, showing a net decrease of $198,500 from the amount outstanding at its commencement.

The financial position and credit of the City is now in an enviable condition. The Report of the Commissioners of the Funded Debt, pages 89–92, shows a balance in the Sinking Fund of $1,023,359 20, applicable to redemption of City 10 per cent. Bonds of 1851, due in 1871, of which as above the amount outstanding June 30th was $1,257,900. These Bonds command five per cent. premium, holders declining to surrender them at less than that rate; yet it is considered probable that, with the disposition existing, the whole amount will be liquidated before maturity, and the Commissioners relieved from the duties of a trust which they have discharged with zeal and fidelity.

TREASURY EXHIBIT.

In Auditor's Report, pages 37 to 44, the Treasurer's Account for the year is presented, which shows—

Cash balance of...	$335,977 86
Loans from Sinking Funds outstanding......................	29,000 00
	$364,977 86
Less demands audited but not presented....................	87,295 53
Carried forward..	$277,682 33

Brought forward $277,682 33

Add to this the balance in hands of the Commissioners of the
    Funded Debt, applicable to redemption of City Bonds... 1,023,359 20

Also, Stock of San Francisco and San José Railroad Company,
    held as collateral with Bond of the Company for redemp-
    tion of $300,000 City Six per cent. Bonds.............. 300,000 00

And the total of assets shown is................... $1,601,041 53

Allowing this sum as an offset to the total of indebtedness outstanding as above, and a net balance is presented of $3,147,623 46.

In addition to the foregoing it is to be noted that after the close of the Fiscal Year the suits of Lucas, Turner & Co. and Felix Argenti, which have been in Court for many years, have been finally decided adverse to the City, and in settlement Bonds are to be issued to the amount of some $320,000, dating from October 1, 1867, payable in twenty years, bearing seven per cent. interest per annum, payable semi-annually on the first days of April and October.

The Order providing for issuance of Bonds as aforesaid finally passed on the 28th of October, and approved on the 29th, reads as follows :

ORDER NO. 791—PROVIDING FOR THE ISSUANCE OF BONDS FOR THE PAYMENT
    OF THE JUDGMENTS OF LUCAS, TURNER & CO. AND FELIX ARGENTI (NOW
    M. ARGENTI, ADMINISTRATRIX, ETC.)

The People of the City and County of San Francisco do ordain as follows :

SECTION 1. The Mayor, the Auditor, and the Treasurer of the City and County of San Francisco are hereby authorized and directed to issue the Bonds of the City and County of San Francisco in an amount which, at par, will be sufficient to pay and satisfy the two final judgments now existing and unpaid against the said City and County of San Francisco, in favor of Lucas, Turner & Co. and Felix Argenti (now M. Argenti, Administratrix, etc.), and to deliver the said Bonds to the owners of the said judgments, in payment and satisfaction thereof, at the rate aforesaid.

SECTION 2. Said Bonds shall be payable in twenty years from the first of October, 1867, and shall bear interest at the rate of seven per cent. per annum. The principal and interest shall be payable in United States gold coin, at the office of the Treasurer of the City and County of San Francisco, and the same shall be so expressed in said Bonds. The interest on said Bonds shall be payable semiannually, on the first days of April and October. Coupons for interest shall be attached to each Bond, and shall be received at par for all taxes due the City and County of San Francisco. *Provided*, no Coupons shall be received unless the same be payable within the fiscal year in which they may be offered in payment of said taxes.

SECTION 3. In all particulars not herein provided said Bonds shall conform to the requirements of Section 6, of Order 547, of the Board of Supervisors, approved September 16, 1863 ; and the provisions of said Order 547, so far as the same are not in conflict with the provisions expressed herein, shall apply to and become a part of this Order.

These Bonds, when issued in conformity with the Order, will augment the total City and County indebtedness to say five millions of dollars ; leaving, however, then unsettled, no floating debt or outstanding claim of any importance.

Following the preceding exhibit of financial affairs for the last and preceding years, other matters, believed to be of public interest, are presented in the succeeding pages, foremost of which, perhaps, is that of.

THE OUTSIDE LANDS.

This subject is one of great interest and importance to the community at the present time. One year ago the general impression prevailed that a long vexed question had been satisfactorily and definitely settled by enactment in Board of Supervisors of Orders Nos. 733 and 748, under provision of which a special committee, consisting of Supervisors R. P. Clement, Frank McCoppin, and Chas. H. Stanyan, were elected by the Board on the 15th of October, 1866, and soon afterward commenced the duties devolved upon them ; and in the month of January succeeding, appointed a Secretary, and gave public notice of their being in readiness to receive applications for confirmatory titles to land, in accordance with provisions of the Orders referred to. The first petition was filed January 28th, 1867 ; since which date the total number referred to the committee is some six hundred and fifty, including some twenty which were withdrawn, in instances where there was conflict to title or erroneous description given of the lands claimed. Of the applications thus submitted, about one-third were for confirmation of title to lands held under the Van Ness Ordinance, the deeds for some one hundred and fifty of which have already been issued, in conformity with the provisions of said Orders.

Action on claims for lands outside the charter line, or west of Devisadero Street, has been deferred, and awaits the completion of survey and map on which such claims are required to be delineated as provided in Sections 2 and 3 of Order No. 733. This map is being prepared by Geo. C. Potter and Wm. P. Humphreys, City and County Surveyors, and when completed, is to be deposited, for public inspection, in the office of Clerk of the Board of Supervisors, where it may be looked for within a short time. By Section 4 of Order No. 733, it was provided that no claim should be delineated on said map unless all taxes were paid thereon for the five years preceding the year beginning July 1st, 1866. Under this provision nearly $60,000 was received by the Tax Collector prior to July, 1867.

The Orders 733 and 748 read as follows :

ORDER NO. 733.

FOR SETTLEMENT AND QUIETING OF THE TITLE TO LANDS IN THE CITY AND COUNTY OF SAN FRANCISCO, SITUATED ABOVE HIGH-WATER MARK OF THE BAY OF SAN FRANCISCO AND THE PACIFIC OCEAN, AND WITHOUT THE FORMER CORPORATE LIMITS OF THE CITY OF SAN FRANCISCO.

The people of the City and County of San Francisco do ordain as follows:

SECTION 1. Immediately after the passage of this Order, the Board of Supervisors shall proceed to devise and adopt a plan for the subdivision into blocks and lots of all the lands not reserved to the United States, situated on the peninsula of San Francisco, and within the present corporate limits of said City and County, and above the natural ordinary high water mark of the Bay of San Francisco and the Pacific Ocean, as the same existed on the seventh of July, 1846, and without the corporate limits of the City of San Francisco as defined in the Act to re-incorporate said City passed by the Legislature of California, on the fifteenth day of April, 1851, so far as said Board may deem such subdivision necessary; and to select and set apart for public uses such lots and portions of said land as said Board may deem necessary, subject to the limitations and provisions hereinafter in this Order contained.

SEC. 2. After the adoption of the plan provided for in Section 1 of this Order, the Board of

Supervisors shall cause to be made a map of said lands according to said plan. Such map shall show the streets and public highways, the blocks formed by the intersection of the streets and public highways, and the lots into which said blocks shall be subdivided; and upon such map shall be designated the lots and portions of land set apart for public uses, and the particular use for which each lot or portion of land shall have been set apart.

SEC. 3. Upon the completion of the map provided for by Section 2 of this Order, it shall be deposited for public inspection in the office of the Clerk of the Board of Supervisors, and there remain for a period of sixty days; and notice shall be published in three of the daily papers during the whole time that said map shall so remain in said office.

SEC. 4. Any person having or claiming any interest in any portion of said lands under and by virtue of any provisions of this Order, may, at any time before the completion of said map, or while the same shall remain in the office of the Clerk of the Board of Supervisors for public inspection, present to the Committee on Outside Lands, hereinafter in this Order provided for, a description and a diagram of the lands in which he shall so claim an interest, and have the same delineated on said map; and may also present to the said Committee in writing his objections to the location or use of any lot or portion of land designated on said map as set apart for public uses and embraced within the description and diagram presented by him; but no claim shall be delineated upon said map by said Committee, unless all taxes have been paid thereon for the five fiscal years preceding the year beginning July 1st, 1866.

SEC. 5. After the said map shall have remained in the office of the Clerk of the Board of Supervisors for the said period of sixty days, as provided in Section 3 of this Order, the Board of Supervisors shall examine the objections, if any are made thereto, and may make such alterations in the location or designation of any lots or portions of lands set apart for public uses as may be necessary to obviate any objections which the said Board shall deem just and proper; provided, that no alteration shall be made which shall affect any person whose claim shall have been delineated on said map, and who shall not have made any objection to the location or designation of the lots or portions of land set apart for public uses.

SEC. 6. As soon as the alterations provided for, in Section 5 of this Order, shall have been made and delineated on said map, the said map shall become and be the official map of said lands; and the portions of land thereon designated as public streets and highways shall become and be dedicated to public use as streets and highways; and the lots and portions of land thereon designated as set apart for other public uses, shall severally become and be dedicated to the uses for which they severally have been set apart.

SEC. 7. No lot set apart for public use, other than for a park, plaza, cemetery or public square, or for the erection thereon of a City Hall, or buildings for a City Library, Hospital, or an Asylum, shall exceed in extent two fifty-vara lots; and no tract or portion of land set apart for a plaza or public square, shall exceed in extent four whole blocks, formed by the intersection of the main streets of the plan; and the tract or portion of land set apart for a cemetery shall not exceed in extent two hundred acres, nor be less than one hundred acres; and the tract or portion of land set apart for a public park shall not be less than three hundred acres.

SEC. 8. In addition to the streets and highways not less than one-twentieth nor more than one-tenth part of any tract which, including streets and highways, does not exceed fifty (50) acres in extent, shall be set apart for public use; but if any tract which by the provision of this Order would pass to one person, shall exceed fifty (50) acres in extent, including streets and highways, there shall be set apart for public use other than for a public park and for a cemetery, and in addition to the streets and highways, not less than one-twentieth nor more than one-tenth part of fifty (50) acres; and not less than one-tenth part of all above fifty (50) acres. from any tract which, by the provisions of this Order, would pass to a number of persons as joint tenants or tenants in common, so much shall be set apart for public use and no more, as by the provisions of this section might be set apart if the interests of the respective tenants were several and divided. If if any tract less in extent than one-half of a block, formed by the intersection of the main streets of the plan, a portion shall be set apart for public use, other than for a public park, or for a cemetery, or for streets and highways, the person or persons to whom said tract would pass by the provisions of this Order, may purchase the amount so set apart for public use, by payment to the City and County, in gold

31

coin, the value thereof; the value to be determined by the Board of Supervisors on the report of the Committee on Outside Lands.

SEC. 9. The tract and portion of land set apart and designated on said map as a public park, and the tract and portion set apart and designated thereon as a Cemetery, and the several portions thereon designated as public streets and highways, shall be deemed absolutely dedicated as such; but persons who, by the provisions of this Order would, but for such dedication, be entitled to any of the lands embraced within such park or cemetery, shall be entitled to receive compensation for their claims to portions to which they would be so entitled less the deductions which might be made therefrom according to the provisions of Section 8 of this Order, such compensation to be made according to the value of the lands taken, the value to be determined by the Board of Supervisors, on the report of the Committee on Outside Lands; but no person shall be entitled to receive, either under the provisions of this section or of Section 8 of this Order, compensation for any lot or portion of land set apart for public use, unless his claim shall have been delineated on the map hereinbefore in this Order provided for, nor until all conflicting claims to such lot or portion of land shall have been finally determined, and no person shall be entitled to receive compensation for any portion of land included on any street or highway.

SEC. 10. No conveyance of any tract of land, or any interest therein made after the eighth day of March, 1866, shall be regarded in the selection and designation of lots and portions of land for public use; but the amount of land that may be reserved and set apart for public use shall be determined by the claims and possessions as they existed on the eighth day of March, 1866.

SEC. 11. All that portion of the land described in Section 1 of this Order, which lies south of a line drawn due south eighty-one degrees and thirty-five minutes east magnetic, through Seal Rock, and west of a line easterly not less than two hundred feet from ordinary highwater mark, is hereby reserved and set apart for public use as a public highway.

SEC. 12. The City and County of San Francisco hereby relinquishes and grants all the right, title, and claim which the said City and County now has or may hereafter acquire as the successor of the Pueblo of San Francisco, or as the grantee or patentee of the United States, in and to the lands hereinbefore in this Order described, and not excepted or reserved, or intended to be excepted or reserved, by any of the preceding sections or provisions of this Order, and which may not be set apart for public use under any of the preceding sections and provisions, and upon which shall be paid previous to the first day of April*, 1867, all taxes which have been assessed thereon, during the five fiscal years preceding July 1st, 1866, unto the persons, or to the heirs and assigns of persons who were, on the eighth day of March, 1866, in the actual *bona fide* possession thereof, by themselves or their tenants, or having been ousted from such possession before or since said day have recovered or may recover the same by legal process. And it is hereby declared to be the intent and object of this section to pass the right, title, and claim of the said City and County in and to every tract or portion of said land, except the portions that are or may be reserved as aforesaid, possessed by one person, unto the possessor thereof in severalty; and every separate tract or portion thereof, except the portions that are or may be reserved as aforesaid, possessed by more than one person jointly or in common, unto the possessors thereof jointly or in common.

SEC. 13. The grant and relinquishment by this Order made, shall be subject to the selections, reservations, and conditions hereinbefore in this Order made and provided for.

SEC. 14. A Committee of three members of the Board of Supervisors shall be chosen by said Board, whose duty it shall be to prepare and report to the Board the plan provided for in Section 1 of this Order, to supervise the making of the map provided for in Section 2, to select, set apart and designate the lots and portions of land hereinbefore provided to be set apart for public use, and generally to superintend the carrying out of the provisions of this Order; all the acts of said Committee to be subject to the approval of the Board of Supervisors.

SEC. 15. Whenever a survey shall be required to determine the boundaries of any claim or portion of any claim, whether ordered by the Committee or requested by the claimants, the

---

* Subsequently extended to July, 1867.

expense of such survey shall be borne by such claimants; and no survey shall be received by the Committee, except it shall have been made by the City and County Surveyor, or a surveyor designated by the committee; and the amount of compensation for such survey shall be fixed by the committee at a reasonable rate, not to exceed the ordinary charges for such services.

SEC. 16. The compensation which may become due, by virtue of Sections 8 and 9 of this Order, shall be made in such manner as the Legislature may hereafter provide.

SEC. 17. This Order shall take effect from and after its passage.

ORDER NO. 748.

TO EXPEDITE THE SETTLEMENT OF LAND TITLES IN THE CITY AND COUNTY OF SAN FRANCISCO.
[APPROVED DECEMBER 22, 1856.]

WHEREAS, The duly constituted authorities of the City of San Francisco, and of the City and County of San Francisco, have, by ordinances and orders, ceded the lands of said city and County to the parties in the possession thereof, subject to the exceptions and reservations in said ordinances and orders contained; and

WHEREAS, It is desirable that all parties should be quieted and secured in the possession of the lands rightly possessed by them, to which the City and County of San Francisco claims title—

Now, therefore, the People of the City and County of San Francisco do ordain as follows;

SECTION 1. Upon receiving a petition from any person or persons, claiming that they by themselves, their tenants, or the persons through whom they claim or derive possession, have been, from and including the eighth day of March, 1866, and still are in the possession of any of the lands described in the decree of Justice Field, of the U. S. Circuit Court, confirming the claim of the City and County of San Francisco, entered November 2d, 1864, in the Circuit Court of the United States, for the Northerh District of the State of California, or embraced within the corporate limits of the City of San Francisco (and above high-water mark), as defined in the act to re-incorporate said city, passed by the Legislature of the State of California, on the 15th day of April, 1851, and that such lands have not been sold, leased, dedicated, reserved or conveyed by authority of the said City and County of San Francisco, or the United States, to any one or for any purpose, asking for a grant from said City and County, the Board of Supervisors shall proceed to act thereon as hereinafter provided. The petition shall be verified by the oath or affirmation of the party in whose behalf the petition is presented, or by some one acting as his agent, and conversant with the facts detailed in the petition.

SEC. 2. All petitions mentioned in the first section of this Order, shall be referred to the Committee on Outside Lands; said committee shall appoint a clerk, who shall be a Notary Public, to perform the duties herein prescribed. The party presenting the said petition may appear before said clerk, and make proof, verbal and documentary, of the truth of the matters alleged in his petition. Copies of the documentary evidence shall be filed with said clerk, and the oral testimony shall be reduced to writing by said clerk, and subscribed by the witness. The proofs of the petitioner being closed, the said committee shall proceed to consider the same, and shall make such report and recommendation thereon as to them shall seem just and proper in the premises. The said committee shall file with the Clerk of the Board of Supervisors the testimony taken as aforesaid, together with the report of the said committee; and said report shall be submitted to the Board of Supervisors for their approval, and if, in their judgment, the claim of the petitioner is well founded, they shall, by an order entered in their minutes, adjudge and award a grant of such lands to the petitioner or petitioners therefor, less the amount reserved for public use. The said Board shall thereupon give public notice of their award, by a notice published at least once a week, for three successive weeks, in some daily public newspaper published in the City and County of San Francisco; which notice shall specify the name of the applicant, the date and filing of his petition, and the tract of land awarded, by a good and sufficient description thereof. Proof of publication of such notice shall be made in the manner now or hereafter required by law for the proof of publication in civil process. The clerk of the said committee shall be allowed the same compensation for taking the oath or affirmation of witnesses, and for reducing the testimony to writing, as is now allowed by law to Notaries Public for like services on taking depositions. The compensation herein allowed the clerk of said committee shall be paid to said clerk by the party presenting the petition.

SEC. 3. Upon receiving proof of the publication of the notice provided for in the 2d Section hereof, it shall be the duty of the aforesaid Committee of the Board of Supervisors, or any two of such committee, to execute, acknowledge and deliver to the party or parties presenting the aforesaid petition, a deed of conveyance of the tract or lot of land as aforesaid adjudged and awarded to the petitioner ; *provided,* the petitioner or petitioners shall, before receiving a deed as aforesaid, be required to quit-claim and peaceably deliver the possession of all land claimed by said petitioner or petitioners reserved by the Commissioners, acting under Ordinance eight hundred and twenty-two (822), and all those lands which shall be reserved by the Committee of the Board of Outside Lands, for the use and benefit of the City and County of San Francisco ; *provided, however,* that in case a suit shall be pending between the petitioner and some third person, involving the right of possession of the tract, or some portion thereof petitioned for, and such third person shall file with the Clerk of the Board of Supervisors a copy of the complaint filed in such action, before the deed shall have been executed and delivered to the petitioner, then, and in that case, the deed shall be withheld until such suit shall be finally determined, and there shall thereafter be executed a deed of conveyance of so much of the tract of land as shall be involved in the said suit, to the party in whose favor the said suit shall be finally determined as aforesaid ; *provided, further,* that the expenses hereinafter provided for shall be paid before such conveyance shall be delivered.

SEC. 4. Upon the filing of a petition as hereinbefore provided, the petitioner shall deposit with the Clerk of the Board of Supervisors a sum of money sufficient to pay for the publication of the notice as hereinbefore provided, notarial fees and other expenses incident to the granting of the prayer of the petition.

SEC. 5. A conveyance executed and delivered in pursuance of the provisions of this Order, shall operate to grant, convey, remise and release to the party, his heirs and assigns therein, the lands in such conveyance described, and all the estate and interest, present and future, of the said City and County of San Francisco in and to such lands.

SEC. 6. The conveyance of any such lands made as hereinbefore provided, shall not be deemed to include the rights of third persons.

SEC. 7. Nothing in this Order contained shall be considered as in conflict with, or as abrogating any of the provisions of Order No. 733.

Subsequent to the passage of these orders, and filing of petitions under them as before narrated, an opinion obtained in the minds of many persons that the proper method had not been pursued or devised to arrive at a just and equitable settlement of the outside land question, or distribution of the Pueblo lands. This idea followed a decision rendered in the Twelfth District Court by his Honor Judge Pratt, in the month of July, in the suit of the Lone Monntain Cemetery vs. the City, upon mandamus to prevent infringement of their possessory title.

The opinion then became prevalent, and was expressed by many, that the Board of Supervisors inherited the powers and prerogatives of the Ayuntamiento under Mexican law, and that in that body the sole power was vested to dispose of the lands in question, but at the same time, under the same law, were restricted from granting to any one person more than one 50 or 100 vara lot. Imbued with such ideas or impressions, and perhaps incited by unthinking or unscrupulous land agents, numerous petitions for grants of 50 and 100 vara pueblo lots were handed in to the Board of Supervisors, commencing with number one on the 12th of July, 1867, and continuing until on the 20th of October the number exceeded twenty-four hundred. The cost of each of these, to petitioners, averaged from five to ten dollars; thus exacting from many poor people a sum which could ill be afforded, and which they were led to contribute, or pay, under the impression that the simple filing of a petition would secure to them the land asked for, provided the same had not been previously granted. Many of the applications thus referred to were trebled or quadrupled for the same locality, particularly for corner lots, which most of the petitioners seemed to prefer. Pertinent to this subject it is to be stated that there are on file in the archives of the Board of Supervisors two thousand petitions to the same purpose, for pueblo lands, which petitions were received in the year 1860–61.

It is not known for what particular lands those petitioners applied for; they are as yet unopened, and are enclosed in sealed envelopes. The effect, however, is to leave recent petitioners ignorant of the selections made by those who can justly claim priority, from locations made years before.

The first of pueblo petitions presented were referred to the Committee on Outside Lands, by which Committee a majority report was presented to the Board of Supervisors on the 5th of August, 1867, to wit :

The undersigned, members of the Committee on Outside Lands, to whom were referred fifty-four petitions for grants of lots claimed to be vacant and unoccupied, have had said petitions under consideration, and now recommend that the prayers of the petitioners be denied.

These petitions have been presented to the Board under an egregious misapprehension of facts and of the law relating to the lands in question ; and the petitioners generally, as we are informed, are people who can illy afford to waste either time or money. And as the preparation and presentation are attended with an expense of from five to twenty dollars, according to the circumstances of the petitioners and the conscience of the person making out the papers—in some instances as high as ten dollars have been received by the agent on the false and criminal pretext that a deposit was required by the Clerk of this Board for advertising and other expenses—it is proper that we should give the reasons which have induced the recommendation we have made.

Twenty-six of the petitions referred to us are *for lots within the charte*r *line of* 1851, being upon or near Larkin Street. It is notorious that the title to these twenty-six lots passed to individuals by operation of the Van Ness Ordinance ; and if any person other than a grantee or successor of some of those individuals, procures title to any of them, it will be by overthrowing the Van Ness Ordinance, and at the expense of the utter destruction of all titles by which any lands outside of Larkin and Ninth Streets are held. If there are any among the petitioners—and we believe there are a few, and but a few—who have presented their applications with a knowledge of the facts and with a view to the means and the consequences we have stated, they surely cannot hope for the cc-operation of this Board. The Board of Supervisors, having in charge the welfare of the city, must do all in its power to protect titles that are good—to prevent disturbance of titles once settled, and to settle those which have not yet become perfect.

These applications have been made upon the theory, probably believed by a majority of the applicants, that the Van Ness Ordinance is void—that the pueblo lands were held by the city "in trust for the inhabitants," and could not be granted except in small parcels ; but every well-informed person, certainly every *lawyer*, knows that the Supreme Court of this State, the tribunal of last resort in the matter, has frequently affirmed the validity of the Ordinance— has repeatedly adjudged that the *fee* of the land passed to the possessors *to the extent of their several possessions, and without limit as to quantity.*

In view of these decisions, affirmed again and again, there is very little danger that any attempts will result in any serious disturbance of the "Van Ness" titles. Indeed, it is doubtful that the profits of the moving spirits will exceed their fees for drawing petitions and their collections for "deposits," as little if any litigation is likely to be incited in regard to so well settled a point. The *principal* evil resulting from the agitation of these matters is, of course, the *wholesale swindling*—for it is nothing less—of those who, through ignorance or thoughtlessness, are led by the false representations of designing and unscrupulous men to spend their money in a hope which is utterly vain, and without so much as a shadow of foundation. These twenty-six petitions would not be more groundless or hopeless or unreasonable if they were for lots along Montgomery Street.

The remaining twenty-eight petitions are for lots outside of the charter line of 1851—for lots not covered by the Van Ness Ordinance. Most of them are for lots in Lone Mountain Cemetery and the lands claimed by the San Francisco Homestead Union.

So much of the "outside lands" as were occupied on the 8th of March, 1866, less the proper reservations for public streets and other public uses, has, by Order 733, been granted by the city (so far, at least, as it has power to grant), to the occupants, upon certain conditions ; and the time for the performance of some of the conditions has not yet passed.

No grants of designated portions of those lands can be made until the streets are laid out and reservations for public use are made.

The work of surveying and platting is progressing, under the provisions of Order 733, as rapidly as possible ; and the work of selecting lots for public use will soon be begun, and will be completed at as early a day as the magnitude of the work will permit ; but, conceding the power of this Board to grant lots in the manner proposed in these petitions, it cannot be expected that any grants will be made until after the extent of the possessions of those entitled under Order 733, shall be ascertained.

It should be distinctly understood that none of the applicants presenting these fifty-four petitions claims to be or is in possession of the land he claims ; and none of them claims any any right except as an "inhabitant" of San Francisco. They all claim simply as *cestuis que trust* of the city ; and they show no reasons why they should be preferred to others in the same situation.

In view of the efforts that are being made by a few individuals to create opposition to the action of this Board in relation to "outside lands," and the erroneous impressions that are obtaining in reference to such action, we, your Committee, deem it proper to state in this report, the *facts*, so that all who wish may understand them.

The question of the city's right to land as the successor of the Pueblo of San Francisco was not finally adjudicated in the United States Courts until during the last year. In early times but few believed in the existence of a pueblo here, and for that reason the lands around the city were entered upon by settlers, in the belief that they belonged to the United States, and steps were taken by the settlers to secure to themselves the rights given by Acts of Congress to settlers on the public lands, and disputes, squatter riots, and litigations were the order of the day. It was of course not desirable that this condition of things should continue, and as it was evident that it would take years to finally determine through the Courts whether the lands belonged to the City or to the United States, it was thought best for the city to assume ownership of those within the then charter limits, and grant them to the parties in the actual possession—thus making them taxable, and causing them to contribute to the support of the Government. This was done ; and the Legislature and Congress having confirmed the Act of the municipal authorities, the title became perfect in the possessors, notwithstanding the controversy as to the existence of the pueblo. The wisdom of this course will not be questioned in good faith at this day; for it is apparent that otherwise the now populous district so disposed of would have remained to this day the same as it was at the time the grant was made—almost a waste, contributing nothing to the treasury and constituting an impassable barrier to the growth of the city.

The concession made to possessors by the Van Ness Ordinance, and the Acts of the Legislature and Congress confirmatory thereof, withdrew a formidable opposition to the claim of the city to four leagues as the successor of the pueblo ; but the controversy was still pending in the Courts of the United States till late in 1866.

On the 8th of March, 1866, for the purpose of ending the litigation and settling the title to these outside lands, Congress passed an Act relinquishing to this city all the right of the

United States in the land described in the decision of Judge Field, in trust to be conveyed to the parties in possession thereof at the time of the passage of the Act—subject to the direction of the Legislature as to terms, conditions and quantities. And in consequence of the passage of that Act, and because the United States had no interest afterwards, and for no other reason, the appeal from Judge Field's decision was dismissed. If that Act had not been passed the appeal would have been prosecuted, and in all probability would have been still undecided.

After the passage of this Act by Congress, and before the dismissal of the appeal by the United States, this Board deemed it important that some action should be taken preparatory to the meeting of the next Legislature. That action, of course, had to be shaped by considerations of public good—the chief public advantages to be sought being settlement of titles, and the increase of revenue by opening up for taxation all lands occupied and claimed by individuals. Now, as the Act of Congress recognized the rights of possessors, it was evident that they would not abide by any action of this Board not in conformity to that Act ; and as the decree of the Circuit Court would not conclude them from questioning the source of title, it was evident that the only disposition of the lands which would not result in almost interminable litigation, would be such as conformed substantially to the terms of that Act.

In that view Order 733 was passed, after having been kept before the public for weeks, for the especial purpose of inviting criticism and comment, after having met with universal approval both from the press and individuals.

This Order does not propose to grant any lands except those which were *bona fide* and actually possessed by claimants on the 8th of March, 1866, and even these it does not propose to *give away*. These lands had been regularly assessed to claimants for the last five years, but the collection of the taxes had not been enforced. And as it was desirable that claimants should pay some portion of their value, no better means could be adopted for equalizing the cost, and proportioning them according to the value of the lands, than to take the Assessor's valuations, and require from each the amount assessed for taxes upon that valuation. This payment is in the form of taxes, but is in fact *a payment of a proportion of the value of the lands*, and probably not less than fifty thousand dollars have been paid into the treasury under this order.

Tht quantity of these lands has apparently been greatly over-estimated. A speaker at a meeting of the Pueblo Land Organization is reported to have said that there were "twenty thousand one hundred vara lots" ; but the truth is, that, exclusive of streets and reservations for a park, plazas, cemeteries, and other public uses, there are not more than *six thousand fifty vara lots*.

The most serious impediment to the permanent prosperity of California and of this city has so far been the uncertain and unsatisfactory condition of land titles, and in view of the public interest, too much encouragement cannot be given to any action calculated to give certainty to such titles and increase confidence in them ; whilst every act tending to an opposite result should be discouraged and condemned by every person desiring the permanent prosperity and happiness of our people.

It is an undoubted fact, that previous to the passage of Order 733, every member of this Board was at great pains to thoroughly inform himself on the subject of these lands. Our best and most intelligent citizens were largely consulted and advised with; and the unanimous opinion and conclusion was, that the plan proposed by the Order was the only practicable plan of settling these titles; and it is confidently believed that, with all who are intelligent upon the subject and fully understand the condition of things, the plan is as acceptable to-day and as highly approved as it was on the day of the passage of the Order. We are so thoroughly satisfied that it is the only plan that will be effective and that would not result in confusion, controversy and litigation, that we feel we cannot urge too strongly upon the good people of the city to give it their encouragement and support, and not to countenance any act or proceeding calculated to impair or prevent its perfect operation.

Respectfully submitted.   R. P. CLEMENT,
                                        CHAS. H. STANYAN.

Following the proceedings narrated, a petition of R. J. Tennent, asking for

a grant of Outside Land, was received in the Board of Supervisors on the 7th
of October, and referred to the Judiciary Committee, by which on the 21st of
the same month a unanimous report as follows was submitted and placed on
file: ·

To the President and Members of the Board of Supervisors of the City and County of San Francisco.

GENTLEMEN—Your committee, to whom was referred the petition of Robert J. Tennent,
asking for a grant of Outside Land, beg leave to make the following report :

The petitions of some three thousand persons, asking for grants of outside land, have been
received and placed on file by this Board. The petitioners do not pretend to be in possession
of the land they covet. They proceed upon the theory that the Board of Supervisors, as successors of the old pueblo, has power to make grants of land to any residents of the city who
may apply for them. It has been represented to your committee that the cost of preparing
the petitions of these misguided people has been from $5 to $15 each ; but assuming that an
amount of five dollars only has been expended in each case, an aggregate of $15,000 has been
uselessly expended. The persons who have been persuaded to make this expensive investment have been swindled, and the time has arrived when the Board should, from considerations of public duty, adopt some efficient measure to prevent a recurrence of the cruel
proceeding. All the powers ever granted to this Board are comprehended in the Consolidation
Act, and whatever powers were exercised by the municipal authorities previous to the passage
of that Act, and not delegated therein, are expressly withheld. We are prohibited from
selling any land belonging to the city ; we cannot even lease city lands for a longer term than
three years ; and no person can point out the authority we have for making grants of land of
the kind we have now under consideration.

It is true that the Board has, by virtue of the provisions of Order 748, ordered deeds to issue
to persons who now are and have been in the peaceable, *bona fide* possession of their land, on
and since the 1st day of January, 1855 ; but all the proceedings under this Order relate to land
held under the Van Ness Ordinance, in cases where no controversy as to title exists.

The controversy, so far as the Van Ness Ordinance is concerned, it is to be hoped, may be
considered as ended forever. One thing, however, was needed to make titles conveyed by
that ordinance perfect, and the need is supplied by Order 748.

Until now the city has never given a written evidence of titles to owners of land under the
Van Ness Ordinance. The deeds issued under Order 748 do not and cannot conclude the
rights of third parties ; but where there is no controversy as to title, they give—not a title
(that was vested long ago), but a written evidence of title. The want of a record title has
long been felt by the holders of property under the Van Ness Ordinance. The evidence
necessary to prove up possession under that ordinance being all parole, it becomes more
difficult to furnish it, each succeeding year, and it is evident that unless some effort be now
made to gather up and preserve in an authentic· form such proofs of possession as the ordinance contemplates and the courts require, the title to all this land will in a short time rest
upon tradition alone. Order No. 748 was framed and passed with the expectation that it
would remedy this apparent difficulty. Its machinery is simple, and the cost of obtaining
deeds under it comparatively small. And although it is true that these deeds confer no new
title on the grantee, but are simply a recognition of one already granted by the Van Ness
Ordinance, yet if the Legislature will make these deeds the starting point for a short statute of
limitations, say of one year, with even the ordinary exceptions in favor of married women,
infants, or insane people, these deeds will become conclusive evidence of the title against all
the world ; and the title searchers need go no further back than the date of these deeds to
ascertain that the claimants under them have a perfectly good and indisputable title.

It has been suggested that a decree against the city to quiet title would dispose of the
difficulty ; but this is a mistake, for the reason that, according to the decision of the Judge of
the Twelfth District Court, following a previous decision of the Supreme Court of this State,
pueblo property cannot be alienated in that way, and all such decrees are void. It has also
been suggested that some further legislation is necessary, in order to put the title to lands
held under the Van Ness Ordinance beyond question. We agree that further legislation is

necessary, but, after mature reflection, we can think of no other effective measure that the Legislature can adopt than the ratification of a city deed, the making of such deed *prima facie* evidence of title, and a short statute of limitations to commence running from the date of the deed. It is just as impossible for the Legislature to make a new title to these lands as it is for the city. Neither can change rights already vested. Under this Order we have already collected together and put upon the record muniments of title that will be invaluable hereafter—invaluable, because those who furnish them are passing, and will soon have passed away.

Order No. 733 grants to the person in the actual possession of the outside lands, upon certain conditions therein named, whatever interest the city may have in such lands—the Order being, perhaps, subject to its ratification by the Legislature. The city pursued the same salutary course in 1855, when the Van Ness Ordinance was passed.

Judge Field decided that the residue of the lands described in the decree (the outside lands) belonged to the city, in trust for the inhabitants thereof; while the Act of Congress of 8th March, 1866, grants these lands to the city "upon the following trusts, namely, That all the said lands not heretofore granted to said city, shall be disposed of and *conveyed by said city to parties in the bona fide actual possession thereof, by themselves or tenants*, on the passage of this Act. in such quantities and upon such terms and conditions as the Legislature of the State of California may prescribe, except such parcels thereof as may be reserved and set apart by ordinance of said city and for public uses."

The language just quoted does not appear to harmonize altogether with that of the decree, and therefore it remains with the courts to determine which is the real source of the city's title—the decree of the Circuit Court or the Act of Congress. We learn that it is contended that the city title is held under the Act of Congress, and that these lands are held in trust for the occupants, subject only to a right in the city to reserve whatever is necessary for public purposes. But it may devolve on the Legislature to prescribe the terms and conditions upon which this Board may proceed to settle the question ; or, it may, in our judgment, determine it without reference to that body. It would appear that the Legislature, and the Legislature alone, has the power to settle the controversy between the city and its occupants, excepting so far as the reservations for public uses are concerned, for these we have the power to make under the Act of Congress.

It is useless in any aspect of the case for us to continue to receive petitions from the deluded persons to whom we adverted at the opening of this report. To receive them at all may seem to imply that we have power to act upon them ; and, as no such power was ever granted to this body, your committee recommend that no more petitions of this character be received, and that the Clerk be instructed to give public notice that those now on file be returned to their authors, and if not called for on or before the 1st December, he will rid his office of them in the most convenient way.

R. P. CLEMENT,
FRANK McCOPPIN,
FRED. G. E. TITTEL.

The matter ended there with passage of Resolution No. 7553, to wit :

Resolved, That no further petitions for grants of lands will be received by this Board, except such as are made in pursuance of Order No. 748, and that the Clerk give notice, by publication in the official paper of the city to those who have heretofore filed such petitions, to call for them within ten days, and that such as shall not be called for and taken away within that time will be destroyed.

It is stated that counsel have been employed to bring the question before the Courts for adjudication; if which is done, it is to be hoped that the matter will be conclusively and decisively passed upon at an early day, even if such result should be contrary to the usages of common practice.

A PUBLIC PARK.

Intimately connected with the final disposition of the outside lands, there is now the important question of laying off a suitable reservation for a great public park. The propriety of a large reservation being made, to the extent of at least one thousand to fifteen hundred acres, is almost universally conceded. This subject received at an early day the attention of the Committee on Outside Lands, appointed by the Board of Supervisors, under the provisions of Order No. 733. That Committee consists of R. P. CLEMENT, FRANK McCOPPIN, and CHAS. H. STANYAN, who have given the matter careful consideration. Their conclusions, with the result of their deliberations and recommendations as to location of the reservation proposed, will be known upon completion of the survey and delineation of the various claims upon the map now making by the City Surveyors, which then is to be submitted, for sixty days, to public inspection, for approval or objections. It is presumed this will be done before the close of the current year.

The magnificent and for many miles extended frontage upon the ocean beach which San Francisco possesses upon the Pacific shore, is believed to be unsurpassed elsewhere; and it may be said by those who have looked upon, or listened to the unceasing waves, as they roll and break upon its sands, that in primitive sublimity and majestic grandeur it is unequalled in the world. Therefore, with such natural advantages, when there shall be provided the adjunct of a grand park, similar in purpose and design to those established in Eastern cities and in Europe, the future dwellers in San Francisco will give deserved credit to those who faithfully and diligently strove to entail such a benefaction upon them.

Under decision of the Supreme Court of the United States, the title to the lands referred to is indisputably vested in the city. There may be some further legislation required to carry out details of the plan devised, but it is sincerely to be hoped that the final result will be the adoption of measures to secure to the citizens of San Francisco a park that shall be worthy of the name.

So long as the question of disposition of the outside lands remains undisposed of, those lands being mainly held only under possessory claims, they are in value comparatively worthless; the frequent conflicts of title between settlers and other claimants deter capitalists from investing in, or on loans accepting them as security. This feature, it is believed, will be to a great extent changed for the better when reservations selected for city purposes shall be definitely settled, and title to the remainder equitably and properly disposed of, for the benefit of the inhabitants, and in pursuance of laws duly made and provided.

WIDENING KEARNY STREET.

Under final decision of the Supreme Court of the State, this great improvement is being rapidly carried out, and within a few months all the buildings required to be removed will be brought to the new western line of the street, making a fine avenue of seventy-five feet wide to its intersection with Third Street; thence running, eighty feet, in width, to the southern frontage on the bay. During the year, the improvements made on the line of the street, as well as Third Street, have been very great, in the erection of buildings, constructed of brick and iron, mostly four stories in hight, the widening of sidewalks, etc., until it has become a notable ornament to the city, as well as greatly enhancing the revenue consequent to the increased value of taxable property. With few exceptions, the assessments for benefits to property made liable for damages for property required to be taken, have been received, the total amount paid into the Tax Collector's office for this purpose, on the 31st of October, being $404.000, leaving about $130,000 then delinquent.

The carrying out of this important measure was not effected without strenuous opposition on the part of many property owners, who deemed the awards made for damages for property taken too small; also, of those considering the sums assessed for benefits too high. The litigation on the part of the city was conducted by Hon. Alexander Campbell, Sr. The Commissioners were E. N. Torrey, C. C. Webb, and A. B. Forbes. The final decision in the Supreme Court in one of the most important cases, viz: that of Wm. A. Piper and others, was rendered July 16th, and is as follows :

IN THE MATTER OF WIDENING KEARNY STREET.

[No. A 1,245.]

This is an appeal from the order of the County Court of the City and County of San Francisco, confirming the report of the Commissioners appointed by said Court to appraise the damages sustained by the respective parties, portions of whose lots were taken for the purpose of widening Kearny Street, and to assess the benefits and apportion the expenses of the work upon the property benefited. For the purpose of the several appeals, we shall, without deciding the point, consider the questions raised as properly arising on the record. The first two points presented are, that the appellant's lot is shown by the proofs taken before the County Court to have been assessed for benefits far beyond what are likely to accrue; but if mistaken in this, that it is assessed too high as compared with the assessments for benefits to other lots, and we are asked to set aside the report as being against the weight of evidence on these points. This Court exercises appellate jurisdiction only, and reviews the action of two other bodies which have passed upon the same questions of fact.

When the verdict of a jury or finding of the Court is based upon evidence in which there is a substantial conflict, the Court will not set it aside on the ground that it is contrary to the evidence. (*Lyle vs. Rollin*, 25 Cal. 440 ; *Ellis vs. Jeans*, 26 Cal. 273 ; *Doe vs. Vallejo*, 29 Cal. 390 ; *Rice vs. Cunningham*, ib. 495.) The rule is not peculiar to this Court ; it is an established principle in the practice of all appellate Courts. The reasons upon which this rule of appellate Courts is founded apply with even greater force to proceedings of the kind now in question than to verdicts. The law requires in the first place three Commissioners to be appointed to make the appraisement and assessment. They are not, like jurors, selected by lot out of all citizens possessing the statutory qualifications, good, bad, and indifferent, and of every grade of capacity and intelligence, but are selected, after the parties interested are heard upon the question, with special reference to their fitness to discharge the particular duties devolved upon them by law in the given case. After having been sworn to faithfully discharge their duties "without favor or partiality," they are required to "proceed to view the lands and tenements mentioned and described in the notice, ordinances, resolutions, and maps aforesaid (of the designated district), and may examine witnesses on oath," etc. In case of doubt respecting any legal principle involved in these proceedings, they are authorized and required "to apply to the said County Court for instruction." It is their duty to investigate the subject thoroughly, examine witnesses if deemed important, obtain all the information within their power, reflect upon the subject, and finally embody the result of their investigation and reflection in their report. Their own observation, their own knowledge, their own reflections and judgment, as well as the testimony of witnesses, constitute important elements in the conclusions attained. The result of their investigations and deliberation having been embodied in a report and filed, a day is appointed by the Court to hear objections against its confirmation, and all parties interested are entitled to be heard, and to "take proof in relation thereto." Upon the facts reported, the report itself would make something more than a mere *prima facie* case, and it would devolve upon the attacking party to overthrow it by proofs, and the proofs should be clear beyond all reasonable doubt or controversy. The report is something more than the testimony of three intelligent and respectable witnessses. It is the judgment of three men selected under the law, in view of their peculiar fitness, after a thorough investigation of the matter committed to them, and embodies the result of their own experience, observation, and reflection, as well as the information received from others. But this question has been fully discussed by eminent jurists, and we shall adopt what they have so well said, rather than attempt to discuss the subject anew.

In the matter of Pearl Street (19 Wend. 652), Mr. Justice Cowan said : "I do not deny that cases may arise in which a reconsideration of the report should be awarded, upon the mere weight of evidence ; but to induce to such a course, the facts should be of a very decisive character, and border strongly on the conclusive. I am not prepared to say that, in reviewing the decision of these Commissioners, even a *prima facie* case against their award, derived from proofs independent of their opinion, should be listened to as a valid objection. It must, in general, be enough to sustain their estimates and assessments, that no positive rule of law has been violated. If we do not find that the legal interest of the tenant, owner, etc., has been misapprehended, their decision then stands as a matter of opinion on the value of an article in the market. So many considerations of time, locality, and other circumstances enter into the estimate, that the only means of finally settling the question is an appraisal. That is committed by the statute to Commissioners appointed by this Court and carefully selected. (2 R. L. of 1813, 409, Sec. 178.) They have power and it is made their duty to view the premises; if necessary, examine experts, to whom they may administer an oath, and explore all the best sources of information. (Ib. 410, Statutes Sess. of 1818, p. 196, Sec. 2.) With these means they generally combine a considerable degree of previous local knowledge. Great differences of opinion may and frequently do exist among witnesses. It is hardly ever safe to disturb the decision of such a question, or any other question of fact made by the tribunal to whom it is primarily committed. Whether it come from a jury, a master, referees or commissioners, we must be governed by the same principle. The very circumstance that it is open to difference of opinion should lead us to conclude that the first decision can rarely be bettered by a reversal founded on the partial and refracted light of an appellate tribunal." Much more is very forcibly said upon the subject in the same case. After much doubt and great hesitation on what appeared to be a perfectly clear case, Mr. Justice Cowan recommitted the matter to the same Commissioners, but he was afterward, evidently, dissatisfied with this determination. (19 Wend. 671.)

Again. In the matter of John and Cherry Streets (19 Wend. 669), the same distinguished jurist says : "Admitting the Commissioners to have acted on correct principles, and that they proceeded regularly (which is denied in respect to the receiving of an unsworn appraisal, made under their direction, a very material paper, which I shall hereafter notice more particularly), I am not satisfied that I ought to remit this report for reconsideration upon any of the objections founded on value. All the proofs mentioned having been regularly before the Commissioners, I would presume that they received due consideration ; and so far as they tended to increase the demands of the claimants beyond what was allowed, were not met with proper grounds of qualification. With the opportunity of viewing the premises, a local knowledge of the business and character of the street, of the market value of lots and buildings, and, indeed, all the elements which go to make up an opinion ; or, at least, the most advantageous means of acquiring the requisite knowledge in all particulars from the best sources ; and then the full means of applying their knowledge on consultation, the Commissioners have come to conclusions differing from those of the deponents whose affidavits were before them, and are now before me. The Commissioners, too, were sworn and had power to examine experts on oath—merchants, surveyors, mechanics, etc., adepts in commerce, values, mensuration, removing, building, repairing, etc., and I must infer that, whenever such examination was necessary to solve doubts, it was had. Men of ordinary capacity can hardly go through with such a laborious estimate and assessment and re-estimate and re-assessment as the one before me without becoming themselves expert in all the departments of knowledge necessary to the business they are about. In regard to a few of the obligations, I admit that the affidavits go into particulars derived from skillful men and other satisfactory sources, which, under my limited means of judgment, lead me somewhat to doubt the accuracy of the Commissioners in the values which they arrived at, but I want more to enable me to disturb their report. I repeat, that the estimate and assessment of values belong peculiarly to them, and I cannot set aside their report on the ground of error in this respect without a case is made against them, clear, strong, and indubitable. I admit that it is very difficult to make out such a case upon *ex parte* affidavits, which are the sort of proof usually before us in street causes, and I believe it has seldom been done. The proof is, in its own nature, open to much objection, and in common experience calls for great reduction, especially when it comes in the form of mere opinion as to price, or benefit, or damage, in respect to a projected improvement. The most candid and skillful entertain opinions on these subjects widely different, and I cannot in this case place the results thus stated by witnesses, or such as I might myself draw from particulars thus stated, in successful opposition to what I must think the more enlightened views of the Commissioners." Mr. Justice Bronson remarked in the matter of Furman Street (17 Wendell, 663), "that the reviews on appeal can, for the most part, extend to error in principle only. When a right rule for making the estimate has been settled, it must very often be impracticable for this Court to ascertain whether too much or too little has been awarded to any individual for damages. In the case under consideration, many of the witnesses differ one half in relation to the true value of the land which has been taken for the street, and the Court has no adequate means of arriving at a true estimate. We can only interfere with the report where, upon the proof as it appears by the affidavits, there is a plain and decided preponderance of evidence against the judgment of the Commissioners. What Judge, Commissioner, or juror ever sat, what lawyer ever practiced in a Court of original jurisdiction where these questions of damage and benefit are daily heard, without witnessing the same conflict and arriving at the same conclusion? The right rule is seldom mistaken. It is the present and future value in cash, of land, rents, materials, and labor. But the premises from which that value is to be drawn are often so complicated, and above all, the views of witnesses so imperfect, their language so obscure, and the subject itself lying so much in the region of conjecture, that an oral examination and cross-examination, and all other the best means of judgment are necessary, (vide *Commonwealth vs. the Justices, etc., of Norfolk*, 5 Mass. R. 435, 437 ; *the same vs. the Justices, etc., of Middlesex*, 9 id. 388; *the same vs. Coombs*, 2 id. 489, 492 ; *Callender vs. Marsh*, 1 Pick. 418, 432-3). * * * These reports of Commissioners, in respect to values, are in the nature of a verdict of a jury upon a question of fact, which is never set aside as against evidence unless it appear affirmatively and clearly to have been unwarranted by the proofs. There is more difficulty in showing this against the Commissioners' report, because from the nature of the proceeding they must make a more free use of their private knowledge than juries are warranted in doing. The latter are confined to action upon their general knowledge, and cannot go on their knowledge of particular facts without being sworn and communicating them as witnesses. (*Rex vs. Rosser*, 7 Carr. & Payne, 648.) Admitting everything, therefore, to have been regular, I should hardly deem the report impeached upon its merits in any matter of valuation." (671.)

And in the matter of William and Anthony streets (19 Wend. 694), Mr. Justice Bronson said : "Courts seldom set aside the verdict of a jury on the sole ground that they may think it against the weight of evidence. And yet there is much less difficulty in such a review than there is in the case under consideration. Jurors do not act upon particular facts within their own knowledge, but upon written documents and the testimony of witnesses submitted to their consideration. The evidence upon which they form conclusions may be put upon paper and submitted to the Court for consideration. But it is not so, or at most only to a very limited extent, in relation to the proceedings of these Commissioners. They are selected not only with reference to their integrity and general capacity for business, but on account of the knowledge which they are supposed to possess concerning the particular duty which they are appointed to discharge. Such information as they have in relation to the value of the property taken, and the probable effect of the improvement upon other property in the same neighborhood—in whatever way the information may have been obtained—they are at liberty to use. The very first thing which is required of them by law, after taking the oath of office, is to view the premises affected by the improvement. (Sec. 178.) They are thus to acquire information, and that, too, of the most important character, which there are no means of bringing before this Court. And beyond this, I entertain no doubt that the Commissioners may take the opinion of others, in whose integrity and judgment they have confidence, without swearing them as witnesses. They may converse with all classes of men concerning the business in hand, and collect information in all the ways which a prudent man usually takes to satisfy his own mind concerning matters of the like kind, where his own interests are involved in the inquiry. The Commissioners must exercise their own judgment at the last, but they may first seek light from other minds, the better to enable themselves to arrive at just conclusions. When the original jurisdiction is exercised in this manner, it is impossible that there should be anything like a regular judicial review.

"We cannot regard the Commissioners as witnesses merely, and then suffer their judgment to be balanced by the opinions expressed in three opposing affidavits, and to be outweighed when a fourth is added. For aught that we can know, the judgment expressed by the Commissioners upon questions of value, may combine the opinions of a hundred men who are in all respects as well qualified to form just conclusions as those who make opposing affidavits. In settling questions of value the Commissioners do not sit as a court and jury and decide upon the evidence of witnesses examined before them. Nothing of this kind was contemplated by the Act of 1813, nor can it be justly inferred from the Act of 1818, which authorized them to administer oaths. (Stat. of 1818, p. 196, Sec. 2.) Estimates from mechanics and builders may become important in the discharge of the duties of the Commissioners, and in these and other cases they may require the sanction of an oath to the estimates which they receive. If, in any case, they make the opinions of others the basis of action without exercising their own judgment, those opinions should be given upon oath. But when they only seek information for the purpose of enlightening their own judgments, they may obtain it in any of the ways in which men usually acquire knowledge. They need not, and in point of practice they do not, sit as a Court. If in any case they take the testimony of witnesses in relation to value, it is but an item in the account, which may go to qualify, but cannot control their own opinions. How then is it possible that we can disturb the report, upon mere question of value, on the single ground that five, ten, or even twenty, respectable men have sworn to opinions at variance with the judgment of the Commissioners?

"A review was given to this Court for the purpose of seeing that the Commissioners exercise their authority in the forms prescribed by law, and for the correction of any error in the principle upon which they have proceeded in making their awards. After what has been done in other cases, I will not say that we cannot go beyond this and examine questions of value. But there must be something more than the opinions of witnesses against the judgment of the Commissioners. We must have facts. There must be something like demonstration that the Commissioners have fallen into error." And in Pryor's Appeal (5 Abb. 275), Mr. Justice Mitchell expresses similar views.

We have to start with, in this case, the report of the three Commissioners selected with reference to their peculiar qualifications for the important and delicate duties intrusted to them, and there is no objection raised as to their fitness. They spent some seven months in their investigations and deliberations, and enough of their doings is shown by the record to make it apparent that they carefully considered the subject, compared one lot with another, and thoroughly studied the various influences which have combined during the last few years to affect the value of the property in the district to be charged with the expense of the work. Upon the filing of the report, according to the statement of the County Judge, some sixteen parties out of the large number affected filed objections, and, so far as the records now before us are shown, they all selected the same two or three lots as standards of comparison, and relied mainly on the fifty vara lot of Main & Winchester, corner of Post and Kearny Streets. If there is any inequality in the assessment it may fairly be presumed that it will be more apparent between that lot and those of the appellants than anywhere else. An investigation was had before the County Court upon these objections, and the evidence was directed mainly to the lots selected by appellants for the comparison. Evidence was introduced both against and in favor of the report, and the County Judge, after an elaborate review of the testimony, in an opinion evincing a critical and thorough consideration of the whole subject, sustained and confirmed the report of the Commissioners; and it is by no means clear to our minds that the reasoning of the County Judge, in his opinion in this case, is satisfactorily answered by the counsel of appellant. However this may be, as a matter of reasoning, there is a manifest and substantial conflict in the evidence introduced upon the two points now under discussion, viz : as to whether the amount of the benefits assessed exceeds the benefits likely to accrue from the widening of the street; and as to whether the amount of the benefits assessed is relatively too high. On both points there is a wide difference in the opinions of appellant's own witnesses, as there necessarily must be in such matters. Some of them evidently do not accurately distinguish between the enhanced value of the property on the south end of Kearny Street, resulting from numerous other causes, and that which results alone from the widening of the street ; while the latter only is to be regarded in assessing the amount of benefits. Some of the testimony is manifestly wild, but if we were to take the testimony of the appellant alone, and carefully scrutinize it, without reference to the report of the Commissioners or the testimony on the part of the respondent, it would appear from it, upon the whole, that there is a large enhancement of value in consequence of the widening of the street—as much at least as the benefits assessed ; while the testimony of the witnesses on the part of the city shows a still greater enhancement of value, and strongly supports the report of the Commissioners, both as to the amount of the enhancement and the equality of the assessment ; and some of it is based upon an actual sale of the property of the appellant claimed to have been assessed too high. It is plain, from all the testimony, that, at the south end of Kearny Street, within the last few years, there has been a very large enhancement in the value of property from other causes, having no reference to the widening of the street— much more so than at the north end ; and if we carefully analyze the appellant's testimony it will be found that the great discrepancy in the testimony lies almost purely in the domain of conjecture rather than in the domain of facts ; that it relates to the cause of the enhancement of value, as whether due to the widening of the street, or other causes, rather than to the fact or extent of the enhancement. Testimony as to the value must necessarily consist very much of opinions, and often be of a very unsatisfactory character, but this is true to a much greater extent with reference to the amount of the enhancement of values, which is due to each of several causes combining to produce a given result. Those witnesses of appellant who attempt to fix the value of the property at the date of their testifying do not vary so much ; for some seven of them estimate the then value of Main & Winchester's lot at from $800 to $1,100 per foot ; or an average of about $985 ; five of them putting it at $1,000 per foot, and six of them the value of the appellant's lot, at from $700 to $1,000 per foot, or an average of $926 per foot. Tested by an actual sale at auction, the value of the latter seems to have been about $960 per foot. But when they come to estimate how much of this value is due to the contemplated widening of Kearny Street, the testimony lies entirely in the field of conjecture; and as might be expected, there is a wide difference in the views of different parties. The Commissioners, in valuing the property for the purpose of obtaining a basis for estimating the benefits, fixed the then value of Main & Winchester's lot at about $770, and appellant's lot at about $740 per front foot—each being somewhat lower than appellant's witnesses placed the value at the time they testified, and relatively about the same. To this, as we understand it, the benefits are added. Thus it is seen that the great discrepancy in the testimony of the appellant's witnesses, and between them and the witnesses of respondent, and the report of the Commissioners, relates, not to the value of the lands, but to the proportion which should be credited to the widening of the street and that which is due to other causes ; and the real contest lies almost entirely in the domain of conjecture.

From considerations before stated, the peculiar qualifications sought in the appointment of the Commissioners, their long personal investigation of the subject, etc., the Commissioners, it would seem, must, in the nature of things, be better qualified to estimate these benefits than witnesses called to the stand for the occasion from among men engaged in active business requiring all their attention, to give, upon the spur of the moment, and upon less comprehensive views of the subject, their ideas, even though such witnesses may be dealers in real estate and generally well informed as to its value. A careful examination of the testimony in the record cannot fail to show that very much of that portion relating to the enhancement of value resulting from the widening of the street as compared with that resulting from other causes, consists of crude and hastily formed opinions.

It is further insisted that the assessment on Kearny Street is erroneous for the reason that it is made upon the hypothesis that all the lots on Kearny Street will be benefited by the improvements in the ratio of their values, whereas the proof shows the fact to be otherwise. This point is really necessarily involved in the second, but is discussed in the briefs as a separate point, and requires more particular notice. We are not authorized, nor are we asked, to assume a legal proposition that the benefits to the several lots fronting on the street will not be in the same ratio as that of their value. It is a question of fact, and must be determined as such on evidence. And so the appellants treat it. But it is, also, one of those facts which lie almost wholly in the field of conjecture. Neither the senses nor our intellectual faculties can fully appreciate it. It cannot be exactly seen, or felt, or weighed; nor can its dimensions or boundaries be accurately measured and defined. It is a fact which the Commissioners were called upon to determine, and after a survey of the entire field, and giving the question the best consideration they could, they did determine that the benefits resulting to the owners of the property from the improvement would be in this case in the same ratio as that of the value of the property. On the hearing of the objections, before the County Court, this was one of the grounds, and the main ground of objection to the report. Testimony was taken upon the precise point, and witnesses, so far as we can judge, equally reputable and equally competent, offered in their opinion upon the question. Two of the Commissioners, Webb and Torrey, testified that in their opinion the benefits resulting to property along the whole line of Kearny street would be in the ratio to its value, and the testimony of Sherman and Burr is to the same effect. If these opinions are correct, as to the equality of ratios between the enhancement of value by improvement, and the value of the property before the widening of the street, the basis upon which the benefits are apportioned on that street is the proper one. It may be true that the repetition of their opinion by the Commissioners upon the stand as witnesses adds nothing to the force of the report. If this be conceded, it still detracts nothing from the weight of their opinions upon the point, whether regarded as their evidence, or their finding upon the question based upon inspection and information obtained as well as their own judgment. It shows, at least, that they still adhered to the opinion, after it had been controverted and counter testimony taken, and the matter had been reconsidered in the light of such objections and testimony. By way of argument, it is said, that any one acquainted with the topography of the city, must see at a glance that the south end of the street must be benefited far more, in proportion to its value, than the north end, and such was our first impression, but the more we reflect upon the matter the more difficult we find it to establish the conclusion by any satisfactory course of reasoning.

The street is simply widened. Every foot of ground upon the entire street to be widened has already been occupied for years. It will open into the same street, after it is widened, as it did before. The same streets cross it—no more and no less—and at the same points as before. The hills at the north and west were there before. The improved portion of the street will occupy the same relative position to the rest of the city, and to the localities toward which the business and population are tending, that it did before. The testimony does not show that the tendency of the population and business spoken of toward the south, has heretofore been owing to the widening of this street. It has manifestly, to a great extent at least, been owing to other causes. A better class of business, requiring better and finer buildings, and inducing greater travel, will undoubtedly seek the street when widened, and it is not easy to see why the better class of business should not seek the entire street. It is said that toward the northern end the main travel comes down Washington and Clay Streets, crossing Kearny into Montgomery. This is at present, doubtless, equally true of the streets crossing south of

Clay. But if the anticipations of the projectors of the widening of Kearny Street are realized, Kearny Street, opening into Third, will become the great thoroughfare through the very heart of the city, from north to south, on the line of greatest travel, and the business of the fashionable world, to a great extent, transferred or extended from Montgomery to Kearny Street, and the travel which now comes to Montgomery Street, instead of crossing, will pass into Kearny. This is the result, to some extent, anticipated by the Commissioners, as appears in the testimony of one of them. There is, it is true, as stated in the argument, a rise of ground from Pacific to Broadway, but it is not so great but that a street railroad passes over it, and when Broadway is reached, Kearny Street opens into the most spacious avenue in the northern part of the city, extending westward with a grade easier than the other, and far lighter than on Washington. Can it be for a moment doubted that when Kearny Street is widened, broad sidewalks constructed, and first-class buildings erected, the favorite line of travel from the north and north-west part of the city will be down Broadway into and through Kearny Street, or that the anticipations of the Commissioners as to this street becoming the leading thoroughfare of the city from north to south are within the bounds of reasonable probabilities? When Kearny Street is widened into the most spacious street in the heart of the city, running in that direction, and the present structures on it are replaced by first-class commercial buildings from Market to Broadway, can it be doubted that much of the travel now coming down Geary, Post, Sutter, Bush and Pine Streets, crossing into Montgomery, will pass into Kearny, and northward on that street toward, and eventually to a considerable extent to Broadway? Or that the building up and occupation for fashionable shops of the southern half of Kearny street thus widened will of itself create a demand for similar structures toward the north, and gradually, at least, force such improvements forward until they reach Broadway?

One of the Commissioners testifies that, after obtaining all they could in respect to travel, "they found the amount of travel about equal at all the crossings from Market to Washington; that the conclusion was, that property opposite the plaza would be as much benefited as any south of it." The property of the appellant is opposite the Plaza, within the district between Washington and Market, and somewhere in the neighborhood of midway between the two termini of the portion of Kearny street to be widened. Should the widening of Kearny street result as anticipated, in making it the leading thoroughfare of the city from north to south, taking much of the travel that now crosses to Montgomery, the appellant's lot must be greatly benefited, and it is not easy to satisfactorily show why it should not be relatively as much benefited by the improvement as any other. Much may be said on both sides of the question, but we do not propose to discuss it at greater length. While we are not entirely satisfied that the rule adopted works with perfect equality, it is not entirely clear from the testimony or argument that it is not; and the question was one peculiarly in the province of the Commissioners to determine. It must also be admitted, we think, that they both had better opportunities of arriving at a correct conclusion, and that they were personally better qualified to determine the question than we. The matter was re-examined by the County Judge, and further testimony taken—the witnesses appearing in person before him, and after a laborious consideration of the case, the report of the Commissioners was confirmed. The testimony is so much in conflict, and consists so entirely of matter of opinion, that we should not be justified in holding that the Commissioners and County Court erred.

It is argued that if the apportionment on Kearny Street is made upon a correct principle, then the apportionment on Third street and the cross streets within the district determined to be benefited, which was made upon a different hypothesis, must necessarily be erroneous. But this conclusion does not necessarily follow. These streets occupy an entirely different relation to the improvement made. It is supposed that the widening of Kearny Street will make it the great thoroughfare, north and south, through the heart of the city, as Montgomery Street now is, and the benefit to the cross streets will result solely from the fact of their close proximity to this great thoroughfare. As the benefit to property on those streets results from its proximity to and not from the fact of its bordering on the improvement, the nearer a lot on a cross street approximates this thoroughfare the greater will necessarily be the benefit derived. It is upon that very theory that the Board of Supervisors fixed upon the limits of the district to be determined to be benefited by the improvement for the purpose of assessing the expenses to be incurred in making it. As the locality recedes from the great artery of travel and business on the cross and secondary streets, the population tributary to it and the travel upon it gradually diminishes till it becomes very small, and the value of the property diminishes in about the same ratio till it becomes valuable only for the purpose of husbandry. On the cross streets this gradual receding from the proximity of the improvement takes place ; but it is not so on that portion of Kearny Street widened. The diminishing scale of benefits as the property recedes from Market Street along Kearny would not furnish the proper rule, for the very obvious reason that the improvement which it is supposed will work the great revolution in the line of travel and business is not at Market Street, and there is no receding from it, as the advancement is made northward along Kearny Street ; but, on the contrary, the advancement is on the very line of the improvement and the line of the increased travel and business throughout the entire distance to Broadway. There is nothing in the testimony tending very strongly to show that the mode of apportionment adopted by the Commissioners for the cross streets and Third Street does not operate equally. The Commissioners found, upon examination, four different classes of lots and property within the district, differently situated with reference to the contemplated improvement : Firstly— Kearny Street, the street to be widened. Secondly—Third Street, on the north side of Market, and virtually an extension of Kearny Street southward from the point where the widened street terminates. Thirdly—The North Beach and Mission Railroads ; and fourthly—Streets crossing. Kearny. The whole amount to be raised was first apportioned among these four classes—a certain amount to Kearny Street, and a certain amount to each of the other classes. No complaint is made that the proper portions have not been assigned to each of these divisions or classes, if the property on Third and the cross streets is liable to be assessed at all. It being assumed that the proper amount has been assigned to Kearny Street, the owner of property on Kearny street is thenceforth interested no further than to have the part assigned to Kearny Street equally apportioned among the property holders on that street according to the benefits. He cannot claim that an error has been made in apportioning the amount assigned to cross streets among the property holders on those streets ; or that the Commissioners adopted a different mode of arriving at the apportionment of those streets. The statute prescribes only one rule of apportionment, and that is according to benefits. But to ascertain the benefits, it may be necessary to apply different principles to property having a different relative situation to the improvement, and presenting different elements affecting the questions of value and benefits. The Commissioners, in this instance, found it necessary to consider different elements in making the apportionments according to the benefits, and it rests with the objectors to show conclusively that they erred in their estimate of the effect of these various elements.

It is next claimed that the Commissioners erred in not assessing the buildings on the lots as well as the lots, and that the buildings were not considered in the assessment The law does not say that the buildings, as such, shall be assessed separately from the lots. The assessment is to be in proportion to the benefit which the owners and occupants of land and houses shall acquire, and is made a lien upon and collected out of the lands through which the benefit is derived. The property enhanced in value and through which the benefit accrues is the thing in respect to which the assessment is made, and the basis on which it rests. Section 7 says that the Commissioners "shall apportion and assess the whole amount * * * upon all the owners and occupants of lands and houses within the territory deemed * * * benefited by such improvement, as near as may be in proportion to the benefits which each shall be deemed to acquire by the making thereof." And Section 16 provides: "The expense of any public improvement herein authorized shall be defrayed by assessment on the owners and occupants of houses and lands, corporations and companies, that may be benefited thereby." And, by Section 8, the report must specify "the sums of money which each and every owner or occupant of houses and lands, corporation or company, deemed to be benefited by such improvement * * * should pay toward the expenses of making the same, and the lands [not lands and houses] in respect to which he shall be deemed by them to be benefited." Section 15 requires the assessment roll to contain, in the proper columns, "the names of all persons   *   *   *   *   *   assessed when known;" "the description of the land [not lands and houses] in respect to which they are assessed ;" "the amount to which such persons shall respectively be assessed," and the amounts are to be collected in the same manner as taxes are collected in said City and County, "and shall in like manner be a lien upon the respective tracts or parcels of land," etc. [not lands and houses]. Thus it appears that when reference is made to the property "in respect to which he shall be deemed by them benefited" as in the eighth section, or "in respect to which they are assessed," or upon which the amount assessed "shall in a like manner be a lien," as in section fifteen, land only is mentioned. Nothing is said about houses. And houses are only mentioned in their sections by way of *descriptio personæ* in connection with lands to indicate the person who is to pay the assessment upon the lands through which the benefit is acquired. Lands include the houses erected on them. The owner and occupant is to pay an assessment in proportion to the benefits received—not upon the valuation of the entire property, including buildings. If he is assessed in proportion to the entire benefit received, it can make no possible difference whether a part of the benefit is credited to the land and a part to the house erected on it, or all credited to the land. It is all taken into consideration somewhere. Nor do the injunctions of the statute require in terms, or by necessary implication, that it should be so distributed.

The land, in the strictest sense of the term, is the only thing of a permanent character. It it cannot be removed, enlarged, diminished or destroyed, and we do not see why the benefit should not all be regarded as accruing to the land alone. It is so regarded in theory by writers upon political economy. Adam Smith, in his great work on the "Wealth of Nations," says: "The building rent is the interest or profit of the capital expended in building the house. In order to put the trade of the builder upon a level with other trades, it is necessary that this rent should be sufficient, first, to pay him the same interest which he would have got for his capital if he had lent it upon good security; and, secondly, to keep the house in constant repair, or, what comes to the same thing, to replace, within a certain number of years, the capital which had been employed in building it. The building rent, or the ordinary profit of building, is, therefore, everywhere regulated by the ordinary interest of money. * * * Whatever part of the whole rent of a house is over and above what is sufficient for affording this reasonable profit naturally goes to the ground rent; and when the owner of the ground and the owner of the building are two different persons, is, in most cases, completely paid to the former. This surplus rent is the price which the inhabitant of the house pays for some real or supposed advantage of the situation. In country houses, at a distance from any great town, where there is plenty of ground to choose upon, the ground rent is scarce anything, or no more than what the ground which the house stands upon would pay if employed in agriculture. In country villas in the neighborhood of some great town it is sometimes a good deal higher; and the peculiar convenience and beauty of situation is frequently very well paid for. Ground rents are generally highest in the capital, and in those particular parts of it where there happens to be the greatest demand for houses, whatever be the reason of that demand, whether for, trade or business, for pleasure and society, or for mere vanity and fashion." (Vol. III., Lon. edition, 1805; 294-5.)

Thus that profound thinker arrives at the same conclusion upon this subject that the Commissioners in this case—three practical business men—attained, after investigating the subject in a practical way, and which, it seems to us, must be attained by every reflecting mind. It would seem that it must be so from the nature of things. How could it be possible that a building, wherever situated, should be worth any more than it would cost to put another there like it, and, say, the rent, or that portion of the net rent over wear and tear, during the period of time required to erect it, and put it in a condition for occupancy? If it were destroyed to-day, another could be erected at actual cost to-morrow, and the destruction and restoration might be repeated *ad infinitum*. If any value accrues in consequence of changes in the surrounding circumstances, it necessarily attaches to the land—to the location. Should the building be destroyed by fire, the land would sell for as much without as with it, less the cost of erecting another like it, and the net rents during the period to put it in a condition to occupy; in practice, probably far more. It would make no difference whether the land was in the hands of the owner in fee, or under lease; for, in the latter case, the enhanced value would, during the term, go to the leasehold estate in the land. The building would actually be worth no more annexed to a leasehold estate, than to the fee. It could be replaced for the same money in one case as in the other. In this case, the Commissioners did take into consideration the entire benefits to buildings, as well as lands. This presumption would arise on the report itself. But one of the Commissioners, Torrey, was called to testify upon the point, and said: "We took into consideration the benefits to buildings and lands. The usual way of assessing is on lands and improvements [probably referring to valuation for the purposes of ordinary taxation]. This differs—it was the benefit to the property we were looking for." And that is precisely what the statute required them to look for. Upon the views before presented, the only enhancement of value to buildings in consequence of the improvement that could in any event take place, would be the increased rents during the time it would take to erect such a building or put a building already there in a suitable condition. A party having a suitable building on his land would hold this advantage—no more. The Commissioners found that, on one side of the street throughout its entire length, it was necessary to cut away the buildings for a distance of over twenty-nine feet—the width added to the street—and that, as a matter of absolute necessity, all the buildings on that side would have to be rebuilt or greatly remodeled. On the other side they found a class of third or fourth rate buildings, some of brick and some of wood, none of which, it is conceded on all hands, are suitable to the condition or contemplated business of the widened street. All, therefore, would have to be entirely remodeled or torn down and new ones erected in their place, or else the owners could not reap the full benefits which would otherwise accrue to their lands. Either the change must be made sooner or later, or the benefits resulting from the widening would not practically accrue. The Commissioners found that it would take about the same time to remodel, so as to adapt these buildings to the new condition of things, as to construct new buildings; and that the owners would therefore, sooner or later, all alike lose about the same amount of time in the interruption of the use of the buildings, and that the only element which could probably give additional value to the building, as such, was therefore wanting. They determined that, under the circumstances of the case, the only benefit accruing to the owners and occupants of the houses and lands accrued in respect to the lands; and we see nothing in the testimony or arguments that would justify us in setting aside the report of the Commissioners, and the order of the County Court confirming it, on that point. There is much less plausibility in this objection than in the second and third.

The fifth point is, that the Board of Supervisors had no constitutional authority to include Third and Market streets, and portions of the several cross streets in the district supposed to be benefited, and, therefore, to be assessed for the payment of the expenses of the improvement. And the sixth point is, that the expense should have been borne by the whole city; and the Board of Supervisors had no constitutional power to impose the burden upon a specific portion of the city supposed to be peculiarly benefited. These points seem to be necessarily inconsistent with each other. But the question has been settled against the appellants in this State, and, by what may be regarded as a uniform line of decisions in other States. (Emery vs. San Francisco Gas Company, 28 Cal. 372; People vs. Mayor of Brooklyn, 4 Const. 430, and cases cited.)

If the facts are correctly ascertained by the Commissioners, no positive rule of law appears to have been violated, and upon the facts there is a manifest and substantial conflict in the evidence upon the points in contest. We are of opinion that the order confirming the report of the Commissioners must be affirmed, and

It is so ordered.   SAWYER, J.
We concur :   SHAFTER, J.
                                                    CURREY, C. J.

EXTENSION OF MONTGOMERY STREET.

Following soon after the successful carrying out of the great improvement made by widening Kearny and Third Streets, there came the important measure of extending Montgomery Street in a direct line to the southward so as to, at the intersection of Channel Street, strike Connecticut Street, which runs thence for a long distance over the Potrero Nuevo in the same direction.

The first proceedings in this matter were had in the Board of Supervisors on the 29th of October, 1866, upon petition of property owners. These were subsequently followed by many petitions for and protests against the measure. Further steps were taken on the 12th of November, by the appointment of a Special Committee to examine and report upon the subject. This Committee was composed of five members, viz :

MONROE ASHBURY, Chairman;

FRANK McCOPPIN,   CHAS. H. STANYAN,
JAS. H. REYNOLDS,   A. J. SHRADER.

Under provisions of the Act of April 4th, 1864, public notice was given for five days, by publication in the Alta California, of notice of intention to condemn the lands necessary to be taken to extend the street through some eight consecutive blocks (irrespective of sub-divisions), the notice specifying time and place for hearing property owners and all others interested in or affected by the proposed extension. Meetings duly set for this special purpose were held on the 21st and 28th of March, and April 3d, 1867, at which the subject was fully investigated, argued pro and con at great length, by lawyers of the highest standing in the community ; was then held in Committee under consideration for several months, until, on the 23d day of September, two reports (the Committee disagreeing) were submitted in Board of Supervisors, to wit :

The undersigned, a majority of the Special Committee appointed to take charge of the matter of the extension of Montgomery and Connecticut Streets, and to whom said matter was referred, report as follows :

Since the hearing of property holders interested in the proposed improvements, and since the determination of the Kearny Street appeals, your Committee have had several meetings, and have carefully considered the matters submitted to them upon the last reference. The undersigned are satisfied that the extension of Montgomery street southwardly to Channel Street and of Connecticut Street northwardly to Channel Street, is, in consideration of the present wants and future growth of the city, a public necessity ; that such extensions would greatly promote the public good, and at the same time add largely to the taxable property of the city ; and that the present is the proper time to carry out the proposed improvement, as the same can be made now at much less expense and much more conveniently than at any future time.

The owners of a large majority of the property within the district to be directly affected by the proposed improvement, and which, in the judgment of the undersigned, ought to bear the expense thereof, are now anxious that it shall be made, and have petitioned the Board accordingly.

The principal opposition to the proposed extension has been made by owners of property fronting on Montgomery Street, as at present laid out, and it has been made not so much on the ground that the extension is not desirable or necessary as upon the ground that it would not benefit the present Montgomery Street, and, therefore, that property fronting thereon ought not to be assessed or taxed therefor.

Upon full consideration of the arguments presented in support of this view, the undersigned have come to the conclusion that no property north of Market Street ought to be charged with any of the expense of the proposed extension.

A final order in accordance with the conclusions hereinbefore stated is presented herewith, and the undersigned recommend its passage.*   J. H. REYNOLDS,
                                                                                  C. H. STANYAN.

----

* NOTE.—Supervisor McCoppin, although not signing, sustained this report.

The undersigned, a minority of your Committee, to whom was referred the petitions and protests in the matter of extending Montgomery Street, across Market Street, in a southerly direction, to Channel Street, beg leave to report :

That, upon the examination of the petitions in favor of the extension, we find represented by the front foot, along the line of the proposed street, or within the district liable to be assessed, 12,100 feet. Also, twenty-eight petitioners, setting forth that they are the owners of land along the line of the proposed street, frontage not given. Also, forty-eight petitioners, setting forth that they are the owners of land on the Potrero, frontage not given.

We find 383 protests against the proposed extension, and represented by the front foot as follows :

	Feet.
Along the line of the proposed street, or within the district liable to be assessed	4,347
On Second Street	2,457
On Third Street	3,300
On Market Street	6,745
On Montgomery Street	3,200
On various streets south of and including Market Street	16,327
Making in all protesting	36,376

If the holders of property through which the proposed street would pass were unanimous in their determination to open the street through it, they could undoubtedly effect their object without applying to this Board. Their want of unanimity, however, prevents them from taking this course, and hence an appeal is made to the power of this Board to effect their object. Such power is given by an Act of the Legislature, approved April 4th, 1864 ; but in the exercise of it the Board is to be governed entirely by a regard to the public wants and convenience. Advantages to be derived by private individuals, however great, have no proper place in our determination. The taking of private property for public purposes can only be justified on the ground of a great public necessity. The opening of a new street, imperiously demanded by the public convenience, justifies such an appropriation of private property ; but the public necessity, which is the justification of the power, should evidently be the limit to its exercise.

The question then to be determined, is whether the public good so imperiously calls for the proposed extension of Montgomery Street as to warrant us in compelling the minority of the property owners to sell their land to the public at an appraised value, against their will. The undersigned are of the opinion that it does not. The following are some of the considerations that have operated on our minds :

1st. The making of the proposed street does not appear to us to be called for by any public necessity whatever. The present streets on the southern part of the city are sufficiently wide and numerous, and no complaint of their insufficiency has been heard from citizens residing in that part of the city, nor from the general public ; nor is it called for or desired by the taxpayers of the city ; but is an enterprise started by a few individuals, owners of property along the line of the proposed street, whose property will be greatly enhanced in value if Montgomery Street is extended as proposed.

2d. The angles at which the proposed street would intersect the lines of streets and lots on the hundred vara survey, the number of gores and angular street crossings it would have, the excessive length of the latter and their disproportion to the amount of house-frontage on the street, are also, in the estimation of the undersigned, very serious objections to the proposed extension.

3d. If Montgomery Street is extended as proposed, the same reasons that led to it may be urged in favor of a like extension of other streets parallel to it. Certainly no great public necessity for a direct communication between the Potrero and the fifty vara survey can be adequately met by the opening of a single street, and nothing less can justify the proposed forcibly taking private property. We must therefore assert a public necessity, and open several parallel streets to supply it, or, denying such public necessity, in which case we find no justification for compelling people to sell their property against their will.

4th. By authority of an Act of the Legislature to establish the lines and grades of streets in the city and county of San Francisco, approved April 26th, 1862, the Board of Supervisors passed an order declaring the map now on file in the office of the City and County Surveyor the official map of the city, thereby pledging the public faith as to the future lines of the streets, which is never to be broken, except a great public necessity requires it, which in this case it does not.

Millions of dollars have been invested in lands and improvements south of Market Street, and within the hundred vara survey, based on the permanence of the present lines of the streets, and the future growth of the city in accordance with them. To change the present lines of the streets, in the hundred vara survey, would, in our opinion, disturb the future prospects and change the relative value of all the lands and improvements south of Market Street, and could not fail to produce extensive mischief and discontent, as well as to impair confidence in the stability and future prospects of the city.

All real estate south of and including Market Street, except that on the line of the proposed street, would be more or less injuriously affected by the proposed extension. So serious a step is not, in our opinion, to be lightly taken, nor unless called for by some urgent public necessity.

Respectfully submitted.   MONROE ASHBURY,
A. J. SHRADER.

After very full consideration and discussion, a final Resolution for extension of the street was passed for printing on the 23d of September, and on the 7th of October, finally passed ; was presented to the Mayor on the next day, and returned without signature and with his objections thereto on the 14th ; was taken up on the 28th of October and finally approved by a requisite two-thirds vote, then becoming valid ; that date just completing one year from the first introduction of the subject into the Board of Supervisors.

The Mayor's Message reads :

MAYOR'S OFFICE, SAN FRANCISCO, October 14, 1867.

To the Honorable Board of Supervisors of the City and County of San Francisco :

I herewith return to your Honorable Body, Resolution No. 7,500, entitled a Final Resolution to extend Montgomery and Connecticut Streets, without my approval, for the following reasons :

1st. The proposed extension would make many acute and obtuse angles at the intersections of the other streets, and thereby greatly disfigure the present 100 vara survey.

2d. It would establish a precedent for the extension of Battery, Sansome, Kearny, Dupont, Taylor, and other streets ; and if such additional extensions followed, it would create so many irregularities that it might become necessary to extend the streets perpendicular to these, such as Ellis, Eddy, Tyler, Turk, and McAllister, in order to restore a rectangular system ; thus the entire 100 vara survey would be obliterated, and such an immense and burdensome expense would be incurred as to greatly impede the future prosperity of the city.

3d. If it is important and necessary for Courts frequently to hold to the doctrine of " *stare decisis,*" and to maintain a certain course of decisions on the ground of perpetuating a rule of property, though such rule were not originally founded in strict law, it seems to me equally important for legislative bodies to adhere as far as possible, consistently with the public interest, to a *settled order of things* in relation to *street lines,* so that the tenure and value of real property may become as stable and reliable as possible, and that the inducements for permanent investments therein may not be discouraged.

4th. A change so great as the one contemplated, and which is to be made in derogation of private rights, by taking private property for public uses, should not, in my judgment depend on a bare majority vote of a single legislative body composed of twelve members ; a two-thirds vote at least should be required.

5th. I have myself been, for the last four years, the owner of lands at South Beach, which ·

would be so largely benefited by the extension of Montgomery street, that I feel myself virtually disqualified for signing the Resolution, on the ground of *interest*.

6th. There appear to be almost insuperable obstacles in the shape of high grades, on the Potrero, to the extension along Connecticut Street, and consequently there cannot be the grand avenue, parallel to the water front for many miles, such as has been frequently de-. scribed, and such as would be really desirable.

7th. Judging by the petitions and protests which have been presented here, the interests in favor of the change seem small in comparison with the vast interests which oppose it.

8th. Finally, there does not appear to be a *clear public necessity* for the contemplated extension—the only reason which in my judgment would justify this Board in a proceeding that will necessarily invade private rights.

All of which is respectfully submitted.

H. P. COON,

Mayor of the City and County of San Francisco.

The next procedure in carrying out this measure, is the adoption of a Resolution directing the City and County Surveyor to make a map showing the district to be assessed ; following that, the serving of notice upon each person liable to be assessed for benefits or damages, and obtainance of descriptions of property to be condemned ; then, upon filing in the County Court a copy of record of the proceedings had, the Judge of that Court has jurisdiction, and appoints three Commissioners of Appraisement to pass upon the benefits and damages referred to. *

An undertaking of such importance as the foregoing naturally elicited a large share of public attention, and was warmly advocated by its friends, and as strenuously contested by its opponents. The latter contended that the cutting through so many blocks diagonally, making thereby acute angles, would destroy the plan or symmetry of the city survey as originally laid out, and seriously damage or deteriorate the value of property on adjacent streets as plotted under the O'Farrell and Eddy surveys. The friends of the measure claimed that the property benefited would pay in full for damages to other, for the property taken; and furthermore, that by the opening of a great street of eighty feet wide, continuous for some three miles, there would be given the citizens of San Francisco a promenade unsurpassed in the world. That such a grand avenue for the people of San Francisco would be agreeable is undoubted. Should the measure be carried out, the street will run, with few variations, in a line close to the eastern frontage of the waters of the bay.

The whole proceedings have been conducted under the advice of the special city counsel in the matter, Mr. Jabish Clement, with whom is associated Hon. Selden S. Wright.

HOSPITAL AND ALMS-HOUSES.

For some years the fact has been known that provisions made for care of the indigent sick and infirm were inadequate to the requirements of the city. In

---

* NOTE.—This was had by the passage, in Board of Supervisors, November 11th, 1867, of two Resolutions, Nos. 7608 and 7617; the latter fixing the 13th of January, 1868, for hearing the matter and appointing Commissioners.

order to provide more suitable accommodations therefor, upon application of the Board of Supervisors, authority was obtained from the State Legislatures of 1863 and 1866 to purchase ground and to erect buildings, under which some eighty acres of arable land, situated some four miles from the City Hall, was purchased (early in the year 1866) at a cost of $30,000. Premiums were offered by public advertisement for plans and specifications for Hospital and Alms-house buildings; the first of these (among eight competitors) was awarded to Messrs. Butler & Bugbee, and the second to Messrs. Kenitzer & Farquharson. The appropriation authorized by law being insufficient for erection of the two buildings, it was determined to proceed with that of the Alms-house, and a Smallpox Hospital, leaving the erection of a new general Hospital until such time as authority for the further expenditure necessary should be obtained.

In the month of September, 1866, after due public advertisement, a contract for erection of the Alms-house was entered into with Kimball Brothers, for the sum of $44,800. This contract was completed, and the building accepted by the city, in September, 1867. The Alms-house has now some one hundred and thirty inmates, and may justly be considered as a manifest evidence of the charitable disposition of the people of San Francisco in thus providing a comfortable home for the poor and unfortunate who are dependent on the public for support. The building, a sketch of which, engraved by Wm. Keith, is given opposite, may be described briefly as follows: Entire front, 187 feet; main center building, 40 by 46 feet; the wings to north and south, each 44 feet by 73 feet six inches; one rear wing, 44 by 64 feet; two one-story side buildings, respectively 15 by 38, and 15 by 26 feet; the elevation of the wings from the ground is some 54 feet, and the center building 66 feet. The whole, it is believed, will furnish comfortable accommodations for from 400 to 500 persons.

The Superintendent is Mr. Geo. F. Harris, who is assisted by some ten subordinates as nurses, etc., and workmen upon the farm; the intention being to make the institution as nearly self-sustaining as possible.

The Smallpox Hospital is located on a remote part of the Alms-house grounds, enclosed with a high fence. Its dimensions are: a center building 41 feet front by 51¼ feet deep, with two wings, each 27 by 21 feet; the whole containing four wards, each 20 by 20 feet, with ample kitchen, dining, store and nurses' rooms, etc., and capable of receiving thirty to forty patients, if necessary.

This Hospital, as well as the City and County Hospital, and Alms-house, is under the supervision of Dr. Wm. T. Garwood, Resident Physician, and Drs. F. A. Holman, Visiting Surgeon, and A. G. Soule, Visiting Physician.

The report of the Resident Physician, pages 286 to 293, presents hospital statistics for the year. The average number of patients provided for yearly, since 1860, has been:

For the year ending June 30th, 1860.......160
For the year ending June 30th, 1861.......176
For the year ending June 30th, 1862.......236
For the year ending June 30th, 1863.......283
For the year ending June 30th, 1864.......322
For the year ending June 30th, 1865.......370
For the year ending June 30th, 1866.......341
For the year ending June 30th, 1867.......308
Remaining at close of the year............291

The expenditures during fourteen years ending June 30th, 1866, were:

1853–4	$213,364	*Brought forward*	$778,040
1854–5	278,328	1861–2	39,292
1855–6	89,478	1862–3	58,049
1856–7	40,360	1863–4	67,314
1857–8	43,880	1864–5	85,127
1858–9	37,653	1865–6	85,441
1859–60	38,591	1866–7	136,567
1860–1	36,386	Total	$1,350,830
Carried forward	$778,040		

In the above expenditures, as given for the fiscal years 1866–7, there is included the sum of $75,393 for cost of land and part payment on erection of buildings. (See Auditor's Report, page 11.) The total cost of the property, including purchase of the grounds, erection and furnishing of buildings, exceeds one hundred and twenty thousand dollars, as follows:

Amount paid—

For ground, eighty acres	$30,000
Kimball Brothers, contract price for main building	44,800
For extra wall and foundation	4,925
Painting, etc	2,119
Erection of stables, building tank, plumbing, etc	11,300
Mantles $750, range $1,200	1,950
Extra work, alterations, etc	1,639
Butler & Bugbee, architect's services	3,340
Furniture for rooms	7,037
Furniture for kitchen, etc	1,540
Stock for the farm	3 968
Contract price for building cistern	938
Thos. Tompson, boring artesian well	384
Francis Lounds, digging well	150
Leason & Hall, digging well	368
	$114,458

The above is exclusive of cost of erection of the Smallpox Hospital building, which was, contract price, $9,150, making a total of nearly $125,000.

· The erection of the buildings was under supervision of the Committee on Public Buildings, consisting of Supervisors F. G. E. TITTEL, CHAS. H. STANYAN and P. H. DALY; the furnishing of building and care of inmates, under supervision of the Hospital Committee, Supervisors MONROE ASHBURY, CHAS. CLAYTON and R. P. CLEMENT.

JUSTICES' COURT.

Under the Act approved March 24th, 1866, there were chosen at the general election, September 4, five Justices of the Peace to compose a Justices' Court in and for the City and County of San Francisco.

The Justices elect are :

JAS. C. PENNIE,	OSCAR T. SHUCK,
T. W. TALIAFERRO.	P. B. LADD,

GEORGE LEVISTON.

Their term of office commences on the first day of January, 1868, and is to continue for two years; one of their number to be appointed yearly by the Board of Supervisors, Presiding Justice. Said Board is also authorized to appoint a clerk of the Court, upon a recommendation of a majority of the Justices, and not more than three constables, severally to hold office for two years, unless sooner removed for cause.

The Court fees are made payable into the Special Fee Fund of the City Treasury, from which the salaries of the Justices, Clerk, and Constables are to be paid. The salaries fixed by the Act are:

Presiding Justice, per annum.......................................$3,000
Four Justices of the Peace, each per annum.......................... 2,400
One Court Clerk, per annum... 2,400
Two Constables, (one additional, if required,) each per annum......... 1,200

In case of three constables being appointed, the salary of each is fixed at $1,000.

The Board of Supervisors are required to provide, in some convenient locality, a suitable building, with rooms for the Clerk's office, Court room, and separate rooms for offices or chambers for each of the Justices of the Peace (the presiding Justice excepted), for the transaction of their official business; or if deemed expedient, to assign separate offices or chambers for the Justices in different buildings and places; also to provide suitable furniture therefor.

The Presiding Justice and Clerk are required to be in attendance at the Clerk's office daily, non-judicial days excepted, from the hour of nine A. M. until five P. M., and at such other convenient hours as may be required by urgent official business; and the other Justices to be in attendance at their respective offices or chambers, for the dispatch of official business, daily, from the hour of nine A.M. until five P.M. Unless otherwise ordered by the Board of Supervisors, leave of temporary absence may be granted by the Mayor to the Clerk or any of the Justices, when such absence will not materially prejudice or delay official business; but absence for more than two hours in a day, or for more than four days in one month, is to be charged with a proportionate deduction of salary.

The Court and Justices have the powers and jurisdiction heretofore exercised by the several individual Justices of the Peace in the City and County; and it is provided that all actions, suits and proceedings, whereof Justices of the Peace and Justices' Courts in said City and County have jurisdiction, shall be commenced, entitled, and prosecuted in said Court. The Court to be always open, non-judicial days excepted, and causes therein to be tried before the presiding Justice, or before any one of the Justices before whom the original process is made returnable, or to whom the cause may be assigned or transferred for trial, or before any three Justices of the Peace constituting the Court in bank; but the Court in bank has exclusive power to hear and determine all applications for new trial.

It is made unlawful for any Justice or Constable to collect or receive any fee or compensation whatever (other than the salary allowed out of the Treasury) for any official services; but all fees or moneys legally chargeable for such services are to be paid into the hands of the Justices' Clerk, and by him paid into the City Treasury, daily or weekly, as may be prescribed by the Board of Supervisors.

THE MILITARY

Organization of San Francisco continues in the same effective and praiseworthy condition in which it was reported in 1866. A just emulation and *esprit de corps* is particularly observable in the various companies composing the Second Brigade of the National Guard of the State.

THE NATIONAL GUARD, organized under the Act of April 2, 1866, consists of six brigades, composed of eighty companies—sixty-four of infantry, of not less than fifty privates, with officers and non-commissioned officers ; twelve of cavalry, of not less than thirty privates, with officers and non-commissioned officers, and four of artillery, officers, etc.—is under command of Major General LUCIUS H. ALLEN ; head quarters San Francisco, whose staff is composed of—

Lieut. Colonel S. C. ELLIS ....Assistant Adjutant General.
Lieut. Colonel A. H. HOUSTON......Commissary.
Lieut. Colonel A. W. VON SCHMIDT. .Engineer Officer.
Lieut. Colonel DANIEL NORCROSS....Paymaster.
Lieut. Colonel S. O. HOUGHTON.....Inspector.
Lieut. Colonel THEO. A. MUDGE ....Ordnance Officer.
Lieut. Colonel J. H. STEARNS.......Quartermaster.
Lieut. Colonel J. W. BRUMAGIM ....Judge Advocate.
Lieut. Colonel GEORGE HEWSTON....Surgeon.
Major S. P. MIDDLETON...........Aid-de-Camp.
Major JAMES L. BEYEA.............Aid-de-Camp.

That portion of the National Guard located in the City and County of San Francisco now consists of two regiments of infantry, three companies of cavalry, and one artillery light battery of six guns, all attached to the Second Brigade ; Brigadier General JOHN HEWSTON, Jr., commanding.

Major G. W. SMILEY...............Ass't Adj. Gen. and Chief of Staff.
Major JOHN HILL..................Inspector.
Major W. F. LADD.................Ordinance Officer.
Major M. M. RICHARDSON ....Paymaster.
Major C. E. HINCKLEY ....Commissary.
Major C. L. WIGGIN ....Quartermaster.
Major A. D. GRIMWOOD ....Judge Advocate.
Major T. J. P. LACY ....Engineer.
Major S. R. GERRY ....Surgeon.
Captain OCTAVIUS BELL...........Aid-de-Camp.

The San Francisco regiment and companies thus referred to are as follows :

FIRST REGIMENT OF INFANTRY.

ROBERT SIMSON............................Colonel.
T. B. LUDLUM............................Lieutenant Colonel.
W. C. LITTLE ....Major.
A. B. WOOD..............................Adjutant.

Company Letter.	Company Name.	Commanding Officer.	Number of Men.
A	State Guard.....................	Captain John G. Dawes..............	60
B	City Guard.....................	Captain George W. Granniss.........	74
C	National Guard.................	Captain Benjamin Pratt	99
D	San Francisco Guard	Captain Edwin Lewis................	No report.
E	Sumner Light Guard	Captain Abram Moger	63
F	Light Guard	Captain Eli Cook	65
G	Ellsworth Rifles	Captain James G. Carson	70
H	California Tigers	Captain Edward McDevitt	81

SECOND REGIMENT OF INFANTRY.

JOHN W. McKENZIE......................Colonel.
JOHN McCOMB ....Lieutenant Colonel.
JOHN STRATMAN ....Major.
H. H. THRALL............................Adjutant.

Company Letter.	Company Name.	Commanding Officer.	Number of Men.
A	Union Guard...................	Captain Harvey Lake	74
B	Veteran Guard	Lieut. Commanding Fred. Harrington.	93
C	Franklin Guard	Captain John McComb	65
D	Liberty Guard.................	Captain Thomas J. Dixon.............	89
E	McClellan Guard	Captain J. W. Wilkinson.............	70
F	McKenzie Guard	Captain R. G. Gillmore.............	94
G	Eureka Guard..................	Captain Frank Harrington............	90
H	San Francisco Cadets..........	Captain C. E. S. McDonald...........	79

FIRST REGIMENT OF CAVALRY.

CHARLES L. TAYLOR ....Colonel.
Vacant ....Lieutenant Colonel.
JOHN H. MARSTON ....First Major.
H. M. LEONARD ....Second Major.
S. B. PIKE..............................Adjutant.

Company Letter.	Company Name.	Commanding Officer.	Number of Men.
A	First Light Dragoons..........	Captain David Moore.................	45
B	San Francisco Hussars	Captain G. G. Brodt	47
C	Jackson Dragoons	Captain P. R. O'Brien	72

LIGHT BATTERY.

Company Letter.	Company Name.	Commanding Officer.	Number of Men.
A	California Guard	Captain Samuel Brannan	92

OFFICIAL FEES.

The following table is presented, showing the returns made by officers in the City and County of San Francisco, for six months ending January and July, 1867, respectively, not payable into the City and County Treasury, being in lieu of fixed salaries :

TABLE OF RECEIPTS.

Offices and names of Officers.	Receipts from July 1, 1866, to January 1, 1867.			Receipts from January 1 to July 1, 1867.			Amount for the Year
	Amount chargeable	Amount Received.	Total.....	Amount chargeable	Amount Received.	Total.....	
COURT COMMISSIONERS.							
John L. Love	$241 00	$1,383 70	1,624 70	233 40	$1,220 80	1,454 20	3,078 90
Robert C. Rogers ...	225 00	973 00	1,198 00	....	735 00	735 00	1,933 00
James M. Taylor ...	38 25	485 25	523 50	189 50	125 75	315 25	838 75
Charles Halsey	....	....	....	186 75	252 50	439 25	439 25
NOTARIES PUBLIC.							
J. H. Blood	52 00	1,546 50	1,598 50	65 00	1,429 50	1,494 50	3,093 00
Henry Dreschfeld ..	....	1,016 75	1,016 75	....	....	....	1,016 75
John Gorman	....	1,027 50	1,027 50	....	869 50	869 50	1,897 00
Samuel Hermann...	....	1,321 50	1,321 50	....	1,781 25	1,781 25	3,102 75
Henry Haight	....	1,834 50	1,834 50	....	1,694 00	1,694 00	3,528 50
William Huefner ...	25 00	1,139 75	1,164 75	....	1,217 50	1,217 50	2,382 25
E. V. Joice.........	....	2,104 25	2,104 55	....	1,282 00	1,282 00	3,386 25
W. W. Lawton......	....	1,243 50	1,243 50	....	1,231 50	1,231 50	2,475 00
T. A. Lynch........	....	1,378 00	1,378 00	191 00	1,351 00	1,542 00	2,920 00
R. P. Lewis	....	1,297 00	1,297 00	....	1,393 50	1,393 50	2,690 50
Samuel S. Murfey ..	....	890 00	890 00	....	1,028 00	1,028 00	1,918 00
J. T. Milliken	191 00	563 50	754 50	....	640 00	640 00	1,394 50
J. W. McKenzie	....	1,000 00	1,000 00	....	1,100 00	1,100 00	2,100 00
Otis V. Sawyer	....	1,123 50	1,123 50	....	1,287 00	1,287 00	2,410 50
E. V. Sutter........	....	750 00	750 00	....	939 50	939 50	1,689 50
N. Proctor Smith...	....	388 75	388 75	....	820 00	820 00	1,208 75
F. J. Thibault......	....	1,993 00	1,993 00	....	1,904 50	1,904 50	3,897 50
Henry S. Tibbey ...	179 00	650 10	650 10	....	1,457 75	1,457 75	2,107 85
George C. Waller ...	179 00	546 00	725 00	138 00	646 00	784 00	1,509 00
John White	....	1,941 80	1,941 80	....	2,782 00	2,782 00	4,723 80
A. G. Randall	....	....	....	....	418 00	418 00	418 00
P. Neumann	....	....	....	6 00	19 50	25 50	25 50
JUSTICES OF THE PEACE.							
R. J. Tobin	139 00	1,755 00	1,894 00	63 00	1,345 75	1,408 75	3,302 75
A. Barstow.........	....	5,100 00	5,100 00	....	3,978 50	3,978 50	9,078 50
James C. Pennie....	240 00	1,902 25	2,142 25	....	1,594 25	1,594 25	4,736 50
E. B. Drake........	1,133 25	3,030 30	4,163 55	....	....	....	4,163 55
J. P. Van Hagan....	388 00	976 32	1,364 32	....	....	....	1,364 32
Wm. H. Bell	....	3,675 00	3,675 00	....	2,108 50	2,108 50	5,783 50
Thomas S. Miller...	....	....	....	454 00	561 00	1,015 00	1,015 00
P. B. Ladd	....	....	....	182 00	251 75	433 75	433 75
CONSTABLES.							
S. C. Harding	161 24	3,641 02	3,802 26	553 86	3,035 40	3,589 26	7,391 52
M. Smith	207 00	895 00	1,102 00	193 61	1,122 65	1,316 26	2,418 26
*J. Hilton	935 30	1,098 80	2,034 10	....	....	....	2,034 10
J. Groesbeck	391 52	415 24	806 76	319 88	265 87	585 75	1,392 51
M. Fennell.........	....	1,921 00	1,921 00	....	1,471 50	1,471 50	3,392 50
M. Harkins.........	....	....	....	366 78	1,126 72	1,493 50	1,493 50

NOTE.—Several resignations and new appointments have been made during the year, which accounts for the difference of receipts of many officers, as returned above.   * No report filed or the last six months.

THE REGISTRY LAW,

Is generally admitted to have proved cumbrous and expensive in its workings or carrying out. Many of its friends, who believe in maintaining the elective franchise in purity, it is said will endeavor to have the Act amended at the ensuing session of the Legislature, so as to preserve its main features, and to accomplish the desired end by the adoption of a simpler and less expensive form. The usual expenses of any election, prior to 1866, seldom if ever exceeded $2,500 to $3,000. The expenses of the election of September 5th, 1866, as given in the Auditor's Report, page 47, were $17,137 81; this, however, included the cost of registration and enrollment. The accounts of expenses of the elections held in September and October, 1867, are not made up; but enough is known to show that the cost of the two is about $25,000, or to say $15,000 for the first, including registrations and enrolments, and $10,000 for the second. The time and trouble necessarily taken to procure registration, and subsequently enrolment for each election, probably prevented numbers from availing themselves of the rights accorded them, and perhaps deterred others from voting at all. For comparison the following figures give the total number of voters in each Ward at each of the three elections referred to, held under the Registry Act; also, the number of votes polled; the number of names enrolled having been furnished by the Clerks of the various Election Districts, and the number voting taken from the official returns.

ELECTIONS.

Wards.	MUNICIPAL—September 5, 1866.		GENERAL—September 4, 1867.		JUDICIAL—October 16, 1867.	
	Number Enrolled.	Number Voting.	Number Enrolled.	Number Voting.	Number Enrolled.	Number Voting.
First Ward	1,056	976	1,736	1,196	1,677	895
Second Ward..	1,053	912	1,533	1,125	1,547	958
Third Ward ...	667	551	1,180	700	1,200	541
Fourth Ward..	1,000	914	1,396	1,201	1,410	988
Fifth Ward....	816	727	948	818	969	684
Sixth Ward....	991	853	1,407	1,004	1,389	889
Seventh Ward.	1,528	1,333	2,556	1,744	2,590	1,387
Eighth Ward ..	1,979	1,756	2,808	2,349	2,775	1,898
Ninth Ward ...	969	834	1,452	1,108	1,477	846
Tenth Ward...	2,749	2,492	4,970	3,339	4,987	2,615
Eleventh Ward	1,343	1,291	1,987	1,705	1,939	1,334
Twelfth Ward.	822	752	1,385	1,183	1,369	836
Totals.....	14,973	13,371	23,558	17,472	23,327	13,871

CITY AND COUNTY OFFICERS ELECTED SEPTEMBER 4TH, 1867.

Mayor .... FRANK McCOPPIN.

Sheriff .... P. J. WHITE.

Treasurer .... OTTO KLOPPENBURG.

County Clerk .... WASHINGTON BARTLETT.

Recorder .... E. W. LEONARD.

Assessor .... BENJAMIN E. HARRIS.

District Attorney.............................H. H. BYRNE.
Surveyor ....WM. P. HUMPHREYS.
Harbor Master...................... ......J. S. HOUSEMAN.
Coroner ....J. LETTERMAN.

OCTOBER 14TH.

County Judge.................................E. W. McKINSTRY.
Probate Judge...............................SELDEN S. WRIGHT.
Police Judge.................................R. R. PROVINES.

THE OVERLAND RAILWAY

Across the continent from East to West, or from West to East, is fast becoming a prominent feature of the day. The indications are greatly growing, going to show that in a very few years more, a tide of pleasure and business travel will flow to and fro along that grand highway of the nation; and in all probability ere long, when the eyes of many tourists or visitors from the old world shall light upon the majestic elevations of the Rocky Mountains or of the Sierra Nevadas, even the snow-clad summits of the Alps may seem somewhat to diminish their lofty heights.

From the East the Union Pacific Railroad is approaching with rapid strides, and from the West with like rapidity the Central Pacific Railroad is being extended over the western range of mountains, so as to meet and make the line complete upon the central plains beyond. That this will be effected within three or four years ensuing is considered certain. The western terminus naturally having been fixed at San Francisco, the advantages to be derived to the city and the State are well said to be almost incalculable. The speedy filling up of the great interior basin or heart of the continent with an active, industrious and intelligent population; the building of the hamlets, the villages and the cities— the very sites or locations of which are, as yet, not known or dreamed of ; the peopling of such a vast extent of territory with a progressive race as is that which now inhabits the eastern and western sides of the North American continent, must necessarily, in the future, exert an immense influence on either side, and perhaps ultimately become a Union-binding tie, guarding and controlling discordant factions or conflicting elements in any quarter.

As giving the most valuable information which can now be shown respecting that vast region soon thus to be traversed and to teem with life and activity, there is presented the accompanying map, engraved by Mr. WM. KEITH, of San Francisco, from a drawing recently published in the City of New York.

And not the overland railroad alone is tending to enhance or promote the coming greatness of the Pacific States. From all directions, north, south, east and west, there has been projected an extensive system comprising many diverging lines of railroad in the interior of the State, and of which about three hundred and fifty miles are complete and in running order. In this respect there has been a marked spirit of enterprise abroad. A railroad line

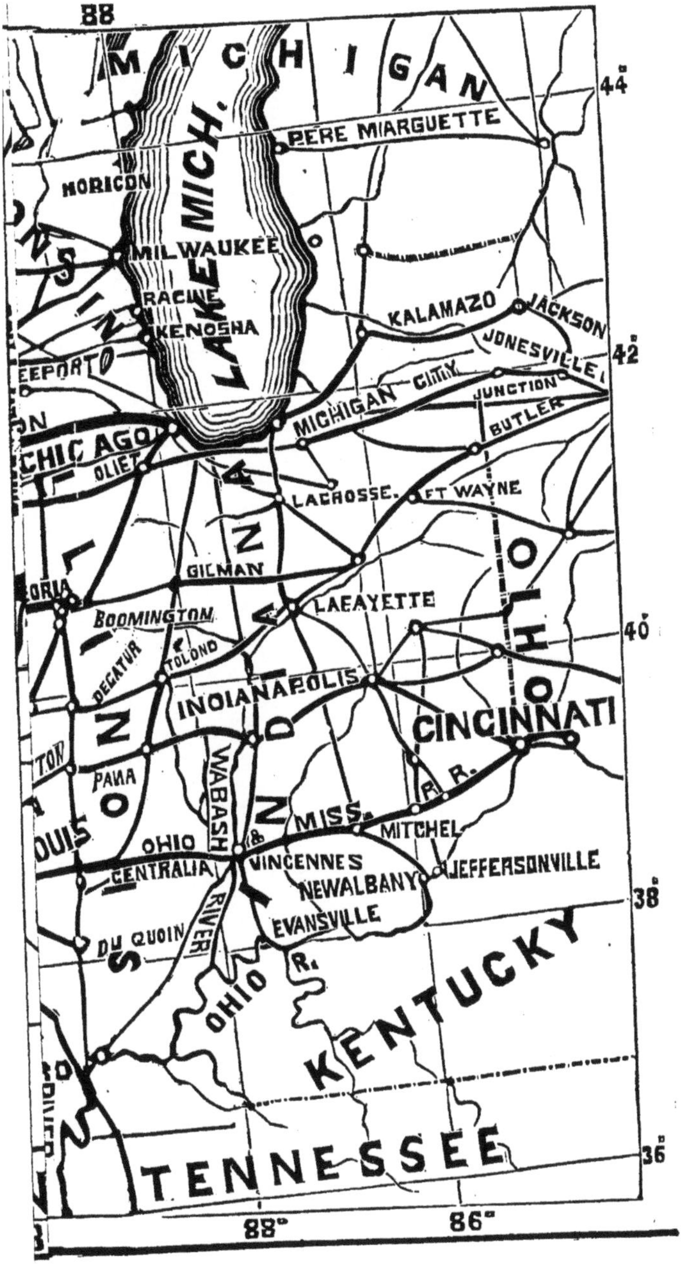

MICHIGAN
LAKE MICH.
PERE MIARGUETTE
HORICON
MILWAUKEE
RACINE
KENOSHA
KALAMAZO
JACKSON
JONESVILLE
MICHIGAN CITY
JUNCTION
BUTLER
CHICAGO
OLIET
LACROSSE.
FT WAYNE
GILMAN
LAFAYETTE
BOOMINGTON
DECATUR
TOLONO
INDIANAPOLIS
CINCINNATI
PANA
WABASH
OHIO & MISS. R. R.
MITCHEL
OHIO
CENTRALIA
VINCENNES
NEWALBANY
JEFFERSONVILLE
EVANSVILLE
RIVER
DU QUOIN
OHIO R.
KENTUCKY
TENNESSEE
ILLINOIS
INDIANA
OHIO
88
44°
42°
40°
38°
36°
88°
86°

from Marysville to Portland, Oregon, some three hundred miles in length, is under survey, and the work already commenced. There is also projected a Southern Pacific road, connecting with the present line at San José, and running thence to the Colorado River, before referred to as likely to become the means of opening a large trade with the interior portion of the country. An immediate carrying out of all the routes or lines now projected is problematical; but it is to be supposed not more so than twenty years ago was considered to be the building of that great series and interwoven fabric of roads which have had such an all powerful influence in contributing to and securing the commercial importance of those great centers of travel and trade, Cincinnati, St. Louis and Chicago, to say nothing of Boston, Baltimore, Philadelphia or New York.

To carry the subject a little further, the following brief compilation is given, showing the names of incorporated companies now organized in California, the lines of routes projected, and the distance done.

NAME OF ROAD.	Length.	Miles Completed
San Francisco and San Jose Railroad, from San Francisco to San Jose......	50	50
San Francisco and Alameda Railroad, from Encinal to Vallejo Mills.........	26	14
Oakland Railroad, from Oakland Point to Clinton...........................	4	4
Napa Valley Railroad, from Vallejo to Calistoga..........................	40	12
California Pacific Railroad, from Vallejo to Sacramento...................	62	
California and Oregon Railroad, from Marysville to Oregon................	300	
Southern Pacific Railroad, from San Jose to Colorado River...............	600	
Copperopolis Railroad, from Copperopolis to Stockton.....................	35	
Sacramento Valley Railroad, from Sacramento to Folsom....................	23	23
Western Pacific Railroad, from Sacramento to San Jose....................	120	20
Placerville and Sacramento Valley Railroad, from Folsom to Placerville.....	36	26
California Central Railroad, from Folsom to Lincoln......................	21	21
Yuba Railroad, from Lincoln to Marysville...............................	24	18
California Northern Railroad, from Marysville to Oroville................	26	26
Central Pacific Railroad, from Sacramento to Fort Bridger................	900	93

The footing of the above statement gives about twenty-three hundred miles of railroad projected or under contract, and nearly three hundred and fifty miles completed.

THE BOUNDARIES OF THE CITY AND COUNTY

As prescribed in Section 1 of the Consolidation Act, are as follows: Beginning in the Pacific Ocean, three miles from the shore, and on the line (extended) of the United States Survey, separating townships two and three, south (Mount Diablo meridian), and thence running northerly and parallel with the shore so as to be three miles therefrom opposite Seal Rock; thence in the same general direction to a point three miles from shore, and on the northerly side of the entrance to the bay of San Francisco; thence to low-water mark or the northerly side of said entrance, at a point opposite Fort Point; thence following said low-water mark to a point due northwest of Golden Rock; thence due southeast to a point within three miles of the natural high-water mark on the eastern shore of the bay of San Francisco; thence in a southerly direction to a point

33

three miles from said eastern shore, and on the line first named (considered as extending across said bay) ; and thence along said first named line to the place of beginning. The islands in said bay, known as Alcatraces and Yerba Buena, and the islands in said ocean, known as the Farallones, are attached to and form a part of said City and County.

The Ward and Election District boundaries are :

FIRST WARD.—Washington Street on the south, Kearny Street on the west, and the bay of San Francisco on the north and east. Islands in the bay attached to First Ward.

SECOND WARD.—Kearny Street on the east, Vallejo Street on the south, Larkin Street on the west, and the bay of San Francisco on the north.

THIRD WARD.—Washington Street on the north, Kearny Street on the west, California Street on the south, and Market Street and the bay of San Francisco on the east.

FOURTH WARD.—Vallejo Street on the north, Kearny Street on the east, Washington Street on the south, and Larkin Street on the west.

FIFTH WARD.—California Street on the north, Kearny Street on the west, and Market Street on the south and east.

SIXTH WARD.—Kearny Street on the east, Pine Street on the south, Larkin Street on the west, and Washington Street on the north.

SEVENTH WARD.—Harrison Street on the south, Second Street on the west, Market Street on the north, and the bay of San Francisco on the east.

Election District No. 1.—Howard Street on the south, Second Street on the west, Market Street on the north, and the waters of the bay on the east.

Election District No. 2.—Harrison Street on the south, Second Street on the west, Howard Street on the north, and the waters of the bay on the east.

EIGHTH WARD.—Kearny Street on the east, Market Street on the south, Larkin Street on the west, and Pine Street on the north.

Election District No. 1.—Post Street on the south, Larkin Street on the west, Pine Street on the north, and Kearny Street on the east.

Election District No. 2.—Market Street on the south, Larkin Street on the west, Post Street on the north, and Kearny Street on the east.

NINTH WARD.—Harrison Street on the north, Seventh Street on the west, and the bay of San Francisco on the east.

TENTH WARD.—Market Street on the north, Seventh Street on the west, Harrison Street on the south, and Second Street on the east.

Election District No. 1.—Harrison Street on the south, Fourth Street on the west, Market Street on the north, and Second Street on the east.

Election District No. 2.—Harrison Street on the south, Seventh Street on the west, Market Street on the north, and Fourth Street on the east.

ELEVENTH WARD.—Seventh Street on the east, by Market Street and Ridley Street in a direct line to the Pacific Ocean on the north, by the Pacific Ocean on the west, and by the line of San Mateo County and the bay of San Francisco to the line of Seventh Street on the south and east.

Election District No. 1.—On the east by Seventh Street to Mission Creek, on the south by Mission Creek and Sixteenth Street to Dolores Street, on the west by Dolores Street to Market Street, and westerly and northerly by Market Street to Seventh Street.

Election District No. 2.—On the north by Mission Creek and Sixteenth Street to Dolores Street, on the east by Dolores Street from Sixteenth to Ridley Street, thence northerly by Ridley Street and a direct line to the Pacific Ocean, thence westerly by the ocean to the line of San Mateo County, on the south by the line of San Mateo County to the bay, and easterly and northerly by the waters of the bay to Mission Creek.

TWELFTH WARD.—Larkin Street on the east, by Market Street and Ridley Street in a direct line to the Pacific Ocean, and the bay of San Francisco on the west and north.

Election District No. 1.—Larkin Street on the east, Bush Street on the south, the Pacific Ocean on the west, and the bay on the north.

Election District No. 2.—Bush Street on the north, Larkin Street on the east, Market Street to Ridley Street, Ridley Street in a direct line to the Pacific Ocean on the south, and the Pacific Ocean on the west.

The assessed value of real estate and improvements thereon, by Wards, is shown by the following exhibit, for which the compiler is indebted to the courtesy of Wm. R. Wheaton, City and County Assessor :

VALUATION OF REAL ESTATE AND IMPROVEMENTS BY WARDS — 1867-8.

Wards.	Valuation.	Wards.	Valuation.
First Ward...................	$1,451,840	Seventh Ward	$3,664,230
Second Ward................	2,170,635	Eighth Ward	5,725,425
Third Ward	7,548,950	Ninth Ward	3,150,580
Fourth Ward................	2,814,380	Tenth Ward	7,234,510
Fifth Ward..................	6,196,400	Eleventh Ward	7,503,345
Sixth Ward..................	2,912,300	Twelfth Ward	4,507,873
Total			$57,880,468

Although the boundaries of many of the Wards, excepting the Eleventh and Twelfth, were materially changed by the re-districting Act of 1864, yet the following table, presented for comparison sake, may not be out of place in showing the increased real property valuation of the city in the short space of seven years. Making note that the designations of Districts is now changed to that of Wards, the valuations were :

COMPARATIVE REAL ESTATE VALUATIONS.

Districts.	Property.	VALUATIONS IN THE FISCAL YEARS				
		1860-1.	1861-2.	1862-3.	1863-4.	1864-5.
First District	Real Estate	$1,381,405 00	$1,416,704 00	$1,324,780 00	$1,469,545 00	$1,448,810 00
Second District	Real Estate	2,177,655 00	2,187,223 00	2,374,191 00	2,681,745 00	2,892,204 00
Third District	Real Estate	2,404,600 00	4,556,150 00	4,119,700 00	4,337,835 00	4,576,875 00
Fourth District	Real Estate	1,887,290 00	2,041,835 00	2,082,465 00	2,258,445 00	2,692,380 00
Fifth District	Real Estate	4,666,500 00	5,408,350 00	5,233,750 00	5,914,650 00	6,164,375 00
Sixth District	Real Estate	1,461,050 00	1,685,526 00	1,706,200 00	1,838,970 00	1,981,295 00
Seventh Dist	Real Estate	1,800,150 00	2,493,600 00	3,288,125 00	3,657,200 00	3,872,600 00
Eighth District	Real Estate	1,277,295 00	1,832,325 00	2,686,311 00	3,240,815 00	3,666,550 00
Ninth Dist	Real Estate	2,272,175 00	3,092,405 00	3,811,970 00	3,856,035 00	3,909,110 00
Tenth District	Real Estate	3,227,295 00	4,742,490 00	6,512,130 00	7,375,715 00	7,906,473 00
Eleventh District	Real Estate	1,572,790 00	2,715,290 00	3,245,596 00	5,459,479 00	6,719,580 00
Twelfth District	Real Estate	{ Included in 11th District. }	{ In cld in 11th District. }	590,032 00	1,017,1 0400	1,562,651 00
Totals		$25,148,885 00	$31,871,897 00	$36,975,250 00	$43,116,558 00	$47,292,903 00

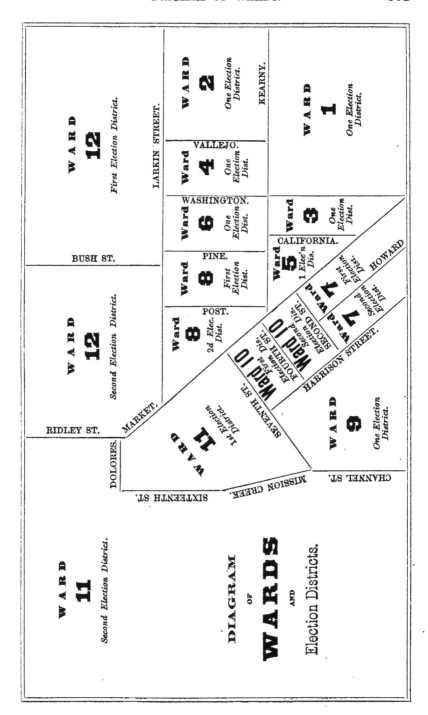

OFFICERS OF ELECTION.

First Ward—Election District	Clerk.............. Judges	Benjamin Shellard. George Munroe. James Harrold.
Second Ward—Election District..............	Clerk.............. Judges	Jeremiah Smith. H. H. Lawrence. M. C. Conroy.
Third Ward—Election District...............	Clerk.............. Judges	J. H. Church. E. A. Robinson. H. G. Langley.
Fourth Ward—Election District..............	Clerk.............. Judges	J. M. Johnson. C. C. Morton. Wm. M. Pierson.
Fifth Ward—Election District	Clerk. .... Judges	Robert Merrill. N. B. Stone. M. Winn.
Sixth Ward—Election District	Clerk.............. Judges	George O. Whitney. J. C. Harvey. H. R. Johnson.
Seventh Ward—Election District No. 1........	Clerk.............. Judges	C. E. Johnson. George T. Knox. R. S. Cutter.
Seventh Ward—Election District No. 2........	Clerk.............. Judges	J. W. Slosson. C. A. Hawley. J. C. Hubbard.
Eighth Ward—Election District No. 1	Clerk.............. Judges	C. J. Snow. Jacob Lynn. Frederick Teese.
Eighth Ward—Election District No. 2	Clerk.............. Judges	Franklin Williams. Joseph Napthaly. Miles Jewett.
Ninth Ward—Election District................	Clerk.............. Judges	J. M. Buffington. Wm. B. Larzalere. Thomas Boyce.
Tenth Ward—Election District No. 1..........	Clerk.............. Judges	T. H. Lawlor. Alfred Miesegaes. N. P. Copp.
Tenth Ward—Election District No. 2..........	Clerk.............. Judges	Bernard Lande. Charles Koen. Herman Rankin.
Eleventh Ward—Election District No. 1.......	Clerk.............. Judges	A. G. Randall. Donald McLennan. Thomas N. Cazneau.
Eleventh Ward—Election District No. 2.......	Clerk.............. Judges	Martin Fennell. M. W. Lamb. John T. McGeoghegan.
Twelfth Ward—Election District No. 1........	Clerk.............. Judges	J. B. Morton. Wm. T. Canham. J. A. Rodgers.
Twelfth Ward—Election District No. 2........	Clerk.............. Judges	Charles P. Kimball. E. Heath. Thomas Bolster.

NOTE.—The term of office of the Clerks and Judges of Elections is two years, unless sooner made elective by the Board of Supervisors, which body also has power to fill vacancies.

FIRES AND FIRE ALARMS.

In the Report of the Fire Commissioners and Chief Engineer of the Fire Department, pages 193 to 250, there is given a very full statement of fire matters since the organization of the new department. The following, presents an abstract of the Report of the Fire Marshal, made to the Board of Underwriters on the 1st of July, showing that the number of fires and alarms during the year exceeded that of the preceding year some forty-four, having been 265 against 221. It appears, with all the vigilance of the Police, materially assisted by the Fire Department and Fire Marshal, it has proved impossible to put a stop to incendiarism, or in many cases to secure arrest and conviction of its perpetrators. The total number of fires reported as incendiary reaches 67, which involved a loss of property to the amount of $250,003.35, or nearly one-third of the total losses of the year, that amount reaching the sum of $883,118.44, as shown, viz. :

Causes of Fires and Alarms.	Nos.	Loss.	Insurance.
Accident..	12	$4,408 85	$112,300 00
Ashes..	15	1,862 17	20,150 00
Attempt at Arson..................................	10	....	7,000 00
Asphaltum Kettle..................................	1	1,750 00	1,500 00
Bonfires...	3		
Carelessness with Fire.............................	21	39,004 00	26,650 00
Carelessness with Candles..........................	5	642 50	10,400 00
Carelessness with Lamps...........................	3	10,170 00	1,500 00
Carelessness with Matches.........................	2	171 66	2,500 00
Coal Oil Lamp.....................................	1	595 00	2,000 00
Children with Matches.............................	4	10,003 00	11,700 00
Chimnies..	20		
Defective Stovepipes...............................	8	3,655 16	62,000 00
Defective Chimnies.................................	6	4,207 00	14,100 00
Defective Stoves...................................	3	3,942 50	9,700 00
Defective Grates...................................	3	52 50	3,500 00
Defective Ranges...................................	2	13,525 00	18,500 00
Defective Furnace..................................	1	350 00	21,500 00
Drunkenness.......................................	1	900 00	
Explosion of Fireworks.............................	1	10,000 00	4,000 00
Fireworks..	1	3,300 00	7,700 00
False..	23		
Gas Lights...	6	3,315 00	26,800 00
Incendiary..	67	250,003 35	402,275 00
Rats with Matches.................................	1	100 00	
Re-kindling..	5		
Supposed Carelessness with Fire....................	5	136,199 80	151,700 00
Supposed Carelessness with Candle.................	1	4,560 63	14,000 00
Supposed Spontaneous Combustion.................	1	26,250 00	25,500 00
Supposed Defective Chimney........................	1	177,503 00	153,500 00
Spontaneous Combustion...........................	2	41,007 75	138,000 00
Sparks from Furnace...............................	1	10 00	
Sparks from Locomotive............................	2	10 00	
Sparks from Chimnies..............................	2	10 00	
Second Alarms.....................................	6		
Unknown..	19	135,609 57	396,550 00
Total..	265	$883,118 44	$1,645,025 00

INCENDIARY FIRES.

Blacksmith Shop....	1	*Brought forward*.............29	
Blacksmith Shop and Saloon......	1	Furniture Stores..................	2
Blacksmith and Wagon Shop......	1	Grocery Store....................	1
Boarding House....................	1	Hay Pile.........................	1
Boot and Shoe Store.............	1	Lodging Houses..................	3
Barn	1	Match Factory...................	1
Barber Shop.....................	1	Machine Shop....................	1
Court House and Store............	1	Paint Shop......................	1
Crockery Crate..................	1	Pile of Wood....................	1
Dwellings........................,	9	Pile of Lumber..................	1
Cabinet Maker..................	1	Restaurant......................	1
Dwelling and Crockery Store......	1	Saloons.........................	2
Dwelling and Second-hand Store...	1	Stores	3
Dwelling and Grocery Store.......	1	Stables	2
Dwelling and Fancy Store.........	1	Stocking Factory.	1
Dwelling and Butcher Shop.......	1	Unoccupied 14	
Dwelling and Fruit Store	1	Undertaker..	1
Distilleries.........	2	Wood and Willow Ware Store......	1
Dry Goods Store..................	1	Wash House.....................	1
Engine House....:.................	1		
		Total.......................	67
Carried forward.:.............29			

ATTEMPTS TO SET FIRE.

Stable	1	*Brought forward*..............	6
Unoccupied..................	3	Dwellings.......................	2
Wash House....	1	Dwelling and Grocery Store.	1
Grocery Store	1	Dwelling and School House........	1
Carried forward..............	6	Total	10

MATERIAL OF BUILDINGS BURNED.

Frame 254		Adobe	1
Brick.............	39	Iron............................	2

SIZE AND STYLE OF BUILDINGS BURNED.

Frame, one story	95	Brick, three story......:........	10
" two " 141		" four "	1
" three "	17	" five "	2
" four "	1	Adobe, two "	1
Brick, one "	9	Iron, three "	2
" two " ..:..........	17		

COMPARATIVE STATEMENT OF MONTHLY LOSSES AND INSURANCE FROM JULY 1, 1864, TO JUNE 30, 1867.

Months.	July 1st, 1864, to June 30th, 1865.		July 1st, 1865, to June 30th, 1866.		July 1st, 1866, to June 30th, 1867.	
	Loss.	Insurance.	Loss.	Insurance.	Loss.	Insurance.
July.........	$4,640 00	$15,000 00	$366,317 75	$261,750 00	$100,488 86	$81,900 00
August......	2,005 00	10,400 00	11,227 00	19,900 00	60,280 75	125,100 00
September...	5,375 00	5,600 00	19,292 00	19,500 00	62,405 38	227,800 00
October......	14,402 93	61,900 00	11,011 50	26,000 00	83,084 68	135,900 00
November....	44,949 12	107,425 00	12,371 00	12,000 00	75,956 75	185,300 00
December....	6,664 75	127,500 00	5,342 10	35,850 00	43,381 27	205,450 00
January......	9,426 00	19,550 00	3,388 50	14,933 34	14,441 81	24,500 00
February.....	38,277 02½	91,150 00	5,070 00	19,000 00	82,974 36	93,300 00
March.......	6,661 25	31,900 00	14,833 00	14,600 00	24,164 99	81,100 00
April........	17,860 00	38,900 00	26,827 42	65,610 00	213,446 99	234,325 00
May.........	55,898 00	143,450 00	79,143 50	161,725 00	107,013 50	194,300 00
June	90,480 00	61,750 00	38,918 00	42,950 00	15,479 10	56,050 00
Total.....	$296,239 07½	$714,525 00	$593,741 77	$693,818 34	$883,118 44	$1,645,025 00

THE GREAT SEA WALL,

Another most important adjunct to the future commercial prosperity of San Francisco, is progressing in earnest. Contracts for two sections, comprising some six blocks, from Union street on the north to Washington street on the south, being about one quarter of a mile frontage, were awarded to A. H. Houston, on the 18th of July, 1867, by whom the work is now being rapidly pushed forward, and it is anticipated that under ordinary circumstances the undertaking will be completed within the reasonable contract time given. The following from the report of WM. J. LEWIS, Superintending and Construct-ing Engineer, made to the Board of Harbor Commissioners on the 1st of November, presents more full particulars as to the progress of the work:

On the 18th of July, the proposition of A. H. Houston, (being the lowest, for building the second section, was accepted, and the contract signed on the 23d of the same month. Under this contract, Mr. Houston agrees to complete said section in accordance with the plans and specifications, for the sum of $206,554, or at the rate of $278 per lineal foot. *On the same day,* a contract was executed with Mr. Houston for the construction of the embankment of the first section. He agrees to complete the dredging, foundation, embankment, and all of said work except the concrete masonry and rip-rap wall, within seven months from that date, and that, as soon after the completion thereof as he shall be notified by the Board, he shall proceed with the building of the residue of said work, and complete the same within six months of the time of receiving said notice. The price to be paid for the first portion of the said work is $72,800, and for the second portion, $68,250, making the total contract price for the first section $141,050, or $217 per lineal foot. By the terms of the contract for both sections, the Engineer is required to estimate the amount of work done every sixty days, and seventy-five per cent. of the value thereof is paid to the contractor, the remaining twenty-five per cent. being retained until the entire work is completed and accepted by the Board.

Work was commenced on the first section in the early part of September, and has been vigorously prosecuted to date.

As sixty days from the time of commencing the work have not expired, no estimate has yet been made, and no money paid on account of contract.

In the progress of the work thus far, nothing has occurred to lessen my confidence in the practicability of the plan adopted by you.

The building of the whole work around the water front, embracing five or six miles in extent, as contemplated to be done, under the Act of April twenty-fourth, 1863, is necessarily to be a work of years, and will cost several millions of dollars, but is now being carried on with as much rapidity as the revenue derived for the purpose from wharf leases, etc., will permit. The undertaking was begun on the northern frontage of the city, at the base of Telegraph Hill, which, close at hand, could furnish ample material for the filling in. The increased facilities to be afforded to the commerce of the port, when the wall shall be completed, can hardly yet be comprehended or appreciated. On such a line of water frontage as San Fran-cisco has on its magnificent bay, there is hardly any limit to be prescribed as the length to which this protection on the eastern line of the city and county may be carried. A few particulars as to the manner in which the wall is being constructed, is presented in the following, furnished the compiler by Mr. Robert E. C. Stearns, Secretary of the Board of Harbor Commissioners:

GENERAL DESCRIPTION.

A pit, or channel, sixty feet wide, at the bottom, at a level of twenty feet below mean low tide, is excavated, and in this channel is placed the foundation of the sea wall, consisting of a rock embankment, thirteen feet in width on top, at level of mean low tide. The outer extremity of the excavation corresponds with the city front, and consequently, at this point the slope of the rock embankment is twenty feet below mean low water. The stones are thrown *pellmell* into the bay, beginning on the center line of the embankment, and are allowed to settle until they reach a firm foundation.

When it is ascertained that the settling has ceased, a body of concrete, two feet in thickness and ten feet in width, is laid upon the embankment, and upon this concrete is constructed a wall of solid masonry.

This wall is seven feet and three inches in width at the bottom, and nine feet eight inches in hight. It is vertical on the land side, and on the harbor side has a batter of two inches to the foot for seven feet and eight inches, where there is an offset of two feet, forming a recess designed to receive the ends of the timbers of the wharf. From this offset the wall is carried up vertically two feet, making it four feet in width on the top.

The top of the wall is four inches below the official grade of the city, and the face of the wall at the top is forty feet distant from the line of the water front.

The face of the embankment on the harbor side is protected by a *rip-rap* wall, no stone in which shall weigh less than five hundred pounds.

The back of the sea wall is forty-four feet distant from the line of the water front, leaving thirty-one feet to the middle of the street. This space back of the wall is to be filled in with earth embankment, the inner side having a slope of one and a half horizontal to one vertical.

RECEIPTS AND EXPENDITURES FOR TWO YEARS.

RECEIPTS FROM NOVEMBER 3D, 1865, TO NOVEMBER 4TH, 1867.

Clay Street Wharf.................................	$30,538 05
Jackson Street Wharf.............................	26,085 65
Washington Street Wharf.........................	18,606 30
Mission Street Wharf	69,973 25
Vallejo Street Wharf..............................	72,773 25
North Point Wharf................................	16,253 15
Folsom Street Wharf..............................	47,750 00
Howard Street Wharf.............................	42,968 22
Pacific Street Wharf..............................	20,010 00
Broadway Wharf..................................	18,000 00
Commercial Street Wharf.........................	7,360 97
Market Street Wharf..............................	18,241 60
East Street Water Front, (north of Market Street)....	14,478 55
East Street Water Front, (Market to Folsom Street)...	32,912 00
Main Street Wharf................................	6,000 00
Front Street, portion of...........................	1,313 00
Stewart Street....................................	3,207 25
Spear and Bryant Streets, portion of.....	4,053 75
Oakland and San Antonio Steam Navigation Company	5,538 97
Vallejo Street Water Front, (Davis to Front Street)...	6,900 00
Davis Street, (portion of Water Front on)..........	240 00
Dry Dock Company...............................	1,200 00
Carried forward........................	$464,403 96

Brought forward.	$464,403 96	
Pacific Mail Steamship Company....................	12,500 00	
Battery Street, portion of.........................	150 00	
Alameda Ferry Company............................	214 95	
Total Revenue from Wharves.................		$477,268 91

RECEIVED IN SETTLEMENT OF SUITS.

Pacific Street Wharf....................	$15,000 00	
Market Street Wharf	15,000 00	
Broadway Wharf.......................................	15,000 00	
Commercial Street Wharf...........................	5,000 00	
		50,000 00
Protest Account—Amount of dockage paid under pro-		
test and withheld heretofore, to abide events......	$3,013 00	
Dredging Account—Amount received from Ferry Com-		
pany, being their proportion of cost of certain		
dredging..	1,368 25	
		4,381 25
State Wharf and Dock Fund—Amount drawn by		
Commissioners, as per Orders Nos. 19 to 29 inclusive		108,414 44
Harbor Protection Fund—Amount drawn by Commis-		
sioners, as per Orders Nos. 1, 2, and 3...........		3,500 00
		$643,564 60

DISBURSEMENTS.

Urgent Repairs to Wharves	$66,468 37
Current Expenses of Wharves; Salaries, etc.....................	42,319 67
Dredging Account...	54,406 50
Salaries and Expense Account...................................	27,983 32
Legal Expenses—Counsel and Litigation.......................	6,793 00
Sea Wall Account—For Surveys, etc...........................	3,873 50
Construction Account..	41,122 83
State Wharf and Dock Fund—Amount remitted State Treasurer...	118,207 62
Harbor Protection Fund—Amount remitted State Treasurer.......	282,389 79
	$643,564 60

The Board is now composed of S. S. Tilton, appointed by the State Legisla-ture ; James Laidley, chosen by the electors of San Francisco ; James H. Cutter, elected by the State at large. Special Counsel, Edward Tompkins.

The biennial report to be rendered to Governor Low at the ensuing session of the State Legislature, will give full information in relation to the transac-tions of the Harbor Commissioners.

PUBLIC STREETS AND SQUARES.

A very full statement of work done in grading and improving streets, during the year, is presented in the Report of the Superintendent, pages 427 to 454.

The summary of cost of the work done, as given on page 453, shows a less cost in assessments issued than in either of the two preceding years. A table following shows in what particulars the variations have been in the year as compared with the preceding, viz. :

	1865–66.			1866–67.		
Work.	Measurement	Amount.	Cost.	Measurement.	Amount.	Cost.
Grading......	Cubic yds.	1,025,482	$404,539 71	Cubic yards	1,191,257	$327,333 39
Paving	Square ft.	483,193	117,763 99	Sq. ft. { Cobbles { Nicols'n	165,883 } 236,005 }	117,594 74
Brick Sewers..	Lineal feet.	24,414	203,920 82	Lineal feet......	21,303.10	156,745 92
Planking......	1000 feet...	2,199,332	81,145 99	1,000 feet.......	2,574,083	96,897 26
Sidewalks	Front feet..	53,765.3	81,061 69	Front feet......	69,725.1	90,154 65
Curbs	Lineal feet.	21,330.6 }	56,345 93	Lineal feet	19,193.9 }	47,423 60
Crosswalks ...	Lineal feet.	7,804.10 }		Lineal feet	6,296.10 }	
Macadamizing	Square feet	992,635	89,491 53	Square feet.....	1,560,119	117,271 89
Piles..........	....	710	16,226 48	....	28 }	884 08
Caps..........	Lineal feet.	6,578	39,068 04	Lineal feet.....	418 }	
Redw'd Sew'rs	Lineal feet.	9,260.5	....	Lineal feet.....	12,137.6	49,578 20
Total Cost..	....	....	$1,089,564 18	Total......	....	$1,003,883 73

It will be seen in the introductory remarks of the Superintendent, page 427, that a different course is being pursued for cleaning the public streets, sewers and street crossings from that usual heretofore in letting out by contract to the lowest bidder. It is admitted that the expense necessarily attendant upon doing the work in the present manner will be greater than under the former system; but the impression prevails that the work will be much better done, and, notwithstanding an increased expenditure, the public will become gainers thereby. The cost as above was payable in United States notes.

From time to time there have been complaints made in regard to the large amount of street work done; and on the other hand more complaints that work considered necessary has not been done. This is to be noted as particularly the case in grading streets through unimproved property, where under the law, if a majority of the property owners object, the work is stopped. The only remedy for this, is by including several blocks in one Resolution of Intention, when a majority in interest favor the proposed measure.

In connection with Street Department affairs, there is also that of the control and improvement of the

PUBLIC SQUARES,

Which, with the single exception of the "Plaza" or Portsmouth Square, are in a condition disgraceful to the city, which cannot expend money required for their proper improvement without further authority from the State Legislature. To further such a desirable improvement the Board of Supervisors, at a meeting held on the 11th of November, adopted a Resolution recommending the San Francisco delegation in the next Legislature to procure the passage of a law granting power to appropriate the sum of $45,000 for such purposes, to be applied as follows: $10,000 each for Washington and Union Squares ; $5,000 for Columbia Square, and $20,000 for Yerba Buena Park.

William Bebee Fairman.

Early in the year 1867 the Board of Supervisors lost by death Mr. Wm. B. Fairman, then in age its youngest member, and who only a short time before had been chosen representative of the Third Ward.

Elected on the 5th of September, 1866, Mr. Fairman took his place in the Board upon commencement of his official term, at the session held on the third of December following, but lived to attend but five meetings, he after a short and painful sickness of six days duration having been taken from life on the 21st of January, 1867.

At a special meeting held on Monday evening, January 23d, convened at call of the Mayor, the sad event was communicated to the Board by Mr. Jas. H. Reynolds, Supervisor of the Tenth Ward, who said:

MR. PRESIDENT—Since our last meeting, one of our members, Mr. W. B. Fairman, the representative from the Third Ward, has gone to his last account. It has always been customary for this Board, under like circumstances, to meet and pass resolutions of respect to the memory of of a departed member. It is for such purpose that we have met here to-night.

Mr. Fairman has been my bosom friend for years, as many of this Board are aware. It was only at my earnest and repeated solicitations that he consented to take a seat in this Body, to which he was returned by a nearly two-thirds vote of his constituents. Had he been spared to serve out his term, he would have left a record of which any member might be proud. He was an honest, upright and straightforward young man. During my long and intimate acquaintance with him, I do not remember any time when he was not interesting himself in assisting some young man to attain an honorable position.

The young men of this city have lost their best friend. He has gone before he had an opportunity to show to the community that where or in that he had been assailed and traduced it was without cause. He was persevering, ambitious, and warm in his friendship. Mr. Fairman was born in the City of New York, in the year 1833; his father dying, left him in early years dependent upon himself for support. At nineteen years of age he came to San Francisco, where he engaged in the employ of W. T. Coleman & Co. as drayman, retaining that situation until 1856; soon after which he engaged in business on his own account, and continued in it until his death. He was an active member of the Volunteer Fire Department up to the time of organization of the present system, and for several years before was Foreman of Knickerbocker Engine Company, No. 5, often risking his life to save the life or property of others.

Mr. Reynolds then presented the following preamble and resolutions, which were unanimously adopted, to wit:

WHEREAS, By a divine dispensation there has been suddenly summoned from the midst of life and an honorable career one of our number, who, during the short period of his official service, had won the regard of his fellow citizens for his devotion to their best interests, and the duties of the position, as well as that of all associated with him in this Board, for the uniform urbanity of his deportment; and

WHEREAS, In his personal relations in life, his generous disposition and kindness of heart endeared him to all with whom he came in contact; therefore, in view of the afflicting event which has deprived the community of a useful citizen, and his associates of a valued friend:

Be it Resolved, That in the untimely decease of William Bebee Fairman, Supervisor of the Third Ward, his family have lost a kind protector, ourselves a valued associate, his constituents an able and industrious representative, and society an energetic and useful member.

Resolved, That the members of this Board sincerely condole with the afflicted family of the deceased in their irreparable bereavement, and that, as a mark of respect, the chamber of the Board be draped in mourning for the space of thirty days.

Resolved, That a copy of these proceedings be transmitted by the Clerk to the family of the deceased, and the same be entered on the minutes of the Board.

Resolved, That this Board now adjourn, to meet in special session at this room at one o'clock to-morrow, to attend as a body the obsequies of our departed associate.

The Board then adjourned.

SCHEDULE OF OFFICERS OF THE CITY AND COUNTY, SHOWING ANNUAL SALARIES PAYABLE FROM THE TREASURY, FEES OR PER DIEMS, IN THE YEAR 1866-67.

Names.	Offices.	How appointed.	Fees, or per Diem.	Annual Compensat'n
H. P. Coon	Mayor, ex officio Pres. Board Sup'rs	Elective		$3,000
Giles L. Wiggin	Mayor's Clerk	By Mayor		1,800
Henry M. Hale	Auditor	Elective		4,000
J. Pettee	Auditor's Clerk	By Auditor		800
Joseph S. Paxson	Treasurer	Elective		4,000
Avery T. Harris	Deputy Treasurer	By Treasurer		2,100
Charles H. Paxson	"	"		1,500
H. C. Simons	Fee Notice Server	"		1,020
Charles Neff	"	"		1,020
James R. Gregory	Tax Collector	Elective	Fees on Poll Tax collections, and	400
John Hanna	Deputy Collector	By Tax Collector	$200 per month	2,400
George B. Bayley	Deputy and Cashier	"	$175 per month	2,100
P. H. Blake	Deputy	"	$150 per month	1,800
	Tax Collector's Deputies, five	"	$150 per month each	4,500
	Poll Tax Deputies as required	"	Commissions on collections	
Thomas Young	City Recorder	Elective		4,000
R. D. Blauvelt	Deputy Recorder	By Recorder		2,100
W. P. Merriam	"	"		1,800
E. Bonnell	Clerk of Recorder	"	Twelve cents per folio	
P. O. Barry	"	"	"	
John F. Sears	"	"	"	
W. L. Cazneau	"	"	"	
C. E. Miles	"	"	"	
E. A. Wilson	"	"	"	
L. P. Davis	"	"	"	
T. B. Simpson	"	"	"	
J. L. Trask	"	"	"	
G. M. Berry	"	"	"	
C. S. Wilcox	"	"	"	

Name	Office	By Whom Elected	Remarks	Salary
T. M. Young	Clerk of Recorder	By Recorder	Twelve cents per folio	$ 900
T. H. Henderson	"	"	"	4,000
J. C. Edwards	"	"	"	2,100
Henry ...	"	"	"	2,100
A. F. Norring	Porter, Hall of Records	Elective		2,100
Wm Loewy	County Clerk	By ... City Clerk		2,100
Jnes E. ...	Deputy Clerk	"		2,100
John F. Boden	"	"		2,100
Octavius Bell	"	"		1,800
L. P. Peck	"	"		1,800
A. D. ...	"	"		1,800
A. J. ...	"	"		1,800
Wm Harney	"	"		
L. J. Lee	"	"		
J. D. Ruggles	"	"		
B. ...	"	"		
W. Ledlie	"	"		
Three Copying Clerks			Six cents per folio	
W. R. ...*	Assessor	Elective		4,000
G. H. Wheaton	Deputy Assessor	By Assessor		2,400
Samuel Gwles	County Judge	Ele...		5,000
M. C. ...	Probate Judge	"		5,000
Alfred Rix	Judge Police Court	By Board Supervisors, to fill vacancy by death of P. W. Shepheard		4,000
John H. Titcomb	Clerk Police Court	By Board of Supervisors		2,400
Davis Louderback, Jr	Prosecuting Attorney	"		3,000
Nathan Porter	District Attorney	Elective	Allowed $600 per annum for assistance in coll'n of delinquent licenses. $300 expe'd 1865-6.	5,000
H. B. Congdon	Clerk of District Attorney	By District Attorney		1,500
H. M. Hastings	City and County Attorney	Ele...		5,000
J. L. Sharpstein	Clerk of City and County Attorney	By City and County Attorney		1,500

34

* Also allowed by Act of 1866, Statutes page 478, one Draughtsman, salary $1,800; twelve Field Deputies for three months, salaries each $150; and four Office Deputies nine months, salaries each $150; or total additional, $12,600.

SCHEDULE OF OFFICERS OF THE CITY AND COUNTY—Continued.

Names.	Offices.	How appointed.	Fees, or per Diem.	Annual Compensat'n
...	Chinese Interpreter	By Board of Supervisors		$1,500
John Lussey	French and Spanish Interpreter	"		1,500
George O'Doherty	Reporter Fourth and Twelfth District	By Court	Fees	2,500
A. J. Msh.	Reporter Fifteenth District	"	"	3,000
S. R. Harris	Coroner	Elective	Fees and	
... Harloe	Harbor Master	"	$75 a mo. for boat hire, office rent	
... Rowell	Health	By Health Officer		2,400
W. P. Scott	Clerk			1,200
S. F. Elliott	Health	By Board of Health		1,200
T. G. Clement	Public Administrator	Elective	Fees not paid from Treasury	1,440
W. A. ...	Clerk of Board of Supervisors	By Board of Supervisors		2,400
... W. Bingham	Deputy	By Clerk, approval of Board		1,200
John A. Russell	Sergeant-at-Arms	By Board of Supervisors		600
B. S. Blitz	City Surveyor	Elective	Fees not paid from Treasury	500
George C. Potter	Superintendent Streets and Highways	By Superintendent		4,000
George Cofran	Deputy Superintendent Streets	"		1,800
D. McLaren	"	"		1,800
D. H. Whittemore	"	"		1,800
D. S. Dikeman	"	"		1,500
D. T. Van ...	"	"		1,500
J. N. Burson	"	"		1,500
H. L. King, Jr	Superintendent Public Schools	Elective		4,000
John C. Pelton	Secretary Board of Education	By Board of Education		1,800
...	Janitor and Assistant Secretary	"		1,200
Joseph Wood	Superintendent Industrial School	Managers Industrial School		1,800
James S. Thomson	Secretary Industrial School	"		1,500
Henry L. Davis	Sheriff	Elective		8,000
Wm. H. Silverthorne	Under Sheriff	By Sheriff		2,400
Justus Struver	Sheriff's Book Keeper	"		1,800

Name	Office	Appointed by	Salary	Notes
Henry D. Lammot..	Deputy Sheriff	By Sheriff	$1,800	
George Childs....	"	"	1,800	
S. C. Ellis......	"	"	1,800	
B. W. Davis......	"	"	1,800	
Z. B. Adams......	"	"	1,800	
R. Colbourne.....	"	"	1,800	
John Hill........	Four Jail Keepers	"	6,000	$1,500 each
Mrs. Emily Short	Matron	By Board of Supervisors	900	
E. P. Buckley...	Collector of Licenses	"	2,100	
Cornelius Hoyer..	Deputy Collector of Licenses	"	1,500	$10 per month for horse feed
R. E. Kerrison..	"	"	1,500	$10 per month for horse feed
Fred. Kilian....	Porter City Hall	"	1,080	$10 per month for horse feed
J. S. Deen......	Assistant Porter City Hall	"	900	
C. J. Morrison..	"	"	900	

HOSPITAL.

Name	Office	Appointed by	Salary	Notes
William T. Garwood	Resident Physician	By Board of Supervisors	2,400	
F. A. Holman....	Visiting Surgeon	"	1,200	
A. G. Soule.....	Visiting Physician	"	1,200	
Charles A. Stivers	Apothecary	Hospital Com'tee and Mayor	1,500	
Mrs. A. E. Nichols	Matron	"	720	
John Lambie.....	Nurse	"	480	
Alexander Basilini	"	"	480	
W. Thayer.......	Seven Assistant Nurses	"	2,520	$360 each per annum
	Nine additional employés—cooks, interpreter, watchmen, etc.	"	3,780	Aggregate Salaries per annum
John Bracken....	Nurse of Small Pox Hospital	"	600	

PAID FIRE DEPARTMENT.

Name	Office	Appointed by	Salary	Notes
F. E. R. Whitney..	Chief Engineer	By Fire Commissioners	3,000	
H. W. Burckes....	First Assistant Engineer	"	1,200	
C. H. Ackerson...	Second Assistant Engineer	"	1,200	

SCHEDULE OF OFFICERS OF THE CITY AND COUNTY—Concluded.

Names.	Offices.	How appointed.	Fees, or per Diem.	Annual Compensat'n
J. P. Jourden	Secretary	By Fire Commissioners		$1,200
Thomas Sawyer	Corporation Yard Keeper	"		600
Fire Alarm and Police Telegraph.				
Monroe Greenwood	Superintendent	By Board of Supervisors		1,800
Chas. F. Simmons	Operator	"		1,200
Stephen C. Field	"	"		1,200
D. W. Swain	"	"		1,200
F. G. Wood	Repairer	"		1,200
John Short, Jr	Pound Keeper	"	Fees and	900
P. J. Cody	Road Master, First District	"	Five Dollars, or	300
J. S. Dyer	Road Master, Second District	"	Five Dollars, or	300
Police Department				
P. Crowley	Chief of Police	Elective		4,000
Wm. Y. Douglass	Captain of Police	By Police Commissioners		1,800
J. M. Welch	" "	"		1,800
I. W. Lees	" "	"		1,800
S. N. Baker	" "	"		1,800
F. L. Post	Clerk	"		1,800
And 79 Officers			$1,500 each	118,500

EARLY DAYS.

The early history of San Francisco is so well known as to require no particular reference in this Appendix, the intention of which is simply to preserve and present in as brief space and concise terms as possible the record of facts accomplished.

In the year 1862, assisted by Mr. Thos. R. Morgan, then Deputy County Recorder, a table showing the early officers of the Pueblo was prepared by the compiler, which is now republished with additions, so as to bring the record up to the present time.

On the third of November, 1834, the Departmental Legislature of California passed an Act authorizing the election of an Ayuntamiento in the Township or Pueblo of San Francisco ; in pursuance of which, Francisco De Haro was elected First Alcalde.

The second election took place November 27th, 1835, when José Joaquin Estudillo was elected First Alcalde. The succeeding Alcaldes under Mexican authority, (but who, in many instances, were Justices of the Peace exercising the functions of Alcaldes,) were :

Francisco Guerrero............1836	Francisco Guerrero...........	{	1842
Y. Martinez...................1837	Jésus Noe.............. ...	{	1842
Francisco de Haro 1838	Francisco Sanchez.............1843		
Francisco de Haro 1839	Guillermo Hinkley..............1844		
Francisco Guerrero.............1840	Juan N. Padilla..............	{	1845
Francisco Guerrero.. 1841	Jesus de la Cruz Sanchez	{	1845
	José de Jesus Noe 1846		

The American flag was hoisted at Monterey on the 7th of July, 1846, by Commodore John D. Sloat, of the United States Navy, who took formal possession of the country in the name of the United States Government. On the 17th of August following, Commodore Robert F. Stockton, successor to Commodore Sloat, assumed command and issued a proclamation, which appeared in an extra of the *Californian*, published in Monterey, on the 5th of September, 1846, which reads :

MONTEREY, Saturday, September 5th, 1846.

To the People of California:

On my approach to this place with the forces under my command, Jose Castro, the Commandant-General of California, buried his artillery and abandoned his fortified camp "of the Mesa," and fled, it is believed, toward Mexico.

With the sailors, the marines, and the California Battalion of Mounted Riflemen, we entered the "City of the Angels," the Capital of California, on the 13th of August, and hoisted the North American flag.

The flag of the United States is now flying from every commanding position in the Territory, and California is entirely free from Mexican dominion.

The Territory of California now belongs to the United States, and will be governed, as soon as circumstances may permit, by officers and laws similar to those by which the other Territories of the United States are regulated and protected. .

But until the Governor, the Secretary and Council are appointed, and the various civil departments of the Government are arranged, military law will prevail, and the Commander-in-Chief will be the Governor and protector of the Territory.

In the meantime the people will be permitted and are now requested to meet in their several towns and departments, at such time and place as they may see fit, to elect civil officers to fill the places of those who decline to continue in office, and to administer the laws according to former usages of the Territory.

In all cases where the people fail to elect, the Commander-in-Chief and Governor will make the appointments himself.

All persons, of whatever religion or nation, who faithfully adhere to the new Government, will be considered as citizens of the Territory, and will be zealously and thoroughly protected in the liberty of conscience, their persons and property.

No person will be permitted to remain in the Territory who does not agree to support the existing Government, and all military men who desire to remain are required to take an oath that they will not take up arms against it, or do or say anything to disturb its peace.

Nor will any persons, come from where they may, be permitted to settle in the Territory, who do not pledge themselves to be in all respects obedient to the laws which may be from time to time enacted by the proper authorities of the Territory.

All persons who, without special permission, are found with arms outside of their own houses, will be considered as enemies, and will be shipped out of the country.

All thieves will be put to hard labor on the public works, and there kept until compensation is made for the property stolen.

The California Battalion of Mounted Riflemen will be kept in the service of the Territory, and constantly on duty to prevent and punish any aggressions by the Indians or any other persons upon the property of individuals, or the peace of the Territory; and California shall hereafter be so governed and defended as to give security to the inhabitants and defy the power of Mexico.

All persons are required, as long as the territory is under martial law, to be within their houses from 10 o'clock at night until sunrise in the morning.

(Signed.)   R. F. STOCKTON,
                         Commander in Chief and Governor of the Territory.
Ciudad de Los Angeles, August 17th, 1846.

A second proclamation of Governor Stockton, dated Los Angeles, August 22d, ordering an election throughout the towns and districts of California, was issued soon after the foregoing, and reads :

To the People of California:

On the 15th day of September, 1846, an election will be held in the several towns and districts of California, at the places and hours at which such elections have usually been held, for the purpose of electing the Alcaldes and other municipal officers for one year.

In places where Alcaldes have been appointed by the present government, they will hold the election.

In those places where no Alcaldes have been appointed by the present government, the former Alcaldes are authorized and required to hold the election.

Given under my hand this 22d day of August, A.D. 1846, at the Government House, Ciudad de los Angeles.

                         R. F. STOCKTON, Commander in Chief
                         And Governor of the Territory of California.

On the eighth day of July, 1846, San Francisco was formally taken possession of by Captain John B. Montgomery, commanding the United States sloop of war Portsmouth, by whom Lieut. Washington A. Bartlett was appointed Chief Magistrate, or Alcalde, which appointment was subsequently ratified by a formal election by the citizens. Mr. Bartlett held the office, with a brief interval, until February, 1847.

Soon after entering upon the duties of his office as First Magistrate of the infant city, Mr. Bartlett issued a set of rules and regulations for government in commercial transactions, which read:

RULES AND REGULATIONS FOR THE TRADE OF THE BAY OF SAN FRANCISCO.

It having come to the knowledge of the Commander of the District of San Francisco, etc., etc., that persons are engaged in stealing and killing cattle, and then selling the produce to any purchaser; and it being necessary to put every possible check upon such practices, and to secure all property to the proper owners thereof;

It is ordered that, from and after this date, no shipments of the products of the country will be permitted to be made in any boat, launch, or other vessel, except under the following regulations:

1st. The points of shipment where boats or launches will be permitted to take freight on board are at "Saucelito," Corte "Madera" (the wood landing between Saucelito and San Rafael), San Rafael, Petaluma and Sonoma; and only at the usual landing of those places, for the north of the bay.

2d. For the Sacramento Valley and River, at Sutter's landing.

3d. For the San Joaquin, Dr. Marsh's landing.

Inspectors will be appointed for all the above-named points, with instructions for their guidance.

4th. For that part of the Bay called the Contra Costa, commencing at the mouth of the San Joaquin River and extending as far as the landing of the Mission of San Jose, hides, tallow, etc., may be shipped under the following regulations: The shipper to give a bill of sale in writing, signed by himself, certifying to the marks in said bill to correspond with the marks on the articles, particularly the marks on the hides and bags of tallow.

5th. An office of inspector of hides and tallow will be established at the pueblo of Jan Jose, and a sub-inspector at the landing of said pueblo. The Inspector General will be at Yerba Buena.

6th. Shipments may be made at any point from the Pueblo of Yerba Buena under the same regulations contained in Article 4.

7th. The Inspector General at Yerba Buena will inspect "all launches or boats on their arrival, and ascertain if the freight corresponds with the bill of lading, and particularly as to the marks being the same as expressed in the bills.

8th. An inspector of tallow will be appointed to ascertain if it is of a merchantable quality, and if it corresponds, that no fraud has been attempted by the introduction of other substances to defraud in weight.

9th. Any person found guilty of selling or disposing of hides that are not legally his own, will be severely punished by fine and labor on the public works, according to the nature of the offense.

· 10th. Any person found guilty of an attempt to defraud by introducing improper articles in bags of tallow, will forfeit the whole package and suffer a further penalty according to the nature of the offense.

11. In order to meet the expenses of the Inspectors, which are intended to protect all who are engaged in a just and honorable trade, a tax of three cents on each hide, and twenty-five cents on each bag of tallow will be assessed.

12th. All such certificates and certified bills of lading will be deposited in the office of the Superintendent of the Port, for the benefit of all concerned.

13th. All boats or launches arriving at the anchorage of Yerba Buena, must be entered for inspection before they can be permitted to unload.

By order of   JOHN B. MONTGOMERY, Esq.,
                                    Commanding Northern District of California.

                        WASHINGTON A. BARTLETT,
                    Collector and Superintendent, Port San Francisco.

Yerba Buena, September 6th, 1846.

MR. BARTLETT'S SUCCESSORS.

Edwin Bryant..................February 22d to June, 1847.
George Hyde...................June, 1847, to April, 1848.
J. Townsend...................April to September, 1848.
T. M. Leavenworth.............September, 1848, to August, 1849.
John W. Geary.................August, 1849, to May, 1850.

The two Ayuntamientos immediately preceding the incorporation of the city were composed as follows :

August 6th, 1849, to January 10th, 1850.

Horace Hawes, *Prefect.*

Joseph R. Curtis, *Sub Prefect.*		Francisco Guerrero, *Sub Prefect.*
John W. Geary, *First Alcalde.*		Frank Turk, *Second Alcalde.*
Thos. B. Winston,	Wm. M. Stewart,	Rodman M. Price,
Samuel Brannan,	Henry A. Harrison,	Stephen Harris,
Alfred J. Ellis,	Bezer Simmons,	John Townsend,
Wm. H. Davis,	Gabriel B. Post,	Talbot H. Green.

Frank Turk and Henry L. Dodge, *Secretaries.*

January 11th, to May 8th, 1850.

John W. Geary, *First Alcalde.*		Frank Turk, *Second Alcalde.*
Samuel Brannan,	Wm. H. Davis,	Mathew Crooks,
Alfred J. Ellis,	Wm. M. Stewart,	A. M. Van Nostrand,
Hugh C. Murray,	F. C. Gray,	Frank Tilford,
Jas. S. Graham,	Jas. Hagan,	Talbot H. Green.
Jonathan Cade, *Sergeant-at-Arms.*		Henry L. Dodge, *Secretary.*

The foregoing needs no comment to present more forcibly to the reader a contrast of existing affairs in the Bay City at the present day, with those of Yerba Buena twenty years ago. Following will be found a list of officers since the incorporation of the city, which, it will be seen, prior to 1856, had two separate sets of officers, for a city and a county government, as follows :

SAN FRANCISCO CITY OFFICERS, 1850 TO 1856.

CITY OFFICIALS.	MAY, 1850.	MAY, 1851.	JANUARY, 1852.	NOVEMBER, 1852.	OCTOBER, 1853.	OCTOBER, 1854.	JULY, 1855.
Mayor	J. W. Geary.	C. J. Brenham.	S. R. Harris.	C. J. Brenham.	C. K. Garrison.	S. P. Webb.	Jas. Van Ness.
Controller	B. L. Berry.	G. A. Hudson.	J. W. Stillman.	R. Matheson.	S. R. Harris.	W. Sherman.	A.J. Moulder.
Assessor	R. B. Hampton and seven others.	W. C. Norris and G. F. Lemmon.	J. C. O'Callaghan. David Hoag and A. Mathews.	M. D. Eyre, J. L. Anderson & J. C. O'Callaghan.	R. Kerrison, J. H. Keller and R. Par.	J. H. Bristow, J. B. Brown & J. Cowles.	W. H. Graham and seven others.
Tax Collector	W. M. Irwin.	T. D. Greene.	D. S. Linnell.	Lewis Teal.	W. A. Mathews.	E. T. Batturs.	E. T. Batturs.
Treasurer	C. G. Scott.	R. H. Sinton.	Smyth Clarke.	Ham. Bowie.	Ham. Bowie.	D. S. Turner.	W. McKibben.
Recorder	F. Tilford.	R. H. Waller.	G. W. Baker.	G. W. Baker.	G. W. Baker.	R. H. Waller.	Jas. Van Ness.
Marshal	M. Fallon.	R. G. Crozier.	D. W. Thompson.	R. G. Crozier.	B. Seguin.	J.W.M'Kenzie	Ham. North.
City Attorney	T. H. Holt.	F. M. Pixley.	C. McC. Delany.	J. K. Hackett.	S. A. Sharpe.	L. Sawyer.	B. Peyton.
School Superin't.	....	....	T. J. Nevins.	T. J. Nevins.	W. H. O'Grady.	W.H.O'Grady	E. A. Theller.
Street Commis'r.	D. McCarthy.	W. Divier.	W. Divier.	W. Divier.	John Addis.	G. W. Ryder.	J. J. Hoff.
Harbor Master	James Hagan.	G. Simpton.	G. Simpton.	W. T. Thomson.	Robt. Haley.	Robt. Haley.	J. B. Schaeffer

SAN FRANCISCO COUNTY OFFICERS, 1850 TO 1856.

COUNTY OFFICIALS.	1850.	1851-2.	1853-4.	1855-6.
Assessor.............	D. M. Chauncey.	H. Vandeveer.	J. W. Stillman.	J. W. Stillman.
Coroner.............	E. Gallagher.	N. Gray.	J. W. Whaling.	H. Kent.
County Clerk.......	J. E. Addison.	J. E. Wainwright.	Thos. Hayes.	Thos. Hayes.
County Judge.......	R. N. Morrison.	Alex. Campbell.	T. W. Freelon.	T. W. Freelon.
County Recorder....	J. A. McGlynn.	T. B. Russum.	James ɛ...	F. D. Kohler.
District Attorney....	A. Benham.	H. H. Byrne.	H. H. Byrne.	H. H. Byrne.
Public Administrator....	J. Henriquez.	D. T. Bagley.	S. A. Sheppard.	Sam. Flower.
Sheriff.............	J. C. Hayes.	{ J. C. Hayes. / Thos. P. Johnson.	W. P. Gorham.	D. Scannell.
Surveyor............	W. M. Eddy.	C. Humphreys.	J. J. Gardiner.	J. J. Gardiner.
Treasurer...........	G. W. Endicott.	J. &h.	G. W. Greene.	R. E. Woods.

The Mayor of the city was *ex-officio* President, and the Board of Aldermen were the Supervisors of the County, from the years 1850, to June, 1856.

MEMBERS OF THE COMMON COUNCIL, 1850 TO 1856.

May 6th, 1850, to May, 1851.

BOARD OF ALDERMEN.

Wm. Greene, *President,*

Chas. Minturn, F. W. Macondray,

David Gillespie, A. A. Selover,

John B. Bispham, *Clerk.*

C. V. Stewart,

M. L. Mott,

W. M. Burgoyne.

BOARD OF ASSISTANT ALDERMEN.

A. Bartol, *President,*

J. Maynard, C. T. Botts,

W. Sharon, L. T. Wilson,

W. A. Grover, *Clerk.*

J. P. Van Ness,

William Corbett,

A. Morris.

May, 1851, to December 29, 1851.

BOARD OF ALDERMEN.

R. S. Dorr, *President,*

E. L. Morgan, A. C. Labatt,

C. L. Ross, James Grant,

E. A. Edgerton, *Clerk.*

George Endicott,

Wm. Greene,

C. M. K. Paulison.

BOARD OF ASSISTANT ALDERMEN.

Joseph F. Atwill, *President,*

T. H. Selby, Jos. Galloway,

H. Meiggs, Wm. D. Conrade,

Robert C. Page, *Clerk.*

Q. S. Sparks,

W. W. Parker,

Jas. Graves.

December, 1851, to November, 1852.

BOARD OF ALDERMEN.

J. H. Blood, *President,*

E. L. Morgan, John Cotter,

Wm. G. Wood, James Grant,

John Crane, *Clerk.*

N. S. Pettit,

Elliott J. Moore,

Caleb Hyatt.

BOARD OF ASSISTANT ALDERMEN.

Nathaniel Holland, *President,*

Jos. Galloway, W. H. Crowell,

Henry Meiggs, John C. Piercy,

Robert C. Page, *Clerk.*

Jas. Graves,

John W. Kessling,

D. W. Lockwood.

November, 1852, *to October*, 1853.

BOARD OF ALDERMEN.

Joshua P. Haven, *President*,   T. H. Selby,
A. J. Bowie,   J. P. Flint,   Chas. L. Case,
Wm. A. Dana,   E. J. Moore,   G. K. Gluyas.
E. A. Edgerton, *Clerk*.

BOARD OF ASSISTANT ALDERMEN.

James De Long, *President*,   J. B. Piper,
H. N. Squier,   H. R. Haste,   Thomas Hayes,
Wm. H. Bovee,   Edward Byrne,   G. W. Bryant.
Robert C. Page, *Clerk*.

October, 1853, *to October*, 1854.

BOARD OF ALDERMEN.

Jos. F. Atwill, *President*,   James Van Ness,
Henry Meiggs,   John D. Brower,   C. O. West,
Richard M. Jessup,   D. H. Haskell,   John Nightingale.
John Crane, *Clerk*.

BOARD OF ASSISTANT ALDERMEN.

F. Turk, *President*,   S. Gardner,
J. T. Hyde,   Geo. O. Ecker,   J. G. W. Schulte,
C. D. Carter,   Wm. H. Talmage,   J. R. West.
Robert C. Page, *Clerk*.

October, 1854, *to July*, 1855.

BOARD OF ALDERMEN.

Jos. F. Atwill, *President*,   G. M. Norton,
James T. Hyde,   Jacob B. Moore,   James Van Ness,
C. H. Gough,   C. E. Buckingham,   J. L. Van Bokkelen.
John Crane, *Clerk*.

BOARD OF ASSISTANT ALDERMEN.

Henry Haight, *President*,   I. M. Merrill,
Jonathan Wilde,   Geo. R. Davidson,   W. F. Story,
Wm. A. Piper,   John Perry, Jr.,   J. C. Maynard.
T. M. J. Dehon, *Clerk*.

July, 1855, *to July*, 1856.

BOARD OF ALDERMEN.

J. M. Tewksbury, *President*,   Robert Rankin,
C. H. Corser,   C. W. Hathaway,   Wm. Greene,
J. Hopkins,   R. W. Slocomb,   J. W. Brittan.
Wm. H. Stevens, *Clerk*.

BOARD OF ASSISTANT ALDERMEN.

H. J. Wells, *President*,		Wm. H. Dow,
Charles Wilson,	E. P. Peckham,	J. C. Beideman,
R. H. Tobin,	John Vandewater,	C. J. Bartlett.
	Robert C. Page, *Clerk*.	

BOARD OF SUPERVISORS.

July to November, 1856.

George J. Whelan, *President.*
Lawrence Ryan, *Justice of the Peace, First District.*
E. W. Smith, *Justice of the Peace, Second District.*
C. M. Chamberlain, *Justice of the Peace, Third District.*
David B. Castree, *Justice of the Peace, Fourth District.*
Robert C. Page, *Clerk.*

OFFICERS OF THE SAN FRANCISCO VOLUNTEER FIRE DEPARTMENT FROM 1850 TO 1867.

A. D.	Chief Engineer.	First Assistant.	Second Assistant.	Third Assistant.
1850.....	F. D. Kohler.	E. A. Ebbets.	T. K. Battelle.	
1851.....	F. E. R. Whitney.	C. L. Case.	W. McKibben.	
	G. H. Hossefross.	W. McKibben.	J. A. Huntsman.	G. P. Kingsland.
1852.....	G. H. Hossefross.	C. P. Duane.	A. R. Simmons.	E. A. Ebbets.
1853.....	C. P. Duane.	E. A. Ebbets.	J. Capprise.	C. S. Simpson.
1854.....	C. P. Duane.	J. Capprise.	W. Free.	F. Wheeler.
1855.....	Jas. E. Nuttman.	W. Free.	J. Capprise.	A. Devoe.
1856.....	F. E. R. Whitney.	D. T. Van Orden.	L. H. Robie.	C. Walsh.
1857.....	F. E. R. Whitney.	D. T. Van Orden.	L. H. Robie.	C. Walsh.
1858.....	F. E. R. Whitney.	D. T. Van Orden.	L. H. Robie.	S. S. Gordon.
1859.....	F. E. R. Whitney.	D. T. Van Orden.	S. S. Gordon.	E. F. Stuart.
1860.....	F. E. R. Whitney.	D. T. Van Orden.	S. S. Gordon.	E. F. Stuart.
1861.....	David Scannell.	S. S. Gordon.	E. F. Stuart.	John G. Corson.
1862.....	David Scannell.	E. F. Stuart.	John G. Corson.	Frank Evans.
1863.....	David Scannell.	John G. Corson.	Frank Evans.	Chas. D. Connell.
1864.....	David Scannell.	Frank Evans.	Chas. D. Connell.	Cornelius Mooney.
1865.....	David Scannell.	Chas. D. Connell.	Cornelius Mooney.	Thomas Finerty.
1866.....	David Scannell.	Cornelius Mooney.	Thomas Finerty.	Chas. McCann.

OFFICERS OF THE SAN FRANCISCO PAID FIRE DEPARTMENT FROM DECEMBER 3D, 1867.

A. D.	Chief Engineer.	First Assistant.	Second Assistant.
1867.......	F. E. R. Whitney.	H. W. Burckes.	Chas. H. Ackerson.

CITY AND COUNTY OFFICIALS, 1856 TO 1861.

City and County Officials.	July to Nov., 1856.	1856.	1857.	1858.	1859.	1860.	1861.
Attorney	Bailie Peyton.	Bailie Peyton.	F. P. Tracy.	F. P. Tracy.	F. P. Tracy.	S. W. Holliday	S. W. Holliday / J. H. Saunders
Assessor	J. Cook.	C. R. Bond.	C. R. Bond.	C. R. Bond.	C. R. Bond.	C. R. Bond.	C. R. Bond.
Auditor	F. D. Kohler	E. Mickle	E. Me	E. Mickle	E. Mickle	E. Mickle	Henry M. Hale
Chief of Police	J. McElroy	J. F. Curtis	J. F. Curtis	Martin J. Burke.	Martin J. Burke.	Martin J. Burke.	Martin J. Burke.
Coroner	H. Kent.	H. Kent.	J. My	J. My	J. McNulty.	J. McNulty.	J. McNulty.
County Clerk	Thomas Hayes	Thomas Hayes	W.	W. Duer	W. Bartlett.	W. Bartlett.	W. Bartlett.
County and Probate Judge	T. W. Freelon.	T. W. Freelon.	M. C. Blake	M. C. Blake	M. C. Blake	M. C. Blake	M. C. Blake
County Recorder	F. D. Kohler	F. D. Kohler	G. W. Beckh	G. W. Beckh	G. W. Beckh	G. W. Beckh	A. M. Ebbets
District Attorney	H. H. Byrne.	H. H. Byrne.	W. K. Osborn	H. S. Brown	H. S. Brown	H. S. Brown	Nathan Porter.
Harbor Master	J. B. Schaeffer	Cheever & Noyes	Amos Noyes	mos Noyes	W. T. Thompson	W. T. Thompson	W. T. Thompson
Police Judge	James Van Ness	H. P. Coon.	H. P. Coon.	H. P. Coon.	H. P. Coon.	H. P. Coon.	Samuel Cowles
Public Administrator	Samuel Flower	R. C. Rogers	R. C. Rogers	L. P. Sage.	L. P. Sage.	L. P. Sage.	A. Hollub
Sheriff	David Scannell.	David Scannell.	aRes Doane.	Charles Doane.	Charles Doane.	Charles Doane.	Charles Doane.
Superintendent of Schools	John C. Pelton.	John C. Pelton.	H. B. Janes	H. B. Janes	James Denman.	James Denman.	James Denman.
Superintendent of Streets	J. J. Gardiner.	B. O. Devoe.	B. O. Devoe.	G. H. Hossefross	G. H. Hossefross	G. H. Hossefross	George T. Bohen
Surveyor	J. J. Gardiner.	J. J. Gardiner.	George R. Turner	George R. Turner	George R. Turner	George R. Turner	George R. Turner
Tax Collector	The Sheriff.	The Treasurer.	W. Y. Patch.	Jonathan Hunt.	Jonathan Hunt.	Jonathan Hunt.	E. H. Washburn.
Treasurer	R. E. Woods.	W. Hooper.	W. H. Tillinghast	W. H. Tillinghast	W. H. Tillinghast	W. H. Tillinghast	W. H. Tillinghast

CITY AND COUNTY OFFICIALS, 1862 TO 1867.

City and County Officials.	1862.	1863.	1864.	1865.	1866.	1867.
Attorney	John H. Saunders	John H. Saunders	John H. Saunders	John H. Saunders	{ J. H. Saunders. / H. M. Hastings. }	H. M. a [illegible]
Assessor	C. C. Webb	{ C. C. Webb / W. R. Wheaton }	Wm R. [illegible]on	William R. Wheaton	William R. Wheaton	William R. Wheaton.
Auditor	Henry M. Hale	Henry M. Hale	Henry M. Hale	Henry M. Hale	Henry M. Hale	Henry M. Hale.
Chief of Police	Martin J. Burke	Martin J. Burke	aMin J. Burke	Martin J. Burke	P. Crowley	P. [illegible]y.
Coroner	B. A. Sheldon	B. A. Sheldon	{ B. A. Sheldon / S. R. Harris }	Stephen R. Harris	Stephen R. Harris	[Ste]hen R. Harris.
County Clerk	Washington Bartlett	{ W. Bartlett / Wm. Loewy }	[illegible] [L]owy	Wilhelm Loewy	Wilhelm Loewy	[Wm] Loewy.
County and Probate Judge	M. C. Blake	M. C. Blake				
County Judge			a [illegible] [Cow]les	Samuel Cowles	Samuel Cowles	Samuel Cowles.
Probate Judge			M. C. [Bla]ke	M. C. Blake	M. C. Blake	M. C. Blake.
County Recorder	Thomas Young	Thomas Young	[T]has Young	Thomas Young	Thomas Young	Thomas Young.
District Attorney	Nathan Porter	Nathan Porter	[illegible]n Porter	Nathan Porter	Nathan Porter	Nathan Porter.
Harbor Master	Charles Goodall	Charles Goodall	[Cha]les [Good]all	{ Charles Goodall / Marcus Harloe }	Marcus Harloe	Marcus Harloe.
Police Judge	Samuel Cowles	Samuel Cowles	P. W. [illegible]	P. W. Shepheard	Alfred Rix	Alfred Rix.
Public Administrator	{ A. Hollub / M. J. Marshuetz }	{ Geo. B. Merrill / J. W. Brumagim }	John W. Brumagim	John W. Brumagim	{ J. W. Brumagim / W. A. Quarles }	W. A. Quarles.
Sheriff	J. S. Ellis	J. S. Ellis	{ J. S. Ellis / Henry L. Davis }	Henry L. Davis	Henry L. Davis	Henry L. Davis.
Superintendent of Schools	George Tait	George Tait	[Geo]ge Tait	{ George Tait / John C. Pelton }	John C. Pelton	John C. Pelton.
Superintendent of Streets	George T. Bohen	George T. Bohen	{ [G]e T. Bohen / George Cofran }	George Cofran	George Cofran	George Cofran.
Surveyor	George C. Potter	George C. Potter	[Geo]ge C. Potter	George C. Potter	George C. Potter	George C. Potter.
Tax Collector	E. H. Washburn	E. H. [Wash]urn	E. H. { Washburn / [Ch]s R. Story }	Charles R. Story	Charles R. Story	Charles R. Story.
Treasurer	Joseph S. Paxson	Joseph S. Paxson	Joseph S. Paxson	Joseph S. Paxson	Joseph S. Paxson	Joseph S. Paxson.

MEMBERS OF BOARD OF SUPERVISORS UNDER CONSOLIDATION ACT, FROM 1856 TO 1862.

Districts.	1856-7.	1857-8.	1858-9.	1859-60.	1860-1.	1861-2.
	E. W. Burr, *President.*	E. W. Burr, *President.*	E. W. Burr, *President.*	H. F. Teschemacher, *President.*	H. F. Teschemacher, *President.*	H. F. Teschemacher, *President.*
First	Charles Wilson	Charles Wilson	ailes S. Bien	Charles S. Biden	Charles S. Biden	Charles S. Biden
Second	William A. Darling	W. A. Darling	W. A. Darling	Joseph Britton	Joseph Britton	Myles D. Sweeney
Third	W. K. Van Allen	W. K. Van Allen	H. S. Gates	H. S. Gates	H. De La Montanya	H. De La Montanya
Fourth	M. S. Roberts	L. B. Benchly	L. B. Benchly	F. W. Brooks	F. W. Brooks	H. L. King
Fifth	Samuel Merritt	Samuel ...	Thas Young	Thomas Young	D. Gaven	D. Gaven
Sixth	ches W. Bond	{Charles W. Bond / Thomas Tennent}	Thas Tennent	Thomas Tennent	H. L. Dodge	Henry L. Dodge
Seventh	H. A. George	H. A. George	Joseph S. ...	Joseph S. Paxson	W. C. Hinckley	William C. Hinckley
Eighth	N. C. abe	N. C. Lane	N. C. Lane	J. S. Davies	John S. Davies	Gerrit W. Bell
Ninth	W. Palmer	W. Palmer	W. 1 Men	W. B. Johnston	Eugene Crowell	{Eugene Crowell / John C. Merrill}
Tenth	R. G. Sneath	R. G. Sneath	R. G. Sneath	James Otis	James Otis	{James Otis / J. H. Redington}
Eleventh	J. J. Denny	J. J. Denny	J. C. Corbett	{Albert G. Randall / John C. Ayres}	Frank McCoppin	Frank McCoppin
Twelfth	S. S. Tilt on	S. S. Tilton	S. S. Tilton	John Lynch	John Lynch	{John Lynch / Jas. W. Cudworth}
	E. W. Playter, / Milo Calkin, } *Clerks.*	Milo Calkin, *Clk.*	[No Calkin, *Clerk.*	Milo Calkin, *Clerk.*	Wm. A. Wells. / J. W. Bingham } *Clerks*	James W. Bingham, *Clerk.*
					B. S. Blitz, *Sergeant-at-Arms.*	B. S. Blitz, *Sergeant-at-Arms.*

MEMBERS OF BOARD OF SUPERVISORS UNDER CONSOLIDATION ACT, FROM 1862 TO 1867.

Districts.	1862-3.	1863-4.	1864-5.	1865-6.	1866-7.
	H. F. Teschenacher, *Mayor and ex-officio Presi't.*	H. P. Coon, *Mayor and ex-officio Presi't.*	H. P. Coon, *Mayor and ex-officio Presi't.*	H. P. Coon, *Mayor and ex-officio Presi't.*	H. P. Coon, *Mayor and ex-officio Presi't.*
First	A. H. Tomb	A. H. Titcomb	A. H. Tomb	A. H. Titcomb	P. H. Daly.
Second	Myles D. Sweeny	John Fay	John Fay	R. P. Clement	R. P. Clement.
Third	H. De La Montanya	H. De La M ntanya	Isaac Rowell	Isaac Rowell	{ W. B. Fairman. / §Edward Flaherty.
Fourth	H. L. King	H. L. King	H. L. King	William S. Phelps	William S. ...s.
Fifth	D. ...sh	{ E. C. Kennedy / A. S. Baldwin / ...e Ashbury	Monroe Ashbury	Monroe Ashbury	Monroe ...ry.
Sixth	{ H nry L. Dodge / Giles H. Gray / Erastus N. Torrey	Erastus N. Torrey	Erastus N. Torrey	Erastus N. Torrey	Erastus N. Torrey.
Seventh	W. C. ...Hay	W. C. ...ey	Giles ...la on	Charles Clayton	Charles Clayton.
Eighth	...it W. Bell	...tt W. Bell	Gerrit W. Bell	{ *Gerrit W. Bell / †Jacob Schreiber / ‡F. G. E. Tittell	F. G. E. Tittel.
Ninth	John C. Merrill	John C. Merrill	A. J. Shrader	A. J. Shrader	A. J. Shrader.
Tenth	J. H. Redington	A. H. Cummings	A. H. ...mings	James H. Reynolds	James H. Reynolds.
Eleventh	Frank ...in	Frank McCoppin	Frank McCoppin	Frank McCoppin	Frank McCoppin.
Twelfth	James W. Cudworth	...iel Cody	...iel Cody	Charles H. Stanyan	Charles H. Stanyan.
	Jam e W. Bingham, *Clerk.*	Jam e W. Bingham, *Clerk.*	James W. Bingham, *Clerk.*	Jas. W. Bingham, *Clerk.* / J. A. Russell, *Deputy Clerk.*	James W. Bingham, *Clerk.* / J. A. Russell, *Deputy Clerk.*
	B. S. Blitz, *Sergeant-at-Arms.*	B. S. Blitz, *Sergeant-at-Arms.*	B. S. Blitz, *Sergeant-at-Arms.*	B. S. Blitz, *Sergeant-at-Arms.*	B. S. Blitz, *Sergeant-at-Arms.*

* Deceased April 16, 1866.   † Took his seat May 21, 1866.   ‡ Took his seat September 17, 1866.   § Took his seat September 16, 1867.

35

MEMBERS AND MEMBERS ELECT OF THE BOARD OF SUPERVISORS—1867-68.

NEW BOARD.

Five new members enter the Board of Supervisors at its session on the second of December. These will represent Wards as follows:—2d, John Harrold; 4th, R. Beverly Cole; 6th, D. D. Shattuck; 8th, J. B. E. Cavallier; 10th, Edward Nunan;—leaving a vacancy in the 11th Ward, to be filled upon nomination of the President, the incoming Mayor, who vacates his seat as Supervisor upon taking that of President, then nominating his successor. The Board, when thus organized, will consist of

Mayor and Ex-Officio President.................FRANK McCOPPIN.

MEMBERS.

1st Ward, P. H. DALY.   7th Ward, CHARLES CLAYTON.
2d Ward, JOHN HARROLD.   8th Ward, J. B. E. CAVALLIER.
3d Ward, EDWARD FLAHERTY.   9th Ward, A. J. SHRADER.
4th Ward, R. BEVERLY COLE.   10th Ward, EDWARD NUNAN.
5th Ward, MONROE ASHBURY.   11th Ward, (Vacancy.)
6th Ward, D. D. SHATTUCK.   12th Ward, CHAS. H. STANYAN.

RESOLUTION No. 6,963.

RESOLVED, That the Heads of the following Departments be, and they are hereby, requested to report to this Board, on or before the first day of August ensuing, the condition of their respective Departments during the fiscal year ending June 30th, 1867, embracing all their operations and expenditures:

Auditor,	Assessor,	Tax Collector,
County Clerk,	Streets,	Fire Department,
Hospital,	Treasurer,	Fire Alarm & Police Telegraph,
Sheriff,	County Recorder,	City and County Surveyor,
License Collector,	Public Schools,	Funded Debt,
Harbor Master,	Pound Keeper,	City and County Attorney,
Industrial School,	Police,	Coroner,
Public Administrator,	Health Officer.	

And that all or portions of said reports be published in a volume, in accordance with the requirements of Section 73 of the Consolidation Act. The Clerk of the Board is hereby instructed to send a copy of this Resolution to the Head of each of the enumerated Departments.

In Board of Supervisors, San Francisco, June 17th, 1867.

Adopted by the following vote :

Ayes—Supervisors Clement, Phelps, Ashbury, Clayton, Tittel, Shrader, Reynolds, Stanyan.

Absent—Supervisors Daly, Torrey, McCoppin.

JAS. W. BINGHAM, Clerk.

Lightning Source UK Ltd.
Milton Keynes UK
UKHW021842070119
335139UK00011B/661/P